Women Artists: 1550-1950

Women Artists: 1550-1950

Ann Sutherland Harris

Linda Nochlin

Los Angeles County Museum of Art
Alfred A. Knopf, New York, 1981

All rights reserved under International
and Pan-American Copyright Conventions.
Published in the United States by the
Los Angeles County Museum of Art and
Alfred A. Knopf, Inc., New York,
and simultaneously in Canada by
Random House of Canada Limited, Toronto.
Distributed by Random House, Inc., New York.

Library of Congress Cataloging
in Publication Data

Harris, Ann Sutherland.
Women artists, 1550-1950.

Exhibition catalog.
1.
Art, Modern — Exhibitions.
2.
Women artists.
I. Nochlin, Linda, joint author.
II. Los Angeles Co., Calif.
Museum of Art, Los Angeles.
III. Title.

N6350.H35
709'.03'074019494
76-39955
ISBN 0-394-41169-2 (hardcover)
ISBN 0-394-73326-6 (paperback)

Manufactured in the United States of America
Published February 25, 1977
Reprinted Three Times
Fifth Printing, March 1981

Contents

Lenders to the Exhibition

Mr. and Mrs. Edward Abrahams, New York
Mrs. L. W. Scott Alter, Cincinnati
Auzou Family, Paris
Mr. and Mrs. R. Stanton Avery, Pasadena
Mr. and Mrs. E. A. Bergman, Chicago
Mrs. Harry Woodward Blunt, Bethesda, Maryland
Julius Böhler, Munich
Robert Peerling Coale, Chicago
S.A.S. la Princesse Leopold de Cröy-Solre, Saint-Benin d'Azy
Sonia Delaunay, Paris
The Marquess of Exeter, Burghley House, Stamford
Leonor Fini, Paris
Mr. and Mrs. Francois Heim, Paris
Jeffrey H. Loria, New York
Alice Neel, Graham Gallery, New York
Dr. Karl Graf von Schönborn-Wiesentheid, Pommersfelden, Schloss
   Weissenstein
Carlo Sestieri, Rome
Earl Spencer, Althorp, Northampton
Private Collectors

Aarhus (Denmark) Kunstmuseum
Thomas Agnew and Sons Ltd., London
Amon Carter Museum of Western Art, Fort Worth
The Baltimore Museum of Art
The Brooklyn Museum
Cá Rezzonico, Museo del Settecento, Venice
Cincinnati Art Museum
The Cleveland Museum of Art
Columbus (Ohio) Gallery of Fine Arts
Corcoran Gallery of Art, Washington, D.C.
The Detroit Institute of Arts
Anthony d'Offay Gallery, London
The Fine Arts Museums of San Francisco
Fitzwilliam Museum, Cambridge
The *Forbes* Magazine Collection, New York
Allan Frumkin Gallery, New York
Galleria degli Uffizi, Florence
Galleria Palatina, Palazzo Pitti, Florence
Gemäldegalerie der Akademie der bildenden Künste, Vienna
Gimpel and Hanover Galerie, Zurich
Hirschl and Adler Galleries, New York
Leonard Hutton Galleries, New York
John G. Johnson Collection, Philadelphia
Kunsthistorisches Museum, Vienna
Kunstmuseum, Basel
Los Angeles County Museum of Art
Marlborough Gallery, New York
The Mauritshuis, The Hague
Luis Mestre Fine Arts, New York
The Metropolitan Museum of Art, New York
Milwaukee Art Center
The Minneapolis Institute of Arts
Musée des Beaux-Arts, Arras
Musée des Beaux-Arts, Bordeaux
Musée des Beaux-Arts, Marseilles
Musée des Beaux-Arts, Villeneuve-sur-Lot
Musée Carnavalet, Paris
Musée Hyacinthe Rigaud, Perpignan
Musée Marmottan, Paris
Musée National d'Art Moderne, Paris
Musée National du Château de Fontainebleau
Musée National du Louvre, Paris
Musée du Petit Palais, Paris
Musée de Picardie, Amiens
Museo del Prado, Madrid
Museum of Art, Carnegie Institute, Pittsburgh
Museum of Fine Arts, Boston
The Museum of Modern Art, New York
National Collection of Fine Arts, Smithsonian Institution, Washington, D.C.
National Gallery of Art, Washington, D.C.

National Gallery of Victoria, Melbourne
Nationalmuseum, Stockholm
National Portrait Gallery, London
Newhouse Galleries, Inc., New York
North Carolina Museum of Art, Raleigh
Palazzo Comunale, Bologna
Palazzo Pitti, Florence
Pennsylvania Academy of the Fine Arts, Philadelphia
Pinacoteca Ambrosiana, Milan
Pinacoteca Nazionale, Bologna
Pioneer Museum and Haggin Galleries, Stockton, California
Radcliffe College, Cambridge
Rojtman Foundation, Inc., New York
San Francisco Museum of Modern Art
The Santa Barbara Museum of Art
H. Shickman Gallery, New York
Staatliche Museen Preussicher Kulturbesitz, Gemäldegalerie, West Berlin
Stanford University Museum of Art, Palo Alto
E. V. Thaw and Co., Inc., London
The Toledo Museum of Art
Victoria and Albert Museum, London
Virginia Museum of Fine Arts, Richmond
Wadsworth Atheneum, Hartford
Peter and Margaret Walch, Albuquerque, New Mexico
Walker Art Center, Minneapolis
Wallraf-Richartz Museum, Cologne
Washburn Gallery, New York
Whitney Museum of American Art, New York
Wildenstein & Company, New York
Williams College Museum of Art, Williamstown, Massachusetts
Yale University Art Gallery, New Haven

Acknowledgments

The idea for this exhibition emerged during the course of some informal after-dinner speeches following the symposium organized in connection with another exhibition, *Caravaggio and His Followers*, held at the Cleveland Museum of Art in 1971. Kenneth Donahue told the story of women artists who came to the Los Angeles County Museum of Art demanding gallery space and exhibition time for women equal to that being given to male artists. During the course of subsequent meetings, when the work of distinguished women artists of the past was discussed, they proposed a comprehensive exhibition devoted to Artemisia Gentileschi, a suggestion that Mr. Donahue greeted with enthusiasm. Athena Tacha, who was seated near me, urged me to respond. I rose and welcomed the suggestion too, but noted that there were many other neglected women artists worthy of exhibitions. The audience responded warmly to both our statements, and Mr. Donahue came over immediately to ask me if I would be interested in being a Guest Curator for such a show. Of course I said yes — how could I have said no — and in the course of our conversation the idea of a historical survey of major women artists emerged. I am therefore grateful first of all to Mr. Donahue for seeing the potential of this conception and for giving me the opportunity to participate in the planning of a major loan exhibition. As soon as it became a serious possibility, I urged Mr. Donahue and his coordinator of exhibitions, Jeanne D'Andrea, to invite Professor Linda Nochlin to be co-curator responsible for the nineteenth- and twentieth-century material. Professor Nochlin and they quickly agreed with this suggestion. Her participation was crucial for she is the only scholar who has been working for a long time on this subject. She has been generous with her time, her knowledge, and her hospitality on the numerous occasions that we have met to discuss our mutual progress and problems. I cannot imagine a better collaborator.

My initial search for women artists active before 1800 was greatly facilitated by a graduate research paper written in 1960 by Dr. Jane Rosenthal for Meyer Schapiro. This essay not only introduced me to the now familiar sociological aspects of our subject but had an impressive appendix of names taken from the standard encyclopedias. Ann Burns assisted me by organizing a card file of women artists and culling basic bibliographies. Stephanie Barron then took over as my first real research assistant, continuing work on the card file and bibliographies and also dealing with much of the huge correspondence necessary to acquire photographs and information about works not discussed since the nineteenth century. I would not have been able to meet any of the preliminary deadlines without her help. She was utterly reliable, generous with her time and, almost as important, constantly cheerful and enthusiastic about the project. She is now Associate Curator of Modern Art at the Los Angeles County Museum of Art.

Several grants made possible the research on which my share of the catalog is based. The Museum supported two essential research trips to Europe in the summers of 1974 and 1975, enabling me to visit museums in England, Holland, Belgium, France, Germany, Austria, and Italy to see works by women artists and to use libraries and photographic archives in Rome, Paris, and London. The award of a Ford Foundation Faculty Fellowship on Women in Society for the academic year 1975-76 enabled me to take a year's leave-of-absence from teaching in order to complete my research and write my part of the catalog. The Ford Foundation requires all its grant recipients to state that the ideas expressed in publications resulting from their support are those of the scholar concerned, which I am glad to do.

I turned to three scholars for special help with three of the artists in my section. Pamela Askew (Vassar College), Peter Walch (University of New Mexico, Albuquerque) and Sally Wells-Robertson agreed to write the biographies and catalog entries for Lucrina Fetti, Angelica Kauffman, and Marguerite Gérard respectively. Their work makes a substantial contribution to our knowledge of these artists; I am much indebted to them for their prompt and generous assistance.

The area of art historical knowledge encompassed by my share of this exhibition has taken me far from my usual scholarly concerns. I have thus found myself turning frequently to others for help. I hope that every significant piece of information passed on to me has been properly acknowledged in the text, but other experts gave help of different kinds, above all help in tracking down works of art in private collections. Eleanor Tufts (Southern Methodist University) was from the beginning a constant source of practical advice and of good company when our paths crossed in Europe. J. J. Wilson and Jan Petersen let me see the manuscript of their book, *Women Artists: Recognition and Reappraisal from the Early Middle Ages to the Twentieth Century* (Harper and Row, New York, 1976). At their suggestion, they avoided illustrating works that we hoped to include in the exhibition, thus making as many different works as possible by these artists available to students. The following people also all gave me vital assistance of one kind or another: Jacob Bean, Evelina Borea, Marco Chiarini, Andrew Ciechanowiecki, De Renne Coerr, Malcolm Cormack, Diane David, Howard Davis, M. Roy Fisher, Ann Gabhart, Dieter Graf, Phyllis Haddas, William V. Harris, John Hayes, Frima Fox Hofrichter, Stanley K. Jernow, Heidi Roehrig Kauffman, Milton Lewine, Thomas McCormick, Deborah Marrow McGuire, Anne-Marie Passez, Donald Posner, Jane Low Roberts, Marianne Roland Michel, Pierre Rosenberg, Susan F. Rossen, Felice Stampfle, Michael Stoughton, Marjorie M. Sutherland, Kathleen Weil-Harris, and Sally Wells-Robertson. I also wish to thank Mary Schmidt and the staff of the art history library at Columbia University, where much of the research was carried out, for their hospitality and helpfulness.

Finally I wish to express my debt to Jeanne D'Andrea, Coordinator of Exhibitions and Publications at the Los Angeles County Museum of Art. She has taken a close personal interest in the exhibition from the beginning. Her advice and assistance have always been available when needed. Since her judgments concerning the choice of works nearly always coincided with my own, the working relationship could not have been easier. Indeed, so closely involved has she been with this project that I do not know how she can have found time to do anything else. Publications Associate at the Museum, Nancy Grubb, read my manuscript more carefully than anyone ever has before and, in doing so, caught many errors and significantly improved the text. They will both deserve a large share of the credit if the exhibition is a success.

Ann Sutherland Harris

An exhibition as extensive as this one is necessarily a cooperative effort. It would be impossible to mention all those who helped make it possible. Among those who did are: the members of my seminars on women and art at Vassar College, Oberlin College, Stanford University, and, most recently, at the City University of New York Graduate Center; the many art historians who generously sent me material on women artists from all over this country and Europe; the many friends and colleagues, including a staunchly supportive group of women artists, who encouraged our efforts from the beginning; and feminist scholars in other disciplines who assisted with their specialized information and general enthusiasm.

Special thanks, of course, go to Kenneth Donahue, who had the courage and conviction to undertake this project. Jeanne D'Andrea, Coordinator of Exhibitions and Publications, and Nancy Grubb, Publications Associate, have been extraordinarily helpful, efficient, and understanding in carrying out the difficult task of getting it all together. My friend and collaborator, Ann Sutherland Harris, has been a pleasure to work with in every way: she is a model scholar and companion, and I have profited greatly from our numerous conversations, our trips to museums, and our general working out of intellectual and practical problems together. Much of the freshest and most illuminating material in the exhibition is due to her efforts. I have had a series of assistants who have worked with me in varying capacities during the long course of the preparation of the show, most notably Maria Walsh, Pamela Brown, Christina Houghtaling, Susan P. Casteras, and Rae Becker. All of them worked extremely hard, remained steady and cheerful under pressure, and helped immensely; to all of them, I am more grateful than I can say.

An exhibition as broad in its historical and geographical boundaries as this one obviously demands a good deal of assistance from experts in specialized fields, and among those who generously shared their ideas and expertise with me were: Lawrence Alloway and Karal Ann Marling, in the field of American art; Robert Rosenblum and Sally Wells-Robertson, as well as Vivian P. Cameron, in the area of French Neoclassicism; Albert Boime, who kindly furnished me with important information about the education, and the obstacles to the education, of women artists in the nineteenth century, as did Judith Stein and Nancy Mowll, the latter in her capacity as research assistant; Ingrid Hutton who was generous not only with paintings but also with information, as was Luis Mestre. Alison Hilton provided me with much-needed material about Russian art, as did John Bowlt; Ellen Oppler was helpful in the area of German art, especially Paula Modersohn-Becker. In the realm of English painting, special thanks are due to Richard Morphet and Alan Staley. For all his efforts on behalf of the exhibition and his support of the French side of our endeavors, Pierre Rosenberg deserves particular mention, as does Geneviève Lacambre, also of the Louvre, who kindly introduced me to Mme. Villers; a special word of thanks is due to Sylvie Béguin for her hospitality and encouragement.

A particular debt of gratitude is owed to those living artists, their work already part of history, who most graciously cooperated in this enterprise. Several of them I have had the added pleasure of meeting; some of them I am honored to number among my friends. They include Mme. Sonia Delaunay, Leonor Fini, Hannah Höch, Lee Krasner, Alice Neel, and Isabel Bishop.

The scholars, mainly doctoral candidates, who so generously lent their talents to the writing of biographies and entries for the catalog no doubt realize how important their contributions have been. For their participation, great thanks are due. These art historians include: Rae Becker, Margaret Betz, Hayden Herrera, Sarah W. Peters, and Judith Wolfe, all doctoral candidates at the City University of New York Graduate Center; Vivian P. Cameron, a member of the Art History Department of the Nova Scotia College of Art and Design and a doctoral candidate at Yale; Susan P. Casteras, also a doctoral candidate at Yale University; Lona Foote, a member of my seminar on women artists at the City University of New York Graduate Center; Professor Karal Ann Marling of Vassar College; Nancy Mowll, a doctoral candidate at the New York University Institute of Fine Arts; Lucy Oakley, a doctoral candidate at Columbia; and Professor Ellen Oppler of Syracuse University.

Still other people, both in this country and abroad, assisted in varied and important ways. They include: Eva Weis Bentzon, Liselotte Camp, Robert Coale, Ronny Cohen, Judith Cousins Di Meo, Patricia Egan, Albert Elsen, William Gerdts, Rosel Gollek, Paula Harper, Heide Grape-Albers, Jill Greenspan, Kurt Grunebaum, Grethe Holmen, Christine Huber, Fred Licht, Anna Lena Lindberg, Simon Lissim, Marianne Marcussen, Gloria Orenstein, Douglass Paschall, Griselda Pollock, Brenda Richardson, Cora Rosevear, Eberhard Roters, M. and Mme. Samoyault, Ann Sargent-Wooster, Gert Schiff, Meier Stein, Aimee Troyen, and Eleanor Tufts. Janis Ekdahl, the Vassar College art librarian, was extremely helpful, as was the Vassar College library staff as a whole.

On the domestic front, my housekeeper, Eleanor Lezon; my mother; my mother-in-law; and above all, my husband, Richard Pommer, were of inestimable assistance. All of them not only helped keep the ship afloat, but preserved morale under sometimes harrowing circumstances.

Linda Nochlin

Authors of Catalog Entries

Ann Sutherland Harris
Teerlinc to Ledoux, unless otherwise
indicated
Linda Nochlin
Charpentier to Tanning, unless otherwise
indicated
Pamela Askew
Fetti
Rae Becker
Beaux, Bishop, Bonheur, Exter biography
and *Grapes in a Vase,* Gonzalès, Höch,
Kollwitz, Krasner, Mayer, Morisot, Moss, Perry,
Valadon
Margaret Betz
Exter costume sketches, Goncharova,
Popova, Rozanova, Udaltsova
Vivian P. Cameron
Auzou, Benoist
Susan P. Casteras
Osborn biography, Peale, Siddal
Lona Foote
Mason
Hayden Herrera
Kahlo
Karal Ann Marling
Tait
Nancy Mowll
Cassatt
Lucy Oakley
Laurencin
Ellen Oppler
Modersohn-Becker
Sarah W. Peters
O'Keeffe
Peter Walch
Kauffman
Sally Wells-Robertson
Gérard
Judith Wolfe
Fini

Preface

Our intention in assembling these works by European and American women artists active from 1550 to 1950 is to make more widely known the achievements of some fine artists whose neglect can in part be attributed to their sex and to learn more about why and how women artists first emerged as rare exceptions in the sixteenth century and gradually became more numerous until they were a largely accepted part of the cultural scene. Neither of us believes that this catalog is the last word on the subject. On the contrary, we both look forward to reading the many articles, monographs, and critical responses that we hope this exhibition will generate.

Our researches have had to focus on potential exhibition material and while the biographies and introduction have allowed us to treat the subject more broadly, the exhibition format necessarily distorts the ideal picture we would wish to present. In fact it has proved extraordinarily difficult to assemble the group of works that we hoped to exhibit here. Many private and public owners are unwilling or unable to part with their possessions for as long as a year; others are reluctant to expose precious works to the risks entailed when an exhibition travels to as many different museums as this one will. In some cases works originally promised had to be withdrawn when their condition proved not good enough for the strain of extended transcontinental travel. In a few cases the remarks of museum directors revealed, we believe, a lack of support for the concept of the exhibition itself and hence an unwillingness to lend major works to the show. These difficulties have meant extensive rewriting of the catalog as promised loans were finally refused. More than a third of Harris' original text and more than half of Nochlin's had to be rewritten, in many cases at short notice close to the final publication deadlines. It will be obvious therefore that the selection of works is far from that originally envisaged. Visitors tempted to ask why a particularly fine work by Anguissola or Kauffman or Cassatt is not here should check with us to learn if it was in fact available before questioning our selections. We in turn would

like to express our gratitude to those lenders, public and private, who greeted the idea of the exhibition with enthusiasm, agreed to lend important works by the artists represented here, and provided much useful information about the works in question.

The inclusion or omission of certain artists from the exhibition was not in every case dictated by the availability of high quality loans. The exhibition could not possibly represent every woman who produced a painting or graphic work of quality between 1550 and 1950. In the case of works dating from 1800 on, problems both of choosing among a multitude of artists and of securing the most significant works by the artist often became acute. For those who still think that small scale characterizes the work of women painters, it might be interesting to know that in several cases — Rosa Bonheur's *Horse Fair* (New York, Metropolitan Museum) and Sonia Delaunay's *Electric Prisms* (Paris, Musée National d'Art Moderne), for instance — sheer size made it impractical to show these prime examples of their author's work in a traveling exhibition. In another case, that of Paula Modersohn-Becker, our exhibition followed the celebration of the 100th anniversary of the artist's birth in Germany, making it impossible to obtain any of the important paintings from collections in her native land. In some cases, one suspects, the rising tide of feminism and the resulting interest in women's art have made museums and collectors reluctant to lend work that might have been thought more expendable four or five years ago; in several cases, museums are organizing their own exhibitions of the work of women artists, including paintings by women in their own collections, thereby making them unavailable to us, even if for the best of reasons. At least one living woman painter was unwilling to have certain aspects of her work shown in the context of an exhibition of women artists, presumably because of the possible misinterpretation of her — admittedly controversial — imagery.

On the other hand, there have been artists and works that have been deliberately, although at times regretfully, excluded. It was decided quite early in the planning of the exhibition to limit it to painting, enriched by some drawing and graphic art, rather than to include the equally interesting areas of sculpture, photography, or crafts. This decision was made partly because the number of painters alone seemed to be growing unwieldy, and partly to maintain a kind of consistency in the subject under investigation; the situations faced by women working in other areas have their own problems, often different from those faced by women painters. The cut-off dates established — 1910 for the artist's date of birth and 1950 for the date of the work — were equally arbitrary but equally deliberate: no good show can do everything at once. Just as we decided that this was to be a show of women's painting, we decided it was to be a *historical* show of women's painting, focusing on the past rather than on the present. Here again our reasons were partly logistical but also theoretical. The issues raised by the art of the past are in many ways different from those raised by that of the present and demand a different approach. This in no way implies any lack of sympathy with the innovative work or the liberating struggle of women artists of today: on the contrary, it is to be hoped that this exhibition will provide an exhilarating sense of expanded perspective for contemporary women artists. And of course one can easily envision future exhibitions of women's art with very different chronological boundaries. The same might be said of national representation. Some countries are obviously better represented here than others: exhibitions already have and no doubt will again explore the work of Latin American women or Canadian ones. Certainly some admirable Scandinavian women painters, like Anna Ancher (1859-1935) of Denmark or Harriet Backer (1845-1932) of Norway, should find a place in future international exhibitions of women artists in this country, as should, for that matter, the work of French women like Nanine Vallain (dates unknown), English ones like Dame Laura Knight (1877-1970), Germans like Ida Kerkovius (1879-?), and, of course, the work of Oriental, African, and Near Eastern women.

All of this suggests not so much that the present exhibition is limited but rather that the possibilities for future ones exploring the work of women in the arts are unlimited: we look forward to future developments.

Ann Sutherland Harris
Linda Nochlin

Women Artists: 1550-1950

1.
Caterina van Hemessen
Self-Portrait, 1548
Oil on panel
12³/₁₆ x 9¹³/₁₆ in. (31 x 25 cm.)
Basel, Öffentliche Kunstsammlung

Introduction

. . . you must know how many women there are in Flanders and in France and even in Italy who paint in such a way that in Italy their pictures are held in high esteem. . . .

Francesco da Sangallo, 1546

In 1548 Caterina van Hemessen of Antwerp signed and dated two small portraits of herself (fig. 1) and of her sister (cat. no. 2). In 1554 Sofonisba Anguissola of Cremona signed a small self-portrait now in Vienna (fig. 2). These paintings mark the debut of the first women artists for whom sufficient work and documentation have been preserved for them to be perceived as artistic personalities. They are not the first women artists recorded in documents, nor the first for whom any works of art have survived, but the amount of evidence available for other women prior to the mid-sixteenth century is scanty and thus hard to evaluate. Why was the Renaissance almost over before any women artists achieved enough fame for their works to be treasured and thus preserved and for their accomplishments to be noted by contemporary biographers? Why did women artists not reach the historical status of Giotto, so to speak, until almost two hundred fifty years after he had become prominent? What made it possible for a small but growing number of women to have successful careers as painters after 1550 but prevented them from having any significant impact before that date?

The Status of European Women in the Middle Ages and Early Renaissance

To answer these questions we must first consider the general position of women in medieval and Renaissance society, although some reasons for the rarity of women artists are obvious enough. As long as women were regarded primarily as bearers and rearers of children, as keepers of the domestic hearth, and as subordinate inferiors of men, both custom and prejudice kept them from even considering careers outside the home. It is also extremely important to remember that the domestic duties of women in pre-capitalist society were extraordinarily varied and arduous and that only a few women married to wealthy men escaped this drudgery. Before the fourteenth century, most clothes were made at home, often from scratch, which meant that wool was carded, spun, and woven into cloth before the sewing could even begin. Women were also responsible for much of the food production. They not only labored in the fields with the men, they also raised vegetables, fruit, pigs, and chickens near the house; milked the cows and made the cheese and butter; cured the slaughtered pigs; preserved meat and fruit; baked the bread; and brewed the beer. Even if a

2.
Sofonisba Anguissola
Self-Portrait, 1554
Oil on panel
7¹¹⁄₁₆ x 4¹⁵⁄₁₆ in. (19.5 x 12.5 cm.)
Vienna, Kunsthistorisches Museum

woman lived in a well-supplied town rather than on a farm, marketing was a daily chore complicated by uneven distribution, seasonal shortages, even famine.

After the thirteenth century, the production of many basic supplies was gradually removed from the home and what had been female domestic industries (the surplus providing useful additional income) became male trades. Brewing beer, making bread, and weaving, all female professions in the thirteenth century, had become male crafts throughout Europe by the sixteenth century. Women remained active only in the carding and spinning of wool, silk, and linen (they dominated the production of silk); in related crafts like dressmaking, ribbon making, and embroidery; and in domestic service and nursing.

With these changes came others pertinent to our subject. The small shop in the master craftsman's home was replaced by a larger shop in a different location, making it impossible for his wife to participate in the business while supervising the house. Historians who have noticed these changes agree that in some respects women filled a greater variety of professional roles, had more responsibility, made a more important contribution to the economy, and had a higher legal status in the Middle Ages than they did during the Renaissance and later. As capitalism made the production of food, clothing, and other daily essentials more efficient it made the business owners wealthy, but at the same time the economic significance of women's traditional sphere of activity was reduced, and women were paid less for the same jobs outside the home than they had previously earned by working at home. These changes contributed to a rapid increase in prostitution as more and more women became unemployed.[1]

Reliable population figures are scarce for all European countries before the eighteenth century but it appears that women outnumbered men during the Middle Ages, a situation exaggerated by the celibate ecclesiastical professions, which employed far more men than women.[2] Women who could not marry or lacked the dowry required to become nuns had to find work. In addition to the jobs already mentioned, women earned their living in a great many ways before the fifteenth century when the craft guilds began to exclude them in order to protect the economic status of male masters and journeymen.[3] Women were wool merchants in fourteenth-century England; they were cutlers and leatherworkers, butchers and ironmongers, glovers and bookbinders, even goldsmiths.[4] One frequently cited source, Etienne Boileau's *Livre des métiers (Book of Crafts)*, written in Paris in the late thirteenth century, lists in a catalog of one hundred crafts five that were a female monopoly and many others in which women were active.[5] Therefore the scarcity of women artists before 1550 cannot be explained simply as part of a pattern excluding medieval women from all craft professions, although in the Renaissance this was certainly to be a significant factor. Nevertheless it is evident that women from the social strata that produced most male artists in the Middle Ages were typically employed in caring for their large families and complex households, even if some also assisted in their husbands' workshops.

In some cases, the wife of a craftsman was proficient enough to supervise the shop in her husband's absence and to take it over after his death. Medieval guild regulations, particularly those in northern Europe, often treated the wife as a business partner with the right to inherit and continue the business if her husband predeceased her. To my present knowledge, however, the wives of painters, sculptors, and goldsmiths rarely participated in a workshop or ran it after their husbands' deaths, for these were highly skilled crafts requiring a long apprenticeship and a very special degree of technical accomplishment for success.[6] Thus we must assume that this practice, while not unusual in less skilled trades, was rare in the professions that concern us.

1.
Alice Clark (*The Working Life of Women in the Seventeenth Century*, London, 1919, passim) documents these changes. See also Eileen Power, *Medieval Women*, ed. M. M. Postan, Cambridge, 1975, especially chap. 3, "The Working Woman in Town and Country," and F. Heer, *The Medieval World*, London, 1961; Mentor paperback edition, 322-23.
2.
Power, *Medieval Women*, 53-55, and Heer, *Medieval World*, 322-23. According to J. R. Hale (*Renaissance Europe, 1480-1520*, London, 1971, 135), the sexual imbalance in the population favored men by 1500.
3.
Clark, *Working Life of Women*, passim, and Power, *Medieval Women*, chap. 3.

4.
Power, *Medieval Women*, 61. E. Staley (*The Guilds of Florence*, London, 1906, 68, 214, 231-32, 235, 353, 373, and 442) publishes documentation for women working as belt makers, silk spinners, lace makers, embroiderers, linen manufacturers, cooks, and bakers. Only in the linen guild, however, did women have full privileges.
5.
Le livre des métiers d'Etienne Boileau, ed. René de Lespinasse and Francois Bonnardot, Paris, 1879.

6.
F. Baron (in *Bulletin archéologique du comité des traveaux historiques et scientifiques*, n.s. 4, 1968, 37-121) reports a few women sculptors in the tax records of several parishes in Paris in the late thirteenth and early fourteenth centuries. Marie de Sainte-Katherine, "la poindresse" (i.e., *peintresse* or painter), was active with her brothers in Lille between 1342 and 1347 (J. Houday, *Etudes artistiques — artistes inconnues des XIVe, XVe, et XVIIe siècles*, Paris, 1887, 4-5). While the lack of such extensive studies of the economic base of the artistic professions explains the rarity of such references, it is still doubtful that complete surveys of Paris, Florence, London, and Bruges, for example, would turn up more than a tiny percentage of professional women artists before 1500. A listing of 525 painters and illuminators recorded in Bologna in the thirteenth and fourteenth centuries includes only one female illuminator (Donzella, active in 1271) and three female scribes (Allegra,

Some late confirmation of how limited women's participation was in the artistic professions is provided by the regulations of a few guilds to which artists belonged. The *Statuti degli Orafi Senesi (Statutes of the Sienese Goldsmiths)* of 1361 simply never mentions women except in the regulation requiring attendance at the funerals of wives, daughters, and sisters of *capomaestri* as well as at the funerals of all their close male relatives.[7] By omitting all mention of women, a passage ruling that guild members "cannot elect themselves, nor their fathers, nor their brothers, nor their friends, nor their sons" as chief officers implies that mothers, sisters, and daughters were never considered qualified for such positions. The *Breve dell' Arte de' Maestri di Pietra Senesi (Brief of the Guild of Sienese Stone Masons)* of 1441 likewise makes no mention of women except in a similar funeral regulation, nor does the *Breve dell'Arte de' Pittori Senesi* of 1355.[8] Both the Sienese goldsmiths and painters had a rule forbidding guild members from working at home, which obviously made it difficult for wives to participate actively had they wished to do so. Only the regulations of the Compagnia di San Luca of Florence, a confraternity of painters founded in 1339, mention women in a context that suggests some were active as painters: dues were to be collected on the first Sunday of the month, when the men would pay three soldi, the women two.[9] According to Reynolds, however, no women's names occur in any of the documents concerning the subsequent history of the Compagnia, nor in those of its sixteenth-century successor, the Accademia del Disegno, founded in 1562.[10] When Artemisia Gentileschi joined the Accademia in 1616, she was apparently the first woman to do so.

Medieval Women Artists
There were a few artistic crafts in which women were extremely prominent before the fourteenth century and in which they continued to be active, although it may be significant that most of the known examples come from northern Europe rather than Italy, as is true of most of the evidence for female participation in the craft guilds. Women were predominant in the production of embroidered vestments and hangings for churches, as they were in tapestry workshops, a control derived from women's traditional association with the spinning and weaving of textiles. Women are also known to have illuminated manuscripts, an art generally restricted to nuns until the late thirteenth century, when lay women illuminators are recorded in Paris.[11]

Women who embroidered, like those involved in the manufacture of silk, were usually members of a higher social class than most male artists. Documents of the tenth and eleventh centuries show that these women were often aristocrats; several were queens. They represent in fact the luxurious summit of the textile industry in which women of all social classes were employed. The women who became nuns were also the daughters of noblemen or at least of merchants wealthy enough to provide them with the requisite dowries.

Unlike most members of medieval society and particularly unlike most women, the aristocratic embroiderer and the nun were usually literate; indeed some were extremely well educated. As members of a privileged class they had the leisure to perfect their education and their artistic talents because the laborious business of running a medieval household concerned them only in an administrative capacity. We will find that the exceptional class status of medieval women artists remains true to some extent of women artists in later periods as well.

Medieval Women Embroiderers
Most of the women who produced the great medieval church embroideries and secular tapestries remain anonymous. Moreover their contribution to the history of art is hard to evaluate now because so much more of their work has perished than of the products of

Flandina, and Uliana) (F. Filippini and G. Zucchini, *Miniatori e pittori a Bologna, documenti dei secoli XIII e XIV*, Florence, 1947, 5, 65, 68-69, and 228; the same authors published a sequel for the fifteenth century which mentions no women at all).
7.
G. Gaye, *Carteggio inedito d'artisti dei secoli XIV, XV, XVI . . .*, Florence, 1839-40, I, 1, 9, and 19.
8.
G. Milanesi, *Documenti per la storia dell'arte senese . . .*, Florence, 1854-56, I, 2ff, and 105ff. The painters' guild of Perugia passed regulations in 1366 that also ignore women completely (L. Manzoni, *Statuti e matricole dell'arte dei pittori delle città di Firenze, Perugia, Siena*, Rome, 1904, 172ff.), as do the rules of the Università dei pittori of Rome passed in 1478 (M. Missirini, *Memorie per servire alla storia della romana Accademia di S. Luca*, Rome, 1823, 5ff.).

9.
Baldinucci, IV, 368-70. Earlier the rules state that "tutti quelli che vengono o veranno a scriversi a questa Compagnia huomini o donne sieno chontriti e chonfessi de' loro peccati. . . ." (all those who enroll or will in the future enroll themselves in this Company men or women should be contrite and confess their sins. . . .)
10.
T. Reynolds, "The Accademia del Disegno in Florence, Its Formation and Early Years," doctoral dissertation, Columbia University, 1974, 24 and 45.
11.
See Baron, *Bulletin archéologique*, 37-121.

scriptoria and metal workshops. Nevertheless the available evidence does allow us to reconstruct a sketchy picture of women whose artistic achievements were recognized and highly valued.[12]

English women were especially famous for their skills, although the names of some German women embroiderers are also recorded. In 1066 a king's sheriff called Godric gave an estate in Buckinghamshire to a woman called Aelfgyth in return for teaching his daughter embroidery. Mabel, an embroiderer employed by Henry III of England, worked from 1239 to 1241 on a chasuble and altar frontal studded with pearls, for which she was paid £11, and was then commissioned to make for Westminster Abbey "a standard of ruby samite well embroidered with gold and with images of the Virgin and St. John." After she had retired to her home in Bury St. Edmunds a few years later, the king paid her the honor of a visit, when he also gave her "six measures of cloth agreeable to her and the fur of a rabbit for a robe."[13] Much earlier, during the reign of Knut (1016-1035), Ealdswith, granddaughter of Brihtnoth, ealdorman of Essex, had been given a village by the abbey of Ely so that she and her women could carry out their embroidery there. She must have been continuing a family tradition, for in 991 her grandmother had given the abbey a hanging embroidered with the story of her husband's heroic deeds and death during the Battle of Malden.[14] One scholar has suggested that knowledge of this embroidered history inspired Odo, bishop of Bayeux, to commission a similar hanging for the nave of Bayeux Cathedral.[15]

The story that Queen Matilda and her ladies made the famous Bayeux "Tapestry" (it is actually a wool embroidery on linen) goes back no earlier than 1803, but it is nevertheless highly probable that this medieval masterpiece was made around 1070 by teams of women following the instructions of a single designer. In producing such a complex political narrative for public display, the designer, whether Queen Matilda or someone else, must have consulted with Bishop Odo or with advisers from the court of William the Conquerer before making the cartoon and ordering the large quantities of linen and matched, dyed wools needed for such a huge undertaking.[16]

Among the noblewomen recorded as fine embroiderers is Queen Aelfflaed (909-916), wife of Edward the Elder, who may have supervised the production of the stole and maniple of St. Cuthbert still preserved in Durham Cathedral and one of the finest surviving examples of early medieval embroidery.[17] Queen Aelgiva, wife of Edward the Confessor, made an embroidered altar frontal in 1016 that was "so richly studded with gems, pearls and thread of gold that it was likened to gold mosaic."[18] Margaret (d. 1083), wife of Malcolm III of Scotland, was also famous for her embroidery, as was Gonorre, wife of Richard I, Duke of Normandy.[19] In other cases queens and noblewomen are recorded as giving magnificent vestments to their churches, but it is not always clear whether they were simply patrons or actually participated in the creation of the garments. Gisela (d. 1031), sister of Henry II and queen of Stephen I of Hungary, documented her responsibility for a gold and purple chasuble that became the coronation robe of Hungary with the following inscription: "Gisela the Queen worked this chasuble and gave it to the church of St. Mary in Civita Alba."[20] The superb vestments given to Bamberg Cathedral by Kunigunde, queen of Henry II, in the early eleventh century may also be the products of a court workshop supervised by the donor, but only tradition and what is known of embroidery production at that date support the attribution.[21]

Women did not completely monopolize the production of embroidery. Monks as well as nuns made church vestments, and by the thirteenth century men were increasingly common in secular workshops as well. Modern scholars note a general decline in the quality of embroidery being produced by the fourteenth century but without commenting on the grow-

12.
The documentary evidence for England has been collected by A. G. I. Christie in *English Medieval Embroidery*, Oxford, 1938 (appendix). See also M. Symonds and L. Preece, *Needlework through the Ages*, London, 1928, 164ff.
13.
R. Kent Lancaster, "Artists, Suppliers and Clerks: The Human Factors in the Art Patronage of King Henry III," *Journal of the Warburg and Courtauld Institutes*, XXXV, 1972, 83-85 (cited by Carr). Lancaster concluded that "except for those who became royal clerks and administrators, no other artist who served the King came so close to escaping the anonymity of the medieval craftsman as did Mabel."

14.
Christie, *English Medieval Embroidery*, appendix.
15.
G. W. Digby, "Technique and Production," in *The Bayeux Tapestry*, ed. F. Stenton, London, 1956; 2nd ed., 1967, 48.
16.
The best modern discussion is Digby's (ibid.).
17.
G. Baldwin Brown and A. G. I. Christie, "St. Cuthbert's Stole and Maniple at Durham," *Burlington Magazine*, XXIII, 1913, 3-17, 67-72.
18.
Thieme-Becker, I, 96, quoted by Carr.
19.
Digby, "Technique and Production," 45, and A. Levé, *La Tapisserie de Bayeux*, Paris, 1919, 8.
20.
Thieme-Becker, XIV, 197, quoted by Carr. P. Lasko (*Ars Sacra, 800-1200*, Pelican History of Art, Har-

mondsworth, 1972, 55 and 137) mentions Gisela only as a patron. The single piece of embroidery illustrated is a cope from the Bamberg treasure. Other general surveys of medieval art seem to pay little attention to embroidery, an oversight one cannot help but attribute to its low status as a female craft.
21.
Lasko, *Ars Sacra*, pl. 133.
22.
See Digby, "Technique and Production," 43ff., for a discussion of the documents that record the production of embroidered hangings in Troyes in 1425. The linen was prepared and finished by a seamstress called Pointsète but the painter and illuminator who made the cartoon were men.

ing role of men in this hitherto female craft. By the fifteenth century we hear of traveling teams of embroiderers, a situation incompatible with extensive female participation.[22]

The history of women as embroiderers, however significant in its own right, is relevant only as background to the later emergence of women as painters. Nevertheless, women's activity as artists throughout recorded history is obviously important even if the baskets, carpets, hangings, and pots that they made and still make in both primitive and advanced cultures have always had less status than the artistic productions of men.[23] This activity meant that many women had the opportunity to discover whether or not they had good manual coordination and a gift for visual expression, which at least increased the chances that some women with special talents might then attempt other kinds of artistic activity. The case of Rosalba Carriera comes to mind. Her mother made lace, a skill that Carriera herself probably also mastered. When the lace market declined, Rosalba turned to decorating the lids of snuff-boxes and from them to painting miniature portraits on ivory, an innovation welcomed by the local tourist trade and from which eventually developed an artistic career of international repute (see cat nos. 41, 42).

Medieval Women Illuminators

With regard to painting at the present time I know a woman called Anastaise who is so skillful and experienced in painting the borders of manuscripts and the backgrounds of stories that no one can cite a craftsman in the city of Paris, the center of the best illuminators on earth, who in these endeavors surpasses her in any way.

— Christine de Pisan, ca. 1405

The scale and intrinsic value of their lavish productions make medieval embroiderers more significant forerunners of the women painters of the late Renaissance and Baroque than the nuns who illuminated manuscripts. Nevertheless, the latter were their real predecessors as painters. Women illuminators can be traced from the tenth until the sixteenth century, and the medium of watercolor on vellum was adopted by at least two women painters of the seventeenth century, Giovanna Garzoni (see cat. nos. 19-21) and Maria Sibylla Merian (see cat. nos. 34, 35), though for quite different purposes. The number of individual women recorded by inscriptions, colophons, and other documentary evidence is nevertheless small compared with the thousands of male illuminators similarly documented.[24]

Two recent short publications summarize most of what is now known about medieval women illuminators, although more work could profitably be carried out in this area. Dorothy Miner's lecture, "Anastaise and Her Sisters," and Annemarie Weyl Carr's article, "Women as Artists in the Middle Ages," both give non-specialists a reliable account of the surviving evidence.[25] According to them, the first known illuminations signed by a woman occur in a Spanish Apocalypse manuscript preserved in Gerona Cathedral. The work, made in 970, is signed: "En Depintrix et Dei Aiutrix Frater Emeterius et Presbiter" (En [Ende] paintress and helper of God and Brother Emeterius Presbyter). The style of Ende's male assistant (it is significant that his name follows hers) is known from another signed manuscript, enabling scholars to isolate his share from hers and to attribute most of the magnificent illuminations in this book to Ende.[26] Miner calls it "one of the most splendid examples of Mozarabic book ornamentation and illustration" known.

Unfortunately the finest medieval illuminations are not usually signed; thus other women's signatures rarely lead us to works of this caliber. The nun Guda from Westphalia, who included her self-portrait in the Homiliary of St. Bartholemew that she decorated in the twelfth century, is "of only modest genius, her meagre stock of models serving as well for herself as for the Virgin Mary" (Carr). Claricia, a lay woman who must have been active in a convent scriptorium in Augsburg during the late twelfth century, has achieved a certain fame

23.
Munsterberg, chap. I. See also Kate McK. Elderkin, "The Contribution of Women to Ornament in Antiquity," *Classical Studies Presented to Edward Capps,* Princeton, 1936, 124-43. I owe this reference to Professor Anne Sheffield. A Hydria by the Leningrad Painter in the Torno Collection, Milan, shows a woman painting decoration on a vase in a pottery workshop (J. D. Beazley, *Attic Red-Figure Vase Painters,* Oxford, 1963, I, 571, no. 73, and II, 1659). It is illustrated in *A History of Technology,* ed. C. Singer et al., Oxford, 1957, pl. 16. This must be the oldest image of a woman artist at work.

24.
Fewer than twenty women are recorded in J. H. Bradley, *A Dictionary of Miniaturists, Illuminators, Calligraphers and Copyists,* New York, 1887-89, and in P. d'Ancona and E. Aeschlimann, *Dictionnaire des miniaturistes,* Milan, 1940, which each contain more than 2,000 names.

25.
Miner's delightful lecture was published as a pamphlet by the Walters Art Gallery, Baltimore, in 1974. Carr's excellent article appeared in *Feminist Art Journal,* V, no. I, Spring 1976, 5-9 and 26. Both should be consulted by anyone using the far less reliable texts on medieval women artists in Munsterburg (chap. 2) and in Wilson and Petersen, although both are useful sources of illustrations.

26.
See the discussion in Miner, 9ff., and Carr, 6.

since the page that she decorated with a portrait of herself swinging from the letter Q as its tail was included in the exhibition *Old Mistresses* in Baltimore, but this work, though charming, is not of exceptional quality (Miner, fig. 2).

The practice among the wealthy of sending their daughters to nunneries for their basic education, which often included copying manuscripts and, on occasion, decorating them as well, helped to establish the idea that knowing how to draw and paint was a suitable accomplishment for well-educated ladies. This idea was to receive far more influential support in the early sixteenth century from Baldassare Castiglione in *Il Cortegiano (Book of the Courtier)*.

The two most famous medieval illuminated manuscripts associated with women were not actually painted by the women concerned, nor do the manuscripts themselves survive. The original *Hortus deliciarum (Garden of Delights)* by Herrade of Landsberg (d. 1195) was destroyed in 1870 while the earliest copy of the *Scivias* by St. Hildegarde of Bingen (1098-1179) has been missing from the Stadtbibliothek in Wiesbaden since World War II. Both women were among the most remarkable and influential of the Middle Ages. St. Hildegarde, "the sibyl of the Rhine," was a mystic who began having visions at the age of forty-three. The *Scivias* records thirty-five of these visions described in a special language of the saint's own invention and provides each with an elaborate illustration. "She saw history as the progress of man, under the guidance of God, towards the Judgment Seat. After five epochs of world history had been run through, and after the gold of man's character had been refined in the fires of time, then would come the final reckoning and fulfillment. Each epoch had its animal emblem: the fiery hound for naked power, the golden lion for the misery of war, the cream-colored horse for frivolity and luxury, the black pig for lechery and schism, and finally the grey wolf for Anti-Christ. . . . When all these ages were done the cosmos would expire in a blaze of light. Before this could happen Empire and Church, Emperor and Pope, must fall, the kings of the West would become independent and heresy spread throughout every land."[27] The lost copy of the *Scivias* seems to have been made not in Hildegarde's own Benedictine convent at Bingen but in Trier, though such original and personal visions can only have been realized visually in close cooperation with their author and must reflect directly her own intellectual concepts and vivid imagination. Hildegarde's terrifying notions of the world's future made her famous throughout Europe and understandably popular with Protestant historians in the sixteenth century.

Herrade of Landsberg was the abbess of a convent in Hohenburg (Alsace) for whose members she composed her *Hortus deliciarum*, "the greatest of the medieval pictorial encyclopedias" (Carr), whose illustrations are now known only from nineteenth-century line drawings made before the manuscript was burned.[28] Some experts, however, date this manuscript a decade after Herrade's death and consider it to have been made in Strasbourg and not in Hohenburg by the nuns themselves, who nevertheless probably did produce the earliest copies of it, now all lost. In this compendium of medieval learning Herrade developed an old theme, the battle of Virtue and Vice, with such vivid imagery that she helped expand and popularize this subject in many later medieval decorative schemes.[29] Unlike most medieval manuscripts, in this the visual images precede and thus dominate the verbal images of the text. Pride is a powerful, confident woman riding sidesaddle on a lion skin draped over her prancing steed and supported by an army of elegant women soldiers in chain mail tunics.[30] In an illustration of the Ladder of Virtue, men and women, secular and church, fall off as they yield to the temptation of immediate worldly gratifications in the form of wealth and power. The Chariot of Luxury is shown overturning, tossing its occupants into thorny bushes. Thus, Herrade's basic moral message is always clear even if the full intricacies of her imagery can be unraveled only by those versed in medieval theology. It is unfortunate

27.
Heer (see note 1), 283; see also 320ff. for some strong feminist statements by Hildegarde. On the last manuscript, see Dom L. Baillet, "Les miniatures du Scivias de Saint Hildegarde conservé à la Bibliothèque de Wiesbaden," *Fondation E. Piot, Monuments et mémoires*, XIX, 1911, 49-149. Additional bibliography is given in Carr, note 18, to which can be added A. Katzenellenbogen, *Allegories of the Virtues and Vices in Medieval Art*, London, 1939.

28.
A. Straub and G. Keller, *Herrade de Landsberg, Hortus Deliciarum*, Strasbourg, 1879-99. For more recent literature and many plates, see G. Cames, *Allegories et symboles dans l'Hortus Deliciarum*, Leyden, 1971. An important new study of the *Hortus deliciarum* and all the extant copies of both text and illustrations will be published later this year.
29.
Katzenellenbogen, *Allegories*, passim.
30.
Ibid., fig. 8a; see also figs. 8b, 25, and 60, and Cames, *Allegories et symboles*, pl. XXXIII.

that neither the *Hortus deliciarum* nor the *Scivias* can be enjoyed in the full glory of their original color and gold but must be imagined from the dry black and white of mechanical reproduction.

Although manuscripts continued to be produced in monasteries until the sixteenth century, lay production was increasingly important from the thirteenth century onwards. Female participation is still found, though in no case can a particular illumination be associated with a particular women. Thus we know that Thomasse, "elumineresse et tavernière" (illuminator and innkeeper) was living in the rue au Foin in Paris in 1292 but we know of no work by her, nor of anything by the eight female illuminators working in Paris during the late thirteenth and early fourteenth centuries that have been traced by Françoise Baron.[31] Somewhat later, in 1454, twelve percent of the Bruges painters' guild (to which illuminators belonged) were women, rising to almost twenty-five percent in 1480.[32] Strangely enough, the records of the painters' guild in nearby Antwerp report only one woman in published records running from 1453 to 1500, and it is by no means clear that later references to widows of masters are proof of professional activity.[33]

Two French women illuminators of the late fourteenth and early fifteenth centuries were famous in their day, although they are now known only to specialists, namely Bourgot, daughter of Jean Le Noir, and Anastaise, who was employed by Christine de Pisan. Bourgot, "enlumineresse," is first recorded in a document of 1358 when she and her father were working for Yolande of Flanders. Later they were employed and paid substantially by Charles V, and subsequently by the Duc de Berry, all three patrons of exceptional stature. Millard Meiss has suggested that Jean Le Noir be identified with a follower of Jean Pucelle's whom he has dubbed The Passion Master.[34] Since father and daughter worked as a team, there must be work by Bourgot among the illuminations linked with Le Noir, although it may never be possible to separate their hands.[35]

Anastaise will probably never be identified with a particular illumination either. She was a favorite of the early feminist writer Christine de Pisan, who converses with Reason about the famous women artists of antiquity in her book *Cité des Dames,* written around 1405. Then, after describing Anastaise in the words quoted at the beginning of this section, Christine adds, "This I know by my own experience, for she has produced some things for me which are held to be outstanding among the ornamental borders of the great masters."[36] As Carr points out, Anastaise was clearly employed in a subordinate role if she was not allowed to paint "yhistoires" but only their "champaigns" and borders. It is possible that such a second-ary role was the lot of other women active in this profession. The citation is nevertheless important as the first extensive tribute to a woman artist in a literary text since antiquity. Not until Guicciardini visited Flanders a hundred years later would the next one appear.

Were the medieval women artists we have been discussing known to their Renaissance successors? Did the former serve as role models, to use a modern term for an old idea, to any extent for the latter? On the whole, it seems unlikely. The only women artists of the past given any publicity during the Renaissance were the legendary women of antiquity recorded in Pliny's *Naturalis Historia* (XXXV, 147) and included by Giovanni Boccaccio in his *De claris mulieribus (Of Famous Women),* written in the late fourteenth century. Judging from the number of women in the Bruges painters' guild, a strong tradition of female participation explains the emergence there of successful women miniaturists like Levina Teerlinc (see cat. no. 1) in the sixteenth century better than the example of any one predecessor. Nonetheless, in literate court circles like that for which Teerlinc's father worked, artists may have known about Anastaise and her ancient forerunners, and the reputation of someone like Bourgot might have been part of the local oral tradition. In France, despite occasional

31.
See note 6. Baron is cited by Miner, 22.
32.
The figures are quoted by Miner, 24, from unpub-lished research by Professor Douglas Farquar.

33.
See Rombouts and Lerius, 20, and F. J. van den Branden, *Geschiedenis der Antwerpsche Schilder-school,* Antwerp, 1883.
34.
Millard Meiss, *French Painting in the Time of Jean de Berry: The Late 14th Century and the Patronage of the Duke,* London, 1967, 168.
35.
Miner, 18-19.
36.
The translation comes from Millard Meiss, *The Lim-bourg Brothers and Their Contemporaries,* New York, 1974, 13-14. The meaning of the word *champaigns* has been debated; some scholars translate it as "landscapes," others merely "backgrounds."

references to women illuminators and even sculptors in fourteenth-century Paris and despite the career of Christine de Pisan, Anastaise is the only woman artist active in the fifteenth century recorded in published sources to my knowledge. There are only three more women recorded in sixteenth-century France, two of whom worked late enough to enter the next century and a third who may be pure invention.[37] In Italy, on the other hand, where the artists' guild regulations imply that women were hardly ever active, some twenty-five women artists are recorded for the fifteenth and sixteenth centuries and for several of these a considerable number of works survive. Italy in fact dominates the history of women painters until the eighteenth century, when France finally overtakes both Italy and the Low Countries as the location of the largest number of recorded women artists.[38]

The Emergence of Women Artists in Renaissance Italy

Various factors explain Italy's prominence in the history of women artists from the fifteenth to the seventeenth century. The Reformation did not sweep away convents in the Catholic South as in the Protestant North, although their numbers and importance declined.[39] Many of the women artists recorded in Italy in the fifteenth and sixteenth centuries were nuns, although none for whom any work survives were very gifted. Copying and decorating texts was by then a commonplace activity, a basic skill expected of most nuns except those devoted to charitable activities such as nursing the sick and dying.[40] In fact the art of illumination practiced in monasteries was in decline, with much of the best work now produced in secular workshops for secular patrons. The nuns, living in a closed world with no strong internal tradition to stimulate them to a high level of competence, let alone to inspire them to new achievements, did not work in an environment likely to produce innovative art.

The best documented Italian nun-artist of the fifteenth century, Caterina dei Vigri (1413-1463), exemplifies many of the general observations just made. She was a well-born Bolognese woman who became a Franciscan nun in Ferrara in the late 1420s and moved to Bologna in 1456 as the superior of a new convent established beside the church of Corpus Domini.[41] Well educated by contemporary standards, she had been taught to play musical instruments and to draw as well as to read and write Latin when she was growing up at the court of Ferrara. Her true profession was not as an artist, however, but as a devoted member of her order; she had visions, performed miracles, and was thought to be the cause of others after her death. She was sanctified in 1703. It is undoubtedly because of her reputation as a saint that her modest artistic efforts have been preserved along with other relics of her life in a room attached to the church where she spent her last years. The style of her work can only be described as naive, provincial, and archaic, for she was essentially a dilettante whose development was not helped by her decision to spend her life in *clausura*.

A Carmelite nun one would like to know more about was Paolo Uccello's daughter Antonia (1446-1491). Vasari tells us that he had "una figliola che sapeva disegnare" (a daughter who knew how to draw), but the only supporting evidence known at present comes from her death certificate, where she is called "pittoressa."[42] The only other fifteenth-century Italian woman artist for whom we have any evidence is Suor Barbara Ragnoni, who signed an *Adoration of the Shepherds* now kept in the Pinacoteca of Siena.[43] Ragnoni was more aware of current developments than Vigri, whose work seems almost a century out of date. The *Adoration* is a charming example of the Sienese school in the late quattrocento when the local tradition was no longer as inventive as it had been in the previous century.

Vasari devotes several paragraphs to the career of a sixteenth-century nun, Suor Plautilla Nelli (1523-1587/88), several of whose works could be traced in and around Florence in the early part of this century but which have disappeared from the modern literature. Vasari reported — and she was alive when he wrote — that she had begun as a miniature painter

37.
A number of splendid Limoges enamels signed by Suzanne de Court prove the existence of one outstanding female master of this craft. There are examples in the Walters Art Gallery, Baltimore; the Frick Collection, New York; and the Metropolitan Museum, New York, including one superb dish in the Lehman Collection, as well as in several European collections (Thieme-Becker, s.v.). She was working at the end of the sixteenth century. Marguerite Bahuche, the wife of Jacob Bunel (1558-1614), is documented working as a portrait painter for the court of Fontainebleau with her husband. On his death, she was given his apartment in the Louvre (E. Giraudet, *Les artistes tourangeaux*, Tours, 1885, 11-12, and J. Guiffrey, *Artistes parisiens du XVIe et du XVIIe siècles*, Paris, 1915, 81ff.). In addition there is the mysterious Isabelle Quattrepomme, who may have been an engraver in Rouen in 1521 (Bénézit, s.v.).

38.
My own card file, which does not pretend to be exhaustively complete since my research had to focus on artists for whom known works were traceable, records roughly 500 women artists active between 1400 and 1800. Of these, 130 are Italian, 212 are French, 67 are Dutch or Flemish, 41 are German, 25 are English, 17 are Spanish, 5 are Swiss, and 3 are Scandinavian. The breakdown by centuries is 15th — 6; 16th — 35; 17th — 209; 18th — 290.

39.
The Council of Trent placed a number of restrictions on convents so that their numbers and influence declined even in Italy (J. Morris, *The Lady Was a Bishop*, New York, 1973, 151ff.).

40.
Creighton Gilbert has drawn my attention to references in the writings of Giovanni Dominici to nuns illuminating texts as a normal chore (*Lettere spirituali*, Fribourg, 1969, letter 35, 174f., December 16, 1402; see also 110, 113, and 128f.). These nuns at the convent of Corpus Domini in Venice were praised by Dominici for their "nobile ingegno nello scrivere e cantare e ancora miniare, che fatto avete del maestro men che discepolo" (noble gifts as writers, singers, and miniaturists, which you exercise rather as masters than as pupils).

41.
Ragg (11ff., especially 150-57) provides a discursive account in which the few facts are discreetly buried. Rightly she devotes little space to Vigri's artistic activities, however odd this seems in a book devoted to the women artists of Bologna. Ragg was puzzled by a *St. Ursula* in the Academy, Venice, inscribed

and copyist but gradually advanced to the production of altarpieces for her own convent, St. Catherine of Siena in Florence, and for outside patrons. The main influence on her work was Fra Bartolommeo, whose style she learned from his pupil, Fra Paolino da Pistoia (ca. 1490-1547). Bartolommeo's restrained classicism was out-of-date by the mid-sixteenth century when she painted her *Last Supper,* an extremely competent essay in his style. As Vasari remarked, her work shows "that she would have done marvellous things if, as men do, she had been able to study and learn to draw and work after living models." She certainly seems to have been the most gifted of the artist-nuns recorded in Italy.[44]

All that the evidence of painter-nuns allows us to conclude is that while taking the veil made it possible for some women to paint, the isolation of the convent combined with the lack of proper training and competitive standards meant that genuine artistic abilities could not flourish there. Further evidence that this was the case comes from the women who did finally emerge as serious, competent painters in sixteenth-century Italy. They were not nuns. Sofonisba Anguissola (see cat. no. 3) was the daughter of a provincial nobleman and Lavinia Fontana (see cat. nos. 5-7) was the daughter of a provincial painter. Different social forces were at work here and we must consider them before examining the case histories of these and other women painters of that period.

The Status and Education of Women in Renaissance Italy

At six or seven put [your son] to learn to read, and then set him either to study or to that craft he most enjoys. If the child be a girl she should be put to sew and not to read, for it is not good that a woman should know how to read, unless you wish her to become a nun.
                                                                    — Paolo da Certaldo, ca. 1320

In Italy during the Renaissance a revolutionary change occurred in artists' images of themselves in relation to society. They struggled to give the status and rewards of an intellectual profession to what had hitherto been classified and rewarded as a craft.[45] This change should have made it even more difficult for women to become artists. A seven-year apprenticeship in a master's shop no longer sufficed. Artists were expected to have a liberal arts education with special emphasis on mathematics and the laws of perspective and to have considerable knowledge of ancient art, both from literary texts and from the objects themselves, which were best seen in Rome. This basic educational program outlined by L. B. Alberti in *Della pittura* was rapidly expanded in the late fifteenth and early sixteenth centuries. It became accepted that the training of every ambitious, serious artist would include the study of the human body, at first from corpses and clothed models but increasingly from the nude male model, and travel to the major art centers to study the achievements of one's rivals and of the best artists of the previous generation or two. Such a level of education and freedom of movement were hardly possible for women in the fifteenth and sixteenth centuries, except occasionally for a member of an aristocratic household whose future would be considered only in terms of the desirable political consequences of her marriage and not of her potential artistic or intellectual attainment. Needless to say, no proper lady could admit to firsthand knowledge of the appearance of the naked male body.

A glance at the considerable literature that concerns itself with the role of women in society — for the most part, women of the upper social classes — will make clear the crippling limitations placed on the development of any artistic or intellectual gifts with which a woman might be endowed. If women of the less privileged social classes, from which most male artists came, had more responsibilities and more freedom of movement, they were always handicapped by the physical strains and dangers of constant childbearing and by the endless hard labor required to provide their families with the basic necessities of life.

Not surprisingly, the ideal woman described in Renaissance treatises corresponds in many

---

"CATTERINA VIGRI F BOLOGNA 1456," whose style differs considerably from her works preserved in Corpus Domini. As she suspected, the signature is a later addition. Current scholarly opinion attributes this work to the circle of Giovanni Bellini (S. Moschoni Marconi, *Gallerie dell' Accademia di Venezia, XV Secolo,* Rome, 1955, 88-89, no. 84).
42.
Vasari, II, 217. Robert Simon drew this document to my attention.
43.
Repr. by Sparrow, 35. Onorata Rodiani, the fifteenth-century fresco-painting *condottiere (condottrice?)* reported by Zaist (I, 29-30, see S. Anguissola bibliography), who is supposed to have worked for Marchese Gabrino Fondolo, the tyrant of Cremona (he was beheaded in 1425), until a courtier tried to rape her, is so far only an extraordinary legend for which

no documentation has been traced. She is supposed to have spent more of her life as a soldier than as a painter, however.
44.
Vasari, V, 79-80. De Dominici has a similar comment about Suor Luisa Capomazza (III, 93). The *Last Supper* of Nelli was made for the refectory of S. Maria Novella. Alinari (31081) photographed it attached to a wall of the Cappella degli Spagnoli. Its present location is not known. Other works of hers listed by Milanesi and Thieme-Becker, for example in the Academy, do not appear in any published catalogs that I consulted.

Tommasina del Fiesco (1448-1534), who became a nun when she was widowed, is recorded as a painter and embroiderer by Soprani (I, 25). St. Catherine de' Pazzi (1566-1607) is also said to have been a painter.

Three nun-painters active in Lucca in the sixteenth and seventeenth centuries are reported by T. Trenta ("Dissertazioni sullo stato dell'architettura, pittura e arti figurative in rilievo in Lucca ne' bassi tempi," in *Memorie e documenti per servire all' istoria del Ducato di Lucca,* VIII, Lucca, 1818, 122-23), along with three women artists who were not nuns. For this reference too I must thank Robert Simon. For one more nun painter, see note 100 below.
45.
R. and M. Wittkower, *Born under Saturn,* New York, 1963, 14ff. See also A. Martindale, *The Rise of the Artist in the Middle Ages and Early Renaissance,* New York, 1972.

respects to the typical female saint, who was nearly always both beautiful and chaste. For many, the only achievement had been to defend their chastity against all pagan assaults, and sometimes from Christian suitors as well. If they had lost their virginity, then they rejected their lascivious pasts and moved to caves where they ended their lives in solitary contemplation. The Church's ideal woman personified the Christian virtue of total self-abnegation combined with the complete rejection of human sexuality. Thus many medieval instructions for the education of women advise against teaching them to read at all lest they discover corrupting texts like Ovid's *Ars amoris (Art of Love)*. Piety, chastity, and obedience to one's husband were considered the goals for all women.[46]

Leon Battista Alberti, a life-long bachelor, put forward a similar model woman in his popular treatise *Della famiglia*. "A woman worthy of praise must show first of all in her conduct modesty and purity." Passivity was not only an ideal; it was, according to Alberti, woman's very nature. "Women . . . are almost all . . . soft, slow and therefore far more useful when they sit still and watch over things." Alberti also wished her to be physically attractive, chaste prior to marriage, and faithful to her husband ever afterwards. And while he mentions many qualities desirable in the woman who is to become "a perpetual mate" — good birth, a decent dowry, the ability to bear sons — he does not mention at all what degree of education he would recommend for his ideal life companion.[47]

Most women in the fifteenth century were illiterate (and so, though to a lesser extent, were most of the male populace). Only girls destined to be nuns were regularly taught to read and write; others, as we noted in the quotation from Paolo da Certaldo, were actively discouraged from such pursuits. The views of San Bernardino a century later are no different. "Make your daughter into a little drudge . . . oh, but there is a maid servant. Make her work . . . to keep her busy . . . [if you do], she won't wait at the windows or be giddy-pated."[48] Francesco Datini (d. 1410), the merchant of Prato whose biography by Iris Origo is a rich source of information about the place of women in early Renaissance society, would have agreed with Paolo da Certaldo too. Datini was upset when his wife, then in her thirties, was taught to read and write by a family friend. "Provide for your household in such a fashion," he wrote her, "as to do you honor and do not pay so much attention to reading that you do other things ill. Order all other matters so that they do well, and then you may read as much as you please."[49] The only women exempted from the rule of minimal literacy were those whose high rank meant that they might one day inherit political power.[50] It was customs and attitudes such as these that provoked Christine de Pisan to exclaim, "Hélas Dieux, pourquoi ne me faiz tu naistre au monde en masculin sexe!"[51]

Most Renaissance men who gave advice to women were patronizingly confident of the inferiority of the female sex and put forward as positive qualities in women those personality traits we now recognize as insuperable barriers to individual achievement. However, a few glimmerings of a more positive attitude can be found in the literature devoted to famous men and women of the past, stories intended to inspire the reader with a desire to emulate past greatness and to avoid past failings. Needless to say, there are more noble examples offered to men than to women and the latter are rarely concerned with professional achievement rather than with good character. Giovanni Boccaccio's collection, *De claris mulieribus*, written around 1370, offered women one hundred four examples drawn mainly from ancient sources but including Eve and a few medieval women rulers as well.[52] Semiramis, Queen of the Assyrians, is praised for proving "that in order to govern it is not necessary to be a man but to have courage." She was not perfect, however, for "this unhappy woman, burning with carnal desire, gave herself to many men," including her own son. Iole reduced the powerful Hercules to the condition of a foolish woman, wearing "girlish garlands and the Maeonian headdress." "We men must therefore be vigilant and arm our hearts

---

46.
Power (see note 1), 80. Confirmation for much of what follows can also be found in Ruth Kelso's splendid study, *Doctrine for the Lady of the Renaissance*, Urbana, 1956, especially chaps. 2-4 and 7. Her appendix (327-424) lists 891 books on women published between 1400 and 1600.
47.
The Family in Renaissance Florence, a translation by Renée Neu Watkins of *I libri tre della famiglia*, Columbia, S.C., 1969, 115ff. and 207ff. Much of the section on the training of a wife reflects the misogyny of its Greek source, Xenophon's *Oeconomicus*.
48.
Both Paolo da Certaldo and St. Bernard are quoted by J. B. Ross in "The Middle-Class Child in Urban Italy, Fourteenth to Early Sixteenth Century," in *The History of Childhood*, ed. L. de Mause, New York, 1975, 207ff. He gives other relevant quotations. See also Sachs, 14ff.

49.
Iris Origo, *The Merchant of Prato*, London, 1957; Penguin edition, 1963, 213-14.
50.
The two kinds of education are exemplified by Georges de la Tour's *Education of the Virgin* (New York, Frick Collection) and Rubens' *Education of Marie de' Medici* (Paris, Louvre).
51.
"Alas, God, why was I not born into this world a member of the masculine sex!" Quoted by Meiss (see note 36), 433. See also 8-15 on Christine de Pisan.

52.
G. Boccaccio, *Concerning Famous Women*, trans. and ed. G.A. Guarino, New Brunswick, 1973, 5, 6, 45, 80, 131, and 144-45 for all the quotations that follow. The Latin text was first printed in the 1470s (Strasbourg, Louvain). A French translation came out in 1493; others followed in 1538 and 1551. The first Italian edition was published in Venice in 1506; others appeared in 1545, 1547, and 1596.
53.
L. B. Alberti, *On Painting*, trans. and ed. J.R. Spencer, New Haven, 1956, 66. "It was also an honor among women [in ancient Greece] to know how to paint"; he then cites the example of Marcia.

with great strength, so that we are not overcome against our wishes" and are not dominated by desires of the flesh. Camilla, queen of the Volscians, who is portrayed as a virginal Amazon, died in battle defending Turnus. She becomes the pretext for a lecture "to the girls of our time:" "I wish that from her example they would learn not to listen to shameful words, to keep silent, to veil their eyes with seriousness, be well-mannered, act with modesty, and avoid idleness, feasting, elegance, dancing and the company of young men. Let young women also know that to desire everything pleasurable and to do everything possible is not in accord with chastity, so that, by becoming more discreet in the flower of praiseworthy virginity, they may attain with maturity to holy matrimony under the direction of their elders."

Buried in all this sermonizing are the brief lives of three women painters of antiquity: Thamyris, Irene, and Marcia. Thamyris (Timarete in Pliny, Boccaccio's source), the daughter of the painter Micon, "scorned the duties of women and practised her father's art." She was known for a picture of Diana kept at Ephesus, where it was preserved for many years. "She should be praised even more if we consider the spindles and baskets of other women." To Irene, also the daughter of a painter, Boccaccio attributes not only a picture of a girl at Eleusis but, confusing Pliny's text, several works by other women artists. "I thought," continues Boccaccio, "that these achievements were worthy of some praise, for art is very much alien to the mind of woman, and these things cannot be accomplished without a great deal of talent, which in women is usually very scarce." Finally Boccaccio mentions Marcia, daughter of Varro (she was actually Iaia of Cyzicus, who according to Pliny lived in the time of Varro's youth, around 90 B.C.), who remained a virgin all her life. He praises her because, "scorning womanly occupations, she gave herself up completely to the study of painting and sculpture so that she would not languish in idleness." He continues to say that she carved figures in ivory as well as painting on it, and also painted her self-portrait by using a mirror. Surpassing Sopolis and Dionysius, the most famous painters of her day, she not only worked faster than they did, but also fetched higher prices. Finally Boccaccio speculates about her tendency to paint women rather than men. "I think that her chaste modesty was the cause of this, for in antiquity figures were for the greater part represented nude or half nude, and it seemed to her necessary either to make men imperfect, or, by making them perfect, forget maidenly modesty. To avoid both these things, it seemed better to her to abstain from both."

It would be hard to exaggerate the importance for the subsequent history of women artists of Pliny's brief paragraph about the women artists of antiquity and Boccaccio's elaborations on it. Most artists' biographers from Vasari onwards mention Timarete, Irene, and Iaia at some point before turning to the lives of their Renaissance and Baroque successors. Alberti even remembers them in passing in *Della pittura*[53] and they turn up in the endless cinquecento debates about the superiority of painting versus sculpture.[54] Baldinucci, aware of the *topos*, declares that he will not provide this obligatory preamble to his life of Sofonisba Anguissola because he is certain that his readers are overly familiar with it.[55] Malvasia, by contrast, gives the most extended account, buttressed with many other examples of notable achievements by women in a passage that has an almost feminist fervor.[56]

In the visual arts ancient precedent had the authority, one can say, of Holy Writ: whatever ancient artists had done was good. Those Renaissance scholars who believed that a new golden age had dawned in the visual arts, that Leonardo, Raphael, and Michelangelo equaled and even surpassed the ancients, were not averse therefore to the idea that this new creative spirit, which they imagined as floating in the air (and of course flourishing particularly in the salubrious atmosphere of Florence, Bologna, Naples, or wherever the writer happened to live), should occasionally infect a woman, as it had in antiquity. It was understood that this was an exception to the general rule that women were not destined by God to become artists, or anything

54.
Paolo Pino's *Dialogo di pittura,* Venice, 1548, in *Trattati d'arte del cinquecento,* ed. P. Barocchi, Bari, 1960-62, I, 109. Benedetto Varchi (ibid., 50) and Francesco da Sangallo (ibid., 77) cite the absence of women sculptors as proof of the greater difficulty and hence superiority of sculpture over painting, an observation I owe to Virginia Bush. Sangallo's statement, partially quoted at the beginning of this essay, continues, "but no where and in no place do you ever find that a woman worked in marble." Obviously he had not heard of Properzia de' Rossi.

55.
Baldinucci, VIII, 207ff. He condemns the practice as patronizing. ". . . but I know not only that it is neither impossible nor very novel that the well-trained genius of a woman can become marvellous in every subject, every so often when it is removed from those humble duties to which for most part that sex is condemned." He goes on to quote Plato on the unused left hand. Vasari includes them in the letter on ancient artists provided for the 1568 edition of the lives by G. B. Adriani (I, 50). Baglione (144) mentions them in his life of Lavinia Fontana (see Fontana bibliography). F. Pacheco (*El arte de la pintura,* Seville, 1649; edition cited edited by F. J. Sánchez Cantón, Madrid, 1956, I, 48) introduces them before his brief discussion of Sofonisba Anguissola, Lavinia Fontana, and Artemisia Gentileschi. De Dominici (II, 327) cites them in his life of Mariangiola Criscuola. P.A. Orlandi's *Abecedario*

pittorico (Bologna, 1704, many later editions) increases the number of women artists in antiquity by misreading some of the men's names in Pliny (e.g., Arcesilea for Arcesilas and Cresilla for Cresilas).
56.
Malvasia, II, 389. Sirani is compared favorably with all her ancient female predecessors. She is said, for example, to have painted faster than Lala Cicizena (Iaia of Cyzicus). Lucio Faberio includes a tribute to Lavinia Fontana in his funeral oration for Agostino Carracci (ibid., I, 307) where she too is compared to the three ancient women painters named by Boccaccio.

else requiring "ingegno" and "giudizio," but the appearance of a talented woman in their midst was always welcomed as evidence of the superabundant creative genius to be found in the city where this phenomenal woman lived. Strangely enough, it was easier for a woman to conform to this new conception of the artist as a divinely inspired genius than it had been for her to emerge from the conservative, traditional medieval workshop.[57]

While artists were winning new status in Renaissance society, there was an important shift in the attitudes toward the education of women that had prevailed in the fourteenth and fifteenth centuries. Early in the sixteenth century at the court of Federigo da Montefeltro in Urbino, Baldassare Castiglione wrote his *Il Cortegiano,* which was first published in 1528. Before the century was out, over thirty editions had been printed in Italy, France, England, and Spain. Castiglione devoted an entire chapter to the ideal female member of an aristocratic household such as Elisabetta Gonzaga, Duchess of Urbino, for whose entertainment and enlightenment the conversations in the book were supposedly held. Almost all the attributes and accomplishments necessary to the male courtier were also declared appropriate to the female, including a high level of educational attainment and the ability to paint, play musical instruments and sing, write poetry, and make witty, stimulating conversation.[58] These ideas were not in themselves new. They can be found much earlier in medieval treatises on courtly behavior,[59] but the invention of printing in the meantime meant that a far wider audience had access to Castiglione's ideas of ideal courtly behavior than could ever have learned about these customs in the Middle Ages. *Il Cortegiano* was enormously popular; its influence on social behavior and educational theory extended far beyond the Renaissance courts, where it originated, to all lesser noble families and to all successful merchants wealthy enough to emulate that way of life. Thus Castiglione helped to emancipate women from the bondage of illiteracy and minimal education, extending the privileges and opportunities of a few women to those of a much wider social stratum. He made it proper, even praiseworthy, for women to engage in a wide range of artistic, musical, and literary pursuits, and if most women only dabbled as amateurs and formal education for women remained poor, there is still no shortage after the mid-sixteenth century of references to women who were regarded by their contemporaries as exceptionally fine artists, musicians, and writers.[60]

Some proof of the influence that Castiglione's ideas had on the women who became painters can be found not only in their family origins but also and more significantly in the ways they were presented to the world by themselves and their biographers. Sofonisba Anguissola, the eldest daughter of a provincial nobleman, fits neatly into the category of daughters of minor aristocrats whose educational horizons were expanded by Castiglione. She and her sisters were all taught to play musical instruments and to read Latin as well as to paint. She signed her works with Latin inscriptions that are always more elaborate than the simple "fecit" formula, and she twice painted herself playing a keyboard instrument (cat. no. 3). Thus she is a good example of the new female courtier, raised outside that closed society but well prepared nevertheless for her life at the court of Philip II in Madrid, where she became a lady-in-waiting to Queen Elizabeth of Valois. Lavinia Fontana could make no claims to noble birth, but she nevertheless presented herself as a well-educated lady in her self-portrait in the Accademia di San Luca in Rome, elegantly dressed and playing the virginals while a servant brings her more music.[61] Caterina van Hemessen painted her sister in a similar guise (cat. no. 2). Indeed a number of portraits of smartly dressed women seated at keyboard instruments can be cited from the late sixteenth century onwards, proof of the spread throughout Europe of more positive educational standards for women. The portrait tradition of showing a woman with her gaze modestly averted and holding a prayer book begins to give way to a variety of more assertive, more individual portrayals of female sitters, an important subject in itself which deserves more attention than it has so far received in the literature.[62]

57.
How far this identification might go is shown by the medal dedicated to Lavinia Fontana, the verso of which shows her seated at an easel, her hair flying in the wind as she works in a fit of creative energy. Galli, fig. 16 (see Fontana bibliography); see also Tufts, 1974, 34 and fig. 14b.
58.
Baldesar [sic] Castiglione, *The Book of the Courtier,* trans. C. S. Singleton, New York, 1959, 201ff., especially 210. There were a few limitations suggested nevertheless. Tennis, fencing, wrestling, and playing loud instruments like trumpets and drums were not thought suitable for women. Some thoroughly traditional attributes are also listed such as grace and beauty (more important for the female than the male courtier) and the ability to manage her husband's estate and household, something on which Alberti had laid great stress. Book III is in fact a good survey of the arguments then current for and

against women, many of which are still popular.
59.
Power (see note 1), 77-78.
60.
This change of climate is also acknowledged by E. Rodocanichi in *La femme italienne avant, pendant et après la Renaissance,* Paris, 1922, 23ff., especially 36-43. Many other factors, especially economic, would have to be considered in any proper discussion of the growth of educational opportunities for women in Europe before 1800.

61.
Alinari 30561; signed and dated 1577. Galli (77, see Fontana bibliography) rejects this work as autograph but does at least think it is an early copy of a lost original. He records another self-portrait of 1577, in the Museo Primoli, Rome, which shows her playing a clavichord, but I have been unable to locate it.
62.
Women playing the lute, on the other hand, are often associated with loose living and illicit sexual relations (see Brussels, 1963, nos. 95, 158, 198, and 252 for a typical sampling).

Since the choice of a professional career was nonetheless highly eccentric for women in six-teenth- or seventeenth-century Italy, it is not surprising that the biographers of these first women artists are careful to stress what proper, ladylike characters these exceptionally accom-plished women were. Vasari describes Properzia de' Rossi (ca. 1490-1530), whom he believed was the first woman sculptor in the history of art, as "skilled not only in household matters, like the others, but in infinite fields of knowledge, so that not only women but men too were envious. She was beautiful and played and sang better than any woman in the city at that time."[63] Sofonisba Anguissola's noble parentage is mentioned by all her biographers; many also list her accomplishments and say that she was beautiful.[64] Malvasia reports of Lavinia Fontana that even though she was made much of by Bolognese society, "she did not become conceited . . . but behaved even more modestly the more favors she received," refusing offers of marriage from noblemen as inappropriate for someone of her class.[65] Malvasia is even more enthusiastic about his heroine, Elisabetta Sirani (see cat. nos. 30, 31). "I lived in adora-tion of that merit, which in her was of supreme quality, and of that virtue, which was far from ordinary, and of that incomparable humility, indescribable modesty, inimitable goodness."[66] The terms of praise are close to those offered by Castiglione to the new duchess of Urbino, Eleanora of Gonzaga: "If ever there were joined in a single person wisdom, grace, beauty, intelligence, discreet manners, humanity, and every other gentle quality, they are so joined in her that they form a chain that comprises and adorns her every movement, uniting all these qualities at once."[67] The idea that male artists should behave like gentlemen was implied already by Cennino Cennini and Alberti, and stated clearly by Paolo Pino in 1548, but male artists were not so frequently complimented in these terms, and their eccentric behavior was often noted by their biographers.[68] By contrast anecdotes about the strange ways of women painters are extremely rare.[69]

The Emergence of Women Artists in Flanders, 1550-1600

Master Gerard, the illuminator, has a daughter about eighteen years old called Susanna. She made an illumination of the Savior, for which I paid one guilder. It is a great marvel that a woman can do so much.

— *Albrecht Dürer, 1521*

We know far less about the first women to make reputations for themselves as painters in six-teenth-century Flanders than we do about their Italian contemporaries. Thus it is more difficult to explain why they emerged into greater prominence at this time. Only for Caterina van Hemessen do certain works survive and only for Levina Teerlinc do we have substantial documentation. The art historian is handicapped above all by the absence of that strong literary-biographical tradition which has preserved a wealth of information about artists active in Italy before 1600 but which began in the North only in the late sixteenth century.[70]

Women seem to have been active in a far wider range of professions in the North than in Italy and their social status in Flemish and German society was probably higher as well. Portraits indicate among other things which members of society were considered important. Thus it is significant that there are far more portraits of women in relation to the total number of portraits that survive in the North than in Italy for the fifteenth, sixteenth, and seventeenth centuries. Even if many of the northern women are presented in their traditional roles as modest wives, mothers, spinners of wool, and readers of prayer books rather than as merchants, scholars, or even cultivated ladies of leisure, Italian women who were not married to ruling princes rarely had their portraits painted at all.[71]

The medieval pattern of wives, and occasionally daughters, following their husbands' and fathers' professions seems to have persisted in Flanders at least until the sixteenth century. Dürer observed a procession in Antwerp one Sunday in August 1520 in which were

63.
Vasari, v, 75. Sabina von Steinbach, who is sup-posed to be the daughter of Erwin (d. 1318), the archi-tect of Strasbourg Cathedral, and the sculptor of the figures of Church and Synagogue, is a legend inspired by a mistaken reading of an inscription recording that a statue was paid for by a donor named Sabina (H. Reinhardt, *La cathédrale de Strasbourg,* Paris, 1972, 101). See note 6 for other early references to women sculptors.
64.
V. Carducho, *Dialogos de la pintura,* Madrid, 1633, 16.
65.
Malvasia, I, 177.
66.
Ibid., II, 386.
67.
Castiglione, *Book of the Courtier,* 287.

68.
Wittkower (see note 45), 93ff.
69.
Rosalba Carriera's increasingly severe spells of depression toward the end of her life are alluded to tactfully by Zanetti (449, see Carriera bibliography). Gentileschi's rape and subsequent trial are not mentioned by any seicento writers.
70.
Karel von Mander's *Schilderboek* (Alkmaar, 1604) is the first extensive collection of Northern artists' biographies but the lives are short and do not com-pare with those of Vasari as historical sources.
71.
A rough census of my own shows that there were three male portraits produced in Italy in the fifteenth and sixteenth centuries for every female portrait; in the North, more than a third of the portraits repre-sent women. The bias is seen in donor portraits as well as in individual and group portraits.

represented "all the guilds and trades, each man dressed according to his rank and most richly. . . . The procession also included a large troop of widows, who keep themselves by the work of their hands."[72] As noted earlier, the painters' guild in Bruges had a substantial number of women members in the late fifteenth century. The custom of sending daughters to convents, where some learned to illuminate manuscripts, should also be recalled, for four of the seven Flemish women artists recorded by Guicciardini in 1567 were miniaturists.[73]

Attitudes toward women also changed in the North from medieval misogyny, which had been inspired largely by a celibate priesthood, to a more positive view of women's role in society as the Reformation gradually established a religion that allowed priests to marry. The Protestant stress on knowledge of the Bible meant that universal literacy became a goal of society, and elementary schools for both girls and boys appeared in the North long before they are reported in Italy.[74] Castiglione's *Il Cortegiano* was read outside Italy too, carrying with it visions of a cultured society in which both men and women were well-mannered and well educated. Perhaps it is less surprising therefore that a few women in Flanders should have become good painters than in Italy, where the Catholic church remained a strong force supporting a patriarchal ideology in which women were strictly subordinate to men.

Levina Teerlinc is the Flemish counterpart of Sofonisba Anguissola. Teerlinc also became a successful court artist, and her fame was still part of the oral tradition when Guicciardini published his account of Flanders almost twenty years after her departure for London. No doubt her example inspired other young women to seek the same path to fame and riches just as Anguissola's evidently did in Italy. Caterina van Hemessen's career was brief but, thanks to Guicciardini, may have had a similar effect. Of the other women artists in sixteenth-century Flanders we know only what Guicciardini tells us, which is about as much as Pliny tells us about Iaia, supplemented by Dürer's famous comment, quoted above, on the miniature he bought from Susan Horenbout.[75]

Women Artists in Italy in the Sixteenth and Seventeenth Centuries
This excellent Painter, to say the truth, in every way prevails above the condition of her sex.
— A patron on Lavinia Fontana, 1588

In the sixteenth century when women first emerged as serious professional artists, their training and education still took place largely in the workshops of established artists. Academies, which would eventually replace to a large extent this essentially medieval training system, did not play an important role in the education of any artists until the late seventeenth century in Paris, when the Académie Royale first assumed such a role with regularity and efficiency.[76] The Accademia del Disegno in Florence, founded in 1562, and the Accademia di San Luca in Rome, revived with a formal teaching program in 1593, were in effect social clubs rather than art schools, for they failed to provide except erratically either drawing sessions with a nude model or debates about the theory and practice of art. Thus exclusion from the meetings of these academies was not a serious handicap for women until the eighteenth century, when the academies in both Rome and Paris finally became serious teaching institutions and their prizes an important indication of future success.[77]

But in the sixteenth and seventeenth centuries the dubious prestige of membership in an academy was less important than the opportunity for a talented woman to study with a good artist, not necessarily her father. Also vital was the chance to attend the private drawing sessions organized in Rome and elsewhere to bring down the cost of hiring a model. The former was sometimes possible but custom and prejudice firmly excluded women from the latter. It was believed that their presence could only ruin the reputation of the woman and give rise to scandal. The first woman to break this barrier was Giulia Lama (see cat. no. 43) in Venice in

72.
Tagebuch der Reise in die Niederlande, Leipzig, 1884, 55 (quoted in *Not in God's Image*, ed. J. O'Faolain and L. Martines, New York, 1973, 157. This collection of sources about women is an excellent selection spliced with lively editorial comment.)
73.
Susan Horenbout, Clara Skeysers, Lavina (Teerlinc), and Ann Smiter.
74.
Sachs, 14ff. and pls. 72 and 73. Rodocanichi (see note 60) mentions no such schools for girls in Italy. See also O'Faolain and Martines, *Not in God's Image*, 194 and 244ff. Jean Luis Vives, *Book of Instruction of a Christian Woman*, first published in Latin in 1523, which appeared in over forty editions in all European languages before 1600, was also influential. He believed that women should be taught to read but should not learn history, logic, grammar, or rhetoric; they should read the Bible rather than Ovid, and so on.
75.
Albrecht Dürer's Tagebuch der Reise in die Niederlande, Leipzig, 1884, 85.
76.
Pevsner, passim.

77.
The rules of the Accademia di San Luca formulated in 1607 forbade women to attend meetings, although they could be elected Academicians ("Le Donne insigni nell'Arte siano accettate Accademiche ma non abbiano luogo in seduta"); Missirini (note 8), 83. In one record of a meeting held on June 16, 1630, the name "Anna Duchela" appears (Archivio di Stato, Trenta Notaii Capitolini, Ufficio 15, vol. 124, f. 866). This sounds like Anna Dughet, sister of Gaspard, who married Poussin a few months later, but even if I have transcribed her name correctly, her attendance was extremely unusual. Giovanna Garzoni never attended any of the meetings at which the conditions of her bequest were discussed.

the early eighteenth century, but she was little known outside her home town and no other woman seems to have tried until the nineteenth century.[78]

Some of the difficulties that women faced in a society unused to their stepping outside traditional roles are exemplified by the experience of Artemisia Gentileschi. Her father, Orazio, was a good painter who could certainly have provided her with a solid training. She had another advantage over those women born in the artistic provinces, so to speak, in being able to study on her own in Rome many major artistic monuments, both ancient and modern. Her father nevertheless believed that she needed additional instruction in perspective and hired a colleague known for his expertise in this area to give her additional lessons at home. Despite the presence of a female chaperone, the result was a now infamous trial in which Orazio accused the teacher of raping her.[79] Sofonisba Anguissola and her sisters, however, were able to study with local Cremonese artists without being seduced. And in the early seventeenth century Giovanna Garzoni, who became famous for her watercolor studies of plants and animals on vellum, left her home in the Marches and did what any talented male artist would have done, traveled to Venice, Rome, and Naples in search of instruction and clients before settling in Florence. Maria Sibylla Merian's biography suggests a similarly independent attitude. Indeed, quite a number of Dutch women studied with masters unrelated to them, even when their fathers were artists. Society may have disapproved of their behaving with such independence, but by the seventeenth century it had clearly become easier for women to control their own lives to some degree.

Boccaccio had not only reminded women artists of their ancient predecessors, he also provided some suggestions about subjects that might appropriately concern them, namely portraits of other women and perhaps portraits of themselves. Women were poorly prepared to take on commissions for altarpieces or any works involving multi-figure compositions as long as their artistic training was limited, though this did not deter some from trying. Thus although Sofonisba Anguissola and Lavinia Fontana found a responsive audience for their portraits, the former for those of herself, the latter for those of Bolognese noblewomen, both women also produced religious works and Fontana made several large altarpieces for public sites as well. If their critics preferred their portraits, neither woman felt constrained to confine herself to painting what she could see rather than what had to be imagined.

Sofonisba's fame was made first as a portrait painter and the demand for examples of her phenomenal skill in this specialty made it difficult, according to Soprani, for her to extend her range to more prestigious categories of painting. By producing one large, full-length portrait of her father with one of her sisters and her brother (Nivaagaard, Malerisamlingen) shortly before she left for Spain, she evidently wished to declare her ability to manage multi-figure compositions and thus perhaps to try history painting at a later date.[80] Nor was she willing to accept the limitations of existing portrait types, for she extended them in her famous conversation piece showing three of her sisters playing chess (fig. 5, see p. 30).[81] Finally, her self-portraits represent an astonishing variety of formats, situations, and sizes (cat. no. 3, figs. 2 and 3). No artist between Dürer and Rembrandt painted so many, but while their extensions of this genre have been the subject of much favorable comment, Anguissola is dismissed instead for looking no further than her mirror.

Anguissola's self-portraits can be explained by the fact that as the first Italian woman artist of note she was the object of much curiosity and admiration. Properzia de' Rossi (ca. 1490-1530) preceded her but died, according to Vasari, just as word of her extraordinary gifts reached Pope Clement VII and thus before she could become the subject of a cult, as Anguissola did. Lavinia Fontana also painted several self-portraits, although nothing like the number pro-

3.
Sofonisba Anguissola
Self-Portrait, ca. 1552
Oil on copper
3¼ x 2½ in. (8.2 x 6.3 cm.)
Boston, Museum of Fine Arts
Emma F. Monroe Fund (60.155)

78.
Ruggeri, pls. 64, 67-70, and ff. (see Lama bibliography). He publishes twenty-three such studies, a few from female models (pls. 86 and 180-82). Gentileschi certainly drew from female models, but while this was important, the male nude had a symbolic significance that made the prohibition to study it an insuperable barrier for women's real advancement in the profession. As Nochlin commented (1971, 33), it is like forbidding medical students from doing dissections or even examining the human body.
79.
See her biography for details and references.
80.
Repr. by Venturi, 926, and H. Olsen, *Italian Paintings in Denmark*, Copenhagen, 1961, pl. XLIIb.
81.
Repr. by Berenson, pl. 1968 (see S. Anguissola bibliography). See R. Edwards, *Early Conversation Pieces*, London, 1954, 14-15.

duced by Anguissola. By the time Artemisia Gentileschi came to maturity, women artists can no longer have been regarded as such extraordinary phenomena for she had to work much harder to find patrons, to whom she sometimes offered a self-portrait as inducement.[82] The first women artists active in northern Europe do not seem to have produced as many self-portraits as their Italian contemporaries, but we do have one by Caterina van Hemessen, and in her still-life paintings Clara Peeters (see cat. nos. 17, 18) made frequent use of the conceit of the self-portrait concealed in a reflection.[83] Self-portraits by women artists again became important in the late eighteenth century when Angelica Kauffman (see cat. nos. 48-51) and Elizabeth Vigée-Lebrun (see cat. nos. 58-61) both enjoyed such spectacular fame that patrons again demanded this double souvenir of genius.

The adulation of Sofonisba by patrons — especially by the Spanish court, which whisked her away from her family, gave her many expensive gifts, a generous annual pension, and a substantial dowry when she married a rich Sicilian nobleman — and the publicity given to these outward signs of success were of great historical importance for later women artists. The fabulous wealth her talents gained for her must have inspired other fathers with talented daughters to think of training them in hopes of similar success. Such dreams of financial glory surely explain why not long after 1560, when Sofonisba left for Spain after almost a decade of activity in Italy, several more women painters appeared in North Italy to emulate their achievements. Lavinia Fontana of Bologna made her debut in the 1570s, Barbara Longhi of Ravenna (see fig. 4) finished her training around the same time, and Fede Galizia (see cat. nos. 8, 9) was reported as a child prodigy in Milan about twenty years later.[84] And not long after Fontana's arrival in Rome in response to a papal invitation, Orazio Gentileschi began training his daughter Artemisia. The compliments and financial rewards given to Anguissola and her successors may have been excessive in relation to their accomplishments but it is extremely important not to forget the historical consequences of their public reception.

Once the breakthrough had occurred, once a few women had become professional artists and had been reasonably well received by patrons and critics, then it is not surprising to find other women following their example. Custom, prejudice, and practical problems such as the lack of safe, reliable contraception continued to make it virtually impossible for a gifted woman to train herself properly, to believe in her gifts as ardently as a man, or to devote herself to her career as completely as a man. Nevertheless a few women overcame most of these obstacles in the sixteenth, seventeenth, and eighteenth centuries, proving that none was insurmountable once the idea had been successfully planted in people's minds that creative genius might on rare occasions be found in a woman. Even if we agree with Nochlin, as I do, that "the golden nugget of artistic genius," which will rise to the surface however unpromising the circumstances, is a myth, it is a powerful myth nevertheless. The belief that women did not even have the potential for artistic genius explains their absence from the earlier history of Renaissance painting more convincingly than any description of housekeeping problems in the fifteenth century.

Once young women with artistic gifts came to believe that the myth of creative genius might apply to them, what kind of reaction did they get from their families, fellow artists, and critics? Every father of a daughter had to worry about providing her with a sufficient dowry to make her an attractive marriage prospect. A woman who could make a substantial contribution to the family income was surely, as far as her father and future husband were concerned, an asset rather than a liability. Indeed we hear of few fathers who opposed their daughters' careers. On the contrary, Anguissola's father promoted his daughter vigorously and not only for financial reasons. At the age of thirty-six he had divorced his barren first wife and remarried, but his new wife produced nothing but daughters, six in a row. We can assume that Amilcare was filled with concern for the preservation of his family's name, and since he

4.
Barbara Longhi
Madonna and Child with St. John the Baptist
Oil on canvas
34⅝ x 27¹⁵/₁₆ in. (88 x 71 cm.)
Dresden, Gemäldegalerie

82.
Bottari-Ticozzi, I, 246.
83.
See below in the discussion of still-life paintings by women.
84.
For information on Fontana and Galizia, see their biographies. We are poorly informed about Barbara Longhi (1552-1638), daughter of Luca Longhi of Ravenna. None of the works attributed to her are dated and no serious research ever seems to have been done on her. Vasari in his brief life of Luca comments on the handicap of a provincial upbringing and career that never took him far from home, a handicap common to several of these first women artists.
According to Minghetti (319ff.), Irene di Spilimbergo (1540-1560), another well-born young woman with a good education, was inspired to try painting after she

was shown a self-portrait by Sofonisba Anguissola. She studied for two years with Titian and is supposed to have made great strides, but she died at twenty. Nothing by her is now known. Tintoretto's daughter, Marietta Robusti (1560-1590), also belongs with this group. Apart from her self-portrait in the Uffizi, none of the works associated with her can be attributed to her with certainty. For a good survey of the situation, see P. Rossi, *Iacopo Tintoretto, I Ritratti*, Venice, 1974, 138-39.
85.
See her biography for details, especially note 10.
86.
Malvasia, II, 386.
87.
For Oosterwyck, see her biography; for Capomazza, see De Dominici, III, 91.

88.
Lavinia Fontana, Fede Galizia, Artemisia Gentileschi, Elisabetta Sirani, Giulia Lama, and Angelica Kauffman are the exceptions to the rule. Two half-length canvases of St. Joseph by Michaelina Wautiers (Woutiers) in Vienna (Kunsthistorisches Museum) hardly qualify her for inclusion in this select group, nor do the genre works of Leyster, Gertruida van Wassenbergh, and Marguerite Gérard.
89.
A *Stigmatization of St. Francis* by Lavinia Fontana (1579, Villa Reverdin, Bologna; Galli, fig. 5, see Fontana bibliography) is essentially a landscape with a few small figures in the manner of Niccolò dell'Abbate. It is one of her most appealing works. The Dutch and Flemish women, whom we might expect to produce a landscape occasionally, rarely do. A few by Caterina van Knibbergen (active 1634-ca. 1670) and Margaretha van Godewyck (1627-1677) are known (see Bernt, 431 and 628), as well as a sea-

seemed to be unable to do this the easy way by producing a son to inherit it, the education and promotion of his talented daughters became his means of endowing the family name with enduring fame. By the time his only son, Asdrubale, was born in 1551, Sofonisba's career was already launched. She was to bring her father more fame than he ever anticipated and a steady annual income of 800 lire a year after she moved to Spain.

Lavinia Fontana was professionally active before her marriage to a minor painter, G. B. Zappi of Imola, who is said to have agreed to assist his wife's career after their marriage.[85] Since his career never developed at all, he apparently did just that. His wife did not simply contribute to the family income; she became its chief source. Elisabetta Sirani's father is said to have been against his daughter's career but was persuaded to change his mind by the biographer Malvasia.[86] When her father's gout later incapacitated him Elisabetta became the main support of the family. Evidently both Rachel Ruysch's father and her artist husband encouraged her career, which made her a rich woman (see cat. nos. 39, 40). Vigée-Lebrun supported not only her own family after her father's death but also the gambling habit and mistresses of her husband.

Other women were unable to continue their careers after they married. Although Caterina van Hemessen, Louise Moillon (see cat. nos. 24-26), Catherine Duchemin, and Judith Leyster (see cat. nos. 22, 23) were established, successful artists, they all painted far less or even stopped completely after their marriages. The option of remaining single, which a number of famous male artists chose (the great triumvirate of the High Renaissance — Leonardo, Raphael, and Michelangelo — for example), was not so easy for women, although we do know a few who managed it, including Giovanna Garzoni, Maria van Oosterwyck (see cat. nos. 28, 29), Giulia Lama, and Marguerite Gérard (see cat. nos. 63, 64). Oosterwyck is specifically reported to have refused offers of marriage in order to dedicate herself to her work and De Dominici tells a similar story about Suor Luisa Capomazza of Naples.[87] But then, as now, women were expected to marry, and with so few role models to suggest either that spinsterhood might be preferable or that a career need not be sacrificed to domestic chores and motherhood, it is not surprising that some of these pioneer women fell by the wayside. No social stigma has ever been attached to women who abandon professional pursuits to become traditional wives and mothers. A move that would be seen as failure for a man is for a woman an accepted course of action for which society expresses only token regrets.

Fathers and husbands who stood to profit from the careers of their daughters and wives were not likely to oppose them, but male artists cannot be expected to have welcomed additional competition. There is little evidence of opposition, however, until the eighteenth century when in Paris at least there were enough women artists to present an economic threat. By and large, women did not attempt to compete with men for the more prestigious public commissions. No woman except the legendary Onorata Rodiani painted frescoes in Italy and very few women in any European country attempted large-scale historical or religious compositions until the nineteenth century.[88] Their limited training confined most women to the less valued specialties of portraiture and still life. With very few exceptions, women did not even try landscape painting until the nineteenth century. It was evidently not possible for women to go on sketching trips and long scenic journeys alone to collect the raw material this new genre required.[89] Thus men not only controlled the most remunerative and most esteemed public commissions as well as landscape, one of the three popular genres, but also had an almost total monopoly over sculpture, architecture, and even printmaking before 1800.[90]

It is probably significant that the few recorded examples of male artists' resentment concern women who made sculpture or religious works for public sites. Vasari reports that although

scape by Caterina Peeters (1615-1676), sister of Bonaventura (Vienna, Liechtenstein Collection, signed and dated 1657). Elizabeth Vigée-Lebrun records making landscape sketches in Naples, Vienna, and Switzerland and making landscape paintings from them but none are known at present.
90.
Properzia de'Rossi (see below) appears to be the only recorded woman sculptor in Italy before 1800. The next one we hear about in Europe is Luisa Roldán (1656-1704), who was a major sculptor in Seville and Madrid in the late seventeenth century (see the fully documented articles by Beatrice Gilman Proske, "Luisa Roldán at Madrid," *Connoisseur*, CLV, 1964, part I, 128-32; part II, 199-203; part III, 269-73). In the eighteenth century Marie Anne Collot (1748-1821), the wife of Falconet, made some superb portrait busts and plaques, though her career was much handicapped by the demands made on her time

by her husband (see H. N. Opperman, "Marie Anne Collot in Russia: Two Portraits," *Burlington Magazine*, CVII, 1965, 408ff., an excellent article with many bibliographical leads). Anne Seymour Damer (1748-1828) also enjoyed a considerable reputation for portraits and animal sculpture. These women, together with Patience Lovell Wright (1725-1786), an American who made wax sculpture, are the only ones known to be active as sculptors before the nineteenth century.
Women architects are even rarer. Plautilla Bricci, sister of Basilio, is said to have helped him design a villa near Porta San Pancrazio for Abbate Elpidio Benedetti in the 1660s (G. Briganti, *Pietro da Cortona o della pittura barocca*, Florence, 1962, 282). The design of a chapel in San Luigi dei Francesi, Rome, is also attributed to her (Filippo Titi, *Descrizione delle pitture, sculture, e architetture eposte al pubblico in Roma*, Rome, 1763, 148).

My files contain the names of about ninety women known to have made prints before 1800 but very little is known about most of them and practically no serious research has been carried out on those for whom a sufficient number of works and adequate documentation are known to make further study rewarding. Among these are Diana Ghisi Scultore (1530-1590); Elisabetta Sirani (one of the few to etch her own designs instead of those by other artists); Sophie Chéron (1648-1711); Susanna Maria von Sandrart (1658-1716); Claudine, Antoinette, and Françoise Bouzonnet Stella (active late seventeenth century); and Françoise Madeleine Basseporte (1701-1780).

everyone else in Bologna, citizens and artists, rejoiced in the talent of Properzia de' Rossi and admired her sculpture, one artist named Amico (Aspertini) "out of jealousy always discouraged her and said nasty things about her to the Operaii [the men in charge of the construction and decoration of San Petronio in Bologna]; and was so unpleasant that she was finally paid a disgustingly low price for her work."[91] Vasari may have exaggerated the degree of her support if Amico's criticisms had so much bad effect. A little later, at the beginning of the seventeenth century, Fontana was awarded an important commission for an altarpiece in San Paolo fuori le Mura in Rome, one of the seven basilicas that every pilgrim hoped to visit. Giovanni Baglione, a painter as well as a biographer, did not approve of the decision. "Even though there were many good painters, the best masters who were then working were passed over and the work was given to Lavinia alone and she painted *The Stoning of St. Stephen Martyr* with many figures and a glory above, shown with the skies open; nevertheless it is true that because the figures are larger than lifesize, she became confused and did not succeed as well as she thought; because there is a big difference between an ordinary picture and machines of that size, which frighten every great intellect. She then made portraits, for which her talent suited her, and she made them quite well."[92] This altarpiece burned in 1823, so we cannot judge to what extent Baglione's criticism was justified, but it is clear that it was motivated by professional jealousy and that his message is that women should stick to small works and portraits. Finally there is the Venetian Giulia Lama, whose drawings prove that she studied extensively from nude male models. According to a sympathetic male witness, she was "persecuted by [other] painters."[93] Her failure to enjoy the kind of success that Rosalba Carriera was then having in Venice must have been due in part to the opposition she faced from other producers of altarpieces in a tight job market. Carriera had generated her own market by creating a new genre — the pastel portrait — and thus was probably not considered a direct threat by local male artists. They may even have welcomed her fame because she brought rich tourists to Venice who might then buy other works of art. Apparently women artists were tolerated by their male contemporaries as long as there were very few of them and they remained at the fringes of the profession.

The reactions of critics to the first women artists are more revealing than those of their families and fellow artists about contemporary attitudes toward women's invasion of what had hitherto been a male preserve. Though much of the earliest criticism is at first sight adulatory, many comments contain the seeds of the standard critical responses to women's art seen up to the present day. One characteristic reaction is amazement and astonishment that a woman can be a competent painter; Dürer's comment on Susan Horenbout quoted earlier is a famous example of this attitude. Another common attitude is the critical double standard — the work is extraordinarily fine for a woman, but does not measure up to the work of men. Finally there is the tendency to see in works by women a "feminine sensibility," although this reaction does not appear until the eighteenth century.

The critical reactions to Sofonisba Anguissola are a special case. In the extensive sixteenth- and seventeenth-century literature on her there are few specific comments about her qualities as an artist. Biographers stress her noble origins, her good education and deportment, her enormous success, the large sums of money and lavish presents given to her by the Duke of Alba and the Spanish crown, and other biographical gossip. There is not one comment of the "good for a woman" variety in any of these early biographies. The reason, I believe, is not simply admiration for her work. Most of the writers had seen very little by her and her artistic reputation was in fact largely secondhand. Vasari's list of works seen in Cremona in 1568 is religiously repeated, along with the story of the drawing of the boy pinched by a crab, which Michelangelo is said to have admired. None of the Italian biographers have any solid information about her Spanish period, except for the more spectacular aspects of her private life

5.
Sofonisba Anguissola
*Lucia, Minerva, and Europa Anguissola
Playing Chess,* 1555
Oil on canvas
27³/₁₆ x 35⁷/₈ in. (69 x 91 cm.)
Poznań, Muzeum Narodowe

91.
Vasari, v, 77.
92.
Baglione, 144 (see Fontana bibliography).
93.
See her biography for Conti's complete statement.

and finances. The explanation is surely that as an artist of noble origins who worked for court patrons who paid her very well she was seen as elevating the status of the profession, a vital concern of artists and their supporters in the sixteenth and seventeenth centuries. Even if her invitation to Madrid was mostly inspired by her curiosity value as that new phenomenon, a female painter, who in a sense could be classed with dwarfs, fools, and other court amusements, her success made her a symbol too useful to be denigrated by pointing out her limitations as an artist.

Thus the negative criticism of Anguissola is only implied and must be reconstructed, so to speak, by comparing her biographies with those of her male contemporaries by the same authors and by references to those authors' aesthetic values as stated elsewhere. Vasari, for example, required far more of the male artists he promoted than the ability to paint lifelike portraits. He expected artists not only to be able to draw from nature accurately but to be able to select from nature according to an inner aesthetic and to be able to add invention, proportion, imagination, and grace. Thus Vasari's praise of Anguissola's portraits as "so lifelike that they lack only speech" does not mean that he ranked her high among cinquecento artists. Indeed his use of the word "diligenza" is a warning signal, for above all he admired artists whose work was not obviously the product of hard work but rather those whose technique was effortless, who displayed "disinvoltura," and he normally paid little attention to portraits.[94] He was far more concerned with large, ambitious compositions full of figures and formal novelties. His references to Anguissola are also relatively brief compared with his discussions of other living artists. To readers able to analyze his language, Vasari's praise of her is polite but limited.

A century later Raffaele Soprani, the Genoese biographer, anticipated comments about Anguissola's failure to produce religious and historical works with many figures. "From simple portraits," he notes, "Sofonisba turned to the composition of 'cose storiate, e d'idea', in which she succeeded quite well, but because she continuously received commissions from people who wanted to be painted by her," she had little time for such works. He cites the picture of her sisters playing chess (fig. 5) as an example of those more ambitious "storied things."[95] Malvasia managed to make a negative critical comment about Anguissola, Fontana, and Galizia by isolating them at the end of a list of male portraitists arranged in a descending order of quality. The same sentence makes clear Malvasia's view that portraiture is a far less demanding art form than history painting.[96]

Lavinia Fontana was patronized by royalty only once but she did work for many aristocrats, including the duke of Mantua, and was invited to Rome by the pope.[97] Whether because she did not achieve the spectacular success of Anguissola or because her prolific output of portraits, private religious works, and public altarpieces (see fig. 6) meant that she was a more familiar figure as well as a more competitive one, Fontana's critics were not so kind. Thus Mazzolari, after commenting favorably on her altarpiece in the Escorial, which he says was especially popular with "ordinary people," continues in this vein: "The things of Lavinia are valued in all Italy, and if it is true that they do not have the excellence and valor to be found in such things by great men, because they are after all by a woman who has left the usual path and all that which is suitable to their hands and fingers . . . they are with good reason much praised."[98] Malvasia has a similar comment about her altarpieces. "No less precious, as coming from the hand of a woman, are those few altarpieces of hers to be seen in some of our churches," he wrote, and another man, a patron of hers, told a friend that a picture of hers he owned was "very diligent and as the work of a woman praiseworthy."[99] Titi, the author of the best eighteenth-century guidebook to Rome, is even blunter about the work of Suor Maria Eufrasia Benedetti, who painted a *Nativity* in S. Giuseppe a Capo le Case, Rome. "There are pictures in this church," he informs the reader, "to be considered not so much for their good-

6.
Lavinia Fontana
Queen Luisa of France Presenting Francis I, Her Son, to St. Francis of Paola, 1590
Oil on canvas
83 13/16 x 54 1/8 in. (213 x 140 cm.)
Bologna, Pinacoteca Nazionale

94.
A. Blunt, *Artistic Theory in Italy, 1450-1600*, Oxford, 1940.
95.
Soprani, 413.
96.
Malvasia, II, 92 (life of Baldassare Galanino).
97.
See her biography for details.
98.
Quoted in Malvasia, I, 180.
99.
For the first quotation, see ibid., I, 178; for the second, Galli, 80 (see Fontana bibliography).

ness as to be admired because they were painted by . . . a nun."[100] The double standard of criticism runs through all these comments.

Perhaps the most open statement of prejudice toward the potential of women as artists made in print before 1800 is G.B. Passeri's introduction to his life of Caterina de' Ginnasi, the only woman he included in his set of artists' lives covering the mid-seventeenth century in Rome.[101] We have noted earlier the custom of prefacing the biographies of women artists with some reference to great women of the past in general and to the women artists described in Pliny in particular, an opening that suggests the writer is sympathetic to women and believes some at least to be capable of achievements comparable to those of men. Passeri's introduction by contrast is openly misogynistic. "Women have never been lacking in intellect, and it is well known that when they are instructed in some subject, they are capable of mastering what they are taught. Nevertheless it is true that the Lord did not endow them properly with the faculty of judgment, and this he did in order to keep them restrained within the boundaries of obedience to men, to establish men as supreme and superior, so that with this lack, women would be more docile, more amenable to suggestion." Not surprisingly, given such an attitude, Passeri finds nothing positive to say about Caterina de' Ginnasi's work. Indeed, her biography is the only one by Passeri containing not one critical judgment throughout. Passeri also selected the evidence to suit his viewpoint. Ginnasi, a nun, was the niece of Cardinal Domenico Ginnasi and a pupil of Giovanni Lanfranco, an artist patronized by the cardinal. Judging by her few recorded works that survive she was not a good artist.[102] The biography that Passeri should have written, of course, was that of Artemisia Gentileschi, who was born in Rome, worked there for part of her career, and died within the period covered by Passeri's work. He might also have considered a life of Giovanna Garzoni. Gentileschi, oddly enough, was ignored by all seventeenth-century biographers except Baldinucci, who tacked a brief life on to that of her father.[103] She was also omitted from De Dominici's lives of Neapolitan artists written in the next century, presumably on the grounds that she was born, trained, and spent much of her life elsewhere.

Women Still-Life Painters of the Seventeenth and Eighteenth Centuries

Although the origins of still life can be traced back to antiquity, it was to all intents and purposes a new art form in the late sixteenth century. Women quickly discovered the suitability of this genre to their social situation. Fede Galizia of Milan, Louise Moillon of Paris, and Clara Peeters of Antwerp were all among the pioneers of the early seventeenth century who helped to establish the formal and iconographical conventions of this new kind of painting. Maria van Oosterwyck and Rachel Ruysch were among the finest flower painters active in Holland during the late seventeenth and early eighteenth centuries, while Maria Sibylla Merian's extraordinary studies of insects and plants have earned her an important place in scientific history as well as in the history of botanical illustration. Finally, Anne Vallayer-Coster (see cat. nos. 52-55) was an outstanding still-life artist in eighteenth-century Paris. Versatile and productive, she produced a stream of sumptuously painted, richly colored, and inventive paintings that illustrate the entire repertoire of the genre in her day. Being female clearly was far less of a handicap to a still-life artist than to a figure painter. Thus it is not surprising that some of the women who chose this specialty had distinguished careers and were more easily regarded as the equal of their male peers than women portraitists and history painters, but since the genre itself was held in low esteem by art theorists and the academies, a successful still-life painter could not expect to have the reputation accorded an artist successful with those reputedly higher forms.

Only Caravaggio's *Basket of Fruit* (Milan, Ambrosiana) predates the still lives of Fede Galizia as an example of pure still-life painting in Italy. All earlier examples by Italian artists include figures inspired by the market scenes of Flemish painters like Aertsen and Beukelaer. Galizia

7.
Fede Galizia
Still Life with Quinces
Oil on panel
14 9/16 x 21 1/4 in. (37 x 54 cm.)
Bergamo, Private Collection

8.
Clara Peeters
Still Life with Fish, 1611
Oil on panel
17 11/16 x 28 5/16 in. (50 x 72 cm.)
Madrid, Museo del Prado

100.
Titi (see note 90), 341. De Dominici (III, 93) makes a similar remark about Suor Luisa Capomazza: "in drawing, to say the truth, Suor Luisa is not perfect; but as a woman she is praised by us."
101.
G. B. Passeri, *Vite de' pittori, scultori ed architetti che hanno lavorato in Rome, morti dal 1614 fino al 1673,* Rome, 1772 (edition cited: J. Hess, ed., Vienna, 1934, 257).
102.
Erich Schleier informs me that the *Last Supper* lunette by Ginnasi from S. Lucia dei Ginnasi is now in the Ginnasi family chapel in Palazzo Ginnasi, Rome. It is a weak copy after Lanfranco's painting of this subject now in Dublin and formerly in San Paolo fuori le Mura, Rome.

103.
Baldinucci, x, 251ff. He introduces her as "valente pittrice quanto mai altra femina" (as good a painter as any woman)!

signed and dated only one of her still-life studies of fruit, however, so that her contribution in this area has only recently been recognized (see fig. 7). She seems also to have worked in isolation, for the fashionable still life in Italy was generally large and elaborate, as if to compensate for its theoretical inferiority. The sophisticated simplicity and restraint of Galizia's still lives appeal far more to us than to her contemporaries. Significantly they are not mentioned by any of the seventeenth-century writers who praised her artistic accomplishments.

Clara Peeters' contribution to the early development of still life is easier to study than Galizia's because, like many Dutch and Flemish artists, she signed and often dated many of her works. Among the works originally selected to demonstrate her style and achievement in this exhibition but too fragile to make the journey were two of her four panels of 1611 in the Museo del Prado, Madrid. The comparatively large size and exceptional quality of this group suggest that it was originally commissioned by an important patron, but there is no evidence at present that either the Spanish court or their representatives in the Spanish Netherlands, Archduke Albert and Archduchess Isabella Clara Eugenia, commissioned it or anything else from Peeters.[104] The panels are among the masterpieces of early seventeenth-century still life, all the more remarkable for having been painted by an artist only seventeen years old.

Each of the four has a different theme. The fish piece illustrated here (fig. 8) is complemented by a game piece (no. 1619); the table set with flowers, dried fruit, nuts, biscuits, and wine (fig. 9) is paired by a meal of meat pie, bread, green olives, and boiled partridges (no. 1622). The choice of objects suggests several of the types of still life that were to become popular — the breakfast piece, the fish piece, and the game piece. Her picture of a dead duck, woodcock, partridge, thrushes, and small birds on a spit all guarded by a falcon is the first dated example of the last, unless one counts Jacopo da Barbari's exceptional panel in Munich of 1504. The genre was to become immensely popular in Flanders in the hands of artists like Snyders and Jan Fyt. Peeters' study of gleaming fish backed by a copper strainer looks forward all the way to Chardin's celebrations of the beauty of ordinary objects in the eighteenth century.

Each of her Prado still lives is a technical tour de force. Her sense of form is secure, her drawing precisely accurate as it defines contours and subtle as it suggests graduated light effects on undulating smooth surfaces. Unlike her own earliest attempts at still life and unlike some other early efforts by her contemporaries, all her objects sit comfortably on the surface, even if it is a little crowded. Peeters made more use of overlap and balanced asymmetries than Osias Beert and selected objects with a greater variety of scale than he did. She also used a lower viewpoint than Beert, Nicholaes Gillis, or Floris van Dijck, perhaps initiating the trend away from the bird's-eye panorama of the first still lives to the lowered viewpoint and diminished table surface favored by the next generation. All early still lives feature objects set on the edge of the table or even projecting beyond it, inviting the viewer to test the illusion of reality. This illusion is hard for us to appreciate, so used are we to the marvels of photography, but to Peeters' contemporaries such creations must have seemed almost miraculous. She trails the leaves of a peony, a pastry, the edge of a pewter dish, and a shrimp's whiskers near our fingers, provoking our sense of touch and admiration simultaneously.

Clara Peeters' masterpiece is an austerely elegant still life of 1612 in Karlsruhe (fig. 10).[105] In marked contrast to her own earlier work and that of her contemporaries, the elements of the composition are extremely simple — two gilded goblets and a cream stoneware vase containing a few flowers. At their base she has laid a tulip, some coins, a golden chain in a pale gray porcelain dish, and four shells. The low viewpoint silhouettes the three vertical objects against the dark background. The central position of the nearest goblet serves to emphasize the many slight asymmetries that enliven the composition by providing a formal counterpoint that works in depth as well as on the surface.

9.
Clara Peeters
Still Life with Flowers, a Goblet, Dried Fruit and Pretzels, 1611
Oil on panel
19 11/16 x 28 5/16 in. (50 x 72 cm.)
Madrid, Museo del Prado

10.
Clara Peeters
Still Life with a Vase of Flowers, Goblets, and Shells, 1612
Oil on panel
23 7/16 x 19 5/16 in. (59.5 x 49 cm.)
Karlsruhe, Staatliche Kunsthalle

104.
They are recorded in the royal palace of La Granja in 1746; at least one was saved from the fire in the Alcazar in 1734 (Museo del Prado, *Catalogo de las pinturas,* Madrid, 1963, 494-95). Dona Isabel Farnese acquired a large group of Dutch and Flemish pictures in Rome in 1735, but the 1734 reference suggests that these four pictures were not part of that purchase, although two are later recorded in her collection (Pedro de Madrazo, Prado catalog of 1910, 289). Peeters is never mentioned in M. de Maeyer's detailed study, *Albrecht en Isabella en de Schilderkunst,* Brussels, 1955. All four works are on panel and measure roughly 20 by 28 in.
105.
Oil on panel, roughly 23 by 19 in.; museum inventory no. 2222. It is signed "CLARA P. ANNO 1612" on the lower left. For bibliography, see J. Lauts, *Katalog alte Meister bis 1800,* Staatliche Kunsthalle, Karlsruhe, 1966, 236.

The tallest object, the goblet on the right, set farthest from us and off center, creates one deliberate and obvious asymmetry. The two goblets furthermore do not frame the vase of flowers, a second obvious asymmetry. Although the flowers reach almost to the level of the lance borne by the figurine on top of the central goblet, it is the solid shape of the container that catches the eye, which views it in relation to the two goblets as a series of three forms rising in height progressively from left to right. This rising line is echoed by shadows below and by the position of the shells in the right foreground. There are other formal contrasts to appreciate — the fragile, linear forms of the flowers in the solid vase, the play of concave and convex shapes of the various containers, the contrast of ceramic and metallic surfaces, and the color scheme of golden neutrals relieved by only a few accents of bright color in the flowers and shells. The shells and the living plants are miracles of nature, the creative skill of God set beside that of man. A composition that appeals at first for its simplicity turns out to contain a highly sophisticated play of formal and even iconographical relationships.

Only in flower paintings with vertical formats can such a low viewpoint be found in still lives of this early date; such flower paintings moreover all feature one vase centered on a ledge or in a niche. Peeters has adapted the format to a still life which has a content clearly inspired by the sixteenth-century *Wunderkammer*, even if the vase of flowers hints at the source of her composition. The *Wunderkammer* (literally a "room of wonders") was a collection of objects which were seen as marvels of nature and of man. Peeters has transposed to a painting some typical exhibits — the shells, the goblets, the chain — thus adding her skill in representing them to the craftsmanship already required for their creation. The result is a kind of miniature *Wunderkammer*, which not incidentally must have been a lot cheaper than a real collection of these items. The chief marvel, however, is the artist's own self-portrait, reflected at least seven times in the bulging forms of the goblet on the right.

11.
Margareta Haverman
Vase of Flowers, 1716
Oil on canvas
31¼ x 23¾ in. (79.4 x 60.3 cm.)
New York, The Metropolitan Museum of Art
Purchase, 1971

She had already included her self-portrait in her dessert piece in the Prado (fig. 9), faintly on the central goblet and in multiple form on the pewter pitcher in the right background. It reappears on a similar pitcher in her still life in the Ashmolean, Oxford. These are not the first artist's self-portraits in reflections. The famous predecessor is Jan van Eyck, who painted himself in the mirror behind the Arnolfinis, witnessing their marriage in 1434 (London, National Gallery), but that picture was then in Spain and presumably unknown to her.[106] Perhaps the idea was suggested to her by Parmigianino's *Self-Portrait in a Convex Mirror* (ca. 1523-24, Vienna, Kunsthistorisches Museum). She cannot have known the original but she could have read Vasari's careful description of it.[107] We have already commented on how frequently some of the first women artists painted themselves, evidence of their awareness of their exceptional character and of their contemporaries' interest in them as a new phenomenon. Peeters' self-portraits, like those of Anguissola, were an ingenious form of self-promotion, though they do not seem to have brought her the success she deserved. However, two of her successors — Maria van Oosterwyck and Rachel Ruysch — also "signed" their pictures in this way so perhaps they had heard of her skills, even though she was ignored by all Northern artists' biographers.[108]

Seventeenth-century France produced a number of women still-life painters, four of whom were elected to membership in the Académie Royale. However, the best of them, Louise Moillon, was not so honored, presumably because her main period of activity, 1629-1641, preceded the founding of the Academy in 1648. The first woman to be admitted was Catherine Duchemin (1630-1698), who submitted a *Basket of Flowers on a Table* in 1663. Her admission was the occasion of a statement by Louis XIV, who declared his desire "to extend his support to all those who are excellent in the arts of Painting and Sculpture and to include all worthy of judgement without regard to the difference of sex."[109] According to one contemporary source, Duchemin gave up painting after her marriage.[110] This would mean that she

106.
It went to Spain in 1556 (M. Davies, *National Gallery Catalogues, Early Netherlandish School*, London, 1955, 39). Another less obvious example is the mirror behind St. John in the left wing of the Werl altarpiece by Robert Campin (Madrid, Prado), which in the seventeenth century was still in the patron's city, Cologne. Tufts (1974, 100) says that Jan van Eyck painted his portrait in a reflection in St. George's armor in the Canon van der Paele altarpiece, but she seems to be mistaken.

107.
Vasari, v, 221-23; see also S. J. Freedberg, *Parmigianino, His Works in Painting*, Cambridge, 1955, 104-6 and 201-2.
108.
For a reflected self-portrait in Ruysch, see Grant, 1956, no. 63 (Ruysch bibliography) and Tufts, 1974, 100 and fig. 55. Sandrart (347 and 424, note 1558) mentions a *Vanitas* by "eine Holländerin" with a self-portrait reflection, a description perhaps known to Ruysch rather than an original work by Peeters.
109.
Quoted by Faré, 1962, I, 68 (see Moillon bibliography).
110.
Florent Le Comte, quoted ibid.

was no longer active as an artist when she was admitted for she married the sculptor François Girardon in 1657. Certainly she cannot have been very productive because nothing by her is now known, except perhaps a vase of flowers in a portrait of her by Sebastian Bourdon.[111]

Geneviève and Madeleine de Boulogne, who came from a large family of artists, seem to have been more active. Both were admitted to the Academy on December 7, 1669, not only because of the quality of their work but "pour encore donner de l'émulation à toutes celles qui s'adonnent à cet art."[112] Nothing by Geneviève (1645-1708) is known today but several pictures by Madeleine (1646-1710) are preserved at Versailles. Among these are four decorative overdoors with armor and military trophies in elaborate compositions. Other works recorded in inventories depicted books, musical instruments, flowers, fruit, and a bust of Louis XIV surrounded with symbols of painting.[113] She would appear therefore to have been a versatile still-life artist and a possible source of inspiration for Anne Vallayer-Coster in the next century.

No paintings by Catherine Perrot, who was admitted to the Academy in 1682, are now known but she wrote and illustrated two books, both dedicated to aristocratic patrons, with instructions for painting flowers and birds in miniature.[114] In addition to these Academicians, we know that Charlotte Vignon (b. 1639), the tenth of twenty-four children born to the painter Claude Vignon, was active as a still-life painter in 1677. One work signed by her has been traced in an English private collection.[115] She was not admitted to the Academy, nor was Marie Blancour, an artist known only from an attractive signed picture of summer flowers in a terra-cotta vase recently given to the National Gallery, London.[116] Moillon and Madeleine de Boulogne were both serious artists; about the others we really know too little to judge their status. At present they are important mainly as an indication of the growth of interest among French women in artistic careers in the seventeenth century. Some twenty-eight women are recorded as active artists, a substantial jump from the three recorded for the previous century. Their numbers were to grow even more rapidly in the next century when France became the dominant country in the history of women artists.

In seventeenth-century Holland and Flanders, where still life was a more popular and respected genre than in France, a number of women specialized in it and one, Rachel Ruysch, became an international celebrity. These women are better represented in the exhibition than their French contemporaries, mainly because more signed works by them have been identified, but in most cases we are dealing with artists for whom only a handful of works survive; in some cases we have only one picture. Thus while historians have an impressive list of names to recite — Margaretha de Heer (see cat. no. 27), Margareta Haverman (fig. 11), Anna Jannsens, Judith Leyster (fig. 12), Maria Sibylla Merian, Jacoba Maria van Nikkelen (fig. 13), Maria van Oosterwyck, Clara Peeters, Helena Rouers, Anna Elizabeth and Rachel Ruysch, Maria Teresa Thielen, Eltje de Vlieger, Maria Weris, Alida Withoos, Michaelina Wautiers, and Caterina Ykens — very few of them will repay further research.[117] The sheer increase in numbers, as in France, is nevertheless significant, and can also be documented in Germany. In Holland we hear too of several women training with artists who were not their fathers — Haverman with Jan van Huysum, Rachel Ruysch and perhaps Margaretha de Heer with Willem van Aelst, Maria van Oosterwyck perhaps with Jan Davidsz. de Heem — an important break from the limiting tradition of family training for women. Painting was, however, an exceedingly competitive profession in seventeenth-century Holland and cases of outstanding male artists supplementing their incomes by taking second jobs are not uncommon. We can guess from the scant remaining visual and archival evidence that most of the Dutch women painters had trouble establishing themselves. Only Rachel Ruysch and Maria van Oosterwyck seem to have had a steady and prestigious clientele for their exquisitely finished flower paintings.[118]

12.
Judith Leyster
Still Life with Tankard, Basket of Fruit, and Roemer, ca. 1640
Oil on canvas
26¾ x 24⅜ in. (67.9 x 61.9 cm.)
London, Brod Gallery

111.
Ibid., and note 208 with further references. Two signed flower paintings by Duchemin were in the Sandor Sale, Vienna, May 2-10, 1918, lots 1151 and 1152. A garland of flowers surrounded an image of the Coronation of the Virgin in the first and a grisaille family scene in the second.
112.
Ibid., I, 68.
113.
Ibid., 68-69, and II, pls. 185-88.
114.
Ibid., I, 69.
115.
Ibid., I, 69-70, and II, pl. 72.

116.
No. 6358, oil on canvas, 25¾ x 20½ in., signed along lower edge, "Marie Blancour." It was bequeathed to the gallery by Captain E. G. Spencer Churchill in 1964; its previous history is not known.
117.
For further information on the women not represented in the exhibition, see Pavière, s.v., and Mitchell. A flower piece attributed to van Nikkelen in old inventories belongs to the Akademie der bildenden Künste, Vienna (no. 895); a flower piece by Rouers dated 1663 is in the Museum of Fine Arts, Copenhagen; a splendid garland of flowers dated 1652 by Wautiers is reproduced in Bernt, no. 1374; finally a flower piece by Caterina Ykens in a private collection was in the exhibition *Le siècle de Rubens*, Musées Royaux des Beaux-Arts de Belgique, Brussels, 1965, no. 307.

118.
Spain's only seventeenth-century female painter should at least be mentioned here, namely Josefa D'Obidos (ca. 1630-1684), for she is at her best as a still-life painter (see the monograph on her by Luis Reis-Santos, Lisbon, ca. 1955; one work is repr. by Mitchell, no. 267). Though born in Seville, she spent most of her life in Portugal. Her work is uneven and some of it is undeniably provincial.

Women Artists and the Academies in the Eighteenth Century

These admissions [of women to the Académie Royale], foreign in some way to its constitution, must not be allowed to become too numerous.

— Statement from a debate at the Académie Royale, Paris, in 1770

The attitude of artists' academies to women members in the eighteenth century and before was contradictory. On the one hand, a few women were elected members by most of these institutions. On the other hand, election did not mean admission to all the privileges enjoyed by male members. Some would not allow women to attend meetings, others did. None allowed them to attend drawing classes or to teach, to compete for prizes or to hold office. Their election was essentially honorific, like the award of an honorary degree. While allowing that some women did achieve a praiseworthy level of artistic accomplishment, despite the disadvantages faced by them, above all the limitations on their training, the academies continued to exclude women from nearly all of their educational facilities and from any responsible role in their administration. This arrangement was accepted with only a minimum of protest by men and women alike until the late eighteenth century.

The Académie Royale in Paris began, as we have seen, with a most liberal statement of intentions from Louis XIV himself, who declared that the Academy should be open to all gifted artists regardless of their gender. The election of Geneviève and Madeleine de Boulogne in 1669 inspired the hope that this event would encourage other women to emulate their good example. By 1682 seven women had been admitted.[119] It was almost forty years before another woman was so honored, however, and in the interim the Academy reversed its original policy and in 1706 declared that no more women could be admitted. The move may reflect the increasing conservatism of the aging Louis XIV, or perhaps a feeling among male members that the presence of so many women, several of them essentially amateurs, lowered the prestige of the institution.[120] Another incident in 1711 indicates the conservative attitude prevalent among Academicians at this time. A friend of the artist Sophie Chéron had prepared a funeral oration in her honor and asked to be allowed to read it at a meeting of the Academy. He was informed that this custom did not then exist for male members and could not therefore be initiated with a speech in honor of a woman.[121]

Despite the rule of 1706, a few women were elected Academicians by the Paris Academy in the eighteenth century. The first of these was a foreigner, Rosalba Carriera, who became a member during her triumphal visit to Paris in 1720. Two years later another foreigner, the Dutch flower painter Margareta Haverman (1693 - after 1750), was elected, but a year later the Academy decided that her *morceau de réception* had been painted by her teacher, Jan van Huysum, and she was expelled. The affair is odd because Haverman's few known signed works (e.g., fig. 11) show that by 1716 she had mastered Huysum's exquisitely detailed manner and certainly did not need to substitute one of his works for hers. He was, moreover, an exceedingly jealous and suspicious man who had no other students because he feared that they might steal his secrets, and so would certainly not have cooperated in such a fraud. It is at least possible that the French Academicians were excessively suspicious of Haverman's talents and expelled her unjustly.[122] With Carriera back in Venice, the Academy thus remained a male enclave until Marie Thérèse Reboul (1729-1805), a miniature painter and the wife of Joseph Marie Vien, was made an Academician in 1757. She was the first French woman so honored in seventy-five years. Her election was certainly due in part to her personal association with a successful male member of the Academy.[123]

The next election of a woman occurred a decade later; once more the candidate was a foreigner, Anna Dorothea Lisiewska-Therbusch of Berlin (see cat. no. 45). In 1770 two more women were admitted, Anne Vallayer-Coster and the pastel portraitist Marie Suzanne Giroust (1734-

13.
Jacoba Maria van Nikkelen
Flower Piece, ca. 1730
Oil on panel
19^5/$_{16}$ x 14^9/$_{16}$ in. (49 x 37 cm.)
Vienna, Akademie der bildenden Künste

119.
Fidière, 10-19. Fidière's book is a useful compilation but American scholars who have trouble obtaining a copy can find all of the information scattered in other nineteenth-century publications of the Academy's archives.
120.
A. de Montaiglon, *Procès-Verbaux de l'Academie Royale de Peinture et de Sculpture, 1648-1783,* Paris, 1875-92, IV, 33-34. It is stated that the motion was passed at a time when several more young women had just applied to become Academicians.
121.
The "Eloge funèbre de Madame le Hay (Elizabeth Sophie Chéron)" by M. Fermel'huis, first published in 1712, was reprinted by A. de Montaiglon in *Archives de l'art français,* 2nd series, I, 1861, 370f. Chéron's *Self-Portrait* (Paris, Louvre, no. 3239) is her only painting known today.

122.
The earliest reference to Haverman's expulsion occurs in somewhat confused terms in J. de Gool, *De nieuwe schouburg der Nederlantsche kunstschilders en schilderessen . . .,* 2 vols., The Hague, 1750-51, II, 33. Her admission but not her expulsion is recorded in Montaiglon, *Procès-Verbaux,* IV, 328. In addition to her painting in the Metropolitan Museum, New York, signed and dated 1716, there is a signed work in Copenhagen (Gammelbo, no. 180, repr.).
123.
For Diderot's comments on Mme. Vien's work, see Diderot, II, 129, and III, 173. Two miniatures by her now in the Musée Fabre, Montpellier, are repr. (III, figs. 33 and 34).

1772), the wife of Alexandre Roslin, a member since 1753. This sudden jump in the female membership to four, when the rules in theory forbade the election of any women, demanded some reconsideration of the statutes. The matter was settled by establishing a limit of four women members.[124] In fact no more women were elected until after the deaths of both Giroust-Roslin and Lisiewska-Therbusch. Only in 1783 were Elizabeth Vigée-Lebrun and Adélaïde Labille-Guiard (see fig. 14 and cat. no. 56) made Academicians. They were to be the last women so honored for a very long time.

Membership in the Paris Academy gave women only two advantages over their less fortunate female colleagues — some prestige and permission to exhibit in the Salons.[125] When women were admitted to the Academy, they were always made full members immediately by being granted the status of *agréé* and Academician simultaneously. While this move regularly was and still is interpreted as a compliment to the superior gifts of the few women granted this honor, in fact it was an arrangement necessitated by the exclusion of women from the Academy's classes of instruction. No woman could really be a proper *agréé* (apprentice Academician) because no woman could attend the life drawing classes and prepare history paintings and proceed thereby to a normal career. During and after the Revolution, the traditional structure of the Academy gradually dissolved, to be revived as the Institut de France with the educational functions taken on by the Ecole des Beaux-Arts. In 1791 Labille-Guiard not only proposed a motion to the Academy that eliminated the limitation on women members to four, making "a well-argued discourse proving that an indeterminate number of women members was the only admissible number,"[126] she also proposed a second motion. Given that women could not teach or hold office, she proposed that in the future they be admitted only as "conseilleurs," an honorary rank to which only the privilege of exhibiting in the Salons was attached. This motion also passed. Thus Labille-Guiard opened up the valuable forum of the Salons to women but at the same time removed them altogether from the ranks of Academicians. Undoubtedly the chance to exhibit in the Salons was of far greater practical value to the majority of aspiring women artists than the chance to dream of becoming an incomplete kind of Academician, but the loss of that rank in effect made official the view that women could not become great artists, while the old system, even if somewhat hypocritical, did tend to create the useful impression that a few immensely gifted women might be ranked with the most important male artists of their day.

There was one alternative institution in Paris that trained artists, licensed them as competent, and held occasional exhibitions, although it was far less prestigious than the Académie Royale, namely the Académie de Saint-Luc.[127] Its origins go back to the medieval painters' and sculptors' guilds of Paris and its members included simple frame makers, gilders and varnishers, fan and sign painters as well as a few serious artists of real ability who also joined the Académie Royale. The rules of the Académie de Saint-Luc make it clear that women apprentices and husband-wife partnerships were common. One statute waived the five-year apprenticeship for wives and daughters of masters. Another gave the admission fee for women not related to a master. Another said that women could not be admitted until they reached the age of eighteen, unless they were the daughters of masters. Between 1617, when reliable records of members began, and 1777, when the Académie de Saint-Luc was abolished by royal decree, some 4500 people were registered as masters. About one hundred thirty women are named, that is, roughly three percent of the membership, all of them admitted in the eighteenth century. Most of them were portraitists, working in oils, pastels, and in miniature. One was a sculptor.[128] Another, Mme. Moreau, admitted by 1776, was a "peintre en cheveux" (hair painter!). According to Le Brun's *Almanac* of that year "she has made several bracelets in this way for the Court, which have brought her much esteem."[129] If most of the artists, male and female, who belonged to this rival of the Académie Royale were rather modest craftsmen, the opportunities that this institution gave to women were nevertheless important. Vigée-Lebrun and Labille-Guiard

14.
Adélaïde Labille-Guiard
Portrait of the Duc de Bauffremont, 1791
Oil on canvas
88³⁄₁₆ x 57⁷⁄₈ in. (224 x 147 cm.)
Musée National du Château de Versailles

124.
Montaiglon, *Procès-Verbaux*, VIII, 53. "L'Académie ayant considéré que, quoiqu'Elle se fasse un plaisir d'encourager le talent dans les femmes en admettant quelques-unes dans son Corps, néanmoins ces admissions, étrangères en quelque façon à sa constitution, ne doivent pas être trop multipliées." (The Academy having considered that while it is pleased to encourage talent among women by admitting a few to membership, these admissions, nevertheless, foreign in some way to its constitution, must not become too numerous.) A limit of four is then stated, "si ce n'est cependant au cas où des talents extraordinairement distingués engageroient l'Académie à désirer d'une voix unanime, de les couronner par une distinction particulière" (unless there is a case of some extraordinarily distinguished talents that inspire the Academy to desire with a unanimous vote to crown them with a particular distinction). On the other hand, the Academy declares itself under no obligation to have four women members at all times.
125.
This was true despite the repetition of the formula about receiving all privileges and obligations when the women were admitted (see, for example, the texts for the admission of Vallayer-Coster and Giroust-Roslin, Montaiglon, *Procès-Verbaux*, VIII, 48 and 51).

126.
Mémoires et Journal de J.-G. Wille, ed. G. Duplessis, Paris, 1857, II, 268.
127.
Jules Guiffrey, "Histoire de l'Académie de Saint-Luc," *Archives de l'art français*, nouvelle periode, IX, 1925, 25ff. (rules) and 161ff. (lists of members).
128.
Marie Rose Daguet Lechartier (ibid., 350), recorded as a widow in 1780. Though these lists always give the profession of every male artist, the women are often listed without this information.
129.
Ibid., 399.

both exhibited with the Académie de Saint-Luc and made a name for themselves there before seeking membership in the Académie Royale, and several other able women took advantage of the occasional exhibitions at the Académie de Saint-Luc and managed moderately successful careers without the help of the Académie Royale.[130] In 1777, however, these opportunities vanished and the defenders of the Académie Royale managed to prevent other alternative exhibitions from being organized on a regular basis. Women had to wait until the end of the century for regular access to public exhibition space when the Académie Royale finally became, in this one respect, a more democratic institution.

If the Paris Academy in effect supported a discriminatory policy toward women throughout much of its existence, it was far more liberal than the English Royal Academy, founded in 1768 by Sir Joshua Reynolds. Its first two women Academicians, Angelica Kauffman and Mary Moser (1744-1819), remained the only women of that rank until this century, when Dame Laura Knight became the third.[131] Provincial French academies could, on the other hand, be far more egalitarian than the Paris Academy. The Académie Royale de Toulouse, for example, had one hundred eleven women students registered between 1751 and 1791; ten women masters exhibited in the Salons of that Academy in the same period, though not all of them were local artists.[132] One of the most active women there was the Marquise de Gauret, who showed genre compositions, portraits, history subjects, landscapes, and flower paintings.[133] The large number of provincial women students does not necessarily mean that all of them were bent on becoming professional artists. From the types of works that they submitted as examples of their skill, it seems clear that we are dealing with amateurs learning to draw as part of an upper-class education. The presence of a number of titled women suggests the same conclusion. The tradition of the lady amateur was well established in France by the late eighteenth century, as it was in England.[134] They soon became a stereotype so prevalent that it became hard for any woman to establish herself as a serious artist. No longer a phenomenal rarity, the woman artist was now in constant danger of being dismissed as a dilettante.

Women Pastel Artists of the Eighteenth Century

Several outstanding women artists of the eighteenth century worked primarily in pastel, a medium that is notoriously fragile because the soft chalks are so easily dislodged from the paper surface. No responsible owner will lend pastels to an exhibition; thus these artists could not be represented here and must be discussed in the introduction instead.

The use of colored chalks other than the standard black, red, and white was a French invention of the late fifteenth century.[135] They turn up occasionally in portrait head studies by Robert Nantueil and others in the sixteenth century, and were employed extensively and elaborately by Joseph Vivien (1657-1734), who was admitted to the Académie Royale in 1701 as a "peintre en pastel." Pastels are also used from time to time in Italian drawings of the sixteenth and seventeenth centuries, for example in the work of Frederico Barocci, Pier Francesco Mola, and Guglielmo Cortese. It was not, however, until Rosalba Carriera adopted them for her portraits and introduced her new technique, much sketchier and more impressionistic than that of Vivien, that the immense possibilities of pastels began to be generally appreciated in France. She herself did not immediately master the special qualities of these soft chalks. Her *Self-Portrait* of 1715 (fig. 15), while an appealingly straightforward portrayal of a plain woman, is technically still an imitation of an oil painting with only a few passages exploiting the unique possibilities of these opaque sticks of color, which can be built up in layers, rubbed into each other with the thumb, and applied with great freedom and with great delicacy and finesse. Only in the application of the lace over the darker skin tones and in a few passages of drapery can Carriera's natural gifts as a painter be seen, as they always are in her sparkling miniatures.

15.
Rosalba Carriera
Self-Portrait Holding Portrait of Her Sister,
1715
Pastel on paper
Florence, Galleria degli Uffizi

16.
Rosalba Carriera
Portrait of Conte Daniele Antonio Bertoli,
1730
Pastel on paper
24½ x 19⁵⁄₁₆ in. (62 x 49 cm.)
Flambruzzo (Udine), Collection Duchessa
Giuliana Badaglio Rota
Photo Alinari

130.
Ibid., 192 (Anne Rosalie Bocquet, later Filleul); 309 (Marie Jacobe van Merle Godefroy); 403 (Mlle. Navarre); 408 (Mlle. Ozanne); and 448-49 (Mlle. de Saint-Martin). Filleul's *Portrait of the Children of the Comte d'Artois* (Versailles, Musée National) was exhibited at Castres (1973, no. 7). A pastel portrait of a woman by Mlle. Navarre was exhibited recently in Paris (1975, no. 6, Collection Cailleux, Paris).
131.
Elizabeth Butler was almost elected in 1879 but the Academy then decided that, despite the precedent set by Kauffman and Moser, the rules formally excluded women members. The first woman to loosen the rules was Annie Louisa Swynnerton, who became an Associate Member (ARA) in 1922, an honor awarded four other women in addition to Knight by 1968. Even Dame Laura, an Academician since 1936, was only allowed to attend the annual members' banquet for the first time in 1967 (see Hutchison, 138, 176, 199).

A flower painting by Moser in the Royal Collection is repr. by Mitchell (185, fig. 257). There are also works by her in the collection of the Royal Academy, London; the Victoria and Albert Museum; the British Museum; and the Fitzwilliam Museum, Cambridge (Broughton Bequest).
132.
R. Mesuret, *Les expositions de l'Académie Royale de Toulouse de 1751 à 1791*, Toulouse, 1972, passim.
133.
Ibid., 582.
134.
Ibid., 257f. In this section of the Salon catalog of 1774, the works by women artists are grouped together. They consist mainly of drawings, copies, and miniatures. For some leads on English women amateurs of high and humble origins, see E. W. Manwaring, *Italian Landscape in Eighteenth-Century England,* New York, 1925, 86-91.

By 1730, when Carriera made the portrait of Conte Daniele Antonio Bertoli (fig. 16) and by the 1740s, when she drew Charles Sackville, 2nd Duke of Dorset (fig. 17), she had perfected and polished her technique to a spectacular level. In these two beautifully preserved examples, we can appreciate her artistic achievement to the full. The image of the Italian count seems to float above the darker layers of background color and a foundation of supporting drapery. Her "dry-brush" technique — an effect created by dragging the flat side of a chalk lightly over a contrasting tone of color — is used here to spectacular effect for the lace jabot of Conte Daniele. The result is a brilliant illusion heightened with a few final dark strokes hinting at the pattern in the lace. The finish of his white wig is equally fine. The confidence with which a lace border is laid along the edge of Lord Sackville's hat and the brocade pattern of his beautifully shaded silk jacket sketched is no less impressive. Carriera's ability to preserve a strong sense of character and personality even while flattering her subjects is also well illustrated by all three works.[136]

17.
Rosalba Carriera
Portrait of Charles Sackville, 2nd Duke of Dorset, ca. 1740
Pastel on paper
Knole, Sevenoaks, Kent, Collection
Lord Sackville

Yet even more than Carriera, it was Maurice Quentin de la Tour who developed the pastel portrait in eighteenth-century France. His pastels do not merely rival oils but even seem to surpass them for all kinds of illusionistic and painterly effects.[137] He did not confine his compositions to busts and half-lengths, as Carriera did, but on occasion made very large pastels with three-quarter and full-length compositions, posing his sitters with striking originality and forcefulness. A far more vivid portraitist than Carriera, he was immensely successful, so much so that his only real rival, J. B. Perronneau, had to spend much of his career outside France in order to make a living.

Unlike la Tour, Carriera produced no outstanding women students. She had neither assistants, apart from her sister, nor pupils, apart from Felicita Sartori, who became a miniaturist. However, her famous example may have inspired Marie Catherine Silvestre (née Herault, 1680-1743), who was born in Paris, to try her hand at pastel portraits, though the results are only competent.[138] Far more impressive are the two known pastel portraits by Theresa Concordia Mengs (1725-1808), the sister of Anton Raphael, whose rigorous childhood training she partly shared.[139] Her portrait of her sister Julia and her self-portrait (figs. 18 and 19) are outstanding examples of eighteenth-century pastel portraiture, with all the immediacy and informal realism associated with the best examples of the genre. Carriera cannot be credited with more than distant influence as a female role model. The careful, highly finished technique of Theresa Mengs belongs to the disciplined, incipient Neoclassical school of her brother, Anton Raphael, who was himself a superb portraitist.

Quentin de la Tour was an irascible, difficult character whose strange habits led to many amusing anecdotes about his eccentric behavior. He hardly sounds like the kind of artist who would have pupils, let alone be an effective teacher, yet the two finest women pastelists of the late eighteenth century were partially trained by him. The first of these was Marie Suzanne Giroust, better known as Madame Roslin (she married the Swedish portrait painter Alexandre Roslin in 1759, after he had settled in Paris).[140] She did not live long enough to fulfill the promise of her first public success at the Salon of 1771, for she died a year later of breast cancer at the age of thirty-eight. Her dated works cover only a five-year period, 1766 to 1771. Her career can hardly have been helped by six pregnancies, her last child being born only five months before her death. Barely a dozen pastels by her are known.

The identified subjects of many of her portraits are family friends and members of her own family. Her portrait of her daughter (fig. 20) is an idealized image of a beautiful child. She is shown holding her pet dog in one arm and a basket of fruit on the other, her hair piled up in a fancy, powdered style, as elegantly costumed and as frivolously occupied as any young aristocrat's daughter.[141] Giroust-Roslin's masterpiece is her portrait of the sculptor, Jean Baptiste

18.
Theresa Concordia Mengs
Portrait of the Artist's Sister, Julia Mengs, ca. 1750
Pastel on paper
16½ x 13⅜ in. (42 x 34 cm.)
Dresden, Gemäldegalerie

35.
A good brief history of the use of pastel chalks in France before Carriera's arrival in Paris is given by Maurice Sérullaz in his preface to Geneviève Monnier's *Pastels XVIIe et XVIIIe siècles*, Musée National du Louvre, Cabinet des Dessins, Inventaire des Collections Publiques Françaises 18, Paris, 1972.
136.
For the dating of these two pastels in the 1740s, see Gatto, 186 (Carriera bibliography).
137.
Louis Vigée, Elizabeth Vigée-Lebrun's father, was far more obviously influenced by Carriera's work than la Tour (see Monnier, *Pastels*, nos. 106-8).
138.
B. Molajoli, *Notizie su Capodimonte: Catalogo delle Gallerie e del Museo*, Naples, 1960, 82 (ten pastel portraits of the Polish Royal family, ca. 1740).
139.
She was in Rome by 1741. There she met her husband, Anton von Maron, whom she married in 1765.

According to P. F. Schmidt (in Thieme-Becker, XXIV, 393), there are works by her in the collection of the University of Würzburg. A good oil portrait of Bernardo Cavaceppi attributed to her is in the Galleria dell'Accademia di San Luca, Rome (no. 40). She and her husband became members in 1765. In addition to the two pastels in Dresden illustrated here (nos. P 178 and P 179), that museum owns two miniature copies by her after Correggio's *Giorno* and *Notte* (nos. M63 and M64).
140.
For more information, see Gunnar W. Lundberg's entry on Giroust-Roslin in Thieme-Becker (XXIX, 29) and his monograph on her husband (*Röslin Liv och Werk*, Malmö, 1957, I, 79, 80, 102, 125f., 140f., and 305). Dr. Lundberg responded generously to my inquiries with information and photographs.

Pigalle (fig. 21), her reception piece when she was elected to the Académie Royale in 1770.[142] This is a far more ambitious work than the portrait of her daughter, for it was intended to display the artist's virtuosity in a difficult medium as well as to stress the stature and achievements of her sitter. Pigalle was then both an officer (*Adjoint au Recteur*) of the Academy and a Chevalier of the Order of St. Michael, whose robes he wears. The black silk suit with moiré lapels and the black cloak with its pale blue moiré borders are magnificently realized, as are his wig, lace jabot, and cuffs. He points discreetly at the cross of the Order of St. Michael lying in his lap and turns to regard us confidently as we gaze past him to a model of his (now partially destroyed) monument to Louis XV in Reims. The background areas are deliberately treated in a rougher, more atmospheric manner to contrast with the crisp, exquisitely detailed finish of the figure in the foreground. The wealth of detail is tempered somewhat by the restricted color scheme which uses only black, gray, white, blue, and flesh tones. In drawing, in lively presentation of character, and in virtuosity of technique, this work is in every way a challenge to the great la Tour.

La Tour's other important female pupil was Adélaïde Labille-Guiard, who studied with him for five years and who worked almost exclusively in pastels until her admission to the Academy in 1783. After that date, she switched to oils.[143] None of her pastel portraits are conceived in quite such an ambitious spirit as Giroust-Roslin's portrait of Pigalle, although her own *morceau de réception,* the *Portrait of Augustin Pajou* (1782, Paris, Louvre), comes very close. Since both works are portraits of sculptors, they make an ideal comparison, but they are conceived very differently. Labille-Guiard shows Pajou working energetically on a bust of J. B. Lemoyne, his teacher. He is dressed in his work clothes, his sleeves rolled up to the elbow, and the contrast with the dignified formality of Pigalle could hardly be greater. The presentations were appropriate in each case. Pigalle was much concerned with raising the status of sculpture in France and therefore attached much importance to the honors he received. Pajou, on the other hand, was a relaxed, easygoing man, far less concerned with the external trappings of success. Labille-Guiard's other portraits of members of the Academy executed shortly before her admission do not seek to dazzle the spectator with technical feats or novel compositions. Most of them are absolutely straightforward bust-length images that concentrate the viewer's attention on the sitter's physiognomy and character. As a group they show how thoroughly she had mastered the art of drawing and of pastel color before she moved on to the medium of oil painting, in which she was to produce her finest works.

Labille-Guiard's best pupil, Gabrielle Capet (see cat. no. 62), also produced some fine pastel portraits in addition to the miniatures for which she is best known. A good example of these, a *Portrait of M. J. Chenier,* belongs to the University of Stanford Art Museum.[144] Vigée-Lebrun also on occasion worked in pastel, although she never used the medium as extensively as did Labille-Guiard. Isolated survivals by other women artists could also be mentioned, for example a *Portrait of a Young Woman* (1727, Amsterdam, Rijksmuseum), by Françoise Madeleine Basseporte (1701-1780), who is better known as a flower painter.[145] Carriera remains, however, the most spectacular and the most influential of women artists who used pastels. Her female successors, either from choice or circumstance, cannot rival her exceptional achievement.

Women Artists, 1550-1800: Conclusions

What can be learned from this gathering of works of art by women and from a study of European women artists active before the nineteenth century? The implication of any exhibition is that the works chosen benefit from their temporary juxtaposition because they share some aesthetic qualities, but these works do not share any special visual characteristics due to

19.
Theresa Concordia Mengs
Self-Portrait, ca. 1750
Pastel on paper
16⁵/₁₆ x 12¹⁵/₁₆ in. (41.5 x 33 cm.)
Dresden, Gemäldegalerie

20.
Suzanne Giroust-Roslin
Portrait of the Artist's Daughter, Augustine Suzanne, 1771
Pastel on paper
23⅛ x 18⅞ in. (59 x 48 cm.)
Paris, Institut Tessin

141.
G. W. Lundberg, *Svenskt och Franskt 1700-Tal i Institut Tessins Samlingar*, Malmö, 1972, 492, no. 1010 and 296f. See also Castres, 1973, no. 29. Her name was Augustine Suzanne.
142.
Lundberg, *Röslin Liv och Werk*, I, 126. See also Monnier, *Pastels*, no. 103. For Diderot's comments on this and her other Salon exhibits of 1771, see Diderot, IV, 202.
143.
Passez, cat. nos. 1 to 54 (see Labille-Guiard bibliography); see also the color pls. opposite 16 (*Self-Portrait*) and 22 (*Portrait of Vincent*). For the portrait of Pajou discussed below, see Passez, no. 37, and Monnier, *Pastels*, no. 57.
144.
The Mortimer C. Leventritt Collection of Far Eastern and European Art, The Thomas W. Stanford Art Gallery, Stanford University, 1941, 105, no. 305 (repr.).

their female authorship. They are best viewed as part of a *musée imaginaire* where, by some extraordinary circumstance, all the artists happen to be women and not men.

If work by women artists has more in common with that by their male contemporaries than that by other women, nevertheless women shared some experiences that affected the kind of work they produced. As has frequently been noted, most women artists before the nineteenth century were the daughters of artists. Those who married often married artists as well. Most women artists before 1800 were trained by their fathers, or by their husbands or some other male relative. Because women could not study the human figure adequately or attend Academy schools, they had to restrict themselves to the arts of portraiture and still life. As portraitists, they painted more women and children than their male contemporaries. Notable exceptions to these general rules can be found throughout the period under discussion but the situation of women artists generally did not change significantly until the nineteenth century.

The most important indication of a changing situation for women artists before 1800 is the growth in their numbers.[146] In the fifteenth century, fewer than ten women throughout Europe are recorded as artists in published documents. In the eighteenth century, almost three hundred women are described as artists in various sources. They still constituted a small percentage of the total population of artists, but by 1750 or so it was no longer exceptionally eccentric for a woman with artistic gifts to decide to earn her living in this way. The exhibition concentrates naturally on the most accomplished and successful women but we should not forget that by the late eighteenth century it was possible for women artists of more modest talents to support themselves, for example by giving drawing lessons, either privately or to groups of students in convent schools.[147]

The existence of female drawing teachers depended on another social development, namely the widespread acceptance of the idea that a well-educated young lady should know how to draw and paint. The practice that had begun in convents in the late Middle Ages and had been encouraged by Castiglione in sixteenth-century Urbino became commonplace throughout the European upper classes by the end of the eighteenth century. References to duchesses, countesses, princesses, and even queens who could draw, paint, and engrave are not unusual,[148] and if some of these women reached a commendable standard, it is also easy to believe that by the nineteenth century George Eliot had reason to condemn "domestic music and feminine fine art" as "small tinkling and smearing."[149] The dabbling female dilettante is with us still, and every woman artist who works at home has experienced the frustration of being dismissed as one.

One intriguing characteristic shared by many of the women represented here has not been commented on previously, namely their precocity. For a surprisingly large percentage of these artists, we have evidence of professional activity before the age of twenty. In many cases, the works themselves survive as proof of their exceptional natural endowment. Fede Galizia's artistic promise was noted publicly when she was twelve. Angelica Kauffman painted her self-portrait at the age of thirteen.[150] Vigée-Lebrun was supporting her family at the age of fifteen. Giovanna Garzoni signed a painting of the Madonna at the age of sixteen. Sirani's own list of her work records five paintings made when she was seventeen, and Artemisia Gentileschi was the same age when she painted her *Susanna and the Elders* in Pommersfelden (cat. no. 10). Leyster had already attracted public comment on her gifts when she was seventeen. Clara Peeters' first dated work was painted when she was seventeen, and those of Rachel Ruysch and Anne Vallayer-Coster when they were eighteen. Susan Horenbout was eighteen when she sold a miniature to Dürer. Louise Moillon's first surviving painting was made when she was nineteen. Caterina van Hemessen and Judith Leyster have both left us works painted when they were twenty. While references to precocious artistic activity by male artists are not

21.
Suzanne Giroust-Roslin
Portrait of the Sculptor Jean Baptiste Pigalle, 1770
Pastel on paper
35 13/16 x 28 3/8 in. (91 x 73 cm.)
Paris, Musée National du Louvre

145.
Museum no. 1925 H 1. It seems possible that it is a self-portrait. According to Faré (1962, I, 136f., see Moillon bibliography), there are a large number of flower studies by her in the Cabinet d'Estampes of the Bibliothèque Nationale. For a pastel by Mlle. Navarre, see note 130.
146.
See note 38 for more figures.
147.
See the section, "Maîtres à dessiner en ville" in J. B. Le Brun, *Almanach historique et raisonné des architectes, peintres, sculpteurs, graveurs et ciseleurs,* Paris, 1776, 154 ("Mlle . . . Machelard, rue de Seine, près le Caffé Royal, donne des leçons dans le Convens avec succès. Sa réputation est faite.") and ff.

148.
The activities of Madame de Pompadour and Queen Marie Leczinska in this respect are well known. A century earlier Honthorst gave lessons to the Queen of Bohemia and her daughters (J. R. Judson, *Gerrit van Honthorst,* The Hague, 1959, xx). A perfect illustration of this social trend is J. A. Pajou's *Portrait of the Mesdemoiselles Duval* of 1814 in the Louvre.
149.
In *Middlemarch* (Penguin edition, 89).
150.
Bregenz, 1968, no. I, Supporting material for statements in this section without footnotes will be found in the catalog biographies of the women named.

unknown, it is by no means usual to be able to discuss works made before they reached their twenties. Gian Lorenzo Bernini is probably the best-documented male child prodigy in the visual arts,[151] while Michelangelo has also left us a few very early works. Raphael signed a contract before he was twenty, and Rembrandt signed and dated a few paintings before he turned twenty. These men remain exceptions, however, to the general rule that precocity is not associated with the visual arts as it is, for example, with musical creativity.

Several possible explanations for the apparently precocious development of women artists before 1800 can be suggested. The phenomenon might indicate that only women who demonstrated extraordinary potential as artists received any encouragement. Women who were late developers or who were less remarkably gifted as children simply never became artists. We can also guess that it was good business to promote women artists while they were young and attractive; their gifts seemed even more astonishing and they attracted not only clients but also suitors. We can even hypothesize that since the kind of works most women were allowed, so to speak, to make required less training than those usually produced by male artists, women could make their debuts sooner than men, who had to master anatomy, perspective, large-scale composition, and special techniques such as fresco. It is also evidently the case that the women themselves and their patrons were anxious to document their amazing careers from the beginning, the artists by dating and selling early works, their patrons by preserving them.

22.
Elizabeth Vigée-Lebrun
Portrait of Charles Alexandre de Calonne, 1785
Oil on canvas
59 x 50½ in. (149.9 x 128.3 cm.)
Windsor Castle, Collection H.M. the Queen

In the sixteenth, seventeenth, and eighteenth centuries a few women artists became international celebrities. Their services were sought by distinguished patrons, including royalty, from many countries. Several of them left their homes to work at the courts of Madrid, Düsseldorf, Vienna, and St. Petersburg. Their works fetched high prices and some of these women became extremely wealthy. In this special group we can place Sofonisba Anguissola, Levina Teerlinc, and Lavinia Fontana in the sixteenth century; Elisabetta Sirani and Rachel Ruysch in the seventeenth century; and Rosalba Carriera, Angelica Kauffman, and Elizabeth Vigée-Lebrun in the eighteenth century. Other women artists, active at the same time and similarly gifted, failed for some reason to catch the public imagination in the same way and led comparatively obscure lives. Clara Peeters, Fede Galizia, Judith Leyster, Louise Moillon, Artemisia Gentileschi, Marie Anne Loir (see cat. no. 44), Françoise Duparc (see cat. nos. 46, 47), Anne Vallayer-Coster, and Adélaïde Labille-Guiard were all successful enough to make a living, and some of them managed to do more than that, but none received the adulation accorded the women in the first group. How can we explain these differences in their public reception?

It was obviously not enough simply to be a talented woman artist at a time when they were rare. While their scarcity gave every woman artist the advantage (possibly dubious) of some curiosity value, only a few women artists were able to build on this foundation and become spectacularly successful. All of the celebrated women named were popular in court and aristocratic circles. This fact suggests that all of them were especially good at social relationships and fitted comfortably into this setting. In fact we have contemporary testimony that this was the case for all the women named except Teerlinc and Ruysch; in their cases, we simply lack firsthand testimony about their personalities rather than have any evidence to the contrary. Gentileschi and Lisiewska-Therbusch, on the other hand, were considerably less successful in this respect although both actively sought the patronage of rulers and powerful noblemen. Neither woman fitted the stereotype of the gracious lady most likely to be a success at court, and their strong, aggressive personalities may have been a handicap in this respect.

The most successful women were not only productive artists but also provided something that appealed to their public. Most of them were excellent portraitists. Sirani continued to work in the manner of Guido Reni, whose style was still extremely popular a generation after

151.
Irving Lavin, "Five New Youthful Sculptures by Gianlorenzo Bernini and a Revised Chronology of His Early Works," *Art Bulletin*, L, 1968, 223-48.
Perhaps Edward Landseer should be mentioned also.

his death. The spectacular flower pieces and nature studies of Ruysch had and still have a strong popular appeal. Clara Peeters, on the other hand, evolved a highly specialized form of still life that went out of fashion in Flanders shortly after its creation. Fede Galizia's austerely simple still lives appeal to us but were not elaborate enough to impress her contemporaries. Gentileschi's Caravaggesque manner was out of favor in Rome by the 1620s. She, too, had to make a stylistic accommodation with new fashions less suited to her artistic temperament. The status of still life in France was not high enough for Louise Moillon to have the éclat she deserved in the seventeenth century; Vallayer-Coster was more successful partly because still life was more esteemed in France by the eighteenth century.

Three women artists of the eighteenth century — Rosalba Carriera, Angelica Kauffman, and Elizabeth Vigée-Lebrun — enjoyed a degree of fame and adulation unparalleled before or since. Does their public reception indicate something significant about eighteenth-century attitudes towards accomplished women or only something about the abilities of these women to express something especially meaningful about the times in which they lived? All three were extremely productive artists, more so even than most of their female predecessors and contemporaries. All three were undeniably good at painting flattering portraits of the upper-class patrons who supported them, and Kauffman in addition produced attractive history paintings of classical subjects much appreciated by all eighteenth-century devotees of classical civilization. All three offered an original and complimentary image to their clients — Carriera her brilliant, elegantly colored, and seemingly effortless Rococo pastels; Kauffman her charming and gentle version of the Neoclassical portrait, and Vigée-Lebrun her equally flattering but more forcefully drawn portrayals (see fig. 22). The influential place of women in the salon society of the eighteenth century must also partially explain why it was so receptive to the talents of these artists. Their careers represent a special historical phenomenon well worth more detailed attention from social historians.

A study of the careers of women artists from 1550 to 1800 inevitably increases our awareness of the effectiveness of the traditional methods of training male artists, either in the studios of established masters or in the academies that supplemented them in the eighteenth century. Those long apprenticeships spent drawing after antique casts, after famous paintings, after engravings, and after the posed nude male model have been suspected of stultifying genius and promoting only mediocre competence, but one has only to consider the limitations placed on the careers of gifted women denied this training to understand how effective in fact it was and how essential to artists of all levels of talent. Though many women managed remarkably well without the benefits of a full-scale training, it is easy to imagine that Lavinia Fontana, Artemisia Gentileschi, Elisabetta Sirani, Anna Dorothea Lisiewska-Therbusch, and Adélaïde Labille-Guiard, for example, would have been even better and more versatile artists had they had a more thorough grounding in anatomy, figure drawing, perspective, and traditional historical composition.

In all those specialties where an academic training matters less, women artists were highly successful. They have equaled their male contemporaries as portraitists in all media and on all scales from the large official icon to the miniature. In still life too we find several outstanding women artists who made significant contributions to the evolution of this genre. Maria Sibylla Merian, one of the finest botanical illustrators of the seventeenth century, also made an important contribution to the history of the biological sciences (see fig. 23). Though rarer, women also made some beautiful and original genre pictures and history paintings. The exhibition should prove, if this is still necessary, that women have always had great potential in the visual arts and that their contribution has grown as barriers to their training and careers have slowly declined.

23.
Maria Sibylla Merian
A Blue Honey Creeper and a Yellow-Winged Bird on a Thistle, ca. 1680
Watercolor and tempera on parchment
Cambridge, Fitzwilliam Museum

What is the place of these women in the history of Renaissance, Baroque, and Rococo paint-ing? To what degree has prejudice resulted in the neglect and inadequate appreciation of their work? Is the relative silence of modern art historical scholarship a just reflection on their merits? Do any of these women deserve a place in the standard survey courses that introduce thousands of students annually to the peaks of achievement in Western art? Should any of these painters be included in undergraduate courses on these centuries? In art historical terms who were the most influential women artists? And what are the most significant points to be made about women artists generally?

These questions must be answered by each visitor to the exhibition and each reader of this catalog for themselves, for there are many possible responses. The catalog contains abundant evidence of neglect by scholars of these painters but the situation will not change unless their exposure here touches a strong chord of response in a wider public. It is not difficult to find negative critical reactions to many of these artists made recently by art historians whose work is justly respected. For obvious reasons, few such opinions have been quoted in this catalog but the exhibition will nevertheless remind us how often the "objective" art historian func-tions as "subjective" critic, as often by the decision to omit an artist as by condemning her work in print.

Given that the choice of monuments and artists touched on in introductory survey courses and in more detailed period surveys is inevitably arbitrary and personal to some degree, the inclusion of a few women can easily be defended. One work now represented in most standard survey texts makes some reference to the early history of women artists easy to include, namely the Bayeux Tapestry. And even if Sofonisba Anguissola's contribution to Renaissance portraiture does not earn her a place in a Renaissance chapter, her historical impact as the first woman artist to become a celebrity and thereby to open up these professions to women certainly does. The growing numbers of women artists and their greater degree of accomplish-ment in the seventeenth century could be mentioned in connection with a work by Maria van Oosterwyck or Rachel Ruysch, who could illustrate Dutch still life as well as Jan Davidsz. de Heem or Willem Kalf.[152] The exceptional popularity of Carriera, Kauffman, and Vigée-Lebrun in the eighteenth century justifies the inclusion of examples of their work, which can also underline the importance of portraiture or clarify the character of Rococo or Neoclassical art. By the time a survey reaches the nineteenth century, major women artists are even more abundant and their neglect harder to justify. The inclusion of a few women artists also allows additional points to be made about the social origins of artists and the growth of institutions that trained them. Detailed discussion of the achievements of some of the artists represented here can surely be justified in any course covering seventeenth- and eighteenth-century art, and even in a Renaissance course some comment on the reasons for their scarcity could be given. Slowly these artists must be integrated into their art historical context. For too long they have either been omitted altogether, or isolated, as even in this exhibition, and discussed only as women artists, and not simply as artists, as if in some strange way they were not a part of their culture at all. This exhibition will be a success if it helps to remove once and for all the justification for any future exhibitions with this theme.

Ann Sutherland Harris

152.
The former was chosen by H. W. Janson for his famous *History of Art,* the latter by the editors of Helen Gardner's survey.

Women Artists after the French Revolution

Why should people prone to pregnancy and passing indispositions be barred from the exercise of rights no one would dream of denying those who have gout or catch cold easily?
— *Le Marquis de Condorcet, 1790*

For women artists, as for women in general, the French Revolution appears to have been a mixed blessing, opening up some doors, shutting others, exhilarating in theory but often exclusive and repressive in practice. While it is certainly true that some of the *philosophes,* the Marquis de Condorcet above all, paved the way for Revolutionary feminism, others, like Jean Jacques Rousseau, made it abundantly clear that marriage and motherhood — and little else besides — were woman's "natural" vocation.

Condorcet, in 1787, had made the first attempt to incorporate the case for the civil equality of women into the liberal political ideology of the Enlightenment.[153] He maintained that if women were to be taxed, they should be able to vote; that domestic authority should be shared; that the professions and, most importantly, educational opportunity should be opened up to the female sex.[154] In essence, Condorcet provided a political theory that justified the principle of equality before the law for everyone, regardless of sex, thus including females in the general term *mankind* for the first time in history.[155]

During the Revolution itself, feminist pamphlets and various proposals for the betterment of women's condition appeared, and women began sending delegations to the government and using the political clubs as a platform. In 1791 Olympe de Gouges, one of the major feminists of the French Revolution, enunciated her "Declaration of the Rights of Women": "All women," she declared, "are born free and remain equal to men in rights. . . . Law is the expression of the general will: all female and male citizens have the right to participate personally or through their representatives in its formation." She also demanded equality of opportunity in public employment, the right to paternity suits, and a general end to male domination.[156] Yet despite the sensational activism of feminists like Olympe de Gouges, Etta Palm, and Théroigne de Méricourt, and a feminist program (rather piecemeal, it is true) of educational, economic, political, and legal change, women were eventually systematically excluded from most Revolutionary benefits, including the right to vote. Their political clubs were outlawed in the fall of 1793.

Although politically advanced, the Revolution was in many ways socially conservative: along with middle-class ideals of political liberty and economic opportunity it espoused the equally middle-class ideal, recently developed at that, of the happy nuclear family, the family as a secure nest offering shelter from the brutality of public or professional life. The Rousseauan notion of woman as the "natural" guardian of the home militated strongly against her achievement of status as an independent being, in the arts as elsewhere.

It is symptomatic of Revolutionary hostility toward the advancement of women that the first act of the Société Populaire et Républicaine des Arts (successor to the earlier Commune des Arts), established in 1793, was to exclude women from its meetings. The arguments raised by the members of the Society in coming to this decision are worth examining in detail, since they were to provide the basis for similar exclusionary decisions in the future. The members decided to close the door to women artists because women were "different from men in every respect." Since the Society, it was maintained, had as its goal the cultivation of the arts rather than politics, and since the law forbade women to assemble and deliberate for any reason, to admit them would be to go against the law. In response to one member's feeble protest that the Jacobin Society had admitted a woman member, another *sociétaire* stoutly maintained that among Republicans, women must absolutely give up the jobs destined to men. Although

153.
K. B. Clinton, "Femme et philosophe: Enlightenment Origins of Feminism," *Eighteenth-Century Studies,* VIII, no. 3, Spring 1975, 295.
154.
See especially Condorcet's "Lettres d'un bourgeois de New Haven à un citoyen de Virginie" in his *Oeuvres,* ed. F. O'Connor and M. R. Arago, Paris, 1847, VIII, 15-19. For an excellent summary of feminism and the French Revolution, see J. Abray, "Feminism in the French Revolution," *American Historical Review,* LXXX, February 1975, 43-62.
155.
Clinton, *Eighteenth-Century Studies,* 295-96 and 298-99.
156.
Abray, *American Historical Review,* 48-49.

admitting that for his own satisfaction, he would be happy to live with a woman who was talented in the arts, still, to do so would be to act against the laws of nature. "Among savage people," he asked (rhetorically to be sure) "those in consequence who are closest to the state of nature, are women ever seen doing the work of men?" The whole issue was blamed on the "Citizeness le Brun" (Mme. Vigée-Lebrun), who exhibited great talent for art and had thereby inspired a horde of other women who "wished to busy themselves with painting although they should only occupy themselves with embroidering the sword-belts and caps of the police." The proposal that only female citizens recognized for their talent and exemplary character should be admitted was countered with the assertion that other popular societies would be angered by the admission of women to the Société des Arts. Finally, despite the fact that their rules made no such stipulation, the Society voted "purely and simply that female citizens would not be admitted."[157]

Yet despite such overt exclusion of women artists from the institutions governing their profession; despite the fact that they were to be denied admission both to the Ecole des Beaux-Arts and the prestigious Class of Fine Arts of the Institute until almost the end of the nineteenth century;[158] and despite the fact that they had to study their craft apart from their male colleagues and under far less favorable conditions, women artists nevertheless made progress, as a group and as individuals, in the years following the Revolution. Whether it was because of the less restricted access to the Salons or the greater emphasis on portraits and genre rather than history painting (despite lip service to the latter),[159] increasing numbers of women painters participated in public exhibitions in the early 1800s. In the 1801 Salon, out of a total of 192 painters exhibiting, about 28, or 14.6%, were women; in 1810, out of 390 painters exhibiting, about 70, or 17.9%, were women; in 1822, out of 475 painters exhibiting, about 67, or 14.1%, were women; and in 1835, out of 801 painters exhibiting, about 178, or 22.2%, were women. Thus, both in terms of percentages and even more dramatically in terms of absolute numbers (since the Salons themselves expanded), the statistical position of women painters improved in the Salons of the first third of the nineteenth century.

Yet such statistics, of course, tell us little about the kind of work women were exhibiting or the attitudes toward women's painting revealed by critics, patrons, and public. It is naturally difficult to generalize about such a varied group of painters; still, one would be safe in saying that the relatively unprestigious genre of the portrait was the most popular among women artists; indeed, critics early in the century recognized the "happy fecundity" of women painters as portraitists.[160] Another type of painting particularly popular with women artists, as indeed it was with many of their male contemporaries, was what might best be termed "sentimental genre": intimate, often domestic, scenes of heart-warming pleasure or, less frequently, heart-breaking minor tragedy, often with moralizing overtones. It must be emphasized that women had no monopoly on this sort of painting, most often associated with Greuze in the eighteenth century and with Boilly, Drolling, and Léopold Robert in the nineteenth; a painting like Ingres' *Henry IV Playing with His Children* (current location unknown)[161] of 1817 is certainly a prime example of the genre under its historical aspect. Nevertheless, in the early nineteenth century, women artists like Marguerite Gérard, Pauline Auzou (see cat. no. 71), Constance Mayer (see cat. no. 72, fig. 24), Eugénie Servières, Elisabeth Chaudet, and Antoinette Haudebourt-Lescot (see cat. no. 75) must certainly be said to have staked out a considerable claim in this popular if not highly respected territory.

Some of these women artists even developed specializations within this already restricted domain as a way of establishing a clearer identity in a highly competitive field, a ploy not uncommon with painters of both sexes before or since. Mme. Haudebourt-Lescot, for example, specialized in — and may even be said to have invented — Italian genre subjects, like *Dancing the Saltarello* or *The Marionette Theater in Rome,* with an emphasis on scenes of

24.
Constance Mayer
The Happy Mother, 1810
Oil on canvas
Paris, Musée National du Louvre

157.
H. Lapauze, ed., *Procès-Verbaux de la Commune Générale des Arts et de la Société Populaire et Républicaine des Arts,* Paris, 1903, L-LI and 183-85.
158.
See Boime, 3-8, for the basic structure, and restructuring, of these institutions.
159.
See Schnapper, "Painting during the Revolution, 1789-1799," in Paris, 1974, 109-10.
160.
G. Wildenstein, "Table des portraits exposés à Paris au Salon entre 1800 et 1826," *Gazette des beaux-arts,* LXI, 1963, 10.
161.
Wherever possible, current locations of works are given. Those not provided are not available.

woman's daily life. Mme. Chaudet, although she did attempt an antique subject in the Salon of 1810 — the now-vanished *Dibutade* — specialized in the genre subcategory of children with animals, a choice well suited to her modest talents, according to Charles Landon.[162] She established her reputation in the Salon of 1799 with a *Little Girl Trying to Teach Her Dog to Read. A Young Girl Feeding Her Chickens* appeared in the Salon of 1802 and *A Young Girl Mourning the Death of Her Pigeon* (Musée d'Arras) in the Salon of 1808.[163] A more dramatic variant of this popular child-and-animal theme by Mme. Chaudet, *A Child Asleep in His Cradle Guarded by a Brave Dog* of 1801 (Musée de Rochefort), in which the sleeping infant seems to have been saved from a serpent by his faithful canine companion, evidently set a precedent. The next year Mme. Villers (see cat. no. 74) presented the even more heart-rending *Baby in Its Cradle Carried Off by the Floods of the Year X*, in which the little victim is accompanied by a faithful dog who paddles along beside the floating cradle — a theme of canine life-saving that ultimately reaches its apotheosis in the English artist Landseer's *Saved* of 1856, in which a giant Newfoundland is represented after having rescued a drowning child.

Yet not all women artists felt themselves restricted to portraits or to genre scenes at the beginning of the nineteenth century: far from it. Nanine Vallain (dates unknown), for example, was a pupil of David's and of Suvée's who exhibited in the Salons from 1793 to 1810. Although she did paint a *Young Woman Seated with a Lamb on Her Lap* in 1788, early in her career, as well as the requisite portraits, she also turned to classical, allegorical, and religious themes. In the Salon of 1793 she showed two Ovidian subjects — *Ceyx and Alcyone* and *Acontius and Cydippe* — both on an ample, if not extravagant, scale. In 1795 she showed a *Spartan Woman Giving a Sword to Her Son;* in 1806, *Sappho Singing a Hymn to Love;* in 1808, *Cain Fleeing with His Family after the Death of Abel;* and in 1810, *Tirzah, Wife of Abel, Crying on the Tomb of Her Spouse and Imploring Mercy.* Most interesting of all, because of its high quality and because it reveals the artist's sympathies with and possible participation in the French Revolution — sympathies rarely embodied in the surviving work of women artists — is Vallain's *Liberty* of 1793-94 (fig. 25), now undergoing restoration in the Louvre. This painting, seized after the closing of the Jacobin Club on 9 Thermidor, 1794,[164] represents an allegorical figure of Liberty dressed in a blue tunic and dark yellow skirt over a red-trimmed white undergarment, holding a red Phrygian cap on a pike in her left hand, the Declaration of the Rights of Man in her right. On the ground at her feet are a symbolic fallen crown and chains as well as the fasces, ancient emblem of authority. The commemorative function of the painting is suggested by an urn to the left, inscribed: "To our brothers who died for her . . ." as well as by the pyramidal cenotaph that looms behind the seated figure. Vallain's work may well be compared favorably with other Revolutionary depictions of the figure of Liberty, such as the one in Jean Baptiste Regnault's *Liberty or Death*, which appeared in the Salon of 1795.[165] Certainly the ambition and scope of her oeuvre and the high quality of the few known works by her hand make Vallain far more than a minor genre specialist or a painter of "women's subjects" in the derogatory sense of the term.

Other women, mainly David's pupils or followers, turned their hands to historical, classical, or allegorical subjects at the beginning of the nineteenth century. Sophie Guillemard (1780-?), a student of Regnault's, exhibited an *Alcibiades and Glycerion* in the Salon of 1802 and a *Joseph and Potiphar's Wife* a year later. Even more ambitious was Angélique Mongez (1775/76-1855), a pupil of David's and Regnault's, who won a first-class gold medal in the Salon of 1804. She painted a *Ulysses Finding Young Astyanax at Hector's Grave,* with life-size figures in the classical style of David, as well as a large-scale *Alexander Weeping at the Death of the Wife of Darius.* In 1806 she showed a *Theseus and Pirithous Cleansing the Earth of Brigands,* a painting with symbolic overtones, and in the 1808 Salon exhibited a complex allegory featuring Orpheus and Euridice with thirteen life-size figures. Still other classical sub-

25.
Nanine Vallain
Liberty, 1793-94
Oil on canvas
Paris, Musée National du Louvre

162.
Ch. P. Landon, *Annales du Musée et de l'Ecole Moderne des Beaux-Arts,* Paris, 1808, II, 16.
163.
See Paris, 1974, no. 20.
164.
M. Furcy-Raynaud, *Nouvelles archives de l'art français,* Paris, 1912, 294.
165.
See Paris, 1974, no. 150, repr. 137.

jects shown by this "art-amazon" were *The Death of Adonis* (1810); *Perseus and Andromeda* (1812); and, in 1814, a much-admired *Mars and Venus*, now in the Musée d'Angers. Mme. Mongez, whose later years were spent in poverty, had a mixed press: although some critics admired her work, others felt that her colors were cold and her style somewhat too obviously dependent on David's.[166] Yet while these criticisms may indeed have been well taken, one suspects that beneath the specific cavils lurks a more inclusive one: condemnation of a woman artist for hubris, for reaching beyond her "natural" sphere and "limited" ability. This is overtly stated by "Le Pausanius Français" in 1805, à propos of Mongez' *Theseus and Pirithous:* "Long ago, someone said: nobody has ever heard of a woman who succeeded in writing a tragedy or in painting a great history painting. Mme. Mongez will at least have the honor of having made the attempt . . . and it may be said of her: . . . *Magnis tamen excidet ausis* [She was overcome by the grandeur of the task]. . . . When you follow the footsteps of men in an art like painting, and above all, those of the history painter, where one must rise above all the petty details which can disturb talent and destroy the work, either you must abandon these great subjects to our sex, or content yourself with sweet, tender subjects, or finally, paint portraits and landscapes."[167]

In a similar way, Mme. Haudebourt-Lescot was tactfully admonished by Landon when she attempted a canvas of unusually large scale, *François Premier and Diane de Poitiers* of 1819, a work that was 6 feet by 3 feet 6 inches. "We believe," declared this critic, "that this [weakness] is not the fault of the painter, whose talent cannot be doubted, but that of the proportions that she has adopted, the use of which demands a more serious and profound command of the brush than that which she has effected up to this time. . . . It is thus to small easel paintings, to charming but popular subjects that Mlle. Lescot should continue to devote her exclusive attention. . . ."[168] Another woman artist, Mme. Benoist (see cat. no. 70), evidently abandoned history painting completely in 1795 after having received adverse criticism, although she continued to draw antique subjects in her sketchbooks.

Still another woman who turned to history painting as well as to the more usual portraits and sentimental subjects was Pauline Auzou.[169] She showed a *Daphnis and Phyllis* in the Salon of 1795 and *Dinomache, Mother of Alcibiades* in 1796. Yet Auzou is interesting from another standpoint as well: like many other artists of her time, some of them women, she was an active participant in what one might call the great Napoleonic pictorial propaganda machine, an enterprise in which Mesdames Godefroid, Benoist, and Chaudet were also involved, as the official portraits of Napoleonic women and children in the Empire galleries at Versailles testify. Indeed, Mme. Benoist was one of the artists (whose ranks included Antoine Gros, François Gérard, Charles Thévenin, and Pierre Prud'hon) who received an annual stipend of from 2,000 to 4,000 francs from the Napoleonic government.[170] Auzou, however, played a major role in a particularly delicate Napoleonic propaganda campaign: the justification of the emperor's marriage to Marie Louise of Austria and, necessarily, of his controversial divorce from Josephine and alliance with France's former enemy. Many artists were summoned to this task. After the final defeat of Austria at Austerlitz, when Napoleon was already planning to marry the Hapsburg princess, Baron Gros was asked to paint the meeting and implied reconciliation of the two emperors on the battlefield. Shortly after, the same artist was commissioned to create a historical precedent for the Austro-French reconciliation by depicting the Holy Roman Emperor Charles v being cordially welcomed by François I at St. Denis (Paris, Louvre).[171] The talents of Marie Louise, the eighteen-year-old pawn in Napoleon's political maneuvers, were celebrated by Alexandre Menjaud in his *Empress Marie Louise Painting the Emperor's Portrait* (Versailles, Musées Nationaux) in the Salon of 1810.[172] This despite the fact that, in the words of one unfriendly historian, "up to the time of her marriage, Marie Louise possessed but one social talent on which she prided herself not a little — the power of moving her ears without stirring a muscle of her face."[173] The elaborate wedding

26.
Pauline Auzou
The Arrival of the Archduchess Marie Louise, 1810
Oil on canvas
Musée National du Château de Versailles

166.
See Nagler, x, 461-63, for a long discussion of Mme. Mongez and her work.
167.
Le Pausanius Français, Salon of 1806, 200 and 203. I am grateful to Sally Wells-Robertson for having brought this passage to my attention.
168.
Ch. P. Landon, *Annales du Musée de l'Ecole Moderne des Beaux-Arts, Salon de 1819,* Paris, 1819, 63.
169.
The career of Auzou is now being investigated by Vivian P. Cameron, a doctoral candidate at Yale University.
170.
R. B. Holtman, *Napoleonic Propaganda,* Baton Rouge, 1950, 164.

171.
For a discussion of these works and the political context in which they were undertaken, see F. Haskell, "The Manufacture of the Past in Nineteenth-Century Painting," *Past and Present,* no. 53, November 1971, 109-20.
172.
Marie Louise evidently took painting lessons from Prud'hon, and some works by her hand still survive. See, for example, her *L'Innocence,* executed while the empress was studying with Prud'hon (oil on canvas, $22^{1}/_{16}$ x $18^{1}/_{8}$ in., now in the depository of the Musée de Besançon).
173.
F. Masson, *Napoleon and the Fair Sex,* London, 1894, 268.

ceremony of the royal pair in the Chapel of the Louvre was recorded by David's pupil and assistant, Georges Rouget. The ultimate political purpose of the marriage — the production of an imperial son and heir, the little King of Rome — was duly glorified by both Rouget and Menjaud, as well as by Baron Gérard in his splendid *Marie Louise and the King of Rome* (Versailles, Musées Nationaux).

But it was Pauline Auzou, in her first attempt at painting contemporary history, who made two of the most original contributions to the iconography of Marie Louise and the Austrian marriage in a pair of works now in Versailles: *The Arrival of the Archduchess Marie Louise in the Gallery of the Château de Compiègne, 28 March 1810*, from the Salon of 1810 (fig. 26), and *Marie Louise, at the Time of Her Departure from Vienna, Distributing Her Mother's Diamonds to Her Brothers and Sisters, March, 1810*, from the Salon of 1812. In an effective and quite appropriate way Auzou has muted the pompous rhetoric of history painting with the intimacy of sentimental genre, especially in the farewell scene, in which that *topos* of feminine virtue, the giving up of jewels, is called into play to celebrate the generosity and family feeling of the young empress-to-be. Although the *Arrival of Marie Louise* is dignified by symbolic bas-reliefs in the background, the work retains a good deal of the freshness and naiveté of Auzou's sentimental scenes: the new empress, who had only met her husband a few hours before (they had been married by proxy in Vienna), is greeted by an excited band of charming white-clad maidens bearing flowers and wreaths. Despite the obvious differences in style, scale, and ambition between Auzou's *Arrival of Marie Louise* and a grandiose work like Rubens' *Arrival of Marie de Medici at Marseilles* — the comparative modesty, restraint, awkwardness, and lack of plastic exuberance of the Auzou work in comparison with the Rubens are obvious — it is nevertheless interesting to find a woman artist, like the seventeenth-century master, participating in that public, ceremonial celebration of the deeds of rulers or the construction of a suitable iconography for the non-events in the lives of the politically prominent which has been one of the important functions of artists over the centuries.

Yet the relative prominence of women artists in the Revolutionary and Napoleonic art world should not blind us to the obstacles that often stood in their way. These difficulties were not merely the obvious ones of second-rate training or patronizing criticism that attempted to keep females in their "proper" place by discouraging ambition and praising minor accomplishment. Women artists of the period, like their counterparts before and since, were also impeded in the conduct of their professional lives by the more general social restrictions that hedged in well brought up women. The case of Mme. Benoist is revealing. A distinguished pupil of both Vigée-Lebrun's and David's, Mme. Benoist (née Leroulx de la Ville) is perhaps best known for her compelling *Portrait of a Negress* (fig. 27), which made her reputation when it appeared in the Salon of 1800. This work, which may well be considered a black equivalent of David's portrait of Mme. Trudaine (ca. 1791, Paris, Louvre), may have been intended as a pictorial manifesto of the 1794 decree abolishing slavery, similar in effect to Girodet's *Portrait of the Deputy Belley* (Château de Versailles) of 1797, in which a distinguished black sitter is also brilliantly represented.[174]

Despite Mme. Benoist's successes and her evident devotion to her profession; despite her reception of a gold medal in 1804 and the numerous commissions she had received from Napoleon; and despite the fact that she had been granted a yearly stipend by the government, at the very peak of her career she was deprived of the opportunity to exhibit in the Salons — a requisite of artistic viability at the time — because of the strictures of feminine propriety. When, after the fall of Napoleon, her husband, Pierre-Vincent Benoist, received the high post of Conseiller d'Etat in the Restoration government, the price was the sacrifice of his wife's career. His position as a high government official required that his wife withdraw from all further public exhibitions of her work. The letter that Mme. Benoist wrote to her husband in

27.
Marie Guillemine Benoist
Portrait of a Negress, 1800
Oil on canvas
31⅝ x 25 ⅝ in. (81 x 65.1 cm.)
Paris, Musée National du Louvre

174.
See London, The Royal Academy and the Victoria and Albert Museum, *The Age of Neo-Classicism*, 1972, no. 26 for Benoist; no. 106 and repr. 11 for Girodet's portrait.

reply to his demand is a cry from the heart, and one that was to be repeated — or repressed — by many women artists in years to come when asked to give up their life's work for the sake of their husbands' careers. After asking her husband to forgive her for "sulking and complaining" Mme. Benoist continues: "Don't be angry with me if at first my heart bled at the course I was forced to take — and ultimately, to satisfy a prejudice of society to which one must, after all, submit. But so much study, so many efforts, a life of hard work, and after that long time of testing — successes; and then to see them almost an object of humiliation — I could not bear that idea. All right, don't let's talk about it any more; I am reasonable . . . my self-respect was wounded too brusquely. Let's not talk about it any more or the wound will open up once more."[175]

France was not the only country in which women artists could receive official recognition at the beginning of the nineteenth century. The small courts and cities of Germany offered them what was perhaps greater security if less wide-reaching reputation. Barbara Krafft (1764-1825), whose father had been a pupil of Anton Raphael Mengs and who herself became a member of the Vienna Academy, painted for the church in Prague and won local fame as a portraitist in Salzburg; she eventually became the Painter to the City of Bamberg, where she had moved in 1812.[176] Of greater interest is the career of Maria Ellenrieder (1791-1863), certainly the foremost woman painter of Germany in the early nineteenth century (figs. 28, 29). Born in Constance, Ellenrieder was granted admission to the Munich Academy through the intervention of a sympathetic bishop and studied there, mainly with Peter von Langer, from 1813 to 1816. While a student, she became interested in old German art, then a source of inspiration for many of her most progressive contemporaries. From 1822 to 1824 she worked in Rome, where she became closely associated with Overbeck and the Nazarenes, Germanic forerunners of the Pre-Raphaelite movement engaged in recapturing the formal purity and moral innocence characteristic of Italian art before the High Renaissance. After completing a *Stoning of St. Stephen* for the high altar of the Church of St. Stephen in Karlsruhe, she was named Bavarian court painter in 1829. Her patron, Grand Duchess Sophie of Baden, gave her numerous commissions for portraits and religious works, of which the most appealing for contemporary viewers are perhaps the least ambitious: the sensitive *Self-Portrait* of 1818, the unabashedly sentimental *Young Girl Picking Flowers* of 1841, both in the Karlsruhe Staatliche Kunsthalle, where many of her works survive. Yet Ellenrieder's religious paintings are certainly not without charm, and her drawings — fresh, direct, both literal and idealized at the same time — certainly deserve consideration as valid works of art in the Nazarene tradition.

The case of Ellenrieder raises an interesting issue associated with women artists, although not irrelevant to many male artists as well: the extent to which women artists must be "discovered" by contemporary art historians. Why do women artists so often seem inaccessible? Obviously that question is closely related to the larger issue of provinciality and to the fact that some artists, many of them women, preferred, or were confined to, local success and reputation rather than activity in the artistic centers of their times. Ellenrieder is an interesting case of the painter who is both "known" and "unknown" at the same time: known, that is, to art lovers in Karlsruhe[177] and in Constance, where she returned in the 1840s, yet virtually unknown elsewhere.

The Nineteenth Century: England, France, and the United States

It cannot be denied that to the average young woman, the study of drawing is a detrimental one. Art is a severe taskmistress, and demands unceasing sedentary toil, giving but grudging rewards in return for drudgery.

— *Ellen C. Clayton, 1876*

In England, women artists participated in imposing, and increasing, numbers in the public

28.
Maria Ellenrieder
The Baptism of Lydia, 1861
Oil on canvas
Zurich, Collection Fred and Meg Licht

175.
Letter from Mme. Benoist to her husband, October 1, 1814, in M. J. Ballot, *La Comtesse Benoist, "L'Emilie de Demoustier," 1766-1826*, Paris, 1914, 212.
176.
See *The Age of Neo-Classicism*, no. 173, repr. 45a (sic:b) for an example of Krafft's work.

177.
Several of her paintings are hung in the galleries of the Staatliche Kunsthalle in Karlsruhe, and her works are fully catalogued by this museum. See *Katalog Neuere Meister 19. und 20. Jahrhundert*, Staatliche Kunsthalle Karlsruhe, 1971, 2 vols. In addition, at least three monographs have been devoted to Ellenrieder: K. Siebert, *Marie Ellenrieder*, Karlsruhe, 1915; M. Zündorff, *Marie Ellenrieder*, Konstanz, 1940; and F. W. Fischer and S.v. Blanckenhagen, *Marie Ellenrieder, Leben und Werk der Konstanzen Malerin . . . mit einem Werkverzeichnis*, Konstanz/Stuttgart, 1963.

exhibitions of the nineteenth century, despite the fact that they were denied membership in the Royal Academy[178] and often had an extremely difficult time getting serious instruction. "In those days," reported a distinguished woman artist of the period, Eliza Bridell-Fox, referring to her student days in the middle of the century, "no advantages whatever were offered in the Government schools to those female artists who desired to attain proficiency in any branch of art, except decorative art. No models were then allowed, no draperies or other accessories. The 'Figure Class' as it was pompously, if ironically, designated, was 'instructed' in one small room, containing a few casts from the antique, the instruction being imparted during one daily visit from the lady superintendent."[179] According to this source, the only decent academy open to women in the early part of the century was Sass's School, about which little is known. In the middle of the century, Bridell-Fox took the unprecedented step of starting an evening class, with an undraped female model, for other women artists. "The class excited intense interest, with different opinions, among lady artists and girl students," declares Ellen C. Clayton, author of the major study of English women artists of the nineteenth century. "Perhaps," she continues, "there is no more vexed subject, or one more difficult of satisfactory solution, than this matter of drawing from the life by ladies studying figure painting."[180] Certainly the lack of adequate opportunity to draw from the nude model presented a grave obstacle to serious women art students during a period when the most esteemed genres of art depended to a large extent on the ability to depict the human body convincingly.

29.
Maria Ellenrieder
Bust of a Young Girl
Chalk
Basel, Öffentliche Kunstsammlung

It was at least partly for this reason that, by 1859, women art students started to storm the very citadel of academic art instruction, the Royal Academy. Although young women by this time had their own "Government School of Art for Females" in Gower Street, they nevertheless sought access to the superior prestige and far more serious instruction offered by the Royal Academy. In April 1859 a memorial was forwarded to each member of the Royal Academy by thirty-eight professional women artists, soliciting their influence "to obtain for women a share in the advantage of the study from the Antique and from Nature, under the direction of qualified teachers, afforded by the Schools of the Royal Academy. But," as William Sandby, the mid-nineteenth-century historian of the Royal Academy, points out, "as this request would necessarily have involved a separate Life School, the Royal Academy could not entertain the proposal in the space to which their schools are at present confined."[181] By 1862, however, five female students were permitted to study in the Antique Schools, following the accidental admission of one of Eliza Bridell-Fox's students, Laura Herford, who had submitted her work identified by her initials alone. Apparently there had never been any specific ruling prohibiting women's entry into the Schools; it was simply, according to Sandby, that none had ever applied before.[182]

Nevertheless, it was slow going for women students, and their admission was marked by considerable ambivalence. By the end of 1863 or the beginning of 1864, a group of female art students from the South Kensington and other art schools was again protesting the Royal Academy's exclusionary policies. They sent a printed memorial to the members petitioning for the right to compete at the Royal Academy examinations, which had been open to women for some years past and then closed to them in June 1863. The text of this boldly phrased memorial makes it clear that the underlying issues were economic even more than aesthetic; at stake was women's right to prepare themselves for self-supporting careers on the same basis as men:

"... The current opinion and feeling of late years, on the part of the educated public, has been strongly in favor of the introduction of women to such callings and pursuits as are, or seem to be, suitable to their sex, capacities and tastes, although the same may have been previously for the most part, or altogether, monopolized by men. ... One channel which in modern times [has] been opened for the enterprize of women, is the pursuit of the Arts of Sculpture and

178.
See note 131.
179.
In Clayton, II, 148.
180.
Ibid., 83.
181.
W. Sandby, *The History of the Royal Academy of Arts,* London, 1862, II, 272.
182.
Ibid., and Hutchison, 118.

Painting, and . . . many women have availed themselves of that opening and are at present earning their livelihood as artists, and many other young women are preparing themselves by study and practice to follow their example. . . . It is well known that the schools of the Royal Academy are of a much higher standard than the other art schools of the kingdom, and are in every way more suitable for advanced students; they are also the only free art schools in this country which is a consideration of moment to some of your memorialists. . . . Your memorialists therefore pray that liberty may be restored to female students to compete for admission into the schools of the Royal Academy, upon the same terms and conditions, in all respects, as are granted to, or imposed upon, male students."[183]

Despite this heartfelt and eminently reasonable plea, by 1868 only 13 women were matriculated, although there had been numerous applications; in 1876, there were 92, and in 1879, 130. As late as the 1880s, discriminatory rules were still in effect. In 1881 it was resolved "that the Male and Female Students work in different Painting Schools,"[184] and in 1888 the rules stated that at the end of Probation, that is, at the end of the second term, the male student was obliged to submit a painting of an entire figure from life, whereas a female student was required to submit a head only. Victorian prudery continued to hedge in women students at the Royal Academy until the end of the century. In 1891, although both men and women were working from live models, women in the School of Painting had to work from the "Draped Living Model" while men worked from the "Nude Living Model." In 1893, after constant petitioning, women students finally were allowed a nude male model — almost nude, that is, for precautions were carefully stipulated in the decision to grant this request: "It shall be optional for Visitors in the Painting School to set the male model undraped, except about the loins, to the class of Female Students," states the relevant passage from the Royal Academy Annual Report of 1894. "The drapery to be worn by the model to consist of ordinary bathing drawers, and a cloth of light material 9 feet long by 3 feet wide, which shall be wound round the loins over the drawers, passed between the legs and tucked in over the waistband; and finally a thin leather strap shall be fastened round the loins in order to insure that the cloth keep its place."[185] Not until 1903 were mixed classes instituted, and even then a separate class of life drawing for females was maintained. And of course, it must be added, the final achievement of equality in art school did little to alleviate the continuing social pressures — the demands of marriage, family, and domesticity — militating against women's achievement in the realm of art. To get a sense of this ultimate impediment one has only to read the reminiscences of Augustus John — hardly a notable feminist despite his great admiration for his sister, Gwen (see cat. no. 113) — about the Slade School in the early twentieth century: ". . . In what I have called the Grand Epoch of the Slade," says John, "the male students cut a poor figure; in fact they can hardly be said to have existed. In talent, as well as in looks, the girls were supreme. But these advantages for the most part came to nought under the burdens of domesticity . . . could be for some almost too heavy to bear."[186]

The situation of women in relation to the Royal Academy has been investigated in detail here because it is paradigmatic, with minor variations, of situations obtaining elsewhere during the same period. The United States, or at least the Pennsylvania Academy, was relatively progressive in this respect, despite the various difficulties women students experienced in gaining access to the nude model. By 1868 the Academy had established a Ladies' Life Class with a female model, a class charmingly depicted by Alice Barber Stephens ten years later in what is perhaps the earliest representation of women artists working from the nude.[187] Nevertheless, it had taken women art students years to achieve this relative equality, and male models were evidently not in regular use until 1877. As late as 1882, and even after, the board of directors of the Academy still received irate letters from those upholders of decency who were horrified that the students' "feelings of maidenly delicacy" were violated by contact with the "persons of degraded women and the sight of nude males in the stifling heat of the Life Class."[188] And of

30.
Unknown Artist (Léon Cogniet?)
Painting Studio for Young Girls, ca. 1830s
Oil on canvas
Musée des Beaux-Arts d'Orléans

183.
J. N. Anderdon [*sic?*] Papers, Royal Academy, XXVI. I am grateful to Professor Albert Boime for having brought this document to my attention.
184.
Hutchison, 143.
185.
Cited ibid.
186.
A. John, Obituary Notice of Lady Smith, *The Times*, February 1, 1958, cited in Holroyd, 1974, 62, footnote (see G. John bibliography).
187.
See Philadelphia, 1973, repr. 4, 17.
188.
Letter signed "R.S." to the President of the Pennsylvania Academy, April 11, 1882. Cited in Philadelphia, 1973, introduction by C. J. Huber, 21.

course, according to legend, it was because Thomas Eakins removed the loincloth from a male model in the Ladies' Life Class that he was asked to resign from his position as professor at the Academy.[189]

Nineteenth-century French paintings of women's art classes (fig. 30)[190] are invariably striking for the absence of what is always the focus of attention in the conventional art school scene of male art students: the nude model. In Paris the only serious class offered to women was at Julien's studio, and according to Marie Bashkirtseff (see cat. no. 102), nude male models were evidently available to women students there by 1877 — whether with or without drapery is not specified. Nevertheless, she complained in her journal that the quality of instruction in the women's class was not as high as in Julien's men's class on the floor below, and nowhere near as thorough as that offered by the Ecole des Beaux-Arts, from which women were completely excluded.[191]

Yet, to return to the situation in nineteenth-century England, the difficulties women artists had in receiving adequate training did not by any means discourage them from participating in the exhibitions of the period. Although their names appear in exhibition records far less frequently than those of their male colleagues, it is nevertheless true that thousands and thousands of women showed their works publicly, many of them participating in the highly esteemed annual exhibitions of the Royal Academy. There are no accurate statistics on the number of women artists represented in the Royal Academy shows of the nineteenth century, but the alphabetical record of Royal Academy exhibitors[192] compiled by Algernon Graves suggests how many there were. Under the letter *A* we find (including Honorary Exhibitors but excluding miniaturists) at least 59 women painters listed, and under the letter *C* at least 215. Granted that some of these women exhibitors showed only one or two flower paintings and that few women equaled the astounding productivity of their more prolific male contemporaries, it is nevertheless true that women artists were very much in evidence at the Royal Academy shows as well as in other, somewhat less important British exhibitions of the time.[193] Many of these women were solid professionals from every standpoint: Mrs. Sophie Anderson, who contributed steadily and substantially to the Royal Academy shows from 1855 to 1896, making her debut with a *Virgin and Child,* contributing a scene of torture in 1876 and a classical *"Evoe, evoe Bacche!"* in 1883; Emily Osborn, who submitted forty-three serious contributions between 1851 and 1884 (fig. 33, cat. no. 82); and Elizabeth Thompson, later Lady Elizabeth Butler, who was widely acclaimed for her ambitious and accurate military paintings (fig. 31, cat. no. 98), of which she showed twenty-two between 1873 and 1903, as well as many more in the twentieth century.

Lady Butler was one of those striking anomalies among nineteenth-century women artists, a woman for whom being female was in many ways an advantage. Like Rosa Bonheur (see fig. 32, cat. nos. 78-80), with whom she was sometimes compared, Lady Butler was astonishing. A woman battle-painter, like a woman animal-painter on the heroic scale, was something out of the ordinary, and the ferocious energy, the "masculine" forcefulness, and the manifest accuracy of their works not only stilled the usual patronizing criticism of women's art, but actually made some die-hard critics — even those as opinionated as John Ruskin — eat their words. "I never approached a picture with more iniquitous prejudice against it than I did Miss Thompson's," admitted Ruskin at the beginning of his panegyric of the artist's *Quatre Bras* (cat. no. 98) of 1875, "partly because I have always said that no woman could paint; and secondly, because I thought what the public made such a fuss about *must* be good for nothing." In the end, the former doubter outdid himself in admiration, maintaining that the righthand corner of the canvas, "where the cuirassier is catching round the neck of the horse as he falls . . . is wrought, through all the truth of its frantic passion, with gradations of color and shade which I have not seen the like of since Turner's death."[194] In many ways, the intrepid Lady

31.
Lady Elizabeth Butler
Scotland For Ever!, 1881
Oil on canvas
40 x 76 in. (101.6 x 192 cm.)
Leeds City Art Galleries

32.
Rosa Bonheur
The Horse Fair, 1853
Oil on canvas
96¼ x 199½ in. (244.5 x 506.7 cm.)
New York, The Metropolitan Museum of Art
Gift of Cornelius Vanderbilt, 1887

189.
See G. Hendrix, *The Life and Works of Thomas Eakins,* New York, 1974, 137-45, for a full account of Eakins' resignation, the position of women art students, and their angry reaction to Eakins' departure.
190.
See also the painting by Grandpierre-Deverzy, cat. no. 76.
191.
Bashkirtseff, 334-35, 351, 407 (see Bashkirtseff bibliography). Accounts of Julien's Women's Class are also given by Anna Klumpke (see Bonheur bibliography), Cecilia Beaux (117-124, see Beaux bibliography) and by Breakell (110-125, see Bashkirtseff bibliography). A thorough study of women students at Julien's and other women's art classes in the late nineteenth century in Paris is now being undertaken by Judith Stein of Temple University.

192.
A. Graves, *The Royal Academy of Arts: A Complete Dictionary of Contributors and Their Work from Its Foundation in 1769 to 1904* (originally published 1905, 1906), New York, 1972.
193.
See, for example, the impressive number of women artists included in Graves' *Dictionary of Artists Who Have Exhibited Works in the Principal London Exhibitions from 1760 to 1893,* 3rd ed., 1901 (reprinted Bath, 1970), which covers not merely the exhibitions of the Royal Academy, but those of the British Institution, the Society of British Artists, the Royal Water-colour Society, the Grosvenor Gallery, the New Gallery, and various other exhibitions.
194.
J. Ruskin, "Academy Notes, 1875," in *The Works of John Ruskin,* ed. E. T. Cook and A. Wedderburn, London, 1904, XIV, 309.

Butler's approach to her work — like that of many of her popular male contemporaries — may remind us more of Cecil B. De Mille than of Cézanne. Like the film maker, she deployed casts of — if not thousands — at least hundreds of figures. And since higher truth was equated with material veracity, she, like De Mille, spared no pains to achieve accuracy of detail: cloth was specially woven and costumes recreated; rye fields were purchased and trampled down (this for *Quatre Bras,* where the encounter depicted had taken place "in a field of particularly tall rye," according to Siborne's *Waterloo Campaign*); horses were made to fall down not once but many times; regiments were sent into action; cannons were fired. Butler's apparently boundless self-assurance, her easy assumption of authority, her unfailing energy, and her passion to control everything down to the smallest detail may remind us of similar qualities in another Victorian superwoman of similar upper-middle-class background: Florence Nightingale. And certainly her privileged background, like Florence Nightingale's, helped her to achieve her chosen goal. Lady Butler's mother had been a noted pianist and a talented painter whose watercolors had captured the attention of a younger Ruskin. Her father, Thomas James Thompson, was a connoisseur, a man of exceptional culture, extraordinary sensitivity, and, of course, an adequate private income. He was firmly committed to women's self-development and devoted much of his life to the education of his two unusual daughters. Lady Butler's sister was the distinguished writer and critic Alice Meynell, a feminist, socialist, and Catholic who wrote discerningly about Mary Wollstonecraft in the *Spectator* as early as 1879, admired Jane Austen, disliked the notion of "feminine style," and contributed to the *Catholic Suffragist.*[195]

It is perhaps the more modest, more intimate works of the Victorian period, like those by Emily Osborn (cat. no. 82) or Edith Hayllar (cat. no. 103), that excite greater sympathy today than Lady Butler's battle pieces, both for their aesthetic quality and for the insights they afford into the actual experience of women at the time. Equally important, a re-examination of the relatively modest domestic scenes by women artists in the nineteenth century, particularly those painted in England, may lead us to question some of the often unstated assumptions underlying art historical judgments. In confronting a work as complex and interesting as Osborn's *Nameless and Friendless* of 1857 (fig. 33), one might well ask why the iconography of fifteenth- or sixteenth-century religious or allegorical art is explicated with such care and subtlety by scholars, while that of nineteenth-century genre painting — often equally intricate and challenging — is so often dismissed as merely "literary" or "sentimental," irrelevant to the major, generally formal, issues raised by the art of the period. Osborn's *Nameless and Friendless* is one of the rare nineteenth-century paintings to deal directly with the lot of the woman artist.[196] Osborn was keenly aware of the economic dimensions of this problem, so often stressed in women's demands for more adequate academic training. For the Royal Academy Exhibition of 1857 she subtitled her work with a verse from Proverbs (10:15): "The rich man's wealth is his strong city, The poverty of the poor is their ruin."

Nameless and Friendless is a fine example of English narrative painting, a mode of expression that Hogarth had made popular in the eighteenth century and that continued to flourish during the nineteenth. The whole point of narrative painting is to tell a story — generally a story with a moral and with clear psychological overtones — within a realistically detailed setting that underscores the implications of the theme as it establishes the social position of the characters. The pictorial elements available to the narrative painter — line, shape, color — are, of course, the same ones available to the staunchest advocate of pure painting; it is just that for the narrative painter, like Emily Osborn, these elements are viewed as means rather than as ends in themselves.

A painting like *Nameless and Friendless* was meant to be "read" rather than merely looked at, to arouse moral feeling rather than simple appreciation of its visual qualities. Indeed, it may

195.
A. K. Tuell, *Mrs. Meynell and Her Literary Generation,* New York, 1925, 5-7, 136, and passim.
196.
The painting is now in the collection of Sir David Scott. For a good reproduction of the original, see J. Maas, *Victorian Painters,* London, 1969, 121. Another nineteenth-century treatment of this rare subject, perhaps known through engraving to Osborn, is Mme. Haudebourt-Lescot's *The Second-Hand Dealer of Paintings* (Salon of 1824), a work almost identical in theme to Osborn's, now known to us only through line-engraving. I am grateful to Sally Wells-Robertson for having brought this work to my attention.

remind us of an episode — visually condensed — from a nineteenth-century novel, which English women above all others excelled at writing. Such a work necessarily employs some of the strategies of literature, or of the theater, or of the sociological study. And, in its emphasis on significant details and meaningful gestures, and in its focus on the "dramatic" moment, it foreshadows similar elements in early films. The heroine occupies the center of the stage, emphasized by the sharp vertical of the shop window and the pallor of the prints behind her, as well as by the light falling on her face and hands. The pathos of her situation — social, financial, professional, and sexual — is clearly established by both the larger elements of the composition and the smaller details of her surroundings. That she is an unmarried orphan is indicated by her black dress and ringless left hand; that she is poor, by her worn-out clothes, unfashionable shawl, and shabby dripping umbrella; that her social position is low is brought out by the eloquent emptiness of the chair against which the umbrella is propped: had she been a wealthy lady client rather than a nameless and friendless woman painter, she would naturally have been sitting down rather than standing up. With downcast eyes and fingers twisting the string from her packet, she awaits the verdict of the dealer, whose skeptical gesture is tellingly contrasted with her nervous one. At the same time, the skepticism or indifference of the dealer and his assistants is contrasted with the insolent, obviously sexual interest aroused in the two wealthy clients to the left, who, in the arrogant nonchalance of their poses and the flashy elegance of their dress, offer a contrast both to the genteel poverty and modest demeanor of the girl and to the more "commercial" appearance and bearing of the shop personnel.[197]

Distinctions of class, wealth, and sex — perhaps the last above all — are thus clearly indicated through the imagery of Osborn's painting. It is certainly significant — or would have been to the mid-nineteenth-century viewer — that the two connoisseurs ogling the vulnerable heroine are looking up from a print of a scantily clad dancing girl: obviously their interest in art, like their attention to the young artist, is motivated more by prurience than aesthetic concern. And while the rainy weather is, perhaps, simply a realistic depiction of English climate, it also helps to suggest the hard life that an unprotected young woman must endure in the city. How different from the mood of Edith Hayllar's *A Summer Shower* (cat. no. 103), in which the rain only emphasizes the cosiness of the home that shelters the players. Implicit in both of these works is the conventional nineteenth-century view of the young lady; a creature safe only in the protected environment of home and family, a being immensely vulnerable once she ventures into the jungle-world of commerce. Although women artists may indeed have been a fact of life in the nineteenth century — and there was simply no way that their presence could be ignored — they were nevertheless to be kept in their place. Both the general rules governing the conduct of women and the critics saw to that, even in the somewhat more relaxed climate of France. During the Second Empire, even quite liberal thinkers like Jules Simon — in his socially progressive study, *The Working Woman*, published in 1861 — condemned women to merely reproductive and repetitive tasks in design and industry, because of their obvious incapacity for any work demanding initiative or imagination.[198] In the same vein, Léon Legrange, in an important article published in the *Gazette des beaux-arts* in 1860, condescendingly delegates to women pastels, porcelains, miniatures, and flower painting: "What more delicate hand could decorate the fragile porcelains with which we love to surround ourselves? Who else could so well reproduce on an ivory cameo, and with a more exquisite feeling of natural tenderness, the features of a beloved child?" demands this author. "And who else but women would have the careful patience to hand-color botanical plates, pious images, and prints of all kinds?" he continues.

Separate but unequal is the leitmotif often repeated in such discussions of the woman artist's accomplishments: "Male genius has nothing to fear from female taste," declares Legrange. "Let men conceive of great architectural projects, monumental sculpture, and the most elevated forms of painting, as well as those forms of the graphic arts which demand a lofty and

33.
Emily Mary Osborn
Nameless and Friendless, 1857
Engraving from the *Art Journal*, 1864, p. 261

197.
Nameless and Friendless has recently been misinterpreted as "A gentlewoman reduced to depending upon her brother's art," by S. Macdonald in *The History and Philosophy of Art Education*, New York, 1970, fig. 9, opp. 96. I am grateful to Judith Stein for having brought this significant misreading to my attention.
198.
C. R. Baldwin, "The Predestined Delicate Hand: Some Second Empire Difinitions [sic] of Women's Role in Art and Industry," *Feminist Art Journal*, II, no. 4, Winter 1973-74, 14.

ideal conception of art. In a word, let men busy themselves with all that has to do with great art. Let women occupy themselves with those types of art which they have always preferred, such as pastels, portraits, and miniatures. Or the painting of flowers. . . . To women, above all, falls the practice of the graphic arts, those painstaking arts which correspond so well to the role of abnegation and devotion which the honest woman happily fills here on earth, and which is her religion."[199] Julie Victoire Daubié, a French feminist and the first woman to present herself for the baccalaureate examination, protested vigorously against this sort of hypocritical rationalization of injustice. In her remarkable study, *La femme pauvre au XIXe siècle (The Poor Woman in the 19th Century)* of 1866, she demanded complete equality in the education of women artists, including access to the Ecole des Beaux-Arts and even to the competition for the Prix de Rome. Like her English contemporaries she based her argument on sheer economic reality: the fact that women artists, granted inferior compensation because of their limited access to education and competition, were thereby denied a living wage.[200]

But bold statements like Daubié's were generally ignored. By the seventies and eighties, women art students from all nations were flocking to Paris in search of instruction in private studios, most notably the one run by the former prizefighter M. Julien (or Julian, as it is often spelled), where they could work from models and receive criticism from such eminent academic artists as Tony Robert-Fleury or the somewhat more "advanced" Jules Bastien-Lepage. Yet they were still hemmed in by the restrictions governing feminine behavior. Cecilia Beaux's cousin suggested that Cecilia (see cat. nos. 99-101) would be "quite *déclassé* if she accepted the invitation of an American friend to escort her to the Salon";[201] and the rebellious Marie Bashkirtseff repeatedly deplored the lack of freedom and opportunity that, she felt, had invidious effects upon her — and all women's — art. "I wrote to Colignon [E. Collignon (1822-1890), a minor artist?] that I wished I were a man," she records in the pages of her journal; "I know that I should become somebody; but with skirts — what can one do? Marriage is the only career for women; man has thirty-six chances, woman has but one, the zero like the Bank. But the Bank gains in any case; we pretend that it is the same with woman; but that is not true."[202] At another time she complains that the men students at Julien's class have three artists to criticize their work while the women have only one;[203] later she angrily inveighs against her lack of opportunity as a woman: ". . . We went to the Ecole des Beaux-Arts. It is enough to make one cry with rage. Why can not I go and study there? Where can I get instructions as complete as there?"[204]

The strictures placed on the freedom of women artists, as well as the overt denial to them of the professional opportunities, rewards, and institutional legitimization offered to their male colleagues, can only be understood in the broader context of women's position during the nineteenth century. To the preservers of the status quo, women's demands for professional equality were often equated with wider assaults on the social framework, with atheism, anarchism, socialism, and free love. Not only were professional women seen as threatening competitors, but their very existence was viewed as inimical to the sanctity of the family, to woman's "God-given" or "natural" destiny as wife, mother, and guardian of the home. The constant references to the woman artist's inborn delicacy and refinement of feeling, the repeated attempts to protect her from exposure to nudity or the hazards of "coarsening" competition, and the establishment of specific restrictions to prevent fully qualified women from being accepted into the most prestigious professional organizations — all of these were responses to what were felt to be very real threats to the status, power, and, not least, the convenience of the men who controlled the various "Establishments." Nor was hostility to women's self-development or professional achievement by any means confined to the ranks of the politically conservative, as a glance at Daumier's lithograph series *The Blue-Stockings* of 1844 or his *Socialist Women* of 1849 will reveal. Seen in this light, the constant solicitude for women's weakness, their sexual purity, their social vulnerability, can be understood as a lightly

199.
L. Legrange, "Du rang des femmes dans les arts,"
Gazette des beaux-arts, October 1, 1860, 30-43. Cited
by Baldwin, *Feminist Art Journal,* 13-14.
200.
Daubié, 292-93. I am grateful to Priscilla Robertson
for calling my attention to this book.
201.
Advice that Beaux evidently ignored. See her *Background with Figures,* 130.
202.
The entry is from 1878. Bashkirtseff, 402 (see her
bibliography).
203.
Ibid., 351.
204.
Ibid., 407.

veiled threat, a way of keeping them in their place by "protecting" them from serious achievement — and independence.

The result of such discriminatory attitudes — whether veiled or overt — was often achievement at a level of competent mediocrity by those women artists tenacious enough to pursue professional careers. The names of Louise Breslau (1858?-1928), Louise Abbéma (1858-1927), and Virginie Demont-Breton (1859-1935), once quite well known, have sunken into oblivion. While one can certainly blame changes in taste for this current neglect, a neglect that until recently obscured even the career of the extraordinarily successful Rosa Bonheur (and of course, those of many of these women's male contemporaries), it must be admitted that women artists were rarely — with the notable exceptions of Berthe Morisot (see cat. nos. 84-88) and Mary Cassatt (see cat. nos. 89-95) — among the most daring or innovative painters of the period. Simply being persistent enough to devote a lifetime of effort to being a serious artist was a considerable accomplishment for a nineteenth-century woman, when marriage and its concomitant domestic duties so often meant the end of even the most promising careers.

Perhaps better than any statistical or sociological study, two novels, one English and one American, cast light on the situation of the woman artist in the nineteenth century. They are interesting not merely for what their authors consciously recount, but for the unconscious attitudes — the ideological assumptions — they unwittingly reveal. In the more conventional of the two — Olive, by Dinah Maria Craik — the fact that the young painter-heroine lives alone, strives for fame and independence, and actually supports herself through the sale of her art is at least partially justified by the fact that she is crippled, and thus automatically considers herself ineligible for woman's "natural" destiny. Yet the book has a "happy" ending nevertheless — happy, that is, by nineteenth-century standards. In the end, to paraphrase Patricia Thomson's discussion of Olive in her provocative study, The Victorian Heroine, Mrs. Craik, having shot her bolts in the course of the novel, is content to let her heroine, whose ultimate greatness the reader has never doubted, sink gently into matrimony. "Of Olive," Thomson states, "Mrs. Craik comments imperturbably that her husband's influence is to deprive the Scottish Academy of 'no one knew how many grand pictures'."[205]

Elizabeth Stuart Phelps' The Story of Avis, published in 1877, is a darker, more unconventional vision. It chronicles the tragic life of a brilliant young woman artist, whose early promise is destroyed, as inevitably as that of any hero in Zola or Dreiser, by the interplay of biological and social forces.[206] Although the novel is often awkward, overwritten, and melodramatic, it nevertheless still has the power to move and convince. The message of The Story of Avis is that the life of the artist and that of the wife and mother are utterly incompatible; in short, that marriage destroys for women any possibility of creative achievement. Avis, a young woman of New England, has recently returned from brilliant successes in Paris, where she had been encouraged to pursue her calling by the great Couture himself. She is determined to dedicate her life to art — great art, this is — to become, in fact, a vestal virgin of painting. In a moment of exaltation, she envisions a mighty mural of feminine experience: "Instantly, the room seemed to become full of women. Cleopatra was there, and Godiva, Aphrodite and St. Elizabeth, Ariadne and Esther, Helen and Jeanne d'Arc, and the Magdalene, Sappho, and Cornelia, — a motley company. These moved on solemnly, and gave way to a silent army of the unknown. They swept before her in file, in procession, in groups. They blushed at altars; they knelt in convents; they leered in the streets; they sang to their babes; they stooped and stitched in black attics; they trembled beneath summer moons; they starved in cellars; they fell by the blow of a man's hand; they sold their souls for bread; they dashed their lives out in swift streams; they wrung their hands in prayer. Each, in turn, these figures passed on, and vanished in an expanse of imperfectly defined color like a cloud, which for some moments she [Avis] found without form and void to her. . . . In the foreground the sphinx, the great sphinx,

205.
Patricia Thomson, The Victorian Heroine: A Changing Ideal, London, 1956, 77. Also see E. Showalter, "Dinah Muloch Craik and the Tactics of Sentiment," Feminist Studies, II, no. 2/3, 1975, 15-17.
206.
For an interesting and illuminating analysis of Elizabeth Stuart Phelps and this work, see Christine Stansell, "Elizabeth Stuart Phelps: A Study in Female Rebellion," The Massachusetts Review, XIII, 239-56. Zola's well-known study of a doomed (male) artist, Claude Lantier in the novel L'Oeuvre, was not finished until 1886.

restored. The mutilated face patiently took on the forms and hues of life: the wide eyes met her own; the dumb lips parted; the solemn brow unbent. The riddle of ages whispered to her. The mystery of womanhood stood before her, and said, 'Speak for me'."[207] Alas for the mystery of womanhood, poor Avis is destined never to speak for it, nor for herself, through her art at all. Forced against her better judgment into a disastrous marriage with a weakling and failure, she is gradually weighed down with the increasing demands of motherhood and housework and brutalized by economic hardship. After the tragic death of her ne'er-do-well husband, when she at last attempts to return to her art — a tired, middle-aged woman — she finds herself no longer capable of anything but the lowest hackwork: her powers have disappeared along with her youth.

Significantly, at the same time that *The Story of Avis* was being written, another young American woman artist was studying in Paris and sending her work to the Salon, but, unlike Avis, feeling increasingly dissatisfied with the conventional ideals of academic art. In the very year that Elizabeth Stuart Phelps' tragic novel was published, Mary Cassatt, whose work had been rejected for the Salon of 1877, was invited by Degas to join a group of "Indépendants." She quickly accepted his invitation, later confiding to her biographer: "At last I could work with absolute independence without considering the opinion of a jury. I had already recognized who were my true masters. I admired Manet, Courbet, and Degas. I hated conventional art — I began to live."[208] Certainly the most important woman artist of the nineteenth century, she is also worthy of consideration as the most significant American artist, male or female, of her generation. Capable of turning her hand to oils, pastels, murals, and, above all, to brilliant printmaking; dedicated to her work throughout a long and productive lifetime; independent in her art, though hardly unconventional in her personal behavior, Cassatt offers the happy example of a nineteenth-century woman artist who bypassed both competent mediocrity and the relatively rare popular notoriety of painters like Bonheur or Butler to reach genuine achievement. Unlike the heroines of *Olive* and *The Story of Avis,* she never married.

The Twentieth Century: Issues, Problems, Controversies
If we must reject the empty fetishes of "The Eternal Feminine," or of "Feminine nature," we must nevertheless recognize the fact that there are women, *and that the fact of being one puts one into a special situation.*
— Sylvie Le Bon, 1975

In the face of the enormous range and variety of paintings by twentieth-century women, it would indeed be futile, if not impossible, to talk of a "women's style" or a "feminine sensibility." There certainly seems to be no mysterious essence of femininity relating Liubov Popova's sharply abstract *Architectonic Painting* of 1917 (fig. 34) to Florine Stettheimer's wittily decorative *Family Portrait II* of 1933 (fig. 35), nor connecting Paula Modersohn-Becker's monumental *Mother and Child* of 1906 (fig. 36) with the staccato audacities of Hannah Höch's *Cut with a Kitchen Knife* of 1920 (see also cat. nos. 141, 142). And surely Gabriele Münter's *Man in an Arm Chair (Paul Klee)* of 1913 (fig. 37), like her other works of this period (cat. nos. 119, 120), can be compared more profitably with those by other members of the Blue Rider group, male and female, than with those by contemporary yet stylistically disparate women artists like the French Marie Laurencin (see cat. no. 131) or the Canadian Emily Carr (fig. 38).

Yet to discard obviously mystificatory, essentialist theories about women's "natural" directions in art is by no means to affirm that the fact of being a woman is completely irrelevant to artistic creation. That would be tantamount to declaring that art exists in a vacuum instead of in the complex social, historical, psychological, and political matrix within which it is actually produced. The fact that a given artist happens to be a woman rather than a man counts for something: it is a more or less significant variable in the creation of a work of art, like

34.
Liubov Popova
Architectonic Painting, 1917
Oil on canvas
31½ x 38⅝ in. (80 x 98.1 cm.)
New York, The Museum of Modern Art
Philip Johnson Fund

35.
Florine Stettheimer
Family Portrait II, 1933
Oil on canvas
46¼ x 64⅝ in. (117.9 x 164.1 cm.)
New York, The Museum of Modern Art
Gift of Miss Ettie Stettheimer

207.
Elizabeth Stuart Phelps, *The Story of Avis,* Boston, 1877, 149-50.
208.
Segard, 8 (see Cassatt bibliography). Translated in *Mary Cassatt, 1844-1926,* National Gallery of Art, Washington, D.C., 1970, introduction by Adelyn Breeskin, 13.

being an American, being poor, or being born in 1900. Like any other variable, little can be predicted on its basis in isolation from the specific context in which it exists.

The artist's sense of the creative self as a woman — her concentration on what is generally considered woman's realm of experience, either because of social pressures or personal choice — may play a greater or a lesser role in women's work, depending on the circumstances. There have been women artists like Gwen John who deliberately restricted herself to a rather narrow range of female subjects (fig. 39, cat. no. 113), or like Frida Kahlo, who turned to herself and her own peculiarly feminine obsessions and dilemmas for subject matter (fig. 40, cat. no. 157). At times when the issues of women's rights, status, and identity have been critical — at present, for example, and in the late nineteenth and early twentieth centuries — this sense of the creative self as a woman could play an important role, not merely in choices of subject matter, but in more subtle pictorial variations, as it seems to have done in the work of Paula Modersohn-Becker (see cat. nos. 114-18) and Käthe Kollwitz (see cat. nos. 105-7). At other times the presence of allegedly "feminine" elements of form or content in the work of art is ambiguous, often, as in the case of Georgia O'Keeffe's flower paintings, hotly affirmed by both admiring and disparaging critics, and as hotly denied by the artist herself.[209] Given the complexity and richness of this field of investigation, it seems wise to restrict the present discussion to a few of the many issues raised by the work of women artists in the first half of the twentieth century: the relation of women artists to the decorative arts; the question of national variation in relation to women's achievement; and the issue of "feminine" subject matter and style.

36.
Paula Modersohn-Becker
Mother and Child, 1906
Oil on canvas
Bremen, Paula Becker-Modersohn Haus

Women and the Decorative Arts
The feminine presence in the field of the decorative arts, more specifically, those related to textiles — weaving, embroidery, stitchery — is a time-honored one.[210] Indeed, women have continued to make significant contributions in this area through the nineteenth and twentieth centuries. For example, exhibits — rather conventional ones, to be sure — of lace, embroidery, tapestry, and needlework were prominent among the works illustrated in the official publication of *Art and Handicraft in the Woman's Building of the World's Columbian Exposition* in Chicago in 1893. Later, the leading weavers and tapestry makers at the Bauhaus — Anni Albers, Ruth Consemüller, Gunta Stölzl, Otti Berger, Benita Koch-Otte — were women.[211] Nevertheless, this traditional relation, or perhaps relegation, of women to the decorative arts was complicated by a variety of social and economic as well as ideological factors at the turn of this century. One complicating factor was the ambiguous status and prestige accorded to the decorative arts themselves, especially in relation to the so-called high arts of painting and sculpture. Another was the complex relationship of the decorative arts to the evolution of abstract painting and the subsequent development of an abstruse mystique to differentiate the latter from the former. Still another factor was the social, political, and moral implications associated with the promotion of the handicrafts and with education in design, especially in Great Britain during the latter part of the nineteenth century.

Have women simply been shunted off into the so-called minor or decorative arts because these were considered less demanding and were certainly less prestigious? It is undeniable that English women were admitted to the Schools of Design, both the Branch Schools and their own Female School in London, long before they were admitted, in any significant numbers, to the teaching facilities of the Royal Academy. The ranks of these schools were swelled not merely by the working-class girls for whom this sort of training, aimed primarily at industrial design, was originally intended, but by vast crowds of impoverished young ladies who were in desperate straits trying to find employment in the arts, primarily as governesses.[212] Even earlier, in France, Mme. Frere de Montyon, a student of Restout's, had founded the Ecole Gratuite de Dessin pour les Jeunes Personnes, a school established in 1805 to help penniless young women become self-supporting, an enterprise perhaps intended as much as an

37.
Gabriele Münter
Man in an Armchair (Paul Klee), 1913
Oil on canvas
37⅜ x 49¼ in. (95 x 125 cm.)
Munich, Staatsgalerie Moderner Kunst

209.
O'Keeffe not only refused to permit any of her flower pieces to be included in this exhibition, but even refused to have them reproduced in the catalog, presumably for fear they would be misinterpreted in the context of a show of women artists.
210.
See pp. 15-17.

211.
M. H. Elliott edited the *Art and Handicrafts* publication of 1893. A sense of the achievement of women textile designers may be gained from a visit to the Bauhaus Archives in Berlin. Although women may have traditionally been involved in handweaving and art weaving, this is by no means true as far as industrial or mass-production of cloth is concerned, as E. Sullerot has pointed out (90): "The industrial revolution was at first characterized by the transfer into the hands of men of almost all the productions which until that time had been feminine." Later, of course, women and children, at considerably lower salaries to be sure, followed men into the textile mills.
212.
Bell, 135-37. K. A. Marling deals with the relation of American women to Arts and Crafts and social uplift in the introduction to *7 American Women: The Depression Decade*, Poughkeepsie, 1976, 10-11.

aid to public morals as to encourage artistic ability. The Ecole Gratuite de Dessin was brought under government jurisdiction in 1810.[213]

The democratizing effort to extend knowledge of the applied arts to the lower classes — and to women — was carried further in subsequent attempts to break down completely the barriers between high art and the decorative arts. The attempt reached a climax in Great Britain during the late nineteenth century with the program of social transformation proposed by John Ruskin and, especially, by William Morris. Interestingly enough, women seem to have served little more than a purely inspirational function for Morris and his followers, although both Janey and May Morris produced embroidery for the cause of arts and crafts. Women in late nineteenth-century England certainly made contributions to porcelain painting, textiles, embroidery, and, often anonymously, to patchwork and other forms of stitchery, and of course Kate Greenaway was active as an illustrator and tile-designer, influencing Gauguin and many other painters. Nevertheless, women as a group were not prominent in the English Arts and Crafts Movement. In Scotland, however, two unusually gifted and productive sisters, Frances Macdonald (1874-1921) and Margaret Macdonald (1865-1933) (fig. 41) made major contributions in design. Margaret later married the innovative architect and designer Charles Rennie Mackintosh, and as members of his circle both sisters created imaginative curvilinear designs for architectural ornaments, metalwork, embroideries, and stained glass, as well as watercolors that often hover on the brink of abstraction.

Although the effort to overthrow the hegemony of "high art" by merging it with the "minor" arts, an effort that has characterized one current of vanguard ideology from Synthetism to Constructivism, is by no means a feminine invention, the extent to which the decorative arts, especially those involving textiles, have played a role in the careers of advanced women artists is striking. Yet even though their achievements in these realms are often brilliant, the fact that painters like Nataliia Goncharova (see cat. nos. 123, 124), Alexandra Exter (see cat. nos. 125-27), Liubov Popova (see cat. no. 143), and Varvara Stepanova; Sophie Taeuber-Arp (see cat. nos. 144, 145) and Vanessa Bell (see cat. no. 122); Marguerite Zorach and Sonia Delaunay (see cat. nos. 128-30) were involved in textile design, weaving, tapestry making, and costume design nevertheless has equivocal implications. On the one hand, for a woman artist to "return," as it were, to her traditional role in the minor arts, generally less conducive to fame and fortune than a career in painting or sculpture, can be viewed as a retrograde step. Yet from another vantage point, we can say that advanced women artists involved in the decorative arts in the early twentieth century were contributing to the most revolutionary directions — both social and aesthetic — of their times.

Marguerite Zorach may indeed have turned from painting to embroidering tapestries after the birth of her second child, when she "no longer had the hours of uninterrupted concentration that she required to work out her personal views on canvas,"[214] and Sonia Delaunay may have moved from monumental Orphist canvases to fabric and dress design (fig. 42) in order to support her husband and herself after the loss of her private income following the Russian Revolution. Nevertheless it is also true that Zorach's needlework, in many ways more original and interesting than her paintings, received more exposure and critical attention than her canvases during the 1920s and '30s,[215] and that Delaunay had had considerable success in the applied arts before the loss of her income[216] and continued to make some of her most original contributions in this area throughout her career. Certainly the experiences of Sophie Taeuber-Arp and Vanessa Bell in the decorative arts exerted a progressive influence on their "high art" creations. Taeuber-Arp, who began as a textile specialist and taught weaving and embroidery at the Arts and Crafts School in Zurich, may well have influenced her husband, Jean Arp, in the direction of greater abstraction as a result of the embroidery and weaving they did together at the time of the first World War. Indeed, it was probably

38.
Emily Carr
Western Forest, ca. 1931
Oil on canvas
50½ x 36⅛ in. (128.3 x 91.8 cm.)
Toronto, Art Gallery of Ontario

39.
Gwen John
Nude Girl, ca. 1909-10
Oil on canvas
17½ x 11 in. (44.4 x 27.9 cm.)
London, The Tate Gallery

213.
Rosa Bonheur's father, Raymond, took over the directorship in 1848, and his daughter took over the following year, after his death. The school, called the Ecole Spéciale de Dessin pour les Demoiselles and later the Ecole Impériale, was headed by Mlle. Nelly Marandon de Montyel after 1860. I am grateful to Professor Albert Boime for much of this information.
214.
National Collection of Fine Arts, Washington, D.C., *Marguerite Zorach: The Early Years, 1908-1920*, introduction by R. K. Tarbell, 1973, 50. The artist was joined briefly in her tapestry work by her husband, the sculptor William Zorach (57).
215.
Ibid., 57.
216.
Cohen, 77 (see Delaunay bibliography).

precisely because of her background in the decorative arts that Taeuber-Arp was one of the first artists to think of abstraction as a natural point of departure rather than the end of a long process of evolution from representation.[217] Vanessa Bell's participation from 1913 to 1919 in Roger Fry's Omega Workshops, for which she designed screens, textiles, and mosaics, seems to have intensified her penchant for abstract colorism and bold surface treatment (fig. 43) which had already been stimulated by contact with the Fauves and Cubists.[218]

For many of the Russian avant-garde artists of the early twentieth century, dedication to the applied arts constituted a revolutionary challenge to the whole mystificatory, reactionary ideology of traditional "high art." "Under pressure from the revolutionary conditions of contemporaneity, we reject the pure forms of art. We recognize self-sufficient easel art as being outmoded and our activity as mere painters as being useless. . . . We declare productional art to be absolute and Constructivism to be its only form of expression." Thus the group of avant-garde artists, including Alexandra Exter, Liubov Popova, and Varvara Stepanova, who met at the Moscow Institute of Artistic Culture in 1921, announced their entry into the world of industrial design — more specifically, in the case of the women artists, into that of innovative clothing and textile design.[219] Artists like Goncharova, Olga Rozanova (see cat. no. 133), and Kseniya Boguslavskaya had made semi-abstract and Suprematist contributions to textile and dress design in the years preceding the Russian Revolution,[220] and both Exter and Mukhina had created more individualistic and elegant fashions and theater costumes in the early 1920s. But Popova and Stepanova, probably the first women artists to be employed as professional designers in the Russian textile industry, attempted even more boldly to adapt mass-produced clothing and fabrics to the new demands of a revolutionary society. Both worked on various kinds of "stereotype" garments: clothing designed to the specification of different jobs or situations — comfortable, functional, and devoid of unnecessary decoration. In so doing, they managed to bring about the extension of art into life that was the leitmotif of the revolutionary art theory of their times, creating fabrics and costumes that still look attractive and contemporary.

A similar impulse to break down the barriers between art and life motivated Russian-born Sonia Delaunay in the creation of her famous *robe simultanée* ("simultaneous dress") of 1914, her collaboration in innovative book-design with the poet Blaise Cendrars (cat. no. 129) in the same year, her creation of avant-garde theater costumes in the early 1920s and of designs for commercially produced fabrics and dresses throughout the twenties (fig. 42). During the same decade Delaunay also turned to furniture design and interior decoration, even having a Citroën automobile painted in colorful rectangles after one of her textile patterns to serve as an appropriate background for the Jacques Heim turnouts executed from her designs.[221] Among her more recent works is an important group of monumental, abstract tapestries.[222]

In attempting to evaluate women artists' contributions to the decorative arts, much depends on one's attitude toward the relative importance of the "high" versus the "applied" arts. If we consider painting the ultimate form of aesthetic expression, then it will be a foregone conclusion that Sonia Delaunay made a sacrifice by neglecting her monumental abstract canvases to produce fabrics and fashions, while her husband, Robert Delaunay, was permitted to continue his calling as a painter and, perhaps even more important, as a theorist of abstract art. If, however, we take a less conventional view of what constitutes value in the avant-garde production of the twentieth century, we can see that women artists, by remaining faithful to their time-honored role as decorative artists, have advanced the cause of abstraction and, at the same time, spread its message beyond the walls of the studio, museum, and gallery into the realm of daily life — a goal devoutly sought by artists — whether "high" or "applied," male or female — from the time of Ruskin and Morris to the Russian Revolution, the Bauhaus, and afterwards.

40.
Frida Kahlo
Self-Portrait with Cropped Hair, 1940
Oil on canvas
15¾ x 11 in. (40 x 27.9 cm.)
New York, The Museum of Modern Art
Gift of Edgar Kaufmann, Jr.

217.
See Taeuber-Arp biography.
218.
See Bell biography.
219.
For a complete discussion of the remarkable contribution of women artists to Constructivist clothing and textile design, see John Bowlt, " 'From Pictures to Textile Prints,' " *The Print Collector's Newsletter,* VII, no. 1, March-April 1976, 16-20.
220.
Ibid., 17.
221.
Damase, 1971, repr. 214-15 (see Delaunay bibliography).
222.
See the catalog *Sonia Delaunay Tapestries,* Aberbach Fine Art Gallery, New York, 1974. For the fabric designs, see Mulhouse, 1971 (see Delaunay bibliography).

Women Artists and the Question of National Origin

Why have women artists as a group seemingly flourished in certain national situations and not in others? What, for example, accounts for the appearance of a remarkable group of innovative women artists in Russia at the beginning of the twentieth century or for the unusual number and productivity of women in the New Deal art programs of the United States?[223]

To study the case of the Russian women — Goncharova, Exter, Popova, Udaltsova (see cat. no. 132), Rozanova, Stepanova, Serabriakova, and others — one must leave the realm of art history and turn to an investigation of the unusually important role played by women in the intelligentsia and the related radical political movements in nineteenth-century Russia. Among left-wing intellectuals of that period, women were generally accepted as complete equals by male colleagues or co-conspirators; among conservatives, women students were viewed as particularly pernicious enemies of the Establishment. With many ups and downs, it is true, determined Russian women pursued professional education in the second half of the nineteenth century, going abroad in relatively substantial numbers when prevented by a nervous and inconsistent bureaucracy from pursuing their studies at home. For example, in the summer term of 1873, there were 96 Russians among the 110 women students at Zurich University, mainly studying to be doctors.[224] Russian women students differed from Western European feminists in that they were almost completely integrated with the radical political movements of their time and were primarily motivated in their search for knowledge and power by a desire to serve the people. From the 1860s on, they began to fill not only universities but prisons and fortresses.[225]

The *kursistka,* or woman student, was a recognizable revolutionary type, in fact the very personification of radical activism, and was painted several times by Nikolai Iaroshenko (1846-1898); his most important version of this subject, exhibited in 1883, aroused a good deal of political controversy. The major nineteenth-century Russian realist, Ilya Repin (1844-1930), painted *A Woman Revolutionary in Prison Awaiting Execution* in about 1884, a subject later identified with a well-known revolutionary martyr, Vera Figner, who had become the leading member of the terrorists' Executive Committee following the execution of another woman "regicide," Sophia Perovskaya. Repin had originally intended to make the exemplary figure of a political dissident returning from exile in his *They Did Not Expect Him* of 1884-88 a young woman, a *kursistka* figure to be precise, representing both the men and women of the new, revolutionary generation.[226]

Among the great pre-Revolutionary heroes were many important heroines, often living in communal quarters with their male counterparts, "going among the people," suffering and making sacrifices on a completely egalitarian basis. In the first of the great political trials of 1877, for instance — the so-called "Trial of the Fifty" — almost half of the accused were women, dubbed the "Moscow Amazons." The names of Sophia Bardina, Lydia and Vera Figner, Betty Kaminskaya, Breshkovskaya, Sophia Perovskaya, Vera Zasulich, and Ludmila Volkenstein, as well as many others, are preeminent in the annals of nineteenth-century Russian revolutionary history. Indeed, one of the Czarist ministers of the 1870s attributed the success of the revolutionary propaganda campaign chiefly to the surprisingly large number of women among the conspirators.[227] Some women, like Valentina Semonovna Serova (1846-1924), mother of the artist V. Serov, were active in both politics and the arts. This talented and energetic woman, an associate of many of the leading cultural figures of her day, including Tolstoi, Turgenev, Repin, Tchaikovsky, and Wagner, wrote five operas that she termed "ideological," one dealing with the condition of the peasantry, another based on the events of the Revolution of 1905.[228]

41.
Margaret Macdonald
Summer, ca. 1893
Pencil, pen, ink, and watercolor
University of Glasgow Art Collections
Mackintosh Collection

223.
The question has been investigated in the realm of women's literature, especially in the field of the novel, more thoroughly than in that of the arts. See for example, most recently, Ellen Moers' interesting and provocative study, *Literary Women,* Garden City, 1976. The situation of Russian women artists of the twentieth century has been discussed in the context of Russian art of the period by John Bowlt *(Russian Art of the Avant-Garde: Theory and Criticism, 1902-1934)* and Camilla Gray *(The Great Experiment: Russian Art, 1863-1922),* and is at present being investigated by graduate students like Ronnie Cohen, who is working on Alexandra Exter at the New York University Institute of Fine Arts, and Margaret Betz at the C.U.N.Y. Graduate Center. The situation of women artists and the New Deal has recently been illuminated by an exhibition organized by K. A. Marling and H. A. Harrison, with their informative catalog, *7 American Women: The Depression Decade.*

224.
F. W. Halle, *Woman in Soviet Russia,* New York, 1933, 36.
225.
Ibid., 40.
226.
This painting was not exhibited until 1896, although it had been painted earlier. See Alison Hilton, "The Revolutionary Theme in Russian Realism" in *Art and Architecture in the Service of Politics,* ed. H. Millon and L. Nochlin, M.I.T. Press, forthcoming.
227.
Halle, *Woman in Soviet Russia,* 50.
228.
I am grateful to Alison Hilton for material on Serova.

Against this background, the vigor, independence, and iconoclastic daring of the Russian women artists of the early twentieth century seem less unprecedented if no less dazzling. Nataliia Goncharova, for instance, seems to have been on a level of complete equality with her avant-garde male colleagues, especially with Mikhail Larionov (1881-1964), with whom she worked closely. At first glance her work seems devoid of any particularly "feminine" qualities that would distinguish it from the work of the vanguard male painters of her time and place. Indeed, the impassioned catalog preface to her one-woman show of 1913 reveals that Goncharova was far more concerned with establishing her identity as a Modernist and a Russian than as a woman.[229] The "masculine" subject of electrical equipment — at that time the very quintessence of the progressive and dynamic — seems to have particularly fascinated her. Canvases like *The Machine's Engine* (1913, Paris, Galerie Loeb), *Electricity, Dynamo Machine*, and *Electric Lamp* (fig. 44),[230] created during her productive Cubo-Futurist phase, express this preoccupation. Interestingly enough, Sonia Delaunay, Russian-born although working in Paris, created her enormous light- and color-filled abstract canvas entitled *Electric Prisms* in 1914 (fig. 45). One recent scholar, Marina Tsvetaïeva, has claimed that Goncharova was the first artist to introduce the mechanical into painting; certainly she was the first to treat mechanical objects as though they had a life of their own, maintaining that "the principle of movement in a machine and in a living being is the same, and the joy of my work is to reveal the equilibrium of movement."[231]

Still, it is interesting to notice how often within the sexually neutral, or even "masculine," and always vigorously avant-garde imagery of Goncharova intrude references — sometimes ironic or rather subversive — to the artist's gender. *The Laundry* (London, Tate Gallery) of 1912 may illustrate the "machine aesthetics," but it does so in terms of a traditionally feminine familiarity with hand-irons, laces, shirts, and collars, and *The Street Wall (Ostrich Plumes and Ribbons)* of 1912, with its elegant ladies' accouterments, is also provocatively "feminine" in its iconography, compared to similar paintings by male artists.[232] One wonders, too, if it was mere chance that led Olga Rozanova to create *Workbox* of 1915, a brilliantly inventive collage — oil, paper, and lace on canvas — using women's traditional sewing materials as both iconography and substance.[233] Like Goncharova, she was concerned chiefly with machine themes at this time, and by ca. 1916, like Popova and Exter, had moved on to pure abstraction of the most architectonic and non-referential sort.

In the case of the remarkable efflorescence of women artists in our own country during the 1930s, the issue is not so much that of radical stylistic innovation as of the sheer numbers of women involved and the range and variety of their pictorial expression. In this case, too, the status of women artists can be properly appreciated only within the larger context of the New Deal art programs and, to a lesser degree, in relation to American women's status in the professions. Just the fact that a 1935 survey of professional and technical workers on relief showed that about 41% of all artists receiving assistance were women suggests their relative importance in the field. Women were also prominent among the professional administrators of the federal art programs, women like Juliana Force, who became the regional director of the Public Works of Art Project, and Audrey McMahon, who acted as director of subsidized art production in New York State throughout the thirties.[234] As K. A. Marling has pointed out, many of the women involved in the Federal Art Project and other government programs had achieved high positions even before the establishment of the New Deal agencies of patronage. Nevertheless, the "gender-blind" consideration of aspiring artists under the New Deal programs not only created an often exhilarating *esprit de corps* — perhaps an unfortunate expression under the circumstances, but still apt — that united artists of both sexes, but at the same time did much to meet the demands of women artists for two kinds of rights: the right to participate and the right to be judged on the same basis as men. In Marling's words: "The

42.
Sonia Delaunay
Fashion Sketches, 1923-28 (detail)
Ink and watercolor
Paris, Collection the artist

43.
Vanessa Bell
Abstract, ca. 1915
Oil on canvas
17¼ x 15¼ in. (143.8 x 38.7 cm.)
London, The Tate Gallery

229.
This preface has been translated by Bowlt, 54-60.
230.
Chamot, 58 (see Goncharova bibliography).
231.
Cited by Chamot, ibid.
232.
See ibid., 51, for a reproduction of *The Laundry;* 53 for *The Street Wall (Ostrich Plumes and Ribbons).* It would be interesting to compare Goncharova's *Picking Apples* of 1909 (repr. Gray, fig. 66) with its formal poses and feminine cast of characters, to Mary Cassatt's vanished mural with this subject at its center, created for the Women's Building of the Chicago World's Fair of 1893.
233.
Repr. in Bowlt, 104.
234.
Poughkeepsie, 1976, 12-13.

catastrophe of the Great Depression, by placing art under the jurisdiction of government for nearly a decade, answered both demands. The art projects sanctioned and consolidated the gains of a century of women's struggles for access to training, and for professional recognition, by coming to the rescue of artists to whose skills and cultural contributions sexual labels were no longer germane. Clearest proof of women's attainment of the right to dispassionate judgment appears in the procedural guidelines followed by the federal Section of Fine Arts. The Section, a non-relief patronage program charged with providing American mural decoration of the highest available quality for public buildings, awarded commissions on the basis of 'anonymous competitions.' Artists were instructed to submit their sketches unsigned. . . . Government juries were not alerted to the gender of the competitors. . . ."[235] The government art programs did not, of course, encourage the highest type of creative endeavor, although, on the whole, they did not stand in its way if it should appear. What they did do was create a relatively democratic, fair — and by implication, fair-to-women — system of supporting and encouraging the arts in this country, a system that managed to patronize artists as different as Marion Greenwood (1909-1970), who created massive Riveraesque murals, and Doris Lee (b. 1905), with her chirpy regional genre scenes, as different as Lee Krasner (cat. no. 155) and Isabel Bishop (cat. no. 151). Indeed, the impact of the New Deal can be seen even in the style and subject matter of women artists who were not really connected with its art programs because they did not need them, like Florine Stettheimer, who nevertheless reveals a decidedly New Dealish social consciousness in her *Cathedrals of Wall Street* (1939, New York, Metropolitan Museum), featuring Mrs. Roosevelt and Mayor La Guardia.

The ultimate impulse behind the creation of greater opportunities for women artists through the New Deal art programs seems to have been not so much feminism as egalitarianism: an ideal perhaps largely mythic, like that of America as a great "melting pot," yet partly effective, too, if only in eliminating a certain *overt* sexual bias in the distribution of largesse. In any case, feminist consciousness does not seem to have played a major role in the conceptions of many of the well-known women artists who participated in the New Deal programs.[236] One can discern occasional references to women's status and condition when these seem appropriate to the circumstances, as in Lucienne Bloch's mural *Cycle of a Woman's Life* (1935, destroyed) for the New York House of Detention for Women, in which she depicted the stages of a woman's life with an integrated cast of characters or, more ambivalently, in Minna Citron's highly satirical "Feminanities" series of 1935 in which the artist, in her own words, attempted "to hold a mirror to the unlovely facets of a woman's mind."[237] Both works are simply individual instances in widely varied oeuvres; few of the major women artists of this period, with the possible exception of Isabel Bishop, seem to have dedicated themselves to themes particularly relevant to women. For most women artists on the Public Works of Art Project, like Agnes Tait (cat. no. 147), it was the American scene, or, even more accurately, as Marling has put it, "an interest in distinctly American forms of artistic expression and a desire to view American art and life in a broader human and historical context"[238] that was the motivating force behind their creations.

The Issue of "Women's Imagery"

The notion that woman's experience *as* woman affords her a special vision of reality and unique imaginative insights, thus providing a source of specifically "feminine" pictorial imagery, is an issue that has been and continues to be hotly debated. Although it would seem obvious from this exhibition that there are no particular stylistic features associated with the work of women artists — "delicate brushwork," for example, or "pastel" colors — it is also clear that in specific historical situations women artists have been encouraged to turn to certain areas of activity more than others: in nineteenth-century England, for example, they were certainly directed more toward the modest realm of flower painting than the ambitious one of the heroic mural. Indeed flower painting seems to have been favored by both amateur and

44.
Nataliia Goncharova
Electric Lamp, ca. 1912
Oil on canvas
Paris, Musée National d'Art Moderne

235.
Ibid., 14.
236.
Ibid., 5.
237.
For a reproduction of the Bloch mural, see ibid., 22.
For one of Citron's paintings from the "Feminanities" series, *She Earns "An Honest Living"* of 1934, see ibid., 26.
238.
See Tait biography.

professional women artists from the seventeenth century down through the nineteenth and even afterwards. Usually one suspects that the reasons are quite practical and unmysterious ones, including accessibility of the subject and demand by the market. Yet even in this case it is obvious that historical and local factors play a greater role in determining style than does the sex of the artist. Rachel Ruysch's flower paintings look far more like those of her male Dutch contemporaries than they do like the flowers painted by Maria Sibylla Merian or by Georgia O'Keeffe, which in turn are clearly related to the stylistic context of their own time and place.

The issue of "feminine imagery" and its complexities may conveniently be examined in the work of two of the strongest German women artists of the early twentieth century: Paula Modersohn-Becker and Käthe Kollwitz. A comparison of their work is revealing precisely because the two painters are so close in time and place, because both are women, and because in addition both created an iconography clearly centered about women and women's experience. Yet what strikes one about these two nearly contemporary artists, both women, both German, and both devoted to the themes of women and children, is the difference in their interpretation of these subjects. This difference is even more striking in that both artists depicted proletarian women, the poor and the outcast, a subject which, in the traditional language of nineteenth-century realism, had been used to convey a deep sense of fatalism, uncomplaining acceptance of a hard destiny.[239]

By the end of the nineteenth century the peasant woman had become the very embodiment of fatalistic conservatism, her major virtue that of endurance — a creature inescapably bound to the unchanging cycles of nature and completely divorced from the dynamic forces of history. Modersohn-Becker's representations of old peasant women, like her *Old Woman from the Poorhouse* of 1903 (cat. no. 115), are a kind of ultimate distillation of this imagery, couched in an original language sparked by contact with the French vanguard — van Gogh, Cézanne, and Gauguin — in which expressive color and daring simplifications of contour become formal equivalents for the awkward, almost animallike endurance of her sitters. The old peasant woman — passive, immobile, unprotesting — is literally at one with her natural setting.

Nothing could offer a greater contrast to this image of static acceptance than Käthe Kollwitz' etching of the same year, *Revolt*, from her series *The Peasants' Revolt*, created between 1902 and 1908.[240] A political activist living among the poor in Berlin and profoundly committed to radical social change, Kollwitz envisioned the anonymous peasant woman as a dynamic force, who galvanizes her fellow oppressed into action. Evidently Kollwitz conceived the protagonist of *Revolt* from reading Zimmermann's classic *Peasants' War*, which gave the account of the peasant woman "Black Anna," who incited her fellow peasants to action. As a young woman, Kollwitz had responded to August Bebel's *Woman under Socialism*, first published in 1883,[241] which connected the struggle for social democracy with women's fight for justice. In four out of the seven prints of *The Peasants' Revolt* a woman figures as the protagonist.

Representations of the political activism of women — real women, that is, and not female allegorical figures — and especially of proletarian women, are relatively rare in the painting of the nineteenth century, although Kollwitz' conception is reminiscent of some of Goya's graphic images of fiercely struggling peasant women in the *Disasters of War*. There did exist a popular, folkloric tradition of the proletarian, female activist — aside from the saintly Joan of Arc, who, significantly, is hardly ever represented in actual combat. The heroines of Auguste Le Barbier's *Jeanne Hachette at the Siege of Beauvais* (1781, now destroyed but known through engravings) and of Horace Vernet's *Scene of the French Campaign of 1814* (1826, New York, private collection) are such figures. Going back even further, there is Pieter Bruegel's representation

45.
Sonia Delaunay
Electric Prisms, 1914
Oil on canvas
98½ x 98½ in. (250 x 250 cm.)
Paris, Musée National d'Art Moderne

239.
For a general discussion of the theme of the peasant in French art of the second half of the nineteenth century, see R. L. Herbert, "City vs. Country, the Rural Image in French Painting from Millet to Gauguin," *Artforum*, VIII, February 1970, 44-55.
240.
See Nagel, repr. 50 (see Kollwitz bibliography).
241.
See A. Bebel, *Woman under Socialism*, introduction by Louis Coser, New York, 1971, for Kollwitz's source of inspiration.

of the legendary Mad Meg (*The Dulle Griet,* ca. 1562-64, Antwerp, Museum Mayer van den Bergh), a virago who has completely thrown off the yoke of male dominance and who, armed with helmet, cuirass, sword, and a kitchen knife, confronts the devil himself with her savage, unleashed energy, at the head of her brigade of women. And indeed, there is something diabolic, like Mad Meg — that not-so-mad embodiment of sexual and social revolt — in the shadowy, sinewy female figure of Kollwitz' *Whetting the Scythe* (cat. no. 105), another plate from the *Peasants' Revolt* series, a figure whose intense concentration on the business at hand contrasts so strongly with the quiet passivity of the old peasant woman by Modersohn-Becker.

Similar contrasts are revealed by Modersohn-Becker's and Kollwitz' approach to the perennially popular subject of motherhood. Maternity is certainly one theme from the Neoclassical epoch (fig. 24) down to the age of Surrealism (cat. no. 158) that can be said to have captured the attention of women artists — those, of course, who have drawn on the experience of their own lives and those of their fellow women for inspiration. This is not to say, of course, that this subject has not appealed to men artists as well or that women artists are in any way "instinctively" drawn to such themes: the whole tenor of this essay argues consistently against such "innate" or "essential" proclivities on the part of women artists, or indeed against the existence of any specifically feminine tendencies whatever, apart from specific historical contexts. That motherhood should have played such an important role in women artists' iconography is hardly remarkable: historically it has been the central life experience for most women, cutting across barriers of class, period, and nationality. Yet even in the case of this most universally popular of subjects, the variations on the theme are more striking than the similarities.

For women artists belonging to and identifying with the cultivated upper-middle classes, like Berthe Morisot or Mary Cassatt, the theme of the mother and child is approached directly and concretely, but with a certain reserved delicacy, a deliberate avoidance of the extremes both of spirituality — i.e., overt references to the traditional Virgin and Child image — and of animal physicality — i.e., Modersohn-Becker (fig. 36). In the work of Cassatt and Morisot, one is made acutely aware of the precise level of elegance and refinement of these mothers and their lovely offspring: indeed, part of the charm of these canvases lies in the subtle but undeniable self-consciousness of distinction of form and of subject they convey to the spectator.

That Käthe Kollwitz' interpretation of maternal feeling should be radically different from Cassatt's or Morisot's is hardly surprising. Less expected, perhaps, is the striking difference between her conception of the theme and that of Paula Modersohn-Becker, a contrast even more surprising in that both of these artists concentrated upon the motherhood of the poor.

Like the old peasant woman, the lower-class mother had been a standard character in the repertory of humanitarian realists during the second half of the nineteenth century. The nursing mother as an image of the life force, of existence sustained at the most primitive level and under the most reduced circumstances — this image was powerfully embodied by Daumier in his Michelangelesque drawing, *The Soup* (ca. 1860-70, Paris, Louvre). It was given more exaggerated expression, at times verging on the ludicrous or the grotesque, in the work of late nineteenth-century Italians like Giovanni Segantini (1858-1899) in his *The Two Mothers* (1889, Milan, Galleria d'Arte Moderna), in which a peasant mother and child are visually associated with a cow and calf, or Teofilo Patini (1840-1906) in his *Mud and Milk* (1883, Rome, Ministero di Agricoltura), in which the ragged mother, a proletarian madonna of humility, nurses her infant while sitting in a stubble-covered field, protected by a battered umbrella. The imagery of the nursing mother was certainly favored by an artist like Fritz Mackensen, painter of *The Nursing Infant* (1892, Bremen, Kunsthalle) and a member of the same Worpswede art colony where Modersohn-Becker worked and lived. In a canvas like *Mother and Child* (ca. 1903, cat. no. 116), Modersohn-Becker has reduced the theme to its

46.
Paula Modersohn-Becker
Self-Portrait, 1906
Oil on canvas
24 x 19^{11}/$_{16}$ in. (61 x 50 cm.)
Basel, Öffentliche Kunstsammlung

242.
For a discussion of the impact of this and related ideas, especially as they pertain to the work of D. H. Lawrence, see Martin Green, *The von Richthofen Sisters,* New York, 1974, particularly 73-100, but also passim.
243.
According to Bachofen, the more recently evolved paternal and spiritual principle belonged, on the contrary, to human beings, more specifically to male human beings, alone. Ultimately, patriarchal civilization, Father Right, the division of labor, the domination of spiritual effort, of change and aspiration — in short, civilized, male-dominated culture as we know it — triumphed; but features of the old, female-dominated realm of nature — immutable instinct and attachment to the forces of the earth — still endure in woman, a creature, he maintained, essentially defined by her instinctive sexual and maternal role. This is a brief and admittedly incomplete summary of

pictorial essentials, and by removing the theme of maternal nourishment from history or social circumstance has implied that motherhood is an instinctive — rather than a social — female function. On the other hand, Käthe Kollwitz, in her etching *Poverty* (1897, San Francisco, Achenbach Foundation), by portraying the poor mother who *cannot* feed her child has inserted motherhood into the bitterly concrete context of class and history. Both these women artists conceived of motherhood and the nurturing of children as the natural destiny of their sex. But Kollwitz set forth the material circumstances that prevent the working-class mother from fulfilling this natural destiny, thereby transforming her into the very personification of the proletarian victim of history. Modersohn-Becker, especially in her extraordinary late works (fig. 36), probably created while she herself was looking forward to motherhood, transforms the mother into a being entirely transcending time or place, a dark, anonymous goddess of nourishment, paradoxically animallike, bound to the earth and utterly remote from the contingencies of history or the social order. While in some ways reminiscent of Gauguin's Tahitian women, which Modersohn-Becker knew and admired (see fig. 46), these late mother and child paintings are actually starker, more reduced to pure function, more boldly divested of any kind of conventional beauty or softening appurtenances than any of Gauguin's female figures.

The dramatic but drastically simplified conception of feminine power expressed in Modersohn-Becker's paintings had a powerful hold on the German imagination in the late nineteenth and early twentieth centuries.[242] One of its most explicit and elaborate formulations was that by the scholar and would-be anthropologist, Johann Jakob Bachofen, who in his book *Mother Right,* published in 1861 but not popularized until the 1890s and then revived in the 1920s, claimed that women had originally dominated during the pre-historic stages of social evolution, when the Divine Mother had been the central cult image, the body had prevailed over the mind, and "the eyes of humanity had been fastened on the earth." Maternity, Bachofen declared, the central feature of this primeval stage of human development, pertained to the physical side of humanity, the only side he felt that humans actually shared with the animals.[243]

Such theories identifying women with the realm of nature and reducing them to their purely sexual dimension had wide dissemination in the early years of the twentieth century. D. H. Lawrence is perhaps their major promulgator in the literature of the English-speaking world, but his is simply the most convincing and coherent voice among many. In the visual realm, it would seem that Georgia O'Keeffe (see cat. nos. 134-40), in her vastly magnified, frontal flowers, like her *Black Iris* of 1926 (New York, Metropolitan Museum)[244] or her suggestively closed and open clamshells of the same year (private collection) is making similar claims for the unity of the feminine and the natural order. In such imagery, the forms of nature, while never losing their own integrity, exist at the same time as strong schematic metaphors of female sexuality, universalized by their separation from any sort of concrete locale or visual context. As such, like Modersohn-Becker's similarly isolated and powerful maternal images — and analogous to the sexually awakened, intuitive heroines of D. H. Lawrence's fiction — they function as potent and vastly attractive mythic projections of essentialist notions of femininity.[245] Such images of female sexuality were basically apolitical if not outright conservative: woman, reduced to her sexual being, conceived of as a part of Nature, was the very antithesis of historical action. Paradoxically, however, in the context of today's feminist activism, such imagery has acquired potent political implications, for woman's control over her sexual destiny is now seen as a central issue in her struggle for self-determination. Nothing could better demonstrate the complexity, and the basic ambiguity, of the issue of what constitutes a valid "feminist imagery" than the recent transformation of the placid iris into a fighting symbol. Having begun this discussion of women artists with one revolution, it is perhaps appropriate that we end it with another, the feminist revolution of today, which, in a sense, has brought into being a new history — a more valid, complex, expansive interpretation of the past — in art, as in every other realm of human experience.

Linda Nochlin

Bachofen's notions. See J. J. Bachofen, *Myth, Religion, and Mother Right: Selected Writings of J. J. Bachofen,* trans. R. Manheim, Princeton, 1967. Also see Green, *The von Richthofen Sisters,* 81-84, on Bachofen. For radically contrasting conclusions based on similar anthropological, or pseudo-anthropological, material (much of it contributed by the American anthropologist Lewis Henry Morgan, whose *Ancient Society* had appeared in 1877), see Bebel's *Woman under Socialism,* and Friedrich Engels' *The Origin of the Family, Private Property and the State,* introduction by E. B. Leacock, New York, 1972, which was first published in 1884. For an excellent critique of mythologizing, pseudo-scientific matriarchal theories, including Bachofen's, see the review by A. Hackett and S. Pomeroy of Elizabeth Gould Davis's *The First Sex* (New York, 1971), entitled "Making History: The First Sex," *Feminist Studies,* I, no. 2, Fall 1972, 97-108.

244.
For a reproduction, see New York, Whitney Museum of American Art, *Georgia O'Keeffe,* catalog by Lloyd Goodrich and Doris Bry, 1970, repr. 40. For a more detailed discussion of the iconography of the iris, see L. Nochlin, "Some Women Realists: Part I," *Arts Magazine,* February 1974, 47-49.
245.
It would seem more than a mere coincidence that O'Keeffe painted *The Lawrence Tree* (1929, Collection the artist, Goodrich and Bry, *Georgia O'Keeffe,* no. 61, repr.) shortly after her first arrival in New Mexico, and that one of her admirers, the New Mexican-by-adoption, Mabel Dodge Luhan, was also one of D. H. Lawrence's most fervent disciples. In the deserts of New Mexico perhaps O'Keeffe — like Lawrence, like Mabel Dodge Luhan, who married a Navaho Indian, and like many other artistic personalities — was also seeking that primordial truth, that dark, timeless unity with and acceptance of nature which seemed for

Lawrence and for Mabel Dodge Luhan, at any rate, inseparably bound with what they considered "true femininity," and as inalterably opposed to the rationality, mutability, and restless ambition of what they thought of as "masculine" civilization. See for example, Mabel Dodge Luhan's *Lorenzo in Taos,* New York, 1932, and the same author's "Georgia O'Keeffe in Taos," *Creative Art,* VIII, June 1931, 407-10. For a recent discussion of the New Mexican art ambience, see S. Schwartz, "When New York Went to New Mexico," *Art in America,* July-August 1976, 93-96.

Color Plates

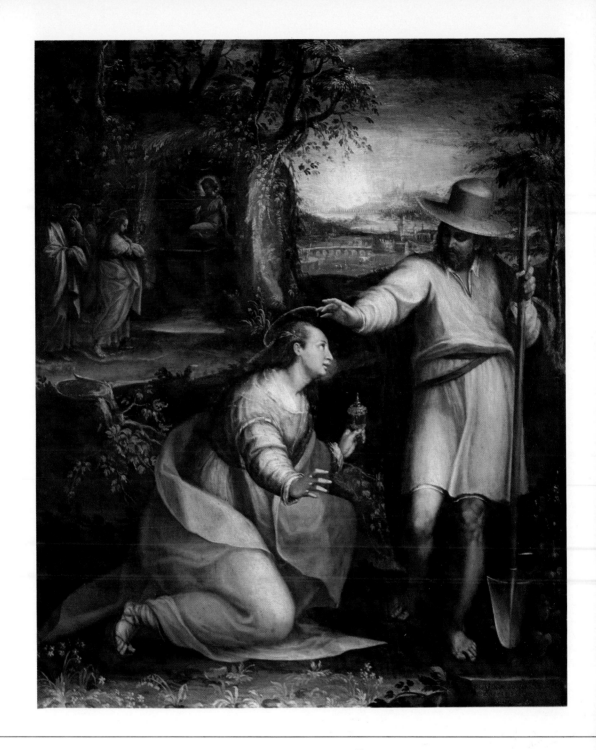

7.
Lavinia Fontana
Noli Me Tangere

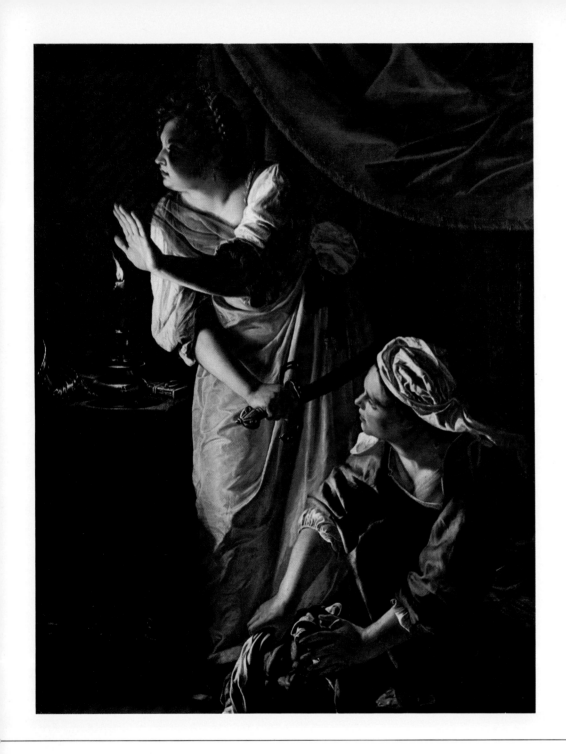

13.
Artemisia Gentileschi
Judith and Maidservant with the Head of Holofernes

14.
Artemisia Gentileschi
Fame

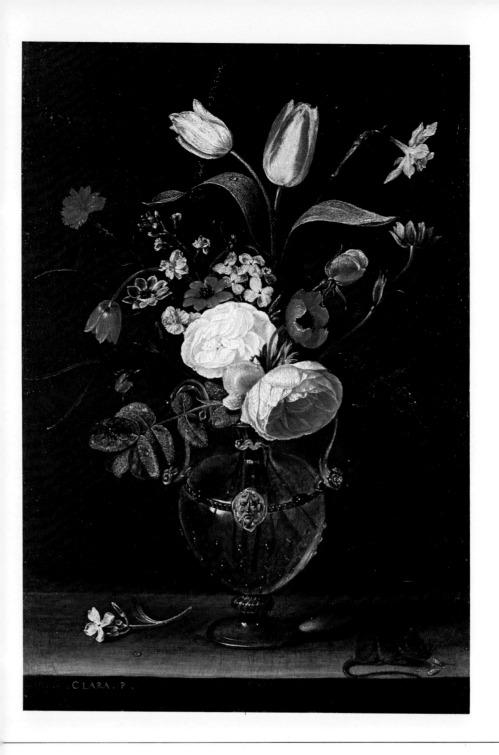

17.
Clara Peeters
Flowers in a Glass Vase

19.
Giovanna Garzoni
Dish of Broad Beans

23.
Judith Leyster
The Proposition

25.
Louise Moillon
Basket of Apricots

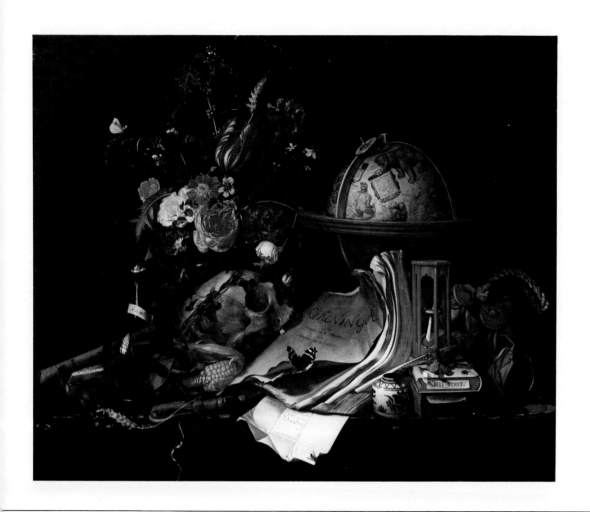

28.
Maria van Oosterwyck
Vanitas

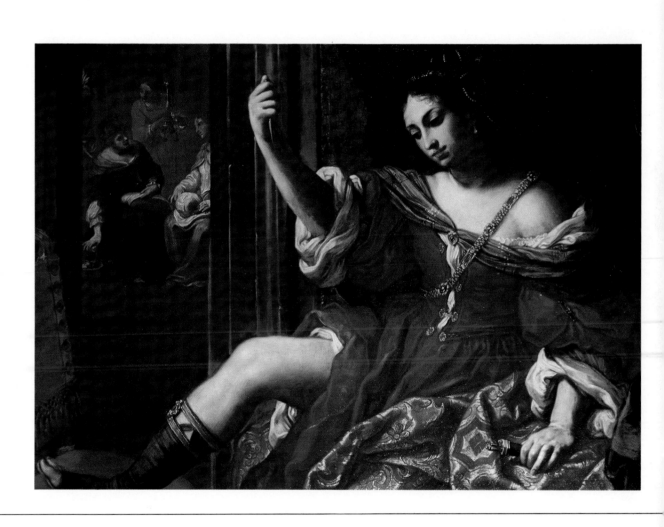

31.
Elisabetta Sirani
Porcia Wounding Her Thigh

40.
Rachel Ruysch
Still Life with Flowers and Plums

45.
Anna Dorothea Lisiewska-Therbusch
Portrait of Jacob Philipp Hackert

46.
Françoise Duparc
The Seller of Tisane

50.
Angelica Kauffman
Cornelia, Mother of the Gracchi

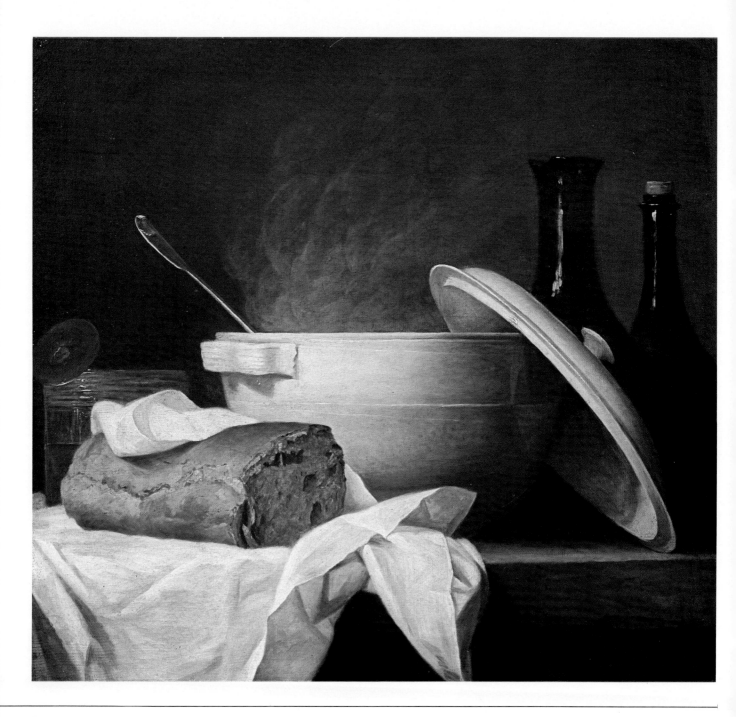

52.
Anne Vallayer-Coster
The White Soup Bowl

61.
Elizabeth Vigee-Lebrun
Varvara Ivanovna Narishkine

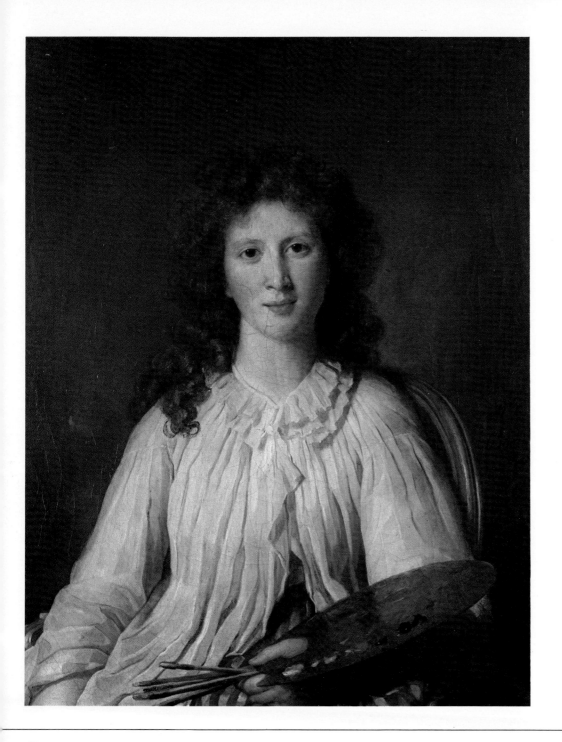

67.
Marie Geneviève Bouliar
Portrait of Adélaïde Binart (Mme. Alexandre Lenoir)

73.
Marie Eléonore Godefroid
The Sons of Marshal Ney

75.
Antoinette Cecile Hortense Haudebourt-Lescot
Self-Portrait

80.
Rosa Bonheur
Gathering for the Hunt

82.
Emily Mary Osborn
Mrs. Sturgis and Children

86.
Berthe Morisot
Mme. Boursier and Daughter

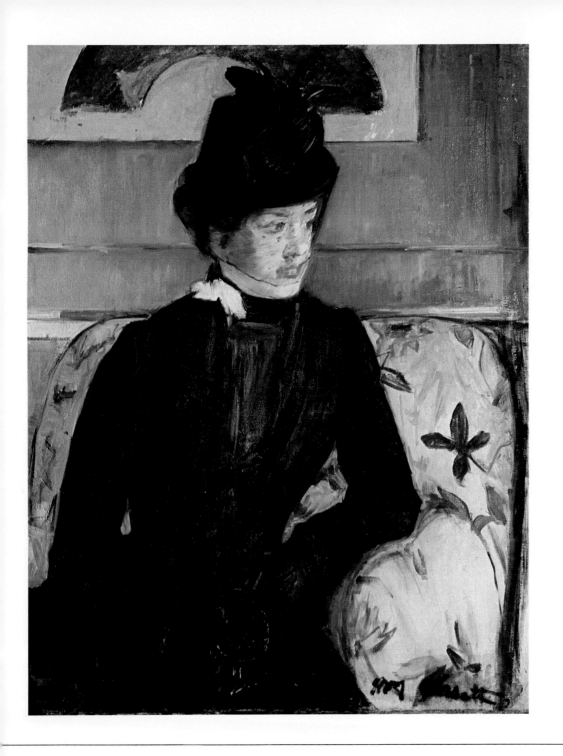

90.
Mary Cassatt
Young Woman in Black

98.
Lady Elizabeth Butler
Quatre Bras

101.
Cecilia Beaux
Sita and Sarita

103.
Edith Hayller
A Summer Shower

108.
Florine Stettheimer
Beauty Contest

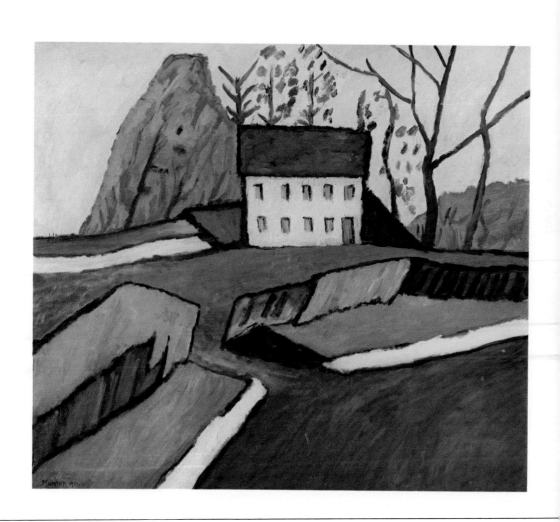

120.
Gabriele Münter
The Green House

124.
Nataliia Sergeevna Goncharova
Portrait of Larionov

130.
Sonia Delaunay
The Flamenco Singer (The Large Flamenco),
detail

152.
Alice Trumbull Mason
L'Hasard

156.
Loren MacIver
Hopscotch

158.
Dorothea Tanning
Maternity

Catalog

Levina Teerlinc
Flemish, ca. 1520-1576

Although the life of Levina Teerlinc is much better documented than those of many women in this exhibition, not one work can be securely attributed to her. She was the eldest of five daughters born in Bruges to Simon Benninck (1483/84-1561), a book illuminator and miniature painter.[1] She and her husband are still recorded in Bruges on February 4, 1545,[2] but soon after they left for London and the court of Henry VIII. In November 1546 she was granted an annual payment of £40 "from the annunciation of our Lady during your Majesty's pleasure."[3] She must have had a considerable reputation as an artist by this date to be invited to work at the English court at a salary that was, as Tufts has pointed out, higher than Holbein's.[4] Even twenty years later she was still famous in the Netherlands.[5] We can thus assume that by 1546 she had not only finished her training but must have been active professionally for a few years. Therefore she must have been born around 1520, and maybe even a few years earlier.

The annuity payments granted her by Henry VIII can be traced in court records almost every year until her death. She worked for Edward VI, for Mary I, and finally for Elizabeth I, whose portrait she first painted in 1551.[6] A number of works are recorded, all miniatures but not always portraits. In 1556 she gave Queen Mary "as a New yaer gift a small picture of the 'trynitie.'"[7] Two years later she gave the newly crowned Elizabeth a small portrait of Her Majesty.[8] In return Teerlinc received expensive presents like a gilded salt cellar and a pair of gilded spoons,[9] and enjoyed high social status at court, as did her husband. With her husband and son Marcus she became an English subject in 1566 and died ten years later in their house in Stepney.[10]

She is only known to have worked as a miniature painter. She was never called upon to paint larger works or stage scenery, to design engravings for books, or to execute any of the other duties given to Tudor court artists. More important for our researches, she was the only portrait miniature painter of Flemish origin known to be employed at court between 1546 and her death, and the only well-documented miniaturist of distinction recorded in England between the death of Hans Holbein the Younger in 1543 and the emergence in the 1570s of her real successor, Nicolas Hilliard. His career as England's first great native-born artist seems to have successfully blotted out memory of her achievements in later records.[11]

There have been several attempts to identify works by Levina Teerlinc but in the absence of any signed works or works that can be firmly linked with documents, the task is a difficult one. In 1934 Simone Bergmans published a group of miniatures that she gave to Teerlinc, but subsequent research has proved that almost all of them are by later artists such as Hilliard and Isaac Oliver.[12] The best summary of the evidence on which any attributions must rest is provided by Erna Auerbach in her study of Nicolas Hilliard. According to her, the work that has the best chance of being an authentic Levina Teerlinc is an oval miniature in the collection of the Earl of Beauchamp showing an Elizabethan Maundy ceremony, which Auerbach suggests might be identified with Teerlinc's New Year's gift to Elizabeth in 1563 of "a Carde with the Queen's Matie [Majesty] and many other personnages."[13] A handful of other miniatures, all portraits (see cat. no. 1), made while Teerlinc was active can also tentatively be assigned to her, pending more careful study. The complete documentation of Teerlinc's life at court also has yet to be fully published. She was certainly, on documentary evidence alone, the most important miniaturist active in England between Holbein and Hilliard. It is hard to believe that her sex has nothing to do with her neglect by scholars, who seem to agree tacitly with Hilliard that "none should medle [sic] with limning but gentlemen alone."[14]

1.

Portrait of a Young Woman, 1549
Watercolor over a dark yellowish carnation ground worked over with gouache, the costume finished with white and powdered gold, on vellum
Diameter: 2⅛ in. (5.3 cm.); the painted area alone: 1¹⁵/₁₆ in. (4.8 cm.)
Inscribed along the upper edge: A : D : 1549[15]
London, Victoria and Albert Museum (P 21-1954)

1.
F. Winkler, *Die flämische Buchmalerei des 15 und 16 Jahrhunderts,* Leipzig, 1925, 139-49, and Paul Durrieu, *Alexandre Bening et les peintres du Breviare Grimani,* Paris, 1891. Her father presumably trained her; she may even have worked on some of his illuminations, but must also have worked independently because it was she, not he, who was invited to work in England. Even Susan Horenbout (Hornebolt) whom Dürer met and admired when she was eighteen, is never recorded working as an artist after she and her family moved to England in the 1520s (H. Paget, "Gerard and Lucas Hornebolt in England," *Burlington Magazine,* 1959, 396-402, especially 401, note 17).
2.
Bergmans, 232 (with no reference to the location of the document or its place of publication).
3.
Auerbach, 1954, 51 and 104. She explains that the confusion about Teerlinc also working as a nurse for Henry VIII is due to a misreading of the word *pitricem* as *nutricem* in this payment.
4.
Tufts, 1974, 43; see note 12 below also for the salary paid to Scrots.

5.
Guicciardini, 20-21. He knew that she was invited to England by Henry VIII and worked subsequently for Mary and Elizabeth.
6.
Auerbach, 1954, 187-88.
7.
Bergmans, 232, for the text quoted, and Auerbach, 1954, 188.
8.
Bergmans, 232.
9.
Bergmans, 232, and Auerbach, 1954, 104.
10.
Auerbach, 1954, 105 and 188.
11.
The women artists mentioned by Tufts (1974, 43), namely Katherine Maynors, Alice Carmillion, and Ann Smiter, are shadowy figures about whom little is known (on Carmillion, see Auerbach, 1954, 157). As noted above, Susan Horenbout is never documented as a painter in England, but she was still alive in 1550 and the possibility exists that she occasionally painted miniatures. Hilliard, who praises

1

Since this miniature portrait of an unidentified young English woman is dated 1549, an attribution to Hans Holbein (d. 1543), Lucas Horenbout (d. 1544), or Nicolas Hilliard (b. 1547) can be excluded. The two English artists then known to be active, John Shute (d. 1563) and John Bettes (dead by 1576) are not known to have worked "in small," making an attribution to them unlikely.[16] It is a work of high quality; on documentary grounds the best candidate for authorship is Levina Teerlinc.

The period between 1545, when Teerlinc moved to England, and 1560, when the precocious young Hilliard signed his first miniature portrait, is crucial to scholars seeking to identify work by Teerlinc, for she was the only significant miniaturist known to be active in English court circles at that time. Four more English portrait miniatures survive from these years — a *Portrait of Queen Mary I* (Collection the Duke of Buccleuch), a *Portrait of a Young Woman* (Collection H.M. the Queen, Windsor Castle), a *Portrait of Katherine, Countess of Hertford* (Collection the Duke of Rutland, Belvoir Castle), and a *Portrait of Robert Dudley, Earl of Leicester* (same collection).[17] In addition a *Portrait of Elizabeth I in State Robes* at Welbeck Abbey belongs in this discussion, for it was painted in the early years of her reign.[18]

The *Portrait of Queen Mary I* is painted in oil on copper, not watercolor and gouache on vellum, the usual medium for miniatures, and is based on a full-scale portrait by Hans Eworth; a connection with Teerlinc therefore does not seem likely. Auerbach found the technique of the remaining three miniatures listed above similar, but there are discernible differences. Our work of 1549 was executed with a light, almost invisible touch. Individual brushstrokes are hard to detect, even under magnification; the contour lines are soft, even those not blurred naturally by the fur of the sitter's costume. The Windsor miniature of a young woman uses a fine, dotted technique, stronger tonal contrasts, and carefully defined contour lines. The latter figure also has more bulk and seems better drawn than the miniature of 1549, in which the head is slightly too large for the body and hands.[19] Finally, the artist responsible for the Windsor miniature appears to have idealized the sitter less than the artist who painted our work.

Judging only from reproductions, the miniature of *Katherine, Countess of Hertford* could be by the same hand as ours. In both the sitter is posed a little stiffly, the arms and hands are included, and the composition is essentially frontal and symmetrical. The slight figure proportions and delicate technique are also common to both. The *Robert Dudley, Earl of Leicester* of about 1565 was thought by Auerbach to be close to the "near-Teerlinc" group although the pose of the sitter, who faces right in three-quarter view, recalls Hilliard. Since he was active by the time this miniature was painted, it is safer to exclude it from the items under discussion as possible works by Teerlinc.

The miniature of Elizabeth I in her coronation robes is a little larger

---

Holbein as "the most excellent painter and limner" and "the greatest master truly in both thosse [*sic*] arts after the life that ever was," never mentions Teerlinc at all in *A Treatise Concerning the Arts of Limning,* written around 1600, nor does Edward Norgate (*Miniatura or the Art of Limning,* London, 1650). The only reference to her in print before the nineteenth century is that of Guicciardini cited above.

12.
The same unfortunately is true of all but two of the works chosen by Tufts to illustrate her lively essay on Teerlinc (1974, 43-49). The so-called *Self-Portrait* (Bergmans, fig. C; Tufts, 1974, fig. 15) must on grounds of costume have been painted around 1615, very probably by Isaac Oliver (C. Winter, *Elizabethan Miniatures,* London, 1943, 30; G. Reynolds, *Nicolas Hilliard and Isaac Oliver,* London, 1947, no. 186). The beautiful miniature of an old woman, dated 1575 (Tufts, 1974, fig. 19), is certainly by Hilliard (Auerbach, 1961, 68ff.). The full-size *Portrait of Elizabeth I as Princess* (Tufts, 1974, fig. 20) is given by the latest scholarly opinion to the circle of William Scrots, who arrived in England in 1545 as Holbein's successor at a salary higher than that of Holbein or Teerlinc (Strong, 74). The attribution to Teerlinc of any part of the Hennessy Hours by her father, now usually dated around 1520 (Tufts, 1974, fig. 16), is obviously highly speculative.

13.
Auerbach, 1961, 53-54 and pl. 6. See also her discussion of an illumination in a Michaelmas Roll of 1553 (1954, 96-97).
14.
A Treatise Concerning the Arte of Limning, ed. P. Norman, The Walpole Society, London, 1911-12, 16. He is of course defending the high social rank that he believed should be accorded to the successful miniaturist. His failure to mention Teerlinc at all, though he must have known her and her work and had to wait until more than a decade after her death to be given the exclusive right to paint the queen in miniature (Reynolds, *Nicolas Hilliard and Isaac Oliver,* 8), suggests a certain reluctance on his part to publicize the achievements of a woman in his domain.
15.
I am indebted to John Murdoch, Assistant Keeper of Paintings at the museum, for this detailed description of the technique of this work and for a correct reading of its inscription. He also read this biography and entry in draft and made several valuable comments.
16.
Auerbach, 1954, 84-85, 153-54, and 185-86.

than the others discussed so far and has an oblong rather than a round format. Auerbach noted its close similarity to a much cruder portrait of Elizabeth in a manuscript of 1559,[20] but concluded that the young Hilliard, to whom all authorities give the work, was influenced by the hieratic traditions of English manuscript illumination in this early work and not that it was the model for the manuscript. In the miniature, the queen is shown wearing her coronation robes, which are described in great detail; the work even includes a real diamond in the scepter. It was surely painted shortly after the coronation in January 1559 and not five to eight years later, as suggested by scholars who give the work to Hilliard, who was only twelve in 1559.[21] Again, Teerlinc seems a more probable candidate. The technique of the miniature also seems close to that of the Windsor *Portrait of a Young Woman,* especially the drawing of the ruff and the dotted touch used to suggest patterned and embroidered fabrics.

Are we dealing with two different artists, one responsible for our miniature of 1549 and the portrait of Katherine, Countess of Hertford, and another who painted the Welbeck *Elizabeth I* and the *Young Woman* at Windsor? Could one artist have painted all four works, changing from the delicate technique seen in the work of 1549 to a stronger, better drawn but slightly less refined technique by the late 1550s? How do any of these portraits relate to the *Maundy Ceremony* miniature with its tiny figures, perhaps painted by Teerlinc in 1563? These are questions that only a specialist with access to the originals can answer. Considerable progress has been made in the last twenty years by scholars who have reconstructed the artistic personalities of other Tudor court artists like Hans Eworth and William Scrots, who once seemed as shadowy as Teerlinc seems now. Perhaps this entry will provoke a qualified scholar into considering in detail the question of Teerlinc and her role in the development of the portrait miniature in sixteenth-century England.

2

17.
All four are illustrated by Auerbach, 1961, pls. 5, 6, 8, and 9. A miniature portrait of a child in the Heckett Collection, Valencia, Pennsylvania, has been attributed to Teerlinc (*Four Centuries of Portrait Miniatures from the Heckett Collection,* catalog by H. Weissberger, Department of Fine Arts, Carnegie Institute, 1954, no. 54 and pl. 1), but the costume indicates a date at the end of the sixteenth century (cf. Auerbach, 1961, pl. 249).
18.
Auerbach, 1954, pl. 35b, and 1961, no. 13 and pl. 13. In the later book, she dates this miniature ca. 1569.
19.
The same faults of proportion can be found in Simon Benninck's *Self-Portrait* miniature of 1558 (London, Victoria and Albert Museum; repr. in color by C. Winter, *Elizabethan Miniatures,* London, 1943, 1b).
20.
Auerbach, 1954, 119-20.
21.
R. C. Strong, *Portraits of Elizabeth I,* Oxford, 1963, 54-56.

Caterina van Hemessen
Flemish, 1528-after 1587

Caterina van Hemessen is one of the first Flemish women artists recorded and the first for whom several certainly authentic works are known.[1] She was the daughter of a painter, Jan van Hemessen (ca. 1500-after 1563), who presumably taught her. Her date of birth is estimated from her self-portrait in Basel, which her inscription indicates was painted in 1548 when she was twenty. Six years later she married Chrétien de Morien, a musician; in 1556 they were both invited to join the court that Mary of Hungary established in Spain after she abdicated her regency of the Netherlands. At her death two years later, she left the couple a generous pension for life. In Guicciardini's *Descrittione dei Paesi Bassi (Description of the Low Countries),* first published in 1567, Caterina is mentioned as one of the women artists then alive. She died in Antwerp some time after 1587. Ten signed and dated works are known, most of them small portraits of women, although she also signed two religious pictures, both oddly archaic works possibly based on prints.[2] All her dated works were made between 1548 and 1552, suggesting that her artistic career may have ended with her marriage.

Her father was one of the liveliest exponents of Flemish Mannerism, but the work of his daughter is carried out in a style of quiet realism untouched by the foreign influences that affected him so strongly. Flemish portraitists of this period usually included landscape views or elaborately described rooms or at least a shadow cast on the wall behind the sitter to suggest surrounding space, but Caterina kept her portraits simple. Except in her self-portrait and in her portrait of her sister at the virginals (cat. no. 2), she provided no indication of setting at all, and even in these two works only the furniture implies space around the figures for the backgrounds are plain. Her best portraits have an appealing intimacy and describe their sitters' features with great sympathy. If they have some obvious anatomical weaknesses (she never seems to have mastered the drawing of hands), the same can be said for a surprising number of her Flemish contemporaries. Since she apparently stopped painting in her mid-twenties after only a brief career she can hardly be said to have reached artistic maturity, yet her works have considerable charm. They are also of great documentary interest as the only surviving evidence, with the exception of works attributed to Levina Teerlinc, of the artistic activity of the ten or so women known to be active in Flanders before the debut of Clara Peeters in 1608.[3]

2.
Young Woman Playing the Virginals, 1548
Oil on oak panel
$12^{11}/_{16}$ x $10^1/_8$ in. (32.2 x 25.7 cm.)
Inscribed upper right: CATERINA DE HEMESSEN/PINGEBAT 1548
Inscribed center right: AETATIS SUAE 22
Cologne, Wallraf-Richartz Museum (654)

Music flourished in Flanders during the Renaissance. Flemish musicians and composers were considered to be the best in Europe and they carried their ideas to the courts of France, Spain, Italy, even Hungary. Women are often shown playing keyboard instruments and lutes in Flemish sixteenth-century paintings. Being able to perform on one or more instruments was considered a necessary social skill, like singing, dancing, and playing chess, in all cultivated upper-class households. One artist, known as the Master of the Female Half-Lengths, even specialized in pictures of attractive young women performing alone or in groups.

Caterina van Hemessen, who married a professional musician, very probably had some musical skills herself. This portrait, however, does not represent her, although it may portray her sister, who according to the inscription would have been two years older than Caterina.[4] The family likeness between this sitter and the young woman in Caterina's *Self-Portrait* (Basel) is obvious. It is also relevant that both works are almost exactly the same size and that the two women face left and right, making the portraits suitable for hanging as a pair.

Caterina van Hemessen's most elaborate compositions, with the exception of her less successful religious works, these are also among the most appealing small portraits produced in sixteenth-century Flanders.[5]

1.
There is no reliable modern discussion of Caterina van Hemessen's career. The facts must be assembled from F. Winkler's entry in Thieme-Becker (XVI, 367), Bergmans' diffuse article of 1955, and the chapter devoted to her in Tufts' book (1974, 51-53), which has several useful large black and white plates.
2.
Both are in private collections in Mons, Belgium. A *Rest on the Flight into Egypt* is dated 1555; the *Christ and St. Veronica* is undated (Tufts, 1974, fig. 23). Bergmans (1955, 136ff.) attributes to Caterina a small picture of *The Concubine of the Levite* (Judges 19:22-29) which has the monogram CVH and the partially legible date 156-. The style suggests what the monogram suggests, namely Cornelis Cornelisz. van Haarlem (1562-1638). The photograph is not clear enough for the monogram and date to be checked.
3.
Bergmans' efforts to attribute the backgrounds of some of Jan van Hemessen's pictures to Caterina and to identify the Brunswick Monogrammist with Mayken Verhulst, a woman miniaturist who supposedly taught Jan Breughel the Elder, and thereby to expand our knowledge of Flemish women artists of the sixteenth century, do not carry conviction (see her articles of 1955 and 1958 and her entries for Hemessen in the catalog for Brussels, 1965).

4.
Tufts, 1974, 51. As she notes, their clothes are almost identical in this work and in the Basel self-portrait. The sister's name was Christina.
5.
An inscription runs round the inner edge of the instrument next to the sounding board. Its text has been identified by Edwin Ripin, who noticed a similar inscription in the same location on the virginals portrayed in Cornelis de Zeeuws' *Portrait of the Family of Pierre de Moucheron* in the Rijksmuseum, Amsterdam. It reads: OMNIA DAT DOMINUS/NON HABET ERGO MINUS. Only the words HABET ERGO MINUS are legible in our painting. (See I. Hiller and H. Vey, *Wallraf-Richartz Museum: Katalog der deutschen und nieder-landischen Gemälde bis 1550,* Cologne, 1969, no. 654.)

Sofonisba Anguissola
Italian, 1532/35-1625

Sofonisba Anguissola was the oldest in a family of six daughters and one son born to Amilcare Anguissola (1494-1573), a Cremonese nobleman, and his second wife, Bianca Ponzona. Her date of birth is not recorded. When Anthony van Dyck visited her in Palermo in July 1624 she told him that she was ninety-six, but scholars have recently come to suspect that she was exaggerating slightly.[1] Her apparent age in several dated self-portraits of the 1550s and other documentary evidence suggests that she was born between 1532 and 1535.[2] Her father encouraged the artistic and musical talents that she and her sisters revealed at an early age. Sofonisba and her next sister, Elena, studied with the local painter, Bernardino Campi, from 1546 to 1549, and after that with another local artist, Bernardino Gatti (Il Sojaro).[3] Her father even corresponded with Michelangelo in 1557, soliciting a drawing that Sofonisba could copy and later thanking the sculptor profusely for his help and encouragement.[4] Her first known work is a *Self-Portrait* in Vienna, dated 1554.[5] Nine signed and dated works survive from the next five years; another twenty-three of her paintings can be dated before 1560.[6] Nearly all of these are portraits of members of her large family and of herself, although she did occasionally paint religious works.

In 1559 Sofonisba was invited to join the court of Philip II in Madrid.[7] She spent at least ten years there with the rank of a lady-in-waiting, painting portraits of the royal family and of herself, but apart from one self-portrait (see cat. no. 3) not one certain work survives from this period of her life.[8] She is said to have married a noble Sicilian, Fabrizio de Moncada, probably by 1570, and to have returned to Italy with him, laden with gifts from the king, to settle in Palermo.[9] When Fabrizio died, she decided to return to Cremona and took a boat to Genoa. Soprani relates that the captain of the ship, a well-born Genoese called Orazio Lomellini, looked after her so attentively that by the end of the voyage she had agreed to marry him and settle in Genoa.[10] This move was made before 1584.[11] She maintained her contacts in Palermo, probably because of her financial interests there, and seems to have settled there again at the end of her life.

Van Dyck interviewed her there in 1624, blind but otherwise well, "avendo ancora la memoria et il cervello prontissimo" (having still a good memory and a sharp mind). She died in Palermo on November 16, 1625, and was buried in the church of her husband's community there, S. Giorgio dei Genovesi.[12]

Sofonisba Anguissola was the first Italian woman to become an international celebrity as an artist and the first for whom a substantial body of works is known. As such, she is a figure of considerable historical importance. The publicity that her spectacular and romantic career attracted must have instilled in the minds of other talented young women the idea that an artistic career was possible. Significantly several of her immediate successors came from the same part of Italy — Lavinia Fontana of Bologna, Fede Galizia of Milan, and Barbara Longhi of Ravenna. Vasari's praise, however brief, of her achievements also insured that her fame was more than local.[13]

Anguissola worked almost exclusively as a portraitist. Her early religious works are not distinguished, revealing the limitations of a training that took place in an artistic backwater and could never, despite the support of her father and the help of Bernardino Campi, have constituted a serious apprenticeship. Her portraits belong to the lively North Italian Renaissance tradition of straightforward realism that is exemplified by the work of Moretto da Brescia and G. B. Morone. While it is true that she was unable to match their grasp of psychology, their variety of presentation, or their confident drawing, she has received an undeservedly poor press since 1900, provoked by the disparity perceived between her level of achievement and the honors showered upon her.[14] No one today would agree with Baldinucci's judgment that in portraiture she was the equal of Titian, but her best works are nevertheless fine examples of late Renaissance portraiture. She helped to create the portrait conversation piece with her picture of her sisters playing chess.[15] Her numerous self-portraits — then a novelty for an Italian artist — display great inventiveness in iconography and composition. There are awkward

1.
Gert Adriani, *Anton Van Dyck: Italienisches Skizzenbuch*, Vienna, 1940, 72-73. His drawing of her and its inscription were first discussed in relation to Sofonisba's career by Cook, 228ff.
2.
Bonetti (1928, 288ff.) proved that her parents married in 1530 very probably and certainly by 1533. They had seven children by 1551. Amilcare's first wife had been barren; it seems unlikely that he waited long after his remarriage to start a family. For this reason I am opposed to recent suggestions (Haraszti-Takács, 59ff., and Tufts, 1972, 53) that she was born as late as 1535-40. The use of the words *virgo* and *adolescens* in some of her inscriptions is of little help. She could have used the former until she married, and *adolescens* in classical Latin can describe someone aged between twelve and thirty.
3.
Lamo, 1584, 35-36, 40, and 49. The documents published by Lamo were used by Baldinucci (VIII, 211-12) to correct Vasari (VI, 498ff.), who said that Sofonisba studied with Giulio Campi. Bernardino left Cremona for Milan in 1549.
4.
Tolnay, 116-18.

5.
A portrait of a Dominican priest signed SOPHONISBA ANGUSSOLA/VIRGO F/M.D.L. II was on the New York art market between 1918 and 1928 (photo in the Frick Art Reference Library, New York).
6.
Berenson (I, 13-14) provides a skeleton catalog of signed and reliably attributed works. To it should be added the two works mentioned in the last paragraph of this biography. A great many more works linked with her name exist in public and private collections. She would make a good dissertation subject.
7.
The date is given first by Baldinucci. Philip II returned to Madrid from Brussels with his new bride, Elizabeth of Valois, in the summer of 1559. Sofonisba is not documented in Madrid until 1561 (Vasari, VI, 499-500).
8.
She mentions working on several portraits in a letter sent to her old teacher Campi from Madrid in 1561 (Lamo, 40). Portraits of Queen Isabella and Prince Don Carlos are recorded in early Spanish sources but neither is traceable today (Tufts, 1972, 50). Holmes (181), attributes to her a *Portrait of Philip II* in the National Portrait Gallery, London.

3

passages in her earliest works — the poorly drawn hand in the *Self-Portrait* of 1554 (fig. 2, p. 13), the spatial relationships of the four figures in the Poznań picture of 1555 (fig. 5, p. 30) — but she had conquered these problems by the time she painted her father with her brother Asdrubale and her sister Minerva in 1558-59. A sympathetic portrayal of three members of one family, this work captures family likenesses and personality differences in an ambitious composition.

The loss of most of her later works makes a final assessment of her artistic achievement difficult. Her *Virgin and Child* of 1588 in Budapest is a far better picture than her *Holy Family* of 1559 in Bergamo.[16] The contrast suggests that she continued to develop in Spain, learning from the Venetian masterpieces in the Spanish royal collections as well as from Luca Cambiaso in Genoa. The *Portrait of Infanta Clara Eugenia* in Vienna, perhaps painted in 1599, is unfortunately in poor condition but seems to have once been a sympathetic interpretation of formal court imagery.[17] On the evidence available, she was a good artist but not a major artistic personality. Her circumstances as a provincial woman artist make her achievements remarkable, however, and her success was of vital importance to the many even more gifted women who came after her, in Italy and throughout Europe.

3.

Self-Portrait, 1561
Oil on canvas
35 x 32 in. (88.9 x 81.3 cm.)
Inscribed lower left: SOPHONISBA ANGUISSOLA VIRGO SEIPSUM PINXIT JUSSU AMI [Icaris] PATRIS 1561 [?][18]
Althorp, Northampton, Collection Earl Spencer

Sofonisba painted more portraits of herself than any artist between Dürer and Rembrandt, a phenomenon best explained by quoting from the letter written to her father by Annibale Caro, who had recently visited the family and was hoping to have a picture by her (he was to be disappointed). "There is nothing that I desire more," he wrote in December 1558, "than the image of the artist herself, so that in a single work I can exhibit two marvels, one the work, the other the artist."[19] Her father used her self-portraits to publicize her gifts, sending one to Pope Julius III (1487-1555) and another to the Este court in Ferrara.[20] The archdeacon of Piacenza Cathedral owned both a portrait of himself by Sofonisba and her self-portrait.[21] At least twelve self-portraits by her are known today. She painted herself in miniature and full size; she showed herself holding a book, a palette, a monogram of her father's name, at work on a picture of the Virgin, playing musical instruments, and being painted by her teacher, Bernardino Campi.[22] This painting of 1561 is her latest accepted self-portrait and her only work certainly produced in Spain. It is thus a document of some importance.

The artist is shown playing a spinet, her performance observed by an old woman who closely resembles the "vecchia donna di casa" noted by Vasari as watching the artist's sisters play chess in the painting now

9.
The Genoese historian Soprani, who seems to have interviewed relatives of her second husband, is the first writer to name Fabrizio de Moncada (414). Documents described by F. J. Sánchez-Cánton ("Los pintores de los reyes Catolicos," *Boletin de la Sociedad Española de Excursiones,* XXII, 1914, 149-50) show that Queen Isabella, who died in 1568, left money for Sofonisba's dowry in a codicil to her will, and that this money was paid to the artist between 1571 and 1574, although the first payment was owed to her in 1569. Thus she would appear to have married in 1569 or 1570, not 1580, as is often stated. No one seems to be able to trace the death date of her husband. De Dominici (II, 237) reports that she executed miniatures and taught others how to paint them in Palermo.
10.
Soprani, 415.
11.
Campi (III, 1) reported in 1585 that "di presente vive in quella nobilissima città [Genoa] honoratissimamente, e con grandissima reputatione" (at present she lives in that most noble city [Genoa], where she is much esteemed and enjoys a great reputation). This hardly sounds as if she had just stepped off the boat.
12.
Her death certificate was traced and published by Cook (228).

13.
Vasari, (V, 81; VI, 498ff.; VII, 133). He did not write a proper life of her; that honor was reserved for artists who were dead. The first published biography of Sofonisba is Soprani's (1684), but the best is Baldinucci's, written by 1681 (Prinz, 181, document 59) but published only in 1688, which makes full use of all the sixteenth-century sources.
14.
The nadir in Anguissola criticism was reached by Claude Phillips, who in 1915 wrote, "Sofonisba painted with something of that tepid rose-tinted sentimentality proper to the woman-painter, then as now" (quoted approvingly by Cook, 235-36). More recently Sydney Freedberg dismissed her portraits as "literal-minded and heavy-handed. . . . [Their] occasional charm . . . [resulting] from what they illustrate, not from any quality of execution or design" (*Painting in Italy, 1500-1600,* Harmondsworth, Middlesex, and Baltimore, 1971, 407).
15.
R. Longhi, "Indicazioni per Sofonisba Anguissola," *Paragone,* no. 157, 1963, 50-52.
16.
Haraszti-Takács, 53ff., and figs. 37 and 42.

in Poznán (fig. 5, p. 30). Presumably this means that her old nurse accompanied her to Spain. A ghostly presence who fits uncomfortably into the space allotted to her, she may have been added as an after-thought. Sofonisba had already painted herself at a spinet (Naples, Museo di Capodimonte). She is clearly several years younger in that portrait, which is also a smaller, less ambitious composition. Even allowing for the damage that affects the left edge of that painting with particular severity, the perspective of the table surface and instrument is not managed with complete success and the background is a flat backdrop rather than suggested space. All of these technical problems are solved in the Althorp portrait, which, as Caro would say, docu-ments her increasing maturity, artistic and personal, in one image. The inscription tells us that she painted this portrait for her father; he should have been pleased with this proof of her continued progress.

Sofonisba's decision to paint herself performing on a spinet is of some sociological interest. In the fifteenth century a very limited education had been given to most women, even those of good families. But thanks to the widespread influence of Baldassare Castiglione's *Il Cor-tegiano,* first published in 1528, a decent education was at last deemed proper for a woman of Sofonisba's social standing. Unfortunately, even though Castiglione helped to make artistic accomplishment in women admirable, his advice also contained the pernicious notion of dilettantism, of ladies dabbling in many arts without perfecting any of them, that pervaded the upper classes by the nineteenth century. Nevertheless, the success of *Il Cortegiano* meant that by the mid-six-teenth century women of good birth were expected to be not merely literate but able to read and translate classical literature, to write poetry, to dance, to play musical instruments and sing, to draw and paint, and to make witty conversation. By showing herself at the keyboard, Sofonisba declared that she was properly educated and thus qualified to be a lady-in-waiting to the queen of Spain. Painting, as Baldinucci put it, was "il suo minore ornamento" (the least of her tal-ents).[23] One of the few women artists active before 1800 who was not the daughter of an artist, Sofonisba came from a higher social class than that of most male artists, and it was her proper education that led to the discovery of her talents. We may guess that her father's failure to produce a son and heir until he was fifty-seven also helped to insure that his daughters' talents were encouraged.

17.
Frederike Klauner, "Spanische Portraits des 16. Jahrhunderts," *Jahrbuch des kunsthistorisches Sammlungen in Wien,* LVII, 1961, 148. Tufts (1974, 23 and 243, note 5) suggests that the sitter is Isabella of Valois, not her daughter. The picture was painted after Sofonisba moved to Genoa because the signature incorporates the name of her second husband, Lomellini. She could have repeated an earlier portrait of the dead queen using her own drawings but it must be admitted that Tufts' suggestion raises some problems.
18.
The text of the inscription is that made by T. Martyn in 1760, quoted by F. G. Grossman (*Between Renaissance and Baroque,* Manchester, 1965, no. 9), but with the date changed to 1561 (Martyn read 1563). All recent authorities give the earlier date. I was unable to examine the picture before the exhibition to check the read-ing of the inscription, which is poorly preserved. The emendation of *ami . . .* to read *amilcaris* is mine.
19.
Baldinucci, 215.
20.
Vasari, VII, 133. The portrait sent to Julius III might be identified with the self-portrait now in the Uffizi, which was bought in Rome in 1666 (Prinz, 176, docu-

ment 39). Her father gave the portrait now in Vienna to the Este in 1556 (Posse in Thieme-Becker, I, 524).
21.
Vasari, VI, 499.
22.
Berenson, I, 14-15. The *Portrait of an Old Woman* in Nivaagaard (H. Olsen, *Italian Paintings in Denmark,* Copenhagen, 36) might be a late self-portrait. The portrait of herself being painted by Bernardino Campi (Siena, Pinacoteca) must have been made after he left for Milan in 1549. Caro's letter of 1558 (see note 19) proves that Campi and the family remained on good terms after her apprenticeship ended.
23.
Prinz, 181, document 59.

Lucia Anguissola
Italian, ca. 1540-ca. 1565

Lucia Anguissola was the third daughter of Amilcare Anguissola and a younger sister of Sofonisba, who is supposed to have been her teacher. According to Baldinucci, "it was generally held that if death had not taken her from the world before her time, . . . [Lucia] would have become a better artist even than Sofonisba."[1] At present only two signed works by Lucia are known: a copy dated 1555 after a *Madonna and Child* by an unidentified Milanese follower of Leonardo[2] and the portrait of Pietro Maria (cat. no. 4), a doctor in Cremona, which Vasari saw when he visited the family in 1568. The copy reveals little about her except that she was a competent painter by 1555, but the portrait of Pietro Maria is an impressive picture for an artist still "adolescens," as the inscription tells us. An appealing small tondo portrait of a child in Brescia has an old inscription on the back identifying it as a portrait by Lucia of Europa, another Anguissola daughter. Attempts have been made to attribute other pictures to her, but her style is so close to Sofonisba's that the exercise is impossible while the latter's work remains unstudied.[3]

Lucia was dead by the time Vasari visited Cremona and he does not report the fact as a recent event. The date of death usually given, 1565, may well be correct, though it is not documented.[4] Elena, the second sister, trained with Sofonisba under Bernardino Campi but gave up her career in order to become a nun.[5] Minerva, the fourth sister, who was said to be a good Latin scholar, also died young before being married.[6] Europa, the fifth born, was married around 1568 to Carlo Schinchinelli, a member of another good Cremonese family, but she was dead by October 1578.[7] Vasari met Europa "ancora . . . in età puerile," and reports that she sent a portrait of her mother to Sofonisba in Madrid, where it was much admired. Baldinucci records two altarpieces by her in the church of St. Elena in Cremona, one of which was still to be seen in the home of one of her husband's descendants early in this century.[8] Finally there was Anna Maria Anguissola, "ancora piccola fanciulletta," when Vasari met her, who by October 1578 was married to Iacopo de Sommi and was still alive in 1585.[9] A *Holy Family* signed by her is in the Pinacoteca in Cremona,[10]

and she was also reputed to be a good portraitist. Their only brother, Asdrubale (1551-1623), inherited his father's various business enterprises and held local political offices, but does not seem to have shared his sisters' artistic interests. Among the works now attributed to Sofonisba are probably some made by her sisters, whose personalities will surely emerge more clearly when more extensive research is carried out on the Anguissola family.[11]

4.
Portrait of Pietro Maria (Pietro Martire Ponzona?), ca. 1560
Oil on canvas
37^{13}/$_{16}$ x 30 in. (96 x 76 cm.)
Signed on the arm of the chair: LUCIA ANGUISOLA AMILCARIS F [ilia] ADOLESCENS F [ecit]
Madrid, Museo del Prado (16)

Vasari records two portraits by Lucia, one of the Duke of Sessa, then Governor of Milan, the other of a doctor, Pietro Maria. The snake twisted round our subject's staff indicates that he is a doctor. This picture was in the Spanish royal collections by 1686; Stirling-Maxwell suggests that it was sent to Spain while Sofonisba was still in Madrid.[12] Amilcare was short of money for Europa's dowry in 1568 and may have sent this picture to Spain shortly after Vasari's visit, hoping to receive a generous gift from the king in addition to the eight hundred lire he received annually for the services of Sofonisba.[13]

Bonetti published a document that calls Bianca Ponzona, the mother of Lucia and Sofonisba, "filiola del quondam M. co [medico] Conte Pietro Martire, dottore."[14] Thus it is possible that the sitter was the artist's grandfather. This identification would explain why the work remained in the possession of the Anguissola family rather than going to the family of a sitter unrelated to them. The names Pietro Maria and Pietro Martire are close and could have been confused.

Lucia has created an impressive, sober image of a distinguished elderly man, although the slightly raised eyebrow hints at a quizzical sense of

---

1.
Baldinucci, VIII, 230.
2.
Caroli, 70 and pl. 68.
3.
Caroli attributes to her rather than Sofonisba a portrait of a woman in the Galleria Borghese, Rome, which has an old inscription glued to the back naming Sofonisba with the puzzling date MDVLI (1546? 1556?). The family likeness is obvious, but the inscription is good evidence in favor of an attribution to Sofonisba. Some less convincing suggestions are made by Charles de Tolnay, 116-19.
4.
Baldinucci, following Vasari, says only that she was dead by 1568. Hans Posse (Thieme-Becker, s.v.) and later scholars give 1565 as her death date, apparently following G. Grasselli (*Abecedario biografico dei pittori . . . Cremonesi*, Milan, 1827, 19).
5.
Vasari does not mention her, but Campi (III, 1) and Baldinucci (VIII, 230) report that she joined the convent of the Holy Virgins at San Vincenzo, Mantua, and was still alive in 1585. A document published by Bonetti (1928, 298) confirms the tradition.

6.
Vasari does not mention her either, but Campi and Baldinucci record her prowess at Latin and her early death.
7.
Vasari (VI, 500), Campi and Baldinucci (see note 5). Her father had trouble raising enough money for her dowry in 1568 and had to appeal to be allowed to give her a smaller sum (Bonetti, 1928, 297). She is referred to as dead in a document of October 1578 (Bonetti, 1928, 298).
8.
Posse in Thieme-Becker, s.v.
9.
Vasari (see note 7), Campi and Baldinucci (see note 5). She is named as the wife of Sommi in her brother's will of 1578 (Bonetti, 1928, 298) and was still alive when Campi published his history of Cremona in 1585.
10.
A. Puerari, *La Pinacoteca di Cremona*, Florence, 1951, no. 205 and fig. 178. He notes the disappointing quality of the work and wonders whether the inscription is not a later addition.

humor. The doctor, nicely placed within the picture format, wears a gray damask coat edged with brown fur. Very little color is allowed into the picture at all — a little green in the foreground on the delicately painted snake, a little gold on the books in the left background. Only the hands betray the immaturity of the artist.

The *Portrait of a Gentleman* at Burghley House, signed by Sofonisba, makes an instructive comparison with Lucia's portrait of Pietro Maria.[15] Both artists used a careful, controlled touch and small brushstrokes, leaving few visible traces of their technique on the surface. Perhaps Lucia observed the features of her sitter with greater precision, especially the eyes, and she made the hands rounder and less structured. Lucia's touch also seems a little softer, her gradation of tone a little subtler than that of her sister. There is only one marked difference in approach. Sofonisba liked to set tables and musical instruments at right angles to the picture plane, creating strong orthogonal lines that lead the eye into the picture space. Lucia instead placed the table and chair at a slight angle and set the books parallel to the picture plane, thus closing off rather than extending the pictorial space. This exhibition will give scholars their first opportunity to study authentic works by both sisters side by side and thereby to clarify the differences between them.

To anyone familiar with the portraits of North Italian artists like Lorenzo Lotto and Moretto da Brescia, Lucia's portrait conveys an impression of conservative caution. We should not forget, as the inscription reminds us, that the artist was "adolescens." Thus it is not quite fair to compare her work with mature masterpieces by contemporaries such as Moretto and Lotto. The first works of the latter are also careful and cautious, and full of the style of his most admired early model, Giovanni Bellini. Lucia's portrait of her grandfather is certainly evidence of a prodigious talent, but there is no way of knowing how she would have developed had she lived a normal life span.

4

11.
For example, a portrait of Margherita Gonzaga aged six, dated 1571, now in the collection of Captain Patrick Drury-Lowe, Locko Park, Derbyshire (exhibited Nottingham, 1968, no. 16). The style resembles generally that of Sofonisba but the inscription, apparently genuine, precludes an attribution to her as she was then either in Madrid or Palermo while the sitter was in Mantua. Either Europa or Anna Maria might be responsible.
12.
Stirling-Maxwell, I, 228.
13.
Bonetti (1928, 292 and 295) published documents concerning the dowry and the annual payment from Philip II.
14.
Ibid., 305 (document of 1578).
15.
Berenson, 1968, I, pl. 1972 (see S. Anguissola bibliography).

Lavinia Fontana

Italian, 1552-1614

Lavinia Fontana had the advantage of being born into the family of a good and moderately successful painter who lived in one of the more vital artistic centers of Italy. At the time of her birth Prospero Fontana (1512-1597), her father, was one of the leading painters in Bologna. He had trained in Genoa with Perino del Vaga and worked in Florence and Rome before settling down at home. Thus her teacher was an artist of cosmopolitan background whose style at the time she was born reflected primarily that of Giorgio Vasari. She could also study masterpieces by Raphael, Parmigianino, Niccolò dell'Abbate, and Pellegrino Tibaldi in local churches and palaces. She was not precocious. Her first recorded works were made in 1575,[1] her first surviving work being a *Dead Christ with Angels* painted a year later.[2] From the late 1570s, however, she produced a steady stream of pictures, usually signed and dated — portraits, small religious works, mythologies, and, after 1589, altarpieces for churches in Bologna, Cento, and Rome. As a patron commented, ". . . this excellent painter to say the truth in every way prevails above the condition of her sex and is a most remarkable person."[3]

Lavinia Fontana is the first woman to have had what might be called a normal successful artistic career, which remained a rare phenomenon until the late eighteenth century. She did not confine her production to the less esteemed categories of portraiture or still life but painted many subjects involving numerous figures, even male and female nudes. She worked on a large scale and executed public as well as private commissions. However, she never worked in fresco, the medium then considered the supreme test of an Italian painter's ability. It is also true that she had to wait until she was almost forty before patrons trusted her with public altarpieces (the Spanish apparently broke the ice by commissioning a *Holy Family* for the Escorial in 1589 for which Pacheco says she was paid the astronomical sum of one thousand ducats.[4] Although several of her public commissions were well received, her contemporary reputation was primarily as a portraitist.[5] Well over a hundred works are documented or recorded in early sources, but only thirty-two signed and dated or datable

works are known today. There are perhaps twenty-five more pictures that are signed or that can be securely attributed to her on stylistic grounds,[6] and a small number of her drawings are also known.[7] This nevertheless constitutes the largest surviving body of work by any woman artist active before 1700.

Fontana was sixty-two when she died in Rome on August 11, 1614.[8] She had moved there in 1603 at the invitation of Pope Clement VIII. Mancini, writing less than ten years after her death, reports that she had been depressed by the death of her artistically talented daughter at the age of fourteen.[9] We might also guess that supporting her family since her marriage in 1577 to a minor artist, G. P. Zappi, and bearing eleven children, only three of whom outlived her, had finally exhausted her.[10]

Seventeenth-century writers did not display the same enthusiasm for Lavinia Fontana's work as they did for that of her famous predecessor, Sofonisba Anguissola. Mancini said that as a portraitist she "valeva assai" (was quite good) which is faint praise indeed. Some twenty years later Giovanni Baglione described her as "quite a good and skillful Master, who was an excellent portraitist . . . and being a woman, in this kind of painting she did quite well." He conveyed some resentment about her receiving the commission to paint *The Stoning of St. Stephen Martyr,* a large altarpiece for one of the major Roman basilicas, S. Paolo fuori le Mura, probably because he wanted the commission himself. He said that better painters were passed over and that the result was not a success.[11] Malvasia always defended the products of his home town, Bologna, and his account therefore is more flattering, but it is clear that he too preferred her portraits to her public commissions.[12] More recent critics have regarded her work with carefully measured enthusiasm. Galli, who published much valuable documentation in his monograph, concluded rather lamely that "without being great, the work of Lavinia Fontana is nevertheless always worthy of consideration." Another comment of his is colored by prejudice: "the fineness of her sensibility manifests

1.
Galli, 64 and 73. Her *Holy Family* in Dresden is signed ". . . vinia Prosperi Fontanae faciebat Ao MD . . ." and was therefore made before her marriage in 1577, after which she dropped her father's name and added "de Zappis" to her signature.

2.
Fern Rusk Shapley, *Paintings from the Samuel H. Kress Collection, Italian Schools, XVI-XVIII Centuries,* London, 1973, no. 1402 and fig. 30. She cites a version, also signed and dated 1576, in the Rollins College Museum of Art, Winter Park, Florida.

3.
Galli, 117, document 8.

4.
Quoted by Tufts, *Art News,* 1974, 64.

5.
When her *Vision of St. Hyacinth* was unveiled in Rome, one writer reported that "il . . . quadro principale, ch'è stupendissimo, è stato fatto per mano d'una gentildonna Bolognese" (the altarpiece, which is stupendous, was made by the hand of a Bolognese lady) (E. Rossi in *Roma,* XII, 1934, 323ff.).

6.
Galli (57ff.) lists 135 works recorded in older sources and modern catalogs. A few of these are known to be errors. Some of the works known to Galli are no longer traceable while others have emerged since his book was published (see note 2). The confused state of knowledge should appeal to a dissertation subject hunter.

7.
J. Bean and F. Stampfle, *Drawings from New York Collections I: The Italian Renaissance,* The Metropolitan Museum of Art, New York, 1965, no. 149 (a group of portrait studies in the Morgan Library, New York); Galli, 68 (a group of studies in the Uffizi).

8.
Galli, 35.

9.
Mancini must be referring to Laodamia, born October 29, 1588, who died in Rome on May 25, 1605, aged sixteen (Galli, 20 and 32-33).

10.
Galli published several documents concerning her large family. Three sons outlived her. Her husband died in Imola in 1615. Malvasia (I, 177), whose information came, he says, from the artist's godson, Alessandro Tiarini, tells us that Zappi was married to her with the understanding that she would continue to paint

itself above all in the exaltation of love and maternity."[13] Freedberg dismissed her as without interest.[14]

Fontana's achievement is not easy to assess. Many of her works are in poor condition and are hard to see, skyed in dimly lit museum rooms or virtually invisible in gloomy churches. Some of her best pictures are concealed in private collections.[15] Her major handicap, however, is being one of the last representatives of a conservative *maniera* style that was to be made obsolete by two artists whose life spans are encompassed within her own, Caravaggio and Annibale Carracci. Thus her work has an old-fashioned air that is unfortunately not redeemed by either a novel personal interpretation of *maniera* or by a consistently high level of quality that would give her work a value independent of contemporary artistic movements. The collaboration of her husband may explain to some extent the uneven quality of her signed productions but she probably also painted too much too fast in order to satisfy the demands of patrons.[16] Her drawing can be superficial in its understanding of form, her portrait compositions often repetitive. Her style however is her own, far less mannered than that of her father with passages of direct realism that suggest she appreciated Annibale even if she did not imitate his more vigorously naturalistic approach.

One of her masterpieces is her *Holy Family with the Sleeping Christ Child* in the Escorial, a complex tribute to the Roman High Renaissance and specifically to Sebastiano del Piombo and Raphael. Her starting point was Sebastiano's picture of the same subject, then nearby in Parma, but she added motifs from Raphael's *Madonna of the Diadem* and *Madonna of the Veil*. Her revival of the subject almost certainly inspired Annibale's slightly later and far more intimate interpretation.[17] Her *Birth of the Virgin* in S. Trinità, Bologna, is an ambitious night rendering full of lively human detail.[18] Her *Vision of St. Hyacinth* of 1599-1600 in S. Sabina, the work that introduced her to the highly critical audience of Roman art patrons, is a beautiful, dignified image in a timeless, ideal style that Baglione called "almost her best work." In the finest of her female portraits her sitters pose serenely and to splendid effect in their richly embroidered costumes and fancy jewelry. Her male patrons are posed with more imagination, as was traditional, in ways that ably suggest their character and flatter their rank.

Fontana is an important figure in any history of the emergence of women artists because she commanded a considerable range of subject matter and was the first to carry out a substantial number of public commissions. Her achievement has nevertheless been underrated. Because she was uneven and because she was overtaken by a major stylistic revolution, she will inevitably be relegated to a backwater of art history; yet at her best she can be very good, as the visitor to this exhibition can judge. It is doubtful, moreover, whether Artemisia Gentileschi's achievements would have been possible a few years later without the pioneering example of Lavinia Fontana.

5.
Portrait of Senator Orsini, 1577(?)
Oil on canvas
46³/₄ x 43⁵/₁₆ in. (119 x 110 cm.)
Inscribed on the chair back: LAVINIA FONTANA DE ZAPPIS FACIEBAT MDLXXV
Bordeaux, Musée des Beaux-Arts (5689)

Lavinia Fontana's contemporary reputation was based primarily on her abilities as a portrait painter. Bologna had no resident portrait specialist in the sixteenth century until Bartolommeo Passerotti returned to Bologna from Rome around 1565, and he was chiefly active as a painter of altarpieces and genre pictures. Before that Parmigianino, who was in Bologna from 1527 to 1531, and Niccolò dell'Abbate, who lived there briefly in the late 1540s, both occasionally painted splendid portraits. There was, however, no local artist with the kind of reputation for this genre that Moretto and Moroni enjoyed in Bergamo and Brescia respectively, or that Pontormo, Salviati, and Bronzino had in Florence. Thus once Fontana's talents became known, her future career was assured. The women of Bologna were said by Malvasia to be especially enthusiastic about her, competing to entertain her and to commission works from her.[19] As a result she painted more portraits of women than most Italian Renaissance artists did, although she also painted many distinguished men, including Pope Gregory XIII and the Persian ambassador to Rome.[20]

The signature and date on the portrait said to represent Senator Orsini are not perfectly preserved. The date has been read as 1575 by the Musée des Beaux-Arts, but since the remains of "de Zappis" seem to follow her name, a date of 1577 or later is probable.[21] It is one of her earliest surviving works. Her subject sits in a room with a view beyond into a series of grand rooms that recall the settings of Florentine cinquecento portraits such as Bronzino's *Ugolino Martelli* (ca. 1535, Berlin, Dahlem Museum) and his two portraits of Lucrezia and Bartolommeo Panciatichi (1530s, Florence, Uffizi). It was basically to the more formal traditions of Florentine portraiture rather than to the more naturalistic presentations favored in northern Italy that Fontana turned for inspiration. She makes a clearer distinction than Bronzino does between the space in which the sitter is placed and the background vista. Her portrait of Senator Orsini comes closest however to the scheme of Giulio Romano's *Isabella d'Este* (Royal Collection, Hampton Court), which was then in Mantua.[22] Her aloof sitters do not usually resemble those of Passerotti or Moroni, though single works by these artists also offer some striking parallels.[23] Perhaps they are fortuitous; perhaps the pose of the senator is better explained as an adaptation of a famous image such as Raphael's *Julius II* (London, National Gallery) or his equally well-known portrait of *Leo X with His Nephews* (Florence, Uffizi).

The identification of the sitter as Senator Orsini is traditional but, as far as I know, undocumented. The Orsini were a Roman, not a Bolognese family, and since the portrait belongs to the artist's

with his assistance. The documents published by Galli (109-10) do not describe such a formal arrangement, but the parents of both parties were well aware of the economic advantages of Fontana's continuing to paint, and since Zappi had no independent career to speak of, we can assume that he did subordinate his career to hers.
11.
Baglione, 144. We cannot test his judgment because the altarpiece was destroyed in the great fire of 1823 that gutted the basilica. It is recorded in an engraving of 1611 by Callot (J. Lieure, *Jacques Callot,* Paris, 1924-26, I, no. 33).
12.
Malvasia, 177ff. He includes the life by Baglione.
13.
Galli, 41.
14.
Sydney Freedberg, *Painting in Italy, 1500-1600,* Harmondsworth, Middlesex, and Baltimore, 1971, 394.
15.
Galli, figs. 2, 6, and 13. The last went from Palazzo Isolani in Minerbio to a Swiss collection, from which it was bought by a Dr. F. Kung in New York in 1931. It is not traceable today. It appears to be her finest female portrait.

16.
Galli, 8.
17.
These sources are discussed by Donald Posner in connection with Annibale's picture (*Annibale Carraci: A Study in the Reform of Italian Painting around 1590,* 2 vols., London, 1971, I, 109-10, and II, no. 110). He illustrates Sebastiano's picture (fig. 93) but overlooks Fontana's which she repeated in several versions (e.g. Rome, Galleria Borghese, dated 1591).
18.
Galli, fig. 8.
19.
Malvasia, I, 177.
20.
Both works, mentioned by Malvasia and Mancini respectively, are lost. Roughly three male portraits survive from sixteenth-century Italy for every female portrait. Women also appear less frequently as donors in Italian altarpieces than in those of Germany and Flanders.
21.
I am grateful to Gilberte Martin-Mery for checking the form of the signature for me. For the change of form after Fontana's marriage, see note 1 of her biography.

5

Bolognese period, the identification is not plausible. It is retained here as a convenience until further research either confirms the tradition or provides a better answer.

6.
Portrait of a Noblewoman, ca. 1580
Oil on canvas
45 x 35½ in. (114.3 x 90.17 cm.)
New York, Rojtman Foundation, Inc.

Although there is now no trace of the customary signature, there can be no doubt that this handsome portrait is correctly attributed to Lavinia Fontana.[24] The meticulous attention to the sitter's embroidered costume and jewels, the drawing of the features and hands, and the type of small lap dog are all characteristic. Fontana's *Portrait of a Woman* (Baltimore, Walters Art Gallery) is especially close in certain details such as the long, tapering fingers, the pattern on the sleeves, and the dog. Other signed portraits of women by Fontana offer similar parallels.[25] The young, clearly wealthy young woman in the work exhibited has traditionally been identified as the Duchess of Mantua, but she does not resemble Duchess Leonora de'Medici as portrayed by Fontana in the painting now in Dublin.[26] Further research into her jewels and clothes might locate some heraldic devices that would allow a more precise identification to be made.

The plain background of this portrait is found in Fontana's other female portraits, while her portraits of male sitters generally include a setting that complements the patron's status and profession. The poses and gestures of her male subjects also tend to be livelier than those of her female sitters and they often look directly at the viewer, in contrast to the modestly averted gaze typical of all female portraits at this time. The portrait makes a splendid impression because of the sitter's beautiful clothes and accessories; her wealth and status, not her personality, are its subject. The conventional pose and mechanical gestures betray little of her character, though comparison with other female portraits by Fontana allows one to guess that her subject on this occasion was a shy young woman who was not yet entirely at ease with her high social status.

7.
Noli Me Tangere, 1581
Oil on canvas
32 x 25½ in. (81 x 65 cm.)
Signed lower right: LAVINIA FONTANA DE / ZAPPIS FACIEBAT / MDLXXXI
Florence, Galleria degli Uffizi (1890-383)
(See color plate, p. 69)

The *Noli Me Tangere* is one of Fontana's most beautiful religious paintings. The soft evening light, the evocative landscape setting with the magical distant vista behind Christ, and the quiet, Parmese color scheme all reveal a sensitive artistic vision not always found in her larger works. The Magdalene wears a golden yellow cloak over a muted pink dress with pink sleeves; her sandals are blue. Christ's robes are a faded pink. To the left in the distance grieving figures

22.
F. Hartt, *Giulio Romano,* New Haven, 1958, pl. 124.
23.
For the Passerotti, see F. Zeri, *La Galleria Spada in Roma,* Florence, 1954, 103-4. no. 88 *(Portrait of an Astrologer);* for the Moroni, see Venturi, 1929, IX, 4, 230.
24.
The attribution has been supported by Antonio Morassi in a document belonging to the owners. A signature may once have existed on the front edge of the table below the dog, an area that is slightly worn.
25.
The Baltimore portrait is illustrated by Tufts *(Hidden Heritage,* 1974, fig. 10). For other comparable works, see Tufts (ibid., fig. 9, *The Gozzadini Family,* 1584, Bologna, Pinacoteca Nazionale) and Sparrow, 40 *(Self-Portrait,* Florence, Palazzo Pitti, signed and dated 157?). The latter work, despite the signature visible in old photographs, has recently been catalogued as School of Moroni (N. Cipriani, *La Galleria Palatina nel Palazzo Pitti a Firenze,* Florence, 1966, 176, no. 1841).
26.
Tufts, *Hidden Heritage,* 1974, fig. 11.

approach the empty tomb where an angel waits to greet them. The golden haze hints at Christ's coming resurrection.

In spirit but not in any precise details Lavinia was here inspired by Correggio, whose *Noli Me Tangere* (ca. 1532, Madrid, Prado) was then in Bologna in the collection of the Ercolani family, one of whom was her godparent.[27] Her Magdalene does not sink to the ground with the sinuous ecstasy of Correggio's figure but kneels firmly, sure of her faith, as she receives Christ's blessing and listens to his instructions. The moment shown must follow the gesture forbidding the Magdalene to come closer that gives the subject its name (John 20:17). Fontana's Christ wears the clothes of an imaginary biblical gardener but Correggio's Christ has laid aside his tools and wears only a blue toga. Fontana's color scheme, though Correggesque, does not follow that of the Prado picture. The subdued lighting is also typical of him. Her landscape is more secluded than that of his *Noli Me Tangere,* but such openings fringed with foliage can be found in other paintings of his.

Fontana had studied other artists than Correggio. The distant view with the winding river, bridge, fortifications, and castles recalls the vistas of Niccolò dell'Abbate. Her sturdy Christ is a Michelangelesque figure but seen through the eyes of Sebastiano del Piombo, whose *Raising of Lazarus* provided her with a schemata for both figures.[28] To name these possible sources is not to accuse Fontana of plagiarism. Knowledge of earlier interpretations of similar themes and emotions, their study, absorption, and reinterpretation, all this was considered essential for an ambitious artist in the sixteenth century. Further, to render homage to the achievements of earlier masters was also to invite comparison with them. The final result in this case resembles no other interpretation of this theme except in the basic iconographical elements — the kneeling Magdalene and the standing Christ. The figures visiting the tomb are seldom included and the landscape is also rarely given such importance.[29]

Fontana reveals here her appreciation of the poetry of Correggio's art, something that no other Bolognese artist was to do until Annibale visited Parma in 1585. She appreciated too the essential simplicity of his composition in contrast to the more complicated designs then fashionable in Bologna. Two years after she finished her *Noli Me Tangere,* Annibale unveiled his first altarpiece in Bologna. His more strongly painted and brilliantly observed realizations of religious drama would finally destroy Bolognese *maniera,* but it is clear too that Fontana was moving, much more quietly, in a similar direction.

6

27.
Vasari records Correggio's picture in the Palazzo Ercolani. At the end of the century, Cardinal Pietro Aldobrandini took it to Rome; it went from his collection to that of the Ludovisi and thence to Spain (P. Bianconi, *Tutta la pittura del Correggio,* Milan, 1953, 37). For the baptismal document, see Galli, 107.
28.
Sebastiano's picture, now in London (National Gallery), was then in Narbonne Cathedral but it was among his most famous works, having been painted in competition with Raphael's *Transfiguration.* Its design was certainly known to Italian artists after 1520, when it was sent to France (C. Gould, *National Gallery Catalogues, The Sixteenth-Century Italian Schools,* London, 1975, 242ff.).
29.
Fontana painted one small picture that is almost pure landscape, her *St. Francis Receiving the Stigmata* of 1579 (Bologna, Villa Reverdin).

FIDES GALLICIA VIRGO PVDICISS·ÆTAT·SVÆ ANN·XVIII OPVS HOC, ·PAVLI MORIGII SIMVLACRVM, ANN·72 GRATI ANIMI ERGO EFFINXIT·ANNO 1596

8

Fede Galizia
Italian, 1578-1630

Fede Galizia was presumably taught by her father, Nunzio Galizia, a miniaturist from Trento in North Italy who was working in Milan when she was born.[1] Her talents were noted in print when she was only twelve years old.[2] By her late teens she had established an international reputation as a portraitist (see cat. no. 8). In 1596 she painted a *Judith and Her Handmaid* now in Sarasota, Florida; an autograph version in Rome was made five years later.[3] A still-life painting made in 1602 proves that she was active in this new genre also (cat. no. 9). She painted the high altarpiece of Santa Maria Maddalena, Milan, in 1616 and several other public commissions for Milanese churches, some of which survive. She made her will on June 21, 1630, and probably died shortly thereafter in the plague then affecting much of Italy.

Stefano Bottari, in a recent useful study of Fede Galizia, has compiled a catalog of works by or attributable to her.[4] The majority of these are still-life paintings, even though her reputation was made as a portraitist who also painted religious compositions. Her few surviving works that are not still lives reveal little impact of the energetic late Mannerist style then practiced in Milan by G.B. Crespi (Il Cerano) and G. C. Procaccini. Instead her work has a restrained simplicity found in a few other late sixteenth-century Italian painters' work and often associated with the Counter Reformation. It is for her still lives, however, that she will be remembered. Among the earliest true still lives made in Italy, the best of them have a powerful impact that belies the simplicity of their design. They have reminded critics of Zurbarán's rare, slightly later still lives, works that are almost primitive in composition by the standards of his time but that are nevertheless acknowledged to be among the most striking produced in the seventeenth century. Galizia's austerely understated designs are only now receiving the appreciation they deserve.

1.
Her date of birth derives from the inscription on her portrait of Paolo Morigia (cat. no. 8) which says that she was eighteen in 1596. Her father was active by 1573 and died after 1621. Very little work by him is known. Thieme-Becker gives a death date "in den ersten Jahren des 17. Jahrh." but he was paid for work in Turin in 1621 (A. Baudi de Vesme, *Schede Vesme; L'arte in Piemonte dal XVI al XVIII secolo,* Turin, 1963-68, II, 490).
2.
G. P. Lomazzo, *Idea del tempio della pittura,* Milan, 1590, 163, reports that she is "dandosi all'imitation de i più eccellenti dell'arte nostra."
3.
Ringling Museums, Sarasota, no. 684 (exhibited in the Worcester Museum of Art, *Woman as Heroine,* 1972, no. 11). Bottari (see note 4 below) did not know this picture, which may be identifiable with the work of the same subject by Galizia recorded in the royal palace, Turin, around 1635 (Bottari, 1965, 28, note 14). For the version in Rome see P. della Pergola, *Galleria Borghese,* Rome, 1952, II, 27-28, no. 30.

8.

Portrait of Paolo Morigia (1525-1604), 1596
Oil on canvas
34¾ x 31 in. (88 x 79 cm.)
Signed along the upper edge: FIDES GALLICIA VIRGO PUDICISS. AETAT.
SUE. ANN. XVIII OPUS HOC, / [G.] PAULI MORIGII SIMULACRUM, ANN. 72
GRATI ANIMI ERGO EFFINXIT. / ANNO 1596
Milan, Pinacoteca Ambrosiana (110)

Paolo Morigia, a Jesuit scholar and historian, was one of Fede Galizia's earliest patrons and supporters.[5] In *La Nobiltà di Milano,* his collection of short biographies of living and dead Milanese notables published in 1595, he declares that she had shown "clear and evident signs of becoming a truly noble painter" in a number of drawings and especially in several portraits, including one of himself. He praises his portrait as being "of such excellence, and such a good likeness, that one could not desire anything more."[6] That portrait is lost, but the one in the exhibition, made a year later, may reflect the design of its missing predecessor.[7] It shows Morigia seated at his desk, looking up after finishing a short poem about the picture and its creator.[8] To the left is a copy of *La Nobiltà di Milano,* with some other books and an inkwell. The crudely lettered inscription above was probably copied off the frame onto the picture at a later date.[9]

Morigia faces us across his desk, only too aware of the fact that his portrait is being painted. He is being most cooperative, holding still for the artist, tolerating this momentary boredom with good humor for the sake of the immortality he hopes the image will provide. The result is effective precisely because Galizia seems to have recorded Morigia just as he presented himself to her, unfiltered by either idealizing conventions or the artist's own personality. She records his wrinkles, his slight squint, and his firmly set jaw and drawn mouth, which suggest a hint of humor nonetheless. The frontal presentation is relieved by the contrapposto of head and body and by the slight asymmetry of his position right of center. The color scheme is almost monochromatic.

There was a strong tradition of naturalistic portraiture in North Italy in the sixteenth century, not just in Venice but also in provincial towns nearer Milan like Bergamo and Brescia, where Moretto da Brescia and G. B. Moroni were active. It is even possible that Nunzio Galizia was inspired to train his daughter to paint by the example of Sofonisba Anguissola, who came from Cremona, some fifty miles southeast of Milan, and was active primarily as a portraitist. The Galizia family came from Trento, just north of Lake Garda, and they must have passed through Brescia and Bergamo on their visits home from Milan. Thus Fede Galizia may have had the example of a female portraitist to inspire her as well as the knowledge of some fine examples of cinquecento portraiture. Indeed the sophistication of her portrait of Morigia proves that she was aware of the achievements of Morone and his contemporaries.

The direct appeal to the spectator, the self-conscious awareness of the sitter, the careful realism, even the still life in the foreground, recall another North Italian cinquecento master even more forcibly than Morone, namely Lorenzo Lotto. He had worked in Bergamo intermittently between 1513 and 1526 on various important public commissions and must have left examples of his striking portraits in local collections. Perhaps she knew his *Giovanni Agostino della Torre* (1515, London, National Gallery), which came originally from a collection in Bergamo.[10] Lotto shows della Torre seated in his study with books on the left, facing us directly, as Morigia does, though not from behind a table. Galizia's composition is closer still to the work of an even more illustrious predecessor, Raphael. His *Fedra Inghirami* (1512-14, Boston, Isabella Stewart Gardner) shows that bishop-scholar seated behind a desk and turned slightly to the left, his hands resting on his manuscript and a book in a pose that is almost a mirror image of Morigia's. It is not impossible that Galizia visited Florence and knew the version of this work then in the Medici collections, though the resemblance may be fortuitous.[11] Certainly it was the vigorously realistic tradition of local cinquecento portraiture that made the greatest impression on her. The high quality of this early work makes it all the more regrettable that so few other portraits by her are now known.[12]

9.

Basket of Peaches
Oil on panel
11 x 16½ in. (28 x 42 cm.)
New York, Newhouse Galleries, Inc.

Only one certain still-life painting by Fede Galizia is known, but not currently located, a small panel signed and dated 1602 published by Curt Benedict in 1938 when it was in the Anholt Collection in Amsterdam.[13] It shows a pear and a half pear on the left, a full-blown rose on the right, and a metal fruit stand filled with apricots in the center. A closely related composition with an old attribution to Galizia is in the Campagnano Collection in Florence.[14] Round these two works Stefano Bottari has grouped almost twenty more paintings that are either by her or close to her in style.[15] Among these is the splendid *Basket of Peaches* in this exhibition.

Paintings of inanimate objects with no human figures present hardly existed in Italy before the seventeenth century, although there were artists like Giovanni da Udine (1487-1564) who were famous for painting fruits, vegetables, and flowers in and around the figure compositions of other artists.[16] Galizia's missing picture of 1602 is in fact the first dated still life by an Italian artist, although Caravaggio's *Basket of Fruit* (Milan, Ambrosiana), which was in the collection of Cardinal Federico Borromeo in Milan by 1607, was certainly painted before 1600.[17] Thus Galizia was, like Clara Peeters in Antwerp and Louise Moillon in Paris, one of the earliest specialists in this new genre. Galizia was probably inspired to try her hand at still life by the presence in Milan of Jan Brueghel, who was working for Cardinal Federico by 1595. Jan, however, rarely painted still lives of anything

4.
"Fede Galizia," *Arte antica e moderna,* no. 24, 1963, 309-60, with two color plates. A more fully illustrated and slightly expanded version of that article has been printed as a small monograph in the series Collana Artisti Trentini (Bottari, 1965).
5.
Morigia, who gets a very brief mention in the *Enciclopedia Cattolica,* wrote at least seventeen books, according to the printed catalog of the British Museum, and was Superior General of his order several times.
6.
Morigia, *La Nobiltà di Milano,* 1595 ed., 282; 1619 ed., 467.
7.
In addition to the two signed versions of the *Judith* mentioned in the biography, there are versions or copies of several of her still lives, suggesting that she repeated successful designs for other clients.
8.
Though perfectly legible, the text has not been published. It reads: "O viatore, ch'miri.' se di saper sei vago, / Chi diè col suo pennel voce a l'imago / Che qui di me si vede, fu già Galizia Fede, / Che per tenermi dopo morte in vita / Qui spirante, e qui vivo, a te m'addita." A literal translation follows: O admiring traveler, if you wish to know whose brush gave voice to this image of me which you see here, it was Fede Galizia, who to keep me alive after death, breathing here and here alive, shows me to you. Bottari (1965, 25-26) publishes two other poems Morigia dedicated to Galizia in 1605 and 1609.
9.
Bottari (1965, 12) gives the variant inscription recorded by Fogolari in 1898. That text gives the letter *G* before the word *Pauli,* implied in our picture by the sign for an abbreviation preceding the word *Pauli* and not needed after *hoc.* Thus our portrait may have been trimmed slightly on the left. Fogolari gives the sitter's age as seventy-four but seventy-two agrees with the known birth date.
10.
C. Gould, *National Gallery Catalogues, The Sixteenth-Century Italian Schools,* London, 1975, 134. Sofonisba Anguissola's *Portrait of a Dominican Astronomer* (Berenson, 1968, I, 14 and pl. 1971, see S. Anguissola bibliography) would certainly have interested Fede, to name yet another possible source.
11.
In 1596 the Boston picture was in Volterra with Inghirami's heirs and thus inaccessible. The portrait is one of the first Italian Renaissance depictions of a scholar at work and as such must be counted an indirect, if not a direct, source.

but flowers.[18] The high viewpoint, planar arrangement, and additive, symmetrical compositions seen in Galizia's first still lives show that she must have been aware of other early efforts, perhaps of northerners like Georg Flegel, perhaps early Spanish *bodegones,* for Milan was then under Spanish political control. At all events, the *Basket of Peaches* exhibited here is a more sophisticated work than Galizia's Campagnano picture, and was almost certainly painted after she had seen Caravaggio's basket set close to the picture surface and filled with grapes, apples, figs, and pears with their leaves still attached.

9

All Galizia's other still lives except that of 1602 show the front edge of the surface on which the fruit has been placed and allow more space around the objects shown as well. In our work leaves and flowers are cut by the edge on all sides. Thus the *Basket of Peaches* (like the 1602 panel) appears to have been cut down slightly. The reduction of the format serves to emphasize the plump, rounded forms of the peaches, which are beautifully realized, and to emphasize the intimacy of the picture. It is so close in conception to her *Still Life with Peaches and Apples* (Heusy, Belgium, E. Zurstrassen Collection)[19] that they may have been conceived as a pair. In both works the color scheme is limited but carefully judged. In the latter the dark green of the glass fruit dish and the pale green of the apples placed beside it are played off against the pale gold flashed with pink of the peaches in the center. In the *Basket of Peaches* the golden tones of the fruit are complemented by the light brown basket and warm brown ground and contrasted only by the dark green leaves emerging from the pile of peaches. In both works a scattering of jasmine blossoms completes the scale of tonal values, inviting us to remember their pungent perfume along with the taste of ripe peaches and the smell of roses and pinks.

The restrained simplicity of Galizia's still lives, which show an increasingly sophisticated play of rounded fruit forms and their elliptical containers against the surrounding space, was not taken up by her contemporaries. Still life in seicento Italy, as if to compensate for its theoretical inferiority, tended to be extremely elaborate, closer to the lavish banquets of Flemish artists like Frans Snyders than to the formal economy of Spanish masters like Juan Sanchez Cotán and Francisco de Zurbarán. Indeed with the exception of Evaristo Baschenis (1617?-1677), who came from Bergamo, no Italian still-life painter made a virtue of simplicity and developed compositions based on a few curved solids. Baschenis' superb orchestrations of the forms of musical instruments, like Galizia's much simpler studies of fruit, were also forgotten until this century, when their formal beauty has at last been recognized.

12.
Bottari (1965) illustrates two others, the *Portrait of Ludovico Settala* in the collection of Mina Gregori, Florence (pl. 4), and another said to be of the same sitter in the Ambrosiana (pl. 5). The latter is in bad condition. A third portrait datable 1622 is said to exist in the collections of the Ospedale Maggiore, Milan (Bottari, 1965, 13, no. 5).
13.
Curt Benedict, "Osias Beert," *L'amour de l'art,* October 1938, 305, fig. 14; see also Bottari, 1965, fig. 6.
14.
Bottari, 1965, fig. 7 and color frontispiece.
15.
A Caravaggesque still life in the Wadsworth Atheneum, Hartford (no. 1942. 353), has been attributed to Galizia but in both composition and technique differs considerably from the group associated with her name by Bottari (S.E. Ostrow, *Baroque Painting — Italy and Her Influence,* New Haven, 1968, no. 6).

16.
A much disputed work by or after Giovanni da Udine is a *Still Life with a Citron Plant* inscribed "G. D. Udine in Casa Spilimberga, 1538" (exhibited in Naples, 1964, no. 3). It may have been part of a wall decoration, although some scholars think it is a later pastiche.
17.
W. Friedlaender, *Caravaggio Studies,* Princeton, 1955, 142-44. The light background paint was certainly applied after the fruit was painted, a fact creating much debate as to whether Caravaggio conceived the work as an independent still life or adapted it at the request of his patron, Cardinal del Monte, who gave it to Cardinal Federico, possibly as early as 1596.
18.
E. Greindl, *Les peintres flamandes de nature morte au XVIIe siècle,* Brussels, 1956, 153, lists only one signed still life in which flowers are not the primary subject. The *Basket of Fruit* attributed to Jan by Bottari (1965, fig. 15) is by no means certainly his work.
19.
Sterling, color frontispiece; Bottari, 1965, pl. 74. Another still life by Galizia very similar to these two was with Leonard Koetser in 1969 (*Apollo,* April 1969, 305-6). It depicts artichokes and asparagus.

Artemisia Gentileschi
Italian, 1593-1652/53

While the life and career of Artemisia Gentileschi were mostly a series of exceptions to the rules about women and women artists, in one respect she was typical — she was the daughter of a painter.[1] Although her father, Orazio Gentileschi (1563-1639), was ten years older than Caravaggio, it is as his follower that he is best known.[2] He adopted the solid realism of Caravaggio's figures, the shallow pictorial space of his compositions, and the natural psychology of his narrative. However, Orazio avoided the extreme tenebroso effects of Caravaggio's mature work, worked in fresco as well as oil, used more extensive interior and exterior settings, and displayed more interest in subtle pastel colors and textural effects. He painted some of the most beautiful works of all Caravaggio's numerous, gifted followers.

Artemisia had the advantage, therefore, of a teacher of real stature. He in turn wanted to ensure that she was properly trained and in 1611 hired Agostino Tassi (ca. 1580-1644), who was then a co-worker on several important commissions, to teach her perspective. Tassi was a violent and disreputable character who had been convicted of arranging the murder of his wife.[3] He raped Artemisia and then tried to soothe her with promises of marriage, never fulfilled. Her father finally took Tassi to court, suing him for the "sverginamento" of his daughter, as well as for the theft of several pictures. The trial, which began in May 1612, lasted five months. Artemisia was tortured with the thumb screw, apparently a contemporary form of lie detector. A month after the trial ended in October, Artemisia was married to a Florentine, Pietro Antonio di Vincenzo Stiattesi; they probably moved to Florence shortly afterwards.[4] Tassi spent eight months in prison but was finally acquitted. The trial must have been a painful emotional experience for her; she has had a reputation as a sexually licentious woman ever since.

By 1615 Artemisia was well known as an artist in Florence. She joined the Accademia del Disegno in 1616 and was one of several artists employed to decorate the Casa Buonarroti in 1617. Several important pictures can be dated to her Florentine period, which ended in 1620. Most of the next decade was spent in Rome, although she may have visited Genoa in 1621 with her father and was in Venice in 1627.[5] Few of her works can be securely placed in this decade, but among them is the marvelous *Judith and Maidservant* in Detroit (cat. no. 13). By August 1630 she had settled in Naples. Despite many hopeful letters to prospective patrons in Rome, Florence, and Modena, explaining that "I have no wish to stay here longer because of the tumults of war as well as the uncomfortable life and high prices," she was to remain there until her death. She left only once, to our knowledge, to go to London to help her aging father finish the decoration of the Queen's House in Greenwich, but after clearing up his affairs on his death in February 1639 she returned to Naples in 1640 or 1641. Her final decade is not well documented, except the years 1648 to 1651 when she corresponded with Antonio Ruffo of Calabria, for whom she painted several pictures. A *Bathsheba* dated 1652 was recorded in the early nineteenth century. She was dead by 1653.

Artemisia Gentileschi is the first woman in the history of western art to make a significant and undeniably important contribution to the art of her time.[6] Her role in the Caravaggesque movement, especially as a transmitter of his ideas to Florence, Genoa, and Naples, although first proposed by Roberto Longhi in 1916, has only recently received widespread recognition, largely thanks to the excellent article by R. Ward Bissell.[7] From the beginning she concentrated on full-scale figure compositions, often of dramatic subjects, and while her contemporaries frequently praised her skills as a portraitist, few examples have come down to us and few are recorded in the early sources. Instead she seems to have preferred biblical and mythological subjects with heroines — Judith, Susanna, Lucretia, Bathsheba, Cleopatra, Esther, Diana — or at least subjects in which women had major roles, such as Joseph and the wife of Potiphar. We might guess that she believed the female nude to be one of her strong suits simply from the number of surviving works employing them. Some of her letters to Ruffo refer to this aspect of her work and the expenses

---

1.
With the exceptions noted, this biography depends on Bissell's article of 1968, to which the reader is referred for full references.

2.
A monograph on Orazio by R. Ward Bissell is nearing completion. A good brief introduction to Orazio can be found in Spear's text in Cleveland Museum of Art, 1971, 100ff.

3.
More information on Tassi is provided by Rudolf and Margot Wittkower, *Born under Saturn*, New York, 1963, 162ff.

4.
Bissell, 154. Her husband is recorded living with her in Florence. They had at least one daughter born around 1618. In 1619 she wrote to the Grand Duke Cosimo II to complain of unfair financial treatment by her husband (C. del Bravo, "Su Cristofano Allori," *Paragone*, 1967, no. 205, 82, n. 11). By 1624 Artemisia was living in Rome with her daughter Palmira, who was then six, and a servant. Letters of 1635 mention her brother Francesco as someone who looks after her affairs and escorts her pictures to clients in Rome and Modena. In 1637, in the postscript of a letter to Cassiano dal Pozzo, she asks for news of her husband. In brief, the marriage did not last and she seems to have lived most of her life in a state of independence rare for a woman at the time.

10

entailed in finding good models. Artemisia must have consciously decided to take advantage of her sex, which made it easier for her than for a male artist to study the female body (and impossible for her to draw the male nude). We can appreciate the vigorous realism of her women and the way her poses stress the psychological drama rather than physical charm. She was enough of a business woman to exploit the taste for pictures featuring the female nude, but she was also flaunting her skill at a branch of painting always assumed to be beyond the capacities of "una donna."

Most of Artemisia's finest pictures were painted before 1630. Despite her firm protestations to Ruffo that she never used the same design twice, she painted repetitions of two of her finest works, the *Judith Killing Holofernes* (Florence, Uffizi) and the *Judith and Maidservant* (cat. no. 13), that are weak shadows of the originals, and a great many pictures of Bathsheba that vary the design only slightly.[8] She received public commissions for the first time in Naples, but traditional subjects like the Annunciation, the Adoration of the Magi, and the Birth of the Baptist did not stir her imagination as Judith and Susanna had. Part of her problem was a shift in taste away from the dark and dramatic realism of Caravaggio to the lighter-toned, ideal style practiced by artists like Guido Reni and Domenichino, both of whom had worked in Naples. Artemisia had to tame her instinctive gifts as a realist, and the results are often literally uninspired.

About twenty letters written to various patrons by Artemisia have been published. In many of them we can sense the strong personality that her paintings also reflect. Artemisia was not a feminist by current standards but her letters reveal her awareness of the problems that professional women face and her determination to be treated fairly. The group of letters sent to Don Antonio Ruffo are especially interesting in this respect.[9] On January 30, 1649, she tells him that when she says her pictures cost one hundred scudi per figure, she means it. She has been paid that sum in Rome, Florence, Venice, and Naples, and Ruffo down in Messina will have to pay it too. She softens the blow with the following: "I have the greatest sympathy for your lordship, because the name of a woman makes one doubtful until one has seen the work." In March she again puts herself down a little after having asserted herself. "As long as I live, I will have control over my being," she declares, but she closes with, "I will not bore you any longer with this female chatter. . . ." On August 7, announcing that she has finished a *Venus and Adonis* for him (the work is lost), she says, "This will show your Lordship what a woman can do." Three months later, she is upset because he has actually felt it necessary to state that he wants a different design of a subject she has previously painted for him. "Thanks to the grace of God and of the most glorious Virgin," she responded in November, "one woman at least has been given that gift, namely to vary the subjects of my paintings, and no one has ever found the same design repeated, not even one hand." Defending her prices once more, she says that pictures with many female nudes are expensive to do and produce "un gran rompimento di capo" (a big headache). And her final remark in this letter, which is

---

5.
Toesca, 89-92.
6.
Perhaps the statement should be qualified as applying only to the post-medieval period, given the contribution of women to the art of embroidery in the Middle Ages.
7.
Tufts (1974, 59) exaggerates when she states that her influence was second only to Caravaggio. The first edition of R. Wittkower's *Art and Architecture in Italy, 1600-1750,* makes only passing mention of Artemisia but the third edition (Baltimore, 1973, 357f.) devotes a paragraph to her.
8.
Bissell (163ff.) discusses several of these, the finest being that now in the Columbus (Ohio) Gallery of Fine Arts (cat. no. 15). The quality of some of the other versions is so low that one wonders whether some are not shop products.
9.
Ruffo, 46-53.

full of that forceful personality that we sense in her best paintings, declares, "You will find the spirit of Caesar in the soul of this woman." We might not approve of a woman today who declared that deep down she was really a man, but we can appreciate Artemisia's declaration in its contemporary context as an exceptional assertion of self-esteem by an extraordinary woman.

10.
Susanna and the Elders, 1610
Oil on canvas
67 x 47⅝ in. (170 x 121 cm.)
Inscribed lower left: Arte [misia] / Gentileschi / 1610
Pommersfelden, Schloss Weissenstein, Dr. Karl Graf van Schönborn-Wiesentheid

This painting comes from a relatively inaccessible private collection near Bamberg and is not well known in the original even to seicento scholars although it has been discussed in print since 1924. The date, inscribed on the step, is partly obliterated and has usually been read as 1610.[10] As long as the artist was thought to have been born in 1597, which meant that she was only thirteen at the time the *Susanna* was painted, scholars disbelieved the signature and attributed the picture to her father.[11] Voss suggested another explanation, namely that the date be read 1619 and the signature accepted, a proposal recently supported by Bissell.[12] I was not able to examine the picture before the exhibition, but the curator of the collection, Wilhelm Schonath, has recently informed me that the most probable reading of the inscription is 1610. Now that we know Gentileschi was seventeen, not thirteen, in 1610, we can reconsider the possibility that the *Susanna* is an early work, painted in Rome only a year after she began her career, according to her father's testimony at the trial.[13]

The form of the signature tends to support the early date. In Florence she signed her works "Artemisia Lomi," reverting to her paternal grandfather's name instead of her grandmother's, probably to emphasize her Tuscan origins.[14] In arguing for the date 1619, when she was in Florence, Bissell suggested that the unusual form of the signature might indicate that the picture was commissioned by a non-Florentine patron. The provenance of the picture cannot unfortunately be traced back to Italy to provide circumstantial evidence in favor of either theory.

The chief argument in favor of the attribution to Artemisia rather than Orazio, apart from the signature, is the heavily built female figure, who is also more emotionally expressive than is usual for Orazio. The chief argument in favor of Orazio's authorship is that the picture is simply too good to be one of her first works. A more defensible argument for his participation is the design, which uses a sophisticated system of flowing, curved lines and carefully balanced volumes that recalls one of his masterpieces of this period, the *Judith with the Head of Holofernes* in Hartford (Wadsworth Atheneum). The folds are not as crisp and angular as they are in Artemisia's *Judith Beheading Holofernes* (Florence, Uffizi) and in her *Magdalene*

(cat. no. 11), both painted a few years after 1610, but the drapery is also less complex and varied in handling than is usual for Orazio in 1610. The painting also lacks the subtle play of reflected light so typical of him. An attribution to Artemisia in 1610 therefore seems to be plausible given some assistance from Orazio with the planning of the design.

Bissell has compared the *Susanna* with a *Cleopatra* and a *Lucretia,* both in Genoese collections, which he attributes to her and dates 1621. Neither work is signed and not all scholars agree with him, some preferring to give them to Orazio. Decisions depend partly on interpretations of Orazio's artistic personality. Usually he is seen as a quieter, more lyrical artist than Artemisia; his women are often slimmer and more elegant and do not convey the earthy sexuality of hers. His beautiful *Danae* in Cleveland is certainly conceived in a very different spirit from the robust Lucretia who squeezes her breast as she prepares to stab herself.[15] Even the daughters of Lot, a subject Orazio painted several times, while heavier than his other women, do not display as much naked flesh as Susanna and Lucretia do.[16] In this respect too the completely nude Cleopatra is striking. Thus I am inclined to support the attribution to Artemisia of all three works.

The Apocryphal story of Susanna and the Elders was already extremely popular with artists in Italy by the late sixteenth century, especially in Venice, but Artemisia's sources seem to be two prints and a painting by the Carracci. Annibale made an elaborate engraving of Susanna around 1590 and a painting of the same subject about ten years later after he had moved to Rome.[17] The basic compositional arrangement with Susanna on the left and the old men approaching from behind on the right could have been adapted from the print as could the heavy build and the pose of Susanna below the waist. The gesture of the man on the right who tells Susanna to keep quiet occurs in the painting, which had a much simpler design that probably appealed to Artemisia too, who may also have considered a print of a nymph by Agostino Carracci.[18]

Two aspects of Artemisia's *Susanna* are original — the concentrated simplicity of the composition and the almost total nudity of Susanna. The contrast of her pale, lonely figure with the darkly sinister pair of plotting elders is brilliantly staged. Formal elegance and psychological truth work in unison. Susanna turns away from the lascivious old men, her raised left arm completing the diamond-shaped unit containing them, a symbol of their mutual involvement, while the rest of her body is silhouetted against the wall, isolated and vulnerable. The composition fuses Artemisia's knowledge of the most advanced trends in Roman painting, albeit with some help from her father, with her own strong feelings about the attitudes of men towards women and her pride in her ability to paint the nude female figure. The problem remains — was this masterly synthesis achieved when she was only seventeen, and if so, to what extent did her father participate in this marvelous painting? By offering scholars an opportunity to see the work, this exhibition may help to answer these questions.

10.
T. von Frimmel, *Verzeichnis der Gemälde in Gräflich Schönborn-Wiesentheid'-schem Besitze,* Pommersfelden, 1894, 75.
11.
Thus Longhi ("Ultimi studi sul Caravaggio e la sua cerchia," *Proporzioni,* I, 1943, 47, note 38); A. Emiliani ("Orazio Gentileschi: nuove proposte per il viaggio marchigiano," *Paragone,* IX, 1958, no. 103, 42); and Moir (100), all cited by Bissell, 157.
12.
Voss, 463.
13.
In 1612 Orazio stated that Artemisia had been painting for three years and had now "reached the point that I can venture to say that today she has no peers. . . ." (Bissell, 154, citing a document published by L. Tanfani-Centofanti in 1897).
14.
Bissell, 157, note 38.
15.
For the *Danae,* see Cleveland Museum of Art, 1971, no. 32 (color pl.); for the *Cleopatra* and *Lucretia,* see Bissell, figs. 5 and 6.

16.
R. Ward Bissell, "Orazio Gentileschi and the Theme of 'Lot and His Daughters'," *Bulletin of the National Gallery of Canada,* Ottawa, XIV, 1969, 16-33.
17.
Donald Posner, *Annibale Carracci: A Study in the Reform of Italian Painting around 1520,* 2 vols., London, 1971, II, nos. 57 and 131a. The painting is known only in a version (copy?) attributed by some scholars to Lanfranco, by others, myself included, to Domenichino.

11

11.
The Penitent Magdalene, ca. 1619-20
Oil on canvas
41¾ x 43 in. (106 x 109 cm.)
Inscribed center left on the chair: ARTIMISIA LOMI and on the right:
OPTIMAM PARTEM ELEGIT
Florence, Galleria Palatina, Palazzo Pitti (142)

This work is one of Artemisia's most beautiful pictures though perhaps not among her more successful in psychological terms. Bissell has suggested that it was commissioned by Grand Duke Cosimo II (1590-1621), whose wife was Maddalena d'Austria.[19] Although the work is not recorded in inventories of the Palazzo Pitti until the nineteenth century, its location, the form of the signature, and the bold Caravaggesque presentation all mark it as a product of Artemisia's Florentine period.[20]

The Magdalene's golden yellow dress is one of the most spectacular passages of painting in all of Artemisia's work; indeed the color is almost her trademark. She sets off this sumptuous display with a dull red chair back, a green tablecloth, and a blue border on the dress. The Magdalene turns away from a mirror, symbol of the vanities of her former, wasted life, and looks to heaven, having now chosen the better part, as the text on the mirror frame explains. The words come from Christ's speech to Martha when she complained that Mary Magdalene was not doing her share of the housework (Luke 10: 42). Artemisia's Magdalene, like all the women she preferred to portray, is conceived as a heroine, and is therefore shown as a woman of heroic proportions. Significantly, Artemisia's interpretation avoids the more obvious suggestions of sexuality so often found in seventeenth-century pictures of this subject, including her father's (Vienna, Kunsthistorisches Museum). The impressive stature of Artemisia's Magdalene also makes a striking contrast with the vulnerable young woman portrayed by Caravaggio (Rome, Galleria Doria). Both these comparisons emphasize the originality and independence of Artemisia's treatment of this common theme.

Despite the splendid rendition of yellow silk and despite the vigorously personal reading of the subject, the picture is not a complete success. Probably it is the lack of dramatic incident that makes the facial expression of studied intensity and the strong gestures of both hands seem rhetorical rather than sincere. Artemisia is still an immature artist who is overstating her case in dramatic terms. By the 1620s she had come to terms with her fiercely expressive artistic temperament, and this psychological maturity, together with even finer pictorial skills, was to produce an authentic masterpiece such as the *Judith and Maidservant* (cat. no. 13).

18.
M. Calvesi and V. Casale, *Le incisioni dei Carracci,* Rome, 1965, no. 178. Another *Susanna and the Elders* attributed to Artemisia belongs to the Marquess of Exeter (Burghley House; Witt Photographic Survey no. B57/1585; see Bissell, 1968, 167). The attribution seems possible and a date in the 1620s reasonable. It shows some impact on her work of Guercino, especially in the background sky and landscape and the color scheme.
19.
Bissell, 156. He also proposes a date around 1620, identifying the picture with the work in progress mentioned by the artist in a letter to Cosimo II of February 10, 1620.
20.
Florence, 1970, 74-75.

12.
Portrait of a Condottiere, 1622
Oil on canvas
82 x 50⅜ in. (208 x 128 cm.)
Inscribed on the back: ARTEMISIA. GETILSCA. FA-/CIEBAT ROMAE 1622
Bologna, Palazzo Comunale

Filippo Baldinucci, the only seventeenth-century artists' biographer to pay more than passing attention to Artemisia, says that she began her career painting portraits and produced many while she lived in Rome.[21] The surviving evidence does not support him. Apart from two self-portraits and this work, no portraits by her exist and there are few references to any in early inventories or other sources.[22] The portraits that she talks of doing in her letters are mainly her own. This large canvas, one of her rare dated works, is an impressive image; the loss of her other portraits, even if they were not numerous, is regrettable.

The subject of this portrait has not been identified.[23] He is shown in military costume standing beside a table covered with a plum red cloth, a flag of lemon yellow and rose hanging to his left. The composition fits a pattern that by this date was standard for conservative patrons all over Europe. The cloth-covered table parallel to the picture plane which supports some iconographically suitable paraphernalia, the one hand outstretched, the other resting on hip or sword pommel, the feet arranged like those of a relaxed ballet dancer, all these details are repeated in hundreds of examples. Given that Artemisia had to work within such a strict formula, she could express herself only in the illusionistic skill with which she depicted textures, accessories, and the subject's features. Geniuses like Titian and Velázquez transcended the limits of this convention by the sheer beauty of their painting and by subtle relaxation of the exaggerated formality inherent in the presentation. Artemisia does not triumph over her limitations to the same degree, but the result is a powerful portrait that conveys admirably the military strength with which the patron surely hoped to impress the spectator.

13.
Judith and Maidservant with the Head of Holofernes, ca. 1625
Oil on canvas
72½ x 55¾ in. (184 x 142 cm.)
The Detroit Institute of Arts
Gift of Leslie H. Green
(See color plate, p. 70)

The compositions of Gentileschi's earlier paintings of this story were heavily indebted either to the work of her father or to that of Caravaggio. This canvas, which scholars believe was painted in the 1620s when she was living in Rome, is a more original and more personal interpretation, stressing the dramatic tension of the heroine's escape from the heart of the enemy camp rather than the violence of Holofernes' death. She employs here the brilliant chiaroscuro effects produced by artificial light sources that were preferred by Caravaggio's

Northern followers, such as Honthorst, and develops the narrative content of her father's marvelous painting in Hartford (Wadsworth Atheneum).[24] Her canvas is more than six feet high; thus the figures are over life-size. Compared to her Uffizi *Judith* the melodrama is much reduced but the final effect is no less powerful.

As well as being a superb piece of pictorial dramatic narrative, Gentileschi's canvas is also quite simply an outstandingly beautiful painting. Passages such as the shadowed violets of the servant's dress set off against the warm ocher of Judith's skirt and the glowing plum reds of the curtain above their heads are especially memorable. The artist's ambition can also be appreciated if we consider for a moment the challenges she set herself — numerous awkward foreshortenings and difficult transitions of light and shade across facial contours and changing fabrics. The artist is at the height of her powers and the result is one of her masterpieces.

14.
Fame, 1632
Oil on canvas
50 x 38⅜ in. (127 x 97.4 cm.)
Inscribed on the book: [1] 632 / [A] RTEMISIA / [fa] CIEBAT ALL IIIS.te M. / SENE. [?] TRosiers [TR in monogram] / SELM . . . DEL / TIQ [?]
New York, Wildenstein & Company
(See color plate, p. 71)

In this magnificent dark-toned picture the deep bluish green robes of Fame are set off by her rust brown sleeves; by the light reflections on her jewelry, on the laurel leaves in her hair, and on the velvet fabric; and by the white of her lace-edged underdress and the pages of the book. Many passages are handled with great bravura, in vivid contrast to the tightly painted, disciplined technique of her earlier works. Once more Artemisia has responded strongly to the theme of heroic womanhood, even though the figure here represents an abstract concept rather than a particular heroine. The features reflect an ideal beauty of classical inspiration but are still full of individual character. The work strikes a perfect balance between the vigorous realism of her work before 1630 and her increasingly elegant, and hence less powerful, paintings of the next two decades.

Unlike her *Self-Portrait* at Hampton Court, which carefully follows the prescription for painting in Cesare Ripa's *Iconologia,*[25] the iconography of Artemisia's *Fame* departs from tradition. Ripa requires Fame to carry a trumpet in the right hand and an olive branch in the left; Fame here does support a trumpet with her right hand, but there is no olive branch, only laurel leaves. Laurel symbolizes triumph and eternity, certainly not inappropriate in this context. Ripa also mentions white wings and a gold chain round the neck from which should hang a heart, all omitted by Artemisia. It would be helpful to know something about the patron for whom she painted this masterpiece, but so far all attempts to identify Mr. Trosiers (Rosiers?) have been unsuccessful.[26]

21.
Baldinucci, x, 251ff.
22.
Bissell, 165-66; for the self-portraits, see Bissell, figs. 18 and 19.
23.
The portrait was given to the city by the heirs of Agostino Pepoli. At the time (ca. 1926), the coat-of-arms on the table seemed to display a Pepoli device, but cleaning removed it and the coat-of-arms now visible has not been identified. The cross on the armor indicates that the subject belonged to the order of SS. Maurizio e Lazzaro.
24.
Cleveland Museum of Art, 1971, no. 30.

25.
Levey, 79-80.
26.
The painting is not in perfect condition. It was painted on canvas but transferred to an oak panel after it entered an English collection. It has recently been restored and returned to its original canvas support. The trimmed inscription suggests that the picture has been cut down at some point on the left and possibly along the top as well. Professor R. Ward Bissell, who is planning to continue his work on Artemisia, tells me that he has been unable to trace the patron's name in any Neapolitan sources.

12

15.
David and Bathsheba, ca. 1640-45
Oil on canvas
98½ x 76½ in. (250.2 x 194.3 cm.)
Columbus (Ohio) Gallery of Fine Arts
Schumacher Fund Purchase and Gift from the Schumacher
Foundation (676)

This painting was a cooperative venture. Artemisia painted the figures; the architectural background was provided by Viviano Codazzi
(ca. 1603-1672), a Neapolitan artist who specialized in such work;
the landscape and sky were provided by another Neapolitan colleague,
Domenico Gargiulo (ca. 1610-ca. 1675).[27] In this context we may
recall Anastaise, the Parisian miniaturist who provided borders and
backgrounds for "yhistoires" by male artists. Almost two hundred
fifty years later we have a documented example of the reverse situation.

At least six paintings of the story of Bathsheba are associated with
Artemisia.[28] Of these the finest is certainly this work, although a
version in Leipzig, which may predate it by a year or so, is a close
second.[29] As Bissell points out, Artemisia's later style is more idealized,
lacking the concentrated drama of her work in the second and third
decades of the century. Her figures become slimmer and their types
less plebeian. Caravaggesque naturalism was out of fashion, and the
ethereal figures of Guido and the stern classicism of Domenichino
were increasingly influential in Naples. Artemisia tempered her
Caravaggesque traits but did not deny her genius for dramatic story-
telling. In the Leipzig version, Bathsheba is busy combing her hair,
attended by her two maids; no messenger comes with the fatal
invitation from King David, nor is he visible on the balcony. In the
Columbus version the figures are slimmer and there is more space
between and around them. Bathsheba turns to look at the jewels
brought by her maid, but when she turns around, she will find the
note from David that will present her with a moral dilemma — to
obey her king or her husband. The pleasant landscape becomes a
symbol of her present peace of mind, the massive building, where
David watches her, a symbol of the tragedy that she is about to
experience because of her physical charms. The story is told with a
clarity that even Poussin might appreciate, while the treatment
retains enough of her vigorous personality for this work to rank
among her best later canvases.

27.
De Dominici, III, 198-99 (for the quote, see Bissell, 163). The handling of the
architecture in both the Columbus and the Leipzig versions (see below) is perfectly consistent with Codazzi's style, as is the landscape with that of Gargiulo.
Benedict Nicolson pointed out that Codazzi was living in Naples between 1639
and 1647, which means that their cooperative works must date from these years.
28.
See Bissell, 163ff. To the four he discusses can be added the version in Leipzig
published here and another in a private collection in Vienna discovered by
Renate Mikula, who hopes to publish it. The latter picture is related to the
version formerly in the Ramunni Collection in Bari (Bissell, fig. 22). I am grateful
to Professor Bissell for telling me about the Viennese picture and for lending
me his photographs of it.
29.
Oil on canvas, size unknown; private collection, Leipzig, on loan to the Museum
der bildenden Künste, Leipzig, in 1968.

15

1.

"Questo Domenico Fetti havea una sorella, che parimente anch'essa dipingeva;
Et il Serenissimo Duca, sommo amatore della virtù, e particolarmente della pittura, fece venire a Mantova non solo lei, ma il padre con tutta la famiglia; & a
tutti provide, e la fanciulla fecela Monaca entro nobile convento, e pur quivi ella
essercitava il talento della pittura, e con buona maniera, e con amore operando,
arricchì non solo quel Monastero di varie figure, ma anche adornò co' suoi colori
altri Monasteri della nobil Città di Mantova." (Domenico Fetti had a sister who
likewise painted. The Duke, a great lover of excellence, particularly of painting,
brought her to Mantua with her father and entire family, providing for them all.
The young girl became a nun in the noble convent where she exercised her talent
for painting in a good style. Working with love, she enriched not only this convent
with various works but also adorned with her painting other convents in the
noble city of Mantua.) Baglione, 155.

2.

As did her brother Domenico whose regular salary as court painter to the duke of
Mantua was established in March of that year. Document of March 24, 1614(Man-
tua, Archivio di Stato, Notai Camerali B. 6. IV), published by Alessandro Luzio,
La Galleria dei Gonzaga venduta all'Inghilterra nel 1627-28, Milan, 1913, 286.

3.

Document of December 3, 1614 (Mantua, Archivio di Stato, P.V. Notai Camerali),
mentioned by Luzio, *Galleria dei Gonzaga,* 286, who identifies Giustina with Lucrina.

4.

This choice was doubtless inspired by the fact that the bodies of four saints, among
them Santa Lucrina, had been obtained from Pope Paul v by Ferdinando Gonzaga.
They were given into the custody of his aunt, Margherita Gonzaga, founder of the
convent of Sant'Orsola to which they were ceremoniously transported in 1614.
(Ippolito Donesmondi, *Dell'istoria ecclesiastica di Mantova,* Mantua, 1616, II,
507; *Vita dell'illustriss.mo et reverendiss. Monsignor F. Francesco Gonzaga,
vescovo di Mantova,* Venice, 1625, 445.

5.

Don Tiberio Guarini, *Breve naratione e vera historia della fondatione del nobi-
liss:o monasterio di S. Orsola in Mant:a fondato dalla Ser:ma Madama Margherita Gonzaga d'este duchesa di Ferrara* (Ms. Biblioteca Comunale, Mantua).

6.

Letter of May 26, 1636, from Arrivabene to Duke Carlo Gonzaga di Nevers
(Mantua, Archivio di Stato, P. VII. 3315. no. 19).

7.

See Luzio, *Galleria dei Gonzaga,* 294, 297.

Lucrina Fetti

Italian, active ca. 1614 - ca. 1651?

Lucrina Fetti, sister of the more renowned painter Domenico Fetti (1589-1623), is first mentioned by Baglione who refers to her as Domenico's "sister who likewise painted." He notes that she was brought from Rome to Mantua with her father and family by Duke Ferdinando Gonzaga who provided for them all. In Mantua she became a nun in the Franciscan convent of Sant'Orsola where, Baglione relates, she exercised her talent for painting, enriching not only her own monastery but others in the city.[1] On December 3, 1614, the year Lucrina arrived in Mantua,[2] it was ordered that 150 scudi be paid to Giustina Fetti, sister of Domenico Fetti "who had become a nun in the Ursuline convent," as a "free gift" from His Highness.[3] It was Duke Ferdinando Gonzaga, therefore, who provided Lucrina with her convent dowry. This order reveals that her given name was Giustina, from which it can be inferred that Lucrina was her adopted name in religion.[4] Since Suor Lucrina is the only Fetti appearing in a list of sisters enrolled at the convent in 1618,[5] Lucrina and Giustina are unquestionably the same person. Two of Domenico's sisters were living in the convent by May of 1636, presumably Lucrina and a sister who must have followed her there sometime after 1618.[6] Neither the given nor the religious name of the sister is anywhere recorded.

That Lucrina Fetti was a painter of some note is attested by Baglione's proportionally lengthy account of her in his discussion of Domenico. Having been active at the Mantuan court in 1621-22,[7] Baglione would have known her work and been a reliable witness to her reputation and achievement. Quite apart from her local fame in Mantua, she continued to receive approval, even acclaim, from Baldinucci,[8] Orlandi,[9] Mariette,[10] d'Argenville,[11] and Nagler,[12] although none of them cites any specific works by her hand. Disparaged by critics earlier in this century,[13] her painting has more recently been singled out again as "worthy of interest."[14]

No works by Lucrina are identified in any literature or inventory before the second half of the eighteenth century. The oeuvre constituted at that time falls into three distinct groups difficult to reconcile with one another in invention and style. Largely based on the observations of Giovanni Cadioli, painter, architect, and founder of the Accademia de Belle Arti di Mantua, Lucrina's pictorial identity remains unclear to this day. In his guidebook to Mantua, published in 1763, Cadioli records a *Deposition* and an *Adoration of the Shepherds* by Lucrina placed on either side of an altar in the small convent church reserved for the nuns of Sant'Orsola.[15] The *Adoration of the Shepherds* has since disappeared; the *Deposition* may be one of the eight scenes from the life of the Virgin and Christ, identical in size, that were judged worthy of removal from Sant'Orsola to the R. Ginnasio di Mantova in 1786, four years after the convent was suppressed.[16] Six of the eight scenes are now with the Hospital of Mantua: the *Adoration of the Magi* and *Deposition* are in the hospital itself; the *Annunciation* and *Crowning with Thorns* are in the hospital chapel; the *Visitation* and *Agony in the Garden* are in the house of Dr. Alfonso Izzo, Mantua.[17] With the exception of the *Deposition* all are signed and dated S.L.F.R.F.S.O. 1629, interpreted as *Suor Lucrina Fetti Romana fece in Sant'Orsola 1629*.[18] In this group of paintings a formal naïveté and stiffness of figural movement are offset by schematized patterns of light and shadow. These create a stylized play of muscles or of sharply creased drapery folds that lend momentum to an essentially "late mannerist" concept of affective posture. Not all of these compositions, however, are original inventions of Lucrina's,[19] and it is possible that the identifying initials may have been added at a later date to a series of her earliest essays, or even copies after them. In any event, it is difficult to believe that Baglione would have considered paintings of this caliber exemplary of what he called Lucrina's *buona maniera*.

A second group of works, notably superior in quality, consists of four life-size full-length portraits of women, now in the Palazzo Ducale, Mantua. Formal state portraits of members of the Gonzaga family, they were all painted for the convent of Sant'Orsola. Represented are Margherita Gonzaga (1564-1618), duchess of Ferrara, widow of Alfonso II D'Este, and founder of the convent of Sant'Orsola;[20] the

---

8.
Baldinucci, IX, 103.
9.
Fr. P. A. Orlandi, *L'Abecedario pittorico*, 1704; rev. ed., Bologna, 1719, 133.
10.
P. J. Mariette, *Recueil d'estampes d'après les plus beaux dessins qui sont en France dans le Cabinet du Roy, dans celui du Duc d'Orléans, et dans d'autres cabinets*, Paris, 1742, II, 38; "Abecedario, Vol. II," *Archives de l'art français*, IV, 1853-54, 246.
11.
Antoine Joseph Dezallier d'Argenville, *Abregé de la vie des plus fameux peintres, avec leur portraits gravés en taille-douce*, Paris, 1745, I, 38.
12.
Nagler, IV, 523.
13.
". . . fu dolcissima pittrice, ma la sua fredda immaginazione non le permise di uscire dalla mediocrità." (. . . [she] was a most pleasing painter, but her cold imagination did not permit her to escape from mediocrity.) Vittorio Matteucci, *Le chiese artistiche del Mantovano*, Mantua, 1902, 374-75. "Der schlechte Erhaltungstand ihrer Bilder beeinträchtigt das Urteil, aber sie schient ein nur mittelmässiges Talent, ohne grosse Entwicklungsfähigkeit gewesen zu sein." (The

poor state of preservation of her pictures impairs judgment, but she appears to have had only a mediocre talent, without great capacity for development.) Endres-Soltmann, in Thieme-Becker, XI, 510.
14.
C. L. Ragghianti, "Codicillo mantegnesco," *Critica d'arte*, LII, 1962, 39. Ragghianti views Lucrina's work as "di deduzioni tutte toscane, dal Sustermans a Cecco Bravo" (of entirely Tuscan inspiration, from Sustermans to Cecco Bravo). Any Tuscan aspects of Lucrina's style could only have been acquired from her brother Domenico who received his early training in Rome from the Florentine painters Andrea Commodi and Ludovico Cigoli.
15.
Cadioli, 72-73.
16.
The Adoration of the Shepherds, The Deposition, The Adoration of the Magi, The Crowning with Thorns, The Annunciation, The Agony in the Garden, The Visitation, and *The Flagellation* (Carlo D'Arco, *Delle arti e degli artefici di Mantova*, Mantua, 1857, II, 214, nos. 43-50). Cadioli particularly admires three *angioletti* among the clouds in the *Deposition;* these are not visible in the *Deposition* now in the Hospital of Mantua. Not all the paintings were, in fact, removed to the R.

Empress Eleanora I Gonzaga (1598-1655), wife of Emperor Ferdinand II;[21] Eleanora II Gonzaga (1628-1686), wife of Emperor Ferdinand III;[22] and Caterina de' Medici (1593-1629), wife of Duke Ferdinando Gonzaga, ruler of the Mantuan court during Domenico Fetti's years of residence.[23] These portraits follow a convention of representation in which each subject is turned slightly to the left in a three-quarter view and is shown wearing a heavy gown that falls in impeccably arranged folds. Variations in pose involve little more than judicious alterations in the placing of hands. A restrained solemnity characterizes these immobile members of the house of Gonzaga whose courtly dignity is further enhanced by the richly patterned materials of their robes and their jeweled ornamentation, precisely described and smoothly painted. A comparison of these portraits with the scenes from the lives of Christ and Mary also attributed to Lucrina reveals no analogies of style. In the portraits, light and shadow as components of modeling and of textural differentiation display a greater sensitivity and refinement. Stiffly falling brocades, elegant fleshy hands, and delicate modulations of light rounding the facial features (all marked by a prominently rounded chin and heavy jowls) find no parallel of achievement in the former group of paintings. The *apparat* of draped cloth in the portraits of the two Eleanoras is painted in a freer, more animated mode than that of the inflexible fabrics clothing the figures. Conically shaped folds of softer surface break into deep irregular indentations assuming rippling, rhythmic, even flamelike configurations. In the background of the portrait of Caterina de' Medici soft feathery trees provide further evidence of the looser brushwork of which the author of these portraits was capable.

There seems no reason to question that Lucrina Fetti executed this group of portraits. As painter-nun in the convent of Sant'Orsola, she was clearly chosen to paint the female patrons of the institution, the women who distinguished the Gonzaga convent and court of Mantua. In providing state portraits, albeit solely of women, she fulfilled a function that her brother Domenico, in the employ of the duke, did not. By revivifying the essentially medieval tradition of the female artist active in the cloister, and through transposing the medieval donor-portrait into the realm of independent easel painting, Lucrina celebrates the individual identities and high destinies of the courtly affiliates of the recently built "noble-convent" of Mantua.

A third group of works associated with Lucrina comprises a miscellany of paintings attributed to her in the guidebooks of Cadioli and his successors. Since they are not consistent in style and some are confused with, or thought in various ways to involve the assistance of her brother Domenico, the question of Lucrina's dependence upon the style and collaboration of her brother is raised. Although Baglione does not mention any working relationship between them, Baldinucci declares that Domenico taught Lucrina to paint.[24] Whether precisely true or not, this would be in line with the prevailing practice regarding the instruction of women in a family craft.[25] Cadioli, in identifying Lucrina's work in Sant'Orsola, assumes a continuing collaboration between Lucrina and Domenico. He considers an *Adoration of the*

Ginnasio. In 1859 the *Annunciation,* the *Visitation,* the *Agony in the Garden,* and the *Crowning with Thorns* are noted to be on the side walls of two chapels of the church of Sant'Orsola (Bartolomeo Arrighi, *Mantova e sua provincia,* Mantua, 1859, 402).
17.
Except for the *Deposition,* these are published by Girolamo Matthiae, *Inventario degli oggetti d'arte d'Italia, Provincia di Mantova,* Rome, 1935, VI, 57, 58, 60, who lists a *Deposition* of smaller dimensions which he attributes to an unknown artist of the late seventeenth century.
18.
Ibid. Matthiae (ibid., 60) questions the authenticity of the initials (because of their wide spacing) as well as the execution of the *Adoration of the Magi,* proposing, on the basis of an excessive hardness of form, that it is an old copy of an original by Lucrina or the work of a late and mediocre imitator.
19.
The *Crowning with Thorns* is a copy after Ludovico Carracci's *Crowning with Thorns,* ca. 1595, Pinacoteca, Bologna.
20.
Listed without attribution by Giovanni Bottani, 1786, as worthy of removal

from the convent of Sant'Orsola to the R. Ginnasio (D'Arco, *Delle arti,* II, 214, no. 25). Inventoried without attribution in the Accademia Virgiliana, 1827 (ibid., 246, no. 40), and 1862 (Mantua, Accademia Virgiliana, ms., "Inventario degli oggetti non compresa dall'atto di cessione rogito Siliprandi 7 Giugno 1862, e che sono di esclusiva proprietà dell'Accademia Virgiliana"). Repr. in Alfonso Lazzari, "Le ultime tre Duchesse di Ferrara," *Rassegna Nazionale,* 190, March-April 1913, 172. Despite the fact that this portrait is paired in the 1827 and 1862 inventories with portraits now attributed to Lucrina, Intra alone has recognized its kinship with them: ". . . ritratto in piedi al naturale di Margherita eseguito dalla monaca Lucrina; appare vestita in una strana foggia, che ha del claustrale e del principesco. . . ." (full-length portrait from the life of Margherita executed by the nun Lucrina. She appears clothed in a strange costume that is evocative of both the cloister and the court.) G. B. Intra, *Il monastero di Santa Orsola in Mantova,* Milan, 1895, 13. A bust portrait of Margherita Gonzaga — with the notation on its back, "Margherita Gonzaga-Abadessa di s. Orsola e Fondatrice di detto convento — di Lucrina Fetti" (Margherita Gonzaga — Abbess of S. Orsola and Founder of said convent — by Lucrina Fetti) — is in the Castelvecchio Museum, Verona (Giuseppe Trecco, *Catalogo della Pinacoteca Comunale di Verona,* Bergamo, 1912, 155, no. 629).

Shepherds to have been retouched by Domenico, and he calls an *Agony in the Garden* a good copy after a work by Domenico.[26] That he did not have a reliable grasp of either Domenico's or Lucrina's style is demonstrated by his attribution of an *Annunciation* painted on two large canvases, now in the Palazzo Ducale, to Domenico Fetti.[27] Since Bottani's inventory of 1786 the *Annunciation* has been attributed to Lucrina.[28] This spirited work, painted for the staircase of the convent of Sant'Orsola, carries the motif of steps into the canvas representing the *Virgin* and is far more pictorially complex and dramatic than any of the biblical scenes dated 1629. Except for a certain corporeal opulence of form, little stylistic relationship to the work of Domenico can be discovered. The textural reality of material properties and the ornate trimmings on draperies present closer analogies to the decorative richness of the Sant'Orsola portraits: in both, draperies endow figures of unostentatious yet dignified bearing with an elegance and courtly stylishness totally lacking in the biblical scenes.

Two other paintings attributed to Lucrina and said by Cadioli to have been retouched by her brother are clearly related to Domenico's work.[29] They are a full-length *St. Margaret* and a full-length *Mary Magdalene* which originally flanked the altarpiece by Anton Maria Viani of *S.S. Margaret and Ursula in Glory with the Trinity*, 1614, in the church of Sant'Orsola. There is good reason to believe that the *St. Margaret* is, in fact, the *St. Barbara* in the present exhibition (see cat. no. 16). The *Magdalene* is lost or unidentified, although a poor and ruined copy hangs in the church of S. Martino, Mantua, and the composition is known through other versions.[30] The known versions reveal a dependence upon many aspects of Domenico's style: the broad-cheeked, full-lipped, heavy-lidded features; the loose décolleté blouse with its rhythmic, sinuous folds, and the soft atmospheric ground of cloud and cherubim.[31] If the eighteenth-century attribution to Lucrina is correct, the closeness of this image to the work of Domenico makes it impossible to deny Lucrina's capacity to emulate her brother's imagery and style. Although most of the known works now attributed to Lucrina neither reinforce nor clarify her working relationship or stylistic affinities with Domenico, they are too few to preclude the possibility of an exchange having existed between them. It would have been customary for her to learn her art from a member of her family, and in the seventeenth and eighteenth centuries such writers as Baldinucci, Mariette, and Cadioli assumed that she did. The supposition that she imitated the style of her brother and that he, in turn, retouched her paintings, has continued into the twentieth century despite lack of corroborative evidence.[32] The *St. Barbara* in this exhibition reopens the question, serving to place it on new visual foundations.

A nun in the convent of Sant'Orsola, Lucrina devoted her gifts as painter primarily to religious subjects and portraits. By tradition, portraiture was the field of art most fully sown with women's talents.[33] Lucrina, by extending her accomplishments into the realm of religious painting, can be joined with the more enterprising women painters of her time. She was undoubtedly held in special esteem by Duke Ferdinando Gonzaga whose passion for art and probable view of a woman painter as a desirable "curiosity" for the court convent[34] may partially have prompted his donation of her dowry. That she was respected by Margherita Gonzaga, founder of Sant'Orsola, is evident from the nature of her commissions and the location of her works in church and convent. There can be little doubt, however, that her position as nun conditioned her art, that the content of her religious paintings is focused on the Virgin or on the female saints held in special veneration by her patroness, while her portraits are exclusively of those women of the court most closely connected with her own convent. If in earlier centuries women painters had found their place in either court or convent, Lucrina synthesizes anew the potentialities and limitations of both milieux. Transforming the vocational heritage of both institutions to meet the needs of her time and place, she succeeded in exalting the authority of women in the worlds of patronage and the religious life, and by her own example, in the arts.

16.

St. Barbara, 1619
Oil on canvas
60¼ x 36³/₁₆ in. (152.5 x 97 cm.)
Inscribed lower left on face of pedestal base: LUCRINA FETTI FECI L'ANNO 1619/ IN S^(ta) ORSOLA
Rome, Collection Carlo Sestieri

The addition of *St. Barbara* to the few known religious paintings ascribed to Lucrina Fetti gains credence, if not proof, from existing documentary evidence as well as from the affinities of style and pictorial vocabulary it shares with the work of her brother Domenico. Although indecipherable in a photograph, the signature of Lucrina emerged, I understand, after a cleaning that removed the previously existing name of Domenico. The painting is not by Domenico.

Lucrina's fame rests on the paintings she provided for the convent of Sant'Orsola in Mantua and its adjacent public church of the same name. The octagonal church of Sant'Orsola, built by Anton Maria Viani, was opened to the public in February 1613.[35] The axial chapel on the left, devoted to St. Margaret, received as altarpiece Viani's *SS. Margaret and Ursula in Glory with the Trinity*,[36] signed and dated 1614,[37] today in the Palazzo Ducale. In 1763 Cadioli noted that beneath Viani's altarpiece were a *St. Margaret* and a *Mary Magdalene* by Lucrina Fetti, both of which he considered to have been retouched by Domenico.[38] Listed as worthy of removal from Sant' Orsola to the R. Ginnasio, Mantua, in 1786 were a "S. Barbara e S. Maria Maddalena, figure intiere in due quadri eguali."[39] Almost certainly these are the same paintings noted by Cadioli (who confused St. Barbara with the patron saint of the chapel). Neither painting appears in the 1827 inventory of paintings in the Accademia Virgiliana;[40] by 1818 the *Magdalene* had been placed in the church of S. Martino, Mantua.[41] A citation in an undated inventory of the Academy enables the *St. Barbara* in this exhibition to be identified with the *St. Barbara* in the 1786 inventory. Listed are "2 quadri di Lucrina

21.
Listed as "dipinta dal Feti" in Giovanni Bottani's 1786 inventory (D'Arco, *Delle arti*, II, 213, no. 23). Inventoried as a work by Lucrina Fetti in the Accademia Virgiliana, 1827 (ibid., 246, no. 38). Catalogued as Lucrina by Nino Giannantoni, *Il Palazzo Ducale di Mantova*, Rome, 1929, 56. The written notation on the back of the portrait: "Suor Lucrina Fetti romana in S. Orsola, Mantua, ha fatto, 1622," is first published by Leandro Ozzòla, *La Galleria di Mantova: Palazzo Ducale*, Cremona, 1949, 4, no. 19.
22.
Inventoried without attribution by Bottani, 1786 (D'Arco, *Delle arti*, II, 214, no. 24). Inventoried as a work by Lucrina Fetti in the Accademia Virgiliana, 1827 (ibid., 246, no. 38). Identified as Eleanora II Gonzaga and cited as a work of Lucrina by Intra (*Il monastero di Santa Orsola*, 19-20), who also notes that Eleanora married Ferdinand III in 1651. This portrait showing Eleanora holding orb and scepter must have been painted for this occasion, from which it can be deduced that Lucrina was still alive and active at this date. Catalogued as Lucrina by Giannantoni, *Il Palazzo Ducale*, 56; and Ozzòla, *La Galleria di Mantova*, 4, no. 18. Eleanora II was brought up in Sant'Orsola until her marriage (Giambattista Intra, *Le due Eleanore Gonzaga imperatrici*, Mantova, 1891, 26).

23.
Listed as "S. Elena," without attribution, in Bottani's 1786 inventory (D'Arco, *Delle arti*, II, 213, no. 22). Inventoried as "S. Elena" without attribution in the Accademia Virgiliana, 1827 (ibid., 246, no. 39). First catalogued as a work of Lucrina with the title, "Sant'Elena Imperatrice," by Ozzòla, *La Galleria di Mantova*, 31, no. 229. That it is Caterina de' Medici represented as St. Helena is beyond doubt since her devotion to the cross is stressed by her confessor and biographer (Fulgenzio Gemma, *Ritratto della Sereniss.ᵃ Principessa Caterina di Toscana Duchessa di Mantova e Monferrato, poi Governatrice di Siena*, Florence, 1737, bk. II, chap. VI), as are her spiritual retreats to Sant'Orsola where she retired after the death of Duke Ferdinando (1626), before returning to the court of Florence (ibid., bk. III, chap. IX). Her features may be compared with a *Portrait of Caterina de' Medici* by an unknown painter in the Uffizi (repr. in Leonardo Mazzoldi et al., *Mantova: La storia*, Mantua, 1963, III, opp. 156), and with a drawing of her by Domenico Fetti, Christ Church Library, Oxford (James Byam Shaw, *Old Master Drawings from Christ Church Oxford*, International Exhibitions Foundation, 1972-73, 27, no. 27, fig. 27). Lucrina's portrait must date between 1617, the year of her marriage to Duke Ferdinando, and 1626, when she returned to Tuscany a widow.
24.
Baldinucci, IX, 103.

Feti rapti S.M.ª Mad.na e S. Barbara con una spada ai piedi."[42] This description of a sword at the feet of St. Barbara leaves little doubt, especially as a sword is an exceptional attribute in representations of this legendary virgin martyr.

Shown slightly *di sotto in su,* St. Barbara stands out of doors on a stepped architectural platform; turning her upper body towards the left, she rests her right arm against a sculptured stone base. The base and background elements, cut off at the sides, give precedence to her corpulent figure, while her right foot, and the sword and martyr's palm lying adjacent to it, project beyond the picture plane, bringing her into immediate spatial proximity to the spectator. Such cut-off effects of setting, defying any logical identification of location, abound in Domenico Fetti's work. Vertical elements of setting used to frame the head and shoulders of a single figure may be seen in his *Melancholia* (Paris, Louvre), while a comparable elimination of the picture plane appears in his *Ecce Homo* (Florence, Uffizi). However, in Domenico's more spatially constructed compositions his figures move and turn three-dimensionally in space-occupying postures, while in the *St. Barbara* Lucrina has conceived her composition in a closer relation to the picture surface, asserting a *horror vacui* and a more ebulliently decorative style.

St. Barbara's amplitude of figure with its curvaceous contours is also indebted to the sensuous fullness of Domenico's figures, so often compared to Rubens'. Lucrina's execution of this ideal, however, is tighter and smoother; her closer brushwork is subordinated to a lustrous clarity of form and surface, and her drapery folds likewise fall in more finely regulated rhythms. A close approximation to the deep indentations and fluctuating curves of Domenico's draperies appears, however, in St. Barbara's sweeping mantle with its dark rivulets of folds and flashing highlights, reminiscent in some ways of the stole worn by Fetti's *Artemisia* (Florence, Palazzo Pitti). The effect of Lucrina's highlighting, however, is more prismatic, for she seeks a sharper vitality of surface and contour than Domenico whose fluid calligraphy of highlights accentuates forms that seem to emerge spontaneously from within an atmospheric space. Although a more abbreviated handling appears in the stone tower and sculptured relief of the architectural base, the gentle bravura and lyrical fantasy of Domenico's optically conceived forms are absent; just as the elusive texture of his pigment, ranging in density from impasto to translucency, is replaced with an execution that effects a clarity and sustains a more consistent substantiality of form throughout. Lucrina's adaptation of her brother's style is nevertheless bold and pictorially accomplished. Most noticeably, she gives it a precise refinement evident not only in the flawless surfaces of St. Barbara's face, neck, and hands, but also in the decoratively patterned border of her mantle and in her carefully waved hair ornamented with a floral wreath. Lingering traces of a Parmigianinesque grace may also be discerned in the placement of St. Barbara's hand across her breast and in the relatively tapering proportions of her figure, although this rhythmic elegance of design is fully assimilated into a natural reality

25.
David Wilkins, "Woman as Artist and Patron in the Middle Ages and Renaissance," in *The Roles and Images of Women in the Middle Ages and Renaissance,* ed. Douglas Radcliff-Umstad, University of Pittsburgh Publications on the Middle Ages and Renaissance, III, Pittsburgh, 1975, 111.
26.
". . . la Natività di Cristo . . .; e l'altro Gesù resvegliato fra la tempesta dagli Apostoli . . ." (. . . the Nativity of Christ . . .; and the other, Christ awakened by the Apostles in the Storm . . .). Cadioli, 73. These paintings have been assumed to be two of the previously mentioned eight scenes of the life of the Virgin and Christ by Lucrina, initialed and dated 1629. None of these scenes, however, could have been invented by Fetti, and his hand is nowhere visible in any one of them. If in 1763 they carried the date of 1629, Cadioli would surely not have postulated the collaboration of Fetti who had been dead for several years. The problem of the 1629 group of paintings is thus compounded. If they were quite other paintings, executed in Domenico's lifetime, they are today lost. Endres-Soltmann in Thieme-Becker, XI, 510, attributes Domenico Fetti's *Adoration of the Shepherds* ("Nativity"), today in the Hermitage, Leningrad, to Lucrina, speculating that it is the painting observed by Cadioli in Sant'Orsola (Mary Endres-Soltmann, "Domenico Fetti," inaugural dissertation, Munich, 1914, 41, 57).

This is not possible since the painting is catalogued in the 1740 posthumous inventory of the Pierre Crozat Collection, no. 223 (Margret Stuffman, "Les tableaux de la collection de Pierre Crozat," *Gazette des beaux-arts,* LXXII, 1968, 67, no. 87, repr. 68). It is not possible to deduce what, if any, *Agony in the Garden* in Mantua in 1763 Cadioli could have thought to be the original from which Lucrina's work was copied.
27.
Cadioli, 76.
28.
D'Arco, *Delle arti,* II, 213, no. 21. Without attribution in the 1827 inventory, Accademia Virgiliana (ibid., 246, nos. 27-28). Listed as a work by Lucrina in Matteucci, *Le chiese Mantovane,* 373, note 1. Catalogued as Lucrina by Ozzòla, *La Galleria di Mantova,* 31, no. 231, fig. 164; 32, no. 240, fig. 165.
29.
Cadioli, 71-72. The *Magdalene* is first recorded in S. Martino in 1818, where it was paired with a St. Francis also attributed to Lucrina by Gaetano Susani, *Nuovo prospetto delle pitture, sculture ed architetture di Mantova,* Mantua, 1818, 53 (1831 edition, 57). The *St. Francis* is, in fact, a copy after Carlo Bonone's *St. Francis,* 1616, Mantua, Palazzo Ducale; pendant to a *St. Anthony,* Mantua,

of corporeal weight. Despite these differences, the similarity of the entire pictorial concept of *St. Barbara* to the work of Domenico is too close to be explained by a "retouching." It can only be assumed that Cadioli found it difficult, understandably, to reconcile the style of this work with other paintings he considered to be by Lucrina's hand (see biography).

Those works by Domenico to which the *St. Barbara* presents closest analogies are his *St. Catherine,* ca. 1615 (London, Hampton Court), from which St. Barbara's features and loosely waved hair seem ultimately derived, and his *St. Margaret,* ca. 1618 (Florence, Palazzo Pitti), in which a single full-length saint is shown in conjunction with an antique plinth carved in a two-tiered relief. In comparison to *St. Margaret* the scale of *St. Barbara* is aggrandized, the proportions changed, and the energy quotient reduced, while the placement of the saint's arm across her body and her extended right arm translate the active posture of St. Margaret into a stance of courtly grace. A *pentimento* in the *St. Margaret* reveals that her face was initially turned at the same angle as St. Barbara's. In both works the reliefs on the sculptured base show the martyrdom of the saint taking place on a platform raised above a pair of spectators occupying the lower tier.[43] The stone plinth in the *St. Barbara* is neatly and crisply carved, however, showing none of the effects of passing time that fancifully mark the similar monument in Fetti's work.

The elements of setting in the *St. Barbara* have been chosen to convey the spiritual precepts that governed her life. For example, the tower her father built to imprison her was planned with two windows, but Barbara insisted upon three in celebration of the Trinity, and these are clearly visible in the painting. After being tormented by her parent and subjected to various tortures and humiliations by the tribunals before which he brought her, she still refused to renounce her Christianity and was finally condemned to execution and beheaded by her own father. In conformity with Counter-Reformation ideals the greatest emphasis is placed upon her martyrdom, referred to in the relief and in the sword crossed by a martyr's palm at her foot. Lucrina has given unprecedented emphasis to those attributes signifying Barbara's defiance of her natural father and sacrifice of earthly life in favor of faith in her heavenly father and life eternal. The design of the sword is virtually identical with that appearing in Domenico Fetti's *Female Saint,* 1613, one of a series of six saints painted on slate, originally made for the convent of Sant'Orsola, now in the Palazzo Ducale, Mantua.

With its reference to the Trinity, the *St. Barbara* would have been a fitting companion for Viani's altarpiece of *SS. Margaret and Ursula in Glory with the Trinity.* Pairing the saint with a *Magdalene* reinforces the idea that both were exemplary "brides" of Christ. This choice of subject not only fully accords with the theme of the chapel of St. Margaret but with the iconographical program of the chapels of Sant'Orsola as a whole. The main axial chapels of the church of Sant'Orsola were dedicated to the three female saints with whom

Margherita Gonzaga felt her community of women to be most closely allied and under whose protection she placed her convent: her namesake St. Margaret; St. Ursula, who embarked upon the religious life with a group of devout female companions; and St. Clare, a woman of noble family who abandoned the world under the influence of St. Francis and became with him founder of the Order of Poor Clares. The religious community of Sant'Orsola, founded by Margherita Gonzaga in 1599, was affiliated with the third order of Franciscans, and the rule of St. Francis and the habit of St. Clare were adopted. Ludovico Carracci's *Martyrdom of Saint Ursula,* 1616 (now lost),[44] adorned the high altar of the church; Viani's altarpiece, as already noted, decorated the chapel of St. Margaret; and Carlo Bonone's *St. Clare Putting the Saracens to Flight,* 1614, Mantua, Palazzo Ducale, was commissioned for the chapel of St. Clare. Lucrina's *Magdalene* and *St. Barbara* further honor Margherita Gonzaga's partiality to female saints. St. Barbara was a singularly appropriate choice, for she was the titular saint of the palatine church of Mantua, where Margherita Gonzaga was buried in January 1618.[45]

St. Barbara, if accepted as a work by Lucrina Fetti, poses again the question of the relationship of her art to that of her brother. Closer to it in style, palette, and manner of execution than any work traditionally associated with her name, this picture provides a new touchstone for a much needed reassessment and reconstruction of her oeuvre.

Palazzo Ducale. Originally they were placed beneath his altarpiece *Sta Chiara and the Miracle of the Sacrament,* 1614, in Sant' Orsola, now also in the Palazzo Ducale (erroneously titled "Il Miracolo di San Gualberto"). The attribution of the *Magdalene* to Lucrina has not remained stable. It is attributed, along with the *St. Francis,* to Domenico Fetti by Arigi, *Mantova e sua Provincia,* 1859, 404. Perina, in Marani and Perina, III, no. 1, 470, refers to a *St. Jerome (sic)* and a *Magdalene* in S. Martino which, through a misreading of Susani, she includes among the works of the Mantuan painter Francesco Borgani. Between 1905 when the *Magdalene* is referred to as "St. Margaret" by Hemore Pescasio (*Guida di Mantova,* Mantua, 1905, 115), and 1965, when both compositions are again cited by Perina, the paintings disappear from all literature. This suggests that the present copy of the *Magdalene* may have been substituted sometime after 1905.
30.
A small copy (8⅗ x 11⅓ in.), painted on copper, is in Milan, the Collection Ing. Arch. Luigi Bonomi. A reduced version, showing the *Magdalene* in three-quarter length, Modena, private collection, has been attributed to Domenico Fetti by Roberto Longhi, "Un altra redazione del dipinto precedente," *Paragone,* IV, no. 41, 1953, 53, repr. pl. 32). A copy of the Modena version, slightly expanded on the right, is in S. Michele in Isola, Venice. A bust-length version, Venice, Collection

Conte Alessandro Zeno, has been attributed to Domenico Fetti by Nicola Ivanoff, "Una Maddalena di Domenico Fetti," *Paragone,* IV, no. 41, 1953, 51-52, pl. 31). Ivanoff and Longhi state that the versions published by them have been cut down from larger compositions. Possibly the Modena version is the painting originally attributed to Lucrina in Sant'Orsola, and the Conte Zeno version a later, more painterly copy executed for the church of S. Martino.
31.
Fetti's *Entombment,* Florence, Galleria Corsini, would seem to lie behind the figure of the *Magdalene,* to the parting of her hair over her shoulders.
32.
Rudolf Oldenbourg, *Domenico Feti,* Rome, 1921, 10. Endres-Soltmann, Thieme-Becker, XI, 510, has attributed other paintings by Domenico Fetti to Lucrina: *The Virgin in Glory,* Leningrad, Hermitage; *The Guardian Angel,* Paris, Louvre; *Six Saints,* Mantua, Palazzo Ducale. These are all by Domenico. *A Madonna and Child,* no. 412, Rome, Galleria Borghese, which she also attributes to Lucrina, has nothing to do with either Fetti. More recently, a *Madonna with SS. Carlo Borromeo and Luigi Gonzaga,* Collection Marchesa Giovanna D'Arco di Bagno, Mantua, has been tentatively catalogued as a work by Lucrina (Mons. Luigi Bosio, *Mostra Iconografica Aloisiana,* Città di Castiglione della Stiviere, 1968, 38, no. 18, fig. 19).

16

33.

See Wilkins, "Woman as Artist and Painter," 113, 115.

34.

Ibid., 111, 115.

35.

Donesmondi, *Istoria eccelsiastica,* II, 1616, 492-93.

36.

Guarini, *Breve naratione,* 73v.

37.

Ozzòla, *La Galleria di Mantova,* 26, no. 180, figs. 93, 94. C. Perina (Marani and Perina, III, no. 1, 483, note 13) remarks that Ozzòla misread the date and that the painting is dated 1619.

38.

Cadioli, 71-72.

39.

D'Arco, *Delle arti,* II, 214, nos. 29, 30.

40.

Ibid., 245-46.

41.

Susani, *Nuovo prospetto,* 53.

42.

Nota dei quadri esistenti nelle stanze dell' Accademia di Mantova, di ragione delle Nazione (last two words crossed out, substitution illegible), n.d., n.p. (Mantua, Accademia Virgiliana, Busta entitled *Vecchia Accademia Inventori degli oggetti e delle carte).*

43.

This motif in both the *St. Margaret* and *St. Barbara* was probably suggested by Ludovico Carracci's *Martyrdom of St. Margaret,* 1616, San Maurizio, Mantua. Annibale Carracci's *St. Margaret,* S. Caterina dei'Funari, Rome, showing the saint leaning against a stone plinth would seem to be the genesis for both compositions.

44.

This painting, sold in 1810 (Intra, *Il monastero di Santa Orsola,* 11), has not reappeared.

45.

In addition, St. Barbara had two namesakes in the fifteenth century, both beatified, of whom Margherita certainly knew and with whom she might have felt akin: Barbara of Bavaria who assumed the Franciscan habit and Barbara of Bergamo who instituted a community of virgins under the rule of St. Clare (for these saints see respectively Pietro Burchi and Rodolfo Tosa da Arenzano, in *Biblioteca Sanctorum,* Rome, 1962, II, 768).

Clara Peeters

Flemish, 1594 - after 1657(?)

Clara Peeters, daughter of Jan Peeters, was baptized on May 15, 1594, in Antwerp.[1] She signed and dated her first known work in 1608, her second in 1609, three more in 1611, and a further two in 1612. All are still-life paintings depicting a great variety of objects — vases of flowers, gilded goblets with delicately chased decoration, Venetian glasses, Delft dishes full of olives or other food, gold coins, rare shells, fish and shellfish, artichokes, grapes, baskets, pewter dishes, stoneware jugs, and knives with fancy handles. A signed work in the Ashmolean Museum, Oxford, can be dated after 1620. At least twenty-five more signed works are recorded as well as a few unsigned examples close to them in composition and technique.[2] On May 31, 1639, Clara married Hendrick Joossen in Antwerp.[3] A work whose present location is not known is said to be signed and dated 1654; another work, not recorded since 1930, is said to be dated 1657.[4] Her death certificate has not been traced. These few facts are all that is certainly known about Clara Peeters. She is said to have been in Amsterdam in 1612 and The Hague in 1617, but no documentary evidence supporting this statement of Bredius'[5] has ever been published. Some of her works suggest firsthand knowledge of contemporary developments in Haarlem, however, so she may well have visited Holland at some point.

Clara Peeters was an astonishingly precocious artist if she signed a work by the age of fourteen or fifteen. We do not know who trained her. There is no evidence that her father was an artist and her name never appears on the lists of apprentices or registered masters of the Antwerp painters' guild. Furthermore, her first works predate almost all known dated examples of Flemish still-life painting of the type she made.[6] Nevertheless the technical polish and compositional sophistication of her first works, seven of them made before she reached twenty, preclude the hypothesis that she was self-taught. She must have had access to first-class instruction in Antwerp, then still the artistic capital of the Netherlands and a city where fine detail and careful finish were stressed more than in Dutch centers like Haarlem or Utrecht. Perhaps Osias Beert, who was registered as an apprentice

in Antwerp in 1596 and became a master in 1602, and whose rare signed works are close to hers in type, introduced the "banquet piece" to Antwerp and to Clara Peeters, but since none of his works are dated, their relationship must remain speculative.[7]

At the time Peeters was learning to paint, there were no artists in Flanders making a living exclusively from the production of independent still-life paintings; indeed the genre hardly existed. Still-life elements in religious works and in portraits assumed greater importance in the late sixteenth century, especially in the work of Pieter Aertsen and his nephew, Joachim Beukelaer, who both made works in which the foreground is filled with heaps of vegetables, fruit, and other produce, and the subject — if there is one — appears as a vignette in the background.[8] From these *fruytmerckten* (literally "fruit markets") came still-life pictures of fruit alone, which are called *fruyktens* in early seventeenth-century Flemish inventories. At the same time pictures of flowers in vases, which in Flemish religious art of the two previous centuries had conveyed theological messages to an audience familiar with flower symbolism, began to be made for their own sake; they appear in early inventories as *bloempotten*. Clara Peeters included vases of flowers in several of her early still lives but rarely painted them alone.[9] The majority of her still lives belong to the categories now called "banquet pieces" or "breakfast pieces," that is, more or less luxurious displays of food, drink, and table settings.[10]

Fewer than ten pictures of flowers and fewer than five of food produced in the Netherlands can be securely dated before 1608, when Peeters painted her first recorded work.[11] Thus she would appear to be one of the originators of the genre. Even if she owed her basic compositional structure and some of her motifs to Beert, she immediately developed a range of special skills of her own. Beert was fascinated by the way light glistens on smooth, translucent surfaces like those of molded glass, wet blackberries, and freshly opened oysters. Peeters was also intrigued by the fall of light but she recorded

1.
Greindl, 37 and 136, note 40. Greindl (34-37 and 178-79) provides the fullest account of Peeters' career. Hairs (1965, 241-44 and 398) catalogs and discusses her flower pictures.
2.
A few more works attributed to Peeters have appeared in sales since Greindl and Hairs prepared their catalogs. The most important of these is a *Self-Portrait* (see note 12 below). A still life dated 1615 was sold by Lempertz, Cologne, on May 8, 1969. A small signed still life of outstanding quality went through Christie's on June 29, 1973 (a detail is illustrated in color in *Connaissance des Arts*, 225-173, 1970, 87). A pair of still lives attributed to her are in the Musée Mouton-Rothschild, Pauillac. Some of the works attributed to her appear to be copies. The whole situation is confused and badly needs the attention of a specialist who can prepare a proper catalog.
3.
Greindl, 136, note 40.
4.
Ibid., 179. A reproduction of the work supposedly dated 1657 can be found in N.R.A. Vroom, *De schilders van het monochrome banketje*, Amsterdam, 1945, 117, pl. 101.

5.
In Thieme-Becker, s.v.
6.
A number of artists with the surname Peeters are listed by Rombouts and Lerius in their study of the Guild of St. Luke, but none are known to be related to Clara. Women are rarely listed as apprentices or masters. At the time she was training, two daughters of artists are listed in 1605 (Rombouts and Lerius, I, 430, "Juana de la Hu" and "Cornelia Rombouts") and a female picture dealer is named in 1602 (ibid., 418, "Maria van Cleve, coomenscap doende met scilderye"). The only evidence that the guild had any contact with Clara Peeters is their hallmark on the back of one of her works (Bergström, 304, note 24).
7.
Benedict, and Hairs, 1951; Greindl, 149-50, provides a list of works and some additional illustrations.
8.
Some characteristic examples are illustrated by Sterling, figs. 31-32, and Bergström, 19-21.
9.
Hairs (1965, 398) lists one dated example in a Danish private collection and three signed examples, all either in private collections or known from sale records.

instead its reflections on metal — coins, gold chains, gilded decorated goblets, and pewter dishes that mirror the bread and pastries set on them. As if to mark this phenomenon as her specialty, she included her self-portrait in these reflections in several works, including those in Madrid and Karlsruhe (figs. 8-10, pp. 32-33), and in her *Self-Portrait*[12] showed herself seated at a table on which are displayed a gilded goblet and salver, coins and jewelry. She also included a vase of flowers, perhaps to publicize her abilities in the best-paid branch of still-life painting.[13]

Not all of Peeters' works depict rare, expensive objects and luxury foods. She also painted a group of works showing large cheeses stacked on top of each other; pewter and Delft dishes holding bread rolls, curls of butter, and pretzels; and stoneware jugs of wine or beer.[14] This type of still life featuring everyday items of food and drink was first developed in Haarlem by artists like Nicolaes Gillis and Floris van Dijck in the first decade of the seventeenth century and was to remain popular there in the form perfected by Pieter Claesz. and Willem Claesz. Heda. Flemish artists, inspired by the Rubensian vigor with which Frans Snyders infused a revived form of the market scenes begun by Aertsen, tended after 1620 or so to paint large, sumptuous displays of produce cascading across tables with cats, dogs, parrots, and even monkeys attracted to the feast. These undeniably decorative displays quickly supplanted the quiet, painstakingly executed images of Peeters, Beert, and Adriaensen. Beert died in 1624; Adriaensen managed to adapt his compositions to the new taste somewhat; but Peeters' later career is obscure. The fact that no still lives attributed to her appear in any published seventeenth-century Flemish inventories suggests that she may have lacked local patronage. Her marriage in 1639 at age forty-five in a time when most women were married before they reached twenty could even indicate that she was in financial difficulties.

Her meticulous delineation of form, her dark backgrounds and brownish monochromes, and her essentially symmetrical arrangements with the objects set on a shallow counter with little overlap would have seemed old-fashioned in both Flanders and Holland by 1630. Her simpler pictures of cheeses and bread may have been designed to appeal to Dutch tastes in the 1620s and 1630s, though the lack of firmly dated works after 1620 in accessible collections makes it hard at present to study this later phase of her career. Peeters' special gift for portraying elaborate goblets and salvers should have appealed to the same clients for whom Willem Claesz. Heda made his *pronkstilleven* ("showy still lives"), but there is no evidence at present that she made this kind of work after 1620. It is even possible that, like Louise Moillon, she gave up painting at one time but took it up again later in life for economic reasons.

While Peeters' later career remains for the moment vague, her important role in the formation of the banquet and breakfast piece in Antwerp at the beginning of the century has long been recognized.

Whether she influenced the Haarlem painters as well as being affected by them is hard to tell, for another Antwerp still-life painter, Hans van Essen, who was training at the same time as she must have been and became a master in 1609, moved to Amsterdam in 1611.[15] He is therefore a better-documented channel of influence than she is. Perhaps she helped to encourage a taste there for the display of more luxurious objects in their humbler breakfast pieces. These and other questions must wait for a longer study of her work, an undertaking now justified by the substantial number of pictures attributed to her and by her significant role in the creation of still life in Antwerp. Perhaps the biggest question of all is how such an exceptionally gifted artist, whose sex, to judge from the experience of many of her predecessors, attracted more rather than less attention to her, could have passed almost unnoticed by the major art patrons and critics of her day. The return to Antwerp of Rubens from Italy in 1609 and the artistic revolution caused by his abundantly energetic genius is certainly part of the story.

17.
Flowers in a Glass Vase, ca. 1615
Oil on panel
16⅝ x 12 in. (42.2 x 30.5 cm.)
Signed lower left: Clara . P .
Pasadena, Collection Mr. and Mrs. R. Stanton Avery
(See color plate, p. 72)

Although Peeters occasionally included a vase of flowers in her still-life compositions (see figs. 9, 10, p. 33) pure flower paintings by her are extremely rare.[16] One example in a Danish private collection is signed and dated 1612; a small signed panel of a vase of flowers belongs to a private collector in Belgium; another signed "Clara P." has not been seen since it was sold in Berlin in 1932. The example in our exhibition is therefore one of four recorded signed examples, only three of which can be traced today. The artist has arranged two roses, two tulips, a narcissus, anemones, pinks, and stock in an unusual glass vase decorated with a strange mask. A sprig of stock, a water drop, and a small mouse chewing petals appear next to the vase.

Independent flower paintings originated in Antwerp and remained a local specialty well into the seventeenth century. Among the first artists known for them was Jan Brueghel, the most gifted son of Pieter Bruegel the Elder, but Osias Beert also painted a few and we can assume that Peeters was familiar with their work. Both artists liked to fill their vases to overflowing with tulips, roses, and other expensive blooms arranged to hide the leaves and avoid overlap. Peeters' vases of flowers by contrast display a limited number of specimens whose leaves and stems play an important part in an arrangement of rhythmic flexibility. The stems curve toward us and away from us; the heads of the flowers rotate in space instead of lying flat in a pattern of lush blooms. The final effect of her flower paintings is pleasingly haphazard and natural, very different from the formal splendor of Jan Brueghel's spectacular displays.[17]

10.
Their origin and development are discussed in Greindl and Bergström. The term "breakfast piece" is an attempt to translate the Dutch word *ontbijt*, meaning a light meal taken at any time of day (Bergström, 303, note 1).
11.
The evidence is culled from the useful lists of works in Greindl and Hairs, 1965, to which can be added the one flower picture known by Gillis van Coninxloo, who died in 1607 (Bergström, pl. 43). The only earlier dated still-life paintings of food are Nicolaes Gillis' *Breakfast* of 1601 (Bergström, 98) and Jerome Francken's *Frugal Repast* of 1604 (Antwerp, Royal Museum). Gillis was active in Haarlem, where he is recorded between 1622 and 1632, but we do not know where he was born or trained. Francken's picture is one of several based on a composition that has been attributed to Pieter Bruegel the Elder and to Aertsen. As Sterling points out (46), the existence of several copies suggests that the original was regarded as a novelty.
12.
The *Self-Portrait* was sold from the J. Hanbury Martin Collection at Sotheby's on November 30, 1966, lot 120 (oil on panel, 14¾ by 19¾ in.). It was sold by the Hallsborough Gallery, London (see their advertisement in *Apollo,* xc, October 1969, p. xlvii) to a buyer of whom the gallery, now defunct, has no record. It is

hoped that the present owner of this important picture will reveal his or her identity and allow the work to be exhibited publicly.
13.
Greindl, 14-15, points out that flower pictures are much more highly valued in inventories than other forms of still life, even when painted by the same artist. Still lives fetched more, however, than landscapes in the first half of the seventeenth century, perhaps because of their novelty and relative scarcity.
14.
A good example of this kind of Peeters still life is reproduced by Gerson and Ter Kuile, pl. 149A (Wetzlar Collection, Amsterdam). A version or copy was with Galleria Lorenzelli, Bergamo, in 1971. What seems to be an even finer example was in the Westerman Collection in Amsterdam (Bergström, 107, pl. 97).
15.
Bergström, 108-9. He does not think that Peeters or Beert influenced the Haarlem breakfast piece.
16.
Hairs (1965, 398) lists all her still-life paintings that include flowers. Our painting appears there as a work sold by Galerie J. Charpentier in Paris in 1951 (June 1, lot 117).

18

18.

Still Life with Cheese, Bread, and Pretzels, ca. 1630
Oil on panel
18 x 25½ in. (45.7 x 64.8 cm.)
London, Thomas Agnew and Sons Ltd.

As explained in her biography, Peeters seems to have changed her style after 1620, moving from the elaborate, exquisitely finished compositions found in her first dated works to a plainer style employing the monochromatic schemes favored in Holland in the late 1620s and 1630s. Most of these later still lives feature a stack of cheeses of various kinds cut open to display the contrast between their porous interiors and smooth, hard rinds. A simple meal is implied by the addition of bread, butter, a stoneware jug of wine, a glass or two, and maybe a folded napkin. Sometimes she also added a few raisins and nuts. The example exhibited here is typical. The same glass appears in similar panels in the Westerman and Wetzlar collections as well as in a version of the latter recently with Galleria Lorenzelli in Bergamo.[18] The same jug is also found in the Wetzlar and Lorenzelli pictures. The finest of this group of four appears to be the Westerman still life, but this work is also one of high quality. The pretzels and bread rolls in the foreground are as carefully drawn and modeled as any similar passages in her famous group of still lives in the Prado (figs. 8, 9, pp. 32-33).

The disciplined austerity of this painting represents a dramatic aesthetic shift from her first works, which she had filled with objects that challenged her virtuosity. Though not richly colored, their palette was varied and attractive. Her later works reject every obvious means of appeal to the spectator. The objects shown are intrinsically humble and relatively simple to paint. There are fewer of them than in her earlier works and the color scheme is even more restricted than in the works of Dutch contemporaries such as Claesz. and Heda. The frequent repetition of a few basic motifs evidently dulled her responses, for the overall quality of her later works does not match that of her spectacular early phase. Nevertheless the best of them are as impressive in their own right and as personal in the context of contemporary still life as any in either Holland or Flanders.

17.
Jacob van Hulsdonck, who was Peeters' exact contemporary, also paints sparser flower arrangements than Jan Brueghel and Beert, but since only one of his works is dated (1617), it would be hard to prove that he influenced her rather than the reverse.
18.
See note 14 of her biography for references to published illustrations of these works.

20

21

Giovanna Garzoni
Italian, 1600-1670

The life of Giovanna Garzoni is not well documented. Even her place of birth is disputed, although most of the evidence points to Ascoli Piceno in the Marches.[1] When she was sixteen, she painted a *Holy Family* that was still in a local collection in 1830.[2] In 1625 she was in Venice where she painted a miniature portrait of a young man that is now in the collection of the Queen of Holland.[3] Between June 1630 and July 1631 she corresponded from Naples with Cassiano dal Pozzo in Rome.[4] These letters reveal that she had only recently arrived there from Rome where she had worked for Cassiano and for Donna Anna Colonna, the wife of Don Taddeo Barberini, prefect of Rome. In Naples she quickly attracted the attention of other powerful patrons, especially the Spanish viceroy, the duke of Alcalà. Pascoli tells us that she was famous for her miniatures in several Italian cities, but especially in Florence, "where she lived for a long time, and was so well liked by those gentlemen, and by the Grand Duke himself, that she sold her work for whatever price she wished. She became therefore quite rich and retired in her old age to Rome."[5] She had settled there by 1654, when she made a contribution to one of the annual feasts of the Accademia di San Luca, of which she may have been made a member as early as 1633.[6] She died in February 1670. She left all her possessions and a useful sum of money to the Academy on condition that they erect a monument to her in their church, SS. Luca e Martina; this they finally did in 1698.[7]

It has been suggested that Garzoni learned to paint in Florence, and in particular that she came under the influence there of Jacopo Ligozzi (1547-1627).[8] There is no proof of this except the stylistic similarity between their studies of plants and animals in the Pitti. Even if she did continue her training in Florence after leaving Ascoli, she can hardly have produced her extensive recorded production for the Medici before she went to Venice in 1625 and to Rome and Naples after that. She must, as Pascoli says, have returned to Florence for a longer visit after becoming famous elsewhere. No doubt the answer to these and other questions could be found in the archives of Ascoli, Florence, and Rome.

Her contemporary reputation was as a miniature painter, but with the exception of the portrait of 1625 mentioned above, none of her known works are miniatures as the term is now understood. It was used then to describe all works executed in watercolor on vellum, which was her preferred medium.[9] In addition to the portraits and studies of plants and animals mentioned in early sources, there are religious works referred to in her letters. One of these, a *St. John* made for Cassiano, was taken instead by the duke of Alcalà despite her protests.[10] The largest group of her works known today is in the Palazzo Pitti, Florence.[11] The Accademia di San Luca in Rome owns an album of twenty-two studies of insects, fruit, and flowers bequeathed to them by the artist.[12] There are four studies by her in Madrid and one of fruit and birds in Cleveland (cat. no. 21).[13] Undoubtedly other works of hers are currently passing under other names.[14]

Her two portraits in the Pitti are technically dazzling but convey no sense of the sitter's personality. Her beautiful studies of plants, elegant in composition, subtle in color, are among the finest of such botanical studies made in the seventeenth century. It would be interesting to know if word of her talents ever reached Maria Sibylla Merian, who was to blend art and science even more extensively in her adventurous career.

1.
A Medici inventory gives her birthplace as Lucca (Naples, 1964, 27), but her funerary inscription (see note 7) says that she came from Ascoli. It is significant also that two artists who came from the same area, Carlo Maratta and Giuseppe Ghezzi, concerned themselves with the erection of her memorial, Maratta providing the portrait and Ghezzi the inscription. In a letter of July 20, 1630, she reports that "... mio padre stia bene in Ancona," further evidence of family connections in that region rather than Tuscany (Bottari and Ticozzi, I, 239).
2.
Carboni, 203-4. It is her only recorded oil painting and suggests that she began her training in her home town.
3.
Colding, 114 and 184, note 91.
4.
Bottari and Ticozzi, I, 238-42. She was not happy in Naples however; by April 1631 she was asking Cassiano to find her work in Rome. She added, "Il mio desiderio è di vivere e morire a Roma."
5.
Pascoli, II, 451.

6.
There are many references to her in the archives of the Accademia di San Luca. She contributed to the Feast of St. Luke (October 18) in 1654, 1655, 1656, 1666, 1667, and 1669 (vol. 42a, f. 40, 43, 48, 73, 77 verso, and 82). It was the custom to bring cakes (*pane di zuccaro*) to members who were ill; she was treated to this luxury in October 1656, again in September 1669, and in January and February 1670 (vol. 42a, f. 149 verso and under dates recorded). She appears on one list of Academicians supposedly created in April 1633 (vol. 69, fasc. 303) but the list may not be reliable. Since she was not elected in the 1650s after her return to Rome, we must presume that she was admitted earlier under the more informal procedures used in the 1620s and 1630s.
7.
She began negotiating for a place in the church in August 1659; the matter was settled by November 26, 1662 (vol. 43, f. 123 verso and 139). Her will, made on June 3, 1666, was opened on February 15, 1670 (the dates given by K. Noehles, *La Chiesa dei SS. Luca e Martina*, Rome, 1970, 116, note 294, are wrong), but the monument was not set up until 1698. It was designed by Mattia de' Rossi, one of Bernini's favorite assistants. Noehles publishes the text of the inscription on page 369.

19.
Dish of Broad Beans
Tempera on parchment
9¾ x 13½ in. (24.8 x 34.3 cm.)
Florence, Palazzo Pitti (1890-4765)
(See color plate, p. 73)
(For comments, see next entry.)

20.
Dish of Grapes with Pears and a Snail
Tempera on parchment
9¾ x 13½ in. (24.8 x 34.3 cm.)
Florence, Palazzo Pitti (1890-4768)

The identification of a group of studies of fruit, vegetables, and flowers as the work of Garzoni we owe to Mina Gregori, who noticed the connection between an entry in a Medici inventory of 1692 and four octagonal pictures of flowers and fruit in the Uffizi, making it possible to attribute other similar studies in the Uffizi to Garzoni.[15] In composition these works are extremely simple. They consist of one type of plant set on a dish or arranged in a vase which she sets in the center of the page on a vaguely defined uneven surface. She adds a few contrasting species — a sprig of hyacinth to a vase of tulips; jasmine blossoms and a few small pears next to a dish of plump, ripe figs; a small pimply gherkin beside smooth, round peaches; and a pink beside the dish of beans. Her selections deliberately contrast or complement textures and shapes, nowhere more obviously than in her picture of tulips in an Oriental vase in which the single pear echoes the shape of the vase standing next to it.[16]

These paintings are not really still lives but rather a blend of still-life and scientific drawing that goes back ultimately to Leonardo and Dürer. Her immediate source of inspiration was probably the work of Ligozzi, whether she saw it as a young woman or encountered it only when she settled in Florence later.[17] It is not surprising that such paintings were made in seicento Florence. The scientific interests of Grand Duke Ferdinand II de'Medici (1610-1670) and of his brother, Cardinal Leopoldo de'Medici (1617-1670), are well known. The former was one of Galileo's friends and protectors, the latter founded the Accademia del Cimento in 1657 to encourage scientific research. The cardinal's art collection also included works by Dutch artists like Otto Marseus van Schriek, whose landscape settings contain a compendium of exotic snakes, butterflies, and plants.[18] It is far more probable that they supported and patronized Garzoni in the 1630s and 1640s than that she worked for other members of the Medici family in the early 1620s, as is usually said.[19] Cosimo II de'Medici died in 1621 at the early age of thirty-one, leaving as heir the eleven-year-old Ferdinand. There was therefore a hiatus in Medici art patronage until Ferdinand and his brothers reached maturity. Additional evidence that this later generation of Medici was responsible for Garzoni's work in Florence is the presence of her works in an inventory of the collection of Vittoria della Rovere, the wife of Ferdinand II.[20] Further research might even reveal a role played as a patron by Vittoria della Rovere, a woman always dismissed in the literature as a bigot interested primarily in religion and pious works.

The simple, symmetrical compositions of Garzoni's beautiful studies explain why they were associated with an early rather than a mature phase of her career. While accurate representation of the species was important to her patrons, Garzoni, to judge by her choice of subject matter, was not simply cataloguing varieties of fruit and flowers, as Bartolomeo del Bimbo was to do later.[21] She followed some still-life traditions in depicting either rare and expensive plants — the tulips, for example — or edible delicacies. Fresh raw *fave* or broad beans are a great favorite in Italy still; the figs, peaches, plums, pears, and grapes are all displayed in peak condition.

Her technique can be seen easily in these works. Faint contour lines are filled in with color laid on in tiny parallel strokes or in stippled strokes that give many of her surfaces a characteristic speckled appearance like that of a bird's egg. Her drawing is assured and her arrangement of the fruit and flowers sophisticated and far more complex than appears at first sight. She creates a feeling of concentrated mass that differentiates her work from that of predecessors like Ligozzi and Balthasar van der Ast.[22] As an artist, she chose to work within strict limits; in her chosen specialty she was nevertheless extremely successful. While we know enough now to appreciate her considerable reputation in the seventeenth century, the full extent of her achievement still awaits proper study. The rich archival material in Rome and Florence and the considerable group of works now identified will make this a rewarding undertaking.

21.
Still Life with Birds and Fruit, ca. 1640
Watercolor on parchment
10⅛ x 16⅜ in. (25.1 x 41.6 cm.)
The Cleveland Museum of Art
Bequest of Mrs. Elma M. Schniewind, in memory of her parents, Mr. and Mrs. Frank Geib

Until Mina Gregori reconstructed the artistic personality of Giovanna Garzoni in 1964, this watercolor was thought to be by Jacopo Ligozzi. As Gregori noted, the technique used here is identical to that found in Garzoni's well-documented group of studies in the Palazzo Pitti, down to the characteristic dotting of the background areas. While Ligozzi always painted one elegant specimen Garzoni combined several, composing them within a setting. This particular sheet allows us to appreciate her skill at drawing animals as well as plants, especially the goldfinches seen from three different viewpoints. The color scheme is pleasantly subdued but has perhaps been altered by some fading of the greens used for foliage.

8.
Naples, 1964, 27.
9.
Maratta's portrait of Garzoni in the Pinacoteca Comunale of Ascoli shows her holding a small portrait (C. Mariotti, *Ascoli Piceno*, Bergamo, 1928, 130). A seventeenth-century collection in Florence was said to have many pictures by her, "si di fiori come di frutti . . . quali sono miniature" (F. Bocchi and G. Cinelli, *Le bellezze della città di Firenze*, Florence, 1677, 503). For another similar description, see Naples, 1964, no. 17.
10.
Bottari and Ticozzi, I, 242.
11.
For this group, see Naples, 1964, 27-28, and the entries below.
12.
The album is mentioned by F. Noack in Thieme-Becker (XIII, 223). I am grateful to Dr. Gaetana Scano, secretary of the Academy, for answering my queries about the album and Garzoni's will.
13.
The four sheets in Madrid (Biblioteca Nacional, nos. 7924-7927) are probably from her Neapolitan period (see note 10). A *Portrait of Amadeo I of Savoy* attributed to Garzoni was with Gallery Lasson, London, in 1966 (panel, 22⅝ x 17⁹/₁₆ in.).
14.
Two still lives of fruit with a sugar caster painted on vellum went through Christie's on July 10, 1973 (lot 60), as Dutch school. They are close to Garzoni's documented work in the Pitti.
15.
Naples, 1964, nos. 12 and 13. All twenty-six works by Garzoni are now in the Palazzo Pitti in a new display arrangement. Dr. Marco Chiarini, the director, to whom I am indebted for information about these works, informs me that one of the group, a study of a lap dog, is signed.
16.
Mitchell, 1973, pl. 161. Three more are illustrated in the catalog cited in note 15.
17.
On Ligozzi, see Mina Bacci, "Jacopo Ligozzi e la sua posizione nella pittura fiorentina," *Proporzioni*, IV, 1963, 53. Ligozzi's studies belong to an early phase of his career; one is dated 1587.
18.
Florence, Palazzo Pitti, *Artisti alla Corte Granducale*, catalog by M. Chiarini, 1969, 31, 34, and 47-50.

Judith Leyster
Dutch, 1609-1660

Judith Leyster is an exception to the rule that women artists are the daughters of artists, for her father was a brewer. She was exceptional too in a century when Dutch artists tended to specialize and when Dutch women tended to paint still lives, for she painted genre subjects and portraits as well as still lives. She conforms to one unfortunate pattern among women artists, however, in that her productivity declined markedly after her marriage.

She was born in Haarlem on July 28, 1609.[1] Her father, Jan Willemsz., had taken the name of his brewery, the *Ley-ster(re)* ("lodestar"), as his own. By 1626-27, Judith was sufficiently well known as a painter to be mentioned briefly in a book praising her birthplace.[2] The following year her parents moved the family to Vreeland, near Utrecht, but by September 1629 they had moved back near Haarlem again. We know that by 1631 she was friendly with Frans Hals (1580/85-1666) because she witnessed the baptism of one of his children. She was a member of the Haarlem guild of painters by 1633 and two years later had three male pupils. When Hals lured one of them to his studio she sued him for the money he owed her as a result and won her case. On June 1, 1636, she married a fellow artist, Jan Meinse Molenaer (1610-1668), with whom she later had three children. They moved to Amsterdam the following year, presumably hoping to do better business in the prosperous capital. They remained there eleven years; Jan Lievens, a Rembrandt pupil, boarded with them in 1644. They moved to Heemstede, now a suburb of Amsterdam, in 1648, and she died there on February 10, 1660, only fifty years old.

Eighty-three years ago the literature on Judith Leyster was nonexistent. Her name first reappeared in a blaze of publicity in 1893, when a work that the Louvre had just acquired as a Frans Hals turned out to be a signed Judith Leyster.[3] Thus she emerged in the shadow of a great and famous Dutch artist. Her documented connections with Hals helped art historians to dismiss her as an imitator and her true artistic personality became blurred by the copies after Hals attributed to her.[4] She is, as we are slowly discovering, a distinct artistic person-

19.
The idea that she was in Florence before 1630 goes back to Carboni, 204.
20.
Naples, 1964, 28.
21.
Detroit, 1974, nos. 105-6.
22.
See, for example, Ast's famous study of fruit, insects, and shells in the British Museum of around 1625 (Jan Gerrit van Gelder, *Dutch Drawings and Prints*, New York, 1959, pl. 31).

1.
In order to avoid attaching a footnote to each sentence in this paragraph, the published sources of this documentary information are given here together: A. van der Willigen, *Les artistes de Harlem*, Haarlem, 1927, 140; Hofstede de Groot, 1893, 192; A. Bredius, *Quellenstudien zur hollandischen Kunstegeschichte: Kunstler Inventare*, The Hague, 1915, 9; Harms, 90, 93, and 94; Elisabeth Neurdenburg, "Judith Leyster," *Oud-Holland*, XLVI, 1929, 28; Wijnman, 63.
2.
Samuel Ampzing, *Beschrijvinge ende lof der stadt Haerlem*, Haarlem, 1628. In 1648 she was again praised in print by Theodore Schrevel, who called her "a leading star in art," a complimentary pun (see Hofstede de Groot, 1893, 192). She is not mentioned in two later compilations about Dutch artists, Cornelis de Bie's *Het gulden cabinet* (Antwerp, 1661) and Arnold Houbraken's *Grosse Schouburgh der niederlandischen Maler und Malerinnen* (Vienna, 1880), although both authors mention several women artists.
3.
See Hofstede de Groot, 1893.
4.
Slive, III, 13 (no. 19); 21 (no. 31); 136-37 (D 24-1); L 3-3; and D 26. The key work for this question is *Two Children Playing with a Cat* (117 and fig. 75), which is said

ality, more versatile than Hals, who made her own contribution to Dutch seventeenth-century painting. After Hofstede de Groot's discoveries of 1893, Juliane Harms made the first serious contribution to our understanding of Leyster in a series of articles published in 1927.[5] Little has appeared since, but a recent master's thesis by Frima Fox Hofrichter clearly establishes that many of Harms' attributions are no longer acceptable and that a great deal of work remains to be done on Leyster.[6]

Haarlem was the town of Frans Hals and many other masters who made attractive small landscapes and genre pictures. Utrecht, near which Leyster lived for a year, had a large Catholic population and supported a school of artists, many of whom had visited Italy, knew Caravaggio's work, and practiced a tenebrist style, painting religious as well as genre subjects with larger figures than was usual in Haarlem. Leyster absorbed ideas from both schools. A number of her early works use candlelight and strong chiaroscuro effects, for example *The Boy with a Wineglass* (Karlsruhe, Staatliche Kunsthalle) and *The Gay Cavaliers* (cat. no. 22), and throughout her career she remained fascinated by the fall of light under different conditions. Her genre subjects can be related to Haarlem traditions but her taste for large figures alone or in small groups instead of the larger groups of small figures preferred in Haarlem can be linked with the Utrecht school as well as with Hals. She obviously admired and studied Hals' extraordinary brushwork and occasionally imitated it quite successfully, but she usually preferred a more controlled, less flamboyant paint surface than his. Virtuoso technique is part of the content of Hals' pictures; Leyster is more concerned with compositional refinements, with the fall of light, and with the psychological interactions of the people she portrays.

Leyster's *Merry Drinker* of 1629 (Amsterdam, Rijksmuseum; on loan to the Frans Hals Museum, Haarlem) raises the issue of her relationship to Hals with particular clarity because her laughing, ruddy-cheeked drinker who invites us to share his pleasure in a beer and a smoke is clearly inspired by works of Hals such as *The Jolly Drinker* (Amsterdam, Rijksmuseum) of 1628-30.[7] There are many differences, however, despite the close similarity of the subject. Hals typically ignores the setting while Leyster includes a table that extends into our space and even allows us to imagine ourselves seated at it. Hals' drinker faces us almost frontally, extending both hands, one to gesture, one to offer us the sparkling illusion of a glass. Leyster's figure seems to pivot on his elbow in the center of the picture as he looks out at us, raises his tankard, lowers the plume of his hat, and smiles. The resulting composition has a complex interlock of curves and diagonals that suggests both space and movement with elegant efficiency. Such compositional subtleties are typical of Leyster, but Hals' single-figure compositions tend to be simple. Her subjects often smile at us, gesture toward us, and invite us to share their life but do so less boisterously than those of Hals.

Perhaps Leyster's most original works are her small domestic genre

scenes. One of these, *The Proposition* (cat. no. 23), is discussed elsewhere; in others she shows mothers combing their children's hair and women sewing by the fireside while their children play beside them.[8] The subject of women at work in the home did not become popular in Holland until the 1650s when a Rembrandt follower, Nicolaes Maes, and a Delft artist, Pieter de Hooch, began to paint women preparing food, cleaning house, and minding children.[9] That such subjects emerged at all is of great interest and deserves more thoughtful analysis than it has received so far. The phenomenon implies a greater respect for the traditional domestic roles of women in Holland than elsewhere in seventeenth-century Europe, even if the pictures are as idealized in their way as modern advertisements showing women with clean, smiling babies and gleaming kitchen floors. That Leyster was the first to paint such themes cannot be proved but she conveys greater sympathy for the daily lives of women and their social situation than do the men in her circle who on occasion also turned to similar subjects.[10]

Most of Leyster's dated works belong to the years 1629 to 1635. Her domestic responsibilities may have handicapped her later career, for only two illustrations in a tulip book of 1643 and a disappointing portrait of 1652 are known to have been made after her marriage. It has also been suggested that she collaborated with her husband, who was principally a genre painter. The ten works by Leyster that appear in the inventory made of her husband's possessions after his death include a flower piece and several pictures of birds, which suggests that she might have switched to painting still lives in order to avoid competing directly with him. Her one known still-life painting could date to this later phase.[11]

It is a commonplace of art history that artists are influenced by other artists and a commonplace of criticism of women artists that they are dismissed as without interest once the influence of their male contemporaries has been identified in their work. Leyster absorbed ideas from many artists besides Hals and never imitated him directly. She was a versatile and ambitious painter who excelled in every area in which she worked. Yet until her career has been studied fully and the copies and imitations weeded out, her artistic relationships with Hals and her husband clarified, and the influence of her work on later Dutch artists considered, we will not be able to evaluate her achievements. All that is certain at present is that she is more than "the most clever painter of her sex in seventeenth-century Holland."[12]

22.
The Gay Cavaliers (The Last Drop), ca. 1628-29
Oil on canvas
35⅛ x 29 in. (89.2 x 73.7 cm.)
Inscribed with the artist's monogram on the tankard
Philadelphia, John G. Johnson Collection

Scenes of men, often with a few female companions or servants, carousing in taverns, drinking heavily, and yielding to the intoxicating pleasures of that new vice, tobacco smoke, were already popular

---

to have Leyster's monogram. In no other signed work does she imitate Hals' brushwork so slavishly and carelessly. I am not at present convinced by Slive's attributions to Leyster with the exception of her *Self-Portrait* (see below).
5.
See Leyster bibliography. The articles are based on Harms' doctoral dissertation of 1926 at the University of Frankfurt.
6.
See Leyster bibliography. The author is now writing her doctoral dissertation on Leyster at Rutgers University.
7.
Slive, III, cat. no. 63 and pl. 105-7.
8.
Dublin, National Gallery of Ireland; Adolph Schloss Collection, Paris (present location unknown); G. Stein Collection, Paris, 1937 (present location unknown).
9.
For example, Maes' *Woman Scraping Parsnips* and *The Idle Servant*, both of 1655, in the National Gallery, London, and Pieter de Hooch's *Woman and Child in a Court* of 1658 in the same collection (Rosenberg, Slive, and Ter Kuile, 1966, pl. 101; see also pl. 100 A and B, 102 and 103).

10.
Compare Dirck Hals' *Household Scene* (Lille, Palais des Beaux-Arts) with Leyster's *Mother Sewing by the Fireside* (Dublin, National Gallery of Ireland).
11.
Harms, pl. 20 (currently with the Brod Gallery, London).
12.
Slive, 1970-74, I, 8.

22

in Holland when Leyster painted this picture in the late 1620s. However, Leyster has chosen a larger format and portrayed fewer figures than was usual for this type of composition and has further emphasized the figures by making the setting almost non-existent. The stress on the human figure and the use of candlelight illumination suggest, as Hofrichter pointed out recently, that this is an early canvas influenced by the work of the Utrecht Caravaggisti, which the artist saw in 1628.[13] A companion piece in a private collection shows three men laughing while one fiddles and another holds a jug of beer behind his back.[14] In it the boundaries of the room are defined and a family peers through a doorway on the left, sharing in the fun. Both works are notable for the emphasis on figures that appeal directly to the spectator, another characteristic of genre works of the school of Caravaggio and another contrast with the typical Dutch "merry company" scenes, where the figures mostly communicate with each other rather than with us.

Although *The Proposition* of 1631 (cat. no. 23) proves that Leyster's use of candlelight illumination continued beyond her first contact with the Utrecht school, only a small proportion of her known works use artificial lighting. Of these, *The Boy with a Wineglass* (Karlsruhe, Staatliche Kunsthalle), which in the past has been attributed to Gerrit van Honthorst, is her most obviously Caravaggesque exercise and hence is probably one of her first works. In *The Gay Cavaliers* and in *The Proposition*, she synthesizes trends current in Utrecht and Haarlem to achieve a more personal result, with much emphasis on the human dialogue between her characters. She was to explore these ideas with even greater sophistication in later works. Her *Self-Portrait* (ca. 1635, Washington, D.C., National Gallery), shows the artist working on a painting of carousing youths similar to *The Gay Cavaliers;* she turns to study our reaction to the half-finished canvas. The work generally acknowledged to be her masterpiece, the *Boy Playing the Flute* (ca. 1635, Stockholm, Nationalmuseum), is more introspective and meditative. Along with a design of great formal sophistication, this work features a marvelously realized play of light and shade across a variety of shapes and textures. The two early works in this exhibition show Leyster laying the foundations for these later achievements.

23.
The Proposition, 1631
Oil on panel
11¹¹⁄₁₆ x 9½ in. (30.9 x 24.2 cm.)
Inscribed lower left with the artist's monogram JLS* and the date 1631
The Hague, The Mauritshuis (564)
(See color plate, p. 74)

The most beautiful and most original of Leyster's small genre pictures, *The Proposition* was the subject of a recent article by Frima Fox Hofrichter in which the imagery is discussed in detail.[15] While paintings and prints showing men making indecent proposals to women were common in the Low Countries in the sixteenth and seventeenth centuries, a work portraying a woman who has clearly not invited

13.
Hofrichter, cat. no. L3.
14.
The Happy Gathering, last recorded in the Von der Honert Collection, Blaricum, Holland, in 1940 (see Harms, 148 and 237).
15.
Hofrichter, 1975.

such an invitation and refuses to accept it is unique.[16] The woman shown here is not a whore. She is a housewife engaged in a domestic chore, and her intense concentration on her sewing as she tries to ignore the man who touches her arm and extends a palm full of coins will instantly engage the sympathy of any woman who has ever been similarly approached by a man who stubbornly refused to believe that his attentions were unwelcome. The contrast with contemporary treatments of this theme by Utrecht and Haarlem artists could hardly be greater. Dirck van Baburen's *The Procuress* (Boston, Museum of Fine Arts) of 1622 is a well-known example of the usual coarse humor characterizing such subjects.[17] The young woman grins at her leering suitor, her plump breasts brimming out of her dress, while the procuress on the right demands payment. The "merry company" pictures of Dirck Hals make equally explicit the willingness of the women to participate by showing embracing couples, lifted skirts, and dishes of oysters, a supposed aphrodisiac.[18] The tone of Leyster's picture is in complete opposition to these boisterously vulgar entertainments. As several scholars have observed, her interpretation looks forward to the quieter, more refined depictions of sexual encounters painted in the 1650s and 1660s by artists like Gabriel Metsu and Gerard Terborch, although in these too, as Hofrichter makes clear, there are still numerous indications that the women are participating willingly.[19] Leyster's *Proposition* is a uniquely personal interpretation with feminist overtones that completely escaped earlier critics, who labeled it *The Tempting Offer.*

24

26

16.
A picture by Dirck van Baburen of 1623 (Würzburg, Residenz) shows an unwilling prostitute with a soldier and procuress pressing their claims, but it is clear that the refusal will be withdrawn when the price is right (Hofrichter, 1975, note 7).
17.
Hofrichter, 1975, fig. 4; Cleveland Museum of Art, 1971, no. 1.
18.
A Party of Young Men and Women at Table, London, National Gallery, 1626, and *A Merry Company,* drawing, Haarlem, Teylers Museum (no. 43 in *Dutch Genre Drawings of the Seventeenth Century,* catalog by Peter Schatborn, International Exhibitions Foundation, 1972).
19.
Gabriel Metsu's *An Offer of Wine* (Vienna, Kunsthistorisches Museum, ca. 1650; Hofrichter, 1975, fig. 7) seems directly modeled on Leyster's picture, as Lawrence Gowing first noted (*Vermeer,* London, 1952, 115).

Louise Moillon
French, 1610-1696

Louise Moillon was one of seven children born in Paris to Nicolas Moillon (1555-1619), a Protestant painter and picture dealer, and Marie Gilbert, the daughter of a goldsmith. Presumably Louise received her first training from her father. Within a year of his death, her mother married François Garnier, also a painter and picture dealer. It is assumed that Moillon's new stepfather was the main formative influence on her style, although his two known dated works, of 1637 and 1644, postdate most of hers and are less refined technically. When her mother died in 1630, an inventory made of her possessions included thirteen finished still-life paintings by Louise Moillon as well as some unfinished works by her. The inventory stated furthermore that the profits from the sale of these works were to be shared equally between her and Garnier, in conformity with an agreement made on June 30, 1620, that is a few months after the death of her father but before the remarriage of her mother. Thus we know that by the time Louise was ten or eleven, she had revealed sufficient talent for her prospective stepfather to make a business arrangement concerning her future production. Her earliest known work is a still life of peaches in a private collection in Paris;[1] her last dated work is a still life of peaches and grapes in the Museum of Strasbourg dated 1682.[2] More than thirty works, nineteen of them signed and dated, are known at present, the majority in French private collections.[3] The only example in an American public collection is the *Basket of Fruit with a Bunch of Asparagus* of 1630 in the Art Institute of Chicago.[4]

Most of Moillon's dated works were produced before 1642, although she lived for another fifty-four years, and apparently resumed her career in the 1670s and '80s. In November 1640 she married a Calvinist wood merchant, Etienne Girardot, by whom she had at least three children. The obvious conclusion is that her domestic responsibilities interrupted her artistic career, although such a course of events was by no means inevitable, as Lavinia Fontana, Marguerite Bahuche, and Rachel Ruysch demonstrated. Moillon's failure to seek admission to the Académie Royale after it opened in 1648 or even later in the 1660s, when her brother Isaac and several women still-life painters were admitted, also suggests that she was inactive after her marriage. We know little about her later life except that she suffered from the persecution of the Protestant community that preceded the revocation of the Edict of Nantes in 1685. She may in fact have resumed her career because of financial difficulties. Two of her children left France for England, a third was converted to Catholicism under pressure.[5] She herself must have been converted, if only to avoid imprisonment and confiscation of her property, for she was given a Catholic burial when she died alone in Paris in 1696.

Louise Moillon is one of the finest still-life painters of the first half of the seventeenth century in France. Like her best-known contemporaries working in this genre——Lubin Baugin, Sébastien Stosskopff, Jean Picart, and Pierre Dubois——she established herself as a specialist in certain kinds of still life, principally studies of fruit, though she did occasionally paint vegetables. Still-life painting originated in the Low Countries with artists like Ambrosius Bosschaert and Jacob van Hulsdonck.[6] A few French examples earlier than hers are known,[7] but until Pierre Dupuis came to maturity in the 1650s, there was no one to rival her exquisitely polished and refined arrangements of grapes, plums, apricots, peaches, cherries, nectarines, strawberries, and gooseberries. She was moreover the only French artist before 1650 who successfully combined still life with the human figure (cat. no. 24). It is a silent tribute to the quality of her work that more of her paintings survive than those of any other French still-life painter active before Jean Baptiste Monnoyer (1634-1699).

Her work and that of her contemporaries is often called archaic, a term perhaps justified when their paintings are compared with contemporary Flemish and Dutch still lives. Moillon, Baugin, Stosskopff, and Linard were, it must be remembered, the pioneers of a new genre in France which was never as popular there as it was in the Low Countries. It was to suffer from its classification as a debased category of art after the founding of the Académie Royale in 1648, for the Academy ranked still life far below history and religious composi-

---

1.
Faré, 1962, ii, pl. 37, and Faré, 1974, 52. *The Fruit Seller* (Faré, 1974, 48-49) is also dated 1629. It is discussed below (cat. no. 24, note 9).
2.
Faré, 1962, ii, 63.
3.
The best discussions of Moillon's career and work are those of Wilhelm and Faré, 1962, i, 41-43 and 98-100. See also Faré, 1974, 48ff. Some of the works these authors mention and illustrate have new locations. Thus Faré, 1974, 54, is now in the Norton Simon Collection, as is the *Still Life of Curaçao Oranges* he illustrates (60, no. 5). The splendid *Still Life with Peaches, Asparagus, Artichokes and Strawberries* (Faré, 1974, 65) is erroneously said to be with Knoedler and Co., New York, who inform me that it never has been in their possession. The superb *Still Life with Grapes, Melons, Squashes and Apples* of 1637 (Faré, 1974, 67) is no longer at the Art Institute of Chicago but was sold and now belongs to a private collector in Bergamo, Italy. Munsterberg (32, lower pl.) illustrates a Moillon that recently went from Parke-Bernet, New York, to Agnew's, London, and has been sold by them to a private collector.

4.
Repr. in color in Faré, 1974, 55. The work listed by Faré, 1962, ii, pl. 53, as with Knoedler and Co., New York, is now at the Grand Rapids Art Museum, Michigan. It is not signed and its condition makes judgment difficult at present but it seems to be a genuine Moillon also.
5.
Faré, 1962, i, 42ff. He cites O. Douen, "Les Girardot à l'époque de la Révocation," *Bulletin historique et littéraire de la Société de l'Histoire du Protestantisme Française,* 3rd series, ix, vol. 39, 1890, 449-64. Douen quotes from a letter of Moillon's daughter written in 1686: "celle que ma mère nous a écrite à mon frère et à moi . . . nous a fait répandre bien des larmes. Dieu la veuille consoler et nous aussi, et nous fasse la grace de nous revoir un jour" (that which my mother has written to my brother and myself . . . has made us shed many tears. May God console her, and us as well, and make it possible for us to see each other again one day). Douen reports that Etienne Girardot died in 1648 but Faré records him present at the funeral of Moillon's brother Isaac in 1673. At all events, her husband was not present at her funeral.
6.
E. Greindl, *Les peintres flamands de nature morte au XVIIe siècle,* Brussels, 1956,

tions and even portraiture. No French artist before 1650 could challenge the sumptuous displays of glistening fish, ripe fruit and vegetables, gilded salvers, and dead game painted by Frans Snyders and Jan Fyt in Flanders, nor even the muted elegance of Pieter Claesz. and Willem Heda in Holland. Yet even if the compositions of early French still life are less sophisticated than those of their Flemish and Dutch peers, they are nevertheless works of great beauty. They project in fact a different aesthetic — quieter, more restrained, more reserved — which many viewers today prefer to the Rubensian rhetoric of Flanders and find as satisfying as Dutch still life of the same period. Among this group of artists, Moillon's works hold a high place.[8]

24.
At the Greengrocer, 1630
Oil on canvas
47¼ x 65 in. (120 x 165 cm.)
Dated lower left: 1630
Paris, Musée National du Louvre (RF 1955-19)

At the Greengrocer shows an elegantly dressed customer considering the purchase of some apricots from a wicker basket presented to her by a young woman. To the left of the shopper is a basket filled with plums, peaches, grapes, and strawberries, presumably the fruit she has already chosen. Ranged along the counter are grapes, plums, apples, melons, cucumbers, artichokes, a cabbage, and a large marrow; behind it is a cat. A shelf to the upper right holds more grapes, some small loaves of bread or pastries, and another basket.

This picture is one of four surviving examples by Moillon that include figures with the still lives for which she is best known.[9] In it she presents many of the subjects in her repertory. The wicker baskets of mixed fruit and of apricots and the bowl of plums are especially characteristic; vegetables rarely appear in her independent still lives. The situation is surely also intended to be read as a parallel to that of the artist herself with a patron deciding what kind of still life to buy.

Large pictures with lavish displays of fresh garden produce being sold to fashionable customers were an established genre in Flanders by 1560 and were still popular in the seventeenth century. Pieter Aertsen and Joachim Beukelaer invented and popularized the genre, but Moillon's work is closer to examples by Lucas van Valkenborch.[10] She departs from Flemish models by placing the scene indoors rather than in an open market place, by having only two figures, and by depicting a smaller stock of goods, most of it fruit. The result is a simpler, more restrained, and in some ways more natural image than the gargantuan displays of perfect vegetables produced by her Flemish predecessors. Her restraint conforms to French taste of the period when Philippe de Champaigne, the Le Nain brothers in Paris, and Georges de la Tour in Lorraine were all enjoying their first successes.

We know that she was an established still-life painter by 1630. In the Louvre picture she seeks to extend her range by working on a larger scale and by including the human figure. This work is important there-fore as an indication of Moillon's artistic ambition at the age of twenty, and also of her artistic independence, for she was the first French artist in the seventeenth century to attempt such subjects.[11] It has been suggested that in composing the figures she used the engravings of Abraham Bosse, a fellow Protestant in the Parisian artistic community, but the examples cited are not especially close to the works named and Bosse's small prints could hardly have been helpful models for such large works.[12] Moillon must have been familiar rather with Flemish genre and still life, as well as with the portraits of Frans Pourbus the Younger, who spent his last twelve years working in Paris, and with the emerging talents of another Flemish emigré, Philippe de Champaigne, who reached Paris in 1622, the year Pourbus died. The careful depiction of the customer's dress recalls Pourbus' meticulous attention to his sitter's economic status,[13] while the simple composition with table and figures placed parallel to the picture plane echoes both Pourbus and Champaigne. Moillon thus aligned herself with those French artists working in a straightforward, realistic tradition that had its roots in Flanders rather than with the fading Mannerist or emerging Baroque styles of Italian origin preferred at court. Like Champaigne and the Le Nains, she probably found her patrons among the wealthy bourgeoisie rather than the aristocracy.[14]

25.
Basket of Apricots, ca. 1635
Oil on panel
15¾ x 20½ in. (40 x 52 cm.)
Paris, Collection Mr. and Mrs. François Heim
(See color plate, p. 75)

This is a still-life masterpiece of deceptive simplicity. The character of the fruit itself — small, plump, speckled, and perfectly ripe — is beautifully evoked. The austerity of the composition draws attention to every slight deviation from the perfect symmetry suggested at first sight. A pair of rounded forms on the left made by one split apricot is matched by the two apricots on the right but broken by the branch of leaves to which they are still attached. The leaf forms are picked up by others crowning the basket, while the slight upwards slope of the basket provides an accent emphasized by the dark vine leaves emerging from it like a green frill. In the foreground the artist entertains us with *trompe l'oeil* water drops and a drinking fly.

Moillon's still lives reveal a constant preoccupation with balancing asymmetries and carefully judged intervals of void and solid while using a basic format of one, two, or three round containers of fruit set on a wooden surface that is always strictly parallel to the picture plane. In a work dated 1630, now in the Norton Simon Foundation Collection, three different types of bowls containing gooseberries, strawberries, and cherries are placed irregularly across a counter.[15] A panel of 1672 in Toulouse contrasts a tall basket of red and purple plums with a small, flat basket of strawberries.[16] When she shows only one container of fruit, she always sets some of the fruit, or fruit of a different kind, on the surface beside the container and breaks the even

pls. 9-12 for Hulsdonck. For Bosschaert, see J. Šíp, *Dutch Painting*, London, 1961, no. 35 (work of 1620 in Prague).
7.
Faré, 1962, ii, pls. 11-14.
8.
In his recent book, Faré reads the dates on Moillon's two panels in Toulouse as 1632 and 1634, instead of the 1672 and 1674 usually given, and reads the date on her Strasbourg panel 1632 instead of 1682 (1974, 56 and 64-66). Faré thus eliminates a late revival of Moillon's career. I have recently examined the two panels in Toulouse and find the traditional reading of the dates the more plausible one.
9.
For the others, see Faré, 1962, ii, pls. 32, 36, and 65, or Faré, 1974, 48-49, 52, and 53. Another was in a Paris sale in 1786; a seventh on panel was cut up in 1947 and has since disappeared (Wilhelm, 10). *The Fruit Seller* (Faré, 1974, 48-49, color pl.) is dated 1629. The fruit is splendid in this work but the figure is stiffer than those in the Louvre picture of a year later. In 1962 Faré attributed a fifth work of this type to Moillon (ii, pl. 35) but now (1974, 18-19) he attributes it to Jacques Linard, as he does two more (22-23) not known to him in 1962. In two of these the women seated at the table hold flowers and contemplate a typical exam-ple of Linard's baskets of flowers. All the figures are noticeably stiffer and flatter than those in the four examples Faré gives to Moillon, two of which are signed and one of which is documented.
10.
See, for example, his scene representing the months of July and August in the Kunsthistorisches Museum, Vienna; another good example was in the exhibition *Le siècle de Breugel*, Brussels, 1963, no. 223.
11.
Perhaps inspired by her example, Sébastien Stosskopff produced a similar blend of genre and still life in *The Five Senses* and *The Four Elements* (Strasbourg, Musée des Beaux-Arts, both signed, one dated 1633). The result is awkward and he did not apparently repeat the experiment. For Linard's efforts in the same vein, see note 9 above.
12.
Wilhelm, 11.
13.
For a typical Pourbus portrait, see A. F. Blunt, *Art and Architecture in France, 1500-1700*, Harmondsworth, 1957, pl. 89. It is possible that Moillon's customer is a portrait, for her features are carefully described whereas the greengrocer resem-

contour of the pile of fruit with leaves. Hers is an art of understatement as satisfying in its infinite variations as the sonatas of Scarlatti.

26.
Still Life with Grapes and Vine Leaves, 1637
Oil on panel
$19^{11}/_{16}$ x 26 in. (50 x 66 cm.)
Signed lower right: Louyse Moillon 1637 (partly effaced)
Paris, Private Collection

In several of her still-life paintings Moillon stresses the decorative character of the leaves, contrasting their irregular contours with the smooth, rounded forms of the fruit. In a beautiful small study of curaçao oranges dated 1634 in the Norton Simon Collection, the oval leaf shapes echo the strange, sectioned forms of the bitter oranges,[17] In an earlier work, *A Dish of Grapes with Figs,* 1631, in a private collection in New York, she first plays with the formal contrast between the glossy, translucent, globular forms of grapes and the large, ragged shapes of vine leaves.[18] She elaborates this theme in two works of 1637. In *Still Life with Grapes and Vine Leaves,* the leaves extend over the ledge, defining the picture plane, and reach into the shadowy background spaces of the composition, almost overwhelming in formal interest the grapes in the center of the composition. This theme is developed to spectacular effect in another, much larger work of the same year now in a private collection in Bergamo, where vine leaves extend in all directions over a harvest festival display of grapes, gourds, and melons.[19] Moillon's sense of pattern and overall design are superbly displayed in these works, proof that she did not confine herself to simple bowls of fruit on ledges.

bles women in other figure paintings by Moillon. A well-known but much later example of a portrait of a woman shopping is Emanuel de Witte's *Adriana van Heusden and Her Daughter at the New Fishmarket in Amsterdam* (ca. 1662, London, National Gallery).
14.
Her only known patron was Claude de Bullion (1570-1640), Louis XIII's Minister of Finance and one of the wealthiest men of his day. For him she painted *The Lunch* at the Chateau de Wideville (Wilhelm, 11, and Faré, 1974, 53).
15.
Faré, 1974, 54.
16.
Ibid., 56, upper left.
17.
Faré, 1962, I, color pl. opp. 88; Faré, 1974, 60, fig. 5.
18.
Faré, 1974, 52 (upper left) and Munsterburg, 32.
19.
Faré, 1962, II, 51, and Faré, 1974, 67 (in both publications the location is wrongly given as the Art Institute of Chicago).

Margaretha de Heer
Dutch, active in the 1650s

At present very little is known about this artist. She is recorded in the nineteenth-century Dutch encyclopedias of artists as a painter of watercolor studies of birds and insects.[1] Kramm guesses that Willem de Heer (1636-1681) was her husband or her brother; there are a few careful pen drawings on parchment signed by him in the British Museum and in the Rijksmuseum in Amsterdam. A work of 1651 by Margaretha is mentioned by Kramm. A *Still Life with Insects, Shells, and a Beetle* in Hartford (Wadsworth Atheneum) is signed by her and dated 1654. Two more signed works are known to the cataloguer, *Return from the Hunt* in Bordeaux (cat. no. 27) and *Two Beggars Fighting*, a small panel in the Leicester City Art Gallery.[2] All three signed works are accomplished paintings but so different in subject and even technique that it is hard to construct a consistent artistic personality from them. *Return from the Hunt* could be later than the other two; it is certainly her masterpiece. She was clearly a gifted painter who did not confine herself to watercolor studies after natural specimens.

27.
Return from the Hunt
Oil on canvas
26¾ x 21¹¹/₁₆ in. (68 x 55 cm.)
Inscribed below the tassel (no longer visible to naked eye): M. de Heer
Bordeaux, Musée des Beaux-Arts (6407)

This beautiful small game piece was attributed to Jan Weenix until Margaretha de Heer's signature was noticed early in this century. The attribution to Weenix is hard to understand since de Heer's interpretation of the game piece is far closer to the work of Willem van Aelst. His elaborately composed heaps of hunting equipment and dead animals always stress the textural contrasts of stone, wood, leather, fur, metal, and cloth. He was especially famous for his ability to paint the plumage of birds. He employed a palette of subtle neutrals relieved with a few accents of cool color — deep blue and green, cream, white, maybe a little orange. The marble ledge and classical architectural detail, which de Heer has used here too, are also typical of Aelst.[3]

After traveling in France and Italy he settled in Amsterdam in 1656. Presumably de Heer came into contact with him after that date, which suggests that this picture is later than her recorded dated works.

Margaretha de Heer has not attempted to rival the baroque intricacies of van Aelst's compositions. Instead she has created a design with a marvelously compact quality, like a well-built brick wall, in which each element is neatly slotted into place. Her restraint recalls the elegant compositions of Willem Kalf (1619-1693), who also worked in Amsterdam, and whose still lives frequently employ a vertical format, although she does not imitate his main stylistic feature — a brilliantly impasted surface that mimics the textures and the sparkle of light portrayed. Only the tassel in her picture hints at the taste for fancy accessories then developing in Amsterdam. The game piece was not popular in Holland, as it was in seventeenth-century Flanders, mainly because there was little good hunting terrain in the United Provinces. This superb example may be de Heer's only essay in the genre. It is further evidence of the astonishing wealth of artistic talent that flourished in Holland's "golden century."

1.
Kramm, III, 658. He also mentions a landscape picture with birds and two myth-ologies, an *Andromeda* and a *Diana*.
2.
Stephanie Barron, who brought the Hartford picture to my attention, and Frima Fox Hofrichter, who told me about the Leicester panel, both deserve my thanks.
3.
A good example is repr. by Bernt, I, pl. 4.

27

29

Maria van Oosterwyck
Dutch, 1630-1693

Some two dozen works are known by Maria van Oosterwyck, a painter of flower pieces and occasionally of still lives.[1] According to Arnold Houbraken's *De groote schouburgh der Nederlantsche konstschilders en schilderessen* of 1718-20 (the first of the few compilations of artists' biographies to mention women in its title), she was born in Nootdorp, near Delft, on August 20, 1630, the daughter of a preacher. Houbraken says that when she displayed artistic gifts at an early age, her father sent Maria to study with Jan Davidsz. de Heem (1606-1683/84), a bit of information doubted by modern scholars because de Heem spent most of his life in Antwerp and only returned to Utrecht, his birth-place, for a brief stay from 1669 to 1672. By then, to judge from her dated works, Oosterwyck was already a fully trained artist. Houbraken also says that she was courted by another still-life artist, Willem van Aelst (1625/26- after 1683), but that he gave up the task as hopeless, so devoted was she to her career. Her first known dated work is of 1667 but she must have been active long before then.[2] There are other dated works of 1668 (see cat. no. 28), 1669,[3] 1685 (Copenhagen, Royal Museum), 1686, and 1689 (Collection H. M. the Queen, Kensington Palace).[4] The small number of surviving works confirms Houbraken's statement that she worked slowly and produced little. She had an international reputation nevertheless; she was patronized by Louis XIV of France, Emperor Leopold, the Stadhouder William III, and the King of Poland.[5] She died in December 1693 at the home of her sister's son in Uitdam.

With the exception of her superb *Vanitas* in Vienna (cat. no. 28) and one still life recorded in sale records, all her known and recorded works are flower pictures.[6] She liked to set her vases on marble table tops and nearly always included grasses with green and white striped leaves. Another favorite motif is a red emperor butterfly perched in the lower foreground with its wings spread. Her works recall in a general way those of de Heem and van Aelst, suggesting that she was familiar with their paintings, even if we cannot prove that she studied or worked with either of them. Her flower pieces are among the best of the period and her *Vanitas* is a masterpiece, one of the finest examples of this genre in seventeenth-century Holland.

1.
The lists of her works in Würzbach and Thieme-Becker are not reliable. To the three works catalogued below and others mentioned in the text can be added the following, all signed flower pieces, in alphabetical order by location: a pair in Atlanta, E. Okarna Gallery (*Apollo,* December 1973); Augsburg, Städtische Kunstsammlungen (Halberstadt Collection); Florence, Uffizi (E. Pieraccini, *Catalogue of the . . . Uffizi Gallery,* Florence, 1906, no. 872. It does not appear in any more recent catalogs); The Hague, Mauritshuis (no. 468); a work with R. Green, London, in 1969 and now in a private collection (*Apollo,* 1969, June, v); Prague, Národní Galerie (no. 0245; oil on copper, 14⁹/₁₆ x 10½ in., information I owe to Dr. Jiří Kotalík); Vienna, Kunsthistorisches Museum (no. 1083 in the catalog of 1884. It does not appear in more recent catalogs); Zurich, U. Brunner Collection (from the Hallsborough Gallery, see *Apollo,* December 1962, and Pavière, I, 47 and pl. 55). A still life in the manner of Kalf signed by Oosterwyck went through Christie's, London, on March 24, 1922, lot 129 (oil on canvas, 27 x 22½ in.; photo in Frick Art Reference Library).
2.
A picture of flowers in a vase with grapes and fruit in a sculptured niche signed and dated 1667 went through Christie's, London, on May 6, 1938, lot 57. It was bought by the Arthur Tooth Gallery, London.

28.
Vanitas, 1668
Oil on canvas
28¾ x 34⅞ in. (73 x 88.5 cm.)
Signed lower right: Maria van Oosterwijck 1668
Vienna, Kunsthistorisches Museum (5714)
(See color plate, p. 76)

This *Vanitas,* painted when the artist was thirty-eight years old, is her first dated work traceable today. Such an ambitious and accomplished work can hardly be one of her earliest commissions. We can guess that she only dated works made for important patrons and that it was in the 1660s that her reputation began to spread beyond Holland. This work is not recorded in the inventories of the Austrian emperors, but its Austrian location and provenance suggests that it might have been made for Emperor Leopold I.[7]

The genre of still life known as a "Vanitas" first developed in Leyden in the 1620s, probably, as Bergström suggests, as a result of the concentration of Calvinist scholars in that city.[8] It is the most intellectual and literary form of still life and the only kind that always has a moral message. There are three classes of objects regularly included. The first are symbols of an active professional and personal life: books, scientific instruments, and artists' tools representing the literary, scientific, and artistic professions; money, purses, deeds of property, account books, and precious objects symbolizing worldly wealth and power; and goblets of wine or beer, cards, dice, and musical instruments recalling the more frivolous pastimes that also consume our days. The next group are objects that stand for the passage of time: clocks, hourglasses, soap bubbles, full-blown roses, dead grasses,[9] skulls, and smoking, extinguished candles. The last group refers to life after death, often represented by a strand of ivy or a laurel branch, but these are frequently omitted, for the tone of most Vanitas paintings is pessimistic.

In Holland such paintings were most popular before 1650. Later examples tend to be larger and more elaborate than those produced in Leyden in the 1630s and 1640s. Oosterwyck's interpretation of the theme is characteristic for its date while also being exceptionally complete in its iconographic range and unusually detailed in its execution.[10] The four most prominent objects in her composition are the large vase of flowers, the globe with signs of the zodiac, the skull wreathed in ivy, and the account book. The smaller objects, reading from left to right, include a flute lying on music books; a mouse eating a stalk of grain; a glass flask of *Aqua Vitae* in which is reflected a self-portrait of the artist; a rattle; a half-eaten ear of corn; a butterfly perched on the edge of a page; a blue and white porcelain inkpot with a goose quill pen lying nearby; an hourglass; a pair of books with a fly, a small bunch of anemones, with a snowdrop lying on them; a knapsack; and some coins. A large stone niche is dimly visible behind the marble table on which these objects are strewn in careful disorder.

The general meaning of all these objects will be clear from the open-

ing discussion of the genre but a few specific identifications may be helpful. The butterfly can symbolize the resurrection of Christ and of mankind generally. The fly is a symbol of sin, the mouse of evil because of its destructive habits. The anemone is associated with sorrow and death and with the passion of Christ, the snowdrop with hope and consolation. The knapsack suggests the journey of life. The various inscriptions are all appropriately moralizing in tone.[11] With the exception of the ear of corn, à recent import from America, none of Oosterwyck's symbols are unusual, although the repertoire is exceptionally complete.

Jan de Heem, her reputed teacher, painted several Vanitas compositions during an early stay in Leyden (1626-29), but they are smaller and simpler than hers and use the monochromatic tones that were to dominate Dutch painting for the next two decades. Perhaps she visited him in Antwerp and learned about his earlier phase there. More probably she visited Leyden, which is not far from Delft, and there saw examples of the local specialty. The moralizing content of the genre may have had a particular appeal for her, since Houbraken tells us that she was extremely pious. The butterflies and grasses so common in her flower pieces may even carry a symbolic message too: because the pleasures and beauties of this life will pass we must follow Christ and look forward to the everlasting delights of heaven.

29.
Vase of Tulips, Roses, and Other Flowers with Insects, 1669
Oil on panel
18⅝ x 15⅛ in. (47.3 x 38.4 cm.)
Signed lower right: Maria van Oosterwijck 1669
Cincinnati, Collection Mrs. L. W. Scott Alter

This small panel is a beautiful example of Oosterwyck's flower paintings of the 1660s. Her favorite striped grasses are here played off against two striped tulips, whose forms reach the limits of the panel. A dragonfly perched on the grasses is placed against a white peony that shows off its transparent wings. The grasses hanging over the ledge on which the glass vase is placed and the butterfly perched above her signature invite us to test the artist's illusion and admire her skill.

The small scale, the simplicity of the design and its extension to all edges of the panel, and the prominent tulips recall much earlier Dutch flower pieces such as Jacques de Gheyn's *Still Life with Tulips* of 1612 (The Hague, Gemeente Museum) and works by the two artists who may have taught her, Jan Davidsz. de Heem and Willem van Aelst.[12] Clearly she was aware of prevailing fashions but she perfected a personal variant that stressed an exquisitely detailed finish, much play with reflections and varied textures, and more symbolism than was usual for flower pictures at that time. In this work, the fly in the foreground can represent sin and the destruction of worldly possessions, the glass vase and the grass the fragility of human life, and the butterfly resurrection. Her flower pieces are not only beautiful and sophisticated examples of this Northern seventeenth-century specialty; their iconographical content makes them more complex in artistic intention than those of most of her contemporaries.

3.
A flower piece of 1669 was with the Leger Galleries, London, in 1961 (*Connoisseur,* October 1961, xxxiii).
4.
C. H. Collins Baker, *Catalogue of the Pictures at Hampton Court,* Glasgow, 1929, III, nos. 691 and 692. They are now kept at Kensington Palace.
5.
Houbraken, II, 214ff. None of her surviving works can be traced back to these owners.
6.
For the still life, see the last item in note 1.
7.
Sandrart (347 and 424, note 1558) records "eine Holländerin," unmarried, who made exceptionally fine miniature paintings, from whom he acquired a *Vanitas* for Archduke Leopold Wilhelm (d. 1662). It included a self-portrait of the artist in a reflection. Pelzer thought that the artist might have been Clara Peeters, but Maria van Oosterwyck, who never married, is a more logical choice, even if the *Vanitas* known to Sandrart, painted before 1662, cannot be identified with the picture in Vienna, although it does contain the artist's self-portrait in a reflection on the vase.

8.
Bergström, 154ff.
9.
"As for man, his days are as grass: as a flower of the field, so he flourisheth. For the wind passeth over it, and it is gone; and the place thereof shall know it no more" (Psalms 103: 15-16).
10.
For comparable examples, see the discussion of Jacques de Clauw, Abraham van Beyeren, and Vincent Lourensz. van der Vinne in Bergström.
11.
The text beneath the word *Rekeningh* ("reckoning") translates: "We live in order to die. We die in order to live." The text on the paper sticking out beneath is identified for us as Job 14: 1 ("Man that is born of a woman is of a few days, and full of trouble"). The tag, *Self-Stryt,* emerging from the book on the right refers to a work of Jacob Cats, the slip below it, *Navolgingh Christi,* to Thomas à Kempis' *Imitation of Christ.*
12.
De Gheyn's work is repr. in color by Mitchell, pl. 157. For comparable examples by de Heem and van Aelst, see Bergström, pls. 178, 179, 185, and 186.

Elisabetta Sirani
Italian, 1638-1665

Elisabetta Sirani's brief career is well documented. Carlo Cesare Malvasia, the seventeenth-century biographer of Bolognese artists, was a personal friend and he wrote a long, embarrassingly adulatory biography shortly after the death of the artist, whom he called "la gloria del sesso donnesco."[1] In it he included a list of about one hundred ninety works that Sirani herself had begun to keep in 1655. She had become a Bolognese culture heroine long before her death, and her funeral was an elaborate affair prompting many trite poems in praise of Sirani and her work, which Malvasia collected and reprinted. Thus the legend of the sweet-tempered, virginal young artist, the equal of all the women artists of the past and heir to the genius of Guido Reni, in whose tomb she was buried, has been associated with Sirani from the beginning. Inevitably such blind adoration and effusive praise has seemed excessive to modern eyes, and while Reni's reputation has risen somewhat from the depths to which it sank in the late nineteenth century, the appreciation of his numerous Bolognese followers is still very much a local phenomenon. Sirani is dismissed outright in most modern writings as a weak imitator of Reni.

She was the daughter of Gian Andrea Sirani (1610-1670), a Bolognese artist whose style was closely modeled on that of Guido Reni, the most admired and most influential Bolognese painter of the seventeenth century. She was not encouraged to paint by her father; it was Malvasia who spotted her gifts and urged her father to develop them. She had the examples of two well-known Bolognese women artists — Properzia de' Rossi and Lavinia Fontana — to inspire her. Malvasia mentions both of them in his life of Elisabetta, as well as some of the legendary women artists of antiquity, and no doubt he told her about them too. She was professionally active by the age of seventeen, as her own list proves, producing two works that year, five the next, and eighteen the next, two of which she also engraved. By 1662 she had recorded about ninety works; she finished at least eighty more before her death as well as fourteen etchings and a number of drawings.[2] Most of her commissions were for private patrons. She also carried out some public commissions, however, including an enormous *Bap-*

1.
Malvasia, ii, 385ff. For the best recent essay on Sirani and her father with full bibliography, see Emiliani, 1959.
2.
A number of apparently genuine works exist that are not recorded in her list, for example nos. 179, 280, and 178 (probably a very early work) in the Pinacoteca Nazionale, Bologna. The largest group of drawings by her is at Windsor Castle (Kurz, nos. 491-516) but there are others in public and private collections, the finest being *The Finding of Moses* in the Metropolitan Museum, New York (J. Bean and F. Stampfle, *Drawings from New York Collections* ii: *The Seventeenth Century in Italy*, New York, 1967, no. 130).

tism for a chapel in the church of the main Bolognese cemetery.[3] She painted portraits, though none survives, religious works, allegorical themes, and occasional mythologies and stories from ancient history. She became a tourist attraction, bringing distinguished visitors from Florence, Mantua, Turin, and even from outside Italy, who all came to see this phenomenal young woman dash off her pictures with the ease of a true virtuoso.[4]

Her death late in August 1665 at the age of twenty-seven aroused immediate suspicions that she had been poisoned. The family's maid was accused and admitted to tipping a packet of powder into her mistress's soup but said that she had been told by the woman who gave it to her that it contained only sugar and cinnamon. After a trial that Malvasia says was not conducted fairly, the maid was exiled. An autopsy revealed that Sirani's stomach was full of holes. Modern medical opinion explains her death as a result of ulcers, but at the time doctors hypothesized that the holes were due to some disturbance of her especially lively female temperament. It was even suggested that the holes were the result of a frustrated love affair!

As can be guessed from her impressive output and from the lively, economical wash technique of her drawings, she worked quickly and easily. She herself records with pride finishing a picture of a Madonna and Child for a visitor to the city in time for it to dry and be taken home with the client.[5] Malvasia describes how one evening immediately after Sirani was told that she had been awarded the commission to paint the *Baptism* for the Certosa, she leaped to her feet, took a sheet of paper, and sketched the composition while her father and Malvasia were chatting, afterwards presenting him with the drawing.[6] Such methods might well result in an uneven level of quality, and indeed some of the works attributed to her are weak, while others are simply copies after Reni. But if judgment is limited to signed works and to works that can be matched to her own careful descriptions on her list, then the standard maintained is high. She is a far better and far more original artist than her father, who actually is only a pale reflection of Reni's later style. Elisabetta's artistic personality is hard to extricate from the legend of the angelic young genius who died before she could reach her prime and from the overwhelming fame of Reni, whose work has only recently been more carefully defined by modern scholarship.

Like every artist working in Bologna in the 1640s and 1650s, Elisabetta was profoundly influenced by the idealized imagery of Reni's art. Moreover, she seems to have decided consciously to model her style on his, a choice that made her extremely popular at the time but that has since worked to her disadvantage.[7] To have mastered the technique and idiom of one of the major Italian artists of the century was no mean feat for a young woman who had no personal instruction from her model, nor, one would think, much help from her undistinguished father. She emulated Reni's elevated sentimentality, his avoidance of any true psychological drama, his preference for subjects with static figures, and above all his intention to create beautiful images rather than to move the spectator deeply or make strong moral statements. To modern eyes, the art of Reni can seem empty, for it does not convey that profound concern for the human condition that the art of Caravaggio and Rembrandt projects so strongly. But Reni nevertheless produced works with a great formal beauty that overcomes the handicap of an alien sentiment. Whether Sirani also managed to cross this barrier is a matter of personal, subjective judgment.

Her art is not simply an imitation of Reni's last manner but is a critical distillation of many aspects of his work. She also seems to have been impressed by the work of Francesco Gessi (1588-1649). Her instant success and the constant pressure to produce works at great speed hardly allowed for a serious, reflective training grounded in the discipline of drawing the human figure. She must have had remarkable facility and a good eye because she mastered certain aspects of Reni's technique with impressive skill. Her drapery forms tend to be more sculptural, more angular, and more complex than his; her tonal range is darker, her colors deeper and richer than his were after 1630; her facial expressions are less bland, more particular. She uses shadowed eye sockets to suggest depth of feeling rather as Andrea del Sarto did in the sixteenth century. She likes patterned fabrics. Most importantly, her compositions are her own. Her Magdalenes, Madonnas, Sibyls, Judiths, and Baptists are never repetitions of Reni's designs, even if her adaptations of his drapery forms and figure types give her work an immediate but superficial resemblance to his. Finally, the brush and wash technique that she uses for many of her drawings is a personal invention, quite unlike the standard methods of drawing current in Bologna at the time.

Sirani died in her late twenties, trapped in her own legend as a kind of reborn, female Reni. Could she have outgrown the myth that enveloped her and used her enormous gifts to develop a more personal style? All the pressures on her were to continue in the same vein. There is, however, visible growth in her surviving works. Her later pictures are stronger technically, better drawn, more firmly constructed. A *Madonna and Child* painted in her last year is beautifully composed.[8] The types are less like Reni than before, the interlocking of the forms of mother and child tenderly expressive of more genuine feeling than he ever conveys. She recorded only nine works in 1665 and her last entry mentions the spring season; she was to die in August. Her early death was a tragedy but her biography must not be allowed to distract us from her genuine accomplishments, which still await serious study.[9]

30.
The Penitent Magdalene in the Wilderness, 1660
Oil on canvas
64¼ x 78¾ in. (163 x 200 cm.)
Inscribed on the rock on the right: Elisab.^ta Sirani/ .F. 1660
Bologna, Pinacoteca Nazionale (750)

Like the *Porcia Wounding Her Thigh* (cat. no. 31), this painting of the

3.
It is still *in situ* (C. C. Malvasia, *Le pitture di Bologna,* Bologna, 1686, ed. A. Emiliani, Bologna, 1969, 342/17 repr.).
4.
Her own list frequently mentions visitors. The last entry is especially touching: "Con occasione, che passò per costà il sig. Duca della Mirandola, venne a vedere le mie opere, e a vedermi operare, e tutti li Principi e principesse, come di Messerano, e altri, e così tutti li Signori, e Personaggi grandi, che sono questa Primavera passati per Bologna ecc." (On the occasion that the duke of Mirandola passed through here, he came to see my works and to watch me work, and all the princes and princesses, like those of Messerano, and others, and in this way all the important people, who passed through Bologna this spring) (Malvasia, II, 400).
5.
Malvasia, II, 399. It was made for the Grand Duke Cosimo III de' Medici in 1664.
6.
Ibid., 402. The drawing is probably the one now in the Albertina (Kurz, 134, fig. 95).
7.
A typical modern reaction is that of Stephen Ostrow: ". . . [she] developed a mannered and feminine version of Reni's style. It was probably her image as a youthful female artist, rather than intrinsic qualities in her paintings, that led to the widespread admiration of her art among Europe's Royal collectors" (*Baroque Painting, Italy and Her Influence,* American Federation of Arts, Traveling Exhibition, 1968, no. 3).
8.
Emiliani, 1959, no. 65. Another *Madonna and Child* dated 1665 is in a private collection in Madrid (Pérez Sánchez, 211 and pl. 50); it seems to be an original of high quality.
9.
Elisabetta's two sisters, Anna Maria (1645-1715) and Barbara (alive in 1678), both painted, but few of their recorded works survive. To Barbara rather than to Elisabetta should be attributed the small *Portrait of Elisabetta* on copper (Bologna, Pinacoteca Nazionale, no. 503; Tufts, 1974, fig. 39). It agrees well with Malvasia's description of Barbara's portrait of her sister (II, 403) and is too weak to be by Elisabetta herself. She had other women students, among them being Ginevra Cantofoli (1608-1672) (Malvasia, II, 407) and Lucrezia Scarfaglia (active ca. 1678), whose *Self-Portrait* is in the Galleria Rospigliosi-Pallavicini, Rome (F. Zeri, *La Galleria Pallavicini in Roma,* Florence, 1959, no. 451).

30

Magdalene is recorded by Sirani in her list of works under the year 1660: "A Magdalene in the Desert reclining on a rough mat contemplating the Crucifix, life-size, for Signore Giovanni Battista Cremonese, the jeweller."[10] Nothing is known about this patron, who is not recorded elsewhere in Malvasia's lives as an art patron. By 1795 the painting was in the collection of a distinguished Bolognese family, the Zambeccari, when it was valued at 250 lire, a high price compared with most works in the inventory.[11] It came to the Pinacoteca Nazionale with the Zambeccari Collection in 1883.[12]

This is a work far more typical of Sirani than the *Judith* (Burghley House, Marquess of Exeter), especially the sweeter facial type, the more delicate figure proportions, and the choice of a traditional religious subject. The penitent saint is shown with all the usual symbols of the hermit's existence — the rough, worn clothing, the skull and religious writings, the knotted rope with which to flail herself, the diet of root crops and water. Her ointment jar lies on its side near the inscription on the right, empty and unused now that Christ has gone to heaven. Its inclusion proves that this is the Magdalene and not St. Mary of Egypt, another female hermit saint who ended her life alone in the wilderness.

The contrast between this interpretation of the theme and that of Artemisia Gentileschi (cat. no. 11) could hardly be greater. Sirani alludes to the Magdalene's legendary past as a woman abandoned to bodily lusts in the seductive pose, the exposed breasts, and the long, golden hair, although the semi-nudity may also refer to the higher truth of her new faith. Artemisia instead covers up her Magdalene, except for the low neckline of the gorgeous dress, and portrays her as a woman of strong personality who is not entirely convincing in the role of abject penitence. To these contrasts may be added others more obvious — the differences in setting, lighting, color, indeed in aesthetic approach altogether. Sirani also painted a more modestly clothed Magdalene (Bologna, Pinacoteca Nazionale, no. 280),[13] a beautiful Reniesque essay with the traditional crimson robes floating around her as she gazes heavenwards from her mountain retreat. In both of Sirani's versions the sweet, idealized expressions, directly inspired by Reni, may not be appealing. Both however are excellent examples of the more classical spirit seen in much Italian seicento art. In the *Magdalene* in our exhibition, the figure has been placed within the setting with great skill. Our eyes rise from her slim legs up to her head, then follow her gaze past the crucifix to the landscape vista beyond. All the details of the setting and the still-life accessories have been painted with far more attention to detail than was usual with Reni, especially toward the end of his career. The *Magdalene* and the *Porcia* set a standard of quality that should be kept in mind by those seeking to link her to the weaker products of Guido Reni's shop.

31.
Porcia Wounding Her Thigh, 1664
Oil on canvas
39¾ x 54¾ in. (101 x 138 cm.)
Inscribed lower left: [Eli] sab. [ett] a Sirani F. 1664
New York, Wildenstein & Company
(See color plate, p. 77)

Sirani's choice of subject on this occasion may be unique. Certainly there are no other representations of this story from Plutarch's *Life of Brutus* (XIII) recorded by Pigler.[14] As the time approached for Caesar's murder, Porcia sensed that Brutus, her husband, was deeply troubled and concerned about matters he was keeping to himself. To test her own strength of character before asking him to share his troubles with her, she took a small knife and made a deep wound in her thigh. When Brutus rushed to her side and showed his great concern at her suffering, she made the following speech to him: "Brutus, I am Cato's daughter, and I was brought into thy house, not, like a mere concubine, to share thy bed and board merely, but to be a partner in thy troubles. Thou, indeed, art faultless as a husband; but how can I show thee any grateful service if I am to share neither thy secret suffering nor the anxiety which craves a loyal confidant? I know that woman's nature is thought too weak to endure a secret; but good rearing and excellent companionship go far towards strengthening the character, and it is my happy lot to be both the daughter of Cato and the wife of Brutus. Before this I put less confidence in these advantages, but now I know that I am superior even to pain."[15] She then revealed the wound and explained her personal trial of courage. Brutus was suitably impressed and after taking care of her wound, did confide in her finally about the plot to kill Caesar.

Sirani's selection of a story from ancient history that has as its point the courage and heroism of a woman can legitimately be described as feminist, especially since the subject is so rare in the visual arts. This was not the only occasion when Sirani combed ancient sources for a new feminist theme for a picture, for she also painted the only recorded example of Timoclea pushing the enemy captain into the well of her house, as opposed to the more usual scene of the captive Timoclea being led before Alexander the Great.[16] Another story of a heroic woman inspired one of her masterpieces, the *Judith Triumphant* at Burghley House of 1658.[17] Indeed, these last two works were made for the same patron. They help to correct the impression that she painted only Madonnas and infant Christs, pliant Magdalenes, and ethereal sibyls.

The *Porcia* was painted a year before her death. It is a skillfully staged narrative that follows Plutarch closely. According to the text, she asked her women to leave her alone; they are shown in the distance in an adjoining room as Porcia prepares to stab her thigh. This well-preserved painting, with its warm color scheme emphasizing red and gold and with many virtuoso passages of lively brushwork, is an ambitious work handled with complete assurance. One of her best works, its theme makes it an especially suitable choice for this exhibition.

10.
Malvasia, II, 395.
11.
Emiliani, 64.
12.
Ibid., 66 and 71.
13.
This work cannot be identified with either of the other two Magdalenes described by Sirani in 1662 and 1664 but seems nevertheless to be a genuine work of high quality.
14.
A. Pigler, *Barockthemen*, Budapest, 1956; 2nd ed., 1974, II, 415, where sixteen representations of the death of Porcia are recorded. Sirani records this work in her list of paintings produced in 1664 as follows: "Una Porzia in atto di ferirsi una coscia quando desiderava saper la congiura che tramava il marito: quadro soprauscio, e di lontano in un'altra camera donzelle, che lavorano, per il sig. Simone Tassi" (A Porcia in the act of wounding a thigh when she wished to know about the conspiracy that her husband was plotting; overdoor painting, and in the distance in another room women, who are working, for Signore Simone Tassi)

(Malvasia, II, 399). Manaresi (129) and G. Cantalmessa ("David Saul o Astolfo" *Bollettino d'arte*, II, no. 1, 1922-23, 43) suggested that the *Lucretia* in the Galleria Borghese be identified with Sirani's *Porzia*, but P. della Pergola (*Galleria Borghese: I dipinti*, Rome, 1955, I, 68-69) correctly dismissed this theory.
15.
Plutarch's Lives, Loeb Classical Library, trans. B. Perrin, London, 1961, VI, 153-54.
16.
Pigler, *Barockthemen*, 1974 ed., II, 362 (eleven examples of Timoclea before Alexander) and 438 (cites Sirani's lost painting of Timoclea pushing the enemy captain into the well). The *Timoclea* appears on Sirani's list of works painted in 1659 (Malvasia, II, 394).
17.
Guide to Burghley House, Stamford, Stamford, n.d. (ca. 1975), 33, no. 304. For the citation in her list of works, see Malvasia, II, 394. There are preparatory studies for this work at Windsor Castle (Kurz, nos. 493 and 494). This important work has never been properly published. Photographs are available from the Witt Photographic Survey, London, no. B57/1656.

32

33

Margherita Caffi
Italian, active 1662-1700

The distinctive style of Margherita Caffi's brilliantly handled flower pictures has become much better known since five works, four of them either signed or recorded in seventeenth-century inventories, were exhibited in 1964.[1] A typical flower picture signed by her and dated 1662 recently passed through the London art market,[2] and a work in a private collection in Milan is dated 1700:[3] at present these two dates are the only firm points of chronological orientation for her career. We do not know when she was born, nor where, although the evidence available suggests that she came from Vicenza.[4] Her father was Vincenzo Volò, also a still-life painter, and she married another one, Francesco Caffi of Cremona, who specialized in flower pictures and tapestries.[5] There are sufficient numbers of her works in Florence, Innsbruck, and Madrid for scholars to suggest that she may have visited and worked at the courts in these cities.[6] Almost thirty pictures by her are now known, all buoyant designs of predominantly blue, crimson, and white flowers set against a dark ground and painted with great bravura.[7] She is also said to have worked as a miniature painter. Her dazzling *pittura di tocco* looks forward to the eighteenth century and in particular to the lighter toned but otherwise very similar decorative flower studies of Francesco Guardi.[8]

32.
Still Life with Flowers, ca. 1680
Oil on canvas
16¾ x 23⅜ in. (42.5 x 59.5 cm.)
Signed lower left: Caffi
Munich, Collection Julius Böhler
(For comments, see next entry.)

33.
Still Life with Flowers in a Landscape Setting, ca. 1680
Oil on canvas
16¾ x 23⅜ in. (42.5 x 59.5 cm.)
Munich, Collection Julius Böhler

1.
Naples, 1964, 112ff.
2.
Sotheby's, London, July 15, 1970, lot 90.
3.
Naples, 1964, no. 262.
4.
One work in a private collection in Genoa is signed: "Marg.ta Vicentina Caffi" (Naples, 1964, no. 265). Mina Gregori has recently drawn attention to a manuscript of ca. 1775 where the artist is called "Margherita Caffi Pittrice della la Vicenzina" (*Antichità viva,* IV, 1965, I, 18, note 5). She is called "Veneziana" in seventeenth-century Medici inventories, however (Naples, 1964, no. 261).
5.
Naples, 1964, 112, and M. Chiarini in Detroit, 1974, 198, with references to nineteenth-century publications not available to me. Chiarini gives Ludovico as her husband's first name.
6.
The catalogs of the exhibitions *La natura morta italiana,* Naples, 1964, and *The Twilight of the Medici,* Detroit, 1974, refer to numerous pictures by Caffi in the Medici collections; at least eight are to be found today in the Uffizi and the

This study of flowers in a dark landscape setting is one of a pair of works by Caffi in the Böhler Collection. The companion piece is signed. Both are typical examples of her lively technique, her strong sense of compositional movement, and her somewhat cavalier description of the species displayed. The arrangement of the flowers into two groups of dissimilar size in an oblong compositional format is also characteristic of Caffi's work. Unlike her Northern contemporaries, Maria van Oosterwyck and Rachel Ruysch, Caffi does not attempt to portray flowers accurately. Indeed she seems to have invented blooms as the decorative spirit moved her. Tulips, peonies, passion flowers, carnations, and convolvulus are popular with her, but their coloring is sometimes eccentric. The use of landscape setting in the work exhibited is unusual and suggests that she was probably familiar with the work of Dutch artists like Otto Marseus van Schriek (ca. 1619-1678), whose work she could have seen if she had worked in Florence for the Medici, as some scholars have proposed.

Caffi's works are almost the only exception in this exhibition to the rule that women artists working before 1800 painted carefully and precisely. A similar brio can be found in some of Vallayer-Coster's smaller flower pieces and in some of Elisabetta Sirani's drawings, but Caffi is the only woman before the nineteenth century who makes a stylistic point of her virtuoso painterly technique.

34

35

Palazzo Pitti. For her Spanish works, see Pérez Sánchez, 343-46; seven works are known, sixteen more are recorded in early inventories.
7.
Three rather weak pictures in her style exist in the Pinacoteca Comunale, Cremona (A. Puerari, *La Pinacoteca di Cremona,* Florence, 1951, nos. 304-6). A number of her works have either passed through sale rooms recently or are in dealers' hands (e.g. Sotheby's, July 12, 1972, lot 108, and June 30, 1971, lot 54; a pair of works were advertised by Romulus, London, in *Apollo,* September 1973).
8.
Charles Sterling (91 and note 210) was the first to appreciate her importance in this respect.

Maria Sibylla Merian
German, 1647-1717

Maria Sibylla Merian's achievements as an entomologist and botanical illustrator have long been recognized by historians of science and students of botanical drawing, but the feminist movement may finally bring her the wider audience that her extraordinary work deserves. Unfortunately, almost all the serious literature on her is in German or Dutch and many of the basic publications are not easily obtainable even in major American research libraries.[1]

Her career synthesized and extended several kinds of professional activity traditional in her family. She was the first daughter of the second marriage of Matthäus Merian the Elder (1592-1650), a Swiss engraver, who specialized in city views and landscapes and who inherited a publishing business from his first wife. His new wife was Dutch; their daughter was born in Frankfurt on April 2, 1647. Three years later he died, leaving his widow with two small children, a stepson, and a business to care for. A year later she remarried. Maria's stepfather was Jacob Marell (1614-1681), a Flemish flower painter who had been trained by Georg Flegel and Jan Davidsz. de Heem. He in turn trained another good flower painter, Abraham Mignon (1640-1679), and Johann Andreas Graff (1637-1701), who was to become Maria Sibylla's husband. She grew up therefore in a household full of artistic and literary activity and received instruction from two well-trained flower painters.[2] In 1641 Matthäus had published a new edition of one of the first collections of engravings of different flower species.[3] This catalog, a product of the new European passion for cultivated flowers of which the most famous manifestation was the Dutch "tulipomania," was our artist's introduction to the scientific study of nature. It eventually inspired Merian's own publications on European insects and plants and on those of Surinam in South America, which made her famous.

Graff studied with Marell from 1653 to 1658, then went to Italy for six years, visiting Venice and Rome in particular, before returning to Frankfurt and proposing marriage to Maria.[4] They were married in 1665; their first daughter, Johanna Helena, was born three years later.

In 1670 they moved to Nuremberg. She was visited there five years later by the German artists' biographer, Joachim von Sandrart, who reported that she made oil and watercolor paintings of flowers, fruit, birds, and also of worms, flies, mosquitoes, spiders, "and other filth."[5] In the same year her first publication, volume one of a three-part catalog of flower engravings, titled *Florum fasciculi tres,* was issued in Nuremberg. The second volume followed in 1677 and both were reissued with the third in 1680. Together they are known as the *Neue Blumenbuch* or *New Flower Book.* They are so rare that many writers on Merian have overlooked them altogether. Rücker and others have pointed out that the plates in several cases depend closely on her father's edition of De Brys' *Florilegium* of 1641 and on Nicolas Robert's *Variae ac multiformes florum species expressae . . . ,* published in Rome in 1665. Perhaps, as Rücker suggested, the *New Flower Book* may have been in part a teaching exercise for the young women, all daughters of local artists or aristocrats, who were set to copying these prints in Maria Sibylla Merian's studio as part of their artistic training.[6]

Her first completely original publication was *Der Raupen wunderbare Verwandlung und sonderbare Blumennahrung (The Wonderful Transformation of Caterpillars and [Their] Singular Plant Nourishment),* of which the first volume appeared in 1679, the second in 1683, and the third not until 1717, shortly after her death.[7] Together they comprise a catalog of one hundred eighty-six European moths, butterflies, and other insects all based on her own research and drawings. Although it was known when she started her research that silkworms must be fed on mulberry leaves, the preferred foods and life cycles of other insects were a mystery, so much so that people believed they emerged fully formed from dirt and mud. Merian collected insect eggs and caterpillars, fed them herself, and recorded the appearance of the egg, caterpillar, cocoon, chrysalis, and adult of each species. The results of her research were represented on a single page, arranged on or near the plant she had learned was the favorite of the animal in question. Her methods seem obvious and logical to us, but then they

---

1.
In addition to the brief chapter in Tufts (1974, 89-93) and "A Surinam Portfolio" in *Natural History,* December 1962, 28-41, see the short account in Blunt, which provides a good general history of the genre. Elizabeth Rücker's catalog of the exhibition devoted to Merian on the 250th anniversary of her death (Germanisches Nationalmuseum, Nuremberg, 1967) is the best short, scholarly account available. I am extremely grateful to Dr. Rücker for answering my queries about Merian and for sending me one of the last available copies of her catalog.
2.
A drawing by Graff of Merian's stepsister, Sara Marell, at work on an embroidery frame gives a vivid picture of their industrious household (J. Stuldreher-Nienhuis, *Verborgen Paradijzen,* Arnhem, 1945, 17).
3.
Johann Theodor de Bry, *Florilegium renovatum et auctum: Das ist vernewertes und vermehrtes Blumenbuch,* Frankfurt a.M.: Mathäus Merian, 1641.
4.
The only way that Merian might have learned about Giovanna Garzoni was from her husband, if he had noticed her or her work while he was in Rome.

5.
Sandrart, 339.
6.
Rücker, 9 and 39.
7.
Copies of the 1679 and 1683 volumes with crudely colored plates are in the library of the American Museum of Natural History, New York, with a copy of the Dutch edition of 1730. The Pierpont Morgan Library in New York owns the Latin edition of 1718.

were, as she proudly declared on her title page, "eine ganz neue Erfin-dung" (a completely new discovery), in contrast to the contemporary practice of studying only preserved specimens in collectors' cabinets. Merian thus revolutionized the sciences of zoology and botany and laid the foundations for the classification of plant and animal species made by Charles Linnaeus in the eighteenth century.

In 1685 Merian left Nuremberg with her two daughters (Dorothea Maria was born in 1678) and returned to Frankfurt to join her widowed mother, leaving her husband behind. In June the four women set off for West Friesland to join Merian's stepbrother, Cas-par, who was living with a colony of Labadists in a castle near Leeuwarden.[8] He died a year later. Her husband visited her and tried to persuade her to return with him to Germany but she refused to leave. They were divorced about seven years later. We do not know why the marriage ended, whether from religious or personality dif-ferences, but she lived with the Labadists until her mother's death in 1690, when she moved the family to Amsterdam. Possibly the need to care for her aging mother had delayed her move to the city, for its flourishing artistic and scientific community must surely have long attracted her attention. She quickly befriended Caspar Commelin, director of the Botanical Garden, and owners of scientific collections such as Frederick Ruysch, whose daughter Rachel we may guess she met too. Ruysch's paintings of insects and reptiles in landscape set-tings might have impressed Merian, but she might also have been critical of their lack of strict scientific accuracy.

It had been during her stay in West Friesland that Merian had first seen specimens of insects from the Dutch colony of Surinam and had conceived her plan to visit that exotic tropical country and study its insects in the same way she had studied those of Europe — in their natural setting. It was not until 1699, however, with the support of the city of Amsterdam — the burgomaster and secretary both had collections of natural curiosities — that she and her younger daugh-ter left on the three-month voyage to Surinam. Johanna Helena was already living there as the wife of a Dutch merchant. For two years, with the help of her daughters, Merian observed, recorded, drew, collected specimens, and interviewed the natives. Her original inten-tion had been to catalog only insects but she enthusiastically gathered information about snakes, reptiles, birds, and monkeys and made many notes on local customs, especially the uses of the plants. In 1701, after falling seriously ill, she and Dorothea returned to Amsterdam loaded down with notes, drawings, and specimens. Four years later her magnificent *Metamorphosis insectorum Surinamsium* was first published. Its sixty large plates, engraved by three Dutch artists after Merian's superb watercolor studies, show bananas, pineapples, lemons, grapes, pomegranates, watermelons, papayas, and other less familiar plants, all supporting the life stages of extraordinarily beautiful moths and butterflies and some extremely large spiders and beetles. Her commentaries on the plates tell the reader how long it took for the insects to hatch, but also, for example, give recipes for cooking bread-fruit and discuss the natives' use of abortifacients.[9] The price to sub-scribers was fifteen guilders with an additional thirty guilders for copies hand-colored by Merian herself. A second volume was planned for the other animals she had observed but it was never published. Her last years were spent preparing a Dutch edition of the first two vol-umes of *Der Raupen wunderbare Verwandlung* and on the comple-tion of its third volume. She suffered a stroke in 1715 and died in Amsterdam on January 13, 1717.

The role of artists in the scientific study of natural phenomena is a subject that embraces predecessors as famous as Leonardo and — more relevant for Merian, who lived in his home town for fifteen years — Albrecht Dürer. Perhaps she was shown some of his extraordinarily detailed watercolor studies of plants and animals. More probably she was familiar with the work of later artists such as George Hoefnagel (1542-1601) and Georg Flegel (d. 1638).[10] She was, as would be expected, a meticulously careful technician who normally worked on parchment, using semi-transparent and opaque watercolors. Her drawings must convey specific information about the structure of blooms, leaves, buds, and insect anatomy. As a result, her composi-tions can seem archaic, the plants artificially turned this way and that as she reveals their form to the eye of the scientist, rather than to that of the connoisseur. Nevertheless she manages, above all in the Suri-nam plates, to provide a great deal of aesthetic pleasure while ful-filling her scientific duties. She has an exceptional sense of surface rhythm and pattern and is willing to curl plant tendrils with slightly artificial elegance and to twist the tails of monkeys and crocodiles in order to enliven the design. Her placing of the specimen on the page is often adventurous. In *Der Raupen* she gives us a spectacular close-up of an iris with a swallowtail butterfly.[11] The banana in the *Metamorphosis* thrusts from the page like a rocket.[12] Other pages simply delight us with their perfect sense of interval and repeated formal elements, for example plate 52 of the *Metamorphosis*.[13] Many of her original watercolor studies for the Surinam volume are pre-served in a bound volume in the British Museum. It could not travel to the exhibition but perhaps its contents can be made more accessible in a facsimile edition. Its finest pages are among the most beautiful scientific illustrations of her period, and the best hand-colored edi-tions of the book are hardly less impressive. Merian is certainly one of the major artists of this genre and deserves to be as famous as Redouté and Audubon. The language barrier partly explains her neglect outside Holland and Germany, but even their scholars have yet to provide a complete catalog of her original watercolors, now scattered in collections from Minneapolis to Leningrad.[14] Such a study would illuminate an important phase of European cultural and scientific history.

34.
Metamorphosis of a Frog
Watercolor and tempera on vellum
$15^5/_{16}$ x $11^3/_8$ in. (38.9 x 28.9 cm.)
The Minneapolis Institute of Arts
The Minnich Collection (66.25.171)

8.
The Labadists were a religious sect founded by a French ex-Jesuit, Jean de Labadie (1610-1674), who had established a sort of Christian commune around the castle owned by the Sommelsdijck family. They rejected infant baptism, denied the presence of Christ in the Eucharist, and paid little attention to study of the Bible. They died out in the early eighteenth century.
9.
The American Museum of Natural History in New York owns the original edition of 1705 with beautifully hand-colored plates and the 1719 edition in Dutch bound with a nineteenth-century manuscript English translation of the text. The plates of this later edition are also hand-colored but not so sensitively as in the 1705 copy. Rücker (nos. 40-99) provides German summaries of many of the plate captions. According to the natives whom Merian interviewed, chewing the seed kernels of a plant called Flos Pavonis (pl. 45) prevented conception and resulted in spontaneous abortions. They did this in order to prevent their Dutch masters, who treated them badly, from increasing the labor force and to avoid having their children born into slavery.
10.
According to Rücker (11), the first plate, which shows the silkworm and mul-berry leaves, is close to the design of Georg Flegel's watercolor of this subject in Berlin (Dahlem Museum, Kupferstichkabinett).

11.
Rücker, pl. 9; she had already used this plate in the first volume of the *Neue Blumenbuch*.
12.
Rücker, no. 51 and pl. 24.
13.
Rücker, no. 91, pl. 27 (the tree belongs to the citrus family).

Merian here sets forth with her usual elegance and clarity a story now known to every schoolchild, though the life cycle of the frog may not have been so well understood in the seventeenth century. Typically she stresses the linear rhythms of the water plant and the delicately varied patterns on the frogs' skins. This page and that from the Morgan Library have every appearance of having been prepared for publication, but neither can be related to plates in her books on European plants and insects, which do include a few discussions of other species. Maybe she intended to produce a book on European amphibians and reptiles, or maybe these studies should simply be taken as an indication of her wide-ranging curiosity about the life cycles and habits of animals other than the insects in which she specialized.

35.
Study of a Painted Lady Butterfly, a Pink Underwing Moth, a Strawberry, A Pea Pod, Two Shells, and a Sprig of White Currants
Watercolor and tempera on vellum
3⅝ x 4⁷/₁₆ in. (9.2 x 11.3 cm.)
New York, The Metropolitan Museum of Art
Fletcher Fund (39.12)

A good many watercolor studies of the plants and animals by Merian that exist in public and private collections cannot be related to any of her published plates. Many of these drawings concentrate on an individual specimen. Others group several related plants and animals on a page, as she does in her published studies of insects and their fodder. In a few cases, however, her purposes seem to be artistic rather than scientific, as with the dish of fruit and nuts in the Albertina (no. 1027), which is signed and dated 1695 and is a perfectly respectable still-life composition. Her fame evidently attracted clients who were more interested in examples of her artistic skill than in her scientific discoveries, for whom such works must have been made.

Her tiny watercolor study in the Metropolitan Museum groups together insects, fruit, and shells but only as a casual study of prize specimens and not as a study of scientific relationships. Butterflies and moths do not feed on strawberries and green peas, as the drawing might imply to someone familiar with Merian's ideas, and the shells are evidently added simply to fill out the design. Though a little worn and faded, this sheet is a good example of the artist's great care and sensitivity when describing the complicated patterns on insects' wings. In some of her later studies of exotic moths and butterflies made in Surinam, she stresses interesting patterning on wings to such a degree that one suspects her of falsifying the model slightly in order to emphasize their spectacular appearance. In our work, which depicts only familiar fauna and flora, a delicate but accurate portrayal is her goal. It should be compared with her wonderful study of a locust and a beetle in Basel (Öffentliche Kunstsammlung, no. B: 387.18).

36

14.
The only American collections with examples of Merian's own watercolors known to the cataloguer are the Minneapolis Institute of Arts (cat. no. 34), the Pierpont Morgan Library, New York, and The Metropolitan Museum of Art, New York (cat. no. 35). Stuldreher-Nienhuis (see note 2, 159ff.) gives a list of the major public holdings of her watercolors then known but the list is neither complete nor reliable (see Rücker, 35ff.) and there are also good examples of her work in private hands (e.g. Rücker, nos. 19-21 and 23-24). There are a few signed and dated watercolors: one of 1684 in Darmstadt (Hessisches Landesmuseum); of 1693 in London (British Museum); of 1695 in Vienna (Albertina); of 1699 in Berlin (Dahlem Museum, Kupferstichkabinett); and of 1706 in Nuremberg (Germanisches Nationalmuseum). Two of a good group of her watercolors in Basel are repr. by Munsterberg (30). Finally, there are two volumes of her watercolor studies in the Royal Library, Windsor Castle, one of them containing studies for all the plates in the *Metamorphosis insectorum Surinamsium* except pl. XXVII, which has so far been noted in print only by Blunt.

Susan Penelope Rosse
British, ca. 1652-1700

Information about Susan Rosse is scant. We do not know exactly when she was born, nor when she married the jeweler Michael Rosse. None of her surviving signed works, which were all made after her marriage, are dated, although a lost portrait of the Moroccan ambassador was dated 1682. According to Vertue, who interviewed her husband after her death, she was first trained by her father, the miniaturist Richard Gibson (1615/16-1690), but she seems to have had access to the studio of Samuel Cooper (1609-1672), whose works "nobody ever copy'd . . . better."[1] With the exception of the miniatures based on Cooper models, none of which are signed and which are probably early works, her portraits tend to be small, even by the standards of the genre. The majority of her sitters are women, including at least two of the mistresses of Charles II (see cat. no. 36). She does not succumb to the tendency of most late seventeenth-century English portraitists to make their female sitters look identical and dim-witted. Instead she both flatters her subjects and suggests a considerable range of character in nuances of facial expression. She died in London in 1700, aged forty-eight, and was buried in St. Paul's, Covent Garden.

36.
Portrait of Eleanor (Nell) Gwyn (1650-1687)
Watercolor on vellum
1⅝ x 1⅜ in. (4.1 x 3.5 cm.)
Signed: SR
Cincinnati, Private Collection

Nell Gwyn was an actress who became the favorite mistress of Charles II, ousting the Duchess of Cleveland, Louise Renée de Kerouaille, from that position and bearing him two sons.[2] Both women were painted by Susan Rosse. Miniature portraits of the duchess exist in the Victoria and Albert Museum and in a private collection.[3] "Pretty, witty Nell," as Pepys described her, was a woman of lively spirit who excelled as an actress in comedy roles. Once she was caught by a mob in Oxford that thought she was the king's French mistress. She is reported to have stuck her head from the carriage window and proclaimed, "Pray good folks, be civil, 'tis the Protestant whore!" The completely frontal presentation of this miniature, which is unique among published examples of Rosse's work, reflects well the sitter's forthright character, while the glint in her eyes and the full mouth suggest her humor and sensuality. Considering the scale, it is a remarkably powerful image and may be Rosse's masterpiece.

37.
Self-Portrait of the Artist, ca. 1690
Watercolor on vellum laid on a rectangular card
Card: 3¾ x 2¾ in. (9.5 x 7 cm.)
Oval miniature: 3¼ x 2⅝ in. (8.2 x 6.7 cm.)
Inscribed on the verso in pencil: Mrs Rosse
London, Victoria and Albert Museum (457-1892)

This miniature is one of fourteen acquired by the museum in 1892 with a tooled leather wallet traditionally known as "Samuel Cooper's Pocket-Book."[4] At that time, all fourteen miniatures were attributed to Samuel Cooper, but G. C. Williamson pointed out a few years later that the costumes worn by many of the sitters indicated a date around 1690, a generation after Cooper's death, and furthermore that many of the miniatures had contemporary inscriptions on the back linking them with Susan Penelope Rosse and her circle. He therefore attributed all fourteen works to her, a suggestion subsequently accepted by other scholars.[5] Recently Graham Reynolds has re-examined the whole subject of the Pocket-Book and its contents.[6] While accepting that the majority of the miniatures are probably by Susan Rosse, including this self-portrait, he reattributes four of the miniatures, all unfinished portrait sketches, to Samuel Cooper. Three of them in fact have old inscriptions on the back associating them with him. Reynolds' conclusions also seem correct on stylistic grounds. Michael Rosse, the artist's husband, sold works by Cooper as well as copies after Cooper by his wife in 1723. Thus it is not surprising to find a few works by Cooper amidst this group of miniatures by her representing herself, her sister, her father-in-law, and some family friends.

Two of the miniatures are inscribed "Mrs Rosse" on the back.[7] Both

---

1.
In addition to Vertue, our primary sources for Susan Rosse are Long, 377, and Foskett, 1972, 481, and pl. 310. Foskett illustrates some additional works in London, 1973, 99-103.
2.
There is a good, detailed account of her life in the *Dictionary of National Biography,* from which all the information here is taken.
3.
No. P 21-1955 for the miniature in the Victoria and Albert; the other is in the collection of Daphne Foskett (Foskett, 1972, 481 and pl. 310, no. 774).
4.
Reynolds, 1 and pl. I.
5.
Williamson, I, 51-52 (cited by Reynolds, 1). Basil Long, Carl Winter, and Daphne Foskett all agreed with his conclusions.
6.
See note 4. I am indebted to John Murdoch, Assistant Keeper of Paintings at the museum, for sending me a copy of this excellent study.
7.
Reynolds, nos. 5 (pl. 18) and 6 (pl. 19).

37

38

are assumed to be self-portraits, although the inscription could mean only that Rosse painted them. In the miniature not shown here the sitter wears her hair arranged with falling corkscrew curls in a style inspired by Queen Catherine of Braganza. In the 1690 miniature the sitter wears her hair pulled back from her face in a plainer style partially covered by a striped scarf that falls over one shoulder onto her low-cut dress. The hair styles suggest that the first miniature dates from around 1680, and the one exhibited from around 1690, when Susan Rosse was in her late thirties. The sitter in question would not seem to be as old as this, but guessing ages in portraits is a notoriously untrustworthy business. The identification must, however, be regarded as tentative.

The miniatures in the Pocket-Book series by Rosse are larger than most of her signed works and more clearly inspired by the unfinished portrait sketches of Cooper, whom we know she admired. She seems to have wished to preserve some of the freshness of Cooper's sketches from life in her finished originals. Thus her modeling is not as detailed, nor are her tonal contrasts as carefully developed, as in Cooper's finished works. As a result, several of her best miniatures in this group have a direct candor and informality, their effect depending on apt characterization rather than polished flattery. Her skillful draftsmanship and her sure sense of design are more easily appreciated in this group than in most of her signed works, which tend to be extremely small. She was an apt practitioner of this demanding and subtle art form and much more than an able follower of England's best seventeenth-century miniature painter.

38.
Portrait of Robert Wignall, ca. 1690
Watercolor on vellum, laid on a card with a prepared gesso back
Card: 3¾ x 2¾ in. (9.5 x 7 cm.)
Oval miniature: 3⅛ x 2½ in. (7.9 x 6.3 cm.)
London, Victoria and Albert Museum (453-1892)

Only two of the nine miniatures by Susan Rosse from the "Samuel Cooper Pocket-Book" (see previous entry) represent male sitters. One of these is inscribed on the back, "My Father / Rosse"; the other is inscribed in the same way "Mr. Wignall Painter." The first inscription was either placed there by Rosse's husband and refers to his father, or by the artist, "father" being short for "father-in-law." The former alternative seems the more probable. Both gentlemen wear the large wigs and long cravats fashionable at the end of the century. The background here is plain; in that of Mr. Rosse, the artist included a landscape vista on the right.

Mr. Wignall, recorded as a "picture-drawer" in the *London Gazette* of April 5, 1697, is otherwise little known. A work signed by him passed through a London sale room in 1909, according to records in the file of the Department of Paintings at the museum. We can only assume that he was friendly with the artist and her husband. Though the final effect is now slightly marred by flaking paint loss around the edges, this is a lively small portrait, neatly composed and lightly but skillfully finished.

Rachel Ruysch
Dutch, 1664-1750

Rachel Ruysch is the first woman who not only achieved an international reputation as a major artist in her lifetime, but also suffered no visible decline in reputation after her death. Her works fetched high prices when she was alive and have remained expensive ever since. Only her decision to specialize in fruit and flower paintings has prevented her from being more widely appreciated. Sterling has called her "outstanding . . . [among] a galaxy of consummate flower painters [who appeared in Holland] in the second half of the seventeenth century."[1] Grant declared that she "is a supreme artist as well as a supreme painter, as great in her line as Rembrandt in his."[2] Not many art historians or collectors take her specialties seriously but even slight acquaintance with the genres to which she devoted her life will make apparent the exceptional quality of her work.

She was born in Amsterdam in 1664 to distinguished parents. Her mother, Maria Post, was the daughter of the architect Pieter Post. Her father, Anthony Frederick Ruysch, was a professor of anatomy and botany and an amateur painter who also collected scientific specimens — shells, fossils, skeletons, rare plants, and minerals.[3] One of her sisters, Anna Maria, also had some artistic talent.[4] Rachel's gifts were detected early, and in 1679, at the age of fifteen, she was apprenticed to Willem van Aelst, one of the finest flower and still-life painters active after 1650.[5] Her first dated works are of 1682; one is a study of insects and a thistle plant in a landscape,[6] the other a painting of flowers, apples, and quinces hanging in a bunch (Prague, Národní Galerie).[7] Her *Still Life with Flowers and Insects in a Landscape* (1685, Rotterdam, Museum Boymans-van Beuningen), which uses a shady landscape setting to display an impressive repertoire of flowers, vegetation, rocks, insects, and reptiles, is a work of complete technical assurance. It reveals too her appreciation of the work of Otto Marseus van Schriek, whose specialty was dark, woodland settings full of exotic fauna and flora, a strange blend of still life and scientific record.[8] She continued to paint both flower pictures and displays of lush fruit and insects, reptiles, and small mammals in wooded settings throughout her career, although flower paintings dominate her production.

She married the portrait painter Juriaen Pool II (1666-1745) in 1693; they entered The Hague painters' guild together in 1701.[9] They had ten children. Despite her domestic responsibilities she made a total of some sixty signed and dated works as well as roughly thirty-five works that are signed only.[10] There are also a few works of apparently autograph quality that are neither signed nor dated. She was court painter to the Elector Palatine, Johann Wilhelm von Pfalz, from 1708 until his death in 1716 and spent some of this period with his court in Düsseldorf. In 1716 the family settled once more in Amsterdam. She was active until three years before her death, proudly adding her age, eighty-three, to the signatures and dates on her last known works, a pair of flower pictures from 1747, now in Lille.[11]

These facts alone are impressive. Ruysch was professionally active before she was twenty, as were several other women represented here. Compared to earlier women artists she managed a substantial output, although it was not particularly notable by the standards of her male Dutch contemporaries, some of whom produced over eight hundred paintings. She had a large family to concern her, even if she had servants to help care for them. And she had almost seventy years of continuous artistic activity. Clearly she was a woman of prodigal physical and artistic energies. However, an accurate perception of her achievement is not yet possible. There are misattributions, copies, imitations, and possibly even some fakes among the two hundred thirty items listed by Grant in his useful monograph.[12] The locations of many of these works are at present unknown; no published illustrations exist of many of them. Even more important, the precise content of her works — the cataloguing of the various species of flowers, fruit, insects, reptiles, and plants that so passionately interested her — is hardly touched on in the literature.

After 1685, when she painted the *Still Life with Flowers and Insects in a Landscape*, Ruysch no longer imitated Schriek but developed a new type of still life from his work. He emphasized the landscape settings in which he placed a few select specimens but she played down the

1.
Sterling, 48.
2.
Grant, 1956, 20.
3.
Jaromir Síp, "Notities bij het Stilleven van Rachel Ruysch," *Nederlands kunst-historisch Jaarboek,* xix, 1968, 157-70.
4.
Her only work traceable today is a signed copy after a work of Abraham Mignon in Karlsruhe (Staatliche Kunsthalle, no. 378; see Mitchell, fig. 317), though other still lives are recorded in older sources.
5.
See Bergström, 220ff. He has already been mentioned as influencing Margaretha de Heer and courting Maria van Oosterwyck unsuccessfully.
6.
Werner Timm, "Bemerken zu einem Stilleben von Rachel Ruysch," *Oud-Holland,* 1962, 137-38. This work in Rostock was previously dated 1681 (Grant, 1956, no. 138).
7.
J. Síp, *Dutch Painting,* London, 1961, no. 40 (color pl.).

8.
See the articles cited in notes 3 and 6. Tufts implies that Ruysch invented wood scenes with snakes attacking smaller animals (1974, 99) but Schriek certainly was the originator of this genre. Two good examples of his work are illustrated by Bernt (nos. 737 and 738).
9.
Grant (1956, no. 8) illustrates a joint portrait signed by both artists last recorded in the G. Stein Collection in Paris in 1938.
10.
These statistics are taken from Grant's catalog of 230 items; see also note 12 below.
11.
Grant, 1956, nos. 197 and 198.
12.
Grant's catalog is uncritical, that is, simply a compilation of works attributed to Ruysch with no discussion of the evidence. It must therefore be used with caution. Some signed works (e.g., Grant no. 1, Hanover, of 1689) and Düsseldorf (not in Grant, museum inventory no. 248) are suspiciously flat and crude in handling. Some works we now know are by other artists (e.g., Grant no. 109, Amsterdam, Rijksmuseum, no. 2086, now given to Walscapelle). The *Flower Piece* in Raleigh

39

background in order to focus on concentrated groupings of plant and animal specimens that are far more complex than his.[13]

Some of Ruysch's paintings of this type use a simpler composition, although the results are nonetheless striking and original. An example in the Fitzwilliam Museum, Cambridge, features an arching cold green thistle plant set against a stone niche, beneath which a lizard crouches as various exotic insects fly past. In another work in the same collection, which may be quite early in date, she paints a stream with its banks, moss, pebbles, a few plants, and insects, all wonderfully fresh and artlessly composed.[14] The Rotterdam picture and its many later variations prove that she experimented with a variety of thematic possibilities and did not progress simply from modest, small canvases to large, complicated designs. Her most sumptuous treatments of this theme, however, were painted in the second decade of the eighteenth century. Her masterpiece in this vein may be the *Still Life with Fruit, Stag Beetle and Chaffinch Nest* of 1717 in Karlsruhe (Staatliche Kunsthalle).[15] It portrays a veritable harvest festival of translucent grapes, velvet-skinned peaches, shiny plums, a melon, a pomegranate, and ripe figs nestled into a dark corner of some fairy-tale garden where they are inspected by a bright blue lizard, a glossy black stag beetle, and other fauna. It is a slightly less elaborate version of her famous picture of 1716 in the Palazzo Pitti. The final effect in all these works of Ruysch is always somewhat surreal to the modern eye but they are no less appealing for that.

Ruysch's flower paintings are often composed around sweeping S-lines of movement marked by curved branches and stems. De Heem already understood the importance of a lively compositional structure for flower pictures; Ruysch continued the tradition but built more elaborate, more sculptural masses of blooms that surge with life. Indeed in the famous large flower piece of 1711 in the Palazzo Pitti she creates a veritable explosion of roses, tulips, sunflowers, carnations, and honeysuckle. She nearly always includes some fruit — dusky plums, a split pomegranate, a fuzzy peach — and always some insects, especially beetles, butterflies, grasshoppers, and dragonflies. The perfection of the specimens, which are seldom available in ideal condition in the same season, reminds us that Ruysch's realism is in fact an ideal representation.[16] She is in effect following the doctrine that it was the artist's duty to select from nature and to portray perfectly what nature could only render imperfectly. Above all the study of her work testifies to her profound knowledge of contemporary botany and zoology. Her works are an extraordinary synthesis of seventeenth-century scientific interest in the range and variety of species found in nature and the artistic traditions she used to display them. The results are beautiful visions of impossible natural perfection.

39.
Flower Still Life, after 1700
Oil on canvas
29¾ x 23⅞ in. (75.6 x 60.6 cm.)
Signed lower right: Rachel Ruysch
The Toledo Museum of Art
Gift of Edward Drummond Libbey (56.57)

The light orange, peach pink, and golden yellow color scheme of this superb flower picture contrasts with the darker tones used by Ruysch for her Viennese canvas (cat. no. 40) and may indicate a date for the Toledo picture well into the eighteenth century, when the trend toward lighter tones and more brilliant colors became apparent in her work and in that of her great rival, Jan van Huysum. Ruysch's strong sense of compositional movement is again apparent in the Toledo canvas. The stalks of poppies in the upper right and the poppies and a carnation along the lower edge establish the main lines of the design around which the sumptuously colored blooms surge like a cresting wave. There are two shells on the marble ledge supporting the vase and a few insects amidst the blossoms but essentially this is a painting of flowers chosen to create a special color effect. A companion picture of fruit, now lost, is recorded in a nineteenth-century sale. It depicted peaches, black and green grapes, apricots, oranges, maize, currants, and a few flowers as well as a bird's nest, a lizard, and insects. The fruits named also suggest a color scheme emphasizing gold, orange, and pink similar to that of this flower piece. Ruysch did not paint many pairs of still-life pictures, presumably because only unusually wealthy patrons could afford such an expensive commission demonstrating her skill in two different specialties.

40.
Still Life with Flowers and Plums, 1703
Oil on canvas
33 x 26¾ in. (84 x 68 cm.)
Signed lower right: Rachel Ruysch 1703
Vienna, Gemäldegalerie der Akademie der bildenden Künste (664)
(See color plate, p. 78)

One of Ruysch's most beautiful flower paintings, this is an excellent example of her compositional skills and especially of her ability to suggest movement, as if a gentle breeze were ruffling the whole arrangement. Long sinuous curves can be traced from the poppy, iris, and grass at the summit to the hanging branch of golden plums at the foot of the vase. The sculptural mass of grouped flowers is powerfully realized, as is the sense of growing life. The color scheme is a subdued harmony of pinks, rose, ocher, gold, cream, and orange set off against the dull greens and browns of the foliage and the dark background. There are more sumptuous, more flamboyant flower pieces by her, notably the gorgeous example in the Kunsthistorisches Museum (no. 572), and there are more modest compositions; but there are few that strike such a perfect balance of design, color, and floral content.

Although any flower piece can be read as a Vanitas, since all flowers can stand for the brevity of human life, any butterfly could mean resurrection, and any caterpillar could be man in his earthly existence,[17] Ruysch did not seem to stress such interpretations in her flower pieces as Oosterwyck did. She conveys rather her own passionate concern with the variety and beauty of nature, and hence of divine creativity.

(Tufts, 1974, fig. 56) is, as Anne Lowenthal pointed out to me, a version with slight variations of Willem van Aelst's signed *Flower Piece* of 1656 in Kassel.
13.
For another similar Ruysch, see Grant, 1956, no. 25 (pl. 13). There are about ten more Ruysch works of this type known.
14.
Grant, 1956, no. 114 (dated 1690) and 122 (undated).
15.
Ibid., no. 106. For the Palazzo Pitti version mentioned below, see Grant, no. 35, and Tufts, 1974, fig. 54. There is an autograph copy of the Karlsruhe picture in Dresden (Grant, 1956, no. 72, dated 1718). All three collections also own companion pictures of flowers by Ruysch.
16.
Sterling, 48.
17.
Bergström, 223-24.

Rosalba Carriera
Italian, 1675-1757

41

Although several women painters of the sixteenth and seventeenth centuries had international reputations, none enjoyed as great a success nor had as much influence on the art of her contemporaries as Rosalba Carriera. She was one of the originators of the Rococo style in painting in France and Italy. She popularized pastel as a medium for serious portraiture. While she introduced ivory as a support for miniatures and revolutionized the genre with her loose, painterly technique, her brilliant pastel technique was even more influential. These achievements have long been recognized by scholars, but with the decline in popularity of Rococo art, the aesthetic value of her art has been questioned.

The eldest of three daughters, she was born on October 7, 1675, to a modest Venetian clerk, Andrea Carriera, and his wife, Alba Foresti, a lace maker.[1] Her early years are not well documented, but she probably began by learning her mother's profession and then, as the lace industry declined, switched to decorating the ivory lids of snuffboxes for the tourist trade. Foreign visitors who discovered her talents are supposed to have encouraged her, first to try painting *tabacchieri* and then to try her hand at pastels.[2] Zanetti, writing in 1771, says that she was taught by G. Lazzari, G. Diamantini, and Antonio Balestra.[3] More recent writers have suggested that she was influenced by S. Bombelli and Fra Galgario.[4] In fact, neither in technique nor in types and composition does she come obviously close to any of her Venetian contemporaries. She was certainly selling miniatures by 1700; her first recorded pastel portrait was made three years later.[5] By 1704 the English amateur Christian Cole had had his portrait painted by her and had shown it to Giuseppe Ghezzi, the secretary of the Accademia di San Luca in Rome. A year later, after she had sent the Academy a miniature of a girl holding a dove, she was made an "accademico di merito," a title reserved for amateur supporters of the Academy and a few special artists, generally not Roman residents, who were not made to pass the normal tests for admission.[6] She had already sent work to Paris. Commissions soon followed from the Duke of Mecklenburg, the Elector Palatine, the King of Denmark,

---

1.
The standard account is Malamani, *Rosalba Carriera,* 1910, of which an earlier version with fuller documentation appeared in *Le Gallerie Nazionali Italiane,* IV, 1899, 27-149. The best account of her career in English is that of Levey in *Painting in XVIII-Century Venice,* 1959, 134ff. *Rosalba Carriera* is the only book on a woman artist included in the useful series I Maestri di Colore (F. Cessi, 1967).
2.
P. J. Mariette, who knew her, says that a French artist called Jean Steve who was living in Venice persuaded her to try painting snuffboxes (*Abecedario . . .,* published in *Archives de l'art français,* II, 1851, 329). This artist has been identified by C. Jeanneret, 772. Cole is usually credited with introducing Rosalba to pastels.
3.
Zanetti, 449.
4.
Gatto, 182-93. For illustrations of works by Diamantini, Balestra, Bombelli, and Fra Galgario, see the exhibition catalog *La pittura del seicento a Venezia,* ed. P. Zampetti, Venice, 1959. The technical freedom and gay palette of G. A. Pellegrini probably had more impact on her art than the work of any other Venetian contemporaries or predecessors. She is said to have admired Correggio greatly but could have seen little of his work in the original until her visits to Paris and Modena.

and the future Elector of Saxony. For the rest of her life she had a constant stream of visitors at her door and more requests for work than she could fulfill.

In 1716 Pierre Crozat, a wealthy Parisian banker and art collector, met Rosalba during his tour of Italy and was greatly impressed by her work and by her person. They became good friends and it was his urging and his offers of hospitality that finally convinced her to visit Paris in the spring of 1720.[7] Her visit was a triumph. She was made a member of the French Academy in October and was feted and entertained by the court and by all the most influential members of Parisian society. She met Antoine Watteau and drew his portrait and was introduced to many other artists as well. Her diary records a daily procession of visitors, sittings, and excursions to local sights and art collections. According to her biographers, Rosalba was not gregarious by nature, and the constant social pressures of Paris eventually became a strain. In the spring of 1721 she returned to Venice, which she left only rarely for the rest of her life. She visited Modena in 1723 to paint the daughters of Duke Rinaldo d'Este and went to Vienna for six months in 1730 to work for Emperor Charles VI. Otherwise she lived quietly in her house on the Grand Canal with her widowed mother (her father died in 1719) and her unmarried sister, Giovanna, who assisted her by taking care of most day-to-day practical matters and also by preparing the grounds, executing draperies, and making copies of her sister's work.

Carriera was said to be an accomplished violinist as well as a literate conversationalist, but the main impression one has from reading her diaries and letters is that of a modest woman totally dedicated to her work who allowed herself few distractions. The death of her sister Giovanna in 1738 caused a depression that kept her from working for several months. In 1741 her sister Angela was widowed and came to live with Rosalba. The loss of her sight, of which she had the first premonitions as early as 1721 but which became serious in 1746, and which several operations in 1749 failed to cure, was her greatest personal tragedy. Rosalba's blindness exacerbated her tendency to suffer from periods of intense depression, and she is said to have ended her life in a state of complete mental collapse.[8] She died on April 15, 1757.

Although she is now best known for her pastel portraits and allegorical paintings, she first made her name as a miniature painter who, in this genre, according to Orlandi, "has surpassed all the other Professors of our time."[9] It was as a miniaturist that she was honored by the Roman Academy in 1705, and it was as a miniaturist that *Il Mercurio Galante* announced her presence in Paris in 1720. Although she was filling commissions for pastel portraits by 1703, she told one patron in 1706 that she was too busy painting miniatures to learn pastel technique properly.[10] On the other hand, it has been said that she gave up painting miniatures quite early in her career once she had established her reputation in the faster, less painstaking medium of pastel.[11] She is nevertheless documented as making miniatures as late as 1736 and seems to have produced works in both media for much of her career, often repeating her pastels in miniatures. She was fastidious about her materials. Friends in Rome and Paris searched out the best manufacturers of pastel chalks for her, even commissioning specially blended tints for her, particularly of flesh colors. One of Mariette's last gifts to her shortly before she became permanently blind was a box of new pastels from Paris.[12]

The most original aspects of Rosalba Carriera's art were her choice of new media for portraits and miniatures and her dazzlingly fresh technique. She was also a superb and subtle colorist and a shrewd judge of character who knew how to pose her sitters, even within her deliberately restrictive format of a head-and-shoulders composition that usually omitted the hands, in ways that suggested their personalities while flattering their sensibilities. In an age when it was far more important for a woman to be physically attractive than it is now, Rosalba's ability to render all her female subjects charming without reducing their features to bland stereotypes was much appreciated. Her male portraits are hardly less idealized than those of her female sitters. Patrons of both sexes hoped to find in their purchases passages of her characteristic virtuoso chalkwork in which lace is suggested by dragging the flat edge of white chalk across a finished underdrawing of darker tones; a similar trick makes the powdered hair seem to float softly round the face. No works show her powers of observation and understanding of human character better than her own self-portraits. She was not an attractive woman, as her contemporaries noted with characteristic disappointment on several occasions, but she does not flatter herself, nor attempt to disguise in her later images her weakening left eye.[13] The finest and most moving of these self-portraits is that made for Consul Smith shortly before she went blind, now in the collection of Her Majesty the Queen at Windsor Castle.[14] She faces us almost directly but her gaze is withdrawn, her lips firmly set. The choice of dark fur robes and the somber mood can be read, in retrospect, as signs of her approaching isolation from her profession and her unhappy last years.

She was always more appreciated by foreign clients than by Venetian patrons. Her brother-in-law, Gian Antonio Pellegrini, who married Angela in 1704, helped to spread Rosalba's fame early in her career during his visits to England, Germany, and France. He was in Paris when she arrived there, working on a ceiling fresco for the Banque de France, and was later responsible for her invitation to Vienna in 1730. Pierre Crozat was only one of her many enthusiastic French patrons. English Grand Tour visitors were regular customers and Joseph Smith, who became their local consul in 1744, was a longtime friend and supporter. The largest collection of her works was that formed in Dresden by Augustus III, Elector of Saxony and King of Poland, who first met the artist in 1712. He amassed more than one hundred fifty of her pastels and miniatures, and when he failed to lure Rosalba to Dresden brought her best pupil, Felicita Sartori, there as the wife of one of his courtiers.[15] This preponderance of foreign

5.
Malamani, 15 and 17. Her first surviving dated pastel portrait is of 1710 (Gatto, 182).
6.
Malamani, 25-26.
7.
Malamani (10), who published the only accurate edition of her Paris diary, points out that it is primarily a list of clients made for business purposes and is not a literary account of her stay.
8.
Zanetti, 449.
9.
P. A. Orlandi, *Abecedario pittorico . . .* , Bologna, 1704 (edition cited: Venice, 1753, 448-49).
10.
Malamani, 31.
11.
She charged 50 zecchini for a miniature but only 20 for a pastel portrait without hands (30 with hands). For a discussion of her later miniatures, see Malamani, 105.

12.
Ibid., 96.
13.
The empress' reaction after first meeting Carriera in Vienna was, "Bertolo mio [he introduced them], questa tua pittrice sàra valente ma è molta brutta" (Bertoli, my dear, this painter of yours may be good but she is very ugly) (Malamani, 78). For a caricature of Carriera by A. M. Zanetti the Elder, see F. Vivian, *Il Console Smith mercante e collezionista*, Venice, 1971, pl. IV.
14.
M. Levey, *The Later Italian Pictures in the Collection of H. M. the Queen*, London, 1964, no. 446. It was painted between 1744 and 1746. Her most elaborate earlier self-portrait is the one now in the Uffizi, made for the Grand Duke Cosimo III de' Medici in 1715 (Tufts, 1974, fig. 57). Another late self-portrait is reproduced by Cessi, pl. XVI.
15.
There are four miniatures by Sartori (ca. 1715-1760) in the Gemäldegalerie, Dresden (1967 catalog, nos. M21, M22, M26, and M31) and one in the Victoria and Albert Museum, London (P30-1955). Her style is closely modeled on that of her teacher.

patrons in part reflected the economic decline of Venice and the shift from Italy to Germany, France, and England of the major political, economic, and artistic power. It was also true, however, that her informal small portraits were not suited to official Venetian taste. The ceremonial traditions of that dying Republic required large, full-length formal oil portraiture, even if there were no artists of distinction to produce them.[16] In France, Carriera established a fashion for pastel portraits that persisted into the nineteenth century. The technical innovations she initiated were taken up and perfected by Maurice Quentin de la Tour, the greatest exponent of this medium in the eighteenth century, and by several talented women.[17] Rosalba's "fancy pieces," her pastels of young maidens with bosoms barely covered by diaphanous veils who ostensibly represent subjects like Air, Spring, and Watchfulness, seem insipidly sweet to modern taste. It is easier for us to appreciate the fact that she was one of the finest portrait painters in a century of great portraiture as well as a brilliant practitioner of that underrated genre, the miniature.

41.
Portrait of Robert, Lord Walpole (1700-1751), ca. 1725
Watercolor on ivory
$3^5/_{16}$ x $2^5/_{16}$ in. (8.4 x 5.9 cm.)
London, Victoria and Albert Museum (P 160-1910)

Since pastels are too fragile to be lent to a traveling exhibition, Carriera can only be represented by her miniatures. As a result, this neglected facet of her artistic achievement can be emphasized, particularly the brilliant draftsmanship of her miniatures, which is otherwise visible only on her best-preserved pastels. This particular miniature is one of her finest representing a male sitter and is exceptionally well preserved.

The decoration of snuffboxes in Venice was not a serious art form but a craft catering to the tourist trade.[18] The exterior of the box, generally oval in shape and most commonly made of ivory, was usually ornamented with small pierced holes filled with a darker color or, in fancier models, with tiny metal pins. The inner surface of the lid was painted with some mythological or genre subject, sometimes of erotic content, which was then varnished to protect the design. That Carriera should not have been content to produce these pedestrian trinkets but instead developed from them a new form of miniature painting says much for both her native talent and ambition and for the perception and support of those who first realized her potential.

The reception of Carriera's miniature of a *Young Girl Holding a Dove* by the Academy is worth recounting in detail. In a letter to the artist, Cole reports that Carlo Maratta held the miniature in his hand for half an hour, finally saying that she had chosen a difficult subject — painting white on white — and that not even Guido Reni could have surpassed this work.[19] Maratta was the most famous and most powerful artist in Rome; his reaction must have helped to establish her reputation throughout Europe. Cole also noted that "a great Spanish virtuoso sculptress" was honored in the same ceremony as Carriera; this can only have been Luisa Roldán.[20]

16.
Levey, *Painting,* 134.
17.
See the discussion in the introduction of Marie Suzanne Giroust-Roslin, Madeleine Basseporte, and Teresa Concordia Mengs.
18.
Jeannerat illustrates some characteristic examples and publishes a miniature by Carriera in the Uffizi, the back of which has the same kind of pierced decoration as the snuffboxes. Colding (125ff.) provides a good discussion of her contribution to the art of miniature painting.
19.
Malamani, 25-26, and Colding, 125. Her admission to the Academy is recorded in the archives of the Academy, volume 46, f. 114, September 27, 1705.
20.
Roldán is not named by Cole but the "grande virtuosa scultrice che sta a Madrid et ha inviato un bozzo bellissimo" must be her. She is not, however, listed as a member by Missirini.

This first documented work of Carriera's is a faintly tinted mono-chrome of cream and white relieved by only a little blue in the sky, a little green in the landscape, a little buff in the skirt, and the slightest tinges of rose in some flesh areas. The brushwork, which tolerates enlargement to several times the size of the original, is of astonishing variety and freedom compared with the normal technique then in use.[21] She uses flicks, squiggles, blotches, and dots as well as exquisitely careful sfumato shading to suggest textures, light, and space. Here, long before Boucher and Fragonard, is the essence of Rococo *pittura di tocco.* As Longhi wrote in 1946, "she knew how to express with incomparable force the evanescent delicacy of an epoch."[22]

The portrait of Robert, Lord Walpole, must have been painted about twenty years later, although we do not know exactly when the sitter, who was the oldest son of Sir Robert Walpole and the older brother of Horace Walpole, visited Venice.[23] The work is recorded at Strawberry Hill in 1784, when it was justly described as being painted "with all the force of oil." It is an informal portrait, an approach best suited to the intimacy of the genre. The sitter does not wear a wig and a hint of a smile lingers in his expression. Her virtuoso technique can be seen throughout. The cloak is shaded with tiny dots but also with a few long bold strokes of dark paint. The eyebrows have been finished off with a few bold blobs that contrast with the fine streaks and spots shading the cheeks and the cravat. The result is one of her most sparkling miniatures.

42

42.
Woman at Her Dressing Table, ca. 1730
Watercolor and gouache on an ivory plaque
3⅜ x 4⅛ in. (8.6 x 10.5 cm.)
The Cleveland Museum of Art
Edward B. Greene Collection (40.1203)

Even more than the *Young Girl Holding a Dove,* this miniature of Carriera's exemplifies Rococo sensibility. The subject has a frivolity that calls to mind the extreme disparities of income in the eighteenth century that allowed some women to surround themselves with silks, flowers, and perfumes while the majority struggled to survive. In fact the image is an ideal fantasy no closer to the daily life of a rich, young woman then than modern advertisements for expensive cosmetics are to the lives of their users.

In technical terms this work is a dazzling achievement, far more sophisticated than her *Young Girl Holding a Dove* of 1705. It is executed with a nicely judged blend of delicacy and brio. Some areas are smooth, others textured with strokes both broad and narrow, others dotted and stippled. She has also let patches of wet color dry without blotting them, thus reinforcing their contours and empha-sizing her casual virtuosity. The color scheme stresses a deep lapis blue and a range of peach and apricot oranges combined with pale and dark neutral tones. No one in Venice could have taught her to paint like that; her technique was very much her own personal invention.

21.
Alinari's photograph (7112a) enlarges it to measure 9 x 7 in., whereas the original is about 3½ by 2 in. For a discussion of earlier techniques on vellum, card, and copper, see Jeannerat and Colding.
22.
R. Longhi, *Viatico per cinque secoli di pittura veneziana,* Florence, 1946, 36.
23.
C. M. Kauffman, Keeper of the Department of Prints and Drawings at the Victoria and Albert Museum, kindly informed me that the following inscription appears on the thin wooden backboard of the miniature: "Robert Lord Walpole / Eldest Son to Sr Robert Walpole / Earl of Oxford./ Drawn by Rosalba / at Venice / H. W." A piece of paper attached to the other side of the board reads: "Robert / Lord Walpole / Eldest Son to / Sir Robert Walpole. Drawn by Rosalba / at / Venice." The initials H. W. are those of Horace Walpole, to whom the miniature belonged, for it appears in an inventory of 1784 of the contents of Strawberry Hill.

43

Giulia Lama
Italian, ca. 1685 — after 1753

The life and career of Giulia Lama are poorly documented. The first evidence we have is an engraved portrait of Pietro Grimani made by Andrea Zucchi in 1719 from a drawing by Lama,[1] which proves that she was a fully trained and accomplished artist by this time. She appears to be about forty years old in her *Self-Portrait* of 1725 (Florence, Uffizi), which suggests a birth date of about 1685.[2] Her father was perhaps Agostino Lama, a little-known Venetian painter who died in 1714, aged seventy. A Venetian guidebook of 1733 mentions three altarpieces by Giulia in Venetian churches, two of which survive — *a Crucifixion with Saints* in San Vitale and a *Madonna in Glory with Two Saints* in Santa Maria Formosa (the latter recently restored). On the basis of these four works scholars have reconstructed her artistic personality, attributing to her some twenty-six paintings previously assigned to artists like Jan Lyss, D. Maggiotto, F. Bencovich, the young G.B. Tiepolo, and, above all, G.B. Piazzetta. Ruggeri has also attributed to her about two hundred drawings, many of them in one private collection in Bergamo, which include studies for her altarpieces and some striking studies of the male nude all in loosely handled black chalk. We do not know when she died, only that she was still alive in 1753.

This bare skeleton of facts was recently fleshed out by the discovery of a letter written in March 1728 by Abbot Luigi Conti to Madame de Caylus.[3] He wrote: "I have just discovered a woman here who paints better than Rosalba [Carriera] when it comes to large compositions. I was much taken by one of her works in miniature, but she is presently engaged on a large work. The subject of the picture is the rape of Europa, but the bull is still in a wood far from the sea; the companions of Europa crowd round the bull on which the laughing Europa is mounting. This group of figures is full of poetry because this woman excels as much in that art as in painting, and I find in her poems all the virtues of Petrarch; her name is Giulia Lama. In her youth she studied mathematics under the celebrated Father Maffei. The poor woman is persecuted by [other] painters, but her virtue triumphs over her enemies. It is true that she is as ugly as she is

1.
Pallucchini, 1933, 400. Pallucchini's articles of 1933, 1968, and 1970 gradually rescued Giulia Lama from total oblivion and pieced together her career, a contribution acknowledged by U. Ruggeri in his useful short monograph on the artist (*Dipinti e disegni di Giulia Lama,* Bergamo, 1973) to which this entry is much indebted.
2.
Perhaps misled by her plain features, scholars exaggerate her age; one would expect her to be younger than Piazzetta (born 1683). Conti (see next note) calls her "fille" in 1728, a word hardly applicable to a woman in her early forties.
3.
Pallucchini, 1970, 161 (reprinted by Ruggeri, 9, note 7). The translation from the French text is mine.

witty, but she speaks with grace and polish, so that one easily pardons her face. She works in lace and has thought much about the machine that Clelia Borromea has thought up for making lace mechanically as one makes stockings and materials. I believe that this machine is not impossible to realize, and the one who invents it will earn a lot of money, and will halve the time now needed by women lace makers. Suggest this idea to your son; perhaps he saw Lama when he was in Venice. She lives, however, a very retired life."

The letter is important not only because it fills in somewhat the background and character of Lama and indicates that she was mathematically gifted, a good poet, a lace maker, and inventor as well as a painter. It also contains the first evidence known to me of outright opposition on the part of male artists to the career of a woman. Since there is no evidence that Carriera was similarly persecuted, the explanation cannot be simply that Lama was a woman practicing a profession traditionally male. Carriera's immunity may be explained by her creation of a new market of her own for miniatures on ivory and pastel portraits, so that she did not compete with the male artists making a living by painting altarpieces and palace decorations. Carriera's huge success, however — she was famous throughout Europe by 1720 — may have suggested to male Venetian artists the disturbing prospect of women becoming similarly successful in the prestigious field of public and private figure paintings, just as Giulia Lama was emerging from Piazzetta's studio in the 1720s. It appears they were not prepared to tolerate such competition. The frankly negative response to Lama's lack of physical charm should also be noted, for this reaction will recur in the biographies of several other eighteenth-century women artists.

The names of the artists with whom Lama has been confused will give an idea of her style and her level of achievement. She chose to base her art on the most eccentric and in some ways the most original of Venetian eighteenth-century painters, Giovanni Battista Piazzetta (1683-1754), instead of taking the easy path to success offered by the lighter, prettier Rococo manner practiced by artists like Amigoni, Pittoni, Sebastiano Ricci, and Tiepolo. Piazzetta's work is characterized by striking chiaroscuro contrasts, by earthy, even ugly figure types, and by novel dramatic interpretations of familiar subjects. He had formed this manner not in Venice but in Bologna, where from about 1703 to 1711 he studied the early manner of Guercino and the work of G.M. Crespi, "whose dusky, glowing amalgams of sober monumentality and wry genre are necessary predecessors to Piazzetta's later accomplishments."[4] Lama's presence in his studio is not recorded, although their friendship is documented by a beautiful portrait of her by Piazzetta.[5] She presumably came into contact with him in the early 1720s (scholars see none of his influence in the 1719 portrait engraving of Pietro Grimani) and was clearly having some public success by 1728.

Comparison of Piazzetta's and Lama's interpretation of the same theme, Judith preparing to decapitate Holofernes, reveals how well she understood the principles of his work and how successfully she could work in the same idiom.[6] In Piazzetta's picture all we see of Holofernes are his massive shoulders in the left corner which are angled toward the figure of Judith, who looks heavenwards for strength and inspiration as she draws her sword. Lama also places the giant on the left and the heroine on the right but she stretches out the body of Holofernes full length across the canvas and shows Judith absorbed in prayer, thus stressing the vulnerability of the victim and the virtue of the heroine, though at the expense of the dramatic tension created by Piazzetta. It is nevertheless a powerful essay in his manner. Her *Crucifixion* in San Vitale (by 1733) and her *Female Saint in Glory* (Malamocco, Parish Church, after 1733?) are impressive large-scale orchestrations of the shifting patches of light and shade typical of Piazzetta and his school. She is uneven, as her drawings reveal very clearly, but she was an ambitious and gifted painter of dramatic narrative and one of the few women active before the nineteenth century whose figure paintings deserve serious study.

43.
The Martyrdom of St. Eurosia
Oil on canvas
23¼ x 15¾ in. (59 x 40 cm.)
Venice, Ca' Rezzonico, Museo del Settecento

This work, like so many by Lama, was called Piazzetta when it entered the collection of the Ca' Rezzonico in 1962, although Goering had suggested an attribution to Lama in 1935. Pallucchini and Ruggeri both gave it to Lama, the latter noting in addition that a drawing in the Metropolitan Museum, New York, also previously called Piazzetta, is certainly connected with this painting.[7] It is a small work and may be a sketch for a larger commission so far unidentified.

The Martyrdom of St. Eurosia has all of Lama's characteristics — a dramatic compositional structure and figure types that recall Piazzetta but with more stress on the homeliness of the physiognomies and on the anatomical distortions produced by the shifting chiaroscuro. The presentation of the story is as brutally frank as *Judith Beheading Holofernes* by Gentileschi. The severed body pours blood towards us, the splayed hand in the foreground still seems alive, the head is held aloft by the triumphant executioner who watches our reaction.[8] Piazzetta himself had trouble making a living as a painter because his works did not appeal to the prevailing taste for light tones, pastel shades, and lighthearted subjects. How much more true this must have been of Lama, whose work seems to emphasize those very qualities in Piazzetta's work that explain his lack of popular acclaim.

4.
Barry Hannegan in *Painting in Italy in the Eighteenth Century: Rococo to Romanticism*, Chicago, 1970, 86.
5.
Thyssen-Bornemisza Collection, Lugano (Pallucchini, 1956, pl. 13).
6.
Piazzetta's picture is in a private collection in Milan (Pallucchini, 1956, figs. 72-73; also no. 32 in the catalog cited in note 4). For Lama's picture, see Ruggeri, fig. 6. Its present location is not known.
7.
J. Bean and F. Stampfle, *Drawings from New York Collections III: The Eighteenth Century in Italy*, New York, 1971, no. 37. It is attributed to Piazzetta in the so-called "Reliable Venetian Hand," which is indeed unusually reliable for both major and minor artists. The chalk stroke used is a little longer and thinner than is usual in Lama's drawings, and the chiaroscuro is hardly noted, which is not typical of her. It is possible that Piazzetta made a drawing which Lama used. On the other hand, the technique of the Metropolitan drawing is not especially close to most of Piazzetta's drawings either.

8.
The cult of St. Eurosia (not Eurasia, the spelling given by Ruggeri) began in Jaca, Spain, in the eighth century, according to *Butler's Lives of the Saints* (June 25), and spread to Lombardy. She was a noble virgin from Bayonne who was slain by Saracens when she refused to marry a Moorish chieftain. She is invoked against bad weather.

Marie Anne Loir
French, ca. 1715-after 1769

Although ten dated portraits of wealthy sitters by Marie Anne Loir are known, her own life and personal circumstances remain somewhat mysterious. She belonged to an artistic family that had been active in Paris as silversmiths since the seventeenth century. Her father was not an artist, though he worked for the king, but her brother was Alexis Loir III (1712-1785), a pastelist and sculptor.[1] Since she received payments for portraits of the Duc de Bourbon in 1737 and 1738, she must have finished her training by then and was probably at least twenty.[2] She was a pupil of Jean François de Troy's (1679-1752), who settled in Rome in 1738 as the director of the French Academy,[3] and it is possible that she went to Rome at this time too. Her brother Alexis was there by 1739,[4] and a portrait by Marie Anne of that year has an identifying inscription on the back in Italian.[5] In any event she is not recorded in Paris between 1738 and 1746, when Alexis returned there to marry and to join the Academy.[6] She was not made a member but was elected to the Academy of Marseilles in 1762.[7] There are portraits by her dated or datable 1745-49 (see cat. no. 44), 1751, 1754, 1756, 1760, 1763, and 1769. She was working for patrons from Pau in the 1760s; another portrait of hers is recorded in Toulouse in 1779.[8] That essentially is all we know about her. The dry facts laid out here cannot be enlivened with gossip from contemporary diaries or with anecdotes from an early biography. Even her date of death is unknown.

She seems to have worked exclusively as a portraitist for wealthy and mostly aristocratic patrons. Her work is similar to that of de Troy, who did not often paint portraits, and of Jean Marc Nattier (1685-1766) and Louis Tocqué (1696-1772), who usually did; among their works are probably overlooked, unsigned canvases of hers.[9] She mastered the contemporary idiom for portraits of fashionable sitters but tempered the prevailing flattery and emphasis on details of dress — the gorgeous velvets and silks, the fragile lace trimmings — with a franker realism than was usual in Paris. She also did not indulge her female patrons with the mythological disguises that now make some of Nattier's ladies look faintly ridiculous. Her few surviving works

are of good quality. Nevertheless it seems clear that by 1740 the mere fact of being a talented woman portraitist no longer attracted special attention in Paris, and what she offered the public was not sufficiently different from the work of her contemporaries for her to achieve a distinct reputation. The fact that several of her last recorded works were made for patrons in Pau suggests that she was having trouble finding commissions in Paris.[10] Perhaps she even moved to the south of France. There must be more information about her in archives in Paris, Pau, and perhaps Marseilles. She is a good example of a woman artist ripe for research and certainly deserves the publicity of a serious article illustrating all her known works, including those known from engravings.

44.
Portrait of Gabrielle-Emilie le Tonnelier de Breteuil, Marquise Du Châtelet, 1745-49
Oil on canvas
39¾ x 31½ in. (101 x 80 cm.)
Bordeaux, Musée des Beaux-Arts (15)

The Marquise Du Châtelet was famous for her erudition and for her friendship with Voltaire, with whom she lived almost continuously from 1734 until her death in 1749. She had displayed exceptional gifts for science, music, and languages as a child, but after her marriage at eighteen in 1725 to Florent Claude, Marquis Du Châtelet, a military man whose intelligence was no match for hers, she established herself in Parisian society, had three children and a couple of affairs. She met Voltaire, twelve years her senior, in 1733. Their relationship brought her back to the intellectual interests of her youth. When the publication of Voltaire's *Lettres philosophiques* in 1734 led to a warrant for his arrest, he retreated to Lorraine, where she joined him after pleading his cause in Paris. They restored his chateau at Circy and made it a gathering place for important literary and scientific figures. She produced three major publications: the *Institutions de physique* of 1740, which helped to make the ideas of Leibnitz known in France; the *Discours sur la nature et la propa-*

1.
The confusion over her family origins can be cleared up by using two recently published collections of documents. The inventory made after the death of Charles Gérin, a curate, on March 7, 1746, was prepared by his nephews and nieces, among them "Guillaume Loir, marchand orfèvre . . ., Alexis Loir, peintre . . ., Marie-Anne et Louise Loir, filles majeures, demeurant rue Neuve-des-Petits-Champs . . . et Jérôme Loir, orfèvre à Pau." A second document makes it clear that the first four named are brothers and sisters (M. Rambaud, *Documents du Minutier Central concernant l'histoire de l'art, 1700-1750*, Paris, 1964, 192-93). The marriage certificate of Alexis Loir, dated June 3, 1746, describes him as "peintre du Roi et son Académie royale de peinture et sculpture . . ., fils de Nicolas Loir, ancien officier du Roi et de Marie-Anne Gérin" (D. Wildenstein, *Documents inédits sur les artistes français du XVIIIe siècle*, Paris, 1966, 98).
2.
The payments were published by G. Maçon, *Les arts dans la maison de Condé*, Paris, 1903, 72-73.
3.
De Troy mentions her in a letter of 1747 as a pupil with whom he was still in touch (F. Aubert, "Joseph-Marie Vien," *Gazette des beaux-arts*, 1867, 283). A

letter of Natoire to Duchesne, written from Rome on May 28, 1751, makes it clear that Loir and de Troy were also good friends. "Personne n'auroit put s'acquitter mieux que vous annoncer la triste nouvelle de la mort de M. de Troy à Mlle. Loir" (No one could have handled better than yourself the task of announcing to Mlle. Loir the sad news of the death of Monsieur de Troy), he wrote; de Troy left a watch and a gold snuffbox to her in his will (*Archives de l'art français*, III, 1852-53, part II, 276).
4.
P. L. Ghezzi made a drawing of Alexis in Rome on September 8, 1739 (F. Noack in Thieme-Becker, s.v.).
5.
G. Guillot, *Catalogue du Musée de Saint-Lo*, Saint-Lo, 1905, 11-12. The inscription reads: "Ritratto del sign. Conte di Matignon fratello del signore principe di Monaco, e sonatore di piva, d'Età 17, Dipinto dalla siga. Loire, 1739." The sitter's full name was Marie Charles Auguste Grimaldi (1722-1749). I have been unable to learn whether he was then in Rome.
6.
See note 1.

167

gation du feu of 1744; and a translation of Newton's *Principia Mathematica*, which appeared after her death. Her end was a tragic misfortune. Always a woman of passionate temperament, she fell in love with a young officer at the court of Stanislas of Lorraine in Lunéville, where she and Voltaire were guests in 1748, and became pregnant. The baby was delivered safely early in September 1749, but she died a few days later from puerperal fever.[11]

In 1745 the marquise and Voltaire were in Paris, where the controversial writer was for once in official favor, thanks to the support of Madame de Pompadour. He was given minor court appointments and was elected to the Academy. At the same time Nattier painted a portrait of the marquise, which was exhibited in the Salon of 1745 but is now known only from engravings. Loir's portrait is said to be based on that of Nattier,[12] and does follow his composition in some respects, but it is by no means a precise copy. The similarities suggest, however, that Loir might not have painted the marquise from life but instead might have made a version of Nattier's portrait for one of the sitter's Parisian admirers.

The iconography of the painting makes obvious reference to the scientific and mathematical interests of the marquise, as well as to her private life. She holds a pair of dividers; behind her to the right can be seen a celestial globe, a set-square, and paper with calculations. A wall of books provides a backdrop. She holds a carnation, symbol of true love. A visitor to the chateau at Circy in 1744 reported that she and Voltaire were extremely happy, "L'un fait des vers de son côté et l'autre les triangles."

Loir respects the idealizing conventions of Nattier's original to some degree but her treatment throughout is far more straightforward and realistic than is usually true of his idyllically pretty productions. Her drapery is more simply arranged and treated. Above all, the painting of the marquise's face is frank, direct, and personal. Her signs of middle age are not disguised. Her splendid dark eyes dominate everything and suggest both her passionate temperament and her intelligence.

44

7.
R. Mesuret, *Les expositions de l'Académie Royale de Toulouse de 1751 à 1791*, Toulouse, 1972, no. 3680.
8.
A *Portrait of a Woman* inscribed on the back, "Agée de 49 ans et peint par Mlle. Loir, en avril 1751," was sold by Parke-Bernet, New York, on November 19, 1955, lot 434. For the works of 1754, 1756, and 1760, see Thieme-Becker, s.v. For the portrait of 1763, see B. Lossky, *Inventaire des collections publiques françaises. Tours, Peintures du XVIIIième siècle*, Paris, 1962, no. 71. The subject, Antoine Duplaa, is shown at the age of nine, according to an inscription on the frame. As transcribed by Lossky, it says that Duplaa was born in Pau, December 4, 1763, and was painted on September 1, 1763; the first year should presumably read 1753. The portrait of Président Bayard of 1769 is in the Musée des Beaux-Arts at Pau (repr. in Castres, 1973, no. 22). For the portrait in Toulouse exhibited in the Salon of 1779, see Mesuret (note 7). It belonged to "M. de Voisins, Associé ordinaire."
9.
A. Doria (*Louis Tocqué*, Paris, 1929, 121, 129, and 148) attributes or associates with Loir three portraits then given to Tocqué. All were then on the art market; none are illustrated, making it difficult to pursue Doria's suggestions.

10.
Jérôme Loir, Marie Anne's brother or cousin, was working in Pau in 1746 (see note 1); his contacts presumably explain the portrait commissions given to Marie Anne and Alexis by the Duplaa family (see Lossky, cited in note 8).
11.
Dictionnaire de biographie française, XI, 1967, 1191f.
12.
P. de Nolhac, *Nattier, peintre de la cour de Louis XV*, Paris, 1910, 228. Nolhac describes Nattier's painting as an oval. The marquise was wearing a fur-edged dress; books and a sphere appeared in the background. He cites an engraving by Haid. Basil S. Long (*Catalogue of the Jones Collection, III, Paintings and Miniatures*, Victoria and Albert Museum, London, 1923, 123, no. 710, a miniature copy of Loir's painting) mentions an engraving after Nattier's painting of 1786 by Langlois, which I have not been able to trace. Haid's print, a homely thing, shows the marquise in a pose and costume close to that of Loir's marquise but with many differences in detail; however the print is so crude that it cannot be trusted as a reliable record of Nattier's original.

Anna Dorothea Lisiewska-Therbusch
German, 1721-1782

Anna Dorothea Lisiewska was born in Berlin on July 23, 1721, into a Polish family of artists who had settled there.[1] Diderot says that she was self-taught but she had lessons from her father and maybe also from Antoine Pesne (1683-1757), who had settled in Berlin after training in France and Italy. Certainly the rough, meaty impasto and loose brushwork that characterize his work made a strong impression on her mature style. Her earliest paintings, however, show her to have been impressed by the French Rococo court style of Watteau and his followers. *The Swing* and *A Game of Shuttlecock* (Potsdam, Neues Palais), a pair of canvases, one of them dated 1741, depict elegantly dressed ladies and gentlemen playing in formal gardens with fountains and avenues of trimmed box hedges.[2] The debt to the *fêtes galantes* of Watteau, Pater, and Lancret is immediately obvious. When Lisiewska married an innkeeper and occasional painter called Ernst Therbusch in 1745, she seems to have given up painting on commission for about fifteen years while she raised her family. She cannot have given up painting entirely, however, because she resumed her public career in 1761 with a style that was more vigorous and more solidly grounded in good drawing and composition than her first efforts. She was invited to the court of Duke Karl Eugen in Stuttgart in 1761, where she made mythological paintings and portraits. Two years later she went to Mannheim to work for the Elector Karl Theodor, returning to Berlin in 1764.

Her successes with the two German princes, as well as with Frederick the Great, whose portrait she had already painted, inspired her to seek her fortune in more prestigious circles. In 1765 she moved to Paris, probably hoping that as that rare phenomenon, the gifted woman painter, she might receive the kind of welcome accorded Rosalba Carriera in 1720. She was not so successful. As Diderot later commented, "it was not talent that she lacked in order to create a big sensation in this country, . . . it was youth, it was beauty, it was modesty, it was coquetry; one must be ecstatic over the merits of our great male artists, take lessons from them, have good breasts and good buttocks, and surrender oneself to one's teachers.[3] Lisiewska-Therbusch was already in her forties and was not a beautiful woman, nor did she have the polish and charm of someone destined for success in court society. On the contrary, she seems to have been somewhat blunt in her manner. She was elected to membership in the Academy, however, despite the rule then officially prohibiting women members, and she sent several works to the Salon of 1767, including her *morceau de réception*, *The Drinker* (Paris, Ecole des Beaux-Arts). This genre figure of a man seen by candlelight was quite well received. "Excellent," commented one newspaper critic; "a lively effect, good chiaroscuro," said another.[4] Diderot was less enthusiastic. "It is empty and dry, hard and red," he wrote, and went on to criticize her failure to realize the true effects of candlelight with its subtle half-tones, though he finished by saying that "it is not nevertheless without merit for a woman, and three-quarters of the artists in the Academy could not have done this much."[5]

The Academy refused to hang an ambitious mythological painting by her depicting *Jupiter and Antiope*. The official reason given was that it was indecent, but there were also misgivings about its quality. Diderot visited her after the decision was taken and found her in a rage. He tried to calm her and to give her some helpful criticism, but the work was not to his taste either. He preferred his gods and nymphs more idealized and thought that her models were plebeian. "If I was Jupiter, I would have regretted going to the trouble of metamorphosing myself," he declared.[6] He admired her ambition, her willingness to listen to criticism, and her determination and went to some lengths to help her career, finding her patrons and giving her advice about Parisian art politics. He bought a *Cleopatra* from her, which he said he worshipped every morning and described as "vraiment fort belle." He also had his portrait painted by her. It was a bust-length work with the shoulders bare. He could see that the artist was having trouble with the neck and nether regions, since he was posing fully dressed, so, "to solve this inconvenience, I went behind a curtain and undressed myself and appeared before her as an academy model. 'I would not have dared to suggest it to you,' she said, 'but you have done well, and

1.
C. Reidemeister provides a solid entry on her in Thieme-Becker (XXIII, 243ff.) based on his unpublished Berlin dissertation of 1924. The exhibition catalog, *Anna Dorothea Therbusch, 1721-1782*, by Gerd Bartoschek, contains a useful biographical essay and a catalog with more than thirty illustrations, mainly of works in East German collections.
2.
Bartoschek, nos. 1 and 2. *The Swing* is also illustrated by H. Wenzel in "Jean-Honoré Fragonard's 'Schauckel,' " *Wallraf-Richartz-Jahrbuch*, XXVI, 198, fig. 149.
3.
Diderot, III, 250.
4.
Ibid., 34.
5.
Ibid., 249.
6.
Ibid., 251.

I thank you.' I was nude, but completely nude. She painted me and we chatted with a simplicity and innocence worthy of earlier times."[7]

Lisiewska-Therbusch's lack of success with French patrons seems to be explained by two factors. Her work was too bluntly realistic for local tastes, and she herself was not an attractive woman, either physically or personally. According to Diderot once more, for he was not an unsympathetic witness and genuinely admired her good qualities, she had an excessively high opinion of herself. She evidently lacked the ability to flatter and to insinuate herself tactfully into high society. But even Diderot finally lost patience with her and denounced her as "the unworthy Prussian," for she blamed him for her failure to gain entry into the court of Louis xv and left him to deal with her numerous creditors when she departed in a hurry in 1768 for Brussels and Holland.[8] By 1771 she was back in Berlin, where she remained for the rest of her life, working mainly as a portraitist, although she did also on occasion paint genre scenes and mythologies.[9]

Lisiewska-Therbusch is a difficult artist to learn more about at present. Many of her finest works are in East European collections and most of the not very extensive literature on her is in German and in relatively inaccessible publications. She and her sister, Rosina Lisiewska-deGasc (1713-1783), certainly deserve to be more widely known.[10] Anna Dorothea can be an uneven artist but she has left us a number of powerful portraits and a few impressive genre pictures. Among the latter is *An Evening Meal by Candlelight* (Moscow, Puschkin-Museum), which shows a young couple dining together watched by a young soldier. Ultimately inspired by Dutch "merry-company" pictures of carousing soldiers and by Caravaggesque candlelight scenes of the early seventeenth century, the human drama presented by Lisiewska-Therbusch is intimate and affectionate without being at all sentimental. The treatment of the light as it falls on the three figures and the various objects on the table is also wonderfully realized.[11] Her portraits rarely seem to flatter the sitters. Indeed, in some cases they are as disturbingly frank as Goya's.[12] A good example of her talents is the *Portrait of a Collector* (Berlin, Staatliche Museen) of 1771. She presents the sitter as a plump, bewigged, elderly gentleman wearing a velvet dressing gown and smiling happily amidst some of his prized possessions. One is curious to know whether the man fitted his self-image as a good-humored devotee of good food, beautiful women, and the fine arts.[13] Her *Self-Portrait* of around 1780 in the same collection is impressive for being a frankly realistic portrait of a plain woman in her late fifties.[14] The artist arouses our interest because she did not fit into the acceptable stereotype of the well-educated, well-spoken lady artist of beauty and charm, and thus her career was not so easy as those of Sofonisba Anguissola and Vigée-Lebrun, for example. Lisiewska-Therbusch's greatest handicap, however, would appear to have been the lack of a solid academic training to prepare her for the career her admirably ambitious character made her attempt.

45.
Portrait of Jacob Philipp Hackert (1737-1805), 1768
Oil on canvas
31½ x 24¾ in. (80 x 63 cm.)
Inscribed on the back: ANNE DOROTHEE THERBUCH DE LISIEWSKA PINX. A PARIS 1768
Vienna, Gemäldegalerie der Akademie der bildenden Künste (113)
(See color plate, p. 79)

Lisiewska-Therbusch was not only a member of the Académie Royale in Paris, she was also elected to membership in the Bologna Academy and, with this superb portrait of the painter Philipp Hackert, was granted membership in the Vienna Academy in 1776 as well. It was painted in 1768, when she and the sitter were both in Paris, where they presumably sought each other out as fellow Berliners. Hackert was a landscape painter who went to Rome shortly after this portrait was painted and eventually settled in Italy.

Hackert wears a lovely sky blue jacket and rests his arms on the curved back of a chair upholstered with yellow satin. The flesh tones are warm, the rest of the color scheme is neutral. His pose is wonderfully relaxed, as if he had stopped drawing to rest and chat for a moment and had turned to look across the room while continuing the discourse. The attractive color scheme and slightly idealized facial expression suggest an attempt by the artist to make her work more appealing to Parisian taste. The competition there certainly put her on her mettle. Her characteristic paint surface with its rough impasto and dabs and strokes of thick paint can be seen especially in the painting of the jacket. She uses a finer touch for the features and flat paint for the background, a contrast that helps to give the figure definition and presence.

7.
Ibid., 252. The portrait of Diderot is known only from an engraving, but there is another small one of him by her in Berlin (Dahlem Museum, no. 3/55).
8.
Ibid., 254.
9.
Bartoschek, nos. 13-15.
10.
See Thieme-Becker, s.v., for the basic biographical leads and a list of works.
11.
Bartoschek, no. 7. There it is erroneously suggested that this candlelight picture was the one she submitted to the Paris Academy.
12.
Ibid., no. 10.
13.
Ibid., no. 11. The sitter might be Johann Julius von Vieth und Golssenau (1713-1784), Master of Ceremonies at the court of Saxony and a friend of Daniel Chodowiecki.
14.
Ibid., no. 25.

Françoise Duparc
French, 1726-1778

47

When Françoise Duparc died in Marseilles in 1778, there were forty-one paintings in her studio. Today only four works certainly by her hand are known. Their impressively high quality has been noted by several writers in this century and selections from this small group have been included in three recent exhibitions, but her painting has not yet struck the chord of popular response that generates the detective work necessary to recover the achievements of an almost forgotten artist from obscurity.[1]

She was born in Murcie, Spain, on October 15, 1726.[2] Her father, Antoine Duparc, was a sculptor who had moved there from Marseilles in 1720 and married a local citizen, Gabrielle Negrela. The family returned to Marseilles in 1730. Françoise's life is poorly documented, and we can only assume that she received the first elements of an artistic education in her father's studio. She is said to have studied with Jean Baptiste van Loo (1684-1745), a painter who settled nearby in Aix-en-Provence in 1731 after studying and working in Italy and Paris, and who was in Marseilles twice, from 1735 to 1736 and again for a longer visit from 1742 to 1745. As Billioud suggests, it was probably during the second of these visits that Françoise worked in van Loo's studio and, according to one source, copied a portrait of his so well that he confused her version with the original.[3] She is said to have then moved to Paris with a sister, also a gifted artist,[4] who died a few years later. After that Françoise is supposed to have moved to London. Some confirmation of this latter visit is provided by records of a "Mrs. Dupart" who exhibited three figure paintings in London in 1763, and of a certain "Duparc," who showed three portraits in 1766.[5] She was back in Marseilles by 1771 and was made a member of the local artists' academy in 1776. She made her will in April 1778, when she was "détenue dans sa maison par infirmité corporelle," and she died almost seven months later, on October 11, at the age of fifty-two.

None of the four paintings that she bequeathed to the town hall of Marseilles and that are now in the local Musée des Beaux-Arts is

1.
The only serious research on Duparc is that of J. Billioud, but see also P. Auquier. Three of her four works in Marseilles were included in the exhibition *Le portrait en Provence de Puget à Cézanne,* Musée Cantini, Marseilles, 1961, nos. 12-14; one was in Castres, 1973, no. 5. *The Old Woman* was in Toledo, 1975, no. 32. See also note 9 below.
2.
Her birth certificate was traced and published by Billioud (173ff.). In the older literature she is said to have been born in 1705 in Marseilles.
3.
C. F. Achard, *Les hommes illustres de la Provence,* 1787, quoted by Billioud, 174ff.
4.
Billioud (175) identifies the sister as Josephe-Antonia, born in Murcie in 1728, and suggests that the move took place after their parents' deaths in 1755.
5.
A. Graves, *A Dictionary of Artists Who Have Exhibited . . . from 1760 to 1893 . . . ,* London, 1901, 3rd ed., 86.

signed or dated. Had she not made the bequest, there would be no way to reconstruct her artistic personality. These four documented works all depict a single, half-length figure — an old man carrying a sack ("L'homme à la besace"), a woman knitting ("La tricoteuse"), a young woman selling herb tea ("La marchande de tisane"), and an old woman seated with her arms crossed ("Femme assise, les bras croisés").[6] They place Duparc with a small group of French eighteenth-century painters who, often inspired directly by Dutch genre paintings of the previous century, chose as their subject matter the daily lives of working-class women and men rather than those of the gilded aristocracy. Chardin (1699-1779) is the most famous of these; Greuze (1725-1805) and Lépicié (1735-1784) are her contemporaries. Of J. B. van Loo's manner — a typical early eighteenth-century mixture of late Roman Baroque rhetoric and Parisian Rococo panache — her work shows no trace. The heavily impasted surfaces of her paintings, the direct and unaffected naturalism of her portrayals, and the profound respect for humanity that her work conveys find a parallel only in the genre paintings of Chardin. Even if the four works in Marseilles were painted after she reached Paris and saw his work, we must presume that she had a basic sympathy for such themes that inspired her choice of such an unusual and unpopular specialty. It is important to note too that, unlike Chardin, she concentrated entirely on the human figure to the almost complete exclusion of implied narrative content or even elements of a setting, something that was not true of any other French eighteenth-century genre painter. The other works described in her will had religious subjects — a Virgin and Child, a miniature of the Magdalene — or were portraits. One additional work depicted a Negro holding a basket of flowers. It would be interesting to know how she approached this last subject, then normally treated in a frivolously decorative vein.

A few works have been attributed to Duparc but only three of these can now be traced. There is an appealing *Portrait of a Young Girl* in Roanne,[7] a poorly preserved *Head of an Old Woman* in Melbourne,[8] and a *Head of a Young Woman* in Perpignan (cat. no. 47), recently recovered from behind its disguise as a Greuze. A *Portrait of a Young Woman* in the Bosc Collection, exhibited in Paris in 1926, is wrongly given to Duparc.[9] Finally there is a photograph of a portrait of a young woman in the files of the Witt Photographic Survey, London, with no indication of past or present ownership, that seems to be correctly associated with her name.[10] Some of those forty-one pictures left to her executor in 1778 must now be hanging unnoticed in private collections in the south of France.[11] Only the kind of publicity generated by the idea of recovering the work of a once neglected but now highly prized genius, like that annually yielding rediscovered masterpieces by Georges de la Tour, can work similar miracles for Françoise Duparc. The human content of her work is of precisely the same kind as that which now makes Caravaggio, de la Tour, Hals, Rembrandt, and Chardin so popular. We must hope that some of this sympathy for artists of the past who showed people as they were rather than as they wished to be will be directed to recovering the work of this original, little-studied painter.

46.
The Seller of Tisane
Oil on canvas
28¾ x 22¾ in. (73 x 58 cm.)
Marseilles, Musée des Beaux-Arts (407)
(See color plate, p. 80)

All of Duparc's surviving paintings seem to blend portraiture and genre. Her subjects appear to be acquaintances whom she has asked to pose; she has captured their slight self-consciousness as they faced her as well as poses and expressions that strike us as spontaneous and characteristic. The *Old Woman* has crossed her arms, reddened by years of washing, in front of her, partly to conceal her worn hands but more as an indication of natural reserve. Her face communicates both affection and trust. Perhaps she was a family servant.[12] The young seller of herb tea is more at ease, regarding us steadily but not without interest as she manipulates a metal strainer(?). These two works are almost the same size; the *Man with a Sack* and the *Knitter* are also about the same size but are slightly larger than the other two canvases. Billioud suggested that the four works were conceived as complementary pairs.[13] Each unit would contrast age and youth but the compositions of the other pair are not as suitably balanced as the two under discussion. It would also have made better iconographical sense to couple the old man and the tea seller, who both made their living in the street, and the old laundress and the knitter, whose professions were domestic. Thus a more casual relationship among the figures seems probable.

Genre painting, especially when it portrayed members of the humblest classes, was never popular in seventeenth- and eighteenth-century France. The Le Nain brothers and Georges de la Tour, who often chose such themes, were rapidly forgotten after their death. Their present high standing is due to a different, more democratic political climate and to different aesthetic values. We no longer require artists to provide ideal images of mankind for our moral edification but rather regard such idealization as a falsification of truth. If the moral tone of much eighteenth-century French art is not exactly elevating, the artist had to at least entertain the audience with technical virtuosity, escapist visions, or comic situations. Thus Lépicié's picture of a young servant girl getting dressed suggests that such a life was blissfully carefree, and if living conditions were simple, they were clean and healthy, as appealingly natural as the current propaganda for life down on the pre-chemical-additive farm.[14] Greuze by contrast uses his picture of a servant woman to preach a moral lesson against that familiar deadly sin, sloth.[15] Duparc gives us no improving message and discreetly tells us little about her subjects. In brief, her works neither entertain nor instruct, which even Chardin's genre subjects always do. This restraint no doubt largely explains her lack of popular success, even if her fine qualities as an artist did not go completely unrecognized by her contemporaries.

6.
The quoted titles of the pictures are those given in her will (Billioud, 178ff.).
7.
Musée Joseph-Déchelette, Roanne, Loire, oil on canvas, 15¾ x 12⁹/₁₆ in.
8.
U. Hoff, *European Paintings before 1800,* National Gallery of Victoria, 1967, no. 551/4; oil on canvas, 16⅝ x 12⁹/₁₆ in. Billioud (184) records the work as in the H. Tonks Collection, London.
9.
Billioud, 184. Only two of Duparc's pictures from Marseilles are in the Castres catalog, nos. 24 and 25, but item 27, a work of Aimée Duvivier, answers the description of the Bosc picture exactly.
10.
I am much indebted to Rupert Hodge of the Witt Collection for answering my inquiries with great promptness.
11.
Billioud (178) has traced the will of her executor, J. B. Chaulier, who died in 1795. Since there is no mention in it of works by her, he presumably sold them after her death.

47.
Head of a Young Woman
Oil on canvas
17⁵/₁₆ x 13 in. (44 x 33 cm.)
Perpignan, Musée Hyacinthe Rigaud (841-2.22)

This work was given tentatively to Greuze in 1884, but Roger Gaud recently attributed it to Duparc. The lack of artifice and the broadly handled, realistic portrayal make an association with Greuze implausible and are typical of Duparc's documented works in Marseilles. The lighting and the frontal presentation of a head and shoulders portrait also resemble the *Head of an Old Woman* in Melbourne given to Duparc, and thus help to confirm that attribution also.[16]

It was rare before the Revolution and not common even afterwards for French artists to depict members of the lower bourgeoisie and working classes. Not surprisingly, portraits of wealthier subjects are seldom as simple and direct as this work of Duparc's. It is significant that exceptions can most easily be found in the work of other provincial artists, such as G. Roques' portrait in Toulouse of Anne Raulet and G. Gresly's enchantingly naive picture of a lace mender and her two children in Besançon.[17] A portrait of Emilie Vernet as a child, made in 1769, and a picture of a young boy with a sketch pad of around 1770, both by Lépicié, also offer a close formal and psychological parallel to Duparc's young woman, but he was ten years younger than she and might even have been influenced by her work in Paris.[18] Duparc's woman bows her head slightly to the left and regards us a little shyly from her shadowed eyes, but a smile lingers on her mouth. The resulting expression is affecting and sympathetic. Duparc had an exceptional gift for capturing a fleeting moment of evocative expression. Her people have the vivid immediacy of Frans Hals' sitters but she achieves these effects with formal means that are by comparison strikingly self-effacing.

12.
See Toledo, 1975, pl. 85, 1710. It is also repr. by Auquier and Billioud.
13.
Billioud, 182.
14.
Le lever de Fanchon, 1773, Saint-Omer, Musée de l'Hôtel Sandelin (Toledo, 1975, no. 65 and pl. 123).
15.
La paresseuse italienne, 1756, Hartford, Wadsworth Atheneum (Toledo, 1975, no. 41 and pl. 87).
16.
See note 8 of Duparc's biography.
17.
Both works are repr. in the exhibition catalog *Paris et les ateliers provinciaux au XVIIIe siècle,* catalog by G. Martin-Méry, Bordeaux, Musée des Beaux-Arts, 1958, pls. XVII and XXXII.
18.
For the first work, see Toledo, 1975, no. 64; for the second, see *Eloge de l'ovale,* catalog by M. Roland Michel, Galerie Cailleux, Paris, 1975, no. 15.

Angelica Kauffman
Swiss, 1741-1807

Angelica Kauffman's career was in many ways typical of eighteenth-century women artists.[1] Her father, Joseph Johann Kauffman (1707-1782) was a minor ecclesiastical muralist and portraitist who oversaw the artistic education of his daughter as they moved about Switzerland, Austria, and North Italy in search of commissions. She was recognized as a child prodigy, assisting her father in church decorations and accepting several independent portrait projects before she reached the age of fifteen. Later the senior Kauffman almost completely retired from active painting to manage his daughter's financial affairs during her long sojourn in London (1766-81).

What sets Kauffman distinctly apart from most women artists of her time is her refusal to accept a career as a painter of portraits, or still lives, or some other minor genre. Instead, she decided to become a history painter. This field, which in the eighteenth century was still by far the most prestigious for a painter, was generally considered unsuitable for a woman. They were, by social convention, not allowed to draw from the nude model, a training thought essential for those who wished to depict historical subjects. Kauffman, with a courage that at the time must have been thought to border on audacity, refused to limit her ambitions. From the 1760s onwards, she painted both history pictures and portraits. Her success can be measured by the international acclaim and clientele that she attracted in her lifetime and by the enduring strength and vitality of her work.

The factual highlights of her career are many and varied. After the early experiences of Switzerland, Austria, and North Italy, she and her father arrived in Florence in June of 1762. There she met for the first time artists who were involved with the newly emerging style of Neoclassicism. Benjamin West, the young American artist who had just recently been studying in Rome, and Johann Friedrich Reiffenstein, a German etcher and a close friend of the chief theoretician of Neoclassicism, Abbé Winckelmann, both knew Kauffman in Florence. In 1763 she and her father traveled on to Rome, then the main center of Neoclassicism, where Winckelmann and such painters as Pompeo Batoni, Gavin Hamilton, and Nathaniel Dance were living. Kauffman quickly established herself in this sophisticated milieu. Her knowledge of several languages helped her to make contacts and gain commissions, especially from the numerous English visitors and residents at Rome.

After a stay at Naples (July 1763 to April 1764), she returned to Rome and in June 1765 was elected to membership in the prestigious Accademia di San Luca. During this period she also studied perspective (probably with Piranesi) and painted her first two extant subject pictures: a *Penelope* (Hove Art Gallery) and a *Bacchus and Ariadne* (Bregenz, Landesmuseum), both signed and dated 1764.[2]

The Kauffmans left Rome in July of 1765. After traveling through Bologna and Parma, they arrived in Venice where Kauffman executed many etchings and drew after the sixteenth-century masterpieces of Titian and his contemporaries. She came to the notice of the wife of the English diplomatic representative in Venice, who invited her to travel to England with her. Kauffman accepted and, separated from her father for the first time, arrived in London in June 1766.

During the early years of the reign of George III, London was second only to Rome as the artistic center of Neoclassicism. Benjamin West and Nathaniel Dance were both there, having preceded Kauffman from Rome. Joshua Reynolds provided the main theoretical voice for painting in the Grand Manner, and it was largely his example that gave rise to the establishment in 1768 of the Royal Academy of Art, whose first president he became. Kauffman's rapid emergence as a leading painter in London may be judged from the fact that she was one of the founding members of the Royal Academy and, along with Mary Moser — a skillful painter of flower pieces — one of the only two women so honored.

Not only was Kauffman a founding member, but the pictures that she sent to the annual exhibitions of the Royal Academy — beginning

1.
Most of the basic facts of her career are given by her excellent and accurate early biographer, Giovanni Gherado de Rossi, *Vita di Angelica Kauffmann, pittrice,* Florence, 1810. The best modern source remains Victoria Manners and G. C. Williamson, *Angelica Kauffmann, R.A., Her Life and Works,* London, 1924. Though (as in these two sources) the artist's last name is usually given in the literature as "Kauffmann," she signed the vast majority of her works with a single final *n* and her spelling has been adopted for this present catalog.
2.
The *Bacchus and Ariadne* was exhibited at Bregenz, 1968, no. 48. Contained in the exhibition catalog (5-17) is Anthony M. Clark's fine essay on Kauffman in Rome, "Roma mi è sempre in pensiero," which is the source for several of the ideas in this biography.

48

with the first in 1769 — gained considerable notice for their striking originality. James Northcote, in his biography of Reynolds, mentions "the pictures which chiefly attracted the attention of the connoisseurs at this the first session of the Royal Academy Exhibition."[3] The first two places he assigns to history paintings sent by West, but third and fourth on his list are Kauffman's *Interview of Hector and Andromache* and *Venus Showing Aeneas and Achates the Way to Carthage* (both now in the collection at Saltram House, Plympton, Devonshire). Kauffman showed two other pictures with subjects drawn from classical antiquity; in fact she and West were the only exhibitors who confined themselves to history pictures — even Reynolds and Dance submitted only portraits. At succeeding exhibitions, she continued to contribute pictures of great originality. For instance, it was she — Swiss-born and Italian-trained — who first exhibited at the Royal Academy a scene from English medieval history, her *Vortigern and Rowena* (1770, no. 116; Saltram House). This subject, like several others that she pioneered, later became popular with British artists.

Kauffman and those of her contemporaries (West, Barry, and Fuseli, to name but three) who wished to bring history painting to prominence in Great Britain never fully succeeded. English collectors steadfastly maintained their preference for portraits — of themselves, their relatives, and even their animals.[4] Without a steady market for history pictures, Kauffman had to earn the greater part of her generous income from portraits.[5] Most of her sitters were female; examples of her London portraits are *The Duchess of Richmond* (Goodwood, Chichester), *The Marchioness Townshend and Her Son* (Burghley House, Stamford), *The Duchess of Brunswick* (London, Buckingham Palace), and *Frances Hoare* (Stourhead, Wiltshire). Many of these portraits were allegorized in some fashion to raise them closer to the status of history paintings. Hence the Marchioness Townshend is shown as Venus to her son's Cupid, while Frances Hoare offers sacrifice to a statue of Minerva. This practice was, of course, very much in the manner of Sir Joshua Reynolds, who was Kauffman's closest friend among the English painters.

Kauffman also produced numerous designs to be used as decorative inserts in the interiors of Neoclassical domestic architecture.[6] Her name is particularly associated with the homes designed by Robert Adam, then the most fashionable architect in England. Though it is doubtful that she personally painted many of the interior decorative panels ascribed to her, she was certainly one of the most prominent of those painters who evolved a gentle, pliant version of the Neoclassical style that was a particularly appropriate complement to domestic interiors. Her most famous, and most successful, decorative project came about in 1778 when the Royal Academy commissioned William Chambers to design a new residence for it. Kauffman contributed four handsome large allegorical ovals for the lecture hall ceiling: *Color, Design, Composition,* and *Genius.* Today these ovals are to be found in the vestibule of Burlington House, the Royal Academy's current home.[7]

3.
James Northcote, *Life of Sir Joshua Reynolds,* 2nd ed., London, 1818, I, 184.
4.
On English patterns of collecting during this period, see David Irwin, "English Neo-classicism and Some Patrons," *Apollo,* LXXVIII, 1963, 360-67.
5.
According to the estimate of Joseph Farington, Kauffman earned about £14,000 during her fifteen years in London (this figure given in an unpublished portion of Farington's *Diaries,* quoted by Manners and Williamson, 51). This was a handsome income, probably surpassed over these same years only by Reynolds, Gainsborough, and West.
6.
On this aspect of her career, see Edward Croft-Murray, *Decorative Painting in England, 1537-1837,* London, 1964-70, II, 227-29.
7.
Sidney C. Hutchison, *The Homes of the Royal Academy,* London, 1956, 9ff., 16, 28, gives the best account of the various installations of Kauffman's ovals.

Another artist who specialized in interior decorative pictures was Antonio Zucchi (1762-1795), born in Venice but resident in England since 1766. In 1781 Kauffman and Zucchi married. This was actually Kauffman's second marriage: in 1767 she had been duped into marriage by an adventurer named Brandt, who had been successfully masquerading in London society as the Swedish Count de Horn. The confused and romantic tangle of this marriage has fascinated several generations of Kauffman's biographers (and, unfortunately, has sometimes tended to overshadow their accounts of her merits as a painter). At any rate, it was not until Brandt died in 1780 that Kauffman — a devout Catholic — was free to remarry. Zucchi was evidently a choice dictated by prudence rather than by passion. As Kauffman's elderly and ailing father had hoped, Zucchi devoted most of his energies to managing his wife's finances.

The Kauffmans and Zucchi returned to the Continent in 1781. After briefly revisiting the place where the elder Kauffman had spent his childhood, they settled in Venice. There, in 1782, Joseph Johann Kauffman died. More happily, it was also there that Kauffman met and enjoyed the patronage of Grand Duke Paul of Russia, the first of the vast numbers of European nobility who would commission works from her in the coming years. Among the clients recorded in the studio book that she kept from 1781 until 1796 are Prince Youssoupoff and Count Kastellai of Russia, Counts Reventlow and Stolberg of Germany, Prince Poniatowski and Count Potocki of Poland, the Duke of Courland, the Prince of Waldeck-Pyrmont, and Emperor Joseph II of Austria. Perhaps only Antonio Canova and Elizabeth Vigée-Lebrun could boast such a glittering international array of clients during this period.

In mid-1782 Kauffman and Zucchi moved on, first briefly to Rome and then to Naples, where she was offered, and declined, the position as Royal Painter to King Ferdinand and Queen Caroline. Nevertheless she did undertake a large group portrait of the royal family (Naples, Capodimonte), which she finished in Rome after her return in November of 1782. She stayed there most of the remainder of her life.

During the next fifteen years Kauffman painted some of her finest works, several of which deserve special mention. Her *Self-Portrait Hesitating between Painting and Music* (ca. 1794, Nostell Priory, Yorkshire) commemorates the point in her early life when she had to choose between promising careers as a singer-musician and as a painter. It is a witty and handsome transcription of Hercules at the Crossroads (between Fame and Luxury), which had been a popular moralizing subject during the seventeenth century. Kauffman's picture was highly praised by her contemporary James Barry in 1802: "Some may say that this is great, since it was executed by a female; but I say, that whoever produced such a picture, in whatever country, it is great, it is noble, it is sublime! How I envy plaintive Music the squeeze she receives; the impression seems deeply imprinted on her hand — all is feeling, energy and grace!"[8]

Of the many pictures that she continued to send back to England, her *Valentine, Proteus, Sylvia, and Giulia in the Forest* (1788, London, private collection), and *Diomed and Cressida* (1788-89, Petworth House, Sussex) are among the most important. They were executed on commission for Alderman Boydell's Shakespeare Gallery, a vast undertaking designed to assemble pictures by all of the best British artists illustrating the works of Britain's greatest author.[9] Kauffman's presence among the participants in this project (some of the other artists chosen were Reynolds, West, Fuseli, Barry, Wright, and Romney) is indicative of the high regard she continued to enjoy in London.

Kauffman also received many honors in Italy. In 1778 she submitted a *Self-Portrait* (Florence, Uffizi) for inclusion in the famous collection of artists' self-portraits in the gallery of the Grand Duke of Tuscany. After the death of Pompeo Batoni in 1787, she was without much doubt the most famous and most successful living painter in Rome. As such she was a central figure in Roman society, and a visit with Kauffman was considered essential for every fashionable tourist or newcomer to Rome. Goethe and Herder spent much time with Kauffman during their respective Italian sojourns, delighting in her company, as did Grand Duchess Ann Amalia of Saxe-Weimar.

After 1795 Kauffman gradually became less active as an artist. Zucchi died that year, and he had largely seen to the management of her financial affairs. During the last dozen years of her life, the Napoleonic campaigns in Italy and the rest of Europe severely disrupted the flow of visitors to Rome. Fewer commissions were available, and it was difficult to arrange international payments from her foreign clients. Nevertheless, Kauffman, who by this time was quite wealthy, continued to work, albeit at a much slower pace. Her home and studio also continued to be a central attraction for artistic residents and visitors to Rome. Local artists gave banquets and wrote poetry in her honor, looking to her as the unofficial head of the Roman school of painting. When she died Antonio Canova assumed charge of the funeral. It was patterned after the ceremonies that had marked the death of Raphael — including the detail that two of her pictures were carried in triumph in a funeral procession made up of all the Academicians of St. Luke along with numerous representatives from other Italian, French, and Portuguese academies.

Kauffman left no real followers. She had rarely had pupils: only Robert Home (in England) and G. B. dell'Era (in Rome) are said to have studied with her. The attempt to introduce heroic-scale subject painting to England was largely a failure, though the prestige of the English school was greatly enhanced by the accomplishments of Kauffman and her generation. In Italy the aesthetic and political shifts caused by the Napoleonic years permanently deflected art from the style in which Kauffman painted, so that again her influence was of short duration. Yet if Kauffman cannot be counted among those artists who decisively altered the course of art history, she must still be awarded a significant place in that history. In their broad range of style and

8.
Quoted by Joseph Moser in an obituary article on Kauffman in *European Magazine*, LV, 1809, 259.
9.
Winifred H. Friedman, *Boydell's Shakespeare Gallery*, New York, 1975, is the most current and most complete source on this subject.

49

iconography, her pictures display a vitality and an ambition characteristic of the best of late eighteenth-century art. With a total oeuvre of over five hundred paintings, some two hundred of which can be traced today, and patrons spread from the British Isles to Italy, Russia, Scandinavia, and even America, she was not only one of the major popularizers of Neoclassicism but also one of the finest exponents of this style.

48.
Cleopatra at the Tomb of Marc Antony, 1770
Oil on canvas
49³/₁₆ x 42¹/₈ in. (125 x 107 cm.)
Burghley House, Stamford, The Marquess of Exeter (286)

According to Plutarch's *Life of Antony*, from which this scene is probably taken, Cleopatra received permission from Augustus to visit the tomb of her lover. Though Plutarch does not specify the time of day, Kauffman has romantically depicted a night scene described within a single pool of torchlight, a device she may have borrowed from her contemporary, Joseph Wright of Derby. Earlier artists had frequently depicted Cleopatra with the dying Marc Antony in her arms, but no prototypes for Kauffman's interpretation of Cleopatra at the tomb have been traced.[10] This concentration upon Cleopatra's more pensive and stoic grief is typical of Kauffman, who often painted similar scenes of women left alone to fend for themselves. Several Neoclassical painters followed Kauffman's example in their treatment of the Cleopatra legend, including François Guillaume Ménageot (Salon of 1785; Musée Angers).[11] Benjamin West's reworking of *Agrippina with the Ashes of Germanicus* from public spectacle (Royal Academy, 1766; New Haven, Yale University Art Gallery) to private grief (Royal Academy, 1773; Sarasota, Florida, Ringling Museums) may well have been suggested to him by Kauffman's *Cleopatra*.

49.
Self-Portrait, ca. 1770-75
Oil on canvas
29 x 24 in. (73.7 x 61 cm.)
London, National Portrait Gallery (430)

Kauffman painted numerous *Self-Portraits*, over a dozen of which survive.[12] The earliest is probably that in the collection of the Tiroler Landesmuseum Ferdinandeum, Innsbruck (no. 303), which has an inscription indicating it was painted when the artist was thirteen years old.[13] From that point on, her *Self-Portraits* were evidently much in demand by her friends and patrons.

This particular painting, showing the artist with sketchbook in hand, is delightfully fresh and informal. It can be dated to the early 1770s more by style than by the apparent age of the artist, for Kauffman continued to portray herself as very youthful well into the 1780s.

10.
See A. Pigler, *Barockthemen*, Budapest, 1956, ii, 351, for a list of paintings showing *Cleopatra with the Dying Marc Antony*.
11.
This relationship between Ménageot and Kauffman was first suggested by Jean Locquin, *La peinture d'histoire en France de 1747 à 1785*, Paris, 1912, 157, note 9.
12.
Some notable self-portraits by Kauffman can be found in the Uffizi; Saltram House (Plympton, Devonshire); Kenwood House (London); and Nostell Priory (Yorkshire).
13.
The Innsbruck *Self-Portrait* was exhibited at Bregenz, 1968, no. 1, fig. 3. Another youthful, and unpublished, *Self-Portrait* is in the collection of the Midland County Historical Association, Midland, Michigan.

51

50.
Cornelia, Mother of the Gracchi, 1785
Oil on canvas
40 x 50 in. (101.6 x 127 cm.)
Signed: Angelica Kauffman
Richmond, Virginia Museum of Fine Arts (75-22)
(See color plate, p. 81)

This picture beautifully displays Kauffman's mature style, particularly in its rich, bold coloring. It was painted for her most faithful patron, George Bowles of the Grove, Wanstead, Essex, who eventually owned forty-nine of her canvases.[14] *Cornelia* was one of her most popular compositions. She painted at least two later versions, one in 1785 for Queen Caroline of Naples and another in 1788 for Prince Poniatowski of Poland.[15] Bartolozzi engraved this, the original Bowles version, in 1788.

Cornelia was the daughter of Scipio Africanus and the widow of Titus Sempronius Gracchus. She gained great renown in Rome for her modesty and for her wise education of her children — a daughter, Sempronia, and two sons, Tiberius and Gaius, who became tribunes. We see here an anecdote relayed by Valerius Maximus,[16] which Kauffman describes in her studio book as follows: "Cornelia, mother of the Gracchi, receiving the visit of a noblewoman a friend of hers who shows her all her beautiful jewels, and asks Cornelia to show her hers. Cornelia then shows her sons Tiberius and Gaius just home from their daily school to her friend together with her little daughter Sempronia saying 'These are my most precious jewels'."[17]

51.
Vergil Writing His Own Epitaph at Brundisium, 1785
Oil on canvas
40 x 50 in. (101.6 x 127 cm.)
Signed and dated: Angelica Kauffman 1785
Albuquerque, New Mexico, Collection Peter and Margaret Walch

Like the *Cornelia,* this picture was painted for George Bowles and shipped to him from Naples in 1785. In her studio book Kauffman described the picture as follows: "Vergil ill and nearing death, writing his epitaph in the presence of his two friends the poets Varius and Tucca who are sorrowful at the approaching loss of their friend. The Muse in sadness guards safely the writings of the Aeneid which the Poet had destined to the flames — the bust of Augustus is on a pedestal as his great protector."[18]

Vergil died at Brundisium in 19 B.C., at the age of fifty. In Kauffman's picture he appears more youthful than that, though his sickly complexion contrasts with the healthier tones of his companions. He is just completing the last word of his self-composed epitaph: "Mantua me genuit; calabri rapuere; tenet nunc Parthenope: cecini pascua, rura, duces." (Mantua gave me the light, Calabria slew me; now holds me Parthenope. I have sung shepherds, the country, and wars.)[19]

The last refers to the subjects of Vergil's three major works: the *Bucolics* (or *Ecologues*), the *Georgics,* and the *Aeneid,* the titles of which can be read on the rolls in the parchment case to the left of Kauffman's picture. Suetonius' *Life of Vergil* is one source for the legend, mentioned by Kauffman, that Vergil wanted his unfinished manuscript of the *Aeneid* to be burned. Instead, Varius and Tucca, operating under the instructions of Vergil's longtime patron and protector, Augustus, had it published.

An interesting comparison can be made between Kauffman's *Vergil* and Jacques Louis David's *Oath of the Horatii* (Paris, Louvre), which the French artist painted in Rome in 1784 and exhibited at the Paris Salon of 1785. David's picture is, on the whole, more archeologically precise than Kauffman's, though one may note in her *Vergil* such correct details as the broken-stringed lyre, prophetic of the poet's impending death, and the purple-stained manuscript case. The difference in sexual typing that separates the two nearly contemporary pictures is intriguing. In the David the women slump passively to one side, while the men dominate the scene with their taut standing poses. Here the only fully erect figure is the female Muse, a counterpoint to the males gathered in a ovoid, receding group drooping at the right.

14.
On George Bowles and his collection, see William Henry Bowles, *Records of the Bowles Family,* London, 1918, 96ff., and Winifred V. Philips, *Wanstead through the Ages,* London, 1949, 116-17. Many of the pictures in this collection descended to Capt. E. G. Spencer-Churchill and were included in the sales of Northwick Park pictures held at Christie's in 1964 after his death.
15.
As recorded in Kauffman's studio book; see Manners and Williamson, 148, 153. For a listing of *Cornelias* by other (mainly French) artists of this period, see Robert Rosenblum, *Transformations in Late Eighteenth Century Art,* Princeton, 1967, 62, note 42.
16.
Valerius Maximus, *Factorum ac dictorum memorabilium,* IV, iv, intro.
17.
Manners and Williamson, 148.
18.
Manners and Williamson, 148. A third picture, *Pliny the Younger at the Eruption of Vesuvius,* was also included in this shipment to Mr. Bowles. It is today in the University Art Museum, Princeton.
19.
J. C. Rolfe, trans., *Suetonius,* London, 1920, II, 479.

Anne Vallayer-Coster
French, 1744-1818

53

Anne Vallayer was the daughter of a goldsmith who worked for the Gobelins tapestry factory; her mother had sufficient knowledge of his business to run the family workshop after her husband's death. Vallayer's childhood was spent in the Gobelins, and she must have been familiar with a whole range of artistic activities as a child. When she was ten the family moved to Paris where her father established himself in his own shop. Nothing is known of her artistic training. Gabriel de Saint-Aubin (1724-1780) was a family friend but not, as far as we know, her teacher, nor is there any evidence that she studied with still-life specialists such as Chardin or Roland de la Porte. Her first recorded work is a portrait of 1762, while her first surviving works are of 1766 and 1767. Only three years later, in 1770, she submitted her *Allegory of the Visual Arts* and her *Allegory of Music* (both Paris, Louvre) to the Académie Royale and was unanimously accepted as a member. One of those who voted for her was Jean Georges Wille, who recorded his feelings in a letter: "I was absolutely enchanted by the talent of this likeable person, whom I saw for the first time and whose talent is truly that of a man perfected in this genre of painting representing still life."[1]

Although she painted some portraits, occasional genre subjects, and a few miniatures, she was mainly active as a still-life painter, and it is as such that she is justly famous. She was both versatile and productive: some four hundred fifty works are recorded. She painted flowers, dead game, musical instruments, military trophies, simple kitchen utensils and fancy porcelain tea services, pink hams, dark orange lobsters, shells and corals, fruit, simple and elaborate compositions, large and small canvases. The works chosen for the exhibition attempt to suggest the range and variety of her repertoire. There is one fancy flower picture, one simple study of plums in a basket, one intricate composition using military trophies, and, finally, one of her masterpieces, an extraordinary essay in white with a steaming tureen of soup as the main motif.

1.
Marianne Roland Michel's excellent study of Vallayer-Coster (Paris, 1970), on which this biography is based, should be consulted for all biographical data and a good selection of the critical reactions to Vallayer's work.

Most of Vallayer's recorded works were produced between 1769 and 1787. Her production declined sharply during and after the Revolution, although she continued to work and submitted one of her most ambitious compositions, a veritable banquet of expensive foods featuring a superb lobster, to the Salon of 1817, a year before her death. The critical response until 1783, when Vigée-Lebrun and Labille-Guiard made their debut in the Salon, was both extensive and complimentary. Though no critic could resist the note of patronizing amazement that a woman should have painted such marvels ("Pour une démoiselle, que d'art! et quel génie"), there is no doubt that some genuine appreciation of her artistic achievement lay behind the gallantry. Diderot, as so often, was the most perceptive observer. He wrote in 1771, "Mlle. Vallayer astonishes us as much as she enchants us . . . no one of the French school can rival the strength of [her] colors . . . , nor her uncomplicated surface finish. She preserves the freshness of tone and a beautiful harmony throughout the canvas. What success at this age!"[2] When, however, she tried expanding her range to include portraits in 1785, the reception was not favorable. Bachaumont advised her "to stick to still-life. The fair sex lacks certain resources without which, in those genres that require more talent, one will never acquire immortality." An anonymous critic calling himself "Le Frondeur" was far ruder. He declared that her portraits had no more value than the achievement "of a man without fingers when he threads a needle, that of doing something badly which the lack of means renders almost impossible." One of the portraits of which these critics disapproved was *Mme. de Saint-Huberty as Dido* (New York, Wildenstein & Co.). It is an ambitious picture with a beautiful color scheme of plum, cream, and turquoise set against a splendid soft gray classical architectural backdrop, but the face is a pretty mask, the actress's gestures are wooden. Vallayer was effectively outclassed as a portraitist by Vigée-Lebrun and Labille-Guiard and wisely concentrated on still life in all subsequent Salons.

Throughout her life Vallayer attracted the support of powerful patrons and of fellow artists in a position to advance her career. Her early and smooth admission to the Academy may have been in part due to the support of Jean Baptiste Pierre, who succeeded Boucher as Premier Peintre in 1770 and seems to have been a family friend. Later, as administrator of the Gobelins, he was probably responsible for commissioning tapestry designs from her. Her patrons included the Marquis de Marigny, the original owner of *The White Soup Bowl* (cat. no. 52), whose position made him in effect Minister of the Arts to Louis xv. She was admired by Diderot, the most influential of all the critics, and was also patronized by the court. Her marriage in 1781 to a wealthy lawyer and member of Parliament, Jean Pierre Silvestre Coster, placed her even more securely in the ranks of the rich and powerful. In the same year, she was given an apartment in the Louvre, a privilege much sought after by Academy members. Her court connections should have made life uncomfortable for her after 1789, but she and her husband remained in Paris until 1793. Probably it was the political neutrality of her subject matter that saved her. After 1789, when Vallayer showed seven paintings, she sent only five works

to the four Salons held between 1793 and 1797. She and the other artists in the Louvre lost their apartments in 1806 because their smoking chimneys annoyed Napoleon. She exhibited in 1810 and then once more in 1817, including the sumptuous *Still Life with a Lobster* mentioned above, which belonged to Louis xvi. It was a fitting farewell from an artist who in no way attempted to change her art to suit the very different political, social, and artistic climate of Paris at the turn of the century.

When Vallayer's contemporaries were not exclaiming over her physical charms and the phenomenon of such talent residing in a female body, they either compared her to Vigée-Lebrun and Labille-Guiard or to Gérard van Spaendonck (1746-1812), the first two because all three were women, the last because both painted flowers. Neither comparison helps us to understand her achievement. Modern critics, perhaps mesmerized by the wit of Diderot, find it hard to distinguish Vallayer from Chardin. Diderot had exclaimed in 1770, "Excellent, vigoreux, harmonieux, ce n'est pas Chardin, mais audessous de ce maitre, cela est fort au-dessus d'une femme." Charles Sterling was among the first to appreciate her real qualities. "[She] is usually written off as a mere imitator [of Chardin], but this is quite unfair. The truth is that, after Chardin and Oudry, she is the best French still-life painter of the eighteenth century."[3] She was certainly fully aware of the traditions of her chosen specialty — of Desportes and Oudry as well as of Chardin, who had greatly expanded the range of the genre and thus increased its respectability. It is important, however, to understand the differences between him and Vallayer. He rarely painted flowers, she painted a great many. He painted many important genre works and some great pastel portraits; Vallayer rarely painted genre and never as far as we know used pastels. Chardin responded above all to simple, familiar objects of daily use in modest kitchens — copper pots, thick ceramic dishes — and to simple foods — eggs, leeks, a crusty loaf of bread, a few ripe peaches. Vallayer also painted such themes with great success — her succulent *Ham with Radishes* of 1767 in Berlin is an ode to good, plain food. However, by instinct she was a royalist, not a bourgeois, and her fondness for elegant porcelain, silver coffee pots, and sumptuous bouquets inspired some of her best canvases. Chardin's thick, impasted surfaces contrast with her thinner, sketchier brushwork. Both artists are exceptionally fine colorists who can be subtle or brilliant as the occasion demands, but whereas the architectural structure of Chardin's tonal masses carries well even in black and white, Vallayer's more even-toned surfaces dissolve in reproduction. There are few artists of her century that it is more essential to see in the original.

Vallayer is now widely acknowledged to be one of the outstanding still-life painters of eighteenth-century France.[4] She suffers, as all others do in our eyes, by comparison with that supreme genius of the genre, Chardin, but she was far more than an able imitator. She was more versatile and more productive, and she reigned supreme in one area that he avoided, flower painting. She is no recorder of specimens, charting every petal and stamen, as van Spaendonck did. Her

2.
Quoted by Roland Michel, 1970, 72.
3.
Sterling, 89.
4.
Levey makes only passing mention of her, however, in his important new survey of French eighteenth-century art (Michael Levey and Wend Graf Kalnein, *Art and Architecture of the Eighteenth Century in France,* Harmondsworth, 1972).

54

vases of blooms are always impressionistic masses of color. Some of her small, spontaneous studies of roses come uncannily close to those of Manet, painted a century later, and she has also been compared to Renoir and Fantin-Latour. She painted ultimately to give pleasure to her spectators, and anyone who responds to good food, beautiful objects, and summer flowers, who is moved by color and visual evocations of the senses, will recognize her achievement and respond to her visions of the *douceur de vivre* of eighteenth-century France.

52.

The White Soup Bowl, 1771
Oil on canvas
19¹¹/₁₆ x 24½ in. (50 x 62 cm.)
Paris, Private Collection
(See color plate, p. 82)

The White Soup Bowl is one of Vallayer's most famous pictures. It was greeted ecstatically by Diderot in the Salon of 1771, belonged to the powerful Marigny, and on his death was acquired by M. Beajon, Conseiller d'Etat. It has been exhibited several times recently by its generous owner. It is certainly one of her masterpieces, but while much admired, it has been little discussed in the literature.

The painting is obviously an essay in white. The large white soup bowl, the steam issuing from its surface, and the crumpled napkin around the loaf of bread dominate the composition. A few neutral grays and browns extend the tonal range, as do the two dark green wine bottles on the right. Paintings stressing white have a quiet history of their own deserving further investigation. One of the first to be recognized as a tour de force in whites was Andrea Sacchi's *Dream of St. Romuald* (1631, Rome, Pinacoteca Vaticana); the Camaldolese habits worn by the monks severely restricted the artist's palette and required masterly control of a limited range of tones to suggest the creamy woolen robes in the shade of a large tree.[5] More to the point, Jean Baptiste Oudry in 1753 had painted a still life of a white duck hanging against a white stone wall, its plumage touching a white china bowl filled with a dessert topped with whipped cream and rows of slivered almonds and its head resting on a partly unfolded white damask cloth on which stands a fancy silver candlestick holding a white candle (London, Marchioness of Cholmondeley).[6] Four years earlier Oudry had delivered a discourse in the Salon on the painting of white, which his astonishing still life illustrates.

Vallayer's *White Soup Bowl* is surely in part an answer to the challenge of Oudry, the appetizing simplicity of her menu a criticism of the luxurious meal he proposes. Diderot was quite carried away by the piece of bread: "Elle [the tureen] est accompagnée d'un morceau de pain qui est vrai comme la nature, mais sans crudité, et vu comme il faut voir pour bien peindre."[7] We can admire too the masterly design that creates the capacious shape of the bowl with only one curved contour set in the shadow of the suggestive ellipse formed by the lid propped up beside it. The meal portrayed — a hearty home-made soup steaming in a cold room, fresh bread, and a good *vin*

ordinaire — seems ultimately more appealing than the elements of Oudry's banquet. Here Vallayer not only pays tribute to the austere dignity of Chardin; she also praises the virtues of domestic thrift as movingly as he ever did. And while coming as close to the spirit of his finest still lives as she ever does, she has also invented a design of bold simplicity unlike anything in his work. *The White Soup Bowl* is one of the masterpieces of still-life painting.

53.

Vase of Flowers with a Bust of Flora, 1774
Oil on canvas
60¾ x 51¼ in. (154 x 130 cm.)
Signed lower left on the drawer: Mlle Vallayer 1774
London, E. V. Thaw and Co., Inc.

This sumptuous composition is less typical of Vallayer's flower paintings than her numerous smaller studies of a single vase of flowers, but it demonstrates her ability to work on a large scale and to organize a complex design, as well as her outstanding gifts as a flower painter. The central motif is a celadon vase with gilded brass mounts filled with roses, peonies, poppies, hollyhocks, and other flowers. To the left is a bust of Flora, the goddess of flowers and plants; near it are the fruits and vines her protection also encourages, a scroll of paper, a red morocco folder, and some books. All these objects rest on a Louis XVI bureau. Green curtains in the background partially obscure a colonnade. They were criticized when the work was shown in the Salon of 1775 by a writer using the pseudonym "la lanterne magique aux Champs-Elysées": "Superbe, en vérité, superbe, mais je ne voudrais point ce rideau dans le fond du tableau, car quoiqu'il ne couvre rien, il en ôte cependant bien de l'agrément."[8]

The *Flora* had a companion picture in the Salon, a *Ceres*, whose present location is not known.[9] In it a bust of Ceres is placed in a landscape setting and surrounded with dead game and harvest produce. The contrast of an interior and an exterior setting is not common in Vallayer's work but it occurs once more in the magnificent pair in The Toledo Museum of Art, which were unfortunately too fragile to be lent to this exhibition. The outdoor still life in Toledo also features game — the centerpiece is a pheasant — while the indoor still life places a huge cooked lobster in front of a silver tureen. All four works positively assault the senses of sight and taste.

The *Flora* illustrates well the difference between the artistic temperaments of Vallayer and Chardin. It conjures up visions of a palace inhabited by noblemen, while Chardin's still lives never suggest an aristocratic ambience. His rare silver pots seem to be the one luxurious possession of a modest family; Vallayer's silver and porcelain tea services are rather the accessories of a marquise's salon. Vallayer tends to be luxurious, Chardin to be restrained. One might almost say that she is baroque and he classical.

5.
A color repr. of Sacchi's *St. Romuald* can be found in J. Held and D. Posner, *17th and 18th Century Art*, New York, 1972, pl. 12. G. P. Bellori (d. 1696) and G. B. Passeri (ca. 1679), both commented on the formal problem posed by the subject and Sacchi's skill in resolving it. Zurbarán also comes to mind as a master of whites, but his extraordinary skills in this area seem not to have been appreciated until this century.
6.
Levey and Kalnein, 1972, 26-27 and pl. 22 (see biography, note 4).
7.
"Beside the tureen is a piece of bread that is as natural as can be, but not crude, and that is seen as one must to paint well." Quoted by Roland Michel, 1970, 165; see also Diderot, IV, 210.
8.
"Superb, in truth, superb, but I do not like at all the curtain in the background, for it covers nothing and besides spoils the harmonious effect." Quoted by Roland Michel, 1970, 102.
9.
Ibid., no. 283.

54.
Still Life with Military Trophies and a Bust of Minerva, 1777
Oil on canvas
44¾ x 62½ in. (114 x 160 cm.)
Inscribed lower left: Mlle Vallayer / 1777
New York, Wildenstein & Company

Around a bust of Minerva the artist has arranged a helmet and
cuirass, a ceremonial baton, a drum, guns, a white flag embroidered
with *fleurs de lys,* and a laurel wreath set beside ribbons to which
crosses of the Order of the Holy Spirit and St. Louis are attached. A
companion piece exhibited with this work at the Salon of 1777 fea-
tured exotic shells and corals.[10] Vallayer made her debut at the Salon
of 1771 with an *Allegory of Music* and an *Allegory of the Visual Arts*
(both Paris, Louvre) and she returned to the theme of musical instruments in a handsome composition that was recently with Julius Böhler
in Munich.[11] These works were certainly painted with knowledge of
Chardin's earlier treatments of such themes, also shown at the
Salon, and must represent a challenge to the older artist.[12] The choice
of such elaborate themes also indicates her ambition and her desire
to create serious still-life compositions worthy of public display
before her fellow Academicians.

Chardin never painted a still life of military paraphernalia, but his
Allegory of Military Music, made for Marigny's Château de Bellevue
in 1767, is a roughly comparable work.[13] His tendency to orient his
composition parallel to the picture plane with the objects arranged to
make a series of firm horizontal and vertical accents is clearly in contrast to Vallayer's preference for strong diagonal lines and a more
casual arrangement of the chosen objects. In her military still life the
strong diagonal is provided by the white flag that stretches across the
canvas. A very similar compositional structure appears in the still life
previously owned by Böhler. She has limited her colors to a careful
harmony of dull red, blue, and gray brightened by the white flag and
bust. Typically she includes the base of a large column in the background, hinting at a setting of palatial splendor. The whole design is
beautifully orchestrated, with Vallayer in complete control of all the
problems posed by the changing perspective of curved forms in space.
The result is an extremely sophisticated piece of decoration hinting
at the past military triumphs of the owner.[14]

55

55.
Still Life with Plums and a Lemon, 1778
Oil on canvas
16⅜ x 18¾ in. (41.6 x 47.6 cm.)
Signed lower right: Melle Vallayer 1778
The Fine Arts Museums of San Francisco
Gift of Mr. and Mrs. Louis Benoist

This is an excellent example of Vallayer's small still-life paintings of
a kind that comes particularly close to the most characteristic productions of Chardin. A pile of plums neatly stacked in a basket, a half-
peeled lemon, a glass with a sprig of orange blossom, and a knife

10.
Roland Michel, 1970, nos. 263 and 264. The companion picture is lost.
11.
Ibid., no. 269. The present owner of this work is not known.
12.
G. Wildenstein, *Chardin,* Zurich, 1963, nos. 86, 340, and 346.
13.
Ibid., no. 345 (pl. 54).
14.
The painting belonged to a Mme. Vissitier when it was shown at the Salon of 1777.
Some research might reveal why she chose this theme.

inviting us to help ourselves to this simple dessert are set on a plain surface. Still-life compositions of this type originated in the Low Countries in the early seventeenth century and were introduced into France around 1630 by Louise Moillon and others. After about 1650 larger, more complicated, more decorative designs became fashionable. Chardin revived this simple formula in the 1730s, and Vallayer apparently found a steady clientele for such works among her less wealthy patrons, for these still lives and her small flower paintings constitute the majority of her production. A good autograph version of this composition with a rectangular rather than an oval format is in a private collection in New York.[15] The same basket of plums occurs in another still life with a glass of water and two sponge cakes in the Cleveland Museum of Art.[16] Chardin had used a similar basket of plums in a still life of around 1758 now in the Oscar Reinhart Collection.[17] If the work of Chardin is studied with those of Vallayer, his appears to be fuzzier, more generalized in its description of the fruit, glass, and almonds nearby. Her interpretations of the motif are more specific and also more freely painted, less mysterious but in their own way just as appealing.

The cultural significance of these small paintings should not be underestimated. The continuing high quality of French food depends upon the ability of the average Frenchman to appreciate the subtle distinctions in the flavors of a particular species of plum or a type of cheese or a growth of wine. It is to such refined devotion to the sense of taste that Vallayer and Chardin respond in these small visual poems in praise of the perfect peach or plum.

56

15.
Roland Michel, 1970, no. 182.
16.
Roland Michel discusses this and other examples of this motif in Vallayer's work in "A Basket of Plums," *Bulletin of the Cleveland Museum of Art,* LX, 1973, 52-59.
17.
G. Wildenstein, *Chardin,* Zurich, 1963, no. 270.

Adélaïde Labille-Guiard
French, 1749-1803

Adélaïde Labille's father, Claude Edmé, ran a fashionable haberdashery shop in Paris.[1] Her mother, Marie Anne Saint-Martin, was a woman of delicate health who had eight children, only three of whom survived infancy. Adélaïde was the youngest. We know little about her early years. Perhaps, like Vigée-Lebrun, she was sent to a convent for a few years to learn to read and write. Perhaps she helped in the family shop when she was a little older. She must have revealed a strong artistic bent, which the family encouraged. Her first formal artistic instruction came from François Elie Vincent (1708-1790), a miniaturist whose shop was not far from that of her father. His oldest son, François André (1746-1816), later became her teacher as well as a close friend and, three years before her death, her husband.

In 1769 Labille's family situation was drastically changed. She lost her mother and one of her two remaining sisters. She also married Louis Nicolas Guiard, a financial clerk employed by Bolliard de Saint-Julien. A legal separation was arranged ten years later; they had no children. Although the marriage was evidently not a success, she signed her paintings "Labille f[emme] Guiard" for the rest of her life.

Already an "agréé" of the Académie de Saint-Luc by the time of her marriage, Labille was not diverted from her ambition to become a serious artist. In order to master the technique of pastels she studied from 1769 until 1774 with Maurice Quentin de la Tour, the greatest master of this medium in eighteenth-century France and a brilliantly incisive portraitist. She herself became an excellent pastel portraitist, although this aspect of her artistic achievement cannot be shown in this exhibition. In 1774 Labille-Guiard exhibited for the first time at the Académie de Saint-Luc, submitting one miniature and one pastel, but she attracted little attention. This was unfortunately the last exhibition sponsored by the Académie de Saint-Luc before this lively and less exclusive rival to the Académie Royale and its official Salon was abolished by royal decree in 1777. She had to wait until the Salon de la Correspondance was organized by Pahin de la Blancherie in 1781 to bring her work to the attention of the general public once more, and by then she was almost ready to storm the citadel of the Académie Royale.

Her childhood friend, François André Vincent, returned to Paris in 1775 after four years of study in Rome. He was made an "agréé" of the Academy in 1777, when he exhibited several works in the Salon, quickly establishing himself as one of the major new artistic talents in Paris. Labille-Guiard began studying oil painting with him (she chose her teachers well, his technique was superb), adding another skill and expanding her artistic horizons in the process. In 1782 she sent pastel portraits of herself and of Vincent along with six other works to the Salon de la Correspondance, where she was extensively praised. She was at last on the verge of real success. She wanted, however, to be admitted to the Academy in order to be able to exhibit in its far more prestigious Salon. To this end, and to counter the rumors that Vincent helped her with her work, she had already begun a series of pastel portraits of Academicians, including Vien, the powerful ex-director of the French Academy in Rome.[2] Opposition was converted to support. On May 31, 1783, by a vote of twenty-nine out of a possible thirty-six, she was made an "agréé" and a full member immediately. Her great rival, Elizabeth Vigée-Lebrun, was admitted on the same day.

In 1783 Labille-Guiard moved to a larger apartment in the rue de Richelieu with several of her pupils, including Gabrielle Capet. Perhaps because she had no family of her own, Labille-Guiard took great interest in the careers of her students and was said to be an exceptionally fine teacher. She also campaigned actively to make the privileges and advantages of the Académie Royale available to other women. Shortly after Labille-Guiard and Vigée-Lebrun were admitted in 1783 the Academy passed a rule limiting the number of women members to four, a quota their admission had filled, for Anne Vallayer-Coster and Mme. Vien were already members. Labille-Guiard circumvented the quota symbolically in her *Self-Portrait* of

---

1.
For all the facts in this biography the reader is referred to the excellent monograph on Labille-Guiard by Anne-Marie Passez.
2.
These rumors were revived recently in the catalog of the exhibition *French Painting 1774-1830: The Age of Revolution*, Paris, 1974, no. 113 (entry by Pierre Rosenberg), where it was suggested that Vincent was partly responsible for her superb portrait of Robespierre.

1785 (New York, Metropolitan Museum) by including portraits of two of her students, Gabrielle Capet and Mlle. Carreaux de Rosamond, who thus appeared on the walls of the Salon, a point not lost on the spectators.

Another obstacle faced by Labille-Guiard took longer to overcome. Her petition for an apartment in the Louvre was repeatedly refused, the argument being that the presence of her young female pupils in the long, dark corridors inhabited by so many male artists with male students would certainly lead to scandalous situations. David had in fact been severely reprimanded in 1787 for letting three women visit his Louvre studio for lessons. Labille-Guiard only obtained an apartment in 1795 and up to then had to make do with an annual pension of a thousand pounds as compensation.

Labille-Guiard was recognized as a major portrait painter throughout Parisian artistic circles by the mid-1780s, her chief competitor being the younger, more precocious, and more socially adept Elizabeth Vigée-Lebrun. Their works had long been compared, sometimes to the advantage of one, sometimes to the other. Some personal enmity was assumed too, perhaps with reason, for Vigée's memoirs contain some cutting remarks about her rival, who is never mentioned by name. Labille-Guiard's views on Vigée are not recorded. They shared some of the same patrons — Hubert Robert, Claude Joseph Vernet, and the Mesdames Adélaïde and Elizabeth (the aunts of Louis XVI) sat for both artists — but only Vigée enjoyed the patronage and support of Marie Antoinette. Labille-Guiard was given instead the title "Peintre des Mesdames." Significantly neither woman was made "Peintre du Roi."

Vigée-Lebrun's highly publicized relationship with the queen meant that she had to leave Paris in 1789. Labille-Guiard, who supported the Revolution, remained in the city, but she had few commissions in 1789 and 1790 and was ill for part of this traumatic period. She gradually found a new circle of patrons among the supporters of the Revolution. She collected her debts from Mesdames and asked Robespierre for a sitting. In 1787 she had shown nine portraits in the Salon, all of members of the royal family or the aristocracy. In 1791 she exhibited eight portraits of Deputies of the National Assembly. Had it not been for one tragic event, she would have survived these devastating political upheavals relatively unscathed. Her personal tragedy was the order to destroy her huge, partly finished painting, *The Reception of a Knight of St. Lazare by Monsieur, Grand Master of the Order,* her most important commission to date, a huge canvas on which she had already worked for two and a half years (Passez, no. 101). She had hoped that it would gain for her the prestigious title of history painter in the Academy but such glorification of the monarchy was not to be tolerated then. In 1793 she saw her greatest dreams and ambitions go up in smoke, and she was never able to summon up the energy to create a comparable work with a less controversial political content. She sent fewer works to the Salons of 1795, 1798, 1799, and 1800 than she had in the past, then stopped exhibiting entirely. Her health, never robust, declined further and she died in 1803.

Although Adélaïde Labille-Guiard never enjoyed the celebrity status of Vigée-Lebrun, many critics have believed her to be the better artist. Her artistic training was longer and more thorough. She was a slow and careful worker who maintained a more consistent level of quality than her rival. She was also a more perceptive student of human character, never indulging her sitters with the superficial flattery that can mar Vigée-Lebrun's productions. Labille-Guiard did not pose her sitters as inventively as Vigée-Lebrun did, but her direct, unpretentious presentations are always thoughtful and appropriate. Finally, she was a beautiful painter who enjoyed describing the colors, textures, and details of her sitters' clothes and who had a remarkable and extremely subtle sense of color.

Labille-Guiard's career is of historical importance because she extended the range of possibilities for all the women artists in Paris who came after her. She herself demonstrated what a determined and gifted woman could achieve by overcoming the obstacles of a nonartistic family background of low social class, of an unsuccessful marriage (the situation at least left her free to pursue her career), and of an Academy that admitted few women and then only grudgingly with limited privileges. She gradually raised her own goals from being a miniaturist, to making full-size pastel portraits, to working in oil, and finally, the ultimate goal of all serious painters of that time, to history painting. Her few large, multi-figure portrait compositions are admirably constructed and suggest that she could have handled even larger canvases, but her training did not really equip her to meet the challenge represented by narrative history painting. It is greatly to her credit, and typical of her character, that she was never satisfied with her achievements and successes but continued to set herself even more difficult tasks. She was a feminist both in theory and in practice, opposing artificial barriers to the fulfillment of women's full potential and working to have those barriers removed. Every later woman artist owes Adélaïde Labille-Guiard a debt of gratitude.

56.
Portrait of Madame de Genlis, 1790
Oil on canvas
29⅛ x 23⅝ in. (74 x 60 cm.)
Inscribed lower left: Labille dme Guiard 1790
Bethesda, Maryland, Collection Mrs. Harry Woodward Blunt

Félicité du Crest de Saint Aubin (1746-1831), the wife of Alexis Brûlart, Comte de Genlis, was well known in Paris society as a gifted musician, brilliant conversationalist, writer, and educator of aristocratic children. After her father, the Marquis de Saint Aubin, lost his money when she was an adolescent she had to complete her education on her own. Her marriage to a wealthy young officer at the age of seventeen solved her financial problems, however, while the marriage of her aunt, the Marquise de Montesson, to the Duc d'Orléans gave her an entry into court society, where her musical and dramatic gifts were much appreciated. She became the mistress of the Duc de Chartres but also a good friend of his wife's, whose "dame d'honneur" she became, while her husband was made Captain of the Guard at the Palais Royal.

In 1777 Madame de Genlis withdrew from society to concentrate on educating her daughters, whom she taught at the convent of the Dames de Bellechasse along with the daughters of the Duc d'Orléans and Paméla, who was born from her liaison with the Duc de Chartres. In 1782 she also took on the education of his three sons, including the Duc de Valois, later King Louis Philippe. It was a move that broke with convention, for boys were normally educated only by male governors. She subsequently published her views on education in *Leçons d'une gouvernante* (1791).

Despite her enthusiastic support of the Revolution (she dropped her titles and became "la citoyenne Brûlart"), her close association with the court made her suspect and she left for England in 1791 where she remained in exile for several years. She returned to favor eventually under Napoleon but lost the pension he gave her in the Restoration and had to live on the proceeds of her writings. She died shortly after her former pupil, Louis Philippe, came to the throne.[3]

This bare outline of the life of Madame de Genlis, which can be filled in by reading her own lively memoirs, is sufficient to prove that she was a woman of considerable character and intelligence whose success at court depended largely on her own abilities. Vigée-Lebrun, who met her a couple of times, reported that her gifts as a raconteur were such that even people who professed to dislike her were enchanted by her company. She was, again according to Vigée-Lebrun, not a beautiful woman but she had a wonderfully expressive face.[4] Labille-Guiard's marvelous portrait admirably conveys the sitter's strength of character and self-confidence at a time when she was about to face considerable personal difficulties once more. The sober, almost monochromatic color scheme of varied grays is relieved only by the green chair back and the red embroidery on her gloves, but the looped ribbons of her hat and the lace trimmings on her costume keep the image from becoming too severe. This work is certainly one of the best produced during the artist's later years.

3.
The biographical material here is drawn from the extensive sketch in Passez's book.
4.
Souvenirs, Paris, 1869 ed., II, 278.

Marie Victoire Lemoine
French, 1754-1820

Marie Victoire Lemoine exhibited some twenty portraits, miniatures, and genre pictures of children in the Salon de la Correspondance in 1779 and 1785 and in the official Salon of the Academy between 1796 and 1814; today the locations of only three self-portraits are certainly known.[1] As with Duparc, Bouliar, and Ledoux, we are poorly informed about her life and training. Her first known teacher was F. G. Ménageot (1744-1816), an accomplished academic history painter and portraitist, who did not establish a studio in Paris until 1774, when Lemoine was twenty. The genre subjects that Lemoine sent to the Salons — "young girl holding a dove," "small boy playing a violin," "young girl cutting lilac" — sound as if they were strongly influenced by the work of Greuze, and thus were pictures of a deliberate sentimentality that would have little appeal for educated modern taste.[2] Yet there is no excess of Greuzian sweetness in her few surviving works, particularly not in her masterpiece, her self-portrait at work in the studio of Mme. Vigée-Lebrun (cat. no. 57). This unashamedly ambitious tour de force declares Lemoine's ability to work on a large scale, to orchestrate an elaborate composition, to combine portraiture and genre, to provide moral instruction, and even to paint still life. Nevertheless she apparently never caught the public imagination, judging from her limited reputation, and can have had only a modest success. With Ménageot in Italy from 1792 until 1801 and Vigée-Lebrun also absent, Lemoine's troubles may be partly attributable to her lack of influential supporters.[3] Once again, we can only lament the absence of the most elementary archival research and hope that scholars will include Lemoine in a long overdue investigation of the numerous women artists who came into prominence in Paris when the Salon was opened to them in 1791.

57.
Interior of the Atelier of a Woman Painter, 1796
Oil on canvas
45⅞ x 35 in. (116.5 x 88.9 cm.)
New York, The Metropolitan Museum of Art
Gift of Mrs. Thornycroft Ryle (57.103)

57

1.
For her Salon exhibits, see Bellier-Auvray, s.v. A *Self-Portrait* in the Musée des Beaux-Arts, Orléans, was exhibited at Castres in 1973 (no. 21). Another *Self-Portrait*, in the collection of Wildenstein & Co., New York, was exhibited in Raleigh, North Carolina Museum of Art, 1972 (no. 11). Thieme-Becker (s.v.) lists a portrait miniature of Daniel Schedvin in Stockholm. A *Portrait of Mme. de Lucqui*, which came from Lemoine's family, was exhibited in Paris, Galerie J. Charpentier, 1926 (no. 69), and sold in London on December 14, 1934 (Bénézit). The *Portrait of the Princesse de Lamballe* shown by Lemoine in the Salon de la Correspondance in 1779 was sold in Paris in 1926 (Vente Mme. x, December 6-7; Bénézit). A version was with Wildenstein in 1945 (Frick Art Reference Library files). Finally a *Portrait of the Vicomtesse d'Angerville* by Lemoine is repr. in R. de la Vigerie, *Généalogie de la Famille Turgot*, Alençon, 1930, 46 (I owe this reference to Vivian P. Cameron).
2.
A painting of a *Young Girl Holding a Cat*, signed by Lemoine and dated 1780, was with the Howard Young Galleries, New York, in 1926 (Frick Art Reference Library files). An excellent analysis of the significance of this phase of European taste is provided by Anita Brookner's *Greuze: The Rise and Fall of an Eighteenth Century Phenomenon*, London, 1972.

The title given above was used for the picture when it was exhibited at the Salon of 1796. When it was included in the historic exhibition of women artists held in Paris in 1926, the two women were identified as Vigée-Lebrun in her studio giving a lesson to Lemoine. There has recently been some debate about those identifications, mostly in the form of letters and oral opinions in the curatorial files of the museum. The features of the standing woman correspond well, however, with those Vigée-Lebrun recorded in her own self-portraits, and, as Joseph Baillio correctly observed, the white gown that she wears agrees with her own descriptions of the clothes she preferred.[4] Lemoine painted two other self-portraits[5] in which her features are shown to be too uneven for the standing figure to be identified as her self-portrait. But, making due allowances for the difficulty of comparing full-face with profile views, the seated figure could plausibly be Lemoine. It must be remembered that in 1796 Lemoine was forty-two and Vigée-Lebrun forty-one. Both portraits are therefore somewhat idealized.[6]

Why should Lemoine paint herself in the studio of Vigée-Lebrun as if she were receiving instruction from this famous artist, who was a year younger than she and never had students except for a brief period early in her career? Was the picture painted before Vigée-Lebrun left Paris for Rome in 1789 and only sent to the Salon at a later date, or was it painted for the Salon of 1796? What is the subject of the painting on the easel and how does it relate to the theme of the whole?

Before scholars realized that this painting was exhibited in the Salon of 1796, it was dated around 1785.[7] The clothes would, however, suggest a date in the early 1790s, according to Stella Blum of the Costume Department of the Metropolitan. The Salon had been open to women since 1791, which also suggests that the work was painted for the 1796 Salon rather than a decade earlier and then kept in reserve.

The subject is clearly some kind of tribute to Vigée-Lebrun, as John Walsh has noted, with Lemoine seated, so to speak, at her feet. The explanation for Lemoine's choice of theme would seem to be the campaign waged by Vigée-Lebrun's husband and others to get her name removed from the list of émigrés, thus making it possible for her to return to Paris safely as well as preventing the confiscation of her property.[8] In 1794 Lebrun had published a defense of his wife; fellow artists signed petitions in 1796 and again in 1799, but only in June 1800 was her name finally cleared. Lemoine's picture makes better sense as part of this campaign than as an isolated tribute painted for private consumption but exhibited at a later date. The simplicity of Vigée-Lebrun's dress and the restrained elegance of her surroundings might be read as a response to the rumors that she had made and hoarded huge sums of money. The white dress even allows us to interpret her as a symbol of innocence.

The unfinished picture on the easel shows a priestess gesturing toward an altar that supports a statue of Athena, goddess of wisdom, and a young woman kneeling before it. The obvious interpretation is that

Vigée-Lebrun had dedicated herself to her profession and is presented as a sort of high priestess of painting, inviting other women to dedicate themselves as wholeheartedly as she to this demanding vocation. Vivian P. Cameron has, however, suggested another reading, namely that the painting was intended by Lemoine as publicity for Vigée-Lebrun's talents as a history painter.[9] Since the latter, unlike Labille-Guiard, never made any effort to be recognized by the Academy as a history painter after submitting her *morceau de réception, Peace Restoring Abundance* (Paris, Louvre), this interpretation is less probable, especially if the work was painted after Vigée-Lebrun had left Paris. The whole work is, however, a bold announcement of Lemoine's ambition to do more than paint portraits and Greuzian half-length genre figures.

One interpretation of the painting can be discarded, namely that it depicts an actual teaching session held by Vigée-Lebrun for Lemoine. There is no evidence that the former ever taught the latter. Not only was Lemoine a year older than Vigée, but Vigée also disliked her brief experience of teaching and quickly abandoned it when she no longer needed to supplement her income. She reported in her memoirs that she was a poor disciplinarian and found it tedious to instruct beginners in the basics of art.[10] The relationship between the two women artists shown here is thus symbolic, not realistic.

This work is an elegant synthesis of Marguerite Gérard's interiors and the compositional clarity associated with Neoclassical painting. Lemoine could have seen Gérard's work in the Salons. The Neoclassical approach she would have learned from Ménageot, whose pictures of subjects like *The Farewell of Polyxena* (1777, Chartres) helped prepare the ground for David's success in the 1780s. Lemoine's earlier *Self-Portrait* of 1777 in Orléans is not only far simpler in conception but is also far less well drawn and composed than that of 1796. A strong desire to make a big impression after not exhibiting in the Salons for ten years evidently spurred Lemoine to surpass herself. The implications of the subject deserve further investigation, but the full meaning of this fascinating self-portrait will not be clear until we know far more about Lemoine herself.

3.
A *Portrait of Pauline Bonaparte*, signed "M . . . Vic . . . Lemoine," was in the collection of Mrs. Theodore Humphrey of New York in 1934 (Frick Art Reference Library photo). It was a big painting (6′7″ x 4′4″) of considerable elegance but with a simpler design than the Metropolitan picture. Perhaps Lemoine was more successful than she now appears to have been.
4.
Letter in the curatorial files of the museum in which he also points out that the artist dressed herself "all'antica" in her *Self-Portrait with Her Daughter* of 1789 (Paris, Louvre).
5.
See note 1 of her biography above.
6.
Baillio noted that Lemoine was a blond and the seated woman in this work appears to be brunette. Vigée-Lebrun also shows herself with darker brown hair than that depicted here.

7.
This was the date given when the painting was exhibited in Baltimore in 1972. A date before 1789 is implied by John Walsh's catalog for the Metropolitan's exhibition, *Portrait of the Artist*, also held in 1972.
8.
For details, see the carefully documented article by M. A. Tuetey, "L'émigration de Madame Vigée-Lebrun," *Bulletin de la Société de l'Histoire de l'Art Français*, 1911, 169-82. Lebrun's pamphlet, *Précis historique de la vie de la Citoyenne Lebrun, peintre* (Paris, 1794), is the first published biography of the artist. His efforts on her behalf began in 1791.
9.
Letter in the curatorial files of the museum. It is only fair to point out that she expressed her views several years ago when she believed that it was painted 1780-85 and may have since changed her mind. There is no known work by Vigée-Lebrun resembling the composition outlined on the canvas.
10.
Vigée-Lebrun, *Souvenirs*, Paris, 1869 ed., I, 35ff. She started taking pupils shortly after her marriage, that is in 1775. Ménageot, who is documented as Lemoine's teacher, had set up his Paris studio only a year earlier.

Marie Louise Elizabeth Vigée-Lebrun

French, 1755-1842

Elizabeth Vigée-Lebrun, as she is now usually called, vies with Angelica Kauffman for the title of most celebrated woman artist of their time. No women artists since have enjoyed the kind of success and admiration that they received. Their careers thus represent a special historical phenomenon that makes it hard in some respects to evaluate their achievements. Vigée-Lebrun was precocious and became a successful portraitist of the Parisian aristocracy before she was twenty. By the time she was twenty-five, she was working for Queen Marie Antoinette. The Revolution interrupted her career in France but her successes continued unabated in other European capitals. Wherever she went — Rome, Naples, Venice, Turin, Vienna, Dresden, St. Petersburg, Moscow, London, Geneva — she was warmly greeted by the *haute société,* deluged with invitations, and given an endless succession of well-paid commissions that would have made her an extremely wealthy woman had she not had the misfortune to marry a chronic gambler when she was twenty.[1] Her *Souvenirs,* written a few years before her death, provide a fascinating, if one-sided, account of European society in the late eighteenth and early nineteenth centuries. She was an artist of extraordinary stamina — she produced roughly eight hundred paintings — and original achievement, whose contribution to the art of portraiture and to the taste of her own time has yet to receive the serious treatment it deserves, despite all the fanfare surrounding her career.

She was born in Paris on April 16, 1755, the daughter of Louis Vigée, a pastel portrait painter who taught at the Académie de Saint-Luc. From age six to eleven she stayed at a convent, learning to read and write and, as she later reported, spending much of her time drawing heads in the margins of her schoolbooks and in those of her friends. On her holiday visits home, her father's friends Gabriel François Doyen (1726-1809) and P. Davesne encouraged her and gave her some instruction in drawing and oils. Doyen continued to encourage her after her father's death in 1767, as did Joseph Vernet. She took more drawing lessons from Gabriel Briard, who had an apartment in the Louvre, and studied the old masters in public and private collections.

She mentions particularly in her *Souvenirs* Rubens' *Life of Marie de' Medici* in the Palais de Luxembourg and, in the Louvre and elsewhere, paintings by Rubens, Rembrandt, van Dyck, Raphael, Domenichino, and Greuze (for "a good lesson . . . in the half-tints to be found in delicate flesh coloring").

By the time she was fifteen, she was earning enough money to support her widowed mother and her younger brother, Etienne, although not in much comfort. Her mother married a rich jeweler, hoping thereby to improve her family's situation, but he proved to be a miser who "displayed his stinginess by limiting us to the absolute necessities of life, although I was good natured enough to hand over everything I earned."[2] Meanwhile Vigée's clientele was improving. She painted Count Shuvaloff (cat. no. 58), the first of many Russian patrons; the Duchesse de Chartres; the Comtesse de Brionne; and the Princesse de Lorraine. After success with such patrons, access to Versailles and the court soon followed. In 1776 she painted the king's brother, Monsieur. Two years later she painted him again and his wife. In 1779 she finally met Marie Antoinette (according to the *Souvenirs,* it was an accidental encounter in the park at Marly) and painted the first of many portraits of her. Pressure from the queen helped Vigée-Lebrun become a member of the Académie Royale in 1783, despite the fact that her marriage to a picture dealer disqualified her.[3] From this point onwards, her career was a succession of international triumphs.

After escaping from Paris the night that the king and queen were arrested, she traveled to Italy, where she lived from 1790 to 1793, mainly in Rome and Naples, though also visiting Florence, Turin, and Venice. She spent the next two years in Vienna, then traveled to St. Petersburg in 1795, where she remained for six years, with a five-month stay in Moscow. She finally returned to Paris in 1801, but despite a warm welcome decided to go to London. She stayed in England for three years, painting the Prince of Wales and arousing the jealousy of many English artists before returning to Paris. From 1808 to 1809 she was in Switzerland, where she met and painted

---

1.

According to the artist herself, she had earned more than a million francs by 1789, almost all of which her husband spent on "les femmes de mauvaises moeurs" and gambling (*Souvenirs,* 1869 ed., I, 34). There is an abridged English translation by Lionel Strachey (New York, 1903) and another, even briefer, by Gerald Shelley (London, ca. 1945). A reprint of the original French edition with at least a good index of proper names is long overdue.

2.

Vigée-Lebrun, 1869 ed., I, 15.

3.

As D'Angiviller noted in his petition to the king for her admission, the wife was identified with the husband's profession, even if she did not participate actively. Lebrun was a prominent dealer who met his wife when he first let her copy the old masters he had in stock. The documents concerning her admission are quoted by Nolhac (37ff.).

58

Mme. de Stael (1808, Geneva, Musée d'Art). She was now in her mid-fifties and less able to tolerate the great hardships imposed by travel at that time, hardships she describes graphically in her memoirs. She settled down in Paris and bought a country retreat at Louveciennes. Her husband, a continual drain on her finances as long as he lived, finally died in 1813. Her daughter returned from Moscow and a bad marriage in 1818, already seriously ill; she died a year later. Etienne Vigée died in 1820, leaving Vigée-Lebrun without the comfort of close family for the last twenty-two years of her life (she was cared for by two nieces). She sent works to the Salon until 1824, but her production had declined by 1810. Her *Souvenirs* were published in 1835 and 1837. She died in Paris on March 30, 1842, and was buried in Louveciennes beneath a gravestone with a relief carving of a palette and brushes, as she had requested in her will.

With no reliable modern catalog of her enormous oeuvre available, any estimation of her artistic achievement can be dismissed as premature. Enough of her work is known nevertheless for it to be clear that many of the existing estimates are patronizingly inadequate. Her portrait of her brother from St. Louis (City Art Museum), painted when she was eighteen, is sufficient proof of her prodigious talent. Not all of her portraits are masterpieces and some of her female sitters are psychologically vapid, but the same can be said of every other portrait painter then active. Enough of her work is of indubitably high quality for her to be ranked with the best portrait painters of the late eighteenth and early nineteenth centuries. The speed at which she worked meant that she did not always produce her best, and it must be remembered that her work is bound to seem uneven as long as there are so many copies, replicas, and imitations parading as authentic pictures.

Her memoirs make it clear that she was interested in the personalities of her clients and was fully aware that a number of her fashionable sitters had little to recommend them but a charming physique. She produced her best work when she painted friends (the *Hubert Robert* of 1788 in the Louvre); when she was dealing with a major client whom she admired (the *Portrait of Charles Alexandre de Calonne*, fig. 22, p. 42); and when she herself was especially struck by the beauty of a customer (the *Varvara Ivanovna Narishkine* of 1800, cat. no. 61). She was endlessly inventive with poses, formats, and settings, though not above repeating a successful arrangement for a different client in another city.[4] She knew the value of a simple, straightforward presentation for some sitters and a more complex bit of staging for others. Mme. Narishkine, the ideal Tolstoy heroine born fifty years too soon, looks straight at us, her perfect oval face, dark hair, and dark, slightly Oriental eyes needing no artifice to win the viewer's attention. Charles Alexandre de Calonne, Controleur-Général des Finances, is given an appropriately rich setting as a foil to his serious, black satin outfit — a sweep of damask curtain, a carved and gilded desk and chair, a fluted pilaster, and a piece of paper inscribed "Au Roi." Hubert Robert, the most amiable of people according to all his friends, is presented instead as a symbol of creative inspiration.

4.
The half-length portraits of Countess Skravonskaia (Paris, Louvre) and of Grand Duchess Elizabeth Alexievna (Montpellier, Musée Fabre) both pose the sitter facing left with their arms resting on a cushion which fills the left foreground (both exhibited at Castres, 1973, 32 and 34). The composition used for the Comtesse du Buquoi (cat. no. 60) was used again for Countess Anna Potacka (J. Mycielski i St. Wasylewski, *Portrety Polskie Elizbiety Vigée-Lebrun, 1755-1842*, Poznań, 1928, opposite 20).

This is a portrait masterpiece of truly romantic fervor, an idealization of artistic genius conveyed with striking realism — the fleshy, ruddy face, the bald head, gray hair, tight jacket, forceful pose — an indelible image.

In many of her portraits of female aristocrats, as in her descriptions of the nobility in her *Souvenirs*, Vigée-Lebrun is inclined to exaggerate their charms and gloss over those imperfections that would give the image some individual character. She is especially prone to giving all her women uniformly large eyes. Her own self-portraits are almost outrageously flattering. There is no doubt that she was herself a beautiful woman, but in her *Self-Portrait* in the Uffizi, painted when she was thirty-five, she barely looks twenty. Her self-portrait with her daughter in the Louvre, painted the year before for D'Angiviller, is equally misleading. This flattery was of course crucial to her success with the rich and well-born, but it would be quite wrong to imagine that her own charms, combined with a modicum of talent, could have won her the kind of reception she received throughout Europe. In spite of everything, one might say, she was an exceptionally fine portrait painter. Her achievement will only be understood, however, after some patient scholar has collected together her scattered oeuvre, weeded out the interlopers, studied the wide range of sources that she absorbed and used, and published the results.[5] Finally, no biography will do her justice if it does not take into account the historical context of her career, a gradually disintegrating aristocratic society of which she was an ardent supporter and for which her work, written as well as painted, provides an incomparable record.

58.
Portrait of Count Shuvaloff, 1775
Oil on canvas
33 x 24 in. (83.8 x 61 cm.), oval
Raleigh, North Carolina Museum of Art
Original State Appropriation (52.9.224)

Count Ivan Ivanovich Shuvaloff (1727-1797) was one of Vigée-Lebrun's first distinguished patrons whose support helped to bring her other influential clients from Parisian society. Shuvaloff (his name is spelled in various ways by English and French writers) was grand chamberlain to Empress Elizabeth II of Russia and also her lover, according to the artist's memoirs.[6] He was the founder of Moscow University and the Moscow Academy of Art. Vigée-Lebrun, who was only twenty when she painted him, later described his character in flattering terms: "He united the most thoughtful courtesy with a perfect manner, and since he was the most excellent of men, his presence was sought by the best company."[7]

The count is shown almost half-length, wearing a fur-edged jacket with two decorations beside the left lapel. He also wears several bands of moiré silk ribbon across his waistcoat, presumably the marks of other honors. His body is turned slightly to the left while he looks out of the picture to the right. The averted gaze gives him an air of reserve appropriate to an important aristocrat. The paint surface seems to be a little thinner and less Chardinesque than in her *Portrait of Etienne Vigée* (1773, St. Louis, City Art Museum), with passages of sketchy brushwork, especially in the areas suggesting hair and fur, that look forward to her mature technique. Altogether the *Portrait of Count Shuvaloff* is a remarkably confident and polished performance for a young artist, demonstrating both her precocious talents and her independence. She has not sought to imitate the detailed finish and surface polish of the best-known portraitists then active — artists like Duplessis, F. H. Drouais, and Greuze. The summary skill seen here was then associated only with the more informal pastel portraits of J.B. Perronneau.

59.
Portrait of the Marquise de Jaucourt, 1789
Oil on canvas
45 x 34½ in. (114.3 x 87.6 cm.)
New York, The Metropolitan Museum of Art
Gift of Jessie Woolworth Donahue (54.182)

Despite the uneasy political situation that forced Vigée-Lebrun to leave Paris in October of 1789, she completed thirty-seven paintings that year according to the list she appended to her *Souvenirs*. This portrait of Marie Charlotte Louise Perrette Aglaé Bontemps (1762-1848) appears among them as "Madame de la Châtre." The sitter had married Claude Louis, Comte de la Châtre, in 1778. She was twenty-seven when she sat for Vigée-Lebrun. Her father was "premier valet de chambre" to Louis XV; her uncle was the financier Beajon, whom the artist also painted. The sitter later divorced her first husband and married François Annail de Jaucourt (1757-1852), which explains the present title of the picture.[8] These biographical details about the men to whom she was related by birth or marriage tell us nothing about the woman herself; for that we have only the image provided by Vigée-Lebrun.

The glory of this portrait is its marvelous composition, which consists of long, sweeping, descending diagonals and curves that begin with the tilt of her hat and are picked up by the sofa back, her arm, the angle of the pillow on which she rests, and the creases of her beautiful white dotted voile skirt. The color scheme is limited almost entirely to flesh tones and neutrals. The gray ground and white dress that dominate the canvas are contrasted only by the blue gray sash and hat ribbons, the dark green velvet upholstery, and the gold embroidery along the cushion seam. The marquise is portrayed as a fashionable lady of leisure. She is reading a small book — a novel perhaps — but the portrait does not imply serious intellectual pursuits, only pleasant distractions. The tinge of melancholy in her expression can be explained as a touch of Greuzian *sensibilité* rather than as a foreboding of the difficult times to come.

We know from her memoirs that the artist wore plain white muslin dresses, which she dressed up with sashes and scarves. She often speaks of persuading her sitters to adopt similar costumes for their

5.
Joseph Baillio is completing a dissertation on Vigée-Lebrun for the University of Rochester. I am extremely grateful to him for discussing my exhibition choices with me and for many pertinent suggestions. For the earlier literature on the artist, see Blum, Hautecoeur, Nolhac, and Helm in the bibliography. Michael Levey (*Art and Architecture of the Eighteenth Century in France*, Harmondsworth, 1972, 187-88) gives a good if slightly grudging appreciation of her work. The catalog for *French Painting 1774-1830: The Age of Revolution* (Paris, 1974, 664-68) provides a scholarly discussion of three works and substantial bibliographical leads.
6.
Vigée-Lebrun, 1869 ed., I, 15-16. See also Nikolenko, no. 46. Nolhac gives his full name as Count Paul Andrewitch Chouwaloff (1908, 161).
7.
Vigée-Lebrun, 1869 ed., I, 16.
8.
All this biographical information was supplied by Joseph Baillio, to whom I am extremely grateful.

59

portraits, the intention being apparently a timeless, classic simplicity. The aim has partly been achieved in this portrait. The enormous beribboned hat we would hide behind the sofa and we would remove or loosen the fichu, but the marquise's dress would still be appropriate for a summer party today. Vigée-Lebrun helped to change French fashion away from the stiff, elaborate dresses favored during the Ancien Régime to the simple, high-waisted, classically inspired white shifts seen in the Directoire portraits of David, for example. None of her female clients, however, adopted a dress as austerely simple as that the artist chose for her own portrait of this year (Paris, Louvre).

60.
Portrait of the Comtesse de Buquoi, 1793
Oil on canvas
53½ x 39 in. (136 x 99 cm.)
Inscribed lower right: L. E. Vigée-Lebrun / à Vienne 1793
New York, Wildenstein & Company

Vigée-Lebrun traveled from Italy to Vienna in 1793 and spent two years there. She records this work in her memoirs as follows: "I remember . . . that Prince Paar, to whom had been brought the large portrait that I had made of his sister, the good and charming Comtesse du Buquoi, invited me to see the portrait at his house. I found the painting hung in the salon, and, since the woodwork was painted white, which generally kills paintings, he had arranged a large green drapery which surrounded the frame and fell below it. In addition for the evening he had arranged a candelabra with many candles and a reflector in such a way that all the light was directed towards my portrait. It is useless for me to say how touched a painter is by this kind of gallantry."[9]

A number of the artist's Italian and Viennese portraits use landscape backgrounds but few as effectively as here, even if the waterfall on the right is geographically preposterous. Vigée-Lebrun recorded her fear and admiration on first seeing large mountains when she crossed from France to Italy in 1789.[10] Her list of works records landscape sketches made in Italy, and later in Switzerland, and she also describes sketching in the parks near Vienna. One passage seems especially appropriate to this work: "[The parks] in the outskirts of Vienna have natural mountains, wooded along their summits; one finds there deep ravines, which one crosses on elegant bridges, natural rivers, and brilliant cascades which descend with rapidity from the heights."[11] The adjective *romantic* springs irresistibly to mind. Beethoven had just moved to Vienna, Schubert was born there four years after this picture was painted. Beethoven's Pastoral Symphony, Schubert's *Winterreise* song cycle, and Vigée-Lebrun's Viennese portraits with their splendid landscape settings are all part of a culture that responds to nature with strong emotions. In her work we sense only rapturous pleasure in the glorious spectacle of mountains, waterfalls, and flourishing greenery, while in their music we obviously find a far more complex range of responses. It is significant that her figures confidently dominate their

9.
Vigée-Lebrun, 1869 ed., I, 282.
10.
Ibid., 135.
11.
Ibid., 284.

surroundings: the rational mood of the Enlightenment is still in control of the visual imagery.

61.

Varvara Ivanovna Narishkine, 1800
Oil on canvas
25 x 21¾ in. (63.5 x 54.6 cm.)
Signed lower left: L. E. Vigée / LeBrun / 1800 / à Moscow
Columbus (Ohio) Gallery of Fine Arts
Derby Fund Purchase (63.19)
(See color plate, p. 83)

"The love of Alexander for a charming Polish woman, whom she married to Prince Narishkine, is known all over Europe. I saw Madame Narishkine, very young, at the court of St. Petersburg. She and her sister arrived after the death of their father, who was killed in the last war of Poland. The eldest of the two might have been sixteen. They were ravishing to see, they danced with perfect grace, and soon one made a conquest with Alexander, and the other with Constantin. Madame Narishkine had beautiful, regular features; her figure was slim and supple, her face, which seemed perfectly Greek, made her quite remarkable; but she did not have, in my eyes, the celestial charm of the Grand Duchess Elizabeth."[12]

Thus the artist recorded her impressions of Madame Narishkine, whom she painted in Moscow in 1800, according to the inscription.[13] The "perfectly Greek" features encouraged the artist to dress the sitter in a classically inspired costume. Her hair is parted over the brow and controlled by ribbons, as is the artist's own hair in her self-portrait with her daughter (1789, Paris, Louvre), also "all'antica." It was a fashion she mentions promoting in Paris, where she once created a sensation by giving a dinner party with herself and many of the guests in improvised classical costumes and with the food served on genuine Etruscan dishes.[14] The cloak looped up over one shoulder and fastened with a simple brooch, the simple dress fastened with a cord reflect the artist's taste. Her judgment was correct. The costume, blue sky, and simple, frontal presentation are perfect foils for the extraordinary natural beauty of this young Polish sitter.

60

12.
Vigée-Lebrun, 1869 ed., I, 336. A portrait by Vigée-Lebrun of Grand Duchess Elizabeth is in the Musée Fabre, Montpellier (exhibited at Castres, 1973, no. 32, repr.).
13.
Nikolenko (98 and no. 19) identifies the sitter as the illegitimate daughter of Countess E. P. Stroganov and Rimsky-Korsakov (not, presumably, the composer), who was given the surname Ladomirsky. She does not cite the passage from the *Souvenirs* quoted above, which would seem to fit the subject of this portrait perfectly. The portrait had previously been said to represent Princess Tufialkin, which is certainly wrong.
14.
Vigée-Lebrun, 1869 ed., I, 67f.

Gabrielle Capet

French, 1761-1817

Gabrielle Capet was born into a family of very modest circumstances in Lyon on September 6, 1761.[1] Her father was described as a "domestique" (household servant) in her baptismal certificate. How she escaped from a life of humble toil in the provinces and came to Paris to train as a painter is not known. She must have displayed such remarkable gifts that some local patron was moved to sponsor her training and her transfer to the capital, where she entered the studio of Adélaïde Labille-Guiard before 1781. Capet's lifelong devotion to Labille-Guiard implies a profound sense of debt to the person who taught her, promoted her, and in every way changed her life. Capet lived in the household of her teacher from 1782 until the latter's death and cared for her during her final illness. It is Capet and her close friend, Mlle. Carreaux de Rosamund, who appear beside their teacher in Labille-Guiard's masterly *Self-Portrait* of 1785 (New York, Metropolitan Museum). Capet is also the subject of one of Labille-Guiard's most restrained and perceptive portraits of the 1790s (Paris, private collection).[2]

Capet began by painting portraits in pastel and oil but eventually became a specialist in portrait miniatures. Doria, in his excellent study of Capet, suggests that she switched to miniatures in order to avoid competing with her teacher and to establish her own artistic identity, but it is worth noting that she continued to paint occasional pastel and oil portraits throughout her career. Her first dated miniature is of 1787. She had made her public debut in 1781 in the Exposition de la Jeunesse, where she exhibited until 1785. In 1787 she was commissioned to paint the royal princesses. When the official Salon was opened to women in 1791, largely thanks to the efforts of Labille-Guiard, Capet was among the twenty-one women represented (there were two hundred thirty-six male exhibitors). She sent works to the Salon fairly regularly until 1814 and ceased working only once, during the last illness and death of Labille-Guiard. Doria catalogs roughly thirty oil paintings, thirty-five pastels, and eighty-five miniatures, the overwhelming majority of them in French private collections. Few of her works are traceable today. The present location of only one of her

oil paintings is known, but a few of her pastels are in public collections,[3] as are some good examples of her superb miniatures, including two in American museums.[4]

Her patrons were mostly educated members of the bourgeoisie; artist friends of Labille-Guiard and of her husband, François André Vincent; writers; politicians; and actors. One of her finest miniatures represented the sculptor Houdon working on a bust of Voltaire; it was stolen from the museum in Caen some forty years ago. The composition was inspired by Labille-Guiard's *morceau de réception* for the Academy, a pastel portrait of the sculptor Pajou (Paris, Louvre).[5] Capet adapted the design brilliantly to the restricted scale of the miniature. Judging from reproductions, it was a powerful image of a sculptor known for the sensitive realism of his portrayals. Her brushstrokes sparkle with life, tiny slivers of color on the ivory surface she preferred. Though she obviously had to work with great care and deliberation when painting miniatures, she nevertheless managed to convey a final effect of spontaneity. In such basic matters as placing the sitter in the chosen format, finding a pose that suggests individual character and avoids clichés, and describing features with that judicious balance of accuracy and flattery required by all portrait patrons, Capet was supremely competent. She was simply one of the best and most popular miniature portraitists active in Paris in the late eighteenth and early nineteenth centuries.

She was also an excellent portraitist on a larger scale, in both pastel and oil. Her *Portrait of a Woman* of 1810, which Doria records in the collection of Félix Doisteau, is superb — cool and direct, beautifully drawn. *Mme. Demetz* (Paris, Collection Henri Philippe in 1934), seated in the shade of her garden, wearing a straw hat and holding a fan, smiling shyly at us, evokes an age as well as an individual. Capet's concentration on the miniature portrait will inevitably limit her reputation, for the genre is not widely appreciated. It has few stars other than Nicolas Hilliard, and perhaps Samuel Cooper, and even then one suspects that their stature is mainly due to the lack of serious

1.
All the biographical information here comes from A. Doria, *Une émule d'Adélaïde Labille-Guiard: Gabrielle Capet portraitiste*, Paris, 1934, except where otherwise noted.
2.
Anne-Marie Passez, *Adélaïde Labille-Guiard, 1749-1803*, Paris, 1973, no. 144.
3.
Her *Portrait of Simon-Charles Miger* (1736-1820) in the Cabinet d'Estampes of the Bibliothèque Nationale (Doria, no. 104, fig. 13) is the only oil portrait traceable. There are pastel portraits by her in the Ecole des Beaux-Arts, the Musée Marmottan, and the Louvre in Paris. The Stanford University Art Gallery owns her pastel of *Marie-Joseph Chenier* (1764-1811), formerly in the collection of D. David-Weill.
4.
In addition to the work in the exhibition and the four Capet miniatures given to the Louvre in 1956 by D. David-Weill, where they joined two others, the following museums have signed examples: *Portrait of an Unknown Man*, 1796, Cleveland Museum of Art (Doria, no. 51); *Portrait of a Woman*, 1797, Musée des Beaux-Arts, Dijon (*Catalogue des pastels, gouaches, miniatures*, Palais des Etats de Bourgogne, Dijon, 1972, no. 154); *Portrait of a Woman and Child*, William Rock-

hill Nelson Gallery and Atkins Museum of Fine Arts, Kansas City (Doria, no. 35 and fig. 32; this work appears to have been retouched since Doria reproduced it — the woman has lost weight and had a face lift!); *Portrait of an Unknown Man*, 1796, Stockholm, Nationalmuseum (Doria, no. 52; it is an autograph version of the miniature in the Cleveland Museum). The *Portrait of a Woman* (Doria, no. 55, fig. 35) now in the Allen Memorial Art Museum, Oberlin, has turned out to be a signed work by F. Dubois.
5.
Both works are illustrated by Petersen and Wilson, 55.

competition from other painters in late sixteenth- and seventeenth-century England. It is the most private, most intimate of art forms. Capet's fame will thus never extend beyond the limits of an educated public that has the time to search her out in the few museums that own her work.

62.
Portrait of Christian-Georg von Schantz, 1796
Watercolor on ivory
Diameter: 3⅜ in. (8.5 cm.)
Signed lower left: M. G. Capet
Stockholm, Nationalmuseum (NMB 157)

This portrait reminds us of the lively cultural contacts that existed between Sweden and France in the eighteenth century. They began with the collector Carl Gustav Tessin (1695-1770), who was a close friend of Watteau's and an enthusiastic patron of French art and artists, and are exemplified above all by the artist Alexandre Roslin (1718-1793). Although born and trained in Sweden, he settled in Paris in 1752, married a French artist, Suzanne Giroust, and became to all intents and purposes a French artist himself.

The subject of this miniature, the Swedish sea captain Christian-Georg von Schantz (1731-1814), was in the French naval service from 1755 until 1780. He is shown wearing his navy uniform with the Cross of St. Louis. The harbor, ship, and fortifications make obvious reference to his profession. Doria estimates the sitter's age as around sixty-five and thus dates the miniature around 1796. He speculates that the sitter either visited Paris or sent a sketch to Paris for Capet to work from.

As with all good miniatures, this work tolerates considerable enlargement. Next to Carriera's boldly handled *Portrait of Robert, Lord Walpole* from London (cat. no. 41), Capet's work will look precise at first, but the deliberately textured surface of the sky and sea; the flickering, impressionistic white and yellow strokes used to indicate lace and embroidery; and the dark strokes modeling the blue jacket all keep the surface alive. The head is a miracle of delicate suggestion. This is a work of concentrated feeling and beauty that is far more than a display of technical virtuosity.

62

Marguerite Gérard
French, 1761-1837

As the daughter of a perfume producer in Grasse, Marguerite Gérard's chances of becoming an artist were infinitesimal; as Fragonard's sister-in-law and a member of the master's menage in the Louvre, impossibility became probability. After she joined her sister in Paris about 1775 Gérard was constantly exposed to the creative process; she was informally apprenticed to one of the most gifted French artists and granted access to the outstanding private collections of the day. Here she could study the masterpieces of the past, particularly the genre scenes of the Dutch seventeenth-century masters whose style she would later emulate with enormous success. Secure in the Fragonard family circle, Marguerite Gérard was not obliged to support herself or to marry to ease the financial burden on her parents. Without monetary worries or a family to care for she was free to devote herself to her art.

Gérard seems to have taken full advantage of her good fortune and soon earned the respect of her colleagues and the critics, becoming the first French woman genre painter to achieve professional success. By her mid-twenties in 1785 she had developed an original genre style inspired by Metsu, Terborch, and the other "petits maîtres hollandais" and had mastered their meticulous technique. Her small-scale, sentimental genre scenes appealed to the prosperous bourgeoisie who could not hang huge academic paintings in their homes, to the critics who could not help admiring their "old-master" ambience, and to the general public who could at least afford to purchase inexpensive engravings of her canvases. According to J. LeBreton's report of 1808 on the fine arts in France, by 1789 Marguerite Gérard's reputation equaled those of the three leading women artists of the period: Vallayer-Coster, Vigée-Lebrun, and Labille-Guiard. All were members of the Academy and were considerably older than Gérard, but they had achieved recognition in the minor fields of still life and portraiture, long the province of women, while Gérard was setting a precedent for more ambitious women artists by succeeding in an area previously reserved to men. Genre painting — the nearest approximation of history painting for an artist lacking the requisite academic education — supposedly required a degree of inventiveness and imagination that placed it a notch above portraiture and still-life painting in the hierarchy of eighteenth-century art.[1]

After the Salons were opened to women in the 1790s, Marguerite Gérard exhibited regularly for twenty-five years and was honored with three medals and the purchase of her canvases by Napoleon and Louis XVIII. In fact, her professional career flourished for nearly fifty years, perhaps in part because of the innocuous, apolitical nature of her genre scenes. She survived every political upheaval from the Revolution to the Empire, from the Restoration to the First Republic, and amassed an impressive personal fortune, investing her earnings from the sale of paintings in real estate and government annuities. Like those of Mary Cassatt, her compositions glorify domesticity and maternity although, like Cassatt, she never married or bore children herself. It seems, however, that Gérard managed to enjoy all the familial pleasures depicted in her paintings. After the death of Fragonard in 1806 and of her sister in 1824 she presided for over a decade as the matriarch of the Fragonard clan, surrounded by the children and grandchildren of Alexandre Evariste Fragonard and of her brother Henri Gérard.

Scholars, connoisseurs, and art dealers usually assume that competent women artists have received clandestine aid from their male teachers, and in Marguerite Gérard's case it has been traditionally presumed that she cohabited as well as collaborated with her mentor, Jean Honoré Fragonard. Neither reliable documentation nor eyewitness evidence exists for either charge. Jacques Louis David, a close friend, described the Fragonards as an honorable family adhering to the "simple, patriarchal habits of our distant ancestors."[2] The notorious "love letters" from Gérard to her "bon ami," her "bon petit papa," were written when she was over forty and Fragonard over seventy years old.[3] Aside from dubious entries and outright misattributions in sale catalogs, the only proof of collaboration between master and pupil consists of two curious engravings after two paintings now in the

---

1.
As a woman artist in eighteenth-century France, Gérard was automatically excluded from the exhibition and educational system of the Academy of Fine Arts, from study of the nude model, from the competitions for aspiring artists culminating in the Prix de Rome, and, ultimately, from history painting, considered the highest form of artistic expression.
2.
J. Thuillier, *Fragonard,* Geneva, 1967, 42.
3.
These eight letters are preserved at the Bibliothèque Doucet, Institut d'Art et d'Archéologie, Paris.

Fogg Museum, Cambridge. Published in 1792, the prints after *The Beloved Child* and *The First Step* both bear the peculiar signatures "Peint par M. Fragonard and Mlle. Gérard" and "Retouché par Regnault and par Vidal." Vidal had already published five other engravings after Gérard's paintings and there exist rare versions of these two engravings bearing only Gérard's name and Vidal's signature alone.[4] Regnault's 1788 engraving of *The Stolen Kiss,* attributed to Fragonard, had been immensely profitable, so he had ample motivation to add the master's name when he "retouched" and reissued Vidal's prints.

Since Fragonard's name seemed to insure commercial success, it is not surprising that the myth of collaboration between Gérard and her brother-in-law has been perpetuated. The small dimensions of her canvases, which rarely exceed 18 by 22 inches, and her painstaking glazing techniques were totally unsuited to collaborative efforts; in fact, the Fogg Museum canvases reveal no evidence of dual brushwork when examined under x-ray and Infra-Red Vidicon machines. The most respected Fragonard scholars voice doubts that the master of dynamic art, of brushwork pulsating with life, would abruptly adopt the precious, static style of Marguerite Gérard, or that he was capable of inventing and executing a stiff, bourgeois genre scene such as *The Stolen Kiss.*[5] It has been suggested that Mlle. Gérard may deserve partial if not full credit for both this painting and *Le contrat,* a similar composition epitomizing her veristic genre style.

Marguerite Gérard was also an accomplished portraitist and miniaturist, employing a freer, more spontaneous manner in these works. In 1796 and 1798 she contributed illustrations for editions of *Les liaisons dangereuses* and *Les amours de Faublas* that demonstrate her awareness of Neoclassical innovations. After 1795 her compositions become flatter, more linear, but she never treated a classical subject nor attempted to reset her genre scenes in fashionable antiquity. However, in her taste for the near past of seventeenth-century Holland and France, Gérard anticipated the romantic nostalgia of the nineteenth century. Not only was she one of the first artists to feature troubadourian detail, costumes, and settings evocative of France's medieval and Renaissance history, she also formulated a stylistic alternative for later artists who were more conservative than Gros or Delacroix but who wished to imbue their historical genre paintings with romantic authenticity. Her example was inspirational not only to the next generation of successful women artists such as Auzou, Chaudet, Haudebourt-Lescot, Mongez, and Servière, who created original genre styles of their own, but her influence on male painters such as her nephew Alexandre Evariste Fragonard, Horace Vernet, Paul Delaroche, and even Jean Auguste Dominique Ingres is also discernible to those familiar with her art.

63.

An Architect and His Family, ca. 1787-89

Oil on panel

12 x 9½ in. (30.5 x 24.1 cm.)

The Baltimore Museum of Art (38.232)

Mary Frick Jacobs Collection

Mistitled *The Architect Ledoux and His Family,* this small-scale panel conforms perfectly to the pattern of Gérard's portraits of the early 1780s. Since the architect Ledoux had two daughters rather than two sons and would have been over fifty years old in the first decade of Gérard's career, to which this work must be attributed, the traditional identification of the sitters is clearly incorrect. In an authentic portrait of Ledoux by Marguerite Gérard (Paris, Musée Cognacq-Jay) the innovative architect of Louveciennes is a portly, elderly man who stands flanked by his drawings for two of his Paris tollhouses, the Monceau Rotonde and La Villette.[6] In contrast, the jaunty patriarch of the Baltimore portrait appears to be in his thirties or forties, despite his powdered hair. He poses with a plan that is not easily identifiable, although scholars of late eighteenth-century French architecture have surmised that it represents a formal garden rather than a building. The stark monumental column behind the sitter may signify his alliance with the architectural avant-garde who admired the simplicity of early classical design. His wife's chic costume with the scarf bodice and top hat worn at a perilous angle was fashionable in the late 1780s and resembles styles depicted in the *Magasin des Modes* published in 1789.

The overall impression of prosperity produced by the rich clothes and direct smiling gazes of Gérard's male sitters is subtly belied by the wistful tilt of the woman's head and her almost melancholy glance. One is reminded of Goya's haunting portraits of the Spanish aristocracy in which one often senses unhappiness and anxiety behind the fashionable façades. Today it is tempting to interpret the lady's enigmatic expression, underscored by the shadowy background, as a premonition of the impending Revolution. In fact, one may date *An Architect and His Family* with assurance to 1787-89 on the basis of the costumes, furniture, and other Gérard portraits of this period such as *Monsieur Mougins de Roquefort,* in which the subject, a delegate from Grasse to the Assemblée and the Convention, is seated in front of a huge placard proclaiming "Droit de l'homme et du Citoyen . . . 1789." Due to their impeccable connections with the revolutionaries — Gérard's godfather Isnard even served as President of the Convention — Fragonard's family never suffered from his former association with the crown and the nobility. Gérard executed several portraits of delegates to the Convention who evidently visited her Louvre studio to sit for a rapidly brushed painting, an appropriate souvenir of their historic role in French history.

It may seem astonishing that Gérard painted both *The Piano Lesson* (cat. no. 64) and *An Architect and His Family* at approximately the same period of her career, but artists of her time often worked in radically different styles according to their subject matter and purpose. In Gérard's genre scenes she emulated the *trompe l'oeil* effects of the Dutch seventeenth-century masters and employed a smooth, glazing technique to eradicate all trace of her brushstroke. In her portraits she adopted a freer, more dynamic technique, applying her colors directly on the surface of her panel or canvas and leaving the tracks of her brush quite visible to the viewer. Her debt to Fragonard

4.

The single-signature engravings appear as early as December 25, 1794, in an anonymous sale of prints under no. 238.

5.

Pierre Rosenberg, "Fragonard: Le Baiser à la Derobée," in Paris, 1974, 42.

6.

A pendant to this portrait, formerly given to Antoine Vestier, exists in a private collection in France. It depicts three women, presumably Ledoux's wife and daughters. Anne-Marie Passez, an expert on Vestier, kindly brought this panel to my attention.

is more obvious in these works and her painterly brushwork might be described as a miniaturization of her master's exuberant manner. The tiny dimensions of *An Architect and His Family* are normal for a Gérard portrait and do not indicate that this panel is merely a preliminary study. In that pre-photography era Gérard was shrewdly producing portraits that were easily transportable but also large enough to display in one's home. It may seem paradoxical that her brushwork is looser and more energetic in these small-scale pictures than in her larger genre scenes, but her portrait subjects were living people, not idealized types or mannikins to be scrutinized at length.

The three-legged table in the Baltimore panel appears in numerous portraits and genre scenes by Gérard during the 1780s and 1790s including her supposed self-portrait, *The Attractive Art Student.* Called a *guéridon,* it was still in the artist's possession in 1824 when she made up a list of family heirlooms that she agreed to safeguard for her nephew Alexandre Evariste Fragonard.

Gérard was surely unfamiliar with the portraits of Goya or Gainsborough, yet there is a curious similarity between the doll-like boys in *An Architect and His Family* and the Spaniard's *Don Osorio* and the Englishman's *Master Buttall.* One may ascribe such affinities to the artists' common period and related subjects, but how does one account for the extraordinary parallel between Gérard's rendition of the cherubic boy in white and Renoir's charming treatment of children a century later? A few flecks of white pigment suffice to suggest the lacy frills on the boy's sleeves, touches of vermilion enliven his hair, and the brushstroke representing a crease in his satin suit casually runs over the dot of his button. To those unfamiliar with Marguerite Gérard's unconstrained portrait style, it might seem extreme to suggest her as an eighteenth-century precursor of Impressionism, but images such as the architect's son in his Sunday suit challenge the traditional assessment of Gérard as an old-fashioned imitator of Terborch. On the contrary, she seems to have been ahead of her time artistically as well as personally, an acclaimed artist whose creations on occasion presage the experiments of the Impressionists and an independent woman whose eschewal of marriage in favor of a career seems comprehensible in light of contemporary feminism.

64.
The Piano Lesson, 1780s
Oil on canvas
18 x 15 in. (45.7 x 38.1 cm.)
Signed bottom left: Mte. Gerard
New York, H. Shickman Gallery

One of the few accomplishments consistently required of a properly educated lady has been the ability to play a musical instrument with reasonable competence. Women's musical skills, like their artistic efforts, were never meant to approach the professional level but were intended to provide light entertainment for the opposite sex and decorous distraction for the ladies themselves. Many of Gérard's genre scenes of the 1780s feature young ladies studying dancing, singing, and the playing of various instruments, including the lute, guitar, harp, and piano. It was felt that proficiency in such social graces not only enhanced one's attractiveness and marital prospects, but would be useful in later conjugal life. Gérard's mothers delight in crooning lullabies to their babies or strumming popular airs for their spouses and children.

In *The Piano Lesson* Gérard reinterprets the familiar theme treated by Fragonard and the "petits maîtres hollandais" of the romantic music lesson in which an admiring male instructor hovers over a fetching female pupil. Eliminating any erotic undercurrent, Gérard presents only the devoted Enlightenment mother who oversees her daughter's music lesson herself rather than delegating this responsibility to a governess or music master. The guitar leaning against the footstool suggests that this maternal paragon is also fully capable of playing and teaching a second instrument. With her sleek hairstyle, porcelain-perfect beauty, and richly glimmering gown the mother exemplifies the bourgeois heroines of Gérard's genre scenes of the mid-1780s. The puppetlike quality of the little girl is characteristic of the artist's peculiar handling of child figures throughout her fifty-year career. Mme. Rousseau of the Institut de Costume in Paris has remarked that the contrast in the dresses of mother and daughter reflects the conservative taste of the bourgeoisie and their reluctance to adopt the daring new high-waisted style during the 1780s. The diaphanous "chemise à la Reine" was formally introduced to society in the Salon of 1783 with Vigée-Lebrun's portrait of Marie Antoinette, which was considered so scandalous that it was removed in the middle of the exhibition. As a result, in bourgeois circles this notorious style was worn chiefly by children until the end of the decade.

The veristic rendering of the mother's white satin gown, a Gérardian cliché, and the quiet intimacy of *The Piano Lesson* are reminiscent of the artist's so-called Metsu Manner, but in this instance there are no overt borrowings from paintings by her idols: Metsu, Terborch, Netscher, Verkolje, and Ochtervelt. Gérard seems to have depended on a draped mannikin to achieve the hyper-realistic reproduction of the cascading fabrics of her ladies' skirts. In fact, the inventory of her estate in 1837 contains a description of four "extremely worn" mannikins of different sizes. During the early 1780s Gérard experimented with the painstaking glazing techniques of the Dutch "petits maîtres" and eventually managed to imitate them with striking success. Contemporary critics almost invariably praised her technical dexterity and favorably compared her magical effects to the work of her seventeenth-century predecessors. Although Gérard relied on the careful layering of transparent glazes to impart an old master ambience to her interiors, she dispensed with this slow, tight technique in her portraits, opting for the more spontaneous painterly style of brushwork visible in *An Architect and His Family* (cat. no. 63).

The date of 1785 or 1786 on the square piano[7] corroborates the attribution of this canvas to the first decade of Gérard's career, the 1780s, when she developed and perfected her Dutch genre style. Since Gérard never dated her pictures, the notation above the piano's keyboard, quite separate from her signature, probably resulted from the artist's scrupulous attention to detail or from a request by the purchaser of the painting. The inclusion of the name and address of the piano maker and the date of the instrument's construction is quite unusual. Although certain pieces of furniture frequently reappear in Gérard's compositions, this square piano is unique in her known oeuvre. On the basis of the accessories alone, this canvas can be convincingly dated to any year between 1785 and 1789. The circular pleated fan, the gold pitcher, the black jewelry box, the bordered screen, and the stubby-legged stool were studio props that Gérard repeatedly rearranged in her compositions of the 1780s.

It is unlikely that *The Piano Lesson* is a portrait as it is executed in the artist's meticulous Metsu Manner, not her more Fragonardesque portrait style, and the figures are Gérardian types utilized in other genre scenes of the period. The brunette mother of *The Childhood of Paul and Virginia* (New York, Wildenstein & Co.) — datable no earlier than 1788, the year Bernardin de St. Pierre's book was published — is the tinted twin of the blond mother in *The Piano Lesson*. The setting with the drapery and alcove behind the piano is similar to the interior in Gérard's *The Letter of Rejection*, on which she also based *The Suicide Vow of Geneviève de Brabant*, an engraving commissioned by Augustin LeGrand in 1789.

According to Carol Duncan, the education of a bourgeois woman in late eighteenth-century France consisted primarily of teaching her to accept her role in life as the unselfish wife and mother who would find emotional fulfillment in pleasing her husband and serving her family.[8] In a letter to Fragonard presumably written in 1802, Gérard complains of the "burden of ignorance" she had born throughout her life, a burden she blames on her femininity and her consequent lack of an adequate education. Despite her success as a professional artist and her sentimental images of womanhood, she clearly resented the limited educational opportunities available to women of her time. Although her heroines usually conform to the behavioral ideals of the Enlightenment, they are nevertheless the dominant figures in her compositions even when depicted in the company of their adoring lovers and husbands. In fact, unlike the artist herself, many Gérardian ladies seem to be relatively learned for their time, dispensing history and geography lessons, translating Ovid, writing poetry, and reading voraciously.

7.
Laurance Libin, associate curator in charge of musical instruments at The Metropolitan Museum of Art in New York, kindly identified this instrument.
8.
Carol Duncan, "Happy Mothers and Other New Ideas in French Art," *Art Bulletin,* December 1973, 582.

63

64

Marie Geneviève Bouliar

French, 1762-1825

The few known portraits by this artist all communicate a warm human sympathy for her subjects, but we know very little about Bouliar's own personal circumstances and little about her career except the dates of her Salon appearances. She was born in Paris in 1762, the only daughter of a tailor, though she may have been related to artists with a similar surname.[1] Greuze, Doyen, Taillasson, and Duplessis have all been named as her teachers, but there is documentary evidence only to support a relationship with Duplessis. Her first recorded work is a portrait of a young woman signed and dated 1785 that has disappeared since being sold in Paris in 1902.[2] Bouliar first exhibited at the Salon of 1791 and sent works there with some regularity until 1817. She won a Prix d'Encouragement in 1795 for her painting *Aspasia* (cat. no. 65), one of her few recorded works that is neither a portrait nor a simple study of a head. She sent what sounds like an even more ambitious composition, *Erminia Carving Tancred's Name on a Tree Trunk,* to the Salon of 1802. Over forty paintings and drawings by her are recorded in the Livrets de Salon and in later sale records; today we can trace to public and private locations only ten paintings and one drawing certainly by her.[3] Not one of her surviving works dates from the nineteenth century. She died at Château d'Arcy (Saône-et-Loire) in 1825.

Joseph Siffred (Siffrein) Duplessis (1725-1802) is named as Bouliar's teacher in the Livrets de Salon of 1796 and 1798. It is probably significant therefore that two of her patrons, Alexandre and Adélaïde Lenoir (cat. nos. 66, 67), were the son and daughter-in-law of Madame Lenoir, who was painted by Duplessis in 1764 (Paris, Louvre).[4] He was, with Alexandre Roslin, the most celebrated portraitist in Paris in the 1770s and 1780s. The poses of his sitters avoid convention and suggest personal idiosyncracies, while his precise technique does justice to the exquisite fabrics and furnishings surrounding his patrons. Bouliar evidently appreciated the underlying informality of Duplessis' polished images, but her portraits are more informal in spirit, generally simpler in presentation, and more freely painted than his. Bouliar often used a frontal presentation for her sitters, and while Duplessis did not especially favor such a pose, he did use it for several of his most impressive half-length portraits, including that of Madame Lenoir.[5] Bouliar's frontal *Self-Portrait* of 1792 (Angers, Musée des Beaux-Arts), which shows the artist with windblown hair, her head tilted slightly to the left as she regards us with a hint of a smile, also seems to reflect some of the sentimental charm of Greuze's female head studies, though Bouliar's picture is far less idealized than the simpering maids of Greuze.

Bouliar's most ambitious surviving portrait is that of *M. Olive, Treasurer of the State of Brittany, and His Family* (Nantes, Musée des Beaux-Arts). Madame Olive dominates the composition, looking directly at the viewer and holding her naked son in her lap. Her husband sits behind her to the left, one arm along the back of the red velvet sofa on which they are posed, his other arm embracing their daughter who, like a young John the Baptist, approaches her brother with a bunch of grapes. The composition is beautifully planned, its obvious formal references to Holy Families suggesting that his family too was a happy one and furthermore subscribed to the new ideals of conjugal bliss and responsible parenthood that emerged in the late eighteenth century.[6] The loose garment round Madame Olive's right breast proves that she is nursing her son herself instead of sending him out to a wet nurse.

Bouliar was a gifted portraitist, one of those rare practitioners of the genre able to present another human personality without seeming to impose her own. She clearly had ambitions to be recognized as more than a portraitist, however, even if she had only limited success in this area. Like several other women in this exhibition, she is long overdue for serious research. Her work is so attractive that a little publicity should be sufficient to start some scholar on the path of collecting it together once more and exploring French archival sources for more information about her family and herself.

1.
This biography could not have been written without the help of Sally Wells-Robertson and Marianne Roland Michel. The discoveries of the latter, incorporated into the biography and catalog entry on Bouliar by Françoise Maison in the exhibition catalog *Trésors des musées du nord de la France: La peinture française, 1770-1830,* Arras, Calais, Douai, Lille, 1975-76, have finally given us the correct birth and death dates of Bouliar (as she spelled her own name, not Bouliard). The previous dates given — 1772 to 1819 — were based on an incorrect reading of a document by H. Jouin ("Mademoiselle Marie-Geneviève Bouliard, peintre de portraits [1772-1819]," *Artiste,* 1891, I, 401-11; reprinted as a book, Paris, 1891, an essay that adds little to the material published by Bellier-Auvray, I, 139). Jouin speculated that her father might have been the engraver Jacques Bouliard, who also exhibited in the Salon of 1791. Perhaps she was related to the wood sculptor Joseph Bouliart, who died in Paris on January 24, 1709, and whose heirs included a Marie Geneviève Boulliart (J. Guiffrey in *Nouvelles archives de l'art français,* 1883, IV, 221-22).
2.
The sale references are given by Maison (see note 1). The inscription reads "Mlle Br 1785."

3.
In addition to the three works in this exhibition, these are (in alphabetical order by location): *Self-Portrait,* 1792, Angers, Musée des Beaux-Arts; *Self-Portrait* (oval version of the Angers picture), Dijon, Musée des Beaux-Arts (Castres, no. 1); *Portrait of M. Olive, Treasurer of the State of Brittany, and His Family* (signed), Nantes, Musée des Beaux-Arts (a *Portrait of the Marquis de Cubieres as a Child* in the same museum is attributed to Bouliar in the 1913 catalog by Nicolle); *Self-Portrait,* drawing, Wildenstein & Co., New York; *Portrait of a Woman with Flowers in Her Hair,* 1791, Paris, private collection (the sitter has the same long face, long nose, large eyes, and small mouth as Madame Olive and might be the same woman a few years earlier); *Portrait of the de With Daughters,* Paris, private collection (two works, exhibited in the Salon of 1793). In addition to the *Portrait of Chevalier Alexandre-Marie Lenoir* (cat. no. 66), four more paintings by Bouliar were shown in the Paris exhibition of 1926. One of these was a work signed and dated 1798 and in the Salon of that year (*Woman with a Black Veil,* photo in Frick Art Reference Library); another was a third version of the Angers *Self-Portrait.* Finally, a *Portrait of Tallyrand,* signed and dated by Bouliar (date not given by catalog and not visible on photograph), passed through the Hôtel Drouot on March 2, 1911, lot 9 (oil on canvas, $9^7/_{16}$ x $7^1/_2$ in.).

65

65.
Aspasia, 1794
Oil on canvas
64³/₁₆ x 50 in. (163 x 127 cm.)
Signed on right above flowers: Mlle. Bouliar / 1794
Arras, Musée des Beaux-Arts

This canvas won a Prix d'Encouragement for Bouliar when she sent it to the Salon of 1795. It is one of the most ambitious of her recorded works and is the masterpiece of her small surviving oeuvre.

Aspasia has been called "the most famous woman in fifth-century Athens."[7] A *hetaera* of exceptional beauty and intellectual accomplishments, she came from Miletus to Athens around 450 B.C., when she was about twenty. She attracted the attention of Pericles, whose mistress she became around 445 B.C., and remained with him until his death in 429. The enemies of Pericles used her as the butt of their attacks on him, accusing her of immorality and of influencing his foreign policy, but he defended her reputation successfully. They had one son. "Socrates came to see her with his disciples, and his intimate friends brought their wives to hear her discourses, although she presided over a business that was anything but honest or even reputable, since she kept a house of young courtesans" (Plutarch, *Life of Pericles,* XXIV). Socrates actually attributes to her Pericles' famous funeral oration on the Athenians killed in the First Peloponnesian War. As recorded by Thucydides, the speech includes one brief word of advice to the widows of these heroes: "Your great glory is not to be inferior to what God has made you, and the greatest glory of a woman is to be least talked about by men, whether they are praising you or criticizing you." It is an odd sentiment for either Aspasia or Pericles to have expressed, in view of their circumstances, but as Pomeroy recently pointed out, Aspasia's liberated lifestyle was not possible for the wives of Athenian citizens, to whom the advice was directed. Aspasia was an exception in the patriarchal world of classical Athens, a woman of influence whose intellect was respected by some of the greatest minds and most powerful men of her day.

Bouliar shows Aspasia seated in an impressive classical interior complete with anachronistic arches and a bust of Pericles in a niche to the left.[8] Garlands of flowers decorate the base of the pedestal and the globe with constellations and signs of the zodiac on the table. Aspasia looks at her reflection in a mirror as if temporarily distracted from the text on the scroll in her left hand.[9] Is she preparing for a visit from Pericles or Socrates? The narrative context is obscure, probably deliberately in this idealized historical portrait. Aspasia would seem to be a somewhat ambiguous example for feminists, especially as presented by Bouliar. Aspasia was certainly more than a high-class *hetaera,* but the exposed breast, flimsy undergarment, flowers, and glance in the mirror all undercut her reputation as a learned woman. We need to recall that in the eighteenth century and before, as we have noted elsewhere, it was a great advantage for any woman seeking a career in male professions to be beautiful as well as talented. The use of subjects from ancient history to point out modern moral

4.
J. Belleudy, *J. S. Duplessis, peintre du roi . . .* , Chartres, 1913, 326.
5.
Ibid., 184 (*Portrait of Vien,* Louvre); 208 (*Joseph Perù,* Musée de Carpentras); and 256 (*Portrait of a Woman,* private collection).
6.
Carol Duncan, "Happy Mothers and Other New Ideas in French Art," *Art Bulletin,* December 1973, 570-83.
7.
S. B. Pomeroy, *Goddesses, Whores, Wives and Slaves: Women in Classical Antiquity,* New York, 1975, 89.
8.
Bouliar has used the portrait of Pericles attributed by some authorities to Kresilas (G.M.A. Richter, *A Handbook of Greek Art,* London, 1959, fig. 155).
9.
The Greek text is barely decipherable and seems to make no sense.

meanings had a long tradition in France and was now in fashion once more, above all in the work of David and his followers. Bouliar's message seems to be that a learned woman can also be feminine, and is thus a gentle plea, couched in the most respectable of artistic language, for the equality of women.

66.
Portrait of Chevalier Alexandre-Marie Lenoir, 1796
Oil on canvas
28¾ x 23⅝ in. (73 x 60 cm.)
Paris, Musée Carnavalet
(For comments, see next entry.)

67.
Portrait of Adélaïde Binart (Mme. Alexandre Lenoir), 1796
Oil on canvas
32¼ x 24⁷⁄₁₆ in. (82 x 62 cm.)
Paris, Musée Carnavalet
(See color plate, p. 84)

Bouliar's portraits of "Citoyen Lenoir" and "Citoyenne Leonir" were exhibited in the Salon of 1796. They belonged to members of the Lenoir family until the late nineteenth century, when the former was acquired for the Musée Carnavalet; in 1945 the latter was also bought for the museum.

Alexandre Lenoir (1761-1839) was a painter and archeologist who had studied in the atelier of Doyen. During the Revolution he became concerned about the many important works of art and monuments being destroyed by angry crowds. With official support, he collected together everything that he could save, hoping to form a national collection. It is due to him that bronze masterpieces of the sixteenth century such as Germain Pilon's figures on the tomb of Henry II in St. Denis still exist. The book Lenoir holds, labeled "Monumens Français," refers to the Musée National des Monuments Français, which he founded.[10] His wife, Adélaïde Binart (1771-1832), was a year older than Bouliar. She too was a painter, who studied with Regnault and exhibited at the Salon from 1795 until 1817. Like Bouliar's, most of her recorded works were portraits; none are traceable today.[11]

As noted above, Lenoir's mother was painted by Duplessis, the master of Bouliar, a personal contact that may explain how she obtained this commission. The warm and sympathetic portrayal of both husband and wife certainly suggests that they were good friends of the artist's. The simple, frontal, half-length composition used for the portrait of Adélaïde Lenoir recalls Duplessis' similar presentation of her mother-in-law even more forcibly than Bouliar's *Self-Portrait* does. Were the authorship of the picture and its subject not known, it would undoubtedly be called a self-portrait of an unknown woman artist. It seems legitimate to sense here a special kinship between the two young women both entering the profession at around the same time. Both works would benefit from cleaning and restoration, but even now, despite the film of old varnish and overly visible craquelure, they are powerfully effective portraits that arouse the viewer's curiosity about the sitters and the artist who painted them.

66

10.
His impressive bibliography is listed by Bellier-Auvray, s.v.; some additional biographical information is in Thieme-Becker, s.v.
11.
Bellier-Auvray, s.v., lists her Salon exhibits.

Jeanne Philiberte Ledoux
French, 1767-1840

68

Jean Baptiste Greuze had several women students who went on to have reasonably successful careers.[1] Of these, Jeanne Philiberte Ledoux is the most closely linked with her teacher in style and subject matter. Their work has been confused in the past and will continue to be confused until a catalog of Greuze's production is available. She was born in Paris in 1767 but did not emerge into public view until 1793, when she exhibited three works in the Salon with the following titles: *Painting at Rest, Little Girls at a Crossroads,* and *Concealed Love.*[2] She exhibited in most of the Salons held between 1793 and 1814, but after showing *Little Girl Holding a Dove* and *Young Boy near an Apple with a Fistful of Sticks* in the Salon of 1819, she disappears from the published sources. Only one of the works attributed to her in public or private collections is signed; none are dated and none can be certainly identified with works shown in the Salons. In short, research on Ledoux is in a primitive state.

The Salon records are our only source of primary documentation about Ledoux. In the Livrets she is identified as a Greuze pupil; the subjects of her works certainly suggest that they were essays in his manner. She did not attempt the elaborate moral tales in genre settings for which Greuze is best known. Instead she exploited the popularity of his head studies of beautiful young women and children, often depicted with animals, whose perfectly rounded features are frequently tinged with melancholy induced by the death of a pet sparrow or the temporary absence of a lover. A work such as Ledoux's *Portrait of a Boy* (Paris, Louvre) displays this blend of idealism and sentiment to perfection. In other works attributed to her, however, she presents her subjects in a more straightforward, unaffected manner. A *Portrait of Greuze* in the Musée des Beaux-Arts, Dijon, attributed to her is based on Greuze's *Self-Portrait* in the Louvre, but whereas that is a finished, formal composition in a painted oval frame, Ledoux's picture is an informal sketch.[3] She uses a rectangular format, simplifies his clothing, lightens the tone, and leaves much of his jacket as sketchy underdrawing. The result is a more accessible, human image. Her *Portrait of a Man* in the Baltimore Museum of Art is a simple head-

1.
Constance Mayer and Marie Geneviève Brossard de Beaulieu both studied with Greuze. The latter was a member of the Paris and Rome Academies. Her *Contemplation* of 1785 is in the Galleria dell'Accademia di San Luca in Rome. Greuze's daughter, Anne Geneviève (1762-1842), and Caroline de Valori were also trained by him.
2.
Bellier-Auvray, s.v., summarizes her Salon contributions. She exhibited a total of sixteen works. Bénézit lists a number of references to works attributed to Ledoux in sales between 1873 and 1945. Four works given to her, all in private hands, were in the exhibition held in Paris in 1926 (nos. 64-67). In addition to the works mentioned in the text, there are paintings attributed to her in Budapest (Magyar Nemzeti Galéria), Dijon (Musée Magnin), San Francisco (The Fine Arts Museums), and Vienna (Akademie der bildenden Künste).
3.
Exhibited in Castres (1973, no. 16) along with her *Portrait of a Boy* (Paris, Louvre), which appears to be her only published signed work.

and-shoulders composition of a middle-aged man wearing a small wig and a crisp lace jabot beneath his dark jacket. The sitter smiles as he looks off to the right. This is portraiture as a souvenir for family and friends, not portraiture as an official record of public achievement.

Ledoux was always a private artist catering to a bourgeois clientele that could not afford large pictures. She was evidently not ambitious for she never exhibited history paintings or even portraits of the famous and influential. Thus her career was not noticed by official sources. Reconstructing her artistic persona presents many practical obstacles, not the least of which is the fact that many of her works remain in unknown private collections belonging to the descendants of her original patrons. Her popularity was not undeserved, however, and her achievements certainly merit the recognition of a serious article.

68.
Portrait of a Boy, ca. 1800
Oil on canvas
16 x 12½ in. (40.6 x 31.7 cm.)
The Baltimore Museum of Art
Gift of The Leonce Rabillon Estate (29.3.9)

The attribution of this work to Ledoux is convincing. The general influence of Greuze is evident, but for Greuze's precise and elegant brushwork Ledoux substitutes a broader, more direct technique. The excess sentimentality of Greuze's children, seen also in Ledoux's *Portrait of a Boy* in the Louvre, is absent here. The appeal of this work to our feelings comes directly from an honest portrayal of its subject. It would be going too far to say that only a woman artist could sense and convey the psychology of children and their vulnerability (Velázquez' touching portraits of the Spanish royal children come instantly to mind), but the expectation that women are more logically employed painting children than are male artists resulted in some fine portraits of children by women artists. Differences in costume suggest that the Louvre portrait is earlier than the Baltimore portrait, and thus that Ledoux did not continue to work in an idiom closely based on that of her teacher but developed instead a style that is unaffected and intimate, especially in her portraits. The quality of this work and of her equally successful *Portrait of an Unknown Man* in the same collection should inspire a student of this area of French painting to investigate Ledoux properly.[4]

4.
The Baltimore Museum of Art owns a third work attributed to Ledoux, also a portrait of a child, but in a style much closer to Greuze than the work in the exhibition.

Constance Charpentier
French, 1767-1849

Mme. Charpentier (née Blondelu) was born in Paris and received her artistic training under Wilk,[1] David, Lafitte, Gérard, and Bouillon. She received a Prix d'Encouragement in 1788 as well as the gold medal of the Musée Royal in 1819. She showed in the Salons quite often between 1795 and 1819, at which point, for reasons unknown, she ceased to exhibit. Like other women artists of the epoch, Charpentier specialized in portrait and genre scenes, such as *The First Cure of a Young Doctor* (Salon of 1808); *A Mother Receiving the Confidences of Her Daughter* (Salon of 1812); and a rather bizarre scene of her own invention, *A Blind Man Surrounded by His Children Being Consoled for His Loss of Vision by the Pleasures of His Four Other Senses* (Salon of 1806). Until quite recently, *Melancholy* and a portrait drawing in the Musée Magnin in Dijon were the only works positively known to be by her hand,[2] and little is known about her personal life.

Mademoiselle Charlotte du Val d'Ognes (New York, Metropolitan Museum), the portrait most frequently associated with Charpentier's name and considered a prime example of women's pictorial talent in the early nineteenth century, is actually a relatively recent attribution. The portrait had been given to David until 1951, when Charles Sterling removed it from David's oeuvre and quite convincingly, on the basis of contemporary documents, drawings, and an engraving of the Salon of 1801, as well as through stylistic analysis, reattributed it to Mme. Charpentier. Yet the attribution is by no means definitive. Neither the vague 1801 Salon catalog description nor the registry of delivery of works to that Salon, nor the scanty commentary possibly related to this work by the critic Ducray-Duminil establishes Charpentier's authorship unequivocally. Stylistic comparisons with the artist's one surviving painting tend, if anything, to weaken the case. Indeed, as Sterling himself admits, further evidence in the form of oil portraits by Charpentier are the only means of providing the necessary evidence for a definitive attribution.[3]

69.
Melancholy, 1801
Oil on canvas
51³/₁₆ x 64¹⁵/₁₆ in. (130 x 165 cm.)
Signed: CM Blondelu/f. Charpentier
Amiens, Musée de Picardie (3213)

The subject of melancholy, detached from a specific literary or religious context and conceived as a generalized visual projection of mood, began to appear in the late eighteenth century in France. As Robert Rosenblum has pointed out, the tradition of the brooding figure isolated in a landscape setting is particularly long and unusually complex in England, and French artists of the period may well have taken the theme from across the Channel. Two works dealing with the theme appeared in the Salon of 1798, in which Mme. Charpentier exhibited. A related subject, a young woman weeping over her father's tomb, by François André Vincent, appeared in the Salon of 1801 in which Charpentier's *Melancholy* was shown. Yet, as Rosenblum has indicated, the most immediate source for the figure of the drooping, slack-armed young woman is David's Camilla, the woman fainting in the right foreground of the *Oath of the Horatii,* a source from which Mme. Charpentier might also have derived the sculptural yet rather softly voluptuous treatment of the surfaces.[4]

A similar juxtaposition of a rather chilly, sculptural, classical figure and a suggestive, emotionally charged landscape had appeared in the Salon of 1799 in Feréol de Bonnemaison's *Young Woman Surprised by a Storm.*[5] The weeping willow and the little pond frequently accompany scenes of mourning, in popular imagery as well as in high art. A similar motif, a mourning woman in a shadowy landscape, appears in a large painting by another woman artist of the period, *The Unfortunate Mother* of Constance Mayer. A closely related drawing of *Melancholy* by Charpentier, with minor variations in the setting, has recently entered a private collection in Paris.

1.
R. Rosenblum suggests that this may be a misspelling of the name J. G. Wille, in Paris, 1974, 75, 345.
2.
A group of works by Charpentier has recently been discovered in the possession of her descendants, but this material has not yet been published. I am grateful to Pierre Rosenberg for this information.
3.
His assertion that the literary rather than plastic poetry of the portrait and "its very evident charms . . . its cleverly concealed weaknesses, its ensemble made up from a thousand subtle artifices" argue for feminine authorship must, however, be greeted with a certain skepticism. Sterling, 121-32.
4.
Paris, 1974, no. 19, 346-47.
5.
Ibid., no. 11, repr. 155.

69

70

Marie Guillemine Benoist

French, 1768-1826

Best known as the author of the *Portrait of a Negress* in the Louvre (fig. 27, p. 49), Marie Guillemine Benoist was one of the most distinguished of Jacques Louis David's female students.[1] In addition to portraits and genre scenes she executed history paintings, but abandoned the last in the late 1790s after these works were criticized.

Born in Paris, Marie Guillemine Leroulx de la Ville was the daughter of an administrative official who encouraged her artistic interests by sending her to Mme. Vigée-Lebrun in 1781 or 1782. She exhibited her first works, a portrait of her father and two pastel studies of heads, in 1784 at the Exposition de la Jeunesse where she continued to exhibit through 1788. While a new atelier was being constructed for Vigée-Lebrun she placed Mlle. Leroulx de la Ville under David's tutelage, a move censured by the Directeur des Bâtiments, the Comte d'Angiviller, since the king had decreed in 1785 that young women artists were not to be trained in the Louvre.

Under David's influence she abandoned the pastel colors and softer modeling favored by Vigée-Lebrun for the more severe, linear draftsmanship and more brilliant colors of David, whose work she emulated throughout her subsequent artistic career. Her appreciation for his work is evident in her first history paintings exhibited at the Salon of 1791 — *Innocence between Virtue and Vice* (cat. no. 70) and *The Farewell of Psyche* (Salon no. 164) — which were so skillfully painted that some critics assumed that David had assisted in their execution.

She married the royalist Pierre Vincent Benoist in 1793. His various anti-Revolutionary activities, which jeopardized their lives in Paris during the Terror, apparently prevented her participation in the Salon of 1793; however, at the Salon of 1795 she exhibited two portraits and a painting representing *Sappho,* her last painting of an antique subject. In the late 1790s and early 1800s she exhibited portraits at the Salons, and from 1802 included sentimental genre scenes, then extremely popular, of children or women with children.

Nevertheless, her sketchbooks from the early 1800s, with drawings of such subjects as the departure of Regulus, testify to her continued interest in history painting.

In 1803 or 1804 Benoist received her first official commission to paint Napoleon's portrait for the Palais de Justice at Ghent, and later she obtained further commissions for portraits of the emperor and his family. She received a gold medal for her work in 1804, then established a studio for women, about which nothing is known. She last exhibited at the Salon of 1812 and painted few works in the years before her death in Paris in 1826.

70.

Innocence between Virtue and Vice, 1790
Oil on canvas
34⅛ x 44⅛ in. (87 x 115 cm.)
Saint-Benin d'Azy, S.A.S. la Princesse Leopold de Cröy Solre

Innocence between Virtue and Vice, exhibited at the Salon of 1791 (no. 273), represents one of Benoist's most ambitious works, which critics praised both for its conception and execution. Benoist had already shown an interest in the theme of seduction and its consequences in two genre paintings inspired by Richardson's *Clarissa* — one representing *Clarissa at the Home of Archer,* the other *Captain Morden at the House of Clarissa* — exhibited in 1787 and 1788, respectively, at the Exposition de la Jeunesse. In *Innocence between Virtue and Vice* the subject was elevated to a more abstract, allegorical plane.

The theme is an adaptation of *Hercules at the Crossroads* (or *Hercules between Virtue and Vice*), a subject made popular in the eighteenth century by the Earl of Shaftesbury's commentary on the topic which he published in his *Characteristiks* (second edition, 1714) and by several paintings, the most famous being Reynolds' variation on the theme in his *Garrick between Comedy and Tragedy*. In most works Vice was represented by a woman, but Benoist portrayed the alle-

---

1.
Ballot, *La Comtesse Benoist, l'Emilie de Demoustier 1768-1826*, provides most of the information on the artist and her work.

gorical figure as a handsome young man whom Innocence reluctantly rejects.

While the composition and the placement of figures in the landscape are clearly Benoist's invention, the painting does incorporate several elements of David's work. The background and the gestures of Vice betray an awareness of David's *Belisarius;*[2] in fact Benoist had earlier represented herself painting a version of Belisarius and his child guide in her *Self-Portrait* of 1786.[3] The poses of Innocence and Virtue can be related to those of the female figures in David's sketches and final version of the painting *Brutus,*[4] a work executed while Benoist was his student and for which she herself did a sketch of one of the female heads.

71

2.
See Michael Levey and Wend Graf Kalnein, *Art and Architecture of the Eighteenth Century in France,* Harmondsworth, 1972, pl. 197.
3.
See Ballot, repr. opp. 32.
4.
See Robert L. Herbert, *J. L. David: Brutus,* London, 1972, color pull-out and for the sketches, pls. 5 and 6.

Pauline Auzou
French, 1775-1835

Recognized by her peers as a versatile, talented, and industrious artist, Pauline Auzou executed portraits, genre scenes, and history paintings. She was especially praised for her ability to produce the last.

Born in Paris in 1775, Pauline Desmarquets entered the studio of Jean Baptiste Regnault, Jacques Louis David's rival, some years before 1793. Her single-minded perseverance there was rewarded, for by the age of eighteen she was exhibiting at the Salon a *Bacchante* (Salon of 1793, no. 777) and a *Study for a Head* (no. 778). Her early style is difficult to determine because many of her early works have not been traced, but one might assume that it resembled Regnault's with its heavy sculptural modeling and strong chiaroscuro.

Auzou's early works are portraits and scenes from Greek history and mythology such as *Daphnis and Phyllis* (Salon of 1795, no. 11) and *Dinomache, Mother of Alcibiades* (Salon of 1796, no. 11). In the late 1790s and early 1800s she added sentimental genre scenes to her repertoire, many representing women in a variety of domestic situations: *Young Woman Reading* (Salon of 1799, no. 10), *Portrait of a Woman Playing a Prelude on the Piano* (Salon of 1800, no. 10), *Two Young Girls Reading a Letter* (Salon of 1802, no. 2).

During the 1800s Auzou, impressed by the work of Jean Auguste Dominique Ingres, modified her painting style by flattening forms and reducing the chiaroscuro, as is apparent in one of her few works in the possession of a public collection, her *Portrait of a Musician* (Manchester, New Hampshire, Currier Gallery of Art).

In late 1793 or early 1794 Pauline Desmarquets married Charles Marie Auzou, a paper merchant, and in subsequent years she gave birth to three children, but her domestic cares never interfered with her professional interests. She obtained a first-class medal for her work in 1808 and continued to exhibit regularly at the Salons up through 1817. In addition, for at least twenty years she maintained an atelier for female students. She died in Paris in 1835 at the age of sixty-71.

The First Feeling of Coquetry, 1804
Oil on canvas
55 x 42 in. (139.7 x 106.6 cm.)
Signed and dated lower right
Paris, Collection Auzou Family

The First Feeling of Coquetry, exhibited at the Salon of 1804 (no. 8), is one of a number of sentimental genre scenes painted by Pauline Auzou that represent an episode in the life of a young girl. Unlike the many paintings by Jean Baptiste Greuze depicting girls with broken objects, which allude to the loss of virginity,[1] this work celebrates the ascendance of a girl to womanhood as the coquette happily appropriates her mother's clothes, jewelry, and makeup during that parent's absence. The implied sensuousness of the subject is heightened both by the lighting and by the inclusion of a trumpet, a perfume bottle, a drinking cup, a mirror, and the fire which might allude to the five senses. Perhaps reacting to this glorification of the loss of innocence, Mademoiselle Desoras exhibited a work in the Salon of 1808 entitled *Coquetry Punished, or the Broken Mirror* (no. 176).

The colors, smooth handling of the paint, and attention to fine detail are all typical of Pauline Auzou's style. The interest in artificial illumination and several light sources, however, is rather unusual in her work and appears in only one other presently known painting, *Ghost Stories* (Paris, private collection), a work never exhibited at the Salons. This depicts an old woman telling ghost stories to children who shy away from the shadows in the room which they interpret as ghosts. Auzou apparently abandoned her preoccupation with artificial lighting because of critical reviews.[2]

Like many other Neoclassical artists such as Jacques Louis David, Auzou made sketches of nude figures for her paintings before their final execution, and for *The First Feeling of Coquetry* there exists a

1.
See Anita Brookner, *Greuze*, Greenwich, 1972, pl. 16, *Les oeufs cassés*, or pl. 49, *La cruche cassée*, for instance.
2.
Reviewing the work, Charles Landon said, ". . . the shadows appear a little exaggerated and the light of the fire reflected on the legs of the figure does not produce a happy effect." *Nouvelles des arts*, IV, 1804, 131-32.

sheet with two drawings of the nude girl. A figure in almost the same pose reappears in a later Auzou work, *The Arrival of the Archduchess Marie Louise in the Gallery of the Château de Compiègne* (Salon of 1810, no. 21; fig. 26, p. 48), while a second coquette makes her appearance on the left in yet another Auzou painting, *Marie Louise, at the Time of Her Departure from Vienna, Distributing Her Mother's Diamonds to Her Brothers and Sisters, March, 1810* (Salon of 1812, no. 22, Musée National de Versailles).[3]

72

3.
Repr. in Georges Lacour-Gayet, *Napoléon, sa vie, son oeuvre, son temps*, Paris, 1921, 437.

Constance Mayer

French, 1775/78-1821

Constance Mayer was born in Paris, where she lived and worked all her life, witnessing the Revolution, the Terror, and the ascendancy of Napoleon. She was the daughter of a customs official to whom she was deeply attached. The closeness of the relationship is evident in her *Portrait of a Father and Daughter* (Salon of 1801), representing her father showing her a bust of Raphael.

From about 1818 until her suicide three years later, the charming, vivacious young woman was subject to periods of depression and anxiety. There is no documented medical explanation for her melancholy, but according to her friend Mme. Tastu, she had an impressionable and sensitive nature and was consistently dependent, personally and professionally, on the men in her life, from her father to her teachers — Suvée, Greuze, and especially P. P. Prud'hon.[1] Suvée's imprisonment during the Terror, Greuze's death in 1805 followed by her father's five years later, the antipathy and even hostility of Prud'hon's children, along with her fear of aging undoubtedly contributed to the sorrow of her last years.

In keeping with the general taste of the period a strong preference for sentimental moralizing appears in Mayer's early works, exhibited in the Salons of 1796 and 1798-1802. Her style and subjects of these years are an outgrowth of her tutelage under Jean Baptiste Greuze, whose fame derives from melodramatic, moralizing genre scenes that feature strong chiaroscuro, theatrical gestures, and shallow, stagelike settings. Mayer's portraits of a young man attired as a hunter, children holding pigeons, or pretty women in pastoral settings are marked with the master's style. Greuze had a large number of students during the 1790s, many of whom, like Mayer and her lifelong friend Jeanne Philiberte Ledoux, were women. According to Mme. Tastu, many of the heads attributed to Greuze are actually by Mayer.[2]

In 1802, during a visit to Greuze's studio, P. P. Prud'hon made the acquaintance of the young woman whom he was later to describe as a "tendre et judicieuse amie," the "chère enfant de mon coeur."[3] That same year, under Prud'hon's guidance, Mayer turned to allegorical subjects, copying his style and his compositions and eventually collaborating with him on a number of paintings. Her hand is discernible in works such as *Abandonment to Pleasure Followed by Repentance, Innocence Seduced by Love,* and *The Dying Laborer,* although the canvases are signed by Prud'hon.[4] The allegorical pictures that are certainly by Mayer, among which are three paintings at the Louvre — *The Dream of Happiness* (cat. no. 72), *The Unfortunate Mother,* and *The Happy Mother* — are almost all from studies or designs by the master.[5] Her paint application and soft coloration, the languishing, meditative qualities of her figures are in the style of Prud'hon.

The relationship between Mayer and Prud'hon is complex although it is certain that while she remained the student and he the master, they shared a strong emotional and professional dependency. From 1810 onwards, Mayer occupied quarters at the Sorbonne near Prud'hon, working in his atelier, taking meals with him in her small apartment, and entertaining mutual friends. Mme. Tastu reports that they addressed each other as "M. Prud'hon" and "Mademoiselle," and that they worked side by side in harmony and with affection.[6]

Mayer was commissioned by Empress Josephine to paint *The Sleep of Psyche,* which appeared in the 1806 Salon as *The Sleeping Venus and Cupid Caressed and Wakened by the Zephyrs.* The picture, along with its pendant, *The Torch of Venus* (exhibited in the 1808 Salon as *The Awakening of Psyche),* was poorly received by the critic Baudry, who compared it unfavorably with Prud'hon's work.[7] Nonetheless, the picture, originally sold as a Mayer, later brought a much higher price as a Prud'hon and, as such, entered the Wallace Collection, London, under the title *The Sleep of Psyche.*

Mayer's personal charm and liveliness emerge in a series of portraits dating from the latter part of her career. Shown at a posthumous exhibition in 1822, the portraits of *Mlle. Trézel, Mlle. Lordon,* and

---

1.
Pilon, 46.
2.
Ibid., 51.
3.
Doin, 140.
4.
See the judgment of Guiffrey and of Charles Clement in Pilon, 52.
5.
For example, see Guiffrey, no. 32, pl. 29, for a pencil design by Prud'hon used by Mayer for *The Happy Mother,* and no. 41, pl. 35, for a sketch for her *Young Naiad Serenaded by Cupids,* shown in the 1812 Salon.
6.
Pilon, 46-47.
7.
Doin, 142.

Young Girl with a Cat are among the most firmly confident pictures of her career. Her work is represented in private collections, in the Louvre, and in the museums at Nancy and Dijon.

72.
The Dream of Happiness, 1819
Oil on canvas
51^{15}/$_{16}$ x 72^{7}/$_{16}$ in. (132 x 184 cm.)
Paris, Musée National du Louvre

This allegorical painting, which originally appeared in the Salon of 1819 under the title *L'Amour et la Fortune conduisant dans une barque, sur le fleuve de la vie, un jeune homme assis a l'arrière de l'embarcation et protégeant de ses bras sa femme et ses enfants endormis (Love and Fortune Steering a Boat on the River of Life, a Young Man Seated in the Rear Protecting His Sleeping Wife and Children in His Arms),* is based on a number of oil sketches, drawings, and preliminary studies by Prud'hon. The basic idea for the painting probably goes back to a wash drawing by Mayer's earlier master Greuze, a work entitled *Allegory of Conjugal Happiness,* representing a young couple rowing a boat with the assistance of a little cupid.[8]

Prud'hon executed fourteen or fifteen studies related to this work.[9] Among the most important of these preliminary studies is a drawing, formerly in the Ferté Collection, and a painted sketch, now in the Musée de Lille, which Mayer herself reworked in an oil sketch formerly in the Rouart Collection.[10] Not only did Prud'hon provide the basis for the painting as a whole, but he also did separate studies of the different figures: the husband, the sleeping wife, the head of the allegorical figure of Fortune rowing the boat, and the helpful cupid who assists her.[11] The finished painting itself, however, is held to be entirely by the hand of Constance Mayer.[12]

She executed several other paintings dealing with the subject of conjugal love and family feeling: *A Mother and Her Children at the Tomb of Their Father* (Salon of 1802); *The Happy Mother* and *The Unfortunate Mother* (Salon of 1810); and the *Unfortunate Family,* unfinished at the time of her death, which was completed by Prud'hon and subsequently shown at the Salon of 1822.[13]

8.
G. Bazin, "Greuze, Prud'hon et Constance Mayer," *Amour de l'art,* 1931, 408, fig. 51.
9.
Guiffrey, 91-106, 32-33.
10.
Bazin, *Amour de l'art,* 407 and figs. 52-54.
11.
Ibid., 407 and figs. 55-58, 410-11.
12.
See, for example, the opinion of Charles Ressort, "Copies, répliques, pastiches" (Dossier du Département des Peintures), *La revue du Louvre,* XXIII, 1973, 399.
13.
Pilon, 128.

Marie Eléonore Godefroid
French, 1778-1849

Marie Eléonore Godefroid was born into a family of artists and art-restorers; her father, François Ferdinand Joseph Godefroid, like many of his contemporaries, had lodgings in the Louvre. His circle of friends included many of the major artists of the pre-Revolutionary period: Joseph and Carle Vernet, David, Suvée, Doyen, Brenet, and Gérard. For about eleven years, from 1795 until 1805, Mlle. Godefroid taught drawing at the exclusive girls' boarding school in Saint-Germain-en-Laye run by Mme. Campan, whose portrait by Godefroid is now at Versailles. Jeanne Louise Henriette Campan, author of a popular volume of memoirs of Marie Antoinette, was later appointed directress of Napoleon's school for the Demoiselles de la Légion d'Honneur. She propounded original theories on female education, which she published under the title De l'éducation, suivi de conseils aux jeunes filles (2 vols., 1824), and has been considered a precursor of feminism. Among the students at Mme. Campan's establishment at Saint-Germain-en-Laye were her two nieces, one of whom was to marry Marshal Ney, and many of Napoleon's female relations, including his youngest sister.

Teaching left Godefroid little time to concentrate on her own work, so in 1805 she entered the atelier of Baron François Gérard, with whom she had maintained friendly relations since her childhood in the Louvre. She devoted herself to portraiture and to assisting the busy Gérard, a prominent portraitist and history painter associated with both the Napoleonic and Restoration regimes. She lived with Gérard's family, and in addition to collaborating with the artist and copying his works, she often helped out in his lively evening salons, filled with notables in the realm of arts, letters, and the theater, "devoting herself to boring guests [and] to smoothing over irritations for her sensitive master." Not only did she submerge herself in her master's style in painting, but she often imitated his handwriting to answer boring letters.[1] She continued to live with Gérard's family even after his death in 1837. She died in 1849 of cholera which she caught while performing a typical act of selfless devotion, supervising the packing of Mme. Récamier's Corinne by Gérard.

Godefroid enjoyed a high reputation as a portrait painter and was commissioned to depict the most socially prominent personages of her time; her specialty was portraits of women and children. Among her most important portraits were: The Children of the Marshal Duke of Enghien; Queen Hortense and Her Children; The Children of the Duke of Rovigo (Salon of 1812); The Children of the Duke of Orléans (Salon of 1827); and The Children of David d'Angers, now in the Musée d'Angers.

Only once, in 1842, did Godefroid actually create a subject painting: for a Senegalese church she executed a Notre-Dame du Rosaire, "in which the figures of the two Christians kneeling at the Virgin's feet, one of the white race and one African, created a graceful composition in an elevated religious style."[2] Particularly interesting in the context of an exhibition of women painters is the subject of a work, after a Gérard composition, that Godefroid showed in the 1843 Salon. It was a portrait of Novella d'Andrea, a brilliant woman scholar of the fourteenth century so well versed in law that she often took the place of her father, a celebrated law professor at the university of Bologna, and so lovely that she had to teach hidden behind a curtain, according to the account of Christine de Pisan, Novella's contemporary, who provided the subject.[3]

73.
The Sons of Marshal Ney, 1810
Oil on canvas
63¾ x 70⅛ in. (162 x 173 cm.)
West Berlin, Staatliche Museen Preussischer Kulturbesitz, Gemäldegalerie
(See color plate, p. 85)

This painting, no. 379 in the Salon catalog of 1810, is listed as Portrait en pied des enfants de M. gr le maréchal duc d'Elchingen. Michel Ney (1769-1815), Duke of Elchingen, Prince of the Moskowa, Marshal of France, was born of lower-class parents in Saarlouis, and rose, through extraordinary military talent, to the summit of the Napoleonic hierarchy. After the victory of Friedland, Napoleon bestowed on him

1.
Arbaud, 512-13.
2.
Ibid., 49.
3.
Bellier-Auvray, I, 670.

the title "the bravest of the brave"; he was active in the Peninsular War from 1808 to 1811, as well as in the 1812 expedition to Russia. Three of his children are represented in the painting; a fourth son, Napoléon Henri Edgar, was not born until 1812. The children in the painting are: Joseph Napoléon, then seven years old, to the right; Michel Louis Félix, age six, to the left, and Eugène, two years old, in the middle. Napoleon himself had helped arrange Ney's socially advantageous marriage to Aglaé Louise Auguié, niece of Mme. Campan and Godefroid's former pupil, in an elaborate wedding ceremony in 1802, directed by the painter Isabey. Indeed, the magnificent sword carried by Ney's eldest son may be the Egyptian weapon that Napoleon won at the Battle of Aboukir and gave to the marshal as a wedding present. The youngest son seems to be pointing to this showy emblem of adult valor, while half-hidden under the table on the left lies a simpler, more practical weapon (possibly a reference to their father's beginnings as a humble soldier). The richly costumed Ney children stand in an elegant interior on a balcony overlooking a landscape with a river, perhaps the Donau in Elchingen.[4] The figure of the little boy with the sword, gazing steadily out at the observer, has its prototype in seventeenth-century works like Zurbarán's *Alonso Verdugo de Albornoz* (1635, erroneously known as "Don Balthasar Carlos," formerly in the Kaiser Friedrich Museum, destroyed in 1945), which was in the Oudry Collection in Paris until 1869; in turn, it looks forward to Manet's *Boy with the Sword* of 1861.

74

4.
I am grateful to Dr. Erich Schleier for generously sharing a great deal of information about this painting with me.

Mme. Villers
French, active late 18th-early 19th century

The little that is known about the career of this artist is confusing and contradictory.[1]

In 1799 (Year VII of the Republic), a "Cne Fme Villers (née Lemoine)," student of "Giraudet,"[2] is listed in the Salon catalog as an exhibitor of three paintings: no. 344, *La Peinture (Painting);* no. 345, *A Sleeping Bacchante;* and no. 346, *A Portrait.* In 1801 (Year IX of the Republic), a Mme. Villers (née Nisa), living at rue Louis-le-Grand, maison Arthur, no. 222, showed three works: no 364, *Study of a Young Woman Seated before a Window;* no. 365, *Study of a Young Woman at Her Toilet;* and no. 366, *A Portrait.* In 1802 (Year X of the Republic), a Mme. Villers, no maiden name specified, living at rue de l'Université, no. 269, showed two works: no. 310, *A Baby in Its Cradle Carried Off by the Waters of the Flood of the Month of Nivôse in the Year X,* and no. 311, *A Study of a Woman from Nature.*

A Baby in Its Cradle was reproduced by Landon in 1803.[3] The painting represented a sleeping infant, modeled after classical prototypes, in a wicker basket with an improvised "sail" made out of bedclothes, that is carried along by a vast torrent; the head of a faithful dog, "his lively eyes riveted on the cradle,"[4] appears to the right. This predecessor of Lassie was probably inspired by Mme. Chaudet's *Baby Sleeping in Its Cradle Being Guarded by a Brave Dog* of 1801, which represented a sleeping infant saved from a serpent by a faithful dog, a work that had been greatly admired in the Salon the previous year.[5]

74.
Portrait of Mme. Soustras, 1802
Oil on canvas
58 5/16 x 44 1/8 in. (148 x 112 cm.)
Signed and dated An 10 (1802)
Paris, Musée National du Louvre

The pose of this charming figure recalls that of the classical "Sandal-Binder," and suggests that the sitter may have been a dancer. This pose, or the similar, if more provocative one of adjusting a stocking, appears in late eighteenth- and early nineteenth-century prints and fashion plates, and, with overtly erotic overtones, in Goya's *Caprichos* 17, *Bien tirada está.* Indeed, the costume of the sitter, especially the beautiful lace shawl, suggests Spain to the modern viewer, although such dress was evidently popular in France as well in the early nineteenth century.[6] The sitter has laid her gloves, which still seem to bear the imprint of her fingers and fingernails, and a rose to one side as she bends to lace up her slipper; her glance, however, is directed not down toward this task, but rather out toward the spectator.

The three-quarter or full-length portrait in a landscape setting, with the sitter frequently set off by an architectural or sculptural motif — a bust, a balcony, or a wall — was popular around the end of the eighteenth and beginning of the nineteenth century. Girodet-Trioson, for example, used this composition for his striking *Portrait of J. B. Belley* of 1797, now in the Musée de Versailles. J. B. F. Désoria employed it for his *Portrait of Elizabeth Dunoyer,* now in the Art Institute of Chicago, of the same year. François Gérard frequently placed his elegant female sitters in this kind of setting — for example, his *Princess Visconti* of 1810 — and of course Ingres raised this portrait type to new heights of cool, poetic eloquence in his *Mlle. Rivière* of 1805, now in the Louvre.

One of the two works that Mme. Villers apparently showed in the Salon of 1802 was *A Study of a Woman from Nature.* Perhaps *Mme. Soustras,* which is dated "An 10" (1802), is identical with that work. Portraits at the beginning of the nineteenth century were often picturesque, anecdotal, and relatively informal; women were frequently depicted putting on their earrings or other jewels, or combing their hair.[7] Mme. Villers herself evidently painted a *Study of a Young Woman at Her Toilet* for the Salon of 1801. Sitters often preferred to hide their identities behind initials;[8] no doubt, some of them — chiefly women — preferred the even greater anonymity of the "Study" when their likenesses were displayed in the Salon: it is possible that Mme. Soustras was one of the latter.

1.
Bellier-Auvray, II, 699. The entry for Mme. Villers states that her maiden name was Lemoine, that she was the student of Giraudet, and that she lived on the rue de l'Université, no. 269. It is then stated that she exhibited works in the Salons of 1799, 1801, and 1802. Yet there is no artist named Giraudet in either this or any other artists' lexicon. Bénézit (VIII, 574), who claims Mme. Villers exhibited in the Salons from 1799 to 1814, lists her as a student of "Girardet," but does not specify which member of this numerous, and predominantly Swiss, artistic family he means. Perhaps "Giraudet" is a misspelling of "Girodet" (Anne Louis Girodet-Trioson, 1767-1824); in any case, there is no record of work by Mme. Villers in the Salon catalogs from 1803 to 1814.
2.
See note 1, above. This information, and that which follows, comes from the Salon catalogs indicated.
3.
C. Landon, *Annales du Musée et de l'Ecole Moderne des Beaux-Arts,* Paris, 1803, IV, 59, repr. 16.
4.
Ibid., 59.
5.
Ibid., repr. 18.

6.
Black might also suggest mourning attire, although it is interesting to note that "in 1801 . . . formal dresses were of black crêpe; black fichus were frequently worn." A.C.A. Racinet, *Le costume historique,* Paris, 1888, VI, n.p.
7.
Wildenstein, "Table alphabétique des portraits . . . exposés à Paris au Salon entre 1800 et 1826," *Gazette des beaux-arts,* LXI, 1963, 11. Men too were sometimes depicted dressing themselves. See, for example, Vien fils' *Portrait of Frion* "coming out of the water after swimming and putting on his clothes" of 1804, ibid.
8.
Ibid., 15.

Antoinette Cecile Hortense Haudebourt-Lescot
French, 1784-1845

Mme. Haudebourt-Lescot was one of the best-known women artists of her time, the only woman artist, in fact, to be included in François Joseph Heim's painting of King Charles x distributing awards to artists after the Salon of 1824. She appears in the left foreground, a little behind her teacher, Guillaume Guillon, who was known as Lethière. A popular history painter, he had been appointed director of the French Academy in Rome in 1807. At that time, the young Mlle. Lescot, an art student who had also acquired a considerable reputation as an amateur dancer, followed her teacher to Rome.

During her Roman sojourn, unusual for a woman of that period although of course almost *de rigueur* for male art students, Lescot developed an interest in scenes of the everyday life and customs of the Italian peasantry. Indeed, she may even be credited with inventing "a new category of picturesque, local-color genre" while living there.[1] Her delight in picturesque yet accurate renditions of Italian scenes parallels, but is more direct and veristic than, that of such contemporary pioneers of genre painting as François Marius Granet and pointed the way for other French specialists in the relatively unexploited theme of Italian peasant life, such as Jean Victor Schnetz and Léopold Robert.

The first Salon in which the artist participated, that of 1810, included eight scenes of Italian life sent from Rome, for which she was awarded a second-class medal. Although many of her genre works have been destroyed and can only be seen in the form of engravings, one of her more ambitious paintings, *The Kissing of the Feet of the Statue of St. Peter in the Basilica of St. Peter, Rome, 1812,* which appeared in the Salon of 1814,[2] is now in the Musée National du Château de Fontainebleau. In this painting of a colorful contemporary Roman ritual, Lescot represents some of the major figures of the Roman art world in the crowd of observers, including the sculptor Antonio Canova. At Fontainebleau, too, are some commissioned works: her scenes from the life of François I and Diane de Poitiers of 1819.

The artist returned from Rome to Paris in 1816 and married an architect, Haudebourt, in 1820. During the next thirty years she exhibited more than one hundred paintings in the Salons, mainly small-scale genre scenes, as well as a good number of portraits later in her career. She received a first-class medal in 1828.

Among her surviving works are an emotional *Vow to the Madonna during a Storm* (Salon of 1817), in the *dépôt* of the Musée Bertrand, Châteauroux, and *A Condemned Prisoner Being Exhorted by a Capuchin Monk Just before Leaving for Torture* (Salon of 1819), a rather melodramatic work, highly praised for its vigorous brushwork, firm color, and fine characterization,[3] but now in bad condition (Paris, Louvre). Among the picturesque genre subjects she treated were: *A Conjurer* (1817); *The Merchant of Relics* (1822); *Dancing the Saltarello* (1824); and *The Marionette Theater in Rome* (1824). Of particular interest in the context of an exhibition of women painters are the many works Haudebourt-Lescot devoted to Italian genre scenes of women's life: women shoppers, dancers, worshipers, and benefactresses, as well as domestic scenes like *The First Steps* (1819), a theme later treated by Jean François Millet, and *The Happy Family.* She also portrayed somewhat darker moments of feminine existence, like *The Abandonment* and *A Young Girl Overcome with Exhaustion on a Trip to Rome* (1827). Haudebourt-Lescot's representation of a young Italian peasant woman attempting to sell a painting, *The Second-Hand Dealer of Paintings* (1824), may well have served as a prototype for a later, more complex and circumstantial representation of a young woman trying to sell her work, Emily Osborn's *Nameless and Friendless* of 1857 (see fig. 33, p. 54).
75.
Self-Portrait, 1825
Oil on canvas
29¼ x 23⅝ in. (74 x 60 cm.)
Signed and dated: Haudebourt-Lescot 1825
Paris, Musée National du Louvre (MI 719)
(See color plate, p. 86)

1.
Robertson, 1973, 5.
2.
Another version had appeared in the Salon of 1812.
3.
A. Jal., *L'ombre de Diderot, Salon de 1819,* Paris, 1819, 177.

Mme. Haudebourt-Lescot attracted considerable attention as a portraitist, as well as establishing a reputation as a specialist in genre. Among those who sat for her were her mother; the Duchess Visconti (ca. 1835-36); and the Comte de Jouy (1839); she was also commissioned to portray various historical notables for Versailles in 1830. The artist had portrayed herself earlier, half-length, in a work now in the Musée des Beaux-Arts, Nancy. She had also been represented in an 1814 drawing by Ingres, now lost, of which a copy by Jean Alexandre Allais exists in a private collection, and in a portrait attributed to Gérard in the Musée Magnin, Dijon.

Her 1825 *Self-Portrait* as a mature woman of about forty is perhaps her most moving work. Although her drawing style has been likened to Ingres', there is little that is Ingresque in the sensuous immediacy and poignant inwardness of this portrait; rather, it may call to mind such early romantic essays in portraiture as those by Gros, or even Géricault. The rich, subdued palette; the shadowy ambience; the expressive pose, at once self-contained and vulnerable, with veiled, inward glance and parted lips; the black velvet beret; and the gold chain all recall Rembrandt's self-portraits. Yet at the same time the delicate impasto of the pearl earrings, the evocative mood, and the feminine details of the costume are reminiscent of his portraits of women, especially *Hendrikje at the Window*. It is tempting to think that Haudebourt-Lescot fused the two Rembrandtian prototypes to create an image that is at once a portrait of the artist and a portrait of a woman.

The artist, who exhibited in the Salons from 1822 to 1855, was born in Tonnerre and studied with her husband, Abel de Pujol (1787-1861), a David pupil and member of the Institute, a painter greatly admired in the early nineteenth century for his religious and historical paintings. Grandpierre-Deverzy, who always exhibited under her maiden name, made her debut in the Salon of 1822 with *The Studio of Abel Pujol in 1822* (cat. no. 76). She seems to have specialized in interiors and literary subjects, showing a *View of a Portion of the Château of Fontainebleau* in the Salon of 1824 and a *Scene from the Novel of Gil Blas of Santillane* in the same exhibition. In the 1827 Salon she showed a canvas of a subject taken from Sir Walter Scott's *Quentin Durward* and one of a subject taken from Mme. de la Fayette's novel, *The Princess of Clèves;* in the Salon of 1831 she showed *The Blind Mother*, a subject taken from a song by Béranger. In addition to numerous portraits, she showed several versions of the interior of her husband's studio. Her style, which displays a certain modest charm, is almost indistinguishable from that of other minor artists of her time; her work is of greater historical than aesthetic interest.
76.
The Studio of Abel Pujol in 1822, 1822
Oil on canvas
37⅞ x 50¾ in. (96 x 129 cm.)
Signed and dated 1822
Paris, Musée Marmottan

This charming painting, which was exhibited in the Salon of 1822 as an *Interior of a Painting Studio*, is the earliest of three versions of this subject shown by the artist. The other two are the *Interior of the Studio of M.A.P. . . . History Painter,* from the Salon of 1836, and the *Interior of the Studio of M. Abel de Pujol, Member of the Institute,* in the Salon of 1855, the last Salon in which the artist exhibited. The latter is now in the Musée des Beaux-Arts, Valenciennes.

Grandpierre-Deverzy gives us a detailed view, in this canvas, of what went on in her husband's well-conducted women's class; women

76

Sarah Miriam Peale
American, 1800-1885

students, of course, studied separately from men until the end of the nineteenth century (see fig. 30, p. 52). On shelves to the left are displayed the antique plaster casts from which the beginning students drew, with the single male nude torso turned modestly to the wall. In the left rear corner an elegantly dressed female model is seated, perhaps a contemporary version of the antique Venus behind her, whose figure is partially veiled by what seems to be the model's cloak, bonnet, and shawl. All around the room, young women are busy sketching, painting, or cleaning their palettes. A group at the right is gathered around the master,[1] who is engaged in criticizing a sketch after the antique; one of the pupils is diverted by another who pulls aside the curtain to observe something on the street. On the walls hang what seem to be reduced copies after important works by Abel de Pujol: *Jacob Blessing the Sons of Joseph,* for which the artist had received the gold medal in the Salon of 1810, hangs in the left foreground; the work in the center of the rear wall would appear to be a version of his *St. Stephen Preaching before His Martyrdom* for the Church of Saint-Etienne-du-Mont; to the left hangs what seems to be a *Deposition* in a pointed "Gothic" format.

Grandpierre-Deverzy's painting is a modest version of a major nineteenth century theme: the painter's studio. More specifically, it is a representation of students at work in a painter's studio. As such, it might well be compared with Mathieu Chochereau's well-known *Studio of David,* of 1814, now in the Louvre, where the male students are shown working from the male model; with Marie Bashkirtseff's *The Studio of Julian* of 1881, now in Leningrad, in which members of Julien's women's class are shown working from a youthful model posed, with fur tunic, as the infant St. John the Baptist; or with Alice Barber Stephens' *Female Life Class,* 1879, now in the collection of the Pennsylvania Academy of the Fine Arts, in which women students are represented working from the nude female model.[2]

The youngest daughter of James Peale, an eminent miniaturist and portrait painter, Sarah Miriam Peale grew up in a culturally enlightened household filled with artists of all ages. Her uncle was the acclaimed natural history painter, portraitist, and scientist Charles Willson Peale, a proponent of equal opportunities and liberal educations for women. His influence and moral support were critical to her development as an artist, as was the rudimentary training she received from her father. In 1817 she exhibited her first works at the Pennsylvania Academy of the Fine Arts, to which she was elected as an Academician in 1824; at that time she and her sister Anna were the only women to be so honored. She studied with her cousin Rembrandt Peale in Baltimore for three months in 1818 and later visited that city intermittently, exhibiting portraits and still lives there before setting up a studio in Peale's Baltimore Museum, where she worked from 1825 to 1829. She rose to prominence as a portraitist rather rapidly, producing at least seventy-five documented portraits before she left Baltimore in 1842. Her celebrated clients included José Sylvestre Revello, the first diplomat from Brazil to the United States, in 1824, and in the following year, the military hero General Lafayette. In 1841-43 she frequently worked in Washington, D.C., painting the portraits of several distinguished political figures, just as Rembrandt and Charles Willson Peale had done earlier. These important commissions included Daniel Webster, the Secretary of State; Abel P. Upshur, Secretary of the Navy; Thomas Hart Benton and many other senators; and quite a few Congressmen. In about 1846 her health began to fail and at the invitation of a family friend she moved to St. Louis, where she remained for the next thirty years, continuing to produce portraits and prize-winning still lives. In 1878 she joined her two artistic sisters, Anna Claypole Duncan and Margaretta Angelica Peale, in Philadelphia and painted still lives there almost until her death seven years later. Because she supported herself throughout her sixty-year career entirely from the sale of her art she is often hailed as the first professional woman artist in America. Her death marked the close of the three-generation dynasty of Peale

---

1.
The portrait of Abel de Pujol in this painting may be compared with his *Self-Portrait* of 1806, now in the Musée des Beaux-Arts, Valenciennes. See Paris, 1974, no. 146, repr., 192.
2.
See Philadelphia, 1973, no. 30 and fig. 4 on 17.

artists and the end of their distinctive contributions to the tradition of American painting.

77.
A Slice of Watermelon, 1825
Oil on canvas
17 x 21^{13}/$_{16}$ in. (43.2 x 55.4 cm.)
Hartford, Wadsworth Atheneum
Ella Gallup Sumner and Mary Catlin Sumner Collection

Although Sarah Miriam Peale produced still lives throughout her career, most of the signed and dated versions were painted between 1820 and 1829, while she was working in Baltimore. Not surprisingly, many of Sarah's works of that decade depend significantly on those by her father and her cousin Raphaelle Peale for their stylistic inspiration. As in numerous still lives by those artists, the fruit in *A Slice of Watermelon* rests on a shallow bowl in a narrow, ledgelike space viewed slightly from above. The simple background, the horizontal emphasis of the table edge, the contrast between the neatly sliced rind and the broken edges of the melon, and the sharp distinction of light and dark follow seventeenth-century Dutch models, yet were more directly influenced by the artist's father and cousin.

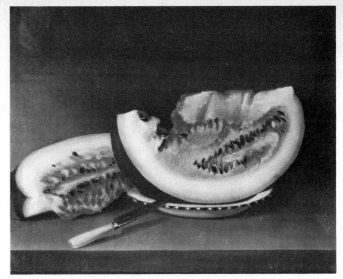

77

The semicircle of the central slice of watermelon is echoed in the curvilinear contours of the other slice and of the bowl; this orchestration of curved shapes is counterpointed by the diagonal thrust of the knife that balances precariously on the rim of the bowl. Within the austere geometry of this tightly composed arrangement the almost haphazard rhythms of the pulp and seeds add a palpable texture.

In about 1860 the artist's approach to still life changed markedly, shifting from the Peale vernacular of tabletop settings to more casually composed vignettes of cherries and other fruits still growing on the branch or in distinctly natural surroundings.

In the late 1840s and '50s, amateur still-life painting enjoyed a great vogue in America among women who created "instant" still lives from ready-made "theorem" or stencil patterns. Occasionally such untrained artists also copied lithographs or works by professional artists; as early as 1828, for example, the naive artist known as the Doty painter made a stiff copy directly from Peale's *A Slice of Watermelon.* By contrast Peale's still lives attest to her technical skill as well as to her highly focused powers of observation.

Rosa Bonheur
French, 1822-1899

Marie Rosalie Bonheur was the first woman artist to receive the coveted cross of the French Legion of Honor, which the Empress Eugénie conferred on her personally in June 1865 at the artist's château at By, on the outskirts of the Forest of Fontainebleau. It was the empress' desire to demonstrate that, for her at least, "genius has no sex."[1] Bonheur enjoyed considerable official success and celebrity in France as well as receiving awards and decorations from Belgium, Spain, Portugal, and Mexico.[2] She was particularly esteemed in England and America where engravings and exhibitions of her work attracted the attention of artists, collectors, and amateurs.

The eldest of four children, all artists specializing in animal subjects, Bonheur received her earliest and most definitive training from her father, Raymond Bonheur, a landscape painter and drawing master in the family's native Bordeaux. By age seventeen she was making substantial contributions to the family income with copies of old masters made at the Louvre; at twenty-seven she became director of l'Ecole Impériale de Dessin for young people. Some years after the family moved to Paris in 1829 she demonstrated her characteristic independence by rejecting an apprenticeship to a dressmaker, electing from the age of ten to spend many hours sketching animals in the still wild Bois de Boulogne, studying the particularities of each species and relating them to human thoughts and feelings. She was interested in both sculpture and painting in these early years, and she continued to make sculptures long after her reputation as a painter had been achieved.

Diligent about anatomical accuracy, Rosa dissected animal parts obtained from a butcher and went regularly to slaughterhouses on the outskirts of Paris during her teens and early twenties. To observe and sketch from life, she attended horse fairs and cattle markets. To avoid the taunts of attendants and observers while she worked, she donned men's clothes, obtaining official authorization for her dress from the prefect of police in 1852.[3] Though her male attire was the subject of much comment, she steadfastly retained working clothes

that were practical, comfortable, and masculine. Rosa Bonheur never married, but devoted herself to her work, to the many animals who found a haven on her large estate, and to a few intimate friends and family members. Her companion for over forty years was the artist Natalie Micas, with whom she shared an independence from convention and a dedication to work.

From her father, an enthusiastic St.-Simonian, a thorough Republican, and a devotee of the new French school of naturalist landscape, Bonheur developed a marked humanitarianism and an enthusiasm for Romantic literature, particularly that of George Sand.[4] Her early contact with the St.-Simonians, who believed in the absolute equality of women as a religious necessity, even postulating a woman Messiah and a female element in the Godhead, was responsible in no small way for Bonheur's emancipation from conventional feminine modes of behavior and the complete freedom with which she undertook large, challenging compositions.

Direct observation from nature, favored by artists in the 1830s and 1840s, remained a principle to which she adhered throughout her life. Like Troyon and Brascassat, with whom her work was often compared, her picturesque compositions were thought to embody the freshness and spontaneity of the Dutch realist school. While she had never visited the United States, before beginning a series of paintings of the American Far West, in 1895, she felt it necessary to obtain a sample of prairie grass, without which, she said, she would not dare to begin her *Bisons Fleeing a Fire* (repr. Klumpke, 19) or *Wild Horses in the Far West.*[5]

From 1841 until her retirement to By in 1853, she exhibited regularly at the Salon with strongly painted compositions of individual or grouped animals in shallow, light- and air-filled spaces. By 1848 she had earned a gold medal for *Red Oxen of Cantal,* a composition based on studies she had made on a recent trip to the Auvergne, and had established a reputation with collectors and critics for a vigorous

1.
Klumpke, 264.
2.
These included membership in the Antwerp Academy of Fine Arts (1868), the Belgian Cross of Leopold, the brevet of commander in the Order of Isabella the Catholic by Alphonso XII of Spain, the Portuguese Order of St. James, and the Mexican Cross of San Carlos from Emperor Maximilian and Empress Carlotta.
3.
Stanton, 364, reproduces a facsimile of the authorization.
4.
She is said to have applauded and accepted as her own goals the following statement from George Sand, "Art for art's sake is a vain word. But art for truth, art for the beautiful and the good, that is a religion that I see." Stanton, 386. See also Emile Cantrel, *L'Artiste,* September 1, 1859, in Klumpke, 198-99, for a critique on the intimate relationship between the work of Bonheur and Sand.
5.
The request was made of Anna Klumpke who records her attempts to obtain the prairie grass on page 37 of her monograph.

technique and charming subjects. She began to devote herself to numerous commissions, including *Plowing in Nivernais* for the French government. Bonheur described herself and her art as "matter-of-fact in everything — American style";[6] nevertheless, the strong sense of movement and the lyrical effects of filtered natural light that inform her most important works demonstrate an innately Romantic spirit.

The Horse Fair (New York, Metropolitan Museum), shown in the 1853 Salon and considered her masterpiece, is more dramatic in conception and broader in brushstroke than her earlier work. The breadth and large manner of Géricault, whose study of horses was in her studio while she painted *The Horse Fair*, is apparent in the dynamic movement, anatomical accuracy, and flickering light that energize the composition.[7]

Bonheur's interest in the American West, her familiarity with engravings such as George Stubbs' *Godolphin Arabian* (1794) and with Catlin's native American subjects, as well as her scrupulous study of photographs, engravings, and life studies,[8] are typical of the Romantic sensibility and realist accuracy that pervade her work. There are some paintings, such as her *Dream of Ossian* (1868), in which both subject and handling are decidedly idealized and dreamlike, but these are rare. The freshness of her observation of both animals and people, the feeling and psychological penetration in her animal portraits are original and dominate her oeuvre. Critics in her own time were particularly impressed with the boldness of her technique and the charm of her color, in some cases labeling her strong style as masculine.[9] She was sometimes thought to be more accurate than poetic and too summary in her handling of landscape,[10] but on the whole her feeling for the harmonies of nature and the creatures that inhabit her landscapes had continuing appeal.

From her earliest days Bonheur was interested in the effects of light,[11] but she was never directly affected by Impressionist experiments nor did she participate in the artistic rebellions of the nineteenth century. Her work, like her life, is strongly individual.

78.
Study of Rams
Oil on canvas
16 15/16 x 25 13/16 in. (43 x 65.5 cm.)
Signed lower right
Musée National du Château de Fontainebleau

In this ten-figure oil study Rosa Bonheur has precisely documented the characteristics of a ram, another example of her dedication to achieving fidelity to nature in art.[12] In such works she presented the subject from a variety of positions and points of view to reveal all aspects of it, often concentrating on showing a specific anatomical part from varied angles, such as the frontal, three-quarter, and profile views of the head in the upper part of this canvas. The subject is frequently presented in one canvas in both vigorous action and

complete repose; usually, as here, more than one model of a particular species is included.

Our study focuses on two different rams, faithfully drawn from direct observation and recorded with linear precision and scientific detail. Bonheur kept these studies for many years, using them at different times in her career as elements in larger works. Although undated, this canvas may be quite early, since, according to the artist herself, she was studying all types of animals in the 1840s in an attempt to understand the muscles, bone, and physiological structure of each species.[13] There are two compositions by Bonheur of this period, *Ram, Ewe, and Lamb* (Salon of 1845)[14] and *Head of a Ram* (1845),[15] in which the ram forms may derive from this oil study. The later and very lively *Herding (Scotland)* of 1860[16] seems also to relate to this study or to similar sketches made during a visit to England and Scotland in the summer of 1855.

79.
Oil Sketch for Haymaking in Auvergne, 1855
Oil on canvas
19 5/16 x 33 7/16 in. (49 x 85 cm.)
Signed lower right
Musée National du Château de Fontainebleau

This oil sketch is a first idea for Bonheur's *Haymaking in Auvergne,* which was exhibited at the Exposition Universelle in Paris in 1855. The painting, commissioned by the French government as a pendant to *Plowing in Nivernais,* which had been painted for the state seven years earlier, was awarded a first-class medal at the exhibition. The commission for *Plowing in Nivernais* had stipulated only that the subject was to be plowing, with payment set at three thousand francs. Bonheur is thought to have taken the idea for that picture from a plowing scene described in George Sand's *La mare au diable (The Devil's Pool)*[17] and to have developed it more elaborately from direct nature studies made during the fall and winter of 1848 in the countryside around Nièvre.

Like *Plowing in Nivernais, Haymaking in Auvergne* is a pastoral scene that pays tribute to the French countryside and the laboring peasant. It was Bonheur's custom to use studies from nature, often made several years earlier, when developing a large composition. During a visit to Auvergne in 1846 she had studied and recorded the life of the province in a series of sketches and drawings that she used for this painting nine years later. Such rural scenes and themes of peasant labor were praised by critics as "those new *Georgics,* in which contemporary artists and writers — modern Virgils — have reinstated and extolled the foster-fathers of the race."[18] The seventeenth-century Dutch masters of similar subjects often served as models for Bonheur and her contemporaries like Troyon, Brascassat, and Millet, while her poetic transcription of country life in both *Plowing in Nivernais* and *Haymaking in Auvergne* was lauded by critics as the equal of paintings by Albert Cuyp and Paulus Potter.

6.
Bonheur, in the 1890s, clarified some mistaken impressions in an earlier monograph by Eugène de Mirecourt (1856). See Stanton, 32.
7.
See Sterling and Salinger, 161-64, for history, provenance, stylistic discussion, and bibliographical references for *The Horse Fair*.
8.
Klumpke, 30, 36-37.
9.
Thore-Burger's review of the 1847 Salon, for example, as quoted in Stanton, 32.
10.
Sterling and Salinger, 161-62, discuss the retouching of *The Horse Fair* due to such criticism.
11.
See Bonheur's correction of the Mirecourt text in Stanton, 32.
12.
A similar study of dogs is repr. in Klumpke, 379.
13.
Quoted in Klumpke, 181.

14.
Repr. ibid., 179.
15.
Repr. ibid., 177.
16.
This painting was exhibited in 1867 and is repr. ibid., 264.
17.
Bonheur's biographer and friend, the artist Henry Bacon, reports that the Bonheur family often read aloud to each other and that Rosa was particularly touched by Sand's masterly descriptions of animals in landscape. Bacon, 833-40. See also a critical comparison of Bonheur's work with Sand's by Emile Cantrel, 198-99, and Roger-Milès, 36.
18.
Henry Peyrol as quoted in *Masters in Art,* 32.

78

Although the composition of the oil sketch for *Haymaking in Auvergne* differs from the finished work it does include all the major components. Pivotal to both is the haywagon with oxen set in a broad meadow, surrounded by men and women loading the hay. There are fewer figures in the preparatory oil and, understandably, a greater sketchiness of setting and figures. Wagon and oxen meet at a right angle on the left and are balanced by reposing cattle and trees on the right; the focus is on the foreground, with a few brief lines to suggest the possible inclusion of middle-ground figures. In the finished painting, the wagon and harnessed oxen are more continuous in line and are placed more centrally in the canvas. This rearrangement permits a broader depth of field in which distant figures, still working in the field, can be seen as part of the haymaking process.

Typical of Bonheur's work of this period are the horizontal arrangement of forms in sparkling, sunlit fields and the concern for anatomical accuracy. Her summary handling of the background landscape sets the foreground forms in relief and focuses attention upon the active and vital figures, both human and animal.

80.
Gathering for the Hunt, 1856
Oil on canvas
30½ x 58½ in. (77.5 x 148.6 cm.)
Stockton, California, Pioneer Museum and Haggin Galleries
(See color plate, p. 87)

Gathering for the Hunt is one of Bonheur's many compositions based on farm and peasant life. Painted in the same period as *Haymaking in Auvergne* it exhibits the same precise rendering of individual forms and a similar compositional emphasis on the interaction of moving figures. The array of hunters, horses, and dogs are aligned parallel to the picture plane, their vitality and motion relieved against a sketchy background of land and sky. Her shallow space stresses the animated foreground action, while the movement of light reinforces the dynamism of the forms. Figures are integrated on the surface of the canvas by the broad, single horizontal sweep of the composition, giving the activity a strong sense of cohesiveness. Bonheur used this compositional arrangement for many multi-figured canvases of similar or related subjects: *The Colliers* of 1875[19] and *In Auvergne* of 1889[20] also exhibit precise foregrounds and atmospheric, sketchy backgrounds. Her forms for *Gathering for the Hunt,* realized with great anatomical accuracy, were undoubtedly studied and sketched in individual studies. This painting combines the vigorous movement and love of horses evident in her popular *Horse Fair* of 1853 (fig. 32, p. 53) with her interest in peasant life apparent in *Haymaking in Auvergne* and *Plowing in Nivernais* (Musée National du Château de Fontainebleau).

79

19.
Klumpke, repr. 189.
20.
Ibid., 365.

Lilly Martin Spencer
American, 1822-1902

Lilly Martin Spencer was one of the most important genre painters in the United States and one of the most popular American artists of the mid-nineteenth century. She was born in England of French parents who emigrated to America in 1830 with their eldest daughter, Angélique Marie, nicknamed Lilly, and two sons, in order to establish a utopian cooperative community. Despite the failure of this plan, the Martins supported progressive causes: the temperance movement, abolition, and women's suffrage.

Lilly grew up in Marietta, Ohio, where her father was a teacher and farmer. Her first important artistic work, undertaken in her teens, was the decoration of the walls of the family home with humorous, life-size representations of the entire household going about familiar activities. The artist may have had help in coloring these wall-drawings from two local artists, one of whom, Charles Sullivan (1794-1869), helped her to hold her first exhibition in 1841. For unknown reasons, she rejected an offer of assistance that would have enabled her to study art in Boston or Europe and instead moved to Cincinnati with her father in 1841. There she did mainly portrait painting, studying briefly with John Insco Williams (1813-1873), one of Cincinnati's best-known portraitists. She married Benjamin Rush Spencer in 1844. Having already broken the conventions restricting women from serious dedication to a career in art, Lilly Martin Spencer broke the conventions of marriage as well: eventually Mr. Spencer devoted himself exclusively to domestic tasks and assisting his wife in her profession. Their marriage was evidently happy and prolific — they are said to have had thirteen children, of whom seven survived —[1] despite the financial difficulties that continually plagued them. In 1847 Spencer exhibited at the first show of the Western Art Union in Cincinnati; several of her works were engraved for distribution to subscribers that year and the two following.

The family moved in 1849 to New York, where Spencer showed and studied at the National Academy of Design, absorbing the manifold influences available to the artist in this metropolitan center. Of particular interest may have been the Düsseldorf Gallery, where the highly finished, often anecdotal productions of this school of German artists were on view. Although she painted some Shakespearean scenes, Spencer gradually turned more and more to her family and to domestic life for inspiration. The middle-class American public preferred genre painting above all other types; anecdotal scenes rich in sentiment and spiced with humor were most popular. During the fifties, Spencer established her reputation as one of America's most important producers of domestic genre, with works such as: *Domestic Happiness* (ca. 1849); *The Jolly Washerwoman* (1851); *Peeling Onions* (ca. 1852, Boston, Postar Collection); *Shake Hands* (1854, Columbus, Ohio Historical Center); *Kiss Me and You'll Kiss the 'Lasses* (1856, Brooklyn Museum); *"This Little Pig Went to Market"* (1857, Marietta, Ohio, Campus Martius Museum); and *The Gossips* (1857), a large-scale, many-figured outdoor work.

After the Spencers moved to New Jersey in 1858, the artist continued to produce domestic genre, although many of her works of the sixties are touched with darker themes related to the Civil War. Her most ambitious painting of this period was a large-scale allegory, probably influenced by French Salon painting of the time, entitled *Truth Unveiling Falsehood* (1869), which, along with the artist's *We Both Must Fade* (1869), a portrait, and several smaller works, was exhibited at the Women's Pavillion of the Philadelphia Centennial Exposition in 1876. Spencer's later style is looser and darker in tonality, lacking the crisp contours, sparkling colors, and sharply defined details of her earlier works.

Although Spencer, unlike her mother, was not an active feminist, it is obvious that as a specialist in paintings of domestic life she concentrated on and sympathized with the everyday experience of women. Many of her paintings have female protagonists, and in her medal-winning allegory, *Truth Unveiling Falsehood*, Truth is protecting a young woman nursing a baby because, as the artist said, woman in particular needs Truth to enlighten and protect her so "that her smile

---

1.
Washington, D.C., 21.
2.
Ibid., 205.
3.
Freivogel, 14.
4.
Washington, D.C., 173. The description was accompanied by an engraving of the subject by A. J. J. Hervieu.
5.
Ibid., 50 and 173.

81

and her words, which are the first that mankind in its innocence looks up to, may not teach it error."[2] Late in life, Spencer painted portraits of two feminists: Ella Wheeler Wilcox and Elizabeth Cady Stanton. In the words of one writer, Lilly Martin Spencer was indeed a "Feminist without politics."[3]

81.
The Young Husband: First Marketing, 1854
Oil on canvas
29½ x 24¾ in. (74.9 x 62.9 cm.)
New York, Collection Mr. and Mrs. Edward Abrahams

The subject of this painting seems to have been directly inspired by a passage in Mrs. Trollope's *Domestic Manners of the Americans,* published in 1832: "It is the custom for the gentlemen to go to market at Cincinnati. The smartest men in the place, and those of the 'highest standing' do not scruple to leave their beds with the sun, six days in the week, and, prepared with a mighty basket, to sally forth in search of meat, butter, eggs, and vegetables. I have continually seen them returning, with their weighty basket on one arm and an enormous ham depending from the other."[4] Spencer's *The Young Wife: First Stew,* ca. 1856, was the pendant to this painting and the two received equally mixed criticism when they were shown together at the National Academy of Design in 1856. The reviewer in *The Crayon* admired the color and lack of "conventionalism" of the pair, but criticized their poor drawing and frozen expressions as well as the frivolity of the incidents depicted with such earnest, painstaking technique.[5]

In actuality, *The Young Husband* seems less coy and mannered than many of Spencer's popular paintings; it is spared the exaggerated grimaces and straining after humorous effect that mar so many of her best-known works. Here the artist has skillfully combined still life with anecdotal figure painting in a piquant city setting. The easy sense of movement and the informal composition may even call to mind some of the city scenes of French nineteenth-century painters like Caillebotte, despite Spencer's far greater emphasis on the anecdotal aspect of the scene.

Emily Mary Osborn
British, 1834-?

Emily Mary Osborn was the first-born child of an Essex clergyman whose curacy took him to London in 1848. There the adolescent girl — with some resistance from her skeptical father — began attending art classes at Mr. Dickinson's Academy on Maddox Street. She studied briefly under John Mogford, a minor landscape painter, and later and more extensively with James Matthew Leigh, a portraitist and history painter whose skills as a teacher were particularly influential. In 1851, at the age of seventeen, she submitted her first entries to the Royal Academy — a few portraits and two genre subjects entitled *The Letter* and *Home Thoughts* — where she continued to exhibit until 1884. In the course of her long career, spent partly in Germany beginning in the early 1860s, her work also appeared in the British Institution, the Society of British Artists, and in such commercial establishments as the Grosvenor Gallery and the New Gallery.

Most of her first financial successes came from portraiture; among her earliest patrons was Queen Victoria, who bought at least two of Osborn's works: *My Cottage Door* of 1855 and the famous canvas hailed at the 1860 Royal Academy show, *The Governess*. Both eminent patronage and public recognition through awards came to her if only to a limited extent; in 1862 she won a silver medal from the Society for the Encouragement of the Fine Arts for *Tough and Tender* and two years later she won a first prize of sixty guineas for the best historical or figure subject at the Crystal Palace Picture Gallery. Conversant with several modes of painting, Osborn produced, in addition to genre pictures (the mainstay of her art), such portraits as *Phillip Gosse, Jr.* and *Madame Bodichon* as well as narrative and literary paintings such as *Isolde, Hero Worship in the Life of Johnson*, and *The Escape of Lord Nithisdale from the Tower in 1716*. Her best-known paintings deal with the theme of the victimized or distressed woman, often the object of callous social treatment and prejudice; two outstanding examples are *The Governess* of 1860 and *Nameless and Friendless* of 1857, one of the rare paintings that represents the plight of the woman artist trying to sell her wares (see fig. 33, p. 54). The prize-winning *Half the World Knows Not How the Other Half Lives,*

1864; *For the Last Time,* 1864; and *God's Acre,* 1868, all deal with related — and similarly bleak — themes of the consequences of death and penury in the lives of young women.

82.
Mrs. Sturgis and Children, 1855
Oil on canvas
90 x 52 in. (228.6 x 132.1 cm.)
Chicago, Collection Robert Peerling Coale
(See color plate, p. 88)

Although the identity of the sitters in this life-sized portrait is uncertain, it is possible that it represents the Bostonian Julia Overing Boit Sturgis. She had come to London in 1848 with her husband, Russell Sturgis, a businessman also from Boston, and three of their children: May; Julian, who would have been seven at the time; and Howard, an infant when the work was painted.[1] The painting, which was no. 266 in the Royal Academy Exhibition of 1855, was commissioned by William Mitchell, who had heard that Osborn wished to produce something of greater importance than anything she had yet attempted. The work was shown at the same time as the artist's small picture, *My Cottage Door,* which was bought by the queen. The artist received two hundred guineas for the portrait, which Mr. Mitchell presented to the Sturgis family.[2]

The composition, which knits mother and children together in a compact, interlocking group, seems clearly dependent upon Leonardo's charcoal cartoon of the *Virgin and Child with St. Anne,* which had been in the possession of the Royal Academy since 1791 or earlier.[3] The portrait type of an upper-class mother and her children in an outdoor setting owes much to the tradition of eighteenth-century British portraiture, as exemplified in the work of Gainsborough, Reynolds, and Lawrence.[4] Yet this work is unusual in that the figures are placed not in the customary landscape setting, but against the foil of a richly painted beach. It is significant that William Powell Frith had exhibited his *Life at the Seaside (Ramsgate Sands)* in the

1.
Militating against this tempting identification is the lack of any specific reference to either the portrait or to the Mitchell brothers in the available documentation about the family of Russell Sturgis. The children are not specifically stipulated as belonging to the sitter in the title. Two of Mrs. Sturgis' children, Julian and Howard, grew up to be fairly well-known writers in England. See E. W. Borklund, "Howard Overing Sturgis: An Account of His Life and Writings Together with His Unpublished Works," doctoral dissertation, University of Chicago, 1959, especially 24-25.
2.
Dafforne, 261.
3.
London, Royal Academy of Arts, *Leonardo da Vinci Quincentenary Exhibition,* 1952, no. 109.
4.
One wonders, for example, how much Osborn's other R. A. picture of 1855, *My Cottage Door,* owed to Gainsborough's various *Cottage Doors.*
5.
Dafforne, 261.

Elizabeth Eleanor Siddal
British, 1834-1862

1854 Royal Academy Exhibition, and that the work had made a strong impression at the time and had been bought by the queen. Frith's detailed, many-figured scene of contemporary seaside activity was therefore shown in the same Academy exhibition in which Osborn had shown her own small *Pickles and Preserves,* which was subsequently bought by Mr. C. J. Mitchell, brother of the man who commissioned *Mrs. Sturgis and Children.*[5] Although the figures in Osborn's portrait are more elaborately dressed and formally posed than those in Frith's genre scene, and lack the protective parasols and bonnets worn by the ladies in the latter's painting, it is certainly likely that the impact of his *Life at the Seaside* accounts for the unusual setting of this ambitious portrait.

Born into a lower middle-class family, Elizabeth Eleanor Siddal rose to prominence as the hauntingly sensuous face with red gold tresses immortalized in numerous Pre-Raphaelite canvases. Discovered in 1849 by Walter Deverell, an artist acquainted with the youthful Pre-Raphaelite Brotherhood, she began posing for several members of the circle, but by 1852 was serving solely as Dante Gabriel Rossetti's model. Her relationship with him intensified on several levels that year: in addition to becoming his exclusive model, mistress, and pupil, she was his romantic ideal and primary muse for the next ten years. Reticent and enigmatic, she was quickly enshrined by the group as a cult object and became an obsessive image in Rossetti's drawings and paintings.

Dependent on Rossetti for her artistic instruction, Siddal inherited numerous stylistic characteristics from him: her awkward drawing, imperfect perspective, and Gothic proportions; her claustrophobically filled interiors; and her predilection for medieval or Arthurian subjects all ultimately derive from his influence. William Holman Hunt, Ford Madox Brown, Alfred, Lord Tennyson, and Rossetti himself all valued her talent highly; and in 1855 the august critic John Ruskin offered her 150 pounds annually as payment for her paintings. The strongest period of her artistic production occurred between 1852 and 1857, after which her health worsened and she painted less frequently, sometimes preferring to write poetry. Her work was exhibited only twice during her lifetime, first at the Pre-Raphaelite exhibition at Fitzroy Square in the summer of 1857 and then a few months later in a show of modern British art at the National Academy of Design in New York.

Continually plagued by bouts of melancholy and lingering illness, she finally married the philandering Rossetti in 1860, but by that time their earlier tempestuous passion had largely been exhausted. Less than two years later she died of an overdose of laudanum. Siddal left behind the dual legacy of her mesmerizing face in the works of Rossetti, Millais, and Hunt as well as approximately thirty of her own drawings and sketches, over a dozen watercolors, and one self-portrait in oil. Long after she died her memory tormented Rossetti; he eventually arranged to exhume the manuscript of his poems he had buried with her as a symbol of grief, self-sacrifice, and guilt.

83.
Clerk Saunders, 1856
Watercolor, gouache, and colored chalks on paper
11³/₁₆ x 7⅛ in. (28.4 x 18.1 cm.)
Signed and dated lower left
Cambridge, Fitzwilliam Museum

Clerk Saunders is one of two works Siddal produced while collaborating with Rossetti on illustrations for a book of old English ballads compiled by William Allingham. She executed several drawings of this subject between 1854 and 1857, although the version closest to this composition was done in May of 1854. The subject comes from a Northumbrian ballad about Maid Margaret and her fiancé Clerk Saunders, who was killed by Margaret's seven brothers for becoming her lover. Unable to rest quietly in his grave until he is freed from his pledge of sexual fidelity and marriage, he comes to her room one night, beseeching, "Give me my faith and troth again,/True Love, as I gied them to thee."[1] Siddal has depicted the moment when the wraith, his bloody wound distinctly visible on his green cloak, obtains release from his vows. Maid Margaret obligingly holds the sacramental bough between her teeth: "She has given it [the bough] him out at the shot-window,/Wi' mony a sad sigh and heavy groan."[2] Yet over her bed hangs a similar sapling branch, possibly alluding to a future lover. The dawn breaking over the city in the background suggests the impending departure of the specter to the now-peaceful realm of death. This shrouded, resurrected figure has a Christ-like quality that is reinforced by other elements in the composition, particularly the Bible on the table and the crucifix behind Maid Margaret.

The features of the young woman bear an uncanny resemblance to those of the artist herself. Given Siddal's stormy and hermetic nature it is not surprising that many of her painted and poetic works embody themes of desolation, jealousy, rejection, and pain. The theme of frustrated love in her poems such as "Love and Hate," "Worn Out," "The Passing of Love," and "Gone" is echoed by her anxiety over the separation of lovers in works such as *The Lass of Lochroyan; The Lady Affixing a Pennant to a Knight's Spear* (London, Tate Gallery); *Sister Helen; Lady Clare* (Cambridge, Fitzwilliam Museum); *The Lady of Shalott* (London, Maas Gallery); and *Sir Patrick Spens* (London, Tate Gallery). The last work, of 1856, the artist based on another ballad, in which melancholy women wait futilely for their dead lovers to return from the sea.

The intentionally archaic and crowded composition and the brilliant gemlike hues of *Clerk Saunders* recall Rossetti's watercolors of about this period, such as his *Tune of the Seven Towers* (London, Tate Gallery); *A Christmas Carol* (Cambridge, Fogg Museum of Art); *The Chapel before the Lists* (London, Tate Gallery); and *The Wedding of St. George and Princess Sabra* (London, Tate Gallery). Several Pre-Raphaelites used themes from early English or Arthurian legends, but the flattening effect and the linear awkwardness of *Clerk Saunders* are peculiarly Rossettian in origin. The theme, however, remains intensely personal, an expression of Siddal's own private fears of rejection, remorse, and tragedy.

1.
"Clerk Saunders," as published in *The Ballad Book — A Selection of the Choicest British Ballads,* William Allingham, ed., London, 1865, 153.
2.
Ibid., 155.

83

Berthe Morisot
French, 1841-1895

Berthe Morisot's career as an Impressionist painter, studded with the frustrations and rejections encountered by this group, is remarkable for a number of reasons. Her social position and sex made Morisot's choice of a profession as an artist unusual; even more astounding for a well-bred young woman was her alliance with the most revolutionary factions of the contemporary art scene. With Mary Cassatt she has the distinction of being one of the first women to challenge the art establishment and to achieve renown outside officially approved circles.

She was born in Bourges, the youngest of three daughters of an upper-middle-class family. In 1848 the family moved to Paris where her father, a civil servant, had been transferred. Berthe and her sister Edma began to draw at a very early age, exhibiting more seriousness and dedication to art than was usual for girls of their class. Encouraged by their parents, they studied for a short time with Geoffroy Alphonse Chocarne, an obscure master, then changed in 1858 to Joseph Alexandre Guichard, a pupil of Ingres' and Delacroix'. As was customary for the era, their training included copying at the Louvre where they tackled Veronese, Rubens, and other old masters with surprising forcefulness. The Morisot sisters admired the work of the Barbizon painters Rousseau, Millet, Daubigny, and particularly Corot, and expressed a wish to paint out-of-doors to the disapproving Guichard.

In 1861 Berthe and her sister were introduced to Corot, who invited them to watch him paint at Ville d'Avray and who became their mentor and a close family friend. They spent the next several summers painting at Pontoise, Normandy, and Brittany, studying with Corot's pupil Achille Francois Oudinot, through whom they met Daumier and one of the earliest painters to work directly from nature, Charles Daubigny. Berthe made her debut at the Salon of 1864 with two landscapes painted the previous summer at the Oise River between Pontoise and Auvers. For the next ten years, until the first Impressionist exhibition in 1874 when she resolved never to

84

show in the official forum again, her work was seen quite regularly at the Salons.[1] Edma married in 1869 and abandoned her career, but Berthe continued to paint, forming new friendships and associations with Degas, Puvis de Chavannes, and particularly Edouard Manet.

She had been formally introduced to Manet[2] in 1868. He already knew and liked her work, and they formed a warm friendship based on mutual respect. It was partly through her efforts that Manet later took up *plein air* painting and Impressionist color. Morisot posed for several portraits for Manet (*The Balcony,* Salon of 1869, Paris, Louvre; *Repose,* 1870, Providence, Museum of Art, Rhode Island School of Design) receiving his encouragement and entrée into the circle of young artists, critics, and poets who met at the Café Guerbois for lively discussions on art.[3] In 1874 she married his younger brother Eugène. It was, however, contrary to Manet's advice and example that she began to exhibit in the independent Impressionist shows.

A cultivated and charming woman who traveled to Spain, Holland, Italy, and England, Morisot was a warm hostess whose home was a center for the best intellectual and artistic minds of the period. Her many friends included Mallarmé, Baudelaire, Zola, and the composers Chabrier and Rossini, as well as a wide circle of artists. After Manet's death in 1883 she was active in arranging a major retrospective and sale of his work. Though free of the financial cares that burdened her colleagues Monet, Pissarro, Renoir, and Sisley, Morisot worked earnestly and loyally as a member of the group, exhibiting in all the group shows except that of 1879, when she was pregnant. Unfortunately, the determination with which she pursued the difficult route of the artistic rebel and her significant contribution to the Impressionist vision have been less emphasized than her supportive and feminine role within the group.

The landscapes that predate Morisot's meeting with Manet exhibit the low-keyed color harmonies of Corot with the freshness of direct observation from nature. Her execution grew freer under Manet's guidance,[4] culminating around 1872-73 in a bolder palette, sketchy execution and elimination of details, and a daring treatment of planes in broad, fluent brushstrokes. She was now clearly devoted to capturing the shifting, evanescent effects of light and atmosphere that also intrigued her Impressionist colleagues. Her brushstrokes became more rapid and loose and her forms dissolved in a shimmer of soft, harmonious color.

For the freshness of her style, the intimacy of her subjects, and the charm of her personality, Morisot was often labeled "feminine" by her contemporaries as well as by more recent critics. Like her friend Mary Cassatt she often portrayed women and children, but her style is quite unlike Cassatt's careful linearity and deliberately flattened figures and spaces. Morisot's work conveys a sense of spontaneity and naturalness. In her interior scenes, for which her daughter and niece were often the subjects, the accidental pose and fleeting impression of a particular moment in time are set down with intimacy, warmth, and serenity. In her later years she turned her attention somewhat more to drawing, giving greater emphasis to the plasticity of her forms. In this she was not unlike Renoir who, after 1883, also sought greater compositional structure, or Degas who had always maintained strong draftsmanship.

Morisot's work, along with that of her Impressionist colleagues, was handled by the courageous dealer Durand-Ruel; though never commercially successful during her lifetime, she did receive better auction prices than Monet, Renoir, or Sisley. Under Durand-Ruel's aegis her work was seen, but poorly received, at group shows in London in 1883, at the Foreign Exhibition in Boston in the same year, in Brussels in 1885, and in the dealer's first successful exhibition in America in 1886. She participated in the Exposition Internationale at Georges Petit's gallery in 1887. Her first one-woman show was held in 1892 at the Boussod and Valadon galleries and in 1894 the French government purchased her *Young Woman Dressing for a Ball* for the Luxembourg collection.

Berthe Morisot's position as a significant artist in the early revolutions of the modern movement is secure. Monographs in several languages and many articles have been written about her work, her correspondence has been published, and her work hangs in leading museums throughout the world. The centennial celebration of her birth was honored with a retrospective at the Orangerie in Paris in 1941; the Council of Great Britain staged a one-woman show of her work in 1950; and her paintings from the Rouart Collection were seen in a traveling exhibition in the United States and Canada in 1952.

84.
The Sisters, 1869
Oil on canvas
20½ x 32 in. (52.1 x 81.3 cm.)
Signed upper right: Berthe Morisot
Washington, D.C., National Gallery of Art
Gift of Mrs. Charles S. Carstairs

Morisot's *The Sisters* is a fairly early work, painted during the first years of her association with the Café Guerbois group. Its subject, two tranquil figures seated in a bourgeois sitting room, was fairly popular in the 1860s and '70s. It was treated by Morisot's friend Fantin-Latour in 1859 (*The Artist's Sisters Embroidering,* St. Louis, City Art Museum) and again by Morisot in 1870 (*The Artist's Sister Edma and Their Mother,* Washington, D.C., National Gallery of Art). As in the 1870 picture, the figures of *The Sisters* sit on a patterned sofa placed against a wall decorated with a fan-shaped painting. Both pictures are representations of commonplace moments in daily life, and in both the figures are immersed in private thoughts or occupations.

During the year that separates the two paintings Morisot began her friendship with Manet and developed a firmer style and greater confidence.[5] The composition of *The Sisters* is essentially symme-

---

1.
In 1865, 1866, 1868, 1870, 1872, and 1873.
2.
By Fantin-Latour while she was copying a Rubens at the Louvre.
3.
It is unlikely that Morisot attended these meetings, but she was certainly informed of the content of the discussions.
4.
See, for example, *The Artist's Sister Edma and Their Mother,* 1870, repr. in Rewald, 243.
5.
The execution of the latter painting nevertheless did cause Morisot some anxiety. See Rewald, 241-42.

trical, although her increasing casualness can be sensed in the subtly varied poses of the figures and the curved, cropped line of the sofa back on the left. Here her figures are still modeled in clear, rounded contours and set in shallow space; they are relieved from their background by a series of receding planes that juxtapose a small-scale dress pattern against the broad floral forms of the sofa and the final flat background plane. In her 1870 painting Morisot's composition is more offhand, and, although the figures are less volumetric, strong tonal contrasts (in the manner of Manet) create a commodious space. In general, the sense of casualness felt in *The Sisters* is dependent upon single forms such as the fan held by the right-hand figure, the relaxed arm of the figure on the left, and the cropped plant in the background. The air of repose that is present in much of Morisot's work is, in this painting, the sum of the sitters' thoughtful introspection as well as the even lighting, broad, simple volumes, and pale harmonies.

Morisot's taste for casually encountered or readily available subjects is reflected in her choice of two local young women as models[6] and in the inclusion of a background painting which, in its fan-shaped form, resembles many of her own compositions.[7] She uses this latter form to unify the composition: its offhand placement between the sisters, its repetition of object and contour in the hand of the right figure, and the echo of its shape along the sofa are the connecting lines between the single parts of the painting.

Morisot's solution to formal problems was soon to gain more ease and her style to become more spontaneous, but her fresh and delightful vision is already apparent in *The Sisters*.

85.
Paris Seen from the Trocadero, 1872
Oil on canvas
18¼ x 32 in. (46.3 x 81.3 cm.)
Signed lower left: Berthe Morisot
The Santa Barbara Museum of Art
Gift of Mrs. Hugh H. Kirkland

The subject of this painting, a panoramic view of Paris, coincides with the then prevailing taste among advanced artists and writers for contemporary subjects and scenes from daily life. Painted out-of-doors with a strong feeling for the effects of light and atmosphere, it is also characteristic of the interest in conveying impressions of nature. The inclusion of figures placed casually in the landscape, treated objectively and with no special accent given to their presence, is also typical of the concern for capturing, on canvas, the accidental and momentary aspects of life. The view as seen from a height was popular with Impressionist artists and adds to the detachment and snapshot effect of the composition. Renoir's *Skating in the Bois de Boulogne,* 1868 (Basel, Collection Robert von Hirsch), and Monet's *Hyde Park, London,* 1871 (Providence, Museum of Art, Rhode Island School of Design), are seen from similar points of view.

Although Morisot is still dependent here on the low-keyed harmonies of Corot's work,[8] the fluid brushwork and freer paint application show new influences from Manet. This scene resembles his *View of the Paris World's Fair* (Oslo, Nasjonal Galleriet),[9] painted four years earlier, but Morisot's composition has fewer figures and makes a clearer distinction between fore-, middle-, and background planes, resulting in a broader perspective and a more tranquil scene. Her execution is sketchier than that of her new mentor and omits detail for a more general and immediate impression. Between the time of Manet's painting and Morisot's, there is a tendency toward freer brushwork and looser composition in the work of Impressionist artists. Beginning about 1872, with this work, spontaneity of handling increased markedly in Morisot's canvases. The defined character of this painting's foreground figures was to loosen considerably in subsequent work; forms were increasingly fused with surrounding objects and dissolved in light and atmosphere. The subdued color of this painting was shortly to give way to the brilliant harmonies of a fully Impressionist palette.

86.
Mme. Boursier and Daughter, 1874
Oil on canvas
29½ x 22½ in. (74.9 x 57.1 cm.)
Signed lower left: Berthe Morisot
The Brooklyn Museum (29.30)
(See color plate, p. 89)

The subjects for this portrait were Berthe Morisot's cousins, Mme. Lucien Boursier and her daughter, the future Mme. Hitier. The choice of family members as subjects is characteristic of Morisot, as is the sense of well-being expressed by the mother and daughter.

In this painting Manet's close-range figural presentations, arrangement of forms parallel to the picture plane, and fluid application of paint have been fully assimilated. That the artist has begun to move toward the accidental composition and sketchy notations of the Impressionists is evident in the broad, loose brushstrokes of the figures. Light flows freely over surface; the color is warm and harmonious. Ambience and sitters are presented casually, without idealization. Morisot's stylistic direction is most apparent in the handling of background. In a setting that suggests a studio or an informal living area, space is more offhand than precise and forms have become malleable and ambiguous as a result of the active, sketchy brushwork. From about the time of this painting, Morisot increasingly subordinated detail and definition of form to color and rapid paint application.

Morisot had painted a more traditional portrait of Mme. Boursier in 1867, in which the seated single figure is presented in a three-quarter view, with a pyramidal composition and compact volumetric planes that suggest Corot's classical simplicity.[10] Although our portrait is more informal, compositional balance and definition of the fore-

---

6.
In a letter to her sister Edma Pontillon, Morisot reports that the models for *The Sisters* posed on three occasions and describes the experience as "a nightmare." Cited in Bataille and Wildenstein, 24.
7.
See, for example, Bataille and Wildenstein, *Le Patinage,* no. 697, fig. 668; *Oies au bord du lac, Eventail,* no. 702, fig. 675.
8.
Rewald, 290.
9.
Ibid.
10.
Bataille and Wildenstein, no. 13, ill. 13.

85

87

88

ground figures are nonetheless retained. The two sitters project a consciousness of the spectator's and, concomitantly, the artist's presence that is quite different from the accidental, snapshot effects of Morisot's fully Impressionist style.

87.
White Flowers in a Bowl
Oil on canvas
18 x 21¾ in. (45.7 x 55.2 cm.)
Signed lower left: B. Morisot
Boston, Museum of Fine Arts
Bequest of John T. Spaulding

In this composition Morisot juxtaposes organic forms with manmade objects, the textures of flowers with the spare surfaces of manufactured products, and the vertical line of the upright jug with the horizontal flow of flowers and bowl. Contrasts in technique underscore her oppositions and enliven the image. Although a relatively small portion of the canvas is devoted to the white blossoms, they are clearly the picture's focal point. Accented by central positioning and a resonant treatment of surface, their small, tight forms are painted with light-filled, thickly textured pigments. In contrast, the broader area encompassing the background, table, jug, and bowl is thinly painted with short, broad brushstrokes. Morisot's flowers stand out in relief against this background, their substantiality and sensuousness reinforced by the richness of the painted surface. The formal tensions of the picture are reconciled by synthesis — the jug and bowl, joined by common brushstroke to background and table, share the volumetric definition of the white flowers. The delight and delicacy of the painting are a result of Morisot's subtle formal resolutions as well as the graceful charm of the subject.

88.
Girl in a Boat with Geese, ca. 1889
Oil on canvas
25¾ x 21½ in. (65.4 x 54.6 cm.)
Signed lower left: B. Morisot
Washington, D.C., National Gallery of Art
Gift of Ailsa Mellon Bruce

Dating from the last decade of the artist's life, *Girl in a Boat with Geese* is painted in Morisot's fully mature style. The unsentimental treatment of nature is characteristically Impressionist, and its simple charm accords with Morisot's general sensibility. Morisot's immediate impressions of the subject, painted out-of-doors as had been her custom for almost two decades, are recorded with a rapid, sketchy technique. Her choppy brushwork produces varied and shifting patterns, making minimal distinctions between trees, water, girl, boat, and geese. Morisot's vision is reflected in the short, staccato brushstrokes, the absence of detail, and the fusion of forms into a single textured surface. Despite the quiet mood of this painting, the high-keyed color harmonies and active surface create a sense of immediacy and vitality.

Mary Cassatt
American, 1844-1926

Mary Cassatt, like many of America's best artists of the eighteenth and nineteenth centuries, lived most of her life in Europe. She went abroad with the wave of art students who, in the second half of the last century, felt it necessary to complete their training in Paris. Unlike the others, however, Cassatt stayed to become a member of one of the most important groups in the history of art, the Impressionists. Most biographies of this artist are sketchy because during her lifetime she was extremely hesitant to be interviewed or to reveal details of her life. She felt that her work should speak for itself. It wasn't until 1913, when she was sixty-nine years old, that she allowed Achille Segard to interview her for his monograph, *Mary Cassatt, un peintre des enfants et des mères*.[1] The information and anecdotes that Segard obtained have been repeated ever since, forming the backbone of all subsequent biographies of the artist.

Mary Cassatt was born in Pittsburgh, spending most of her childhood in various places around Pittsburgh and Philadelphia and traveling in Europe. Her family was middle class at a time when a middle-class income allowed leisure and travel. She decided early to become an artist. Segard reports that Cassatt's father, on hearing her plans to study art in Europe, responded by saying "I would rather see you dead."[2] But family resistance did not deter her from pursuing her career. She entered the Pennsylvania Academy of the Fine Arts in Philadelphia in 1861 and spent four years there. In the late 1860s she took extensive trips to Europe to study, returning home only for the duration of the Franco-Prussian War (1870-71). In 1872 she was back in Europe for serious study of the old masters in Italy, Spain, and Holland. At the same time she began to exhibit regularly at the annual Paris Salon and to show at the National Academy of Design in New York.

Works from this period show that although she considered the old masters her teachers, she admired and wanted to be part of the newest trends in French painting. Her first three Salon entries (1872, 1873, 1874) were of Spanish subjects à la Manet; the first, *On the Balcony*

during the Carnival (Br. 18[3]) is close to Manet's painting of the same subject exhibited at the Salon of 1869. Her grasp of the essentials of the new Realism was recognized by Degas, when her entry in the Salon of 1874 was pointed out to him by a mutual friend. She recalled to Segard that he was impressed: stopping in front of it, he said "C'est vrai. Voilà quelqu'un qui sent comme moi."[4] Degas and Cassatt later met and their admiration for each other's work led to a close and fruitful association. From her first appearance in the Impressionist exhibitions, which he invited her to join in 1879, the critics linked her work to his. But her stature as an artist in her own right, and the wealth of inspiration that she drew from many artistic sources, prevents her from being called a follower.

During the period from 1879 to 1886 she was an active member of the Impressionists, exhibiting with them in 1879, 1880, 1881, and 1886. In the lightness of her palette, the quality of her brushstrokes, and the intimate contemporaneity of her subject matter, she explored all the aspects of the Impressionist aesthetic. Most of her models in these years were taken from her family, especially her parents and her sister Lydia who all came to Paris to live with her in 1877. Her brothers, Gardner and Alexander (later president of the Pennsylvania Railroad), visited often during their European voyages, bringing their families. They were also pressed into service as models, and the children became subjects of their aunt's earliest mother and child paintings.

By the Eighth Impressionist Exhibition in 1886, Impressionism was under attack by the new generation of radical artists and was undergoing transformations by its original adherents. Cassatt's work at this time shows that she too was evolving a new style. She began to achieve a more monumental effect by relying less on "spontaneity" and "contemporaneity" and more on fine drawing and a simple, stable composition. The search for a more timeless image led her to devote more and more time to the mother and child theme, applying her modern vision to a traditional subject.

1.
Achille Segard, *Mary Cassatt, un peintre des enfants et des mères*, Paris, 1913.
2.
Ibid., 5.
3.
Adelyn Breeskin, *Mary Cassatt, A Catalogue Raisonné of the Oils, Pastels, Watercolors and Drawings*, Washington, D.C., 1970.
4.
"It's true. There is someone who feels like me." Segard, 35.

89

91

92

At the end of the 1880s Cassatt came to artistic maturity in a variety of media. In printmaking she created two series of etchings and dry-points, one in black and white, one in color. The series of color etchings, exhibited in 1891, was inspired by Japanese woodcuts and is considered one of her greatest achievements. She designed and executed a large mural for the Woman's Building at the 1893 World Columbian Exposition in Chicago on the subject of "The Modern Woman." Also in 1893, she was given a one-woman show in Paris by her dealer, Durand-Ruel, indicating that her paintings and pastels were finally accepted by the general art world. But in spite of the fact that she was becoming part of the "Establishment" (as were the other Impressionists), many aspects of her work link her to the newer movements like the Symbolists and the Nabis.

The late period of her work, 1900-14, consists mainly of portraits of friends and many more versions of the mother and child theme. Her fame as a mother and child painter is at its height in this period; the nostalgia and sentimentality of the pre-war era made her popular. She opposed the radical art trends of this decade, just as her art had been opposed thirty years before. Failing eyesight forced her to stop painting in 1914, but she maintained her artistic interests until her death in 1926.

89.
Mother about to Wash Her Sleepy Child, 1880
Oil on canvas
39½ x 25¾ in. (100.3 x 65.4 cm.)
Signed lower left: Mary Cassatt/1880
Los Angeles County Museum of Art
Bequest of Mrs. Fred Hathaway Bixby (M.62.8.14)

In many ways this work is a prime example of Mary Cassatt's painting style in the early years of her participation in the Impressionist group. She had admired their art before she officially joined the group in 1879 and had already begun assimilating elements of the new style into her own work. In particular she was interested in the effects of the light palette and the vigor of the visible brushstroke. A profile view of her sister (*Lydia Reading the Morning Paper,* 1878, Omaha, Joslyn Art Museum) shows the new approach she took to the quality of the paint, giving it an independence and life that are so characteristic of Impressionist painting. *Mother about to Wash Her Sleepy Child* is in this same style of vigorous brushwork that captures, especially in the draperies, a scintillating brightness.

Also Impressionist in character is the casualness of the two figures engaged in a perfectly unexceptional everyday activity. This casual effect is primarily conveyed by the pose of the child, sprawled in her mother's lap in the most unselfconscious, "unposed" way. This sense of a subject caught unaware in the middle of an action is found in other works of this period, like *Susan Comforting the Baby* (1880, Columbus Gallery of Fine Arts). A later work of the same subject, known as *The Bath* (1892, Art Institute of Chicago), shows that as Cassatt's work matured it diverged from this "temporary" quality in

order to convey an image of greater stability and timelessness. But around 1880 the influence of Impressionists like Berthe Morisot, who had exhibited mother and child paintings in earlier Impressionist exhibitions, was very strong.

The pose of the child, with her legs spread apart over her mother's lap, is one that instantly conveys the physical reality of a young child, giving the picture an intense believability. It also conveys, by its extreme relaxation, the intimacy and ease in the relationship between the two figures. Such an expressive pose, in addition to being a favorite of Cassatt's, has a long history in images of the Madonna and Child going back to the Gothic period.

Cassatt gave special attention to children as subject matter in 1880. Her brother came to Europe that year with his wife and four children, and the artist devoted the summer to *plein air* painting and the special effects of bright light, using all members of her family as models. The resulting group of paintings was exhibited the next spring in the Sixth Impressionist Exhibition and earned widespread acclaim. One of her most fervent admirers was the writer and critic Joris-Karl Huysmans who commended her on her masterful control of the mother and child theme. Often exasperated by such paintings ("Ah! les Bébés, mon Dieu!"), he recognized Cassatt's talent for conveying the pleasurable aspects of the subject without trite sentimentality. Encouragement from such a source probably contributed to Cassatt's frequent use of the theme in her later work.

90.
Young Woman in Black, 1883
Oil on canvas
31½ x 25¼ in. (80 x 64.1 cm.)
Signed lower right: Mary Cassatt
Lent by The Peabody Institute
Courtesy of The Baltimore Museum of Art (L.64.18)
(See color plate, p. 90)

Cassatt's *Young Woman in Black* embodies many of the tendencies of the Realist/Impressionist movement which she joined in 1879. It shows that Cassatt was a "painter of modern life" in the Baudelairean sense, interested in capturing the moment through its fashions, manners, and poses. The technique is fresh, giving the impression that the scene was recorded quickly, before the moment was lost. She presents her model as an elegant woman of poise, a female dandy. The young woman is dressed simply in a black sporting costume, perhaps as an equestrienne like Courbet's *L'Amazone* of 1856 or Renoir's *Horsewoman* of 1873. Although posed casually in the flowered armchair, she conveys a sense of energy by the uprightness of her figure and by the crisp silhouette of her dark costume against the bright whiteness of the chair.

The broad handling of the paint indicates Cassatt's loosening of technique in response to the more painterly styles of her contemporaries. The creaminess of texture recalls Manet, whom Cassatt admired from her earliest days in Paris, especially in a work like *The Plum* of 1877. Renoir and Morisot might have also inspired her to experiment with the visible brushstroke as a means of expressing spontaneity, but she avoids the extremes of the broken brushstroke that became the trademark of Impressionist painting.

In several ways the background setting of the painting is also typical of the Impressionists. First, certain broad shapes of the background are used to echo the pose of the sitter. For instance, the curve of the chairback parallel to the woman's right shoulder and the curve of the fan over her head add emphasis to the lines of her body. Also, the flowered upholstery of the armchair provides a lively decorative design which plays an active role in the painting's composition. Finally, the painted fan (perhaps by Degas) mounted on the wall behind her is an example of a popular way to add interest and intimacy with a "picture within a picture."

This painting also suggests Cassatt's study of Degas's work during this period. The silhouette of the costume conveys a sense of the body and creates an interesting abstract design. Degas used this device in the several versions of a work that Cassatt herself posed for: *Miss Cassatt and Her Sister in the Louvre,* 1880. Both Degas and Cassatt admired and were inspired by Japanese prints, from which this artistic device originated.

Achille Segard speaks of this work as a portrait. But it is often difficult to determine whether Cassatt's figure paintings are portraits or works for which a friend or relative was used as a model. Seldom does she make the physical appearance of the sitter the main objective of the work, and she tends to be interested in only a few facial types which she uses again and again. Certainly in this painting, the elegance of the figure and the sense of energy it conveys supersede the portrayal of an individual woman's features.

91.
Two Children at the Seashore, 1884
Oil on canvas
38½ x 29¼ in. (97.8 x 74.3 cm.)
Signed lower right: Mary Cassatt
Washington, D.C., National Gallery of Art
Ailsa Mellon Bruce Collection

Modern art historians are slightly embarrassed by Mary Cassatt's interest in painting children. But the fact is that children were such a popular subject in the late nineteenth century that we are still in a period of reaction to it. Although the majority of child paintings were produced by artists of limited vision and ability, many of the most objective figure painters considered children worthy subjects. Manet, Renoir, Morisot, and Degas all painted their youthful models with straightforwardness and Cassatt's first attempts in this genre were hailed as unusually unsentimental. These artists even used child subjects in works intended for major exhibitions. Cassatt's first major child painting was exhibited in the Salon of 1875; the famous *Girl in*

the Blue Armchair (Washington, D.C., National Gallery of Art) was submitted to the American Exhibition of the Exposition Universelle of 1878; and she exhibited paintings of her young relatives in the Impressionist Exhibition of 1881.

Cassatt used the marine setting only one other time, in *The Boating Party* (Washington, D.C., National Gallery of Art) of 1892, but the theme of children on the beach was common in contemporary European and American art. There were two major traditions in the use of this theme, and Cassatt's image incorporates elements of both. The first tradition, the view of nature as a vast pleasure ground for stylish tourists, is best known to us through the marinescapes of Boudin. Degas's version of a beach scene, *Bains de Mer,* shown in the Impressionist Exhibition of 1877, might have been Cassatt's immediate source. Also important was the influence of English versions of this theme, such as W. P. Frith's *Life at the Seaside (Ramsgate Sands),* which was shown at the Royal Academy in 1854 and bought by Queen Victoria.

The other tradition of seaside children was perfected by Winslow Homer in American art. Homer was a contemporary of Cassatt's, probably well known by her, whose work was also susceptible to modern European currents. Views of children in the great out-of-doors were common in his paintings and wood engravings of the 1870s. Capturing a contemplative mood, he depicted children in twos and threes, each absorbed in his own activity with a vast landscape setting. There is a striking similarity of mood between Homer's groups of children outdoors and Cassatt's *Two Children at the Seashore.* They share a seriousness not found in the usual "charming" approach to children. Also similar is the breadth of the marine setting with the distant horizon suggesting the boundless world of the child's imagination. But Cassatt's children are not the hardy country variety found in Homer's work; they belong to the well-dressed tourist class of Frith and Boudin. The isolation of the figures does not express independence as it does in Homer's work, but merely indicates that their parents or nurses are somewhere outside the limits of the picture. Cassatt combines the two traditions by extracting two of the figures normally seen as part of the stylish seaside panorama and monumentalizing them so that they have unusual psychological and compositional importance.

92.
Baby in Dark Blue Suit, Looking over His Mother's Shoulder, 1889
Oil on canvas
29 x 23½ in. (73.7 x 59.7 cm.)
Signed lower right: Mary Cassatt
Cincinnati Art Museum (1928. 222)

By the end of the 1880s Cassatt's reputation as a painter of *maternité* was well established, and her use of this theme was recognized for its variety and special quality of directness. Throughout her career she was interested in the formal and expressive aspects of compositions involving two figures, and the mother and child subject allowed wide experimentation in this area. As a rule, the figures are presented as the basis of the painting's composition. Pushed forward to the extreme foreground, the gestures and poses of the figures overshadow the sketchy setting. In this painting Cassatt has used a mother and child combination that she found particularly interesting: the mother holding the child upright in her arms so that the child's head is on the same level as hers. This allows an interplay between the two heads, the psychological centers of the two bodies. Cassatt's mastery of this device can be seen in the 1884 portrait of her brother Alexander Cassatt and his son, Robert, where the two black suits merge and the two sets of dark eyes form an intense psychological pattern.

In this painting, the interest is not in the juxtaposition of the two faces, but in the opposition of direction; the child looks out, obscuring most of his mother's face, which is directed into the background. The boldness of a design that obscures the face of the most important figure is as impressive today as it was in the late nineteenth century. Most of the Impressionists experimented with this radical device as they attempted to heighten the expressiveness of other aspects of the composition. At the same time, of course, obscuring the face created a new and ambiguous psychological mood. Cassatt experimented with partial covering of the face in *Five O'Clock Tea* (1880, Boston, Museum of Fine Arts) where the teacup covers all but the eyes of one of the figures, and with obscuring the faces of both figures in *A Goodnight Hug* (ca. 1880, New York, Estates of Stephen R. and Audrey B. Courrier).

One finds this mother and child arrangement (mother's back to the viewer, child looking out) used by other artists, but not for the same purpose as Cassatt's. The mother and child are either a small part of a larger composition, as in Ford Madox Brown's *Work* (1852-65), or they convey an anecdotal message, as in William Mulready's *Brother and Sister,* 1857, where the children play literally "behind their mother's back." Cassatt's figures, instead, exist in monumental isolation, devoid of any anecdotal interest. Our back view of the mother is explained only in terms of the pictorial effect, not in terms of any discoverable human drama. The sense that the figures are at rest eliminates even the possibility that the poses are temporary, in the manner of an Impressionist "captured moment." Cassatt's mature style, around 1890, has eliminated the Impressionist effect of spontaneity in favor of a more iconic effect where the figures are static, unresponsive to time and environment.

The only aspect of the painting that seems to belie this timelessness is the gesture of the child with his finger in his mouth. The gesture is so typical of children and so undignified that it gives the effect of casual realism, almost to the point of genre. It would be "cute" if it weren't depicted with such seriousness, showing that an artist with strict control over emotional effects can create a profound image with elements that could become trite if not handled carefully. Masaccio used a similar finger-sucking baby for his monumental *Madonna and Child* of the Pisa altarpiece in the early fifteenth century.

93.
The Coiffure, 1891
Color print, with drypoint, soft-ground, and aquatint
14⅜ x 10½ in. (36.5 x 26.7 cm.)
Pittsburgh, Museum of Art, Carnegie Institute
94.
The Fitting, 1891
Color print, with drypoint, soft-ground, and aquatint
14¾ x 10¹/₁₆ in. (37.5 x 25.5 cm.)
Pittsburgh, Museum of Art, Carnegie Institute
95.
Peasant Mother and Child, ca. 1894
Color print, with drypoint and aquatint
12½ x 10 in. (31.7 x 25.4 cm.)
Los Angeles County Museum of Art
Graphic Arts Council in memory of Ruth Sprecher (M.76.42)

Mary Cassatt's interest in printmaking and graphic techniques continued throughout her career. According to Segard, she learned the etching process from an older Italian artist, Carlo Raimondi, while she was in Parma in the early 1870s. Her interest in etching was shared by most of her friends in the Impressionist circle and was in tune with the etching revival in the mid-nineteenth century. In 1879, in addition to exhibiting in the Impressionist exhibition, she, Degas, Pissarro, and some others worked on a projected journal of prints that was to be called *Le jour et la nuit.* By experimenting with new aquatint techniques with Degas, she attempted to capture in the black and white medium the effects of lighting and environment that she had achieved in her paintings of theater and interior subjects. Her drawing style of this period is less concerned with a strong linear treatment than with creating pictorial form with light and dark.

Throughout the 1880s, however, Cassatt's style underwent a process of technical simplification, aided by study of Japanese prints, that resulted in the strong linear design of the color prints of the 1890s, such as *The Coiffure, The Fitting,* and *Peasant Mother and Child.* Prior to 1891, when she first exhibited her color prints, she had been showing black and white etchings and drypoints at the yearly Exposition des Peintres-Graveurs at Durand-Ruel's gallery. A series of twelve drypoints of unusual delicacy and simplified design was shown in 1890. However, in 1891 the Société des Peintres-Graveurs Français excluded her from their exhibition, which they opened only to native-born French artists. Therefore, she and Pissarro, who was born in the West Indies, put on individual exhibitions of their work in rooms adjacent to those of the Société at Durand-Ruel.

Cassatt's works in that exhibition included paintings, pastels, drypoints, and the series of ten colored prints that represented her first attempt at this new technique. Her experimental works received mixed reactions, but they had high praise from such important sources as Degas, Pissarro, and Félix Fénéon, the famous Symbolist critic. Today, of course, Cassatt's colored prints are considered among her most creative and interesting works. Often, Cassatt's work in black and white paralleled the paintings and pastels she was working on at the time. Occasionally they would be created as an exercise, in the manner of a sketch, to work out a particular pictorial effect to be used in a painting. But the colored prints were intended as major works in and of themselves, and the scale and monumentality of the subjects reflect this intention.

The Fitting and *The Coiffure* were both in this series of ten prints that was printed in an edition of 25. They are a combination of etching, drypoint, and aquatint, which was further enriched by the special effects of the application of the ink onto the plate that Cassatt did herself. Each print was colored separately in a technique called "*à la poupée,*" meaning that various colored inks were applied to the plate at one time and then printed simultaneously. Usually color printing is a process of sending the paper through the press several times, each time printing a different color. Cassatt's process, *à la poupée,* was more like "painting" the plate. Accidental bleeding of the colors into one another, variations of color from one print to the next, variations of wiping the plate, made each print different, creating a variety of images within a medium that is ordinarily characterized by standardization.

Cassatt's colored prints were inspired by the Japanese prints that had become so popular in the Western world in the second half of the nineteenth century. By 1890, when a large exhibition of Japanese prints was held at the Ecole des Beaux-Arts in Paris, the initial novelty of Oriental pictorial effects had subsided and European artists could study the techniques with the benefit of long familiarity. Many artists such as the Nabis and the ex-Impressionists Renoir, Cézanne, Sisley, and Pissarro followed Cassatt's lead in experimenting with colored prints in the 1890s. But none was as successful as Cassatt in combining the Japanese quality of design and subject matter with the French late Realist tradition.

Peasant Mother and Child, not a part of the series of ten, was probably done later as Cassatt continued her study of this medium. It is related to a pastel of the same composition that was done before 1894. The title *Peasant Woman* refers only to the fact that Cassatt frequently used women from the village near her summer home as models, preferring a sturdy, unsentimental figure type for her maternal scenes. It is interesting to note that at the same time the young Käthe Kollwitz was also using the etching medium to create her very distinct images of peasant life.

93

94

Lilla Cabot Perry
American, 1848?-1933

Lilla Cabot Perry — poet, painter, lecturer, and promoter of Impressionism in America — was born to the socially prominent Lowell and Cabot families of Boston. Educated according to the convention for cultivated Boston ladies, she was at ease in the foremost social and intellectual circles of her native city. In 1874 she married Professor Thomas Sergeant Perry, a scholar and teacher of eighteenth-century English literature and the grandnephew of the renowned Commodore Matthew C. Perry. The Perrys were hosts to a large circle of writers, artists, and socialites, including William Dean Howells, Henry James, and Lilla's brother-in-law John LaFarge.

Perry received her professional training in the mid-eighties at the Cowles School, Boston, under Robert Vonnoh and Dennis Bunker, and in Paris at the popular Julien and Colarossi academies. She also studied with Alfred Stevens. During these years she published *Heart of Weed* (1886), the first of four volumes of poetry.[1] Like many affluent Americans during the last two decades of the century, the Perrys traveled to Europe often and frequented artistic and intellectual circles in their host countries.

Perry's meeting with Claude Monet in the summer of 1889 was to have an extraordinary impact on her personal and professional life. His fidelity to nature, his candid transmission of method, and his personal warmth and honesty impressed her. She spent the next ten summers at Giverny with her family in a house beside his, forming a close friendship with Monet and with Pissarro, who was living close by. Although Monet did not take pupils, he talked freely of his goals and techniques and encouraged her to work directly from nature.

Particularly in her landscapes and her figural compositions in outdoor settings, the high-keyed palette, broken brushstrokes, flickering lights, and loose composition adopted from Monet are unmistakable. Around 1896 Perry painted *Haystacks, Giverny*[2] which in subject and style is patently an homage to the master. Her style, however, varies; although her subjects are almost always casually arranged in space and involved in commonplace activities, thus reflecting the Impressionist style, she retained a clearer draftsmanship and a relatively greater concern for detail and volume than appear in French Impressionist work.[3] Linear clarity and the projection of mood became increasingly evident in her portraits after about 1912 when she had stopped spending extended periods of time in France and was working in Boston and at her summer home in Hancock, New Hampshire. Her late landscapes, painted in New Hampshire, are atmospheric, brilliantly lit, and fully Impressionist in character.

Perry enjoyed a solid reputation as a painter and poet in her own time.[4] She exhibited at the Paris Salon (for the first time in 1889), at the International Art Exhibition in Dresden in 1897, and at the Exposition Universelle in Paris in 1900. She won a silver medal in an 1893 Boston exhibition held at the Massachusetts Charitable Mechanics' Association and bronze medals at the 1904 St. Louis Exposition and at the 1915 Panama-Pacific Exposition in San Francisco. Her several one-woman shows in Boston and New York were always received enthusiastically by the critics,[5] and she had a sizable following as a portraitist.

Along with efforts by Mary Cassatt and a few other perceptive artists and connoisseurs, Perry's enthusiasm for Impressionism was instrumental in introducing the new style to America. When she returned to Boston from Giverny in the fall of 1889 she brought one of Monet's paintings of Etretat back with her and was astonished to discover that no one liked it but John LaFarge.[6] She began a campaign to publicize the new art, encouraging collectors and lecturing on Monet and Impressionism at the Boston Art Students Association (1894). Her own work, popular with critics and public, was perhaps her most successful means of promotion, and it is no accident that her third volume of poetry, published in 1898, was entitled *Impressions*. A founding member and first secretary of the Guild of Boston Artists, Perry joined with American Impressionist painters Frank W. Benson, J. J. Enneking, A. C. Goodwin, Philip Leslie Hale, and Maurice B. Prendergast[7] in exhibitions at the guild. She exhibited in museums and art societies along the eastern seaboard, and in 1927 she pub-

---

1.
Anthologia Graeca (called *From the Garden of Hellas*) in 1891; *Impressions*, 1898; and *Jar of Dreams*, 1923.
2.
New York, 1969, no. 9, repr. in color.
3.
For examples see ibid., no. 14, *Mrs. John LaFarge;* no. 18, *The Widow;* and no. 19, *In the Studio.*
4.
See Frank W. Benson's enthusiastic comments on a 1931 show, ibid., introduction, n.p.
5.
Ibid.
6.
Perry, 119.
7.
New York, 1969, n.p.

lished "Reminiscences of Claude Monet from 1889 to 1909."

Perry died at her home in Hancock, New Hampshire, in February 1933. She is now remembered best for her association with Monet, and her own work has been eclipsed by a taste for more avant-garde styles. Nevertheless, it is charming and quite characteristic of the American version of the Impressionist aesthetic. A 1969 retrospective of her work at the Hirschl and Adler Galleries in New York certainly re-established her as an artist worthy of independent consideration.

96.
Little Angèle, 1889
Oil on canvas
25½ x 32 in. (63.8 x 81.3 cm.)
Signed and dated upper right: Lilla C. Perry/Giverny '89
New York, Hirschl and Adler Galleries

Little Angèle demonstrates Perry's more reserved approach to subjects painted indoors as contrasted with her spontaneity in capturing a passing moment in nature. Even though it was painted at Giverny during one of the summers that the artist was under Monet's influence, the picture is more conservative and less Impressionistic than might be expected. Monet's high-keyed colors, his obsessive interest in the effects of light, and his use of colored shadows do appear here: Perry employed a brilliant palette for the potted plant, the sun-bleached landscape, the window ledge, and the costume of the model, and the shadows cast to the right of the figure are decidedly blue. Nonetheless, the artist is still using value contrasts and linear modeling, particularly in the flower pot and the face and torso of the figure. The overall single tone and dissolving forms of fully Impressionist pictures are minimized here, while the brushwork is flowing and smooth rather than choppy and rapid. The picture's ambiguous space results less from the fusion of forms by light than from the placement of the angular window and wall forms parallel to the picture plane.

Perry sometimes hired local Norman peasants to model for her, as she did in this case, but more often one or all of her three daughters were the subjects of her pictures. Like Monet, she portrayed specific locales and times of day and seasons.[8] In *Little Angèle* the subject and lighting effects convey the atmosphere of a summer afternoon in Normandy; country life is presented as picturesque and harmonious. The charm of the peasant and the serenity of the countryside are formally equated in a carefully balanced juxtaposition of the costumed child with the colorful flowers and background landscape. Just as the young girl's outward gaze reflects her awareness of the viewer and her own role as model, Perry's undisguised concern for compositional balance and linear clarity betrays the picture's artifice and gives greater importance to the formal elements of picture making than to Impressionist recording of objective optical phenomena.

There are two versions of *Little Angèle* dating from about the same time and varying only slightly. Perry's reason for painting the same composition twice is unknown, but both pictures were in the artist's possession and then in her estate until they were bought by the Hirschl and Adler Galleries.

8.
L. C. Perry lived in Japan between 1898 and 1901 while her husband occupied a chair in English literature at Keiogijika College in Tokyo. During this time she devoted herself to painting specific aspects of Japanese life and topography. For examples of her fidelity to time and place see New York, 1969, nos. 20-22.

96

97

Eva Gonzalès
French, 1849-1883

Eva Gonzalès was introduced into sophisticated literary and art circles at an early age by her father, Emmanuel, a well-known novelist and, from 1870, a delegate and honorary president of the Comité de la Société des Gens de Lettres. On the advice of the director of *Siècle,* Philippe Jourde, and the poet/dramatist Théodore de Banville, Eva began art lessons at age sixteen with the fashionable master Charles Chaplin.[1] She worked seriously in a small atelier in the rue Bréda and became acquainted with young, unknown writers and artists, including the painters soon to be known as the Impressionists.

Gonzalès is best known for her association with Edouard Manet, to whom she was introduced by the painter Alfred Stevens in 1869. Discouraged by the poor reviews of his Salon entries, Manet hesitated to discuss his work or to ask anyone to sit for him,[2] but Eva's striking beauty apparently revitalized his courage. He asked her to pose, to which she promptly agreed, becoming his model, his student, and a benign rival of Berthe Morisot. From 1869 until both died in 1883, a warm friendship and student-master relationship existed between them.

In Manet's large *Portrait of Eva Gonzalès,*[3] finished in 1870 and exhibited in the Salon of that year, the model sits before an easel, applying paint to a still life. Formal characteristics such as the pale figure relieved against a dark background, the limited middle tones, and the fluid brushstrokes were soon to appear in Eva's own work. She also shared Manet's desire to achieve success through the official organ of the Salon rather than through independent exhibitions and declined invitations to participate in Impressionist shows.

From 1870, when she exhibited *The Little Soldier, The Passer-by,* and a pastel of her sister, Jeanne, her work was seen at the Salon with regularity (except for a rejection in 1873). Although she was first listed as a pupil of Chaplin's, Manet's influence was apparent, troubling critics who were divided between aversion to Manet and loyalty to Emmanuel Gonzalès. However, Eva was usually treated kindly by the critics, receiving accolades in advanced art circles and being celebrated by Edmond Duranty, Philippe Burty, and Zacharie Astruc. Her clientele was small, but loyal — the newspaper *L'Art* bought her pastels and she was recognized in England and Belgium as well as in France.[4]

Gonzalès' style, closely allied to that of Manet's Spanish period, changed little through the years — her forms remained disciplined, her palette sober. Her subjects, like those of the advanced painters of the period, were selected from everyday life, a predilection that had been evident even under Chaplin's guidance. When, after 1871, Manet pursued the more brilliant color and active surfaces of the Impressionists, Gonzalès retained the neutral color schemes and precise contours of the sixties; only in her pastels did her tones soften and her palette lighten. While her work is not innovative, it has charm and a sense of sincere personal expression. It is significant that despite her attachment to Manet she did not follow where he led, but continued in the direction she believed best suited her temperament.

In 1879, after a three-year engagement, Gonzalès married the engraver Henri Guérard. A son, Jean Raimond, was born to the couple in April 1883, shortly before Gonzalès learned of Manet's death. She lived only five days longer, leaving her son to be raised by his father and her sister, Jeanne, who became Guérard's second wife.

Since her death, exhibitions of Eva Gonzalès' work have been held at the Salons de la *Vie Moderne* (1885), at the Salon d'Automne (1907), at several galleries in Paris, and at the Musée National des Beaux-Arts in Monte Carlo (1952). Her paintings have been purchased by the French government as well as by private collectors, but the broadest representation of her oeuvre is in the collection of her son and his heirs.

1.
Chaplin also taught Mary Cassatt for a short time in 1870.
2.
According to Berthe Morisot's mother. See Rewald, 218 and note 47, 237.
3.
Ibid., repr. 225.
4.
Paris, 1885, 14.

97.
The Little Soldier, 1870
Oil on canvas
51½ x 38⅝ in. (130 x 98 cm.)
Signed lower right
Villeneuve-sur-Lot, Musée des Beaux-Arts

The Little Soldier, painted the first year Eva Gonzalès was associated
with Edouard Manet, is patently an homage to his *Fifer* of 1866. Her
subject, a young boy in military attire holding a disproportionately
large bugle, left hand poised on hip, face turned toward the spectator
with a frank and open gaze, is handled more traditionally than its
celebrated model. Gonzalès' child stands more firmly in space and
is modeled in more realistic volumes than Manet's flattened young
soldier, whose form and spatial surroundings are simplified to heavy
contours and a few cast shadows. The artist's academic training under
Chaplin is revealed in the formal pose, the controlled brushstrokes,
and the gradual modulations of tone through most of the painting.
Manet's more radical influence is particularly apparent in the elimination of intermediate tones around the areas of the face and left leg
and in the use of cast shadows to define space. It has been suggested
that the face of the little soldier strongly resembles the sitter for several
of Manet's pictures, Victorine Meurand,[5] although Gonzalès actually
selected her model from the barracks of a nearby firehouse. Though
less bold than *Olympia* or the nude in the *Luncheon on the Grass,*
Gonzalès' figure is handled with the same reportorial detachment
that characterizes Manet's subjects.

The Little Soldier was shown in Gonzalès' first Salon in 1870, the
same year that her portrait by Manet also appeared. Despite the
fact that she was listed as a student of Chaplin's, there was no doubt
of the link to her new mentor, and the picture was criticized for following the principles of Manet more than those of Chaplin. Even the
advanced commentator Castagnary, who was impressed with the
painting, disliked the lack of half-tones and warned Gonzalès against
lapsing into "mannerism."[6] Nonetheless the brilliance of the work by
a twenty-one-year-old artist astonished several critics and evoked
favorable comparisons with earlier celebrated women painters.[7]

Emmanuel Gonzalès' connections in government circles were instrumental in the purchase of *The Little Soldier* by the state immediately
after the Salon. The associations of the painting with controversial art
circles, however, kept it from being assigned a permanent locale until
1874. It was then allocated to the Musée des Beaux-Arts at Villeneuve-
sur-Lot, but was hung in a relatively unfavorable position in the town
hall rather than placed in the museum. More recent recognition
of the charm and worth of the painting and the artist resulted in its
transfer to the museum's Salle du XIXe in 1970.

5.
Roger-Marx, n.p.
6.
Salon de 1870, reprinted in *Castagnary: Salons (1857-1870),* Paris, 1892, 429, as
quoted in Rewald, 241.
7.
These critics were Duranty, Burty, and Astruc. See Roger-Marx, n.p.

Lady Elizabeth Butler
British, 1850?-1933

An extremely prolific and successful painter of military subjects, Lady Butler was the British equivalent of such French specialists in this genre as Ernest Meissonier (1815-1891), Alphonse de Neuville (1835-1885), and Edouard Detaille (1848-1912). She was the sister of the well-known poet and woman of letters Alice Meynell (1847-1922). Elizabeth Thompson was born in Lausanne of British parents and traveled extensively on the Continent, where she studied briefly with an academic draftsman, Giuseppe Bellucce, in Florence and then painted in Rome. She received the major part of her academic training, however, at the South Kensington School of Art, under headmaster Richard Burchett. She supplemented her life classes, anatomy lessons, and study from antique casts with private classes in painting and the study of the "undraped" female model. She was a member of the Society of Lady Artists and was elected to the Royal Institute of Painters in Water Colour.

From the time of her earliest adolescent sketches she seems to have been attracted by the military and she determined on her specialty at the same time she decided to become a serious art student. Although her first painting exhibited at the Royal Academy, *Missing*, 1873, attracted positive notice, it was not until the following year that her *Calling the Roll after an Engagement, Crimea*, more commonly known as *The Roll Call*, created a major sensation. So popular was this work (for which she had sought out old uniforms from the Crimean epoch and managed to secure a Crimean veteran as a model) that it had to be protected by a policeman at the Royal Academy Exhibition of 1874. *The Roll Call* was transferred from its original purchaser, a Mr. Galloway, to Queen Victoria upon the latter's request.

Lady Butler followed this youthful success with a long series of representations of important British military engagements, historical and contemporary: she generally preferred to depict the moment before the battle rather than the bloody actuality of the encounter itself. Among her best-known works, which received wide distribution in the form of engravings, were: *Quatre Bras* (1875); *Balaclava* (1876); *Inkermann* (1877); *The Remnants of an Army* (1879, London, Tate Gallery); *Scotland for Ever!* (fig. 31, p. 53); *Floreat Etona!* (1882); *After the Battle, Tel el Kebir* (1885); *Steady the Drums and Fifes* (1897); and *Tent Pegging* (1902).

The artist married a military man, Colonel, later General, the Rt. Hon. Sir William Francis Butler, G.C.B., in 1877 and traveled with him to such far-flung outposts of Empire as Egypt and South Africa, recording her experiences in writing as well as sketches. But her accurate knowledge of military uniforms, accouterments, and battle formations, to which she owed the verisimilitude of her paintings, was more generally obtained from firsthand observation of maneuvers in England as well as from close questioning of veterans and military experts. One suspects the possible use of photographs, a practice current among her French contemporaries, in some of her later works. Butler's technical expertise, her careful rendering of detail, her clever compositions, as well as her choice of emotional incidents helped to establish and maintain her reputation in her chosen field. She exerted an influence on British military painting, on such artists as Ernest Crofts,[1] Walter G. Horsley, and especially on Richard C. Woodville.[2] She was sometimes called the "English Rosa Bonheur," a comparison Butler did not appreciate.

In 1879 Lady Butler narrowly missed — by two votes — election to the Royal Academy; despite the inclusion of Angelica Kauffman and Mary Moser in the original foundation, the Council of the Academy declared that by the letter of the law, the election of females was not provided for, and, as a result, women were not elected until the 1920s.[3] 98.

Quatre Bras, 1815, 1875
Oil on canvas
38¼ x 85⅛ in. (97.2 x 216.2 cm.)
Melbourne, National Gallery of Victoria
(See color plate, p. 91)

1.
See, for example, Crofts' *Capture of a French Battery at waterloo* in Q. Bell, *Victorian Painters*, London, 1967, repr. III.
2.
I am grateful to Professor Howard P. Rodee for this information.
3.
Hutchison, 138.

This painting, under the title *The 28th Regiment at Quatre Bras*, was shown as no. 853 in the Royal Academy Exhibition of 1875. It represents the British regiment, in square formation, at the Battle of Waterloo, receiving a furious charge of French cuirassiers and Polish lancers. Lady Butler had been deeply impressed by a visit to the battlefield at Waterloo in Belgium and was to represent another important encounter there, the charge of the Scots Greys under Captain Baswood, in her *Scotland for Ever!* of 1881 (fig. 31, p. 53). As usual, she made careful preparations for the final painting, which was promised to Mr. Galloway for £1,126.

Her methods of preparation may strike us as more like those of a movie producer than of a painter. On July 4, 1874, three hundred men of the Royal Engineers in full dress, with knapsacks, were formed in the old-fashioned four-deep square for Lady Butler at her request, firing in sections to create the requisite smoke; the artist then went down the ranks, choosing suitable, youthful looking models. She and her mother then selected a rye field at Henley-on-Thames as a plausible setting, bought it, and immediately trampled it down, with the aid of a lot of children. All the figures were taken either from individual military models or from appropriate policemen; the colonel of the Royal Engineers had the Waterloo uniforms made for the artist at the government clothing factory, uniforms accurate down to the old "brickdust" red and baize cloth of the period. The horses lying down, floundering, and rearing to the left and right of the painting were studied from life at Sanger's Circus; later, the Horse Guards, directed by their surgeon, had a magnificent black charger thrown down for her to see; at another time, the artist had herself charged by two young troopers on horseback, to give her a sense of what the young men in her painting must have felt. In the midst of preparing the canvas, Lady Butler went to Paris with her father. While there, she visited Goupil's gallery where she much admired Alphonse de Neuville's *Combat on the Roof of a House,* which seems to have inspired her in the composition of her own painting. She also visited the studio of Edouard Detaille, another prominent military painter.[4]

Quatre Bras was extremely popular at the Royal Academy Exhibition, where it was inevitably compared with its opposite number, the popular *La charge des cuirassiers français à Waterloo* by F. Philippoteau (1814-1884). John Ruskin praised *Quatre Bras* highly in his "Academy Notes" of 1875: ". . . It is amazon's work this; no doubt of it, and the first fine Pre-Raphaelite picture of battle we have had; — profoundly interesting, and showing all manner of illustrative and realistic faculty . . . Camilla-like the work is — chiefly in its refinement, a quality I had not in the least expected, for the cleverest women almost always show their weakness in endeavours to be dashing."[5]

4.
Butler, 1923, 110-46, passim.
5.
The Works of John Ruskin, ed. E. T. Cook and A. Wedderburn, London, 1904, XIV, 308-9.

Cecilia Beaux
American, 1855?-1942

Cecilia Beaux grew up in a tightly knit Philadelphia family that stressed seriousness of purpose and exposure to the arts. Shortly after her birth, her mother died, and she and her sister were raised by maternal relatives. From her French father she developed an interest in European culture, and from her aunts and uncle she received moral and financial support during her formative years.

Beaux began drawing lessons at age sixteen in the studio of a distant relative, Katherine Drinker, a painter of historical and biblical subjects. She had no thought then of pursuing a career in art, but she was an apt student and her diligent attention to any task resulted in work that was clearly promising. For a short time she studied with a Dutch artist, Adolf van der Whelan, who had opened a small class in Phila-delphia, and later with William Sartrain who came to Philadelphia from New York City every two weeks to oversee a small number of students. She may also have studied at the Pennsylvania Academy of the Fine Arts between 1877 and 1879;[1] she later taught drawing and painting there.[2] Motivated by a desire for financial independence while she continued her studies, Beaux put her talents to work draw-ing for a United States geological survey and making overglaze paintings on china plaques for a commercial manufacturer. She also made intimate portraits of family members and friends.

Her first important painting, *Les derniers jours d'enfance,* 1883-84 (*The Last Days of Childhood,* Merion, Pennsylvania, Collection Henry S. Drinker),[3] was an immediate success, heralding her lifelong concern with both stylistic means and expressive content. The color and composition of this early painting, for which her sister and nephew were the models, are related to Whistler's *Arrangement in Black and Grey: The Artist's Mother,* but unlike Whistler's more formal con-cerns, Beaux's interest centers in the tenderness between mother and child.

In portraits of family and friends, such as *Dorothea and Francesca* (1899-1900, Art Institute of Chicago), there is a strong sense of inti-macy and of the artist's fondness for her subjects. Yet she believed that the true source of valid and beautiful art was the imaginative handling of design and color. In her portrait of Fanny Travis Cochran (1887, cat. no. 99) and *New England Woman,* 1895 (Philadelphia, Pennsyl-vania Academy of the Fine Arts), the creation of form by means of delicate tonal oppositions and nuances of spare color reveals the art-ist's subtle handling of formal elements and creates a lively pictorial surface that reinforces the vitality and presence of the subjects. Beaux sometimes selected unusual points of view to underscore the character of her subject. In *Ernesta with Nurse* (1894, New York, Metropolitan Museum), the youth of the subject is emphasized by a child's-eye perspective that suggests the closeness of the ground and gives only a partial view of surrounding objects.

In 1888 Beaux made the first of many trips to Europe. She worked at the Académie Julien under Tony Robert-Fleury and William Bouguereau, traveled to Brittany and then to Switzerland, Italy, southern France, and England. She admired the work of Monet and other moderns,[4] but her greatest enthusiasm was reserved for the old masters, particularly Rubens, Titian, and Rembrandt.

By 1900 Cecilia Beaux was settled in New York and established as a leading portraitist. Her circle of friends included the publisher Rich-ard W. Gilder and his wife, Helen McKay Gilder, through whom she met some of the most prominent figures in the arts, finance, and gov-ernment. Among the many celebrities who commissioned portraits were Mrs. Theodore Roosevelt, Mrs. Andrew Carnegie, Dr. John Shaw Billings,[5] and the Honorable Serene E. Payne.[6] She knew many noted people in the arts; some, like Augustus St. Gaudens and John LaFarge, were close friends; others, like Henry James, Frederic Chopin, and the violinist Jan Kubelik, were acquaintances.[7]

Beaux's fluid, painterly style has been compared with the work of John Singer Sargent, which she admired, but she was generally more objec-tive than he and rarely attempted to flatter her sitters. In her more

---

1.
Beaux was registered during these years, but she never acknowledged studying at the academy. The period covers the years of Thomas Eakins' incumbency there.
2.
Between 1895 and 1915.
3.
Exhibited at the Pennsylvania Academy of the Fine Arts in 1885 for which it received the Mary Smith Prize. The painting was also shown at the Paris Salon in 1887.
4.
Through Lilla Cabot Perry she met Monet at Giverny in 1896. See Beaux, 201.
5.
Dr. Billings was in charge of the Army-Navy Library between 1865 and 1895 and the New York Public Library, 1896-1913. The portrait is presently in the Army-Navy Library in Washington, D.C.
6.
Chairman of the Ways and Means Committee of the U.S. House of Representatives.

academic portraits, such as those of the war heroes Georges Clemenceau; Admiral, Sir David Beatty; and Cardinal Mercier, commissioned by the United States government in 1919, the artist's goal is clearly a dignified portrayal of office and position rather than a flattering likeness. Her best work is characterized by simplicity of form, a casual placement of figures in space, and original, sometimes dramatic, composition. Her work became increasingly sensuous in texture and subtle in color as she matured.

The first sizable exhibition of Cecilia Beaux's work took place at the St. Botolph Club in Boston in 1897. Between that year and 1933 she had fourteen one-woman shows and had works exhibited at the Pennsylvania Academy of the Fine Arts, the MacBeth and Knoedler galleries in New York, and the Paris Salon. She received numerous prizes and awards: the Mary Smith Prize from the Pennsylvania Academy of the Fine Arts in 1885, 1887, 1891, and 1892, and a gold medal in 1898; bronze and gold medals from the Carnegie Institute of 1896 and 1897, respectively; and a gold medal at the Paris Exposition of 1900. She was elected to the Academy of Arts and Letters, the National Academy of Design, and the Society of American Artists, and was presented with an honorary degree (Ll.D.) from the University of Pennsylvania. She was the first American woman to be asked by the Uffizi to paint a self-portrait for the Medici Gallery of prominent artists (1925). She lectured frequently, traveled widely, and maintained a summer home in Gloucester, Massachusetts. She published her autobiography, *Background with Figures*, in 1930 and three years later was hailed as "the greatest woman painter of America."[8] The Metropolitan Museum of Art, the Corcoran Gallery, and the Philadelphia Museum of Art are among the many public and private collections in which her portraits may be seen.

After her death in 1942 Cecilia Beaux's reputation waned rapidly and by the time her nephew, Henry S. Drinker, catalogued and published her work in 1955 she was relatively unknown to the public. In an era devoted to radical innovation, the relatively conservative style of her art obscured its charm, vitality, and personal nature. Fortunately, a 1974 retrospective at the Pennsylvania Academy of the Fine Arts has rescued her oeuvre from the oblivion still enveloping the work of many other women artists.

99.
A Little Girl (Fanny Travis Cochran), 1887
Oil on canvas
35½ x 28½ in. (90.2 x 72.4 cm.)
Signed upper left: E. C. Beaux; upper right: Cecilia Beaux
Philadelphia, Pennsylvania Academy of the Fine Arts
Gift of Miss Fanny Travis Cochran, 1955

This painting is one of the finest examples of Cecilia Beaux's handling of color as an expressive vehicle. Executed in brilliant hues and sharp tonal contrasts, it predates her first trip to Europe in 1888. It is representative of her early style, acquired through her studies with the

Munich-trained William Sartrain, and is the outgrowth of the combined expressive-aesthetic efforts already present in her *Derniers jours d'enfance* of 1883-84. It is also the first in a series of predominantly white paintings in which the artist was to introduce subtle gradations of tone and small areas of intense color to enrich and vivify basically neutral surfaces.

Here the opposition of the white in the sitter's dress to the rich red brown background is echoed in the contrast of complementary yellows and purples in the sash and pansies. The controlled use of brilliant color in limited areas of the composition underscores the vitality of the young subject. Beaux uses other color contrasts quite subtly here. The broad strokes of brown that represent the child's long hair and the curving dark frame of the chair against which she rests rise discreetly in relief against an equally dark background. Beaux achieves a sense of three-dimensionality in these forms by grading her tones with utmost sensitivity and by adding warm highlights to an otherwise single hue.

The artist has chosen a simple composition to reinforce the youthful innocence of her ten-year-old subject, reducing the design of the picture to the compact forms of the child and the sinuous line of the chair frame. The basic elements of the composition were outlined in a small oil sketch which, except for detail, differs very little from the finished work.[9]

100.
Portrait of Bertha Vaughan, 1901
Oil on canvas
57 x 37 in. (144.8 x 94 cm.)
Signed lower right: Cecilia Beaux
Cambridge, Radcliffe College

One of many commissions executed by Cecilia Beaux during her long career as a portraitist, this picture was painted in 1901 after Beaux's reputation was already firmly established in the Philadelphia, Boston, and New York areas. She had made two trips to Europe, six of her portraits had been exhibited in 1896 at the Société Nationale des Beaux-Arts in Paris, and a sizable presentation of her work had appeared at the St. Botolph Club in Boston (1897).

Throughout her career Beaux's goal was to combine basic character traits with physical likenesses. Here the forthright personality and conservative outlook of a member of Boston society are captured through formal devices and carefully selected accessories that suggest the ease, affluence, and traditional values of Bertha Vaughan's world. Intrinsic to the characterization of the standing figure is the inclusion of simple, elegant objects: the brass candlesticks on the mantelpiece, the mirror over the fireplace, the casually held white feather fan, the fur-trimmed cloak. These articles, no less than the upright posture and the candid glance of the sitter, project her worldliness and confidence. The stable pyramidal form of the figure and its comfortable

7.
There exist impromptu drawings by Beaux of James (New York, Collection Rosamond Gilder), Chopin (Gloucester, Massachusetts, estate of the artist at Green Alley), and Kubelik (formerly in the Whitney Museum of American Art, current location unknown; repr. in *Century Magazine*, 1901).
8.
The occasion was the presentation of the Chi Omega medal. *New York Sun*, April 17, 1933, and *New York Times*, April 23, 1933.
9.
See Philadelphia, 1974, no. 23, repr.

disposition in space provide the portrait with a sense of balance and stability that supports the solid character of the subject.

In this example, as in Beaux's work as a whole, paint is applied in broad, sweeping brushstrokes and color harmonies can be enjoyed for their independently sensuous and painterly qualities. The primary role of the brushwork, however, is the revelation of form, and the warm brown, red, fleshy pink, and yellow green palette is, like the subject herself, traditional and conservative in character.

101.
Sita and Sarita, ca. 1921
Oil on canvas
37⅜ x 25⅛ in. (94.9 x 63.8 cm.)
Signed lower left: Cecilia Beaux
Washington, D.C., Corcoran Gallery of Art
(See color plate, p. 92)

The sitter for *Sita and Sarita,* also known as *Girl with the Cat,* was Sarah A. Leavitt, a maternal relative of the artist's. Beaux's portraits of family and friends are among her most successful pictures, for the freshness and warmth that characterize her best work depend on a rapport with her subject. While her portraits are not incisive, her impression of the sitter's character is of paramount importance to the picture, and she insisted on some personal knowledge of her subject before she would begin a portrait.

Here, as in all of Beaux's work, the surroundings as well as color and composition are used to suggest the artist's response to her subject. A sense of mystery infuses this double portrait of the green-eyed girl and the black cat poised on her shoulder. Her arm raised to support the animal, her black hair fused with the cat into one compact mass of black brushstrokes, the girl and the animal share an animal grace. Their eyes, in a continuous horizontal line, stare silently out at the spectator, their thoughts veiled, their emotional unity made apparent by the composition.

One of Beaux's several monochromatic compositions, here the forms are defined by a careful manipulation of the white tones of the dress against the lightly patterned sofa and by the gray brown background that sets the forms in relief. Tonal relationships are subtle and paint is applied in broad brushstrokes that minimize the figure's volume and texture. Beaux's usually active surfaces give way here to a rhythmic flow of line. Though this portrait dates from 1921, it is an autograph replica of a painting made in 1893 or 1894 and is related to the artist's development during the last decade of the century.

In the pre-Paris *A Little Girl (Fanny Travis Cochran)* (cat. no. 99), the artist used a similar monochromatic color scheme but with warmer tones, sharper contrasts, and more brilliant accents of color. In *Sita and Sarita* the flatter forms and paler palette suggest a concern with more formal pictorial qualities that may have resulted from

99

100

Beaux's trip to Paris. The inclusion of the black cat as well as the flatness of this composition recalls Manet's work of the 1860s. It is likely that Beaux, who was in Paris in 1889 when a fund was taken up to purchase Manet's *Olympia* for the French government, was somewhat influenced by his style. She may also have been influenced by Whistler's series of women in white.

In portraits designed somewhat later, such as *New England Woman* (1895) or the *Portrait of Henry Sturgis Drinker* (1898, Washington, D.C., National Collection of Fine Arts, also known as *Man with a Cat, At Home,* and *Man in White*), Beaux eliminated the dark background and replaced the opposition of whites with gradations of tone in subtle, glowing color. In both pictures the white clothes, objects, and walls of the room are bathed in colored lights and shadows that animate the monochromatic color scheme. The more vigorous brushwork of these portraits, as well as the vitality of their color and surfaces, extend the formal experiments of *Sita and Sarita*.

A first version of *Sita and Sarita* was exhibited at the Champ de Mars Salon in Paris in 1896 and was bought by the Luxembourg Gallery. It is in the Paris collection at present. Our painting entered the Corcoran Gallery collection in 1923 where it was first shown in an exhibition of contemporary American paintings.

Marie Bashkirtseff
Russian, 1859-1884

The career of this short-lived Russian-born artist has been so highly romanticized, chiefly as a result of the posthumous publication of her *Journals,* that it is extremely difficult to separate fact from fiction in Bashkirtseff's career. Even her birth date has recently been contested.[1] Bashkirtseff, known also as Bashkirtzeva, was born in Poltava, Russia, to a family of very minor nobility; she was quite well educated.[2] Her parents were estranged, and Marie, with her grandfather, mother, aunt, brother, sister, and a cousin, settled in Nice in 1872. There they lived luxuriously, making trips to Rome, Florence, and Naples. It was in Nice that the fourteen-year-old Marie fell in love (unreciprocated, needless to say) with the Duke of Hamilton. In 1877, following the artist's trip to Russia, she and her family moved to Paris, where Bashkirtseff enrolled in the women's class at the Académie Julien. There she studied chiefly with Tony Robert-Fleury and later with Jules Bastien-Lepage, who was still considered daringly realistic at the time. Among her fellow students in the women's class was the Swiss Louise Breslau, whom the ambitious Bashkirtseff marked out as her arch-rival almost from the beginning.

Afflicted with tuberculosis, which caused her death a few years later, and weighed down by the demands of a social life she by no means entirely rejected, Bashkirtseff nevertheless worked diligently. In 1880 she exhibited a portrait of her cousin Dina at the Salon under the signature "Marie Constantinowna Russ." Competing with a Spanish classmate who painted the same scene, she prepared for the 1881 Salon a large-scale group portrait of about sixteen of her fellow students in the women's class working from a model (a child posed as the little St. John the Baptist).[3] In 1883 Bashkirtseff exhibited a *Parisienne,* a pastel, under her own name as well as an oil painting, *Jean and Jacques* (Chicago, Newberry Library), representing two scruffy urchins strolling by a city wall.[4] *A Meeting* (cat. no. 102), exhibited in the Salon of 1884, is her best-known work and attracted considerable attention.

1.
Moore, 14. The author, one of the rare objective scholars of Bashkirtseff, maintains that the artist was born on January 12, 1859, neither in 1860, as has generally been accepted, nor November 11, 1859, which was her Saint's Day.
2.
Moore, XXIV.
3.
Breakell, 111-14. The painting, *L'Atelier Julian,* is reproduced in *Beaux-arts,* VIII, May 20, 1930, 12.
4.
Repr. Moore, frontispiece.

102

Bashkirtseff managed to produce a substantial body of work in the course of her brief and often interrupted career. Her mother gave eighty-four paintings, two pastels, fifty-five drawings, and three pieces of sculpture to the Russian Museum of St. Petersburg in 1908. These were exhibited in 1930.[5] Nevertheless, the artist is rightly known best as the author of the popular *Journals,* first published in "bowdlerized, abbreviated" form in 1887.[6] D. L. Moore asserts that there are actually eighty-four manuscript volumes of Bashkirtseff's diaries in the Bibliothèque Nationale in Paris, of which only a portion has been published in highly selective, expurgated form.[7] As a result of the publication of the *Journals* and the efforts of various admirers, including William Ewart Gladstone and Maurice Barrès, a cult of false soulfulness sprang up around the memory of the artist, a cult satirized in 1911 by Stephen Leacock in his parody, *Sorrows of a Super Soul: or, The Memoirs of Marie Mushenough.* Yet even the published *Journals* provide invaluable factual information about the life of a woman art student in Paris and about Julien's class specifically. In addition, they give a vivid picture of a lively, willful, sometimes divided and often rebellious young woman, a young woman attracted if not dedicated to contemporary feminism and keenly aware of the injustices faced by women artists. Bashkirtseff was angry at the fate that prevented her from working at the École des Beaux-Arts; above all, she bewailed her lack of liberty: "What I long for . . . is the liberty without which one cannot become a true artist," she wrote in 1879. "Do you believe that we profit by what we see when we are accompanied, or when going to the Louvre we must await our carriage, our *chaperon,* or our family? . . . That is one of the great reasons why there are no women artists."[8] Her fantasies of success, in the unpublished passages of her diaries, are often couched in even stronger terms: "When I have the *Prix de Rome,*" she declared, "all the Tabanias, all the Lardarels, all the Mercuards [men acquaintances] will lie down like a carpet and I shall walk over them, not to crush them — but — it will be they who wish it from the moment when I am what no woman artist has ever yet been."[9]

5.
P. Ettinger, "Exposition Marie Bashkirtseff à Leningrad," *Beaux-arts,* VIII, May 20, 1930, 12.
6.
Moore, xvii.
7.
Moore, xv-xvi. This author appends a useful chronological list of publications relating to Bashkirtseff, 293-95.
8.
Bashkirtseff, *Journal,* trans. A. D. Hall, pt. 1, 1908, 416.
9.
Cited in Moore, 276. I am grateful to Judith Stein for having brought this passage to my attention.

102.
A Meeting, 1884
Oil on canvas
74^{15}/$_{16}$ x 68^{15}/$_{16}$ in. (190 x 175 cm.)
Signed and dated: M. Bashkirtseff, 1884, Paris
Paris, Musée National du Louvre

The painting, which was exhibited in the 1884 Salon, represents a group of street urchins meeting on an empty lot after school. The boy on the left, older than the others, seems to have attracted their attention with something he has drawn or written on a slate. To the right, in the background, a little girl carrying a basket walks into the distance. The broken wood fence in the background is decorated with chalked graffitti and peeling posters. Colors are generally subdued, the highest tones reserved for the rose-colored stockings of the boy on the right and the blue smock of his friend in the center.

Although the artist listed herself as a student of Tony Robert-Fleury's in the Livret of the Salon, both the style and the subject matter of *A Meeting* are very close to a work by Bashkirtseff's other master, Jules Bastien-Lepage — his *Nothing Doing (Pas mèche)* of 1882 (Edinburgh, National Gallery of Scotland). Indeed, when the painting was exhibited, with considerable success, in the Salon of 1884 it was even rumored that Bastien-Lepage had assisted the artist. Bashkirtseff herself was aware that her earlier painting *Jean and Jacques* resembled Bastien-Lepage's representations of children,[10] but she indignantly repudiated all suggestions of actual assistance.

Although the *Meeting* did not receive a medal, it was bought by the government for the Musée du Luxembourg and several engravings and lithographs were made after it. Her fellow student at Julien's, the English painter Mary Breakell, criticized *A Meeting* for being "a mere gallery transcript of the surface of things, seen through the eyes and put down on canvas, in the borrowed manner of another, even though that other might be a Bastien-Lepage."[11]

10.
Bashkirtseff, *Journal,* 234.
11.
Breakell, 121.

Edith Hayllar
British, 1860-1948

Edith Hayllar was probably the most talented of the four Hayllar sisters: Edith, Jessica, Kate, and Mary. All four daughters of the painter James Hayllar (1829-1920) received a thorough academic training from their father, and all chose to concentrate on the domestic genre scenes popular with many Victorian artists, specifically on subjects drawn from daily life in their home at Castle Priory. Afternoon tea, for example, was a favorite subject with all the Hayllar girls. They used each other and members of their family as models and the rooms and garden of their home as settings for their paintings. All four created a visual record, at once engaging and precise, of Victorian upper-middle-class life in the 1880s and '90s.

Jessica, the eldest, accidentally crippled in about 1900, was the most prolific: she exhibited in the Royal Academy from 1880 until about 1915. Kate and Mary seem to have had much briefer and less significant careers than their two older sisters. Edith, like Jessica, depicted the daily life of Castle Priory and frequently portrayed children, usually members of the family, but she particularly favored subjects relating to sport, or more precisely the relaxation following athletic exertion rather than the sporting event itself. She painted boating, shooting, and tennis parties in natural, unforced compositions within meticulously accurate settings.

Edith Hayllar seems to have been a successful artist. She exhibited twelve works at the Royal Academy from 1882 to 1897 and also showed at the Society of British Artists, the Institute of Oil Painters, and the Dudley Gallery: the latter was evidently very popular with women artists.[1] She also sold a painting to the Walker Art Gallery in Liverpool.

Despite her success as a professional artist, Edith Hayllar completely abandoned painting when she married the Rev. Bruce MacKay in about 1900. Although it has been plausibly suggested that the artist simply lost interest after leaving Castle Priory and the family life there that had inspired so many of her paintings,[2] it seems more likely that a career in art was viewed as antithetical to women's "natural" destiny as wife and mother, and therefore had to be given up. A striking parallel has been pointed out between Edith Hayllar's renunciation of art after her marriage and that of the heroine of Mrs. Craik's Victorian novel, *Olive,* who was, in addition, crippled like Jessica Hayllar.[3] So deeply did Edith Hayllar hide the evidence of her artistic career that her own granddaughter did not realize that she had been a painter until after her death.

103.
A Summer Shower, 1883
Oil on board
20 x 16¾ in. (50.8 x 42.5 cm.)
New York, The *Forbes* Magazine Collection
(See color plate, p. 93)

Exhibited at the Royal Academy in 1883, Edith Hayllar's *A Summer Shower* represents Victorian genre painting at its best. It conveys a sense of abiding satisfaction, spiritual and visual, and of tranquil domestic pleasure akin to that created by the Dutch little masters in the seventeenth century and, on a somewhat more worldly level, by James Tissot in the nineteenth. A tennis party has been interrupted by a sudden shower and the players wait for the rain to stop. Indoors and outdoors are effectively combined in the view through the arched entrance to the wood-paneled refreshment room, where one of the players is pouring himself a drink of lemonade, and out to the rain-filled garden beyond, marked by a dark-clad figure with an umbrella.

A Summer Shower is also an engaging reminder of the state of the game of tennis in England in the eighties. The perfection of rubber and the subsequent development of a tennis ball capable of bouncing on grass had opened the way to the invention of lawn tennis in 1873. The game quickly became popular, and by 1875 the All-England Croquet Club set aside one of its lawns at Wimbledon for the new tennis. The racquet was square-topped, relatively heavy, and had a wooden handle.[4] Obviously, men had the advantage as far as com-

1.
Wood, ii, 6.
2.
Ibid.
3.
See Minneapolis, University Gallery, University of Minnesota, *The Art and Mind of Victorian England: Paintings from the Forbes Magazine Collection,* introduction by Melvin Waldfogel, 1974, 41.
4.
Minneapolis, University Gallery, University of Minnesota, *The Art and Mind of Victorian England: Paintings from the Forbes Magazine Collection,* introduction by Melvin Waldfogel, 1974, 42.
5.
Wood, 1974, ii, 6.

Suzanne Valadon
French, 1865-1938

fortable dress was concerned, but the costume of the young woman in the foreground seems remarkably casual, loose, and informal for the period. There is the slightest, most decorous suggestion of mutual interest between the two young people in the foreground.

The colors are light and fresh, the paint handled delicately if somewhat dryly, and the poses marvelously natural; that of the young man pouring lemonade could only have been envisioned by eyes free from the stereotypes of academic training. All in all, one can only agree with Christopher Wood's estimation of the painting when he calls it: "One of the most charming genre scenes of the nineteenth century . . . wonderfully redolent of an English summer afternoon, with sets of inconsequential tennis, showers, lemonade, and tea doubtless to follow."[5]

Suzanne Valadon, born Marie Clémentine Valadon in Bessines-sur-Gartempe, the illegitimate daughter of a laundress, began her career in the Montmartre section of Paris, frequenting the bohemian cafés and the circles of the artistic avant-garde. She had little formal schooling but a native intelligence and a resourceful spirit helped her to survive independently from about age ten or twelve. She worked at various jobs from waitress to circus acrobat, lived freely outside conventional moral standards, and in 1883 bore an illegitimate son, the painter Maurice Utrillo.[1]

In the early eighties Valadon became an artist's model, posing for Zandomeneghi, di Nittis, the Czech artist Inaïs, Henner, Puvis de Chavannes (*The Sacred Forest*, 1883), Toulouse-Lautrec (two portraits of 1885 and 1886 and *The Drinker*, 1889), and Renoir (*Dance in the City* and *Dance in the Country*, 1883; *The Braid*, 1885; and several bathers). True to her inquisitive nature, she began to produce drawings and pastels in a bold linear style from about 1883 onwards, using the opportunity to learn by listening to and observing the painters for whom she modeled.[2] Through Toulouse-Lautrec or Bartolomé she met Degas; she never posed for him but he admired her work and purchased several drawings. Valadon's strong personality appealed to Degas; he referred to her affectionately as his "terrible Maria" and they corresponded from about 1890 until his death in 1917.[3]

Valadon's earliest known paintings, dating from 1892-93, are portraits of children and of Bernard Lemaire and Erik Satie,[4] who was then her lover. Two years later, in Degas' atelier, she first began her rich production of prints, and in 1894 she exhibited at the Société Nationale des Beaux-Arts. While she was intrigued by the techniques of the School of Pont-Aven[5] and drew on its simplification of form and bold color, from the outset she preferred forceful realism to pure aestheticism.

1.
Utrillo's father may have been the Spanish painter and journalist, Miguel Utrillo y Molins, although other names have been advanced, among them the singer at the Lapin Agile, Boissy.
2.
Valadon claimed to have been drawing since the age of nine. Tabarant, 628.
3.
Undated letters, published in part in Rey, 8-10.
4.
Cat. nos. 1-4, Paris, 1967.
5.
Valadon, 53.

In 1896 she married the wealthy businessman Paul Mousis, dividing her time between Montmartre and a country home outside Paris. She produced nudes, portraits, and still lives in varied media, but particularly in drawings and prints. Her work was sold at Lebarc de Bouteville, and by Vollard, who also published her engravings in 1897. But not until 1909, when the forty-four-year-old Valadon left Mousis for the twenty-three-year-old painter André Utter, did her fully mature style begin to emerge as she devoted herself exclusively to painting. During her marriage to Mousis, Utrillo, who had been raised by his grandmother, was diagnosed and treated for alcoholism and Valadon taught him to paint as a distraction and a form of therapy. Despite his frequent bouts with alcoholism and mental illness, Utrillo was artistically successful and he exhibited with Valadon and Utter in joint shows from 1917 on.

Valadon's strong and original style has kinships with that of other artists whose work she admired. Her drawings and pastels of young women bathing and dressing rely heavily on similar subjects and attitudes in Degas' work, and her *Black Venus,* 1919 (Musée Municipal de Menton), exhibits the taste for exoticism and rhythmic arabesques found in Gauguin's Tahitian themes. Valadon's canvases are frequently charged with a nervous energy that recalls van Gogh, whose work she knew and whose *Portrait of Mme. Roulin* (Otterlo, Kroller-Mueller Museum) may well have inspired the crude contours, flattened spaces, and intense expression of her *Portrait of Mme. Levy,* 1922 (private collection). In her mature work of the twenties and thirties, she combined bold color and pattern with sensitively handled plastic form in rhythmic, unified surfaces in the spirit of Matisse.[6] It is, however, the earthiness and robustness of Valadon's images that stamp them as uniquely hers. Her many nudes sit, stand, or recline with sensuous abandon amidst richly colored objects in limited and often ambiguous space. The vitality of objects in her still lives and floral pieces, as in her figure paintings, is the result of their uncompromising plasticity. The convergence of living and decorative energies in Valadon's work greatly appealed to critics and collectors, and from 1921 until the end of her life she enjoyed wide acclaim and financial success.

Valadon showed at the Indépendants and at advanced private galleries such as Berthe Weill and Bernheim-Jeune. The first of her many one-woman shows was held at the Clovis Sagot Gallery in 1911, and the following year her work was seen in a group exhibition in Munich.[7] In 1920 she was elected a *sociétaire* of the Salon d'Automne where she had exhibited regularly since showing *Summer* there in 1909. Valadon was the most productive and critically successful during the 1920s and early 1930s. Her international reputation was affirmed in 1928 with the publication of an important illustrated article in the German periodical *Deutsche Kunst und Dekoration* and with a monograph by Adolphe Basler the following year. Major retrospectives were held in 1927, 1929, 1931, and 1932;[8] her work was solicited for numerous group shows in France and abroad; and from 1933 until

104

6.
For example, compare Matisse's work of the same period with Valadon's *Still Life with Violin,* 1923 (Musée d'Art Moderne de la Ville de Paris).
7.
Organized by Clovis Sagot.
8.
At the Berthe Weill Gallery; the Galerie Bernier; the Galerie le Centaure, Brussels; and the Galerie Georges Petit, respectively.

her death, she participated in the Salon des Femmes Artistes Modernes.

In the early thirties, Valadon, Utter, and Utrillo agreed to live separately, although they continued to exhibit together and saw each other frequently. From this time on she experienced periods of depression and fatigue, but continued to paint.

Noting the "masculine" power and virility of her work, critics sought an explanation for her strong style in her rebellious, "primitive," and strong-willed personality.[9] The unfailing self-reliance developed in her earliest years is frequently echoed in the forthright glance of her figures and in the firm handling of form, color, and content. She relied upon intuition rather than intellect and her canvases transmit the felt sensations of a highly charged, personal vision.

104.
The Blue Room, 1923
Oil on canvas
$35^{7}/_{16}$ x $45^{11}/_{16}$ in. (90 x 116 cm.)
Signed and dated lower left
Paris, Musée National d'Art Moderne (Lux 1506-P)

The Blue Room represents Valadon's fully mature, expressive style. In the same year she painted three nudes *en plein air,* a self-portrait, and several still lives;[10] this picture combines elements of all three genres and summarizes her frequent use of a large-scale figure in a domestic setting. The body of the clothed model in this painting is as forcefully felt as the nudes of the same period. Volumes are defined in broad, sculptural masses that assert the solidity of the figure beneath the garments. Also present are the highly charged components of contemporaneous still lives and the expressive intensity of the artist's portraits of the same years.

This work is a conjunction of solid form and decorative surface. The edges of individual parts are established with heavy contours that reinforce volume and weight and flow rhythmically from model to surrounding objects in a unifying ornamental pattern. Set in relief against a sonorous, overall blue background, the staring model dominates the shallow space around her while fusing with the richly decorative motives of settee, fabrics, and objects. Bold color and energetic surface-depth relationships are woven into a luxuriant texture reminiscent of Matisse's canvases.

The aggressive gaze, dangling cigarette, and languorous pose of the model recalls the women of Toulouse-Lautrec's brothels, although the compositional centrality of the figure and its steady, outward stare suggest a control and stability that are Valadon's own. If the figure is bluntly available, she is also self-reliant and conscious of her sensual power. She is kin to Romantic odalisques and to the voluptuous nudes of Renoir, but Valadon has foregone the passivity of such models for a more dominant and aggressive image.

The motif of *The Blue Room* had appeared eleven years earlier in *The Future Unveiled* (1912, Vaux-sur-Seine, France, Collection Adolphe Aynaud). Although similar in composition, pose, and arrangement of masses, the integration of décor, figure, color, and line into an expressive decorative surface and the strong definition of volume are not as forceful in the earlier work.[11] Valadon's emotionally charged responses to her environment and to her subjects led her to return to earlier themes in order to amplify and enrich their expressive content. According to her own comments her artistic impulses sprang less from a desire for novelty than from a determined will to capture and intensify a moment in life.[12]

9.
Mermillon, n.p. François Mathey (*Six femmes peintres,* Paris, 1951, 10) points out that other famous women artists are customarily referred to as "Berthe Morisot," "Eva Gonzalès," or "Marie Laurencin," while Valadon, like Picasso or van Gogh, is called "Valadon."
10.
Three nudes of 1923 were exhibited in the 1967 Suzanne Valadon retrospective at the Musée National d'Art Moderne, nos. 57-59. One nude (no. 994) and a still life (no. 995) appeared at the Salon des Indépendants in 1923, and a still life (no. 1956) was shown at the Salon d'Automne of the same year.

11.
Paris, 1947, 62.
12.
Valadon, 53.

105

106

Käthe Kollwitz
German, 1867-1945

Käthe Kollwitz was one of the finest and best-known graphic artists working in the first half of the twentieth century. Her prolific output of etchings, lithographs, and woodcuts, while conservative in style, is nonetheless radical in content, bold and forceful in imagery. The strength of her work lies in its compassion and humanity: her subjects were drawn from the same reservoir of the poor and oppressed that inspired Rembrandt, Goya, and Daumier. The sensuousness of oil or the solution of purely formal problems held little interest for her; she intended her art to be one of urgency and social purpose. Her statements, like the clear and articulate lines she used to express them, are sharp, uncompromising, and somber. Early in her career Kollwitz chose to work in graphic media, drawings as well as prints, a decision in keeping with the German tradition of linear art. Her first major print cycle, *The Weavers' Uprising* (1895-97), based on Gerhardt Hauptmann's play of the same name, takes up the themes of poverty, suffering, and rebellion. She was also active as a sculptor, and in 1933 her sculpture of grieving parents, bearing her own features and those of her husband, was unveiled at Roggevelt Military Cemetery in Belgium. The work was a war monument commemorating her son, Peter, who was killed in battle during World War I.

Kollwitz' vision is earthbound and tragic, with human vulnerability and death at its core; yet underlying her work is an almost Christian sense of ultimate salvation. As the wife of a doctor in a poor, working-class district of Berlin she was a constant witness to the struggles of proletarian life, and what she saw she put into her art.

Born Käthe Schmidt to a large family, the artist's reminiscences of her childhood in East Prussia are records of warmth, freedom, mutual respect, and social and spiritual dedication. Her family, particularly her father, recognized her talent at an early age and encouraged a career in art. She began training at age fourteen in her native city of Konigsberg (now Kaliningrad) under the engraver Rudolf Maurer. In 1884 she moved to Berlin to continue her studies with Karl Stauffer-Bern, who introduced her to the work of the engraver-sculptor Max Klinger. While Klinger's fantastic vision differs considerably from her own, his work left a deep impression upon the young woman, and it may have been his example that caused her to combine etched outlines with soft aquatint backgrounds, as in her *Peasant's War* cycle. In 1885 she returned to Konigsberg, studying for a short time with Emil Neide, then spent the years 1889-90 in Munich under the tutelage of Ludwig Herterich. In 1891, one year after she had completed her first etchings (K 1-3),[1] she married Dr. Karl Kollwitz and settled permanently in Berlin. Studying sculpture at the Académie Julien in 1904, she met Steinlen and Rodin; in 1907 she spent a year in Florence as the winner of the Villa Romana prize, also visiting Rome; and in 1927 she was an official guest of the Soviet Union on the tenth anniversary of the revolution.

Kollwitz was the first woman to be elected a member of the Prussian Academy of Arts (1919) where she held the directorship of graphic arts from 1928 until her resignation in 1933 during the Nazi era. She attended exhibitions, visited the studios of other artists, many of them women, and read voluminously, particularly Goethe. Kollwitz concentrated on the working class and showed a marked awareness of women's role within that milieu, clearly identifying with their varied responsibilities and pleasures. In her frequent and tender images of mothers with children, which obviously stem from personal experience, the burden of survival is set aside for joyous intimacy and pleasure.

She first exhibited in 1893 at the Berlin Free Art Exhibition, where she continued to show regularly until her work was banned by the Nazis in 1936. Her *Weavers' Uprising* cycle was recommended for a gold medal in 1898, but the Kaiser ordered it withheld because of the strong political content of the work. Two years later the cycle was bought for the Dresden state collection and the medal awarded. In 1917, under the aegis of the Berlin Secession, she was given a fiftieth-birthday retrospective at the Paul Cassirer Gallery.

1.
Klipstein.

In addition to the *Weavers' Uprising,* Kollwitz' graphic cycles include the *Peasant War* series of etchings (1902-8) and two woodcut cycles, *War* (1922-23) and *Proletariat* (1925), which were inspired by the work of Ernst Barlach. The death of Kollwitz' son as well as the unstable political climate of Germany after World War I helped generate the two later series, which express the moral and ethical issues that are the mainstay of her art.

Neither the stylistic innovations nor the experimentation with new media that interested many of her fellow artists during the early decades of this century held any attraction for Kollwitz. Her early prints and drawings are in a naturalist style, using traditional spatial and compositional arrangements and careful detail. In general she retained these basic stylistic tenets throughout her life, but she grew increasingly sensitive to the expressive potential of reduced forms and simplified composition. Although from the 1890s she exhibited regularly at the Berlin Secession, which favored the Impressionism of Max Lieberman and Lovis Corinth, she was also aware of and admired the high-pitched emotional images of the Expressionists. As early as 1892 Edvard Munch's Expressionist treatment of themes of human suffering made a deep impression on Kollwitz.[2] Her forms became increasingly compact, her style more condensed and expressionistic. It may be that her sculptural studies in Paris in 1904 increased her feeling for massive volumes and more abstract large-scale forms. In 1909 she expressed a wish "to do etchings so that all the essentials are strongly stressed and the inessentials omitted."[3] The power of her later work resides not only in its emotional themes, but in its concentrated, generalized forms. Kollwitz' gripping imagery and her stylistic direction towards reduced composition and monumental sculptural forms are particularly effective in her last print cycle, *Death,* of 1934-35. Here, in eight powerful lithographs, the obsessive motif of mortality is combined with self-portraits in a fully realized broad, bold style.

The last ten years of Kollwitz' life were difficult and tragic. Under the Nazis she was unable to exhibit, although she worked in her studio in Berlin until the last months of the war, when she was evacuated to Moritzburg, outside of Dresden. In 1940 she suffered the loss of her husband, and in 1942 her grandson was killed in battle. When death came on April 22, 1945, her last words were, "My greetings to all."[4]

107

105.
Whetting the Scythe, 1905
Soft-ground etching
$11\frac{13}{16}$ x $11\frac{5}{8}$ in. (30 x 29.5 cm.)
Palo Alto, Stanford University Museum of Art
Given in memory of Jane Desenberg Lyons by Professor and Mrs.
James L. Adams and Dr. and Mrs. Jud R. Scholtz

Whetting the Scythe is the third of seven compositions in the *Peasants' War* cycle, images based on the sixteenth-century uprising of the German peasantry. For this series, which was published in a single issue for the Society of Historic Art in 1908, Kollwitz carefully

2.
Munch's work was first exhibited in Germany at the Union of Berlin Artists in 1892.
3.
Quoted in Hans Kollwitz, 1955, 42.
4.
H. Bittner, *Käthe Kollwitz,* New York, 1959, 15, as quoted in Munsterberg, 113.

researched the economic and social conditions of the period and the actual events of the rebellion. As in her earlier *Weavers' Uprising* series (1897), cause, protest, and defeat unfold sequentially. The first two prints, *The Plowmen* and *Assaulted,* are graphic descriptions of the economic and social plight of the peasants; in *Whetting the Scythe* and *Munitions' Vault* the preparations for battle are outlined; *Outbreak, Battlefield,* and *The Prisoners* chronicle the rebellion and its tragic consequences. Kollwitz gave particular emphasis to the vital character of Black Anna, an actual participant in the events of 1523-25. In *Outbreak* and *Battlefield* she is portrayed as both a historical figure and as a generating force in the rebellion.

In *Whetting the Scythe* the single waist-length figure with a large farming implement is conceived on a monumental scale that elevates the simple subject into a symbol of the potential power of the peasant class. Using bold forms and a dramatic interplay of light, Kollwitz focuses on the work-worn hands and rugged features of her peasant subject. The interlocking planes of scythe and figure form a tight compositional bond. With the eyes barely visible and the mouth — the traditional instrument of protest — replaced by the sharpened blade of the scythe, Kollwitz' figure acquires the ominous character of Death the Reaper. The scythe she holds assumes a dual meaning as an instrument for both nourishment and destruction.

While Kollwitz' message is unequivocally social and political, her sensitive handling of light and form not only sharpens the message, but is a means of purely aesthetic communication. Several studies for this composition exist in pencil and chalk drawings,[5] and impressions are in collections in Berlin, London, Dresden, as well as in the United States.

106.
Home Worker, 1909
Charcoal
16 x 22 in. (40.6 x 55.9 cm.)
Signed in pencil, lower right: Kollwitz
Numbered in pencil, lower left: '14'
Los Angeles County Museum of Art
Museum Purchase with Graphic Art Council Funds (M.69.69)

This is a preliminary study for the red crayon drawing *Home Worker,*[6] which first appeared in *Simplicissimus* in September 1909. It appeared again two months later in the same publication as the first composition in the series *Images of Wretchedness,* and may have inspired a touching contemporary poem, *Song of the Shirt.*[7] Kollwitz used this subject again in 1925 for a lithograph.

Kollwitz' bold sweeping lines and dramatic chiaroscuro give plastic definition and a strong sense of presence to the sleeping figure. In this sympathetic portrayal, the overwhelming weariness of the worker is underscored by the sprawling, horizontal arrangement of forms, the limp arms, and the partially open mouth. The image is made particularly poignant and immediate to the viewer by the carefully limited space and the close-focus view.

107.
Self-Portrait, 1934
Charcoal
17 x 13¼ in. (43.2 x 33.7 cm.)
Signed and dated in pencil, lower right: Kathe Kollwitz 1934
Los Angeles County Museum of Art (69.1)

This drawing, executed when the artist was sixty-seven years old, is one of the many self-portraits that span Kollwitz' long career. Her first etched self-portrait dates from 1891 and presents a serious, vigorous young woman who looks confidently out at the spectator. Here, forty-three years later, the taut expression and lined features bear witness to a long and difficult life.

Kollwitz' self-portraits are usually stark records of the physical and psychological effects of aging and sorrow. As in analogous full-face compositions — a self-portrait of 1923[8] or a lithograph of the same year as this drawing[9] — the staring features are seen as if in a close-range mirror. The portrait is both a representation of the artist and a forum for self-examination; its expressive force derives from the shadows concentrated around the nose and mouth and the studied expression in the eyes. While less tense than the cropped image of 1923 or a head of 1924,[10] it is candid, direct, and emotionally charged.

In keeping with the generalized forms to which the charcoal medium lends itself and with Kollwitz' later stylistic direction, this portrait is rendered in broad, free strokes and few details. The strong plastic qualities of the head result from a sensitive handling of light and shadow and a repetition of form-defining lines. The broad linear sweep and severe frontality of the form give the image both dignity and monumentality. As in Kollwitz' other self-portraits from the last decade of her life, sadness and aging are mitigated by a determined spirit.

5.
Nagel, nos. 394-98, 262.
6.
Nagel, no. 498, 284.
7.
Mentioned in Heilborn, *Käthe Kollwitz,* 1924, and Nagel, 284.

8.
Klipstein, no. 168, 223.
9.
Ibid., no. 252, 340.
10.
Ibid., no. 198, 271.

Florine Stettheimer
American, 1871-1944

Florine Stettheimer, the second youngest of the three daughters and one son of Rosetta Walter and Joseph Stettheimer, was born in Rochester, New York, in 1871. She studied art with Kenyon Cox at the Art Students League and then, between 1906 and 1914, traveled abroad with her mother and two sisters, Ettie and Carrie, studying art in Berlin, Stuttgart, and Munich. The Stettheimers — or "Stetties," as they were known to their friends — returned to New York City at the outbreak of World War I. They quickly established a salon that attracted the liveliest members of the avant-garde to their New York apartment and to their summer home, André Brook. Among those they entertained were Marcel Duchamp, Gaston Lachaise, Carl Van Vechten, Albert Gleizes, Elie Nadelman, Alfred Stieglitz, Edward Steichen, and the critic Henry McBride. Later, Marsden Hartley, Charles Demuth, Virgil Thomson, Cecil Beaton, and Pavel Tchelitchew joined the Stettheimer family circle. Florine's sisters were both accomplished. Ettie, whom the artist portrayed in 1923 against a dark, spectral background illuminated by a combination burning bush and Christmas tree, received a doctorate in philosophy from the University of Freiburg and published two novels under the pseudonym "Henrie Waste." Carrie devoted herself to the perfection of an elaborate dollhouse, with a miniature art gallery containing small-scale replicas of works by Duchamp, Nadelman, Lachaise, and Archipenko, executed by the artists themselves; she was depicted with her masterpiece by her sister in 1923, the same year that the artist created her memorable self-portrait, floating weightlessly on a flower-petal couch.

After a disastrous exhibition at Knoedler's in 1916, Florine Stettheimer largely withdrew from public exposure although she did participate in the annual exhibitions of the Independent Society of Artists from 1917 to 1926, showed occasionally at the Carnegie International Exhibitions in Pittsburgh, and, beginning in 1931, exhibited with the American Society of Painters, Printers, and Gravers. Her major public success of the thirties was the sets and costumes she created for the Gertrude Stein-Virgil Thomson opera, *Four Saints in Three Acts,* which opened at the Wadsworth Atheneum Theater in Hartford in 1934.

Following the death of their mother in 1935 the Stettheimer sisters separated and Florine moved to her own studio apartment in the Beaux-Arts building, which she decorated largely in lace and cellophane; there she continued painting, entertaining, and having "unveilings" of her works. She died in 1944. A posthumous exhibition of her work was held at the Museum of Modern Art in New York in 1946; her flower paintings were shown at Durlacher Bros. in 1948. More recently, in 1973, Columbia University exhibited a number of the artist's paintings, watercolors, and drawings, with special emphasis on the earlier, relatively unknown works.

Florine Stettheimer's mature paintings are a unique expression of what might best be considered camp sensibility at its highest. Both highly sophisticated and willfully naive, they display, with calculated artificiality and a vivid sense of theatrical distance, family and guests in their natural habitat; public amusements like beauty contests or fashion sales at Bendel's; and friends like Marcel Duchamp, Henry McBride, Carl Van Vechten, or Alfred Stieglitz portrayed in settings of sly relevance. Later in her career, Florine honored the city she so deeply admired with the four monumental *Cathedrals of New York,* now in The Metropolitan Museum of Art: *Cathedrals of Broadway* (1929); *Cathedrals of Fifth Avenue* (1931); *Cathedrals of Wall Street* (1939); and *Cathedrals of Art* (unfinished, 1942). Her style, diaphanous, androgynous, and deftly incisive, was probably influenced by the ideas of her friend, the Mexican artist Adolofo Best-Maugard, whose book, *A Method for Creative Design,* was published in 1926. In addition to painting, Florine Stettheimer wrote poetry, published posthumously as the *Crystal Flowers* in 1949. Her unpublished diaries are in the Beinecke Library at Yale.

108.
Beauty Contest, 1924
Oil on canvas
50 x 60¼ in. (127 x 153 cm.)
Signed and dated 1924
Hartford, Wadsworth Atheneum
Gift of Miss Ettie Stettheimer
(See color plate, p. 94)

This painting, dedicated to the memory of P. T. Barnum, is one of a series of depictions of public or private entertainments, with friends and family often included as either participants or spectators, that Florine Stettheimer created in the late teens and early 1920s. Other works of this type include *Lake Placid* (1919, Boston, Museum of Fine Arts), which represents the Stettheimers and their friends engaging in water sports; *Natatorium Undine* (1927, Poughkeepsie, Vassar College Art Gallery), similarly aquatic in motif, though far more fantastic in conception, with Carl Van Vechten's wife, the actress Fania Marinoff, as well as the Stettheimer sisters among the cast of characters; and *Asbury Park South* (1920, Nashville, Fisk University), where Van Vechten looks down on the lively scene on a segregated beach from a reviewing stand not too different from the one to the right in *Beauty Contest,* while Marcel Duchamp, Fania Marinoff, Avery Hopwood, the photographer Paul Thévenaz, and the artist herself appear among the merrymakers at the beach.

Beauty Contest bears witness to Florine Stettheimer's ongoing engagement with an exuberantly personal variant of baroque or rococo theatricality, the style identified with the circus itself, and with Barnum, its ultimate impresario. Although the artist noted in her diary that "Beauty contests are a blot B.L.O.T. on American something — I believe life — or civilization,"[1] she nevertheless obviously relished the free play of pictorial inventiveness the subject afforded her; she even included herself to the upper left, accompanying Edna Kenton and Edward Steichen, who is photographing the contest. The latter

was a most appropriate choice, for at the time Steichen was photographing famous beauties displaying themselves in fantastic costumes and "exotic" poses. In 1923 he began his *Vanity Fair* series of reigning stars of the film and theater, with performers like Gilda Grey in Javanese costume and Gloria Swanson in a setting as lacy as anything Florine Stettheimer ever dreamed up. The figure typing Florine's name to the far right may be Carl Van Vechten.

The androgynous, or at least ambiguous, physiques of the contestants, as well as the inclusion of blacks among its decidedly variegated personalities, may call to mind the famous Harlem drag balls of the time. Indeed, Carl Van Vechten and Avery Hopwood occasionally served as judges at integrated transvestite costume parties at the Rockland Palace Casino in about 1924 and 1925, beauty contests at which the "Astors and the Vanderbilts sat regally in boxes to observe the parades of pretty boys in gilt and feathers and elegant gowns."[2] The unusually "hot" palette adds to the sense of sultriness and excitement.

Although the real P. T. Barnum was far more portly than the white-haired judge in the box to the right, it may be relevant to note that a major biography of the circus impresario, M. R. Werner's *Barnum,* had appeared in 1923, a year before the completion of this painting. And, while speculating about the identities of the participants in this gala occasion, one might point out the resemblance of the svelte, Hispanic silhouette of the man leading a white horse in the center of the painting to that of Rudolph Valentino, one of the more flamboyant cinematic inventions of the time.

1.
Tyler, 71.
2.
B. Kellner, *Carl Van Vechten and the Irreverent Decades,* Norman, Okla., 1968, 201.

Romaine Brooks
American, 1874-1970

Romaine Brooks, a painter best known for her portraits, was born in Rome of an extremely rich but eccentric American mother. The early years of her life, recounted chiefly in her unpublished memoirs, *No Pleasant Memories,* sound like a farfetched Gothic novel. Although one may well doubt the total accuracy of this account, probably begun in about 1930,[1] it is nevertheless true that the artist's mature life was haunted by the complicated miseries of her youth. Her peripatetic and unbalanced mother (deserted before Romaine's birth by her husband, Major Harry Goddard), insisted that Romaine become the companion-keeper of her mad brother, St. Mar. Mrs. Goddard kept Romaine in a state of terror and apparently deserted her daughter completely when the child was about six or seven, leaving her in the care of their laundress. The latter took the child to a New York slum apartment and had her selling newspapers in the street until she was rescued by her grandfather's secretary. Yet it was in this unlikely environment, according to Brooks' own account, that she first discovered the consolation of drawing.

After schooling in New Jersey, Italy, and Geneva, with summers spent in various villas along the Riviera, Brooks studied voice in Paris and finally prevailed upon her mother to grant her a monthly allowance of three hundred francs, which gave her independence.

In 1896-97 Brooks went to Rome to study art. There she had her own studio and worked at the Circolo Artistico and the Scuola Nazionale, where she was the only woman student. In the summer of 1899 she rented a studio on the island of Capri, at that time a refuge for an artistic and sexually liberated group that included Axel Munthe, E. F. Benson, Somerset Maugham, the Compton MacKenzies, and Norman Douglas, who commemorated the Capri "Beautiful People" in his novel *South Wind* (1917). After the deaths of both her brother and mother in 1902, Brooks inherited a fortune. She contracted a "white marriage" with John Ellingham Brooks, a homosexual dilettante from Capri, and continued to paint, first in London and then in St. Ives in Cornwall. In England she became friendly with the popular painters Charles Conder and Augustus John. Brooks finally established herself in a luxurious apartment on the present Avenue du Président Wilson in Paris. She studied briefly with Gustave Courtois and quickly became part of the Parisian *haut monde;* the aesthetic, Whistlerian black, white, and gray color scheme of her apartment established her as a popular interior decorator as well as a portraitist.

Brooks' first one-woman exhibition in 1910 at Durand-Ruel's in Paris, consisting for the most part of Whistlerian figure studies, was extremely successful. In subsequent years her portraits recorded, directly or indirectly, her attachments and relationships with the world of French arts and letters as well as with high society and the homosexual elite of the period, worlds that often overlapped. Among those she portrayed were the dancer Ida Rubinstein, whose elongated, extravagant good looks set a new standard of androgynous elegance (1917); Gabriele D'Annunzio, the stormy Italian poet and playwright (1912 and 1916); Jean Cocteau, literary figure and fashionable avant-gardiste (1914); and Natalie Clifford Barney, the aphorist and *salonnière* (1920), with whom Brooks established a forty-year liaison.

Among Brooks' most interesting portraits are those of lesbians. *Una, Lady Troubridge* (1924) — the close friend of the author Radclyffe Hall and a major figure in the latter's scandalous novel of lesbian life, *The Well of Loneliness* — is incisively represented in severe masculine attire, with monocle, clipped hair, and dachshunds. In *Renata Borgatti at the Piano* (ca. 1920), the mannish yet subtly feminine musician seems lost in the world of her own creation. Brooks herself figured, under a fictitious name, not only in *The Well of Loneliness* but in a more lighthearted novel of lesbian life, Compton Mackenzie's *Extraordinary Women,* in which the artist served as model for the heroine, Olympia Leigh.

Brooks' mature portraits are often mannered in conception and austere in execution. They may be characterized as generally "symboliste" in style; for the most part the palette is reduced to Whistler's scale of

---

1.
Doubts about the veracity of the memoirs have been expressed by Sir Harold Acton, who knew Brooks in Florence; by Professor Norman Holmes Pearson of Yale University; and by Carl Van Vechten; as well as by her recent biographer, Meryle Secrest. See Secrest, 10-11.
2.
G. Annan, review of Secrest, in *Times Literary Supplement,* January 30, 1976, 102.
3.
"Catalogue of an Exhibition of Original Drawings by Romaine Brooks," The Arts Club of Chicago, January 11-31, 1935, in *Romaine Brooks, "Thief of Souls,"* Washington, D.C., 1971, 26-27.

109

black, white, and gray tonalities, which tends to dramatize — perhaps overdramatize at times — the bloodless, fashionable remoteness of her sitters. Yet at its best, for example in her *Self-Portrait* of 1923, Brooks' portrait style, with its deft yet canny suggestion of inner life through nuances of form; its sense of rejection of the physical conveyed by tense pose, simplified contour, and thin, relatively colorless pigment; and the human isolation suggested by compositional diffidence — can be intensely moving. Equally interesting, although less well known than her portraits, are Brooks' line drawings (see cat. nos. 111, 112) — over one hundred of them — originating mainly from the 1930s, drawings which, in the words of one critic, "appear to be by Thurber out of Beardsley."[2] Each drawing consists of a single, unbroken line; they are related to Surrealist automatic drawing in their strategies and their revelation of internal fantasy, conflict, and desolation. Of them, the artist herself commented: "These drawings should be read. They evolve from the subconscious. Without premeditation they aspire to a maximum of expression with a minimum of means. Whether inspired by laughter, philosophy, sadness or death these introspective patterns are each imprisoned within the inevitable encircling line. But the surety of outline and apparent freedom from technique are the unconscious evolution from a more material and direct form of art."[3]

Brooks returned briefly to the United States in 1935-36, when her drawings were exhibited at the Arts Club of Chicago. In New York she painted portraits of Carl Van Vechten and Muriel Draper. When World War II broke out Romaine Brooks and Natalie Barney, who had been living on the Riviera, left for Florence and then settled for a time in Fiesole. The artist probably painted her last portrait when she was eighty-seven, and died in Nice on December 7, 1970, at the age of ninety-six.

109.
The Crossing, ca. 1911
Oil on canvas
45⅜ x 75⅜ in. (115.2 x 191.4 cm.)
Signed Romaine Brooks/1900 (date appears to have been added later)
Washington, D.C., National Collection of Fine Arts
Smithsonian Institution
Gift of the artist

Ida Rubinstein, the probable model for this painting, had first appeared before the Parisian public in 1909 in Diaghilev's *Cléopâtre,* in which she was carried on stage in a mummy-case and then unswathed until she emerged in a fantastically exotic costume designed by Bakst. Her specialty was mime rather than dancing. In this nude study, *The Crossing,* Brooks has assimilated Rubinstein's lithe, otherworldly, androgynous physique to the theme of the mingling of death and eroticism, a favored motif in both art and literature of the turn-of-the-century Symbolist movement. A similar dark, elongated nude model had appeared in Brooks' earlier *White Azaleas* (1910), which had been exhibited at Durand-Ruel's the year it was painted. In the earlier painting the figure is less expressively attenuated and the

110

tasteful décor, with its *japonaiserie* and carefully balanced accouterments can be more easily related to the expressive reticence of the British Aesthetic Movement, and especially to Whistler, than to the wilder excesses of International Symbolism. In *The Crossing*, the setting is more abstract and evocative; instead of lying on a couch, the nude seems to float on a large white wing hovering over an immeasurable black background. The downward fall of the black hair of the model effectively evokes the inertia of impending mortality. This slender, often emaciated, and always provocative nude ideal was certainly not Brooks' alone. At the turn of the century, it was favored by such artists as Beardsley, Toorop, Minne, Delville, Klimt, and many others related, however marginally, to the Symbolist movement. Later, Gwen John preferred this type in her choice of nude models as well, and certainly it has been preferred by the world of fashion ever since.

Rubinstein posed, dramatically cloaked, for her portrait by Brooks in 1917. Earlier she had appeared, nude once more, in the guise of St. Sebastian in *The Masked Archer* (1910-11). There she is being shot at by a dwarfish D'Annunzio, who created his scandalous drama, *The Martyrdom of St. Sebastian,* with music by Debussy and sets and costumes by Léon Bakst, specifically for Rubinstein. She may also have inspired Brooks' later nude, *Weeping Venus,* of 1916-18. Interestingly, Rubinstein adopted the décor and pose of Brooks' *White Azaleas* in a nude photograph she had taken of herself in 1917.[4]

110.
Miss Natalie Barney, "L'Amazone," 1920
Oil on canvas
33⅞ x 25⅝ in. (86 x 65 cm.)
Signed: Romaine 1920
Paris, Musée du Petit Palais

Natalie Clifford Barney (1877-1971), Brooks' companion for over forty years, was, like the artist, an American expatriate who lived most of her long life in Paris. A writer known for the elegance and lucidity of her French style, Barney published several volumes of aphorisms, essays, poetry, and a novel, in English, *The One Who Is Legion,* privately printed in London, with illustrations by Romaine Brooks. Her major theme in all these works was androgyny, conceived of in its largest sense: the utopian vision of a world of sexual and intellectual harmony achieved by the elimination of sexual differentiation and antipathy; the very intensity of Barney's ideals made her view the position of her women contemporaries with ironic compassion, and at times, with scathing bitterness. Among her major works are: *Pensées d'une Amazone* (1918); *Aventures de l'esprit* (1929); *Nouvelles pensées de l'Amazone* (1939); and *Souvenirs indiscrets* (1960).[5]

Perhaps even more important than Barney's writings was her famous salon at her "pavillon de l'amitié" on the rue Jacob. Among the many guests who gathered there over the years were Anatole France, Au-

guste Rodin, Pierre Louys, Rainer Maria Rilke, Gabriele D'Annunzio, Sinclair Lewis, Marcel Proust, Paul Valéry, Colette, Ford Madox Ford, Guillaume Apollinaire, and Rémy de Gourmont. It was the last who addressed her as "the Amazon" in his *Lettres à l'Amazone,* published in the *Mercure de France*. The horse in the foreground of the portrait by Brooks is probably a reference to this sobriquet, as well as to Barney's strength of character and her fondness for riding. Brooks often included a symbolic animal image in her portraits: aside from the dachshunds in *Una, Lady Troubridge,* one finds a significant ocelot in the portrait of *La Baronne Emile d'Erlanger* (ca. 1924) and an enigmatic figurine of a white goat in *Elsie de Wolfe* (1920). The energetic silhouette of the jade figurine in the painting of Barney contrasts strikingly with the placid, blond form of the sitter herself and with the misty pallor of the background, through which emerges an adumbration of the house on the rue Jacob. It is possible, given Brooks' predilection for sly allusions in her portraits, that her choice of this snowy background refers to both friends' interest in androgyny and hermaphroditism. Balzac had used the whiteness of snowy mountain peaks as a potent symbol of purity and the mystical union of the sexes in his famous story of hermaphroditism, *Séraphita;* Brooks herself employed a similar, though more fantastic, snowy setting in her *Chasseresse* of 1920.

111.
It Makes the Dead Sing, ca. 1930
Pencil on paper
18⁹⁄₁₆ x 12¼ in. (47.2 x 31.1 cm.)
Washington, D.C., National Collection of Fine Arts
Smithsonian Institution
Gift of the artist

112.
Sorrows of Departure, ca. 1930
Pencil on paper
18 x 12³⁄₁₆ in. (45.7 x 30.9 cm.)
Washington, D.C., National Collection of Fine Arts
Smithsonian Institution
Gift of the artist

4.
For this photograph see Secrest, opp. 151.

5.
For the richest source of information about N. C. Barney, including translations of some of her work, see *Adam International Review: A World Tribute to Natalie Clifford Barney,* London, 1960, and J. Chalon, *Portrait d'une séductrice,* Paris, 1976.

111

Gwen John
British, 1876-1939

Gwendolen John was born in Pembrokeshire, Wales, the older sister of the flamboyant and prolific painter Augustus John. Despite a far more public and profitable career, Augustus is said to have maintained late in his life: "Fifty years from now I shall be known as the brother of Gwen John."[1] Certainly Gwen John's reputation, strong though relatively restricted in scope during her lifetime, has expanded considerably in recent years. The artist's introverted character, her deliberately limited choice of subject and painstaking style, and her intense need for privacy offer a striking contrast to her brother's technical facility and bohemian exuberance.

Gwen John, like Augustus, attended the Slade School in London. She studied there from 1895 to 1898, mainly under Henry Tonks, who stressed sound drawing, winning the Nettleship Prize for figure composition. In 1898 she and two women friends from the Slade (one of whom, Ida Nettleship, was to become her brother's wife) went to Paris and attended the Académie Carmen, where Whistler taught twice weekly and where painting rather than drawing was emphasized. After returning to England in 1899 and creating a few works that have been related both to the intimate style of Vuillard and to the more naturalistic approach of the New English Art Club, John returned to France in 1903 and remained there, except for brief visits to England, for the rest of her life. She posed for, and evidently had a love affair with, the sculptor Auguste Rodin, and established an important friendship with the German poet Rainer Maria Rilke.

In about 1910 Gwen John's work began to show the impact of Picasso's emaciated, Blue-Period figural style; at the same time she met one of her strongest supporters, the American collector of avant-garde art, John Quinn, who ultimately acquired a large number of her paintings.[2] In 1914 John moved to the Parisian suburb of Meudon, where Rodin lived; she had converted to Catholicism the previous year and painted a great many watercolors and gouaches of the Sisters and orphans at a neighboring convent, as well as a series of portraits of the founder, Mère Poussepin. Intense devotion to her art, her reli-

112

1.
Holroyd, 1974, 61.
2.
New York, 1975, 7.

gion, her cats, and to a neighbor, Véra Oumançoff, sister-in-law of Jacques Maritain, and an increasing insistence on privacy mark the years of the artist's maturity. She seems to have stopped painting in about 1932, and died in Dieppe on September 18, 1939.

John's works are usually small. Rarely signed and never dated, they concentrate on the theme of the isolated woman sitter. The woman or young girl is generally represented three-quarter length, occasionally nude (fig. 39, p. 60) although more usually clothed. Sometimes these representations are portraits, or at least repeated studies of known models. The figures are generally immobile, drained of specific expression although expressive as images because of the intensity of their mood, the subtle psychological effect of the restrained composition, and the characteristically exaggerated eloquence of bone structure, hands, and features. Contours are handled with refinement and surfaces are built up in painstaking yet rich, muted harmonies. In the mature works, those after about 1915, color saturations are extremely reduced, brushstrokes become at once smaller and more evident, and surfaces achieve a chalky, frescolike quality reminiscent of that of Puvis de Chavannes, whom the artist greatly respected. Her later works have been, quite correctly, likened to those of Modigliani and Cézanne.[3]

113.
Girl with a Blue Scarf, ca. 1915-20
Oil on canvas
16¼ x 13 in. (41.3 x 33 cm.)
New York, The Museum of Modern Art
Gift of Nelson A. Sears in memory of Mrs. Millicent A. Rogers, 1963

113

This painting, originally in the collection of John Quinn, is quite typical of John's mature style. The unknown sitter is depicted three-quarter length, in a self-contained, rather withdrawn pose. The subtle irregularities of the contours of the figure play against the muted complexities of the grayish white background. A tenuous sense of pictorial diffidence so characteristic of the artist; the asymmetry of the scarf, the slightly ruffled coiffure, the clasped hands all contribute to that sense of intermingled tension and impassivity characteristic of some of John's most successful representations. There are several variants of this image of a dark-haired girl wearing a lilac jacket and a full, bunchy skirt with a flowing dark scarf knotted about the neck: *Young Woman in a Mulberry Dress* in the collection of Mrs. Iola S. Haverstick; *Young Woman in a Mulberry Dress* in the collection of Thomas F. Conroy; *Study of a Young Woman in a Mulberry Dress,* in a private collection (nos. 13, 14, 15 in New York, 1975). The same young woman also served as the model of *The Concièrge* in the collection of the Lady Elizabeth Montagu; still another version of the model, in the "Mulberry Dress" series, is in the Southampton Art Gallery.

3.
Ibid., 9.

Paula Modersohn-Becker

German, 1876-1907

In her native land and especially in the Bremen area where she worked, Paula Modersohn-Becker has long been recognized as a pioneer of modern art. She was the first German painter to assimilate the Post-Impressionist currents she discovered for herself in Paris and to forge a very personal, expressive style, creating some unquestioned masterpieces during her brief career.

She was born in Dresden into a cultured home open to artists and men of letters. After the family moved to Bremen, she took drawing lessons from a local painter and, when she was sixteen, attended a professional art school while staying with relatives near London. Her father, a retired engineer of the railroad bureaucracy with five other children, worried about the uncertainties of an artist's life. Only after Paula had dutifully completed a two-year teachers' training program and acquired a more conventional and reliable means of self-support could she continue her art studies. From 1896 to 1898 she attended the Berlin school for women artists, where Käthe Kollwitz had studied also and was soon to teach. During a summer vacation at home, Paula discovered the artists' colony in nearby Worpswede and settled there in 1898 to continue her studies and work on her own.

The young Worpsweders had achieved considerable fame after exhibiting in the Munich Glaspalast in 1895 and again in 1896. Rejecting their academic backgrounds and life in modern industrialized cities, they called for a return to nature and the simple rural life. They found their Barbizon in Worpswede. Paula studied with the one figure painter among them, Fritz Mackensen, winner of the gold medal in Munich for an ambitious large canvas of peasants worshiping outdoors (clearly indebted to Courbet's *Burial at Ornans*). Otto Modersohn's lyrical approach to the typical north German landscape appealed to her, and she learned graphic techniques from the *Jugendstil* illustrator and designer Heinrich Vogeler. Before long, however, she began to sense the limitations of this provincial group and escaped to Paris on New Year's Eve of the new century.

It was the first of four such trips to the French capital. From January to July 1900 she attended the independent Académie Cola Rossi and took anatomy lessons at the Ecole des Beaux-Arts; her diaries and enthusiastic letters home suggest that she was even more inspired by her frequent visits to museums, galleries, and the art exhibitions at the Exposition Universelle. Although in 1901 she had married Otto Modersohn, who had recently been widowed and left with a young child, she returned to Paris in the spring of 1903, again studying at Cola Rossi. During her third visit, from February to April 1905, she enrolled at the Académie Julien, made contacts with the Nabis, and discovered other contemporary tendencies. "Curiously, this time the old masters don't affect me so much but primarily the very, very moderns," she wrote to Otto.[1] Accordingly, she planned to visit Denis, Vuillard, and Bonnard in their studios where she could further study their work — certainly an audacious practice for a young woman at that time. An extended Parisian stay from February 1906 to April 1907 then produced extraordinary artistic growth and a crisis in her personal life: separation from her husband. In the fall of 1906 Otto followed her to Paris and persuaded her to try anew to reconcile the demands of art and of domestic life. Pregnant, she returned with him to Worpswede in 1907. She painted very little that summer, gave birth to a baby daughter in early November, and on the 20th suffered an embolism and fatal heart attack as she got up from childbed. She was thirty-one.

Unlike many of the successful and long-lived women whose art is exhibited here, Modersohn-Becker compressed extraordinary productivity into the shortest period: some four hundred paintings and studies and one thousand drawings.[2] Much of this she considered student work; she first expressed satisfaction with her growing abilities in 1902, after painting her stepdaughter, Elsbeth.[3] On July 6, 1902, Paula wrote her mother how pleased she was with this painting in which she saw how her power of expression had grown and would continue to develop: "I am going to amount to something! . . . I feel

---

1.
Modersohn-Becker, 211.
2.
Her several premonitions of early death (Modersohn-Becker, 1900, 122-23; 1902, 169; 1906, 237) to some extent may explain her productiveness and sense of urgency (comparable to van Gogh's); or her recognition that domestic life would absorb her energies.
3.
Bremen, 1976, no. 71, color pl. 9.

that soon the time will come when I don't have to be ashamed and keep quiet, but feel with pride that I am a painter." She knew very clearly the direction that her art was to take, stating her aims first in writing and then realizing them in painting during her mature Worpswede period: 1903-5. Mackensen's way had been "not broad enough, too genre-like for me," she noted in her diary in late 1902. Inspired by a book on Mantegna, she tried to capture essence with monumental form. She thought less about nature during the conception of the picture, later adding the required realistic details: "my personal sensation is the main thing," she concluded.[4]

Modersohn-Becker continued to trust her own sensations as she learned her craft by studying the moderns and old masters in the museums. Holbein, Titian, and Böcklin, etchings by Rembrandt and Goya, antique and Gothic sculpture, Coptic mummy portraits, and Japanese scrolls are among the various sources she mentions. Her last letter to Clara Rilke recalls how at Vollard's gallery in 1900, she had discovered Cézanne, "one of the three or four artistic forces which struck me like a thunderstorm and a great experience."[5] She does not identify the others, though she records the impact of Rodin's personality and art in his studio, while her paintings speak of van Gogh and Gauguin.

Her magnificent still lives of 1905 in the museums of Bremen, Wuppertal, and Cologne pay homage to Cézanne — not by facile imitation of his characteristic brushstroke, but by their color harmonies and dynamic pictorial organization. Like Cézanne, she learned to translate into paint the intensity of her visual response and to distill the essence of a few pieces of fruit or of another human being. "The strength with which a subject is grasped (still-life, portrait, or imaginary pictures), that's the beauty of art."[6]

Upon returning from Paris in April 1903 she saw how deeply the "great Biblical simplicity" of the country people affected her: "The desire burns in me to achieve grandeur through simplicity."[7] This she achieved in her great peasant portraits. Encouraged by the example of van Gogh (see cat. nos. 114 and 115), she painted such masterpieces as the *Old Woman from the Poorhouse in the Garden,* in Bremen, and the *Old Peasant Woman Praying* (cat. no. 117), her only major work in an American museum. She had gone far beyond Mackensen's anecdotal naturalism; though retaining some individual likeness, she portrayed broad humanity.

In Paris in 1906, she went even further, literally stripping her models of their mundane clothing. She painted them not as depersonalized studio nudes, however, but as naked maternities. The tender peasant madonnas, such as the one exhibited here, have become genuine earth mothers. In a Bremen painting (fig. 36, p. 59), the woman lies on the ground, curled around her baby like a protective animal. Other pictures in Bremen and Dortmund become fertility icons, with tropical fruit and plants as attributes.[8] With her infant at her breast,

one woman kneels in a circle of pale light as in a mysterious ritual; another ceremonially presents us with a pagan Christ child.

Modersohn-Becker also dared to paint herself naked. At age thirty, on her wedding anniversary in May 1906 (duly inscribed on the canvas), having left her husband, she depicted herself pregnant (which she was not): her maternal potential confronting her artistic self. In another nude self-portrait with amber beads (fig. 46, p. 66), joyful vitality and creativity are symbolized by some flowers, butterflies, and a screen of lush foliage. Similarly, she holds a camellia branch in her most famous self-portrait, the haunting image in the Folkwang Museum of Essen; like the Coptic mummy portraits she admired she evokes spiritual, even otherworldly mysteries.

In these last paintings, Modersohn-Becker explored an amazing range of styles. From the solid realism of her mature Worpswede period, she approached the lighter palette of Impressionism without relinquishing her usual forceful drawing and modeling. At the end of 1906, she had been inspired by Gauguin, whose vast retrospective she saw at the Salon d'Automne,[9] and she ultimately created a classical synthesis of Post-Impressionist styles, even approaching the primitivism and proto-Cubism of the young Picasso.[10]

Regret of her untimely death need not detract from recognition of her impressive achievements — any more than it does in the case of Seurat, who also died at thirty-one. In 1906 she experienced an exhilarating surge of artistic energy: "I'm going *to be* something — I am experiencing the most intense, happiest time of my life," she wrote her sister.[11] The productivity and experimentation of that final year indicate that she had not yet fulfilled her potential nor exhausted her powers, and that she would continue to grow and to create. But she had reached her goals, "to be something," and "to achieve grandeur through simplicity."

114.
Peasant Woman, 1898-99
Charcoal on paper
19 x 27½ in. (48.2 x 69.8 cm.)
Signed lower right: Paula Modersohn-Becker
(posthumous authentication, probably by the artist's daughter)
New York, Allan Frumkin Gallery

Modersohn-Becker has given us an almost photographic yet sympathetic likeness of a Worpswede peasant woman who is leaning forward tensely, posing somewhat self-consciously. Every physiognomic peculiarity is recorded, from the furrowed brow and bulbous nose (their shapes echoed in the lapel), to the wart on her chin. Such meticulous naturalism, the careful drawing, and painterly modeling of light and shade make this unusual among Modersohn-Becker's approximately one thousand drawings. It is entirely characteristic, however, of a specific brief moment in her career: the fall and winter of 1898-99 when she studied with Fritz Mackensen.

4.
Modersohn-Becker, 177-78.
5.
Hetsch, 49. Clara Westhoff, a talented sculptor and Rodin student, married the German poet Rainer Maria Rilke in 1901.
6.
Modersohn-Becker, 216.
7.
Ibid., 200.
8.
The paintings in the Becker-Modersohn Haus in Bremen and in the Museum am Ostwall in Dortmund are illustrated in color in the exhibition catalog of the Kunsthalle Bremen, 1976, pls. 29 (poor color) and 28. The self-portrait as if pregnant is illustrated in Stelzer, pl. 52, as is the first version of the self-portrait with amber beads (the final version is in the Kunstmuseum Basel) and the Essen self-portrait, color pls. 73 and 83.
9.
Especially in the two primitive maternities described above, and the *Seated Nude Girl with Flowers,* in the von der Heydt-Museum, Wuppertal, color pl. 25 in the Bremen catalog.

10.
Petzet first related Modersohn-Becker's work to Picasso's of 1906 in *Das Bildnis des Dichters: Rainer Maria Rilke — Paula Becker-Modersohn: Eine Begegnug* (Frankfurt, 1957; rev. paper ed., 1976, with increased comparative illustrations); see also Christa Murken-Altrogge, "Der französische Einfluss im Werk von Paula Modersohn-Becker," *Die Kunst,* LXXXVII, 1975, 145-52. Modersohn-Becker need not, however, have seen Picasso's self-portrait or his portrait of Gertrude Stein, both of 1906, to have developed in this direction, but could have drawn on the same, or similar, prototypes as Picasso. For a discussion of Paula Modersohn-Becker's relation to Expressionism and her inadequate evaluation in this country, see also Oppler, 364.
11.
Modersohn-Becker, 227.

114

Mackensen, a product of the Munich Academy, wrote condescendingly about Paula's two years at the "ladies' school" where she allegedly had lost her sense of direction, which he intended to restore to her; nevertheless, he was greatly impressed by how energetically she tackled her studies of nudes and portraits.[12] "Devoted copying of nature, that's what I am supposed to learn. I allow my own little person to get too much into the foreground," she wrote in her diary on December 16, 1898. The meticulous drawing, careful observation of tonal values, and studious, pedantic finish of the *Peasant Woman* are quite typical of conservative academic training. The drawing is thus a valuable document of Paula's last student days with Mackensen in Worpswede, just before she took off for Paris to find new artistic directions.

Already in a letter of February 12, 1899, she announced that she felt herself moving away from the constricting atmosphere of Worpswede, and by late summer she was making much freer drawings and painting broadly executed landscapes. She evidently included some of these in her first group exhibition of December 1899 — judging by the derogatory newspaper criticism and by her future husband's comments on her work as "not intimate enough, too poster-like."[13]

While this portrait cannot be identified or dated specifically, we have other drawings of this period that are comparable in style and subject matter: children and old people from the poorhouse who gladly posed for the young artist for a few pennies and a brief respite from their monotonous lives. She recorded several drawing sessions with "Old Man Bredow" (October 4, 1898; November 29, 1898) which resulted in two well-known drawings. And when she writes to her family (November 25, 1898) that this is "the season of the spinning-room," one visualizes the handsome drawing of a peasant woman seated in profile, spinning, which is particularly close to our drawing in mood and execution.[14]

At first glance these drawings suggest possible kinship with work by Käthe Kollwitz, and indeed her very earliest academic drawings and Kollwitz' self-portraits of around 1889-90 are comparable. The latter's more famous graphics contemporaneous with our drawing, such as the *Weavers* cycle of 1898, however, already use modified forms to express intense social outrage, a quality quite foreign to Modersohn-Becker. In her objective but quietly sympathetic image of this patient, tired woman she is closer in spirit to van Gogh, specifically to his many preparatory drawings for the *Potato Eaters* of 1885.[15] Both artists portrayed the simple country people of the lowlands — whether of Worpswede or Nuenen — with respect and compassion. When Modersohn-Becker discovered van Gogh's paintings later in Paris, she responded to his humanity and to his art, and during 1905, especially, created her own impressive peasant portraits "with that something of the eternal which the halo used to symbolize" (see cat. no. 117).[16]

12.
Clearly these are later recollections, in Hetsch, 40.
13.
Some of Otto's diaries are reprinted as an appendix to Modersohn-Becker, *Briefe*, entry of January 27, 1901, 248 (important first recorded description of his future wife). For discussion of newspaper criticism, see Oppler, 364-65.
14.
Old Man Bredow drawings, repr. in Pauli, nos. 57 and 58; *Peasant Woman Spinning* in Frankfurter Kunstkabinett exhibition, *Paula Modersohn-Becker,* Wolfgang Werner KG, 1975, no. 19. For other examples and discussion of the "regressive quality" (*Rückgriff*) of these drawings, see Bremen, Worspwede 1898-99 period. For examples of her mature drawing style, see Günter Busch, *Paula Modersohn-Becker: Handzeichnungen,* Bremen, 1949, pls. 31-37, with excellent introduction; see also Bremen, 1976, nos. 389, 390, and also illustrations in Günter Busch, *Paula Modersohn-Becker: Aus dem Skizzenbuch,* Munich, 1960.
15.
J. B. de la Faille, *L'oeuvre de van Gogh, catalogue raisonné,* Paris/Brussels, 1928, iv. 1189-94.
16.
Vincent van Gogh, letter to Theo (no. 531), September 3, 1888.

115.

Old Woman from the Poorhouse, 1903
Oil on cardboard, cradled
21½ x 15¾ in. (54.6 x 40 cm.)
Monogrammed and dated lower right: 03
New York, Private Collection

This small oil sketch is of greatest interest as an early exploration of a theme that fascinated Paula Modersohn-Becker for several years, culminating in the remarkable *Old Woman from the Poorhouse in the Garden.*[17] During her second trip to Paris in 1903, Modersohn-Becker had admired the French "impromptus," the small color sketch "which often says more than the [finished] painting."[18] Upon her return to Worpswede, she painted many such "impromptus," including this old peasant of the drab heath and peat bogs. She must have been pleased with this dark image, since she dated it herself — not her general practice.

Paula had first described this "ancient" peasant woman from the poorhouse, Old Mother Schröder, in September 1898, and for many years she remained her favorite model and a solicitous friend, last mentioned in 1907 when she worried about the artist's long pregnancy like a midwife.[19] The old woman kept Paula entranced with jumbled childhood memories and "hallucinations," speaking colloquial Plattdeutsch in her "sibylline voice" — much of it strange and at first incomprehensible to the city-bred girl.[20] In June 1902 Modersohn-Becker reported sketching her even after supper, this "three-legged old woman" who never walked without that third leg, her cane — hence, "Dreebeen" in the local dialect. In his journal, Otto enthusiastically described Paula's painting of Dreebeen with her goat and chickens: "marvelous in color, really remarkable in conception, the surface roughed up with the brush handle. Amazing, how grand these things are, how grandiose as painter's vision."[21]

The entry is dated June 15, 1903, a period when we have several Dreebeen studies, including one quite close to ours in pose and landscape background.[22] The version exhibited here, however, is especially intriguing for its blue green glass bottle on a stick, a type of garden decoration popular in Worpswede then, and even now. Modersohn-Becker evidently enjoyed these colors and reflections: she placed a silvered glass ball, "a gleaming jewel," in her own flower garden.[23] She gradually transformed this ordinary country woman posing stolidly in her Sunday-best hat, with the glass bottle and scrawny tree perfectly natural to Worpswede, into some supernatural creature: an ancient witch or a primeval Norn of Germanic mythology. The metamorphosis is completed in the final great work in Bremen. The dark peasant face appears foreboding, even malevolent; foxglove and huge poppies seem endowed with magical powers, and the glass bottle looms like an ominous crystal ball. In less than three years, Modersohn-Becker created an undisputed masterpiece from the initial conception of our modest oil sketch.

116.

Mother and Child, ca. 1903
Oil on cardboard, cradled
28¼ x 20 in. (71.7 x 50.8 cm.)
New York, Private Collection

For any number of reasons — cultural and social, personal as well as artistic — the mother and child motif fascinated Modersohn-Becker. Observations about motherhood filled her letters and diaries as she sketched the ever-pregnant country women and the nursing mothers of Worpswede,[24] contemplated the mystery of Christmas and its message of motherhood,[25] and thought of her own future family.[26] Brought up with conventional expectations of marriage and raising children, "the ultimate purpose of woman,"[27] she nevertheless postponed her own pregnancy for the sake of her art.

In 1892 Mackensen had painted a peasant woman sitting on a wheelbarrow in the peat fields, nursing her infant.[28] Reminiscent of Millet — whom the German artists greatly admired — it is his finest work, celebrated in Munich and promptly acquired by the Kunsthalle Bremen. His sitter was quickly dubbed the *Worpswede Madonna* or *Madonna of the Peat-Moor.* A comparison of the *Mother and Child* exhibited here with the older prototype proves dramatically how far Paula Modersohn-Becker had developed. While a respectful distance separates Mackensen's subject from the painter and spectator, Modersohn-Becker's seated half-length figure nearly touches the picture frame, creating an effect of immediacy and involvement. She applied paint freely to broad, simplified shapes within a flattened space, brushed the garments sketchily, and used emphatic impasto for the faces. Her technique reinforces the personal impact of the composition.

Mother and infant are intimately united by strong, rhythmic lines and recurring colors and shapes; the baby's shoulder, sleeve, and features echo the mother's. Formal means link the two with their natural setting of gently swaying birches, which for the artist had early symbolized young women.[29] The network of cool silvery tree trunks relates to the emphatic lines below, the light neutrals subtly harmonizing with the deeper shades. Warm earth tones predominate: the soft reds, ochers, burnt sienna, and umbers of local sand, earth, and freshly cut peat moss. The human group is one with nature, the mother is part of nature, an ideal which all the Worpswede artists sought but few realized so fully.

The precise dating of our painting is problematic, although it can best be related thematically and chronologically to two famous works in Hanover and Hamburg generally considered to be of 1903. In the Hanover painting, a gaunt peasant stares into space, preoccupied with her own thoughts, nursing her infant without joy; it could have been painted by Käthe Kollwitz as a protest against the many unwanted children of the poor. By contrast, our young woman gazes

17.
In the Paula Becker-Modersohn Haus, Roselius Collection, in Bremen. Frequently repr. in color: Bremen, 1976, no. 178, pl. 21; Stelzer, pl. 77.
18.
Modersohn-Becker, 183 and 197, with references to Degas, Daumier, Millet.
19.
Ibid., 242.
20.
Ibid., 57.
21.
Ibid., 249.
22.
Bremen, 1976, no. 91, fig. 42, also dated "03," and no. 92, also on wood. Number 136 is possibly somewhat later; nos. 176, 177, the drawing no. 360, and Pauli no. 30 lead up to the great no. 178 (Pauli, no. 27). Since the latter is such a mature accomplishment, it is generally dated, "around 1906," though a date of mid- or late 1905 appears more likely to me. It is quintessentially Worpswede in theme and somber style (Paula Modersohn-Becker was in Paris throughout 1906 and began to use a lighter palette); it is clearly indebted to van Gogh's *Berceuse,* frequently noted in the literature, hence it is interesting to know that *two* versions were shown

at the 1905 Indépendants which Paula Modersohn-Becker visited.
23.
Modersohn-Becker, 168 and 187.
24.
Modersohn-Becker, 1898, 61, 70.
25.
Ibid., 1900, 135.
26.
Ibid., 1900 and 1901, 128, 149.
27.
Ibid., May 1900, 111.

tenderly at the child at her breast. It is probably Modersohn-Becker's most loving image of motherhood, possibly signifying expectations about her own future role (from Paris she had written in March 1903 of recurring reveries about "babes in swaddling clothes, nursing, and so on"[30]). The other 1903 painting, in Hamburg, approximates our picture compositionally and may even portray the same young woman, judging by her profile and clothing. Somewhat awkward in execution and still indebted to Mackensen's example, it certainly precedes our version.

Because the *Mother and Child* shown here is clearly superior to these two paintings in the German museums, C. G. Heise concluded that it must have been finished later, perhaps after the 1905 trip to Paris. Yet there are already several studies dated 1903 that show the same amazingly spontaneous brushwork and bold simplification of forms. Predominantly warm earth tones and a special interest in people within nature, in women and children placed against trees, are now considered characteristic of Modersohn-Becker's 1903-4 production. Indeed, in one such study dated "03" a young peasant leaning against a birch tree strikingly resembles our young mother, even in such particulars as her red dress and hair style.[31]

Later in Paris, in 1906 and 1907, an Italian mother with a young child inspired Paula Modersohn-Becker to create again several outstanding paintings of her favorite motif. The series reaches an artistic climax with the nursing mother in Bremen (Becker-Modersohn Haus) who has ceased to be an ordinary individual and has become the very embodiment of a primitive life-giving force. Our picture, however, remains a masterpiece of Worpswede at midcareer and a warm human document of universal appeal.

117.
Old Peasant Woman Praying, ca. 1905
Oil on canvas
29¾ x 22¾ in. (75.5 x 57.7 cm.)
The Detroit Institute of Arts
Gift of Robert H. Tannahill (58.385)

This splendid portrait exemplifies Modersohn-Becker's highest achievement of her Worpswede years which had begun with drawings such as the one exhibited here (cat. no. 114). From the beginning, the painting was recognized as a masterpiece. It was reproduced in the earliest catalogs of her work, acquired in 1919 for the distinguished collection of modern art in the Kunsthalle Hamburg, and illustrated in Modersohn-Becker's letters and diaries, thus becoming one of her best-known paintings. The Nazis confiscated it in July 1937, during Operation *Entartete Kunst* ("Degenerate Art"), when they removed modern art from German public collections (and sold the best for valuable foreign currency). Since Modersohn-Becker did not idealize her peasant women and maternity figures, they were judged ugly, unfeminine, subversive.[32]

28.
All works are illustrated in Heise's excellent little booklet, *Paula Becker-Modersohn: Mutter und Kind,* Stuttgart, 1961, including Mackensen (fig. 2), the Hamburg (fig. 6) and Hanover (fig. 7) pictures, our version (fig. 8), and some related drawings. A very lovely charcoal drawing of a mother hugging her child, close to our painting in affectionate feeling, is reproduced in Stelzer, pl. 36. Illustration of the Hanover painting (no. 95, pl. 21) is also in Bremen, 1976, with extensive discussions of the mother and child theme and its religious implications.
29.
Modersohn-Becker, 1897, 25.
30.
Ibid., 194.
31.
See Bremen, 1976, no. 103, color pl. 18; color pl. 29 of the *Kneeling Mother and Child* in Bremen (no. 211) is far too light. Good discussion of Worpswede peasant and nature themes, people in nature, etc.
32.
See the literature below and Oppler, note 38.

The old peasant woman is seated in a dark interior that opens up to stylized green foliage lightened in a radiant halo around her head. Her hands are crossed on her chest in an ancient gesture of meditation and prayer;[33] their V-shape emphasizes the face itself. The wrinkled, weathered yellow skin, prominent nose, and heavy-lidded, melancholy eyes help identify this woman as a favorite model, perhaps, like old Dreebeen, from the poorhouse.[34] While it is a recognizable likeness, the face and figure are generalized, depicted in forceful outlines and broad paint application; we are again reminded of Modersohn-Becker's aim to achieve grandeur through simplicity.

The sprig of wild flowers in the woman's lap is an unexpected detail, although flowers frequently appear in the artist's portraits. They fulfill decorative or symbolical functions, as they do in contemporaneous *Jugendstil* works and in older art, such as Philipp Otto Runge's group portrait of his parents and children (1806) and his allegorical *Phases of the Day* — familiar paintings in the Kunsthalle Hamburg. Furthermore, wild or cultivated flowers were ever present in Modersohn-Becker's studio and in her writings, where she delighted in their seasonal beauty and recorded personal associations or traditional flower symbolism. The fragile blossoms in this portrait have been plucked from the fields and will soon fade and wither, in contrast to the robust leaves outside. Like the birch trees behind the mother and child (cat. no. 116), the little flowers and luxuriant foliage underscore the peasant woman's part in the eternal rhythm of the seasons, her patient endurance of growth and decline, her stoic acceptance of the passage of human life as well.

The devotional subject is unusual in Modersohn-Becker's work and one suspects that she was thinking of certain artistic prototypes:[35] the religious peasant pictures of Millet and of her teacher Mackensen (his award-winning canvas of outdoor worship, for instance); Wilhelm Leibl's famous *Three Women in Church* (1878-82); or Charles Cottet's triptych of Breton fishermen which she had admired in Paris. Perhaps she had also seen some of Gauguin's Breton peasant folk at prayer or works by his Pont-Aven circle; the heavy "synthetic" outlines indicate stylistic similarities. She has avoided certain defects that frequently occur when the sophisticated artist seeks to portray the primitive faith of "the noble peasant": images that appear patronizing, anecdotal, romantic, and sentimental. Modersohn-Becker has captured the old woman's dignified presence with respect and empathy. It is primarily the old peasant's personality that affects us; the artist, the outside observer, remains discreetly in the background.

Again we are reminded of van Gogh. Modersohn-Becker probably completed our portrait in 1905, the same year as the final version of *Old Woman from the Poorhouse in the Garden,* after returning from Paris where she had seen the van Gogh retrospective.[36] When Rainer Maria Rilke visited her at the end of that year, he was finally impressed by her work, and described her as "painting things that are very Worpswede-like, but which nobody has yet been able to see and to paint, and in this quite individual way, strangely approaching van Gogh and his tendency."[37]

118.
Still Life with Fruit and Flowers, ca. 1906-7
Oil on canvas
12 x 13¾ in. (30.5 x 34.9 cm.)
New York, Private Collection

Modersohn-Becker painted still lives throughout her career; this most personal of genres suited her temperament. In the privacy of her studio she could concentrate on problems of form and content, selecting objects to express purely artistic concerns or personal and symbolic meanings: a sensuous arrangement of tropical fruit or earthenware pottery with peasant bread and vegetables, or family heirlooms and a favorite necklace.

This still life which at first appears so simple is a rich play of dualities and opposites. Against the two-part division of the background in muted complementaries of dark blue and yellow, Modersohn-Becker has arranged two pieces of fruit, two vegetables, and two large flowers, as deliberately as figures in a chess game. The exotic orange and lemon balance the two locally grown deep red tomatoes below, creating a cross pattern with the flower vase. A tiny wild daisy mediates between the two showy, cultivated asters, their sharp pinks and lavenders presenting a daring contrast to the orange and dark red colors.

Cézanne's lessons of composition and the balancing of colors and shapes are still evident, but the colors are now heavy and dense, no longer modulated; space is flattened to appear almost two-dimensional and contours are simplified. Modersohn-Becker had been looking at paintings by the Gauguin circle, artists of the Pont-Aven school, the Nabis, and perhaps even the Fauves. The bright flowers express the very essence of *flower,* as if taken from a child's primer, suggesting yet another artist who at this very moment was being discovered by the French and German avant-garde: the Douanier Rousseau. Modersohn-Becker may have noticed his work at the Indépendants where he exhibited, as did the artists of the other groups mentioned. In 1906 she met Rousseau through Bernhard Hoetger, a German sculptor who emulated various exotic and primitive styles. She portrayed Hoetger's wife with a certain artless frontality, surrounded by a riot of brilliant flowers that could have been plucked from this still life or from a painting by Rousseau.[38]

Our still life is undated, but it may well have been painted during the final year of Modersohn-Becker's life when she rapidly took inspiration from several modern sources. Yet the picture does not look derivative nor especially complicated. Rather, it is haunting in its apparent simplicity — the quality toward which the artist worked throughout her life — a sophisticated work of art that appears naive.

33.
Probably taken not so much from life as from art, from Fra Angelico's *Annunciation,* for instance.
34.
The Kunsthalle Hamburg owned another fine portrait of this same woman, wearily resting her head on her hand, which also was confiscated in 1937 and reacquired in 1951 (Stelzer, fig. 27); a smaller head is in the von der Heydt Museum in Wuppertal (Pauli, nos. 70 and 98, with the comment that they depict the same woman as ours).
35.
See Bremen, 1976, for interesting discussion and comparative materials in the appendix, under "peasant life" and "life in nature." For Modersohn-Becker's religious compositions of 1907, possibly inspired by Bernard and Denis, see nos. 202, 203.
36.
For discussion of the problem of chronology, see entry for *Mother and Child* (cat. no. 116) and note 22 for *Old Woman from the Poorhouse* (cat. no. 115).
37.
Rilke's letter of January 15, 1906, to Karl von der Heydt, his new patron, who would later become an important collector of Modersohn-Becker's paintings.

38.
In the Becker-Modersohn Haus, Bremen, where there is also an important study of Lee Hoetger in a very different primitive style, close to Picasso's proto-Cubism even (pls. 33-35, Bremen catalog, with discussions of these various contacts: the Hoetgers, Rousseau, Nabis, etc.). For some examples of other late still lives that can be related to our version, see Bremen, 1976, pls. 26, 31, and the 1907 figure composition pl. 30 (all in color); also pl. 50.

115

116

117

118

Gabriele Münter
German, 1877-1962

The style and career of Gabriele Münter are closely bound up with the artistic innovations of the Blue Rider group in Munich and with the general atmosphere of vigorous creative activity that made that city a center for the avant-garde in the early years of the twentieth century. Yet although Münter's work is certainly a recognizable manifestation of Blue Rider ideas — the notion of color as an independent expressive element rather than a representational vehicle, for instance — nevertheless, her achievement of formal organization through color relationships, as well as her subjective yet controlled sensibility, brings her closer in some ways to the French Fauves, or to the Gauguin of Pont-Aven, than to the more abstract or expressive extremes of German Expressionism.[1]

Münter was born in Berlin to a German father who had emigrated to the United States, married the daughter of a fellow German emigrant there, and then returned to Germany at the time of the American Civil War. In 1897, at the age of twenty, she went to Düsseldorf where she studied first with an elderly painting teacher, then at the Ladies' Art School; women were still not admitted to the official Art Academy at that time. In 1898 she and an older sister traveled to the United States. On her return to Germany, in 1901, at the relatively advanced age of twenty-four, Munter set off for Munich and began studying art, although without deep conviction, at the School of the Association of Women Artists. In Munich, as in Düsseldorf, the leading art school — in this case, the Royal Academy — was closed to women. For a term she drew heads, chiefly under Angelo Jank, who was impressed by her work and quickly moved her up into the life class. Bored with traditional academic teaching, she became one of the first students to attend the avant-garde Phalanx School, which had been organized by Wassily Kandinsky in 1902. There she studied first with the sculptor Wilhelm Hüsgen (1877-1952) and then with Kandinsky himself, who was evidently a stimulating teacher. In Münter's own words: ". . . Kandinsky, quite unlike the other teachers, explained all problems thoroughly and intensely and accepted me as a human being with conscious aspirations and capable of setting herself tasks and aims."[2]

From the end of 1903 through 1908, Kandinsky (who had separated from his wife) and Münter traveled together, spending the period from 1906 to 1907 in Sèvres and visiting nearby Paris frequently. Both artists exhibited in the Salon des Indépendants and the Salon d'Automne; both must have been impressed by the bold formal innovations of the Post-Impressionists and the Fauves, especially the pure, openly brushed color of the latter.[3] Kandinsky and Münter also visited the Riviera, North Africa, Italy, Austria, and Switzerland. In 1908 they settled in Murnau, a picturesque village in the foothills of the Bavarian Alps, where they lived with Alexej Jawlensky and his companion, the painter Marianne von Werefkin (1860-1938), a couple with whom they remained closely allied. Jawlensky especially was imbued with ideas of Gauguin's Synthetism — the use of color and decorative shapes as expressive equivalents for responses to nature — and had also been greatly impressed by Matisse whom he had encountered in 1907.

In 1909 Kandinsky and Münter, Jawlensky and von Werefkin were among the artists founding the New Artists' Association of Munich, a group that also included Alfred Kubin. In 1911, after disagreement had arisen within this group, Kandinsky, Münter, Kubin, and Franz Marc withdrew, and in December of that year Kandinsky and Marc organized the first Blue Rider exhibition, named after the "Blue Rider Almanac," a publication containing folk and medieval art as well as avant-garde work. In addition to Kandinsky, Marc, and Münter, who showed six paintings, August Macke and the Frenchman Henri Rousseau participated in the first Blue Rider show, which was marked more by a variety of anti-naturalist styles than by any precise formal characteristics. Münter showed fourteen works in the second Blue Rider exhibition in 1912, a show that included a sizable number of works by Paul Klee, whom Münter was to represent in her *Man in an Armchair* (fig. 37, p. 59) of the following year. In 1913 she also took part in the momentous First German Autumn Salon in Berlin. When World War I broke out, Münter and Kandinsky left Munich for Switzerland and in 1915 went to Stockholm. In 1917 Kandinsky, who had returned to Russia, married a young woman

---

1.
S. Terenzio, "Gabriele Münter in 1908," *The William Benton Museum of Art Bulletin,* the University of Connecticut, Storrs, I, no. 3, 4.
2.
Undated note by Gabriele Münter, "Blue Rider" Archives, Städtische Galerie, Munich, cited in H. K. Röthel, *The Blue Rider,* New York, 1971.
3.
See Terenzio, *The William Benton Museum of Art Bulletin,* 9 and note 8.

there; his relation with Münter came to an end, as did the most interesting part of her career as an artist, although she continued to paint for many years afterward.

Münter, like other members of her circle, was deeply impressed by folk art and executed a certain number of *Hinterglasmalerei* ("under-the-glass paintings"), the earliest of which are copies of old Bavarian peasant works in this demanding technique, and the later ones her own inventions.[4]

In 1957, when she was eighty, Münter gave one hundred twenty early Kandinsky paintings and about thirty of her own to the Städtische Galerie of Munich, an impressive gift that enriched art historical knowledge of the evolution of the pre-1914 styles of both artists.[5]

119.
Portrait of a Young Woman, 1909
Oil on canvas
27⅝ x 19 in. (70.2 x 48.3 cm.)
Milwaukee Art Center
Gift of Mrs. Harry Lynde Bradley

Throughout her career, Gabriele Münter, in addition to painting many landscapes and some highly personal still lives, addressed herself to the subject of the human figure. Sometimes she might represent a group of friends out-of-doors, as in her *Jawlensky and Werefkin* (1908-9, Munich, Lenbachhaus), in which the couple reclines in a colorful landscape setting, or her *Boating* (1910, Milwaukee Art Center, Collection of Mrs. Harry Lynde Bradley), in which Kandinsky is represented standing in a boat, rowed by a woman and accompanied by another woman and a child. The latter composition recalls, if in greatly simplified form and with a woman substituted for the male rower, Mary Cassatt's *The Boating Party* (1893, Washington, D.C., National Gallery). At other times the figures are represented in an intimate, indoor setting, as in her *Kandinsky and Erma Bossi at the Table* (1912, Munich, Lenbachhaus), in which he is represented with raised hand, obviously making a point in a discussion with the woman artist, who listens attentively, with folded arms.

More often, though, the artist turned to the individual human subject, generally a friend, and often with a somewhat humorous effect: her *Listener (Portrait of Jawlensky)* of 1909 (Munich, Lenbachhaus) is almost a caricature in its drastic simplifications. Although she claimed that both her *Man at the Table (Kandinsky)* of 1911 (Munich, Lenbachhaus) and her *Man in an Armchair (Paul Klee)* (fig. 37, p. 59) of 1913 were intended primarily as studies of form, color, and mood rather than as individual likenesses, a strong sense of character and presence emerges from each canvas.[6]

Our painting, although more modest in scale, can perhaps best be compared with the artist's magisterial *Portrait of Marianne von Werefkin*, also of 1909, now in the Lenbachhaus in Munich.[7] In the latter, Münter portrayed her fellow artist, who had painted an intense, almost grotesque, *Self-Portrait* the year before,[8] in a magnificent, multicolored flowered hat and a violet scarf, against a gold background; the work is strangely reminiscent of, although less coloristically violent than, Henri Matisse's *Woman with the Hat (Mme. Matisse)* of 1905 (San Francisco, Haas Collection), which Münter might have seen or heard about during her stay in Paris. In our *Portrait of a Young Woman,* the sitter looks down and sideways rather than up and out; her costume is more severely tailored, and the color harmonies are somewhat less extreme than those of Münter's Werefkin portrait. Nevertheless, both works are characterized by similar degrees of abstraction and simplification of the human form into salient color areas and by the use of heavy black outline in place of modeling. In both works, as in all of Münter's best figure studies, a remarkable sense of authentic personality and poignant mood arises, almost unexpectedly, from the flattened surface of the canvas.

120.
The Green House, 1911
Oil on canvas
34¾ x 39½ in. (88.3 x 100.3 cm.)
Milwaukee Art Center
Collection of Mrs. Harry Lynde Bradley
(See color plate, p. 95)

Münter was devoted to the depiction of nature throughout her career: some of her most ingratiating works are landscapes. Among her earliest paintings of 1904 are several richly painted impressionistic landscape views. The scenery around Murnau especially inspired her, from the time she arrived there in 1908 — see, for example, her *View of the Murnau Marsh* of that year (Munich, Lenbachhaus)[9] — until the 1930s, in works like her *View of the Mountains* of 1934 (Munich, Lenbachhaus).[10]

Our painting is somewhat less lyrical and flowing, more rigid and centralized than some of her landscape canvases. The original composition — which plays off the strict frontality of the light turquoise house, with its blue green windows and brown roof, against the vigorous asymmetrical diagonals of the landscape forms in the foreground and the mountains behind — is reminiscent of Post-Impressionist landscapes, those of Cézanne and van Gogh above all; but the daring color combinations are decidedly Fauve or post-Fauve in their intensity. The combination of greens, yellow ochers, and blue violets recalls similar sharp-toned, offbeat harmonies in other of the artist's landscapes of the period: her *Houses on a Wintry Road* (1910-11, Milwaukee Art Center, Collection of Mrs. Harry Lynde Bradley), for example, or her *Village Street in Winter* (1911, Munich, Lenbachhaus).[11] In our work the starkness of the forms and the intensity of the colors are mitigated by the delicate silhouettes of the tree branches framing the little house, softening its intransigent rectangularity.

4.
See Gollek, 243-46, for reproductions of Münter's work in this medium.
5.
For an account of Münter's bequest and its implications in relation to Kandinsky's early style, see L. Eitner, "Kandinsky in Munich," *Burlington Magazine*, ic, June 1957, 193-98.
6.
For Münter's own account of the genesis of the latter work, in a letter to Dr. H. K. Röthel of 1950, see Munich, 1962, no. 67 and repr. 18.
7.
For a color repr., see Gollek, 70.
8.
The work is in the Lenbachhaus in Munich. See Gollek, repr. in color, 80.
9.
Gollek, color repr., 69.
10.
Ibid., color repr., 76.
11.
Ibid., color repr., 73.

119

Vanessa Bell
British, 1879-1961

"Fascinating, brilliant and formidable,"[1] Vanessa Bell was the older sister of novelist Virginia Woolf; the daughter of Sir Leslie Stephen, a prominent man of letters; and the great-niece of the Victorian photographer Julia Margaret Cameron. She studied art under Sir Arthur Cope, R.A., from 1899 to 1900, and then attended the Royal Academy Schools, working under Sargent from 1901 to 1904. Following the death of her father and a trip to Italy in the spring of 1904, Vanessa, her brothers Thoby and Adrian, and her sister Virginia established themselves at 46 Gordon Square; in so doing, they formed the nucleus of the so-called Bloomsbury Group, a loosely defined but often tightly knit circle of writers, artists, and intellectuals that made an enormous impact on British cultural life in the years before and after the First World War.

Vanessa Stephen married Clive Bell, art historian and aesthetician, in 1907; her two sons, Julian and Quentin, were born soon after, in 1908 and 1910 respectively. Another child, Angelica, was born in 1918. The artist traveled to Turkey in 1911 with her husband and Roger Fry, the most important apostle of European avant-garde art in England. Fry had organized the influential, and scandalous, First Post-Impressionist Exhibition at the Grafton Gallery in London in 1910-11, an exhibition that seems to have had a considerable effect on Bell's style, as it did on those of other British artists. In 1912 Bell herself exhibited four works in Fry's second Post-Impressionist show, along with a young friend, Duncan Grant, with whom she was to be associated for more than fifty years, and such modern masters as Braque, Cézanne, Derain, Vlaminck, Goncharova, Herbin, Larionov, Lhote, Matisse, and Picasso. Matisse, and perhaps Cézanne and Picasso as well, seems to have impressed her deeply; in fact, she made an oil sketch of the Matisses hanging in the Grafton Gallery.[2]

The increasingly daring abstraction of Bell's style in the years around 1914, including the production of a few totally abstract works, was no doubt affected by her participation in the decorative arts program of the Omega Workshops from 1913 to 1919. For the workshops, founded

1.
She is thus described by Denys Sutton in the introduction to the *Letters of Roger Fry*, New York, 1972, I, 47.
2.
London, 1964, 6.

by her friend Roger Fry, she designed screens, textiles, and a mosaic floor.[3] In addition, she designed embroideries for Mary Hogarth, carpets for Allan Walton, pottery for Foley China, and bookplates and illustrations, especially for her sister's works, for the Hogarth Press.[4]

The work of Vanessa Bell's early maturity (ca. 1910-20) "identifies her as one of the boldest innovators in British art of this century," in the opinion of Richard Morphet. This authority continues: "In these dramatic early years, no British artist's work represented more purely and outspokenly than hers and Duncan Grant's a fully fledged Post-Impressionism, carried to the point of total abstraction."[5] Landscape, figure studies, still lives, and portraits attracted her almost equally. Her style of this period, Fauvist in inspiration, was marked by a decorative inventiveness and free use of flat, often unmodulated, color areas. Bell's works from the late 1920s on tend to be more representational and less decorative yet equally, if not as overtly, controlled by underlying formal relationships. In the artist's own words: "It is . . . so absorbing, this painter's world of form and colour, that once you are at its mercy you are in grave danger of forgetting all other aspects of the material world."[6] Vanessa Bell died on April 7, 1961, at Charleston, her home in Sussex since 1916, which had provided inspiration for many of her paintings, as well as serving as a meeting place for those friends and family members who constituted the later flowering of the long-lived Bloomsbury circle.

121.
Street Corner Conversation, ca. 1913
Oil on board
27 x 20 in. (68.6 x 50.8 cm.)
London, Anthony d'Offay Gallery

The subject of this work, with its boldly simplified figures and angular composition, may have been inspired by the artist's trip to Italy in 1912, but its style certainly reflects the impact of the two Post-Impressionist exhibitions at the Grafton Gallery in London in 1910-11 and 1912-13. The sharp, uptilting perspective of the street to the right was anticipated in Bell's *Street Scene in Tuscany* (London, Anthony d'Offay) of 1912, and the abstract treatment of the figures in her *Bedroom, Gordon Square* (London, Anthony d'Offay) of the same year, both of which already reflected Matisse's Fauvism. Yet *Street Corner Conversation* is more audacious and more original than either of these works. The austere yet bold color combination — grays set off against oranges and ochers — may well suggest Picasso's palette of the early Cubist period. Indeed, the Spanish artist's *Still Life (Carafe and Bowl)* of 1908, then in Leo Stein's collection, now in the Museum of Modern Art in Moscow, was no. 60 in the Second Post-Impressionist Exhibition; the impact of this work is perhaps even more clearly evident in Bell's *Still Life on Corner of Mantelpiece* of 1914, now in the Tate Gallery.

Yet it is clearly Matisse, and Fauvism generally, that are most relevant to the general conception of the work: the expressive though impersonal use of color; the deliberate "crudeness" of the brushwork; the schematic treatment of the figures; and the planar intensification of the background. The Second Post-Impressionist Exhibition was particularly rich in Fauve works: in addition to more than thirty paintings by Matisse, including his *Conversation* of 1909, then in the Tschoukine Collection, it contained substantial contributions by Braque, Derain, Vlaminck, Friesz, Marquet, and Van Dongen. *Street Corner Conversation* also displays Bell's peculiar predilection for architectonic design, what Richard Morphet has called "her obsession with verticals," which "operates as one means of directing attention to a representational picture's equal reality as a two-dimensional design, tied to a flat, rectilinear surface."[7]

122.
Portrait of Iris Tree, 1915
Oil on canvas
60 x 48 in. (152.4 x 121.9 cm.)
London, Private Collection

The subject, a voluminous figure in a black dress, is seated on a brilliantly patterned sofa, with her hands folded on her lap. The painting would seem to reflect Matisse's portrait style of ca. 1906-10: for example, the *Young Sailor,* a version of which appeared in the Second Post-Impressionist Exhibition, or his *Portrait of Marguerite with a Black Cat* of 1910, also in the same show. In both paintings, the large, simplified, flattened forms of rather darkly clad sitters are placed against the foil of a bright, insistent background.

Iris Tree (1897-1968), the daughter of the famous actor Sir Beerbohm Tree, was a poet: she contributed to Edith Sitwell's *Wheels* anthology and published *Poems* in 1919, the latter having as its frontispiece a photograph of the *Head of Iris Tree* by the sculptor Jacob Epstein. Bell's *Portrait of Iris Tree* is one of three versions painted simultaneously by herself, Duncan Grant, and Roger Fry at 46 Gordon Square. Fry's version is now in the collection of his daughter, Mrs. Pamela Diamand. Grant's *Portrait of Iris Tree,* now in the Reading Public Museum and Art Gallery, is extraordinarily similar in conception to Bell's, although somewhat less bold in its decorative flattening of the human form: his version is also somewhat more three-dimensional, partly because the figure is turned slightly to the right and partly because the right arm is strongly foreshortened.[8] The same three friends had painted Lytton Strachey together in 1913.

Although not primarily a portraitist, Bell painted many portraits throughout her career, mainly of friends and relatives. Many of her subjects were important figures in their own right, and, for the most part, members of the Bloomsbury circle, conceived of in its largest sense. Her portraits reflect the change from her earliest, more naturalistic style, to the bold flattening, simplification, and decorative colorism of her more abstract period, to the lyrical, sometimes monumental, and often psychologically penetrating intimacy of her later works. Among those who sat to her were: Saxon Sydney-Turner; her sister, Virginia Woolf, most notably on a deck chair in 1912; Lytton Strachey; Helen Dudley; David Garnett; Duncan Grant;

3.
London, 1973, 15.
4.
London, 1964, 3.
5.
London, 1973, 5.
6.
Cited by Morphet, London, 1973, 11.
7.
London, 1973, 7-8.
8.
See London, Wildenstein & Co., Ltd., *Duncan Grant and His World,* 1964, no. 28, repr. 6.

Aldous Huxley; Roger Fry, depicted playing chess with Bell's son, Julian, ca. 1933; her brother-in-law, Leonard Woolf; and E. M. Forster. Among her most moving portraits are two of herself: one, with spectacles, looking out uncompromisingly at the spectator, of 1926 (New York, Collection Carolyn Heilbrun); the other, magisterial, now in the possession of Lord Clark, in which the artist, an old woman, has depicted herself in sun hat, shawl, and eyeglasses, of 1958.

121

122

Nataliia Sergeevna Goncharova
Russian, 1881-1962

Born in the Tula region of central Russia, Goncharova left in 1892 to study at the Fourth Gymnasium in Moscow; in 1897 she finished her secondary schooling and took courses in history, botany, and zoology for several months. At this time she also began to study painting and was admitted in 1898 to the Moscow School of Painting, Sculpture and Architecture, where she studied sculpture with a disciple of Rodin, Pavel Trubetskoi. In about 1900 she met Mikhail Larionov, a student of painting with whom she began to paint. In 1903 Goncharova completed her courses at the Moscow School, winning a gold medal for sculpture; then began the real flowering of her talent for painting. In 1903-6 her art reflected, as did Larionov's, Impressionism and Neo-Impressionism. In 1906 she sent four pastels to the exhibition of Russian painters organized by Serge Diaghilev at the Salon d'Automne in Paris. Although Goncharova did not accompany Larionov to Paris that year, as is sometimes thought, her work after 1906 does reflect the influence of Gauguin, Cézanne, and Matisse (especially after Matisse's visit to Russia in the autumn of 1911). She participated in numerous other exhibitions, including: The Wreath (Moscow, 1907-18); Link (Kiev, 1908); Golden Fleece (Moscow, 1908, 1909, 1909-10); Union of Youth (St. Petersburg, 1910, 1911, 1911-12, 1912-13); Jack of Diamonds (Moscow, 1910-11); the first Izdebsky Salon (showing only in St. Petersburg, 1910); the second Izdebsky Salon (Odessa, 1910-11); Donkey's Tail (Moscow, 1912); The Blue Rider (Munich, 1912); Roger Fry's Second Post-Impressionist Exhibition (London, 1912); the Herbstsalon at the Der Sturm galleries (Berlin, 1912, 1913); Target (Moscow, 1913); No. 4 (Moscow, 1914); Galerie Paul Guillaume (Paris, 1914); and The Year 1915 (Moscow, 1915). Goncharova also held large solo exhibitions in 1910 and 1913 (Moscow) and 1914 (Petrograd) which caused public scandals; in 1910 her works, especially the religious ones, were called pornographic, a charge that caused Mikhail Larionov to defend her in what is possibly his first published statement (signed M. L., in *Zolotoe runo,* no. 11/12, 1909, which actually appeared in 1910). Goncharova published her own statement at her second solo exhibition in Moscow, 1913 — the most complete showing of her art ever held (761

works). In 1912-13 she published graphics in Futurist booklets that expanded the concept of the illustrated book (the 1912 edition of Kruchenykh's *Igra v adu* [*Game in Hell*] and *Pustynniky* [*Hermits*], 1912; S. Bobrov's *Vinogradari nad lozami* [*Gardeners over the Vines*] and K. Bolshakov's *Le futur,* both 1913). In 1915 she and Larionov left Russia to work with Diaghilev on décor and costumes for his Ballets Russes, traveling with the company to Spain and Italy in 1916 and 1917, before settling permanently in Paris. Among the ballets Goncharova designed for Diaghilev are: "Le coq d'or," 1914; "Liturgie," unrealized, 1915; "España and Triana," unrealized, 1916; "Les noces d'aurore," 1922; "Les noces" and "La nuit sur le Mont Chauve," 1923; "L'oiseau de feu," 1926; "Légende," 1929. She continued to design for the theater, to paint, and to exhibit to the end of her life. After a period of neglect, her reputation is now growing throughout the world, and her work has been almost totally rehabilitated in the Soviet Union.

123.
Fishing, 1909
Oil on canvas
44 x 39¼ in. (112 x 100 cm.)
New York, Leonard Hutton Galleries

One of the three leaders of the Russian Neoprimitivist movement,[1] Goncharova, with Mikhail Larionov and David Burliuk, responded to the vitality of native arts and crafts and of the *lubok* print, a naive form of graphic art similar to the *images d'Epinal* in France. The three artists also acknowledged the importance of contemporary French art — the work of Gauguin, Matisse, and Henri Rousseau — to the Russian movement.[2] *Fishing* is a mature example of the blending of these two trends, Western and native, in Goncharova's work of the period. The theme from Russian peasant life is combined with the flat colors and thick outlines that characterize both Fauve paintings and *lubok* prints. That Goncharova was especially attracted to the decorative and monumental aspects of naive art[3] is evident in the strong composition and the glowing, vital colors of *Fishing.*

1.
For an evaluation of the Neoprimitivist movement in Russian art, see John E. Bowlt, "Neo-primitivism and Russian Painting," *Burlington Magazine,* CXII, 1974, 133-40.
2.
E. Eganbiuri (23) discusses Goncharova's primitivist peasant scenes and states: ". . . I would say they correspond to the work of Henri Rousseau, which introduced fable into the painterly formula."
3.
Goncharova, in a preface written with Larionov for the exhibition of native and Oriental art they organized in Moscow, 1913. The preface is commented on in Khardzhiev, 307.

123

Due to the existence of a similarly named Goncharova painting, it is somewhat difficult to pinpoint early exhibitions of this version of *Fishing,* and therefore difficult to date the work with complete certainty. The 1961 British Arts Council exhibition noted that the title of our version of *Fishing* is inscribed on the back of the canvas along with the artist's signature. Since this title is distinguishable in the original Russian from the title of the other version (*Rybnaia lovlia* and its variant *Lovlia ryby,* "Fishing," as distinct from *Rybolovy,* "Fishermen"), both titles are cited in the list of exhibitions. Due to this ambiguity, Eganbiuri's date of 1909 for a painting entitled *Fishermen* does not necessarily refer to this painting. Gray's date of 1910 for *Fishing,* though undocumented, is equally probable.[4]

124.
Portrait of Larionov, 1913
Oil on canvas
41½ x 31½ in. (105 x 78 cm.)
New York, Luis Mestre Fine Arts
(See color plate, p. 96)

In late 1912 Mikhail Larionov developed Rayism,[5] an optical theory built on the theories of Cubism, Futurism, and Orphism whose object was to render in colored line and texture the rays of light that the artist sensed between himself and the subject of his painting. These rays both emanated from the subject and were reflected by it, often producing complex intersections of these colored lines on the surface of the canvas.[6] The ultimate aim of depicting these light rays was to capture the various physical and psychological properties of a subject. In her *Portrait of Larionov,* Goncharova uses the Rayist style to portray him as the creator of a new dynamic mode of painting. Here, as in all of her Rayist paintings, she retains vestiges of a recognizable subject. Her *Portrait of Larionov* also incorporates features from naive Russian woodcut prints and from cartoons; for example, she has depicted the brim of Larionov's bowler hat twice, a device familiar in cartoons even today as a symbol of motion. Cubism, as it was then understood (i.e., as an attempt to represent an object on the painting surface by rendering it from different viewpoints), informed Goncharova's approach, but it is Cubism adapted to her particular, deliberately naive bias. Larionov's face is flayed and spread across the canvas like a primitive mask; his right eye merely suggested by a few crisp strokes and by the unmistakable arch of his brow; his mustache summarily rendered by seven quick stabs of paint. The ruddy strokes of nose and brow suggest a profile that is belied by the flesh-colored band that sweeps through it and across the canvas.

The most evanescent and puzzling areas of the canvas hug the corners: the brilliant red, yellow, and orange are set off against deep cobalt and black in the upper part of the canvas; these corners are Goncharova's pictorial signature as a Rayist painter. The light rays are evident in more modest form in the intersecting and tangential lines of the facial features and hat. The black and white shape in the lower left is open to numerous interpretations; whether newspaper or symbolic wing, what the form is does not matter so much as much as the fact that it is highly streamlined and dynamic.

4.
Gray's implication that *Fishing* was hung in the first Jack of Diamonds exhibition (Moscow, December 1910-January 1911) must yield to the painting's documented showing in the concurrent second Izdebsky Salon in Odessa. Gray, 1972, 127.
5.
The term usually encountered for this style, "rayonism" is a direct transcription from the French; the English translation of the Russian word *luchizm* is better rendered "rayist."
6.
M. Larionov. "Luchistaia zhivopis' " [Rayist painting], *Oslini Khvost i Mishen',* Moscow, 1913, 93, 98; translated by John E. Bowlt in *Russian Art of the Avant-Garde: Theory and Criticism 1902-1934,* New York, 1976, 96, 98.

Alexandra Exter
Russian, 1882-1949

Alexandra Exter (née Grigorovich) was a pioneer in modern abstraction whose reputation rests primarily upon her brilliant innovations in the field of scenic and costume design for the Russian theater. Her originality in this medium not only shaped and synthesized plastic and dramatic arts, but also defined the major part of theatrical design in the USSR during the 1920s. During the crucial years 1908-14, when a revolutionary new perspective was developing in the plastic arts, Exter played an important role as liaison between the Parisian and Russian avant-garde movements. Her contribution to twentieth-century vision was greater than her reputation might indicate, and it is only in recent years that an assessment of her work as a whole has been attempted.[1]

Born in Bielostock, Exter grew up in the conservative city of Kiev in a milieu that encouraged intellectual originality and artistic creativity. In 1906, when she had completed her training at the Kiev Academy of Fine Arts, she began a lifelong commitment to the newest and most advanced art currents. She associated with artists, poets, and composers in advanced circles in Moscow and St. Petersburg, exhibiting in Moscow in 1907 with Larionov, Goncharova, and the Burliuk brothers in a show called The Wreath, which was to serve as a model for group exhibitions of the Russian avant-garde for the next decade. In 1908 she and David Burliuk organized the street exhibition Zveno in Kiev, which included the work of The Wreath artists as well as other little-known painters, including Lentulov, Denisov, and Fonvisin. Her work at this time was devoted to delicate, tonal landscapes, French in feeling and related to the Symbolist currents present in the work of advanced Moscow painters. It was also in 1908 that she married her cousin, Nikolai Eugenovich Exter, a wealthy lawyer, and made her first trip to Paris. There she worked for a short time at the Académie de la Grande Chaumière, receiving instruction from the portraitist Carlo Delvall, but her temperament very quickly led her to abandon academic pursuits for more challenging directions.

She came to know Picasso, Max Jacob, and Apollinaire in the Soirées de Paris, a salon for the avant-garde of Munich, Rome, Moscow, and Barcelona that was financed by the collectors Serge Jastrebloff (Férat), whom Exter had known in Kiev, and the Baroness d'Oettinger. She also developed a close friendship with Ardengo Soffici, who was later active in Italian Futurist circles, and with Fernand Léger, in whose Académie d'Art Moderne she taught Constructivist theatrical décor from the time she settled permanently in France in 1924 until the early '30s. Between 1908 and the beginning of World War I, Exter traveled regularly between Kiev, Moscow, St. Petersburg, and Paris, bringing photos and publications of Russian Futurism to the West; she also traveled to Italy in 1912. She participated regularly in Russian group exhibitions such as the Union of Youth (1908-14) and Tramway v (1915) in St. Petersburg and the Moscow Jack of Diamonds, as well as in the Salon des Indépendants and the Salon de la Section d'Or (1912) in Paris, and in the Free Futurist exhibition in Milan (1914). In Moscow she was considered the emissary of Parisian Cubism, contributing illustrations to Russian Cubo-Futurist manifestos until 1916 and introducing members of the Russian avant-garde such as Liubov Popova and Nadezhda Udaltsova into the French Cubist circles of Le Fauconnier and Metzinger. It was also through Exter's efforts that Goncharova and Larionov came to know Apollinaire and the Parisian Cubists.

In 1910 and 1911 Exter worked in the monochromatic palette and formal vocabulary of Analytical Cubism. Influenced by the Futurists and Léger and the robust sensibility of her Russian heritage, she then turned to boldly colored cityscapes, composed in broad geometrical planes and wedges. Between 1912 and 1916 she worked in a variety of styles and media, making collages, easel paintings, and spatial constructions.[2] Whether producing theatrical designs or illustrations for literary works such as I. A. Aksenov's *Picasso and His Circle* (1917) and Futurist poetry and theory,[3] the problem of controlling dynamic, disjunctive, non-narrative forms in a formal equilibrium was basic to her stylistic experiments. Her work grew increasingly abstract and, under the influence of Malevich and Tatlin, she took the final step to

1.
See Paris, 1972.
2.
Hilton, 34-39, 56-62.
3.
For the illustration for the cover of the Aksenov book see Paris, 1972, 12.
Futurist poetry and theory illustrated by Exter in 1914 was Benedict Livsic's *Wolves' Sun* and *Moloko Kobylic*.
4.
New York, 1975.

non-objective painting at the close of 1915.

Exter's return to Russia at the beginning of World War I marks the start of her association with the anti-Realist theater and particularly with the director Alexander Tairov, with whom she was to collaborate in several radical theatrical productions. In his Kamerny Theatre, which opened in Moscow in December 1914 with curtains designed by Exter, Tairov strove for non-literary, extemporaneous theater and the creation of a dramatic arena in which a dynamic interaction between audience and stage would occur. For his 1916 production of Inokenti Annenski's *Famira Kifared,* Exter created a theatrical ambience in which minimally costumed actors, painted to underline their natural musculature, were set into a scenic construction of suspended three-dimensional geometrical forms, animated by electrical motors and saturated with continuously moving colored lights. The impression of dynamic living reliefs achieved by this integration of setting and actors was hailed by avant-garde critics as a true revolution. Exter worked with Tairov in the fall of 1917 on a production of Oscar Wilde's *Salome* and again in May 1921 on *Romeo and Juliet.* For each production she sought a distinct unity of form, color, movement, and sound in a non-representational space.

From 1917 until 1924 Exter taught non-objective painting in Odessa, designed for the Moscow Atelier of Fashions and for the Moscow Children's Theatre, and began work on the symbolic science fiction film *Aelita* (see cat. no. 127), for which she employed a variety of metallic and synthetic materials related to the kinetic sculpture of Naum Gabo. Her easel painting became increasingly experimental, and construction her primary artistic activity.

Exter continued to work as a Constructivist artist in Paris from 1924 until her death in 1949 at Fontenay-aux-Roses. She worked in experimental film with the Russian poet Evreinov in the late twenties, made marionettes intended as *dramatis personae* for an unrealized film by Peter Gad in 1929, continued to exhibit and to teach, and published a book of stage designs in 1930.[4] She knew the major avant-garde figures in all the arts, worked closely with many, and continued, until the end of her life, to originate and create in a plastic vocabulary equally rich in both two- and three-dimensional forms.

125.
Grapes in a Vase, 1913
Collage and oil on canvas
20⅛ x 24 in. (51.1 x 61 cm.)
Labeled and signed by the artist on the back of canvas
New York, Leonard Hutton Galleries

Grapes in a Vase, one of Exter's several collages of the years 1913-15, assimilates Parisian Cubist currents with a bold colorism distinctly Russian in character. Broad forms consisting of wedges and planes of flat, opaque color are combined with newspaper fragments and stenciled letters to shape the still life. Along with *Still Life with*

125

126

Bottle and Glass, 1913,[5] and *Wine,* 1914,[6] the composition differs
from Western Cubist work in its jewellike color, lack of transparency,
and greater breadth of planes. Exter has organized her forms in a
tightly structured composition that generally adheres to the vertical-
horizontal axes of the canvas; the diagonal forms to the right of the
composition, controlled and contained by the shape of the canvas,
suggest her Futurist affinities of the same period. The subject matter
of *Grapes in a Vase* conforms to Cubist paintings by Braque and
Picasso of 1912-13; the composition is strongly allied to Braque's
collage of September 1912, *Still Life with Fruit Dish and Glass.*[7]

A series of cityscapes, more dynamic in movement but equally
controlled compositionally, exist from this same period. One such
work, *Town with Flags,* 1913,[8] recalls in subject and arrangement of
forms the explosiveness of Futurist compositions and Robert
Delaunay's experiments in simultaneous colors in his window and
city paintings of 1909-12. Surface-depth tensions, weight and rhythms
of color, tight construction, and the formal control of moving
energies which, after 1915, were detached from representation, are
already suggested in Exter's work of 1913-14.[9]

Grapes in a Vase affirms Exter's cosmopolitanism and dedication to
avant-garde ideas, but it does not yet establish the free and infinite
space nor the dynamic, architectonic constructivism that were to
mark both her painting and theater design from 1915 onwards.

126.
*Costume for "Entremeses" (?), Farcical interludes, by Cervantes,
project for the Moscow Art Theater,* 1921
Pencil on paper
17¾ x 14½ in. (45 x 37 cm.)
New York, Luis Mestre Fine Arts
127.
Costume for the Protozanov film "Aelita," 1924
Gouache on paper
19 x 12 in. (48 x 30 cm.)
New York, Luis Mestre Fine Arts

Exter's designs were instrumental in transforming Russian theater
décor and costumes in the 1920s. Rejecting the archeological and
ethnographic exactitude achieved by "World of Art" designers like
Golovin and Bakst, Exter instead focused attention on the material
construction of space in the theater. In this design for the costume of
the chief of atomic power in Protozanov's Martian fantasy, *Aelita,*
Exter has expressed twentieth-century concepts in contemporary
materials — celluloid and metal sheeting. Still photos of the finished
film indicate that the costumes were entirely successful in conveying
the impression of robots and machine men. In our second costume
design, the amusing contrast of massive forms with extremely thin
ones conveys a sense of the comic, almost of the grotesque, like that
found in another sketch[10] for an unrealized production of Cervantes'
Entremeses, on which Exter was working in 1921.

127

5.
Repr. in New York, 1971, no. 17, 34.
6.
Ibid., no. 18, 35.
7.
Repr. in Edward Fry, *Cubism,* New York, no. 38, 112.
8.
Repr. in Compton, 101.
9.
See nos. 19, 20, 21, 22, *Colored Tension, Colored Contrasts, Colored Rhythm,*
and *Colored Rhythm* in New York, 1971, 36ff.
10.
No. 8 in the New York Public Library catalog for *Artist of the Theatre:
Alexandra Exter,* repr. 27.

Sonia Delaunay
French, b. 1885

Throughout a long and productive career, Sonia Delaunay has contributed not only to the art of painting, but has made significant innovations in the decorative arts as well. In both areas, to borrow the words of Arthur A. Cohen, "The liberation of color is the theme of her creativity."[1]

Born into a Jewish family in the Ukraine, Sonia was adopted in 1890 by her maternal uncle, Henry Terk, and lived in his cultivated household in St. Petersburg. Her artistic education began at the age of eighteen, when, in 1903, she traveled to Karlsruhe to study for two winters under the academic draftsman Ludwig Schmidt-Reutte (1863-1909). She arrived in Paris in 1905, with four other young Russian women, and studied there at the Académie de la Palette, where she met a group of youthful innovators, including Amédée Ozenfant and André Dunoyer de Segonzac. By 1907, influenced by folk art, Gauguin, van Gogh, and the Fauves — perhaps Matisse above all — she was creating strong, original paintings in the Fauve manner, works like her *Philomène* (Paris, Collection the artist), in which the flattened, red-bloused figure is sharply outlined against a decorative, brilliantly flowered wallpaper. She met Picasso, Braque, Derain, and Vlaminck in 1908, and encountered the work of the Douanier Rousseau the same year. She contracted a marriage of convenience in 1909 with the art critic Wilhelm Uhde, who had organized her first one-woman exhibition at his gallery on the rue Notre-Dame-des-Champs the previous year. She was not to exhibit her paintings again until 1953.[2] She had met the painter Robert Delaunay in 1907 and, after divorcing Uhde, married him late in 1910. Their mutually supportive relationship was paralleled, in the field of the arts, perhaps only by that of Jean Arp and Sophie Taeuber-Arp, who were later to become their close friends. With the birth of the Delaunay's son, Charles, in 1911 came another stimulus to Sonia's artistic inventiveness: she designed a baby blanket out of bits of colored fabric, like those of Russian peasants, which seemed to her to evoke Cubist conceptions — "and we tried then to apply the same process to other objects and paintings."[3]

By 1912 the poet Guillaume Apollinaire had baptised Robert Delaunay's coloristic, light-filled Cubism "Orphism" and Sonia Delaunay had painted her first "simultaneous" works (cat. no. 128). For the Delaunays and their friends, Simultanism — at once an art style, a theory, and a way of life — was the very essence of the modern, involving a harmonic unity of abstract, or nearly abstract, forms, color, and motion. Sonia Delaunay applied their discoveries not only to painting, but to pastels, collages, and book bindings as well. In 1913, a key year in her, and Robert's, career, she collaborated with the poet Blaise Cendrars (b. 1887) on the creation of the first Simultaneous book, *La Prose du Transsibérien et de la Petite Jehanne de France (The Prose of the Trans-Siberian and the Little Jehanne of France)* (cat. no. 129). In addition, she created Simultaneous dresses and other articles of clothing that she and her husband wore to the popular Bal Bullier, a nightspot frequented by artists and poets that in turn inspired her to create an enormous — $38^3/_{16}$ by $153^9/_{16}$ inches — colorful, friezelike semi-abstract painting (Paris, Musée National d'Art Moderne),[4] as well as numerous smaller studies of this theme. In the same year she exhibited at the Berlin Autumn Salon, where her "cubist" book bindings may have influenced Paul Klee to move in the direction of greater abstraction.[5] One critic, Michel Hoog, has recently suggested that by creating brilliantly colorful works like the *Bal Bullier* in 1913, Sonia Delaunay led her husband back to the creative possibilities of color that were to mark his subsequent — and highly influential — art and theoretical writing.[6]

At the 1914 Salon des Indépendants, Sonia Delaunay exhibited her other major work of the period, *Electric Prisms* (fig. 45, p. 65), presumably inspired by the halo of moving colors radiating from electric light globes, an effect that had earlier inspired Blaise Cendrars to create his "Nineteen Electric Poems." At the outbreak of the First World War, the Delaunays left France and did not return until 1920. They visited Spain but settled down in Portugal for most of their exile. Both countries inspired Sonia Delaunay to create a series of

1.
Cohen, 16.
2.
For discussion of the reasons why she did not exhibit, see Cohen, 37, and Nemser, 38.
3.
Cited in Cohen, 49-50.
4.
Repr. in Damase, 74-75.
5.
Cohen, 167.
6.
"In 1910, when Robert was getting a bit lost in a monochrome cubism in which he did not feel at ease, it was the presence of his wife, in our opinion, which led him back to color. The language, so innovative in every way, of the *Bal Bullier* (1913) of Sonia, seems indeed a direct preparation for that which Robert was to develop in the *Merry-Go-Round with Pigs, Blériot,* or *The Cardiff Team.*" M. Hoog, introduction to *Robert Delaunay (1885-1941)*, Orangérie des Tuileries, Paris, 1976, 17 (my translation).

paintings on Iberian themes, subjects like flamenco singers (cat. no. 130), the market at Minho, and Portuguese still lives. In addition, she executed four projects for a semi-abstract religious work, never carried out: an *Homage to the Donor,* for the Jesuit Convent of Valença do Minho, in 1916.

After the Russian Revolution wiped out her income in 1917, Sonia Delaunay increasingly concentrated on commercial projects, including costume and fabric design and interior decoration. In 1918 she designed the costumes for Serge Diaghilev's revival of the ballet "Cléopâtre"; in 1919, she executed the interiors for the Petit Casino in Madrid. Upon their return to Paris in 1920, the Delaunays became friendly with members of the Surrealist group, including André Breton, Louis Aragon, Philippe Soupault, René Crevel, and the Dadaist Tristan Tzara. Sonia executed the costumes for Tzara's scandalous theater performance, *Le coeur à gaz,* in 1923.

From the mid-twenties on, Sonia Delaunay became more and more involved with fashion and textile design, establishing an atelier for the creation of Simultaneous fabrics and woven-tapestry coats in 1924, the year she created the costumes for Joseph Delteil's poem, "The Coming Fashion," which was presented with her costumes at the Hotel Claridge in Paris. The next year, at the famous Exposition des Arts Décoratifs — the "Art Deco" Show — she and the couturier Jacques Heim presented their joint creations in a boutique; her Simultaneous fabrics were subsequently exhibited at the Salon d'Automne. Sonia Delaunay voiced her strong feelings about the interaction of art, contemporary fashion design, and democracy in a lecture she delivered at the Sorbonne in 1927. A few years later, in 1932, she published some of her ideas on the subject in an article for Jacques Heim's *Les artistes et l'avenir de la mode (Artists and the Future of Fashion),* in which she predicted the success of imaginative mass-produced, ready-to-wear clothing and the resultant democratization of aesthetic values.[7]

In 1936-37 the Delaunays were commissioned to execute large mural paintings for the Palais de l'Air and the Pavillon des Chemins de Fer, with the cooperation of fifty unemployed artists, at the Paris Exposition of 1937, an undertaking for which she received a gold medal from the government. Shortly before this time, she had begun once more to concentrate on painting. After the death of her husband in 1941, Sonia Delaunay continued to develop as a painter as well as to devote considerable attention to the consolidation of the oeuvre and theoretical contributions of her husband. She held her first major solo exhibition since 1908 at the Galerie Bing in Paris in 1953 and has continued to show her works with great frequency ever since in museums and art galleries throughout the world. In 1964 she donated 117 works by herself and Robert Delaunay to the Musée National d'Art Moderne in Paris. Her most recent achievements have included large-scale tapestries woven at Aubusson, book illustrations, gouaches, and drawings, as well as oil paintings.

The protean, yet stylistically consistent career of Sonia Delaunay deserves, and certainly has received, consideration as a major contribution to twentieth-century modernism. Although a few critics have tended to belittle her achievement because of her involvement and commercial success in the decorative arts, such a narrow construction of her status is highly questionable. As Arthur Cohen has put it: "Delaunay's decision to apply the principles of abstract art to the redecoration of modern life, at the same time as it withdrew her from any tutelary relation to her husband, expanded the horizon and possibilities of modern art."[8]

128.
Simultaneous Contrasts, 1912
Oil on canvas
21⅝ x 17¹⁵⁄₁₆ in. (55 x 45.5 cm.)
Paris, Musée National d'Art Moderne

Although relatively small in scale, *Simultaneous Contrasts* is a fine example of the effort to achieve a dynamic equilibrium of light and color with circular or disclike abstract — or nearly abstract — forms that occupied both Delaunays from 1911 to 1914. The title of the work derives ultimately from Michel Chevreul's *Concerning the Laws of the Simultaneous Contrast of Colors* of 1839, a scientific treatise on the interaction of colors that had most recently exerted considerable influence on the Neo-Impressionists, as well as on the Delaunays and their circle. Although the conception of the painting is related to that of Robert Delaunay's *The First Disc* (1912, Meriden, Connecticut, Tremaine Collection) and his series of *Circular Forms* of 1912-13,[9] Sonia Delaunay's approach to the abstract formulation of color-movement on the plane surface of the canvas is more lyrical and less systematic than Robert's.

The investigations of coloristic abstraction undertaken in *Simultaneous Contrasts,* painted early in 1912, come to a climax in major works such as the *Bal Bullier* of 1913 (Paris, Musée National d'Art Moderne) and its related studies. In the monumental *Bal Bullier,* the abstract movement of pure pigment, characteristic of the earlier canvas, is penetrated by the swaying rhythms of boldly simplified human forms, or rather, of colored shapes and planes that suggest the movement and excitement of the patrons of the popular Montparnasse dancehall. In *Electric Prisms,* on the other hand, the culminating work of 1914 (fig. 45, p. 65), the square format tends to emphasize the abstract circularity of the broken-colored haloes of light, with their glittering transparencies and dynamic intersections. The sense of constructive artifice in this work is underscored by the insertion of a reduced replica of a poster advertising Delaunay's and Cendrars' *Prose du Transsibérien* (cat. no. 129), a use of the printed word in painting as a witty reminder of the conventional nature of both pictorial and verbal signs that is reminiscent of the slightly earlier Cubist works by Picasso and Braque.

7.
Cited in J. Damase, ed., *Robes et gouaches simultanées, 1925: L'art et le corps, rythmes-couleurs en mouvement,* Brussels, 1974, 44 and 46.
8.
Cohen, 82.
9.
See Paris, Orangérie des Tuileries, *Robert Delaunay, 1885-1941,* 1976, 69-74, for discussion and reproduction of these important paintings.

128

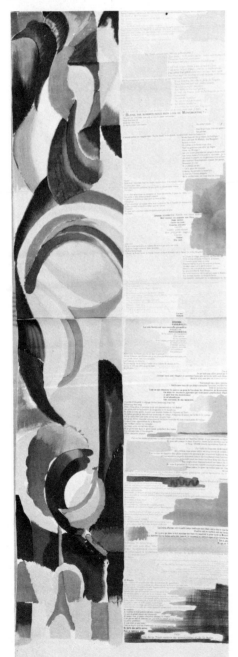

129

129.

Decoration for "La prose du Transsibérien et de la Petite Jehanne de France" (The Prose of the Trans-Siberian and the Little Jehanne of France) by Blaise Cendrars, 1913
Gouache and ink on printed text
81½ x 13⅞ in. (204.5 x 35.2 cm.)
New York, The Museum of Modern Art

The poem of Blaise Cendrars with Simultaneous color by Sonia Delaunay ("Delaunay-Terk" in the title) is indeed "one of the early miracles of the modern movement in poetry, painting, and design," to quote from Arthur Cohen's perceptive analysis of this work.[10] Innovative artists and writers had already been testing the conventional barriers separating the meanings of works from their physical existence as forms on a surface. Both Stéphane Mallarmé in his *Un coup de dés jamais n'abolira le hasard (A Throw of the Dice Never Will Abolish Chance)* of 1897 and the Futurists had gone far in radical typographical innovation, as, in a more overtly pictorial way, had — and would — the Delaunay's friend, the poet and art-theorist Guillaume Apollinaire, in his verbally and visually experimental *Calligrammes* (ca. 1913-16).

La prose du Transsibérien, however, constituted a unique undertaking. Cendrars, a close friend and admirer of Apollinaire's, had met Sonia Delaunay at the beginning of 1913; shortly afterwards, following a reading of Cendrar's *Les Pâques (Easter),* in the Delaunay home, she bound a copy of the text in the poet's presence with an abstract collage binding intended as a visual equivalent of the poem.[11] It was probably as a result of this action that the two decided on a more complex and innovative mode of collaboration, which yielded the "first Simultaneous book."

The very form of the book is original: the long poem is printed on a single sheet of paper that unfolds to a length of about 6½ feet. At the top left is the equivalent of a title page; to the right, a map of the route of the Trans-Siberian railway, the purported theme of the evocative, free-flowing text. The text itself unfolds on the right-hand side of the continuous central fold in a richly variegated typographical composition. The poet and artist collaborated on the typography, using twelve type faces in different colors that at times are linked together or interrupted by blocks of pigment. The artist's equally innovative abstract composition runs down the left-hand side of the sheet: in no sense can Delaunay's colorful, dynamic inventions be considered "illustrations" to the text, although the energies of the words and painting are carefully calibrated to match or contrast with each other. The curvilinear formal movement unfolds from an ethereal blue and green arc at the top down to a brilliant red Eiffel Tower at the bottom, an image that corresponds with the reference to Paris in the closing lines of the poem itself. The Eiffel Tower was, of course, a favored image — suggestive of both Paris and modernity — with the Delaunays and their friends. Robert Delaunay had done a series of thirty paintings

---

10.
Cohen, 32.
11.
This binding was exhibited at the Berlin Autumn Salon of this year, where it impressed Paul Klee. Cohen, 28.

based on the Eiffel Tower beginning in 1909, including the *Red Tower* of 1911,[12] and had represented the structure prominently in the background of his summarizing *La Ville de Paris* of 1912 (Paris, Musée National d'Art Moderne); Apollinaire had constructed the words of one of his "calligrammes" in the shape of the tower, with "O Paris" at its center;[13] and Sonia Delaunay made red Eiffel Tower designs intended as letterheads for the Delaunays' personal writing paper in 1913, the same year that she executed her paintings for *La prose du Transsibérien.*[14]

The book was published in an edition of 150, of which only 62 were evidently assembled, the printed text being attached to a *pochoir* (a stencil process for making colored prints) binding. As an ultimate, witty homage to the Eiffel Tower, the two collaborators intended that the complete assembled edition, laid end to end, would reach the top of that edifice![15] Unfortunately, the project was not a commercial success at the time, although today examples are much sought after.

The poem-painting was, however, highly regarded in the avant-garde circle in which Cendrars and the Delaunays played such an important role. In the words of Apollinaire: "Blaise Cendrars and Mme. Delaunay-Terk have realized a unique experiment in simultaneity, written in contrasts of colors in order to train the eye to read with one glance the whole of a poem, as an orchestra conductor reads with one glance the notes placed up and down on the bar, as one sees with a single glance the plastic elements printed on a poster."[16]

130.
The Flamenco Singer (The Large Flamenco), 1916
Oil, sizing, and encaustic on canvas
68½ x 56¾ in. (174 x 144 cm.)
Paris, Collection the artist
(See color plate, p. 97)

After the relative abstraction of the works of about 1911 to 1914, Sonia Delaunay's canvases of her Spanish and Portuguese period are marked by a return to representation of a sort, or, more exactly, a kind of adaptation of Simultanism to Iberian intensities of mood and local color. In both the large *Market at Minho* (Paris, Musée National d'Art Moderne), created in Portugal in 1915, for which there exist several studies, and in this work, presumably inspired by Madrid, the costumes and customs, even a little folkloric naïveté, seem to have been absorbed into the pictorially sophisticated world of Simultanism.

In the *Market at Minho,*[17] for example, through the judicious addition of horns and legs, a "Simultaneous disc" becomes a cow seen head on. In *The Flamenco Singer* a guitar is suggested by the familiar, multicolored, circular targetlike bands; it is as though the actual performers grew organically from the abstract discs of color at the heart of the painting, discs of color whose energy fades in intensity and brilliance as they move away from the center of activity toward the margins of the work. The interaction of the circular rhythms of color in this canvas becomes a visual equivalent for the sensual movements — whirling, stretching, and clapping — and the pulsating, haunting melodies of this highly stylized form of Spanish folk culture.

There exists another version of this subject, far more representational and expressionist in character, known as *The Small Flamenco* (35¹³/₁₆ x 35¹³/₁₆ inches), painted in Madrid (?) in 1915 (Paris, Collection the artist) in the same wax medium that Delaunay used for the large version.[18] In the smaller work, the singer and his female companion are shown as definite personalities, and their vigorous expressions, achieved through bold exaggerations of color contrasts and forms, are not so far from those of figures executed by a Blue Rider artist like Jawlensky, with whom the Delaunays were certainly acquainted. There exist several studies for these works, like the watercolor and gouache *Flamenco Singers* of 1916 (private collection), in which the theme is again almost entirely reduced to equivalences of abstract color movement, or the similarly non-objective gouache of 1916, *The Dancer* (Paris, Musée National d'Art Moderne, Donation Delaunay); there also exist some more representational watercolors of the dancer theme executed during this period. The artist had in fact turned to the subject of flamenco singers as early as 1913, in a charming, effervescent pastel (New York, Collection André Emmerich), and of course had been preoccupied with dance themes, though of a somewhat different kind, in both her *Bal Bullier* and *Tango Magic-City* paintings of that year. With its palpitating motion, its transformation of static color into visual energy, the dance was a theme of long-lasting appeal to Sonia Delaunay.[19]

12.
Paris, Orangérie des Tuileries, *Robert Delaunay, 1885-1941,* 1976, no. 30, repr. 55, and 56-57.
13.
See G. Apollinaire, "2e Canonnier Conducteur," *Calligrammes,* in *Oeuvres poétiques,* ed. M. Adéma and M. Décaudin, Paris, 1956, 214.
14.
See Damase, repr. 365-67, of which one is dated 1914.
15.
Cohen, 30-31.
16.
G. Apollinaire, June 15, 1914, *Les soirées de Paris,* cited by Cohen, 35.
17.
See Damase, 108-9, for a color repr. For a study of this painting, see Charles Georg, *Le marché au Minho de Sonia Delaunay,* Geneva, 1965.
18.
Repr. Damase, 116.

19.
The hot wax method employed by Sonia Delaunay in the *Flamenco Singer* enabled her to achieve great strength and brilliance of color. Although she had learned the technique from the Mexican painter Angel Zarraga in Paris, she did not use it until her stay in Spain and Portugal (Cohen, note 65, 95).

Marie Laurencin
French, 1885-1956

131

Born in Paris, Marie Laurencin was an illegitimate only child who never knew the identity of her father. She maintained an extremely close relationship with her mother, with whom she lived until the latter's death in 1913. Laurencin was educated at the Lycée Lamartine and studied drawing at the Académie Humbert, where she met Georges Braque. In 1907 Picasso recommended her as a fiancée to the poet Guillaume Apollinaire, who subsequently met her in the shop of the art dealer Clovis Sagot. The objections of Apollinaire's mother to Laurencin's illegitimacy (ironic in light of the fact that Apollinaire himself was illegitimate) prevented them from marrying, but they had a long and stormy love affair. Laurencin inspired some of Apollinaire's best-known poems, including "Le Pont Mirbeau," a reflection on lost love, and "Le poète assassiné," in which she appears in the guise of Tristouse Ballerinette. Henri Rousseau commemorated their relationship in a full-length double portrait entitled *The Poet and His Muse,* painted in 1909.[1] Laurencin's friendship with Apollinaire provided her entrée into the Cubist circle, and Apollinaire used his prominence as an art critic to promote her work. In his 1913 treatise, *Les peintres cubistes: Méditations esthétiques,* he classified her as a "scientific cubist," although her naive and decorative style bore little resemblance to the work of the other Cubists. Laurencin acknowledged her debt to Apollinaire in a pen and ink drawing entitled *Apollinaire Teaching Me,* executed in 1907-8.[2]

By 1913 the affair with Apollinaire was waning, and in June 1914 Laurencin married Otto von Waetjen, an aristocratic German painter working in Paris. During their honeymoon on the Atlantic coast, France declared war with Germany and Laurencin, technically a German by virtue of her marriage, escaped across the border into Spain, where she and her husband settled in Barcelona. There she encountered a set of exiles from the war, including Albert Gleizes, Max Goth, and Francis Picabia. An accomplished poet as well as a painter, Laurencin contributed illustrations and poems to the first four issues of *391,* Picabia's Dada review. The alienation she felt among the exiles in Barcelona and her deep depression during this prolonged

1.
First version, Museum of Modern Art, Moscow; second version, Kunstmuseum, Basel.
2.
Collection of Mme. Pierre Roché, repr. in Steegmuller, 162.

separation from Paris are expressed in several of the poems in her *Petit bestiaire*, published in 1926.

By 1920 she had divorced her husband and returned to her native city. There she began a successful career as a designer, providing illustrations for many books, including André Gide's *La tentative amoureuse*, published in 1921, and a deluxe edition of Lewis Carroll's *Alice in Wonderland*, published in Paris by the Black Sun Press in 1930. As a member of the circle surrounding the avant-garde young French composers called "The Six," she designed the sets and costumes for the 1924 Ballets Russes presentation of *Les Biches*, produced by Serge Diaghilev, choreographed by Bronislava Nijinska, and with music by Francis Poulenc, one of "The Six." Laurencin also designed wallpaper and textile patterns for Art Deco designer André Groult, who often hung her pictures in the rooms he decorated. She collaborated on dress designs with Groult's brother-in-law, the leading couturier Paul Poiret. A social celebrity in her own right, Laurencin's portraits of society women were much in demand, although her sitters are practically indistinguishable from one another, their individual features having been replaced by the large eyes and tiny noses characteristic of her later style.

Laurencin was also a prolific printmaker. Her first prints date from 1903-4; she continued to produce lithographs, etchings, and woodcuts throughout most of her life, many of which are preserved in the Bibliothèque Nationale in Paris. Her painted works, executed in the naive and decorative style established by 1909, consist primarily of self-portraits, portraits, and fantasy subjects from literature or from her imagination, rendered in delicate pastel colors.

131.
Group of Artists, 1908
Oil on canvas
24¾ x 31⅛ in. (62.9 x 79.1 cm.)
Signed lower left: Marie Laurencin/1908
The Baltimore Museum of Art
Bequest of Miss Etta and Dr. Claribel Cone

Through her relationship with Apollinaire, Laurencin joined the circle of artists and writers who met frequently at the Cloiserie des Lilas café and in Picasso's Montmartre studio, the Bateau-Lavoir. The sitters depicted here were all members of that group. From left to right they are: Picasso, Laurencin herself, Apollinaire, and Picasso's mistress Fernande Olivier. The lamblike white animal at lower left is Picasso's dog Frika. Apollinaire was a close friend of Picasso's, who made several humorous portrait drawings of the poet. The relationship between Laurencin and Olivier seems to have been more restrained, and Olivier's comments about Laurencin in her 1945 book, *Picasso and His Friends*, are less than complimentary.[3]

All of the sitters in the *Group of Artists* were present at the famous banquet given for the primitive painter Rousseau in 1908, the year this portrait was painted. *Group of Artists*, one of Laurencin's earliest paintings, is executed in a style that combines the naive simplifications of form characteristic of Rousseau with the more self-conscious primitivizing of a sophisticated painter like Picasso. Although it lacks the radical dissonance of composition and the scandalous subject matter of Picasso's 1907 *Demoiselles d'Avignon* (New York, Museum of Modern Art), the simplified, almost caricatured faces in Laurencin's picture do recall the treatment of several of the faces in Picasso's *Demoiselles*. The extreme flattening of all of the figures and the disjunctions between head and body in the figures of Picasso and Olivier may also derive from *Demoiselles*. Despite Laurencin's obvious dependence on the work of other artists, the *Group of Artists* remains unmistakably her own; her subtle and decorative use of the arabesque pervades every corner of the picture, from the features of the sitters to their sinuous arms, extending even to the curving tendrils in the bouquet of flowers at the upper right.

A small bust-length oil portrait of Picasso by Laurencin, possibly a preliminary study for *Group of Artists*, is in the collection of Mrs. Donald S. Stralem in New York.[4] That representation of Picasso closely resembles his image in the group portrait, except that in the bust his profile is reversed and he is nude.

According to Gertrude Stein, who bought *Group of Artists*, it was the first picture that Laurencin ever sold and marked the beginning of her career as a professional artist.[5] In 1909 Laurencin painted another portrait of the same group, expanding it to include portraits of Gertrude Stein, the poet Maurice Cremnitz, a young woman,[6] and a blonde angel. Laurencin gave this second group portrait, entitled *Reunion in the Country*,[7] to Apollinaire, who cherished it even after his marriage; it hung above his deathbed in 1918.

3.
Olivier, 69, 85-87, 108-9, 182.
4.
Repr. in Nochlin, 1971, 32.
5.
Stein, 76-77.
6.
The young woman is possibly Cremnitz' wife; see Laurencin's 1908 portrait of Cremnitz, his wife and daughter, entitled *The Family*, illustrated in *Sale Catalogue, Helena Rubinstein Collection*, pt. 1, Parke-Bernet, New York, April 20, 1966, no. 37, color pl.
7.
Repr. in Mackworth, following 132.

132

Nadezhda Andreevna Udaltsova
Russian, 1885-1961

Very little is known of Udaltsova's life apart from her friendship with Liubov Popova and her professional association with the Russian vanguard. Apparently she met Popova in 1912-13 at the Paris studios of Metzinger and Le Fauconnier where they both were studying. Upon her return to Russia in 1913 Udaltsova continued her close association with Popova and became friendly with Tatlin and Aleksandr Vesnin. With Popova, Udaltsova modestly began exhibiting with the Russian avant-garde by sending a single painting to the 1914 Jack of Diamonds exhibition in Moscow. Because of her firsthand experience with French art she was inclined at first to exhibit with the group of artists who continued to invite French artists — who, in fact, broke with Larionov over this very issue. Udaltsova participated in almost all the major exhibitions in Russia: Leftist Trends and Tramway v (Petrograd, 1915); 0.10 (Petrograd, 1915-16); The Store and the fifth Jack of Diamonds (Moscow, 1916). By the November 1916 Jack of Diamonds, Udaltsova was showing her "painterly constructions" which, like the contemporary work of Malevich, Tatlin, and Rozanova, eschewed figurative subject matter. Udaltsova worked at Svomas/ Vkhutemas in Petrograd in the 1920s with Popova, Malevich, Rodchenko, and Kliun. Along with paintings by these artists, Udaltsova's were purchased for the prestigious Museum of Artistic Culture in Moscow, and she participated in the Erste Russische Kunstausstellung, 1922, in Berlin. Most likely during the 1920s, Udaltsova married the painter Aleksandr Drevin, whose work was also purchased for the Moscow Museum of Artistic Culture.

132.
At the Piano, 1914
Oil on canvas
42 x 35 in. (107 x 89 cm.)
New Haven, Yale University Art Gallery
Gift of Collection Société Anonyme

Though seen frequently throughout the United States since its acquisition directly from the Erste Russische Kunstausstellung in 1922, Udaltsova's *At the Piano* has received scant notice. Yet the obvious comparison of this painting with Jacques Villon's *Little Girl at the Piano,* 1912 (New York, Collection Mrs. George Acheson) — which Udaltsova would surely have seen in Paris — is most instructive. Villon's oval format complements the soft, curved forms of the girl and her languorous, pastel environment; the forms of Udaltsova's pianist are angular, the colors vigorous and gaudy primaries. In contrast to the generalized forms of Villon and the majority of the French Cubists, Udaltsova's are quite detailed, from the lampshade to the foot pedal of the piano. Her "decorative coordination of flat planes of color"[1] radiates from the center of the canvas, eliminating any suggestion of depth. In accord with the strong lines that angle up and out from the base of the composition, the central vertical axis seems to swing from side to side, suggesting the pendulum of a metronome; if Udaltsova used the device with this intention, then *At the Piano* might indeed have been the canvas entitled *Music,* shown at the 0.10 exhibition.

1.
Camilla Gray, *The Russian Experiment in Art: 1863-1922,* New York, 1972, 184.

133

Olga Vladimirovna Rozanova
Russian, 1886-1918

Born in the Vladimir Province of Russia, Rozanova attended the Bolshakov Art College and the Stroganov Art School in Moscow from 1904 to 1910. In 1911 she moved to St. Petersburg and began exhibiting with the Union of Youth, a group of vanguard artists. In 1912-13 she attended Zvantseva's Art School and began illustrating the booklets published by Russian Futurist poets, including Aleksei Kruchenykh. During this time Rozanova contributed to the Union of Youth exhibitions (St. Petersburg, 1911, 1911-12, 1912, 1913-14); the International Futurist exhibition in Italy (Rome, 1914); Tramway v and Leftist Trends (Petrograd, 1915); 0.10 (Petrograd, 1915-16); and the fifth Jack of Diamonds (Moscow, 1916).

In 1916 Rozanova worked with Malevich and Matiushin, among others, on the (unpublished) journal *Supremus*. Two years later she was selected to be a member of IZO Narkompros and of Proletkult, and with Rodchenko headed the art-industry subsection of IZO. The First State Exhibition (Moscow, 1919) contained a posthumous showing of Rozanova's works, as did the Erste Russische Kunstausstellung (Berlin, 1922).

133.
Man in the Street, 1913
Oil on canvas
32⅝ x 24¼ in. (83 x 61.5 cm.)
New York, Leonard Hutton Galleries

Until one finds the tall, dark cylinder of a top hat in the upper center, it is virtually impossible to identify the subject of Rozanova's *Man in the Street;* the top hat becomes the key which then allows the other pieces — tan face, gray coat, gray and black buildings, and blue violet windows of an automobile — to fall into place around it. Though there is only a minimal attempt here to depict speed or motion, the device of slightly shifting all the parts of the composition (in the vocabulary of Russian Futurism, *sdvig*) forces to the surface the tension and dynamism of this typical scene of modern city life. Rozanova had exploited this device in other work of 1913, in particular her canvas *Factory and Bridge* and her lithographs for the 1913 issue of *Soiuz molodezhi (Union of Youth).*

Georgia O'Keeffe
American, b. 1887

Georgia O'Keeffe, a major figure in the evolution of American art of the twentieth century, was born on November 15, 1887. She grew up in a large family, of Irish-Hungarian-Dutch lineage, on a dairy farm near Sun Prairie, Wisconsin. Her strong interest in music developed first, but by age ten she had decided to become a painter. Formal art training from plaster casts began in 1901 when she entered a convent school in Madison.

In 1905 O'Keeffe studied anatomical drawing with John Vanderpoel at the Art Institute of Chicago. She has always valued his emphasis on line and structure, even though figures were early omitted from her art. During 1907 she worked at the Art Students League in New York, learning the elegant Munich method of using rich pigments then taught by William Merritt Chase. She won his class prize for a still life, but soon lost interest in imitating academic European styles and quit painting to work as a commercial artist in Chicago.

During the summer of 1912 she took a course in the principles of abstract design given by Alon Bement — a follower of the art educator Arthur Wesley Dow.[1] Dow combined the Oriental mode of composition (space structured from the flat relations of shapes and color) with the Kantian viewpoint (using nature's forms to express emotion rather than for imitation).

During the next four years she taught Dow's principles in Virginia, South Carolina, and the public schools of west Texas. Just before her thirtieth birthday she held a secret exhibition of her work, saw that it all had been influenced by others, and destroyed it. Starting over, she vowed to please herself — putting down only "what was in my head."[2] With eyes reschooled by the art of Mexican children, and, most of all, by the eerie skies and landscapes of the Texas Panhandle, O'Keeffe began using charcoal to put down abstract shapes that contained her own thoughts and feelings.

On January 1, 1916, a batch of these private symbol drawings arrived in New York addressed to her art student friend Anita Pollizer. No one else was supposed to see them, but remembering that O'Keeffe had once written she would rather have Alfred Stieglitz like something she had done than anyone else, Miss Pollizer took them straight to Stieglitz.[3] The story is often told that Stieglitz, without O'Keeffe's permission, decided to exhibit ten of these abstractions at his avant-garde 291 Gallery in the spring of 1916, and that the irate artist tried to make him take them down — which he refused to do. Whatever the truth of this account, the meeting drastically changed both their lives. In 1917 Stieglitz gave O'Keeffe her first solo show at 291 and a year later gave her the financial aid she needed to abandon teaching and paint full time. He also began his "composite portrait" of her — which consisted of some five hundred photographs taken over a twenty-year period.

Stieglitz and O'Keeffe were married in 1924.[4] Until his death in 1946, he exhibited her work almost yearly. By her own account, the men of the inner "Stieglitz circle" — which included Charles Demuth, Arthur G. Dove, Marsden Hartley, and the photographer Paul Strand — did not want her around at first. But when her paintings of Manhattan (a male artists' preserve) sold well and received a good press, as indeed all her work did from the start, she won their respect. Dove told Stieglitz, "That girl is doing without effort what all we moderns have been trying to do."[5]

At the instigation of Mabel Dodge Luhan, O'Keeffe visited Taos, New Mexico, in 1929. Always happier in the country than in the city, she found herself able to work better in the desert than anywhere else.[6] Until Stieglitz died she spent several months a year in New Mexico, but in 1949, when her large task of dividing the Stieglitz art collection among public institutions was completed,[7] she settled in Abiquiu. She has said that when she finally began to travel the world in the 1950s, she did it just to see if she'd chosen the right place to live. It is perhaps not surprising that the words commonly used to describe O'Keeffe's art — "vast," "lucid," "spartan," "epic," "austere," "healthy,"

1.
Dow may have picked up some Synthetist theory from Gauguin at Pont-Aven, and he was a close student of both Japanese and Chinese art, but he was in no sense a modernist — the 1913 Armory Show was a shock to him. O'Keeffe came to New York for periods during 1914 and 1916 especially to study with Dow at Columbia Teachers College.
2.
Quoted in Lloyd Goodrich's introduction to *Georgia O'Keeffe Drawings*, New York, 1968.
3.
The extraordinary letter written to Georgia O'Keeffe by Anita Pollizer in which she confesses and describes this visit to Stieglitz — quoting his excited words about the drawings (he did not then say "Finally, a woman on paper") — is at the Beinecke Rare Book and Manuscript Library, Yale University.
4.
She kept the name O'Keeffe. "Why should I take on someone else's famous name?"
5.
Herbert Seligmann, *Alfred Stieglitz Talking: Notes on Some of His Conversations, 1925-1931*, New Haven, 1966, 44.

6.
For an account of O'Keeffe's first reactions see Mabel Dodge Luhan, "Georgia O'Keeffe in Taos," *Creative Art*, June 1931, 407-10.
7.
Stieglitz was the primary sponsor of the modern art movement in America. His own collection was composed of 850 modern paintings — both European and American — as well as sculpture, photographs, prints, and drawings. Although he did not collect systematically, a primary aim was to keep a visual record of the evolving work of Dove, Marin, and O'Keeffe. Because the collection was too large for any one museum to hang, major works were divided between The Metropolitan Museum of Art, the Art Institute of Chicago, and Fisk University at Nashville, Tennessee. For O'Keeffe's account of this dispersal, see "Stieglitz: His Pictures Collected Him," *New York Times*, December 11, 1949. For an examination of the material in the Metropolitan, see George Heard Hamilton, "The Alfred Stieglitz Collection," *Metropolitan Museum Journal*, no. 3, 1970, 371-90.

134

135

136

137

"clean-cut," "unsentimental," "pristine" — should also describe the area she has loved for half a century.

Her work since 1915 has been labeled "feminine" by many critics because of its many associative connections with the female body.[8] But the wide range of her artistic language would seem to gainsay this simple description. Although O'Keeffe has rarely made a cause out of being a woman artist (she did give a speech in 1926 to the National Women's Party in Washington), her ability to go it alone has become a contemporary feminist model for freedom of thought and action. To her, the important thing has always been to carry out her own decisions about how to make art — and to satisfy herself. In the process of doing this, she anticipated the diverse concerns about color and shape of Rothko, Louis, Noland, and Ellsworth Kelly.[9] ("When I first saw Kelly's work I thought 'I could have done that'."[10])

O'Keeffe's first full-scale retrospective (which showed the different musical elements of her work, as well as her free-wheeling attitude toward the American abstraction/representation issue) took place in 1943 at the Art Institute of Chicago. It was followed by another in 1946 at the Museum of Modern Art in New York; one in 1960 at the Worcester Art Museum in Massachusetts; one in 1966 at the Amon Carter Museum of Western Art in Fort Worth, Texas; and the most recent in 1970 took place at the Whitney Museum of American Art in New York. She was elected to the National Institute of Arts and Letters in 1949, the American Academy of Arts and Letters in 1963, the American Academy of Arts and Sciences in 1966. In 1970 she was awarded the National Institute of Arts and Letters' Gold Medal for Painting. Since that time she has continued to observe the remote place she lives in, using the evidence of her eyes and ears to make images that seem at once formal, particular, and transcendent.

"When I think of death I only regret that I will not be able to see this beautiful country any more, unless the Indians are right, and my spirit will walk here after I'm gone."[11]

134.
Blue No. 1, 1916
Watercolor
15⅞ x 11 in. (40.3 x 27.9 cm.)
The Brooklyn Museum
Museum Purchase (58.73)
135.
Blue No. 2, 1916
Watercolor
15⅞ x 10¹⁵/₁₆ in. (40.3 x 27.8 cm.)
The Brooklyn Museum
Museum Purchase (58.74)
136.
Blue No. 3, 1916
Watercolor
15⅞ x 10¹⁵/₁₆ in. (40.3 x 27.8 cm.)
The Brooklyn Museum
Dick S. Ramsay Fund (58.75)

8.
Among those who first described the content and style of O'Keeffe's work as feminine: Alfred Stieglitz, in his 1919 notes to Stanton McDonald Wright on "Woman in Art," quoted by Dorothy Norman in *Alfred Stieglitz: An American Seer,* New York, 1973, 136-38; Marsden Hartley, *Adventures in the Arts,* New York, 1921, 116-19; Henry McBride, *The Herald,* February 4, 1923; Paul Rosenfeld, *Port of New York,* New York, 1924, 199-210; Lewis Mumford, "O'Keeffe and Matisse," *The New Republic,* March 2, 1927; Helen Appleton Reed (a fellow student of O'Keeffe's at the Art Students League), "Georgia O'Keeffe — Woman Artist Whose Art Is Sincerely Feminine." *Vogue,* June 15, 1928. For criticism from the recent feminist point of view see Miriam Schapiro and Judy Chicago, "Female Imagery," *Womanspace Journal,* Summer 1973, ii; Linda Nochlin, "Some Women Realists: Part i," *Arts Magazine,* February 1974, 47-49; Lawrence Alloway, "Women's Art in the '70s," *Art in America,* May-June 1976, 64-72.
9.
For discussion of how O'Keeffe's work adds to our understanding of the origins of recent styles, see Goossen, 224.
10.
Eldredge, 189.

137.
Blue No. 4, 1916
Watercolor
16 x 10¹⁵/₁₆ in. (40.6 x 27.8 cm.)
The Brooklyn Museum
Dick S. Ramsay Fund (58.76)

Georgia O'Keeffe has said almost nothing about how and why she made her sudden bold leap into abstraction during 1915 and 1916. There is only her well-known statement: "I realized that I had a lot of things in my head that others didn't have. I made up my mind to put down what was in my head."[12] In the extraordinary experiments of those two years can be found the genesis of her later morphology.

Her earliest series of abstractions were done with charcoal on paper during the fall of 1915 in Columbia, South Carolina, where was teaching at Columbia College.[13] The four *Blues* represent some of her first attempts to deal freely in color with "the things in her head." Apparently these were not preliminary studies for a more advanced oil painting, but were considered by the artist as an independent series — successive reductions of a single theme.[14]

Most, if not all, of O'Keeffe's abstract paintings come from her perceptual experience of the real world. In *Blue No. 1,* the most complex in color and shape, we can see the penciled composition underneath the exquisitely controlled puddling of black, blue, and yellow, a composition that suggests derivation from elements in the natural world, veiled and stripped of all naturalism. It is this veiling and reduction of natural motifs — so prevalent in O'Keeffe's work of the late teens — that suggests that she was familiar with Kandinsky's unique grammar of abstract painting, as defined and diagrammed in part II of his *Concerning the Spiritual in Art.*[15]

Although the transition from *Blue No. 1* to *Blue No. 2* seems very abrupt compared to those between the others, no record exists of any intermediate studies. Missing in *No. 2* is the upper border of aquatic forms, with their delicate references to conch shells, sea foam, and ripples. Also eliminated are the inchoate silhouettes of leaping human figures and heads with eyes that emerged from the depths of the earlier watercolor. Only two of the ovoids have survived — their outlines smoothed and rounded — and they are now suspended, one above the other, on the bare onion paper, with a thick calligraphic cluster of diagonal lines acting as their base. The metamorphosis of the shapes shared by both paintings is easy enough to trace, but in its simple, cannily balanced symmetry *No. 2* seems much closer to Dow's Oriental principles of design than *No. 1* does. Perhaps O'Keeffe painted the latter just before she came to New York in February to work with Dow again. There is also a difference in the way watercolor is handled: most of the shapes in *No. 1* are outlined and then filled in with quite thin wash; in *No. 2* the blues and deep green appear to have gone on directly in a modulation from thick opaque color to thin transparent stain — again, closer to Dow's adaptation of the

Japanese theory of *Notan* (the harmony of tonal relationships). In *No. 3* and *No. 4* the green has been dropped, and the strict forms of *No. 2* presented with ever increasing condensation. It is color that determines the construction of these two last paintings.

What was the implication of blue for O'Keeffe in 1916? Perhaps, like Kandinsky, she equated blue with the intellectual/spiritual sphere; or perhaps she believed, as he did, in the absolute equivalence between colors and music. Despite the fact that O'Keeffe was evolving her own vocabulary of form during this period, it seems obvious that she was open to, and actively reinterpreting, complex influences.

138.
Lake George Barns, 1926
Oil on canvas
21 x 32 in. (53.3 x 81.3 cm.)
Minneapolis, Walker Art Center

Lake George Barns is one of O'Keeffe's austere meditations on buildings she knew intimately from her long summers on the Stieglitz estate at Lake George, New York. Her barn portraits span approximately fifteen years (1918-33) and she worked on them in three very different locales: Lake George; central Wisconsin (the landscape of her childhood); and the Gaspé region of Canada. This painting was done toward the end of her Lake George summer period, and it immediately precedes her more impressionistic New York skyscraper series painted between 1926 and 1929.

Martin Friedman puts *Lake George Barns* into the "measured rural architecture" category of Precisionism.[16] Lloyd Goodrich sharply dissociates O'Keeffe's work as a whole from this style, but he does say that her country buildings are the most Precisionist of her paintings.[17] O'Keeffe has never considered herself to be part of the Precisionist movement. When interviewed by Katharine Kuh in 1962 she said, "I'm not a joiner and I'm not a precisionist or anything else . . . it's curious that the show [*The Precisionist View,* 1960] didn't stress what really might have been called precise in my work — the Canadian barns."[18]

Certainly *Lake George Barns* is difficult to accept as a Precisionist work. It is not "icily defined," nor does it have a "flawless finish" (the variety of brushstrokes is highly visible): the lines of the barns are not ruler straight, the light is atmospheric rather than brilliant, and the mood expressionistic rather than impersonally formal. Stieglitz's photographs of the same barns confirm it to be based on direct observation, but O'Keeffe has rendered those particulars in ways that are acutely disturbing.

In this rectangular canvas, whose shape is echoed by interior horizontal lines, our eyes are forced to concentrate on the complex size, line, and color relationships among three barns and their landscape. Only the essence of these forms has been given. Details like slatted walls and shingled roofs (the focus of Stieglitz's camera lens) are

11.
Quote from an interview with O'Keeffe by Henry Seldis, *Los Angeles Times West Coast Magazine,* January 22, 1967.
12.
Quoted in Lloyd Goodrich's introduction to *Georgia O'Keeffe Drawings,* New York, 1968. O'Keeffe's own first book, scheduled for publication late in 1976 by Viking Press, may fill this gap in our knowledge, and many others besides.
13.
One roll of these drawings was sent from Columbia, South Carolina, to Anita Pollizer for criticism — arriving in New York on November 16, 1915. The famous second batch, which Miss Pollizer took straight to Stieglitz, came to her on January 1, 1916.
14.
A rare photograph, formerly in the estate of Abraham Walkowitz, appeared in the exhibition *Abraham Walkowitz and Alfred Stieglitz: The 291 Years — 1912-17,* at the Zabriskie Gallery, New York, 1976. It is labeled "Georgia O'Keeffe Exhibition, May-July, 1916, 6⅛" x 9"," and it plainly shows *Blue No. 1* and *Blue No. 4* hanging together on the wall. If the 1916 date of this photograph is correct, the *Blues* appeared in O'Keeffe's first 291 exhibition, and must have been made early in 1916 — probably in New York — for O'Keeffe was working there with Dow at Columbia Teachers College during the winter-spring term.
15.
The English translation of this book was published in London and Boston in 1914 under the title *The Art of Spiritual Harmony.* Anita Pollizer's letters to O'Keeffe during the summer of 1915 speak of Kandinsky and of her own interested study of *The Art of Spiritual Harmony.* In all likelihood, O'Keeffe had digested it as well. She could also have seen Kandinsky's paintings exhibited at 291 at various times, for Stieglitz considered Kandinsky extremely important to the future development of painting. He bought the only Kandinsky at the 1913 Armory Show (*Improvization no. 27*) because he wanted to save it for New York. And as early as 1912 he published an excerpt from *Concerning the Spiritual in Art* in his *Camera Work* (no. 39, July 1912, 34).
16.
In Friedman's view, O'Keeffe and Charles Sheeler represent the two main currents of the Precisionist movement. He cites "Extreme simplification of form, unwavering, sharp delineation, and carefully reasoned abstract organization" as the stylistic qualities common to both artists. Minneapolis, Walker Art Center, *The Precisionist View in American Art,* catalog by Martin Friedman, 1960, 14.
17.
Goodrich, 20-21.
18.
Kuh, 201-2.

missing, but there is no mistaking the farm character of these buildings. They dominate the land and interfere with the skyline — as real barns do.

O'Keeffe's art is resolutely non-metaphoric. We perceive the integrity of these barns (they do not stand for forms other than themselves) but they are, nonetheless, equivalents for the artist's feelings. There is something crowded and stifling about these three shuttered buildings; they deprive us of a sense of distance, and there is no exit at either end. The low gray sky adds to our sense of being completely hemmed in. The only escape offered is through the blue crack in the clouds — but this suggests a metaphysical rather than a physical escape. It is well recorded that O'Keeffe felt increasingly restless in the close greenness of upstate New York. Three summers after this picture was painted, she escaped to New Mexico.

Different kinds of openings are a major thematic preoccupation in both the artist's abstract and realist paintings. The right square window of the gray barn, with its open (missing?) pane, is a geometrical motif that dates back to O'Keeffe's early work, as so much of her distinctive vocabulary does. Perhaps the best-known prototype for this motif is *59th Street Studio* of 1919, while the most evolved examples of it are to be found in her *Patio* series of 1946-60. In the last, the most severely reduced of all her works, she examines over and over — at different ranges, from different angles — the mesmeric impenetrable door of her Abiquiu home.

139.
Ranchos Church, Taos, New Mexico, 1930
Oil on canvas
24 x 36 in. (61 x 91.4 cm.)
Fort Worth, Amon Carter Museum of Western Art

O'Keeffe made several series of paintings of the eighteenth-century mission church at Ranchos de Taos in 1929 and 1930. She was fascinated with the oddly buttressed west end and in this work has put us as close to it as we can get and still see the whole structure. The earth seems to have risen of its own accord into these bulging, sheared-off shapes that suggest geology rather than architecture. O'Keeffe also relates this handmade adobe building to its natural environment by means that are strictly formal. The intervals between the turbulent gray sky, the distant sand hills, and the stretch of mesa on the right are rhythmically repeated — vertically as well as horizontally — by the roof and walls. Actually, the more we look at this representational painting the more gridlike and abstract it becomes. This frequently occurs in O'Keeffe's work — not surprisingly, because for her (as for her teacher, Arthur Wesley Dow) the principles of composition are always the same.

The slightly elevated vantage point and the contrast of near and far — with the middle ground eliminated — are found in many of O'Keeffe's

Southwest landscapes. These characteristics can be understood as both a factual rendering of local optical conditions and an expression of the artist's own vision.

Among O'Keeffe's most persistent investigations are her shelter shapes, which come in many guises, including those protecting the fetus (pelvic bones) and lower forms of life (clamshells); those offering protection from the weather (barns); and those providing sanctuary for the spirit (the Ranchos Church). Clearly these forms illuminate some important aspect of existence for the artist. It is easy to assume that they relate to the sexual and psychological experience of being a woman, and to womb imagery in particular — but O'Keeffe has consistently denied that she ever deliberately evoked genital shapes in her work.[19]

Stieglitz, however, wrote some notes on "Woman in Art" in 1919 that emphasize the explicitly feminine sexuality he saw in O'Keeffe's work: "Woman feels the World differently than Man feels it . . . the Woman receives the World through her Womb. That is the seat of her deepest feeling . . . if these Woman-produced things [O'Keeffe's] which are distinctly feminine can live side by side with male-produced Art — hold their own — we will find that the underlying aesthetic laws governing the one govern the other — the original generating feeling merely being different."[20] Certainly this sort of sexually dichotomized view of O'Keeffe's art is highly debatable, but it represents a type of interpretation — or misinterpretation — current during the earlier part of the twentieth century and not unknown today.[21]
140.
Pelvis with Blue (Pelvis I), 1944
Oil on canvas
36 x 30 in. (91.4 x 76.2 cm.)
Milwaukee Art Center
Gift of Mrs. Harry Lynde Bradley
(Not illustrated)

This painting[22] is one of O'Keeffe's many explorations into the way line is affected by light. Her pelvic bonescapes were begun in 1943, and in the 1944 catalog for the show *An American Place*, where they were first seen, the artist wrote: ". . . When I found the beautiful white bones on the desert I picked them up and took them home. . . . I have used these things to say what is to me the wideness and the wonder of the world as I live in it. . . . For years in the country the pelvic bones lay about the house indoors and out — always underfoot — seen and not seen as such things can be — seen in many different ways. . . . I was most interested in the holes in the bones — what I saw through them. . . . They were most wonderful against the Blue — that Blue that will always be there as it is now after all man's destruction is finished. I have tried to paint the Bones and the Blue."

Although these shapes may come directly from the artist's experience

19.
O'Keeffe's best known rebuttal to viewers' and critics' continuing belief in the vaginal iconology of her enlarged flowers was written in 1939 for the *An American Place* exhibition catalog: "Well — I made you take the time to look at what I saw and when you took time to really notice my flower you hung all your own associations with flowers on my flower and you write about my flower as if I think and see what you think and see of the flower — and I don't."
20.
Notes on "Woman in Art" written to S. MacDonald Wright on October 9, 1919. Quoted by Dorothy Norman in *Alfred Stieglitz: An American Seer*, New York, 1973, 137.
21.
For a thorough discussion of sexual and "feminine" interpretations of O'Keeffe's art during the twenties and thirties, as well as the artist's reaction to such criticism, see chap. VII, "O'Keeffe and the Critics," in Eldredge, especially 148-59.
22.
A letter to the Milwaukee Art Center from the artist dated June 27, 1976, says: "The Pelvis was a painting I liked very much and had it hanging in the part of the house where I lived most, so I missed it when it was gone. But I suppose it is good for others to see it." The Art Institute of Chicago has *Pelvis 3*, also of 1944.

138

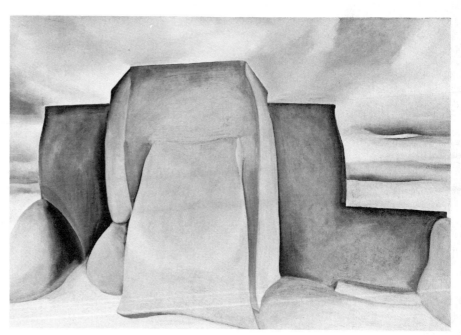

139

of holding a pelvis bone up to the sky, their origin is not easily seen in the final image. Distorting the scale of an object by isolating it has been a primary characteristic of O'Keeffe's work since 1924 — the year she began her celebrated flower paintings. O'Keeffe's turn toward sharp line and the close-up early in the 1920s indicates that she had adapted the linear accuracy of Stieglitz's sharply focused photography to her own artistic ends and was familiar with the camera work of Paul Strand as well.[23]

What is apt to strike the contemporary eye first in *Pelvis with Blue* are the multiple tensions between the two blue patches — tensions between part and whole, centrality and asymmetry, convexity and concavity, largeness and smallness, nearness and farness. The divisions between blue and white are complex, with edges that are sharp, flat cutouts; edges that curve with perfect three-dimensionality; edges that are broken; and edges that puzzle perceptual logic (for example, the slim white halo at the upper left of the ovoidal form). Because we have difficulty in locating the light source, this virtuoso display of edges seems arbitrary at first. But O'Keeffe is a painter deeply concerned with visual truth. Once she has extracted the essential qualities from natural forms, she can be, in her own words, "ridiculously realistic." Thus, this is probably an accurate rendition of desert sunlight on bleached bone.

The shimmering, weightless blue appears to be lit from within. Floating shapes, often found in O'Keeffe's work, are created by explicit formal means. In this case, the blue, most intense at its edges, is gradually, unevenly lightened toward the center, with fine, regular brushstrokes that follow the circularity of the form. The effect is that of a precarious airy suspension.

Pelvis with Blue is an exceptionally beautiful variation on the artist's recurring theme of motion and stillness. Inevitably, O'Keeffe's bones have been associated with the symbolism of death and transfiguration, in spite of her statement that "the bones seem to cut sharply to the center of something that is keenly alive on the desert even though it is vast and empty and untouchable and knows no kindness with all its beauty." Whatever the artist's intent, her particular way of viewing infinite space through the microcosmic hole of an animal's pelvic bone sets up a network of rich correspondences between the optical, the biological, and the spiritual.

141

23.
Actually, the question of who influenced whom, and when, in the Stieglitz circle, is not easy to pin down, and there seems to have been a good deal of cross-fertilization. For example, Strand's *Forms (Bowls)* close-up dates from 1916, but his microscopic studies of ferns and irises were done in 1927 and 1928, respectively — thereby following O'Keeffe's first painted flower close-ups by at least three years. That Stieglitz himself was influenced by O'Keeffe's abstractions after 1917 has been noted by Doris Bry in her book *Alfred Stieglitz: Photographer*, Museum of Fine Arts, Boston, 1965, 18.

Hannah Höch
German, b. 1889

Hannah Höch is one of the last surviving members of the Berlin Club Dada and the only woman of the group. In a reaction to the political and social corruption of post-World War I Germany, she played an active role in the club's bitterly satirical, anti-establishment events, sharing fully the sentiments and explosive activities of her masculine colleagues. With Raoul Hausmann she is thought to have invented photomontage, a medium for which she is best known and which she still favors. Since 1939, when Nazism forced her retirement to the country, Höch has lived in a modest cottage at Heiligensee, on the periphery of Berlin, where she spends her time tending a rich garden and quietly continuing her production of art.

Höch's garden provides the tranquility necessary to her temperament and serves as an alternate field for artistic expression. The wildly profuse and cherished plant life that dominates her physical surroundings is not unlike the rich variety of textures and multiple objects in her collages or the seemingly disparate images of her photomontages and oils. She has always worked simultaneously in varied media and styles, using the broadest range of available imagery, testing, pruning, and rearranging her material. Her work is often satirical, sometimes whimsical, but her chief concern (according to a recent statement) has always been to utilize art in support of her personal ideas and the expansion of her own vision.[1] Her guiding principles have been free experimentation, craftsmanship, and intellectual control.

She was born Johanna Höch in Gotha at Thuringen, the daughter of an insurance executive who taught her gardening during his lunch hours and tried to discourage her expressed desire for a career in art. In 1912 she left Gotha and enrolled in the Berlin School of Decorative Art where she learned glass painting, soldering, and craft techniques under Harold Bengen. In 1915 she became the pupil of Emil Orlik who taught her woodcut and linoleum block techniques and corrected her work in miniatures, academic painting, and near-abstract drawings. Orlik encouraged her enthusiasm for experimentation

with style and media. In the same year Höch met and began a seven-year liaison with the fiery young poet, painter, and philosopher Raoul Hausmann. Together they entered into the charged spirit of protest that permeated German society, politics, and art. In 1918 Höch joined with Hausmann, Richard Huelsenbeck, George Grosz, John Heartfield, Johannes Baader, and Walter Mehring in a new, aggressive Berlin Dada movement, participating in the stormy poetry readings, exhibitions, and theatrical events that frequently ended in violence.

Between 1915 and 1918 Höch painted her first abstract oil (1916), made her first abstract collage with bits of lace and leaf patterns (1917), and created a series of stuffed dolls that exhibit a playful spirit and a taste for the absurd. She and Hausmann were struck with the creative possibilities offered by photography while they were vacationing on the Baltic Sea in 1917. Shortly afterwards they began to arrange photographs and fragments cut from newspapers, magazines, and picture postcards into extraordinarily forceful compositions.

Höch participated in the first Dada exhibition held at the J. B. Neumann Gallery in 1919 and in the International Dada Fair held at the Otto Burchard Gallery the next year; collaborated with Kurt Schwitters in his Merzbau projects in 1922 and 1925; and worked with Hans Arp on a series of photomontages in 1923. Photomontage served particularly well for her satirical images in *Dada-Journal*, 1919 (Rome, Achille Perilli)[2] and for *Cut with a Kitchen Knife* (Berlin, National-galerie).[3] The latter, exhibited at the International Dada Fair, is typical of Höch's aesthetic handling of a polemic theme. Black and white photos of cogwheels, gears, auto and locomotive parts are arranged in an uneasy equilibrium with the heads of government officials and members of the contemporary art and theatrical world. Here, as in her paintings and other photomontages and collages, she works within a context of manipulated scale, oppositions of organic and inorganic matter, discordant and seemingly chaotic multiplicity, and startlingly singular relationships between objects

---

1.
Paris, 1976, 23.
2.
Repr. 62, ibid.
3.
Repr. 61, ibid.

and images. The explosive anti-art sentiments of the Dada movement never destroyed Höch's essentially aesthetic impulses; her work is carefully constructed and her juxtapositions of opposing materials are light in spirit. Despite the pessimism of many of her themes the lyrical and formal currents in her work reveal an optimistic faith in the power of art.

Höch has also dealt forcefully with the feminine experience, using objects traditionally associated with women — bits of lace, buttons, clothing patterns. While she admits to the irony of such works as *The Engaged Couple,* 1920 (Paris, Edouard Roditi); *The Union,* 1922 (private collection); and *The Bride,* 1924 (Berlin, Nierendorf Galerie), she claims no overtly feminist intentions for her work.[4]

There is a purely abstract and lyrical current that runs through Höch's oeuvre in works as varied as her lace collages; her series of abstract watercolors built around the figure *5,* begun in 1919; many of her oils; and in the spidery calligraphy of a work like *Drawing for a Monument of an Important Lace Shirt,* 1922 (Kunsthalle, Hamburg). In oil as well as in collage her work has the air of construction, and her painted objects, in imaginative fantasies such as *Vegetations,*[5] 1928 (Gelsenkirchen, State Collection), retain their sense of tangibility despite the irrational perspectival and contextual relationships.

Höch made a final break with Raoul Hausmann and Berlin Dada in 1922. In *Personal Mottoes*[6] (Berlin, Nierendorf Galerie), a collage of the same year, she wove the photos, lettering, poetry, mechanical imagery, lacy fabrics, and the names of her colleagues into a souvenir of personal experiences, friendships, and formal concerns that summed up her life and personal credo. During the twenties and early thirties she continued to work simultaneously in various media, producing several series — ethnographic collages that were inspired by a visit to the Leyden ethnographic museum in 1927 and symbolic landscapes between 1920 and 1930. Höch made two trips to Paris in 1924 and 1925 and spent three years in Holland between 1926 and 1929 in close contact with the De Stijl group. She maintained her friendships with old colleagues, particularly Kurt Schwitters and his wife, and continued her exhibitions with the Berlin November Group (begun in 1919) throughout the twenties and early thirties.

The years between 1935 and 1945 were arduous; she was unable to exhibit and although she did work, much of her time was spent in her garden raising food for survival. Since 1946 she has had eleven one-woman exhibitions in Berlin, Milan, Rome, Turin, London, and Cassel. It was not until 1947 that she introduced colored photographs into her photomontage work. She continues to experiment, working largely in oil and collage and in themes that combine current events (*Homage to the Men Who Have Conquered the Moon,* 1969, Collection the artist) with abstract beauty (*Beauty, Wisdom, Energy,* 1969/70, Collection the artist).

142

4.
Ibid., 27.
5.
Repr. 50, ibid.
6.
Repr. 59, ibid.

141.
Tailor's Daisy, 1920
Collage on paper
12⅛ x 9⅝ in. (30.8 x 24.4 cm.)
Chicago, Collection Mr. and Mrs. E. A. Bergman

The light and lyrical side of Hannah Höch's work reveals itself in this collage, as does her penchant for turning ordinary objects and mundane experiences into imaginative and surprising arrangements. Here she has gathered the elements of tailoring — wedge-shaped planes of clothing patterns, flowing lines that trace the scissors' cut, and broken lines that mark the direction of seams — against a gridlike background of uncut fabric. Included also are snaps, hasps, needles, and a zipper that runs the length and breadth of the image, holding and framing the still unsewn garment.

Like many of her collages — *White Clouds*, 1916 (Berlin, Nierendorf Galerie), and *White Form*, 1919 (Collection the artist), which this composition resembles — and the photomontages that predate 1947, this work is in black and white. Its strong linearity and absence of color have a graphic quality that recalls Höch's early interest in printmaking. Her strong feeling for handicrafts is also evident in her choice of subject and in the way she weaves dancelike rhythms of interpenetrating lines and shapes into a tightly controlled ornamental motif. By juxtaposing the tailor's patterns with the artist's, Höch puns on the nature of pattern and playfully fuses craft with art, humor with serious purpose.

Although made during the high point of her Dada activities, this collage has none of the sharp social criticism of the photomontages of the same years. It points, instead, to the more whimsical inventions, present from the outset of her career, that were to become freer and more apparent after 1922.

The unlikely combination of materials or images that gives Höch's work its quality of fantasy is less obvious here than in her more thickly textured collages (*Hommage to Arp*, 1923, Basel, Collection Marguerite Arp-Hagenbach, or *Fetishes*, 1971, Collection the artist). Like her lace collages (*L'Astronomie*, 1922, Collection the artist) that juxtapose three-dimensional solidity with the pierced voids of filmy fabric, *Tailor's Daisy* depends upon suspension of normal associations. The individual components of an article of clothing have been extracted here from their usual context and assume a novel identity. They are no longer objects with a specific purpose, becoming instead forms and textures that are carefully integrated into a work of abstract art.

Although this is a fairly early work, it reveals the aesthetic preoccupations that have engaged Höch throughout her career — a serious concern with formal construction and an effort to combine experience and art, humor and lyricism.

142.
The Tamer, 1930
Collage on paper
14 x 10¼ in. (35.6 x 26 cm.)
Chicago, Collection Mr. and Mrs. E. A. Bergman

In *The Tamer*, as in much of Höch's work, commonplace elements are combined to produce a troublesome, disquieting image. The central figure, comprised of both male and female parts, emerges through a tear in the background. With its feminine, conventionally beautiful head played off against powerful, masculine arms, the sex of the figure remains ambiguous. Also vague, but clearly an issue, is the question raised by the presence of the seal, an animal form that sets in relief the hybrid nature of the human. Running along the opening and around the figure are a series of upholstery nails that seem to hold the background in place and are echoed by a vertical line of similar nails at the left edge of the composition.

The Tamer is an outgrowth of Höch's satirical Dadaist work, but unlike some of the earlier collages it seems, at first glance, to make sense. Its parts are arranged in logical scale relationships without the spatial ambiguities prevalent in much of her work, and there is a single focus on one central, monumental image. The large seated figure inhabits its space like an icon, detached, distant, but strongly human in its references, recalling the scale and pose of traditional Madonnas. The work has a quality of the absurd that also characterizes Höch's Dada dolls and the constructions of her friend Kurt Schwitters. Assimilated into one concentrated image, Höch's usual juxtaposition of contradictory parts here achieves a kind of perverse reconciliation. Like the images of Surrealist artists of the same period — Jean Arp, Max Ernst, and Joan Miró — and Höch's concurrent portrait collages (*English Dancer*, 1928, Collection the artist; *Russian Dancer, My Double*, 1928, Collection A. Dörries, Braunschweig; and *Deutsches Mädchen*, 1930, Collection the artist), *The Tamer* taps sources of fantasy and the unconscious. However, it relies less upon spontaneity than upon deliberate construction and intellect. The work is conceived first as a broad, unified image and then composed from carefully chosen single parts. The contextual contradictions that give *The Tamer* its air of fantasy ultimately derive from the artist's intellectual concern with selection and arrangement.

Liubov Serbeevna Popova

Russian, 1889-1924

Born of a cultured family near Moscow, Popova was enrolled first
in Yaltinskaia's Women's Gymnasium, then in Arseneva's Gymnasium
in Moscow, in 1907. At about the same time she also began to study
painting seriously with Stanislav Zhukovsky and Konstantin Yuon
in Moscow. In 1912-13 she worked in Paris, attending the studios
of the Cubist painters Le Fauconnier and Metzinger, where she met the
Russian painter Nadezhda Udaltsova. Popova returned to Russia in
1913 and began to exhibit with the avant-garde: she sent work to the
Jack of Diamonds (Moscow, 1914); Tramway V and 0.10 (Petrograd,
1915-1916); The Store and the fifth Jack of Diamonds (Moscow,
1916); and 5 x 5 = 25 (Moscow, 1921). She was appointed to teach at
Svomas/Vkhutemas in 1918 and two years later was chosen a member
of Inkhuk, a post she left in late 1921 to devote herself to utilitarian
design. In 1922 Popova designed sets and costumes for Meyerhold's
production of Crommelynck's *The Magnanimous Cuckold,* and the
following year for S. Tretyakov's *Earth on End.* In her last year,
Popova worked on textile designs at the First State Textile Factory,
Moscow.

143.
Untitled (Human Bust), 1912
Oil, sand, and collage on canvas
$20^9/_{16}$ x 17⅛ in. (52.2 x 43.5 cm.)
New York, Luis Mestre Fine Arts

Popova's paintings of 1912-13 demonstrate a full arsenal of Cubist
devices: the subdued palette, the combed texture of hair, the sand
and wallpaper elements, and the simplification of certain shapes to
cylinder, plane, and cone. From Futurism Popova had absorbed the
formal fascination of the interpenetration of figure and environment;
in our picture, Popova has exploited the analogy of the intersecting
planes of the cheek with the intersecting planes in the corner
of the room. In comparison with her slightly later works such as the
Traveler, 1915 (Los Angeles, Norton Simon, Inc., Museum of Art),
and *Violin,* 1914 (Moscow, Tretyakov Gallery), this painting is
relatively simple, almost schematic in both composition and in the
use of collage elements.

In the absence of reliable documentation, it is tempting to suppose
that this early canvas might be a memento of Popova's study with
Le Fauconnier and Metzinger that she brought back to Russia in
1913. Although there are no exhibition references to this painting at
that early date, its theme does correspond to a painting entitled
Figure + House + Space, which Popova exhibited in Tramway V.

Sophie Taeuber-Arp
Swiss, 1889-1943

143

The work of Sophie Taeuber-Arp, who was born in Davos, Switzerland, and received her professional training in the decorative arts at
Saint-Gall in Munich and at the Kunstgewerbeschule in Hamburg, is
generally associated with that of her husband, the sculptor Jean
Arp. At times, indeed, the two artists collaborated: on works such
as *Duo-Collage* (1918) or *Duo-Drawing Torn and Rearranged* (1947)
and, most notably, in the creation, with Theo Van Doesburg, of the
modernist café-restaurant complex, L'Aubette, in Strasbourg (1927-28).

Taeuber-Arp became a member of the Schweizerischer Werkbund in
1915, the year she met Jean Arp; she taught weaving and embroidery
at the School of Arts and Crafts in Zurich from 1916 to 1929 and
published a small book on her specialty in 1927.[1] At the same time she
participated, mainly as a dancer (she studied with Rudolf von Laban),
in the lively Dada activities at the Café Voltaire in Zurich. There her
fellow Dadaists included Arp, Hugo Ball, Emmy Hennings,
Richard Huelsenbeck, Marcel Janco, and Tristan Tzara.

Although she turned to abstract, or rather, as she and her colleagues
preferred to think of it, "concrete" painting as early as 1915, and to
relief sculpture in 1931, Taeuber-Arp continued her work in the
decorative arts throughout her career. She created the imaginative
marionettes and décor for Carlo Gozzi's *Le roi cerf* in 1918 and the
interior decoration of abstract rectangular designs for the tearoom of
L'Aubette, where she was also responsible for the stained glass, the
billiard room, and several other aspects of this ambitious collaborative
project. When she and Arp moved to Meudon, outside Paris, in 1928,
Taeuber-Arp planned the house and designed the furniture. In 1937
she founded the short-lived review, *Plastique*.[2]

Yet Taeuber-Arp managed to devote a great deal of her attention to
the formal problems of pure painting and relief; indeed, she is one of
the first artists, perhaps because of her background in the decorative
arts, to have envisioned abstraction as a point of departure rather
than seeing it as the result of a process of evolution.[3] Both she and

1.
Sophie Arp-Taeuber and Blanche Gauchat, *Dessin et arts textiles*, Zurich, 1927.
For detailed information on Taeuber-Arp's advanced ideas about the decor-
ative arts and teaching, see Staber, 83-86.
2.
Ibid., 103.
3.
See J.-L. Daval, "Lettre de Suisse romande," *Art International*, xv, 1971, 83.

Arp created abstract work in embroidery and weaving in about 1914-18; at the same time both were experimenting with the effects of the "laws of chance" in torn-paper works. Her first paintings, in 1916, were watercolors and drawings of colored rectangles, sometimes enriched with little curvilinear figures. In succeeding years she reduced her repertory almost completely to rectilinear forms and triangles, achieving a climax in this mode with the majestic *Triptych* of 1918, subtitled *Vertical-Horizontal Composition with Reciprocal Triangles.* Her most distinctive creations, however, both in the paintings and in the wood reliefs of the 1930s, are marked by the use of the circle and of circular forms. Indeed, in the words of one critic, Hugo Weber, she may be called "the artist of the circle."[4]

Although the individual forms of her mature works may be simple, their deployment, their suggestion of space and movement, and their subtle interplay of color-rhythms are often extremely complex, suggesting the existence of underlying mathematical permutations. These works are strict, pure, and geometric, with little of the organic evocation or metamorphic whimsy of her husband's sculpture.

In Paris, Taeuber-Arp was associated with the Cercle et Carré group, founded by Michel Seuphor and Torrès-Garcia, as well as with the Abstraction-Création group, in which she participated with Herbin, Kupka, Vantongerloo, Gleizes, and other proponents of non-figural art from 1931 to 1936. In 1940 she and Arp left Paris, settling in Grasse from 1941 to 1942. In 1942 the couple returned to Switzerland, where Sophie Taeuber-Arp died in Zurich, as the result of a flaw in the heating system of her bedroom.

144.
Little Triptych, Free Vertical-Horizontal Rhythms, Cut and Pasted on a White Ground, 1919
Watercolor on paper
8¼ x 12³⁄₁₆ in. (21 x 31 cm.)
Basel, Kunstmuseum
Gift of Marguerite Arp-Hagenbach

The title of this lyrical, modestly scaled, yet compelling work may well refer back to the powerful, large-scale triptych of 1918, *Vertical-Horizontal Composition with Reciprocal Triangles,* each section of which measured 44⅙ x 20⅞ inches. In the *Little Triptych,* the parts have softer, more wavering boundaries, the colors are more fluid, and the spatial relations suggest a weightless equilibrium among the blunted squares and rectangles, as opposed to the sharply defined relationships among firm, hard-edged shapes of light and dark color in the larger work of the previous year. An effect of randomness, of relaxation of the rules, is created by the structure of the *Little Triptych;* a similar effect of softened yet meaningfully coordinated rectangular color relationships is created in the artist's *Free Vertical-Horizontal Rhythms,* a gouache of 1919 in the collection of Max Bill.

Both Taeuber-Arp and Jean Arp worked in gouache and watercolor in their earlier abstract experiments. Both also worked in watercolor and pasted paper, sometimes in collaboration, to capture the chance effects sought by the Dadaists. Arp himself gives Taeuber-Arp priority in devising (in 1916) watercolors in which squares and rectangles of brilliant color are juxtaposed horizontally and vertically.[5] Among Taeuber-Arp's most successful works of this type is the gouache *Composition in Quadrangular, Polychrome, Dense Spots,* created in 1920.

145.
Activated Circles, 1934
Oil on canvas
28⁹⁄₁₆ x 39⅜ in. (72.5 x 100 cm.)
Basel, Kunstmuseum
Gift of Marguerite Arp-Hagenbach

In both the paintings and wood reliefs made by Sophie Taeuber-Arp during the 1930s, the circle has an important position, sometimes segmented, sometimes as a conical projection, and sometimes played against rectangular forms. Despite the hermetic strictness of the composition of *Activated Circles,* there is a latent element of dynamism, a sort of abstract choreography, suggested by this abstraction and reiterated by its title. Indeed, because of the very strictness of the composition, the slightest deviation from geometric regularity creates an intense sense of movement.

The sculptor Max Bill has analyzed the *Activated Circles* in a series of diagrams that reveal the underlying vertical and horizontal relationships of the painting, the deviations from strict verticality and horizontality that enliven it, and the complex interplay of the four subdued colors — black, gray, light blue, and dark blue. Says Bill: "One might be tempted to see in these colored dots the balls of a juggler or the dice of a gambler, but quickly one notices that they have a different meaning and create a rhythm. . . . A more careful examination reveals an order."[6]

4.
Cited in Staber, 54.
5.
H. Read, *The Art of Jean Arp,* New York, 1968, 38.
6.
Max Bill, cited in Staber, 73.

144

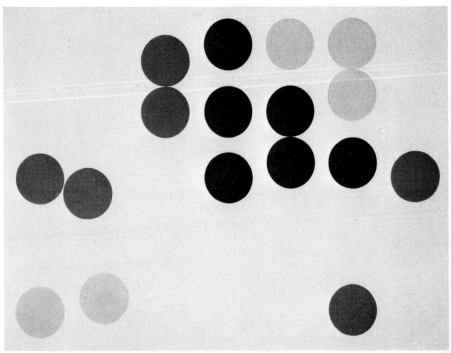

145

Marlow Moss
British, 1890-1958

Marlow Moss, an extraordinary woman and important twentieth-century artist, is relatively unknown to the general public. In part her obscurity is due to the loss of a major part of her output in a bombing that destroyed her house and atelier at Glauciel, France, in 1944. It is also true that she rarely sought publicity and was content to live and work quietly in France or in the English countryside at Penzance in Cornwall. During the 1930s her Neo-Plastic style was familiar to artists and connoisseurs of the Abstraction-Création group, of which she was a founding member, and from 1946 onwards she exhibited regularly at the Salon des Réalités Nouvelles and in group shows in London, Paris, Holland, and Switzerland. Her work, on occasion, was mistaken for that of Piet Mondrian, her mentor and the wellspring of her inspiration; it is, however, original. Unlike Mondrian, she sought a solution to the problem of translating physical energies into abstract equivalents by mathematical rather than by intuitive means. Using arithmetic equations and other materials in addition to paint, Moss transformed the elusive processes of nature into concrete and original works of art.

She was born Marjorie Jewell Moss to an upper-class English family whose values and way of life were to conflict with her own tastes and temperament. Music, which was later to play an important role in her art theory, was her all-engrossing interest in the early years. By age twelve she had reached a high level of accomplishment as a pianist. Her adolescence was marked by a series of difficulties and emotional tensions, particularly her family's strong opposition to her serious involvement in the arts. Tuberculosis curtailed her musical studies and forced a long period of inactivity. After her recovery she turned first to ballet and soon after expressed her desire to study art. The resulting objections led to a final rupture with her family and emotional conflicts that were not to be resolved for several long and difficult years.

Moss spent one year at the St. John's Wood School of Art, probably 1916-17, then transferred to the Slade School. She was more interested in controversial Post-Impressionist and Cubist art than in the academic training that seemed to her imitative and meaningless. Frustrated and suffering from the rejection of her work, she left the Slade School in 1919. In a state of emotional distress, she shut herself away in a cottage in Cornwall. A fortuitous encounter with a biography of Marie Curie helped to revitalize her energies,[1] and she returned to London to create a new life and direction.

She now began a period of emancipation, attempting to purge herself of emotion, to develop the broadest intellectual capacities, and to free herself of conventional mores. She took the name Marlow Moss and began to steep herself in philosophy and literature, among other subjects. Her spiritual sustenance derived from Nietzsche, Rimbaud, Marie Curie, Rembrandt, van Gogh, and Mondrian. Until the crucial year 1927, when she spent a short holiday in Paris and decided to establish herself permanently in France, she attended sculpture classes at the Municipal Art School in Penzance and worked in her London atelier in styles varying from Impressionist to Cubist.

Moss sought a mathematical formula by which to choreograph on canvas the essential relationships of space, movement, and light. Mondrian's work, which she first saw in the original in Paris in 1927, directed her quest. She met him personally in 1929 and saw him frequently until his departure from Paris nine years later. She studied with Amédée Ozenfant and learned Constructivist technique with Fernand Léger at his Académie Moderne.[2] In 1929 she produced her first Neo-Plastic paintings. She eliminated illusionistic space and curves, adhering to the flat surface of the canvas and using only angular geometric shapes; she limited her palette to red, yellow, blue, gray, white, and black. Moss strove for open, reduced form in order to interpret space and movement through rhythmic line and color. The problem of light as a vital energy obsessed her from her earliest awareness of its function in the canvases of Rembrandt, the Impressionists, and van Gogh. In her own work she experimented with layers of extremely thin coats of white paint, sometimes mixed with a touch of

---

1.
In gratitude she left a legacy to the Marie Curie cancer fund in her will.
2.
She later said, "All I understand of the art of painting I owe to his [Léger's] criticism." Zurich, 1973, n.p.
3.
Ibid.
4.
Ibid., nos. 36 and 38.

one primary, to achieve a luminous and radiant surface. To realize her carefully balanced compositions she worked with compass, ruler, and pencil, arranging precisely drawn colored forms on sketch paper.

Moss introduced the double-line composition at the Salon des Surin-dépendants in 1930, two years before its appearance in Mondrian's work. In a letter to the master she explained that she had found the single line too static, anti-rhythmic, and compositionally limiting.[3] In an attempt to retain the constructive element in her work without depending upon the counterpoint of black line against white ground, she began, about 1935, to add pieces of linen, thin plastic wire, cord, and other materials to build up a relief effect in all-white composi-tions. In her work after World War II, Moss returned to black lines and color, sometimes substituting rectilinear white slats for lines in order to achieve the sparest suggestion of form. In the final six compositions of her life the superstructure of Moss's Constructivist scheme for space, movement, and light became all but invisible and was carried by color alone.

Moss returned to England via Holland in 1940 at the outbreak of World War II. In Cornwall she began the study of architecture that was to serve as the inspiration for her three-dimensional metal constructions. The departure point for some of her sculpture is the continuous loop of Max Bill and the elegant, polished surfaces and curved geometric shapes of Hans Arp. She also made constructions that are sculptural equivalents of her angular Neo-Plastic paintings.[4]

During the last years of her life Moss worked toward an economical and increasingly reduced use of form while maintaining tight com-positional structure. In 1953 and again in 1958 she was presented in one-woman shows at the Hanover Gallery in London. Posthumous exhibitions of her work were held at the Stedelijk Museum in Amster-dam in 1962, at the Municipal Hall at Middleburg in 1972, and at the Gimpel and Hanover Galerie in Zurich in 1973-74.

146.
White and Blue, 1935
Oil on canvas with red thread
24⅞ x 17¾ in. (63 x 45 cm.)
Zurich, Gimpel and Hanover Galerie

White and Blue is an example of the delicate balance and sovereign purity of Moss' Neo-Plastic compositions. This canvas dates from the beginning period of her experiments with relief. Here slender lines of red thread, set against a luminous white ground, replace the thicker black and gray grid patterns of earlier work. Reduced to the barest suggestion of form, the narrow lines intersect at right angles and meet, at center left and lower right, the resistance of rectangles overlaid in white. The lines are suspended in space, midway between rhythmic continuity and abrupt arrest. The tension between move-ment and stasis, the materiality of thread and the void of open space is an arrangement of the abstract forces of energy. Moss uses color in a complementary sustention of flow and recession, balancing the thinness of red against the solidity and weight of the blue rectangle at lower right.

In an attempt to create an analog in painting for the forces of nature, Moss used line and color as equivalents of plane and volume. Wanting to achieve the purest expression of movement, space, and light, she continuously attempted to reduce form, replacing it with color and rhythm. The prevailing harmony and refinement of *White and Blue* derive from the pure plasticity of Mondrian's canvases. Here, however, Moss' own vision is evident in the inclusion of concrete, three-dimensional material; the suspension and reduction of line; and the spatial resonance of her ground.

146

147

Agnes Tait (Mrs. William McNulty)
American, 1897-?

A native of New York City, Agnes Tait received her training at the National Academy of Design. Until the onset of the Depression, she exhibited on a regular basis in New York and was particularly noted for decorative panels that exploited lacy friezes of tree forms and elegant profiles of animals or flowers poised against flat metallic backgrounds.

Throughout the Depression years Tait was active in a number of federal art agencies and, perhaps as a consequence of her involvement with "Art for the Millions," her attention turned to narrative and figural painting, which still retained an emphasis on decorative values. During the winter of 1933-34, she became an easel painter for the Public Works of Art Project in New York. While serving with the WPA's Federal Art Project, she was introduced to mural painting as a member of a collaborative team charged with the decoration of Bellevue Hospital in 1937. In 1939 her canvas *Olive Grove, Mallorca*, a decorative study of figures and animals in a tree-filled landscape, was selected for inclusion in the Gallery of American Art Today at the New York World's Fair. Sketches that Tait had submitted to earlier mural competitions of the Treasury Department's Section of Fine Arts resulted in an independent commission to decorate the U.S. Post Office in Laurinsburg, North Carolina, in 1941. Her mural frieze in the lobby of that building was entitled *Fruits of the Land*.

After World War II, Tait moved to the artists' colony at Santa Fe, New Mexico, where she divided her time between printmaking and illustrating children's books. Her best-known lithograph of the period, *The Old Friend* of 1950, combines a decorative interplay of delicate profiles of kittens and the spare branches of trees in winter with a strong, humane interest in the elderly woman who befriends homeless animals. Tait's illustrated storybooks include *Peter and Penny of the Island* (1941), *Heidi* (ca. 1950), and *Paco's Miracle* (1961).

147.
Skating in Central Park, ca. 1934
Oil on canvas
34⅛ x 48¼ in. (86.7 x 122.5 cm.)
Washington, D.C., National Collection of Fine Arts
Smithsonian Institution

Agnes Tait's *Skating in Central Park* was executed early in 1934 while the artist was employed by the first of the federal art programs of the Depression years, the Public Works of Art Project. Because the PWAP represented the earliest formulation of what would become a massive New Deal relief and patronage effort on behalf of destitute artists, that agency's stylistic and iconographic guidelines were still tentative. Artists were merely informed by Juliana Force, director of operations for New York's Region No. 2, that "the American Scene" was the subject matter preferred for works of art to be allocated to federal facilities.

Tait conformed to "the American Scene" proviso with a view of skaters in Central Park. Her canvas, however, is far from an artless slice of urban life served up to fill the demands of relief employment. Instead, *Skating in Central Park* reflects many of the complex stylistic trends informing the art of the period, trends that the catchall phrase "the American Scene" has all but obscured. There is, for example, a strong abstract and decorative sensibility at work in Tait's crisp patterns of bare tree limbs silhouetted against snow and sky, and in the flattened, stereometric figures making rhythmic patterns across the canvas. These swelling patterns are subtly reinforced by the countervailing curves of hillocks and the bridge at the right. The treatment of the boy with two dogs, just below the tree that marks the center of the painting, defines Tait's aesthetic. The splayed figure controlling two heraldic animals — the Gilgamesh motif, in fact — is a traditional staple in the repertory of the textile designer and the decorative artist, and its use here recalls Tait's own decorative screens of the twenties. This sense of strong, clear surface pattern can also be said to form the basis for the nascent American mural movement of the late twenties, which came into full flower when the catastrophe of economic depression prodded the government into making work for unemployed artists. Tait's concern for the integrity of the canvas surface and her emphatic, rhythmic movements across that surface relate her to Thomas Hart Benton and Boardman Robinson, the instigators of the American mural renaissance of the early thirties.

The narrative flavor of *Skating in Central Park* allies Tait with the main current of American genre painting, buried by the impact of the Armory Show but quietly revived as the Depression approached. The subject chosen here places Tait in a sequence of fun-filled glimpses of wintry New York at play that runs from Winslow Homer's illustrations for *Harper's Weekly* through William Glackens' *Central Park, Winter* (1905). Kenneth Hayes Miller, who returned to the skating theme repeatedly in the twenties, lending it a timeless heroism through calculated compositions derived from Signorelli and the Renaissance masters, may have influenced Tait's handling of her figural types. Her closely shaped costumes, which conform to and stress the bulbous outlines of heads and bodies, recall the dress of Miller's swaddled ladies and children.

Skating in Central Park, with its animated cast of scattered characters deployed for decorative effect, also suggests Tait's familiarity with American "primitive" art, especially the newly discovered work of Joseph Pickett. Primitivism, as a native and unspoiled form of American expression, attracted scholarly attention and achieved mass popularity just before the Depression, thanks to the efforts of Holger Cahill and The Newark Museum. A neo-primitive school of American art quickly developed in the years after 1930. Doris Lee is the best-known painter of this group, and her *April Storm, Washington Square* (ca. 1933) is virtually identical to Tait's painting in its surface rhythms and decorative emphasis. The salient difference is that whereas Lee stresses the antic behavior of her figures, to the point of creating a caricature of both New Yorkers and the American primitive style, Tait retains respect for the dignity of her subjects and the integrity of her art.

This respect is reinforced by the obvious similarity between *Skating in Central Park* and the works of Pieter Bruegel the Elder. Tait's trees, animals, and silhouetted figures are closely related to Bruegel's *Return of the Hunters,* while her golden, glowing palette duplicates that of Bruegel's peasant dances and weddings. Although Miller and his 14th Street School followed old master examples compositionally, Tait's procedure seems to derive from Grant Wood's deliberate use of Flemish conventions and techniques to link the life of everyday American types to an ongoing historical continuum, and thus to insinuate America's right to a place in the ongoing art historical tradition of the West.

Agnes Tait's *Skating in Central Park* therefore embodies, at a remarkably early date, a number of distinct and crucial factors at work beneath the rhetoric of "the American Scene": a mural quality, a renewed concern for the power of native iconography, an interest in distinctly American forms of artistic expression, and a desire to view American art and life in a broader human and historical context. Tait's message was not lost on her contemporaries. This painting was selected for inclusion in an exhibition of the best of PWAP work across the nation, held at the Corcoran Gallery in April of 1934, and was subsequently chosen by Frances Perkins for display in the Department of Labor. Throughout the Great Depression, *Skating in Central Park* spoke to those most directly concerned with the plight of suffering Americans of the human grace and dignity of their fellow citizens.

Kay Sage
American, 1898-1963

148

The Surrealist painter Kay Sage shared with her husband, Yves Tanguy, a predilection for abstract, suggestive, sometimes biomorphic, sometimes architectural forms, often in deep spatial vistas. Though small in scale, her paintings are often surprisingly monumental in their effect. Her oeuvre includes objects and collages as well as paintings. The artist also published several volumes of verse, and her autobiography, as yet unpublished, entitled *China Eggs,* was completed in 1955.[1]

Born in Albany, New York, of wealthy parents, Sage lived in Europe, mainly Italy, during the early part of her life, with a short visit home to the United States during World War I, when she attended the fashionable Brearley and Foxcroft schools. In 1925 Sage married Prince Ranieri di San Faustino, whom she divorced in 1935. The artist studied briefly at the Scuolo Libera delle Belle Arti in Rome and had her first solo show in Milan in 1936 at the Galleria del Milione. While in Italy, she wrote and illustrated a book of children's poetry, called *Piove in Giardino,* under the name of K. di San Faustino.

At the outbreak of World War II, she returned permanently to the United States, and in 1940, the year she married the French Surrealist Yves Tanguy, she had her first American exhibition at the Pierre Matisse Gallery. The couple settled in 1941 in Woodbury, Connecticut, where their circle included such art world figures as Hans Richter, the Surrealist artist and film maker; the sculptor Naum Gabo; the painter Peter Blume; and the critic James Thrall Soby, who was one of Sage's strongest admirers.

Tanguy had developed a unique Surrealist style of abstract, deep-spaced illusionism, in which the paint was applied with a tight, invisible facture that played up the ambiguity of the visual statement. Like Tanguy, Sage evolved a manner in which the minute realism of the descriptive surface is played against the patent unreality of

1.
This manuscript is in the Archives of American Art, Washington, D.C. I am grateful to Stephen R. Miller, who is at present engaged in writing a definitive study of the artist, for this information.

the motif. At times, her mat surfaces and self-contradictory vistas, articulated by means of architectonic forms, are reminiscent of similar strategies in the style of the Italian Scuola Metafisica, which had played a role in the formulation of Surrealist imagery. In 1947 Sage, along with Tanguy, Arp, Duchamp, Matta, Giacometti, and many others, took part in the last major group show of the Surrealist movement, organized by André Breton and Marcel Duchamp at the Galerie Maeght in Paris. In 1950 the artist exhibited at the Catherine Viviano Gallery in New York, where she was to exhibit in 1952, 1956, 1958, 1960 — the year of a retrospective show of her work from 1937 to 1958 — and in 1961. Her painting was included among the works of American artists shown at the American Pavilion at the Brussels World's Fair in 1954.

A joint exhibition of her work and Tanguy's at the Wadsworth Atheneum in 1954 revealed the substantial differences between the two artists' styles despite their superficial similarities.[2] Sage's formal language is characteristically rather angular and harsh, her compositions illuminated by a mysterious, melancholy light. Her colors are subdued and earthy, lacking the jewellike preciousness of Tanguy's, and her motifs characteristically suggest scaffolding of some kind, sometimes molded into perversely organic or even anthropomorphic forms as in the unlikely, eerily metamorphic head of *Small Portrait* (1950, Poughkeepsie, Vassar College Art Gallery). A major retrospective of Sage's work was held at the Mattatuck Museum, Waterbury, Connecticut, in 1965.

148.
Page 49, 1950
Oil on canvas
18 x 15 in. (45.7 x 38.1 cm.)
Signed and dated: Kay Sage '50
Williamstown, Massachusetts, Williams College Museum of Art
Bequest of Kay Sage Tanguy

This work is typical of a group of Sage's canvases from the mid-forties through the fifties in which an architectural scaffolding or framework is combined with drapery in order to suggest an equivocal windowlike motif. Other works with this melancholy, at times vaguely threatening, iconography are *Hyphen* (1954, New York, Museum of Modern Art); *Quote-Unquote* (1958, Hartford, Wadsworth Atheneum); and *No Wind No Birds* (1958, Washington, D.C., Monagan College). The drawing that defines the complexly interrelated forms is clean, the brushwork almost imperceptible, the imagery at once modest yet compelling in its austerity and its evocation of continuing space and incident beyond the literal boundaries of the small frame. The image, though authoritative, ultimately escapes exact definition. In the words of the artist herself: "There is no reason why anything should mean more than its own statement."[3]

2.
B [uckley], 4.
3.
Sage, 1961, quoted in Waterbury, 1965.

Franciska Clausen

Danish, b. 1899

In the important international exhibition of avant-garde art organized by the Société Anonyme in 1926 and held at The Brooklyn Museum, Francisca (*sic*) Clausen was one of the two artists representing Denmark. Accompanying the reproduction of her abstract, architectonic canvas in the elegant catalog was the information that she had recently "come to Paris and joined the group of young artists who have gathered around Léger. However," continued Katherine Dreier, author of the text and prime mover of the Société Anonyme, "she has kept her own personality intact and is considered by Leger [*sic*] as one of the most gifted of the group."[1]

Franciska Clausen was born in the Danish city of Aabenraa, which, until 1920, belonged to Germany. She studied art in Weimar, Copenhagen, and Munich, where she attended Hans Hofmann's school from 1921 until she went to Berlin in 1922. There, at the avant-garde gallery Der Sturm, she encountered Laszlo Moholy-Nagy, then one of the leaders of the movement toward pure abstraction. Under his influence Clausen moved in two not unrelated directions: toward reduction of formal elements through the medium of collage and, at the same time, toward extremely objective, if simplified, representational painting, such as *The Ladder (Moholy-Nagy's Studio in Lutzowstrasse, Berlin)* (Collection the artist), which was exhibited under the auspices of the radical November Group at the Great Berlin Art Exhibition of 1923.[2]

In 1922 a major exhibition of Russian Constructivist art in Berlin brought such figures as El Lissitzky and Natan Altman to that city. Particularly impressed by Altman's pictorial self-discipline and innovative social ideas, Clausen began to see art more and more as an objective solution to purely formal problems rather than as a kind of individual self-expression.[3] In 1923 she studied for a time with Alexander Archipenko, a leading Constructivist. She went to Paris in January 1924, where she became one of the first women students in Fernand Léger's studio at the Académie Moderne. She was followed there by several other Archipenko students, including a group that soon became known as "The Scandinavians," including, as well

as herself, Otto Carlsund and Erik Olson; these "Scandinavians" soon became Léger's most outstanding pupils. He encouraged them to exhibit, participating with them in a show at the Maison Watteau, the Swedish House of Culture in Paris; financing Otto Carlsund's first solo exhibition; and, in 1928, expressing a wish to do the same for Franciska Clausen; she, however, refused his offer, doubting that her works were good enough.[4]

Léger's pupils worked in a communal atmosphere, often collaborating on joint projects or executing works conceived by the master. In the mid-1920s Clausen, like the rest of this group, turned her attention to various problems of composition. Perhaps the main issue, at least from 1924 to 1926, was the enrichment of abstraction by means of representational, or even *trompe l'oeil,* elements. Clausen played a quite literal role in one of Léger's paintings that achieves this objective: hers is the profile to the left in his important *Composition with Profile: Knife and Figure* of 1926 (Paris, Fondation Le Corbusier), which was one of Léger's most controlled and powerful Purist statements, and a cherished possession of Le Corbusier's.[5] She worked on various problems of composition involving the interaction of simplified, purified shape-elements, derived from contemporary life, within abstract pictorial contexts. At the same time, she was still attracted by purely formal issues of architectonic construction, as exemplified by her *Composition* of 1925 (formerly in the collection of the Comte de Noailles, Paris).[6] This tendency toward pure abstraction was emphasized by her contact with Mondrian, Arp, and Taeuber-Arp, and her joining the Cercle et Carré group, with whom she exhibited in 1930. The impact of Neo-Plasticism and *art concret* may be seen in many of her works of ca. 1928 to 1930, such as her *Neoplasticist Composition* (ca. 1928, Lund, Prof. Oscar Reutersward) or her *Vertical-Horizontal Composition,* a gouache of 1930 (Stockholm, Moderna Museet); her *Circles and Squares* of 1928 (Collection the artist) might well be compared with Sophie Taeuber-Arp's related works of the same period (see, for example, cat. no. 145, although it is somewhat later).

1.
International Exhibition of Modern Art Arranged by the Société Anonyme for the Brooklyn Museum, text by Katherine S. Dreier, New York, 1926, 10. Dreier and the Société Anonyme consistently supported the work of avant-garde women artists: the Collection of the Société Anonyme at the Yale University Art Gallery contains work by: Tour Donas (Tour D'Onasky, ca. 1896-?), purportedly "the first woman abstract painter"; Nadezhda Udaltsova; Ragnhild Keyser (1889-1943); Jacoba van Heemskerck (1876-1923); Sophie Taeuber-Arp; Suzanne Duchamp (1889-?); and several other women artists. See the *Collection of the Société Anonyme: Museum of Modern Art 1920,* Yale University Art Gallery, New Haven, 1950, 17-18, 38-39, 49, 52-53, 68-69, 131.
2.
See Andersen and Hansen, repr. 40.
3.
Ibid., 168.
4.
Ibid., 169.
5.
See London, The Tate Gallery, *Léger and Purist Paris,* 1970, 80 and repr.

After her return to Denmark during World War II, she executed an
important series of collages, beginning in 1950, but has devoted
herself in recent years mainly to the production of quite conventional, realistic portraits.[7]

149.

Vase with Pipes, 1929
Oil on canvas
24³/₁₆ x 18⁵/₁₆ in. (61.5 x 46.5 cm.)
Aarhus (Denmark) Kunstmuseum

Vase with Pipes is an important example of Clausen's oeuvre at a
moment when Surrealist ideas may have begun to infiltrate and soften
her Purist stylistic formulations. The various elements of the painting
can be related to similar ones habitually used in the twenties by Léger
and the members of his circle. Léger himself, for example, had
depicted pipes in a similar sort of sharply divided abstract space in his
The Two Pipes of 1925 (private collection);[8] the same kind of stylized,
floating flowers figured in his *Still Life* of 1927 (Bern, Musée des
Beaux-Arts);[9] and the classical shapes of the urn relate to any number
of similar forms in his works of this period.

Clausen, too, had been working with the formal contrasts resulting
from the insertion of quite solidly three-dimensional objects into pictorial contexts dominated by schematic reductions of standardized
objects or abstract elements. Her *Bar* of 1927 (Lyngby, Collection the
Commune), for example, combines a convincingly shaded flask and
piled up saucers with a schematized pipe and glass and sweepingly
abstract architectural shapes. In her monumental *Screw-Propeller* of
1926 (Skive Museum),[10] one of a series of representations of
machine parts, she surrounds the relatively realistic principal element
with a variety of abstract and relatively representational sub-themes,
within a precisely delineated planar, non-representational, yet
somehow suggestively nautical, context.

Vase with Pipes is peculiarly Clausen's creation and unique to this
period of the very late 1920s and early '30s, when, in both her work
and Léger's, the impact of Surrealism was softening forms, loosening
composition, increasing ironic and incongruous juxtapositions of
objects or spatial disposition, and, at times, interjecting an unexpected
sense of organic growth.[11] Here, the diagonal, upward-shooting
rhythm of the colorful, rather strongly modeled pipes emerging from
the jagged, torn "pouch" contrasts strongly both with the — equally
colorful — abstract background and with the softer, drooping curves
and rhythms of the extremely different right-hand side of the painting.
This side is dominated by the serene gray form of the classical urn profile against an equally gray background, enlivened by the simplified
flowers and, above all, by the sprightly, lyrical butterfly. Ironically,
the world of inorganic objects to the left seems far more vigorous and
energetic than that of organic nature to the right, from which it is so
sharply distinguished, despite the triangular element at the base of the
painting that cuts across both areas. In a semi-Surrealist context of implicit
sexual overtones, it might not be too far-fetched to see subtle references
to masculine versus feminine qualities in the exaggerated "contrast of
objects" between the left-hand and right-hand portions of the painting.

149

6.
Andersen and Hansen, repr. 46.
7.
See ibid., 160-61, for reproductions.
8.
Paris, Grand Palais, *Fernand Léger,* 1971, no. 89, repr. 83.
9.
Ibid., no. 99, repr. 82.
10.
Andersen and Hansen, color repr. 57 and on cover.
11.
See Paris, 1971, nos. 106, 107, and 110, for example. John Golding, however,
makes well-taken distinctions between the basic intentions of Léger's art and those
of the Surrealists in London, The Tate Gallery, *Léger and Purist Paris,* 1970, 22.

Alice Neel

American, b. 1900

"My choices perhaps were not always conscious, but I have felt that people's images reflect the era in a way that nothing else could."[1] The artist's statement succinctly defines the scope of her career, which has emphasized the portrait above all other subjects. Born in Merion Square, Pennsylvania, Neel attended the Philadelphia School of Design for Women (now Moore College of Art), completing her studies there in 1925. Following her marriage to a Cuban, she came to New York City in 1927. After various personal disasters, including the loss of a child in infancy, a nervous breakdown, and attempted suicide, Neel settled permanently in New York in 1932, participating in the New Deal Public Works of Art Project in 1933 and joining the WPA easel project in 1935. In 1938 she moved to Spanish Harlem, where she remained for twenty-five years. Her sons were born in 1939 and 1941.

Neel's earliest works are marked by an unusual mingling of social commitment and subjective intensity; forms are shaped by feeling in works like *Futility of Effort* (1930), a schematic rendering of the death of a baby, or in the overtly dreamlike, surrealist *Subconscious* (1942). At times it is her own experience that is depicted with sharp social satire, as in a work like *Well Baby Clinic* (1928), or with quiet pathos, as in the memory portrait, *Dead Father* (1946), which is, despite its personal rather than public inspiration, strangely reminiscent of Ben Shahn's image of the martyred Sacco and Vanzetti.

Neel is, however, best known for the portraits of art world figures and of her children and their families that she has made during the sixties and seventies. In works like *Henry Geldzahler* (1967), *Andy Warhol* (1970), and *Isabel Bishop* (1974), she reveals the inner reality of her sitters within a framework of incisive social and temporal accuracy; her pictorial edge is cutting yet honed for external fidelity at the same time. Neel's portraits of mothers and children, sometimes nude, often tense, are peculiarly satisfying. Works like *Carmen and Baby* (1972) or *Mother and Child (Nancy and Olivia)* (1976) are completely devoid of the sugary sentimentality usually associated with this sub-

ject. Her open-minded depictions of the male nude (*Joe Gould,* 1933; *John Perrault,* 1972) are equally unconventional.

An outspoken advocate of the rights of women and an enthusiastic supporter of recent feminist activism — Neel did a *Time* magazine cover portrait of Kate Millet in 1970 and designed an announcement for the National Organization of Women in 1973 — the artist nevertheless maintains: "Injustice has no sex and one of the primary motives of my work has been to reveal the inequalities and pressures as shown in the psychology of the people I painted."[2]

150.
T. B., Harlem, 1940
Oil on canvas
40 x 40 in. (101.6 x 101.6 cm.)
Signed lower left
New York, Alice Neel, Graham Gallery

Traditional images of martyrdom — Christ, a dying saint, Marat — are inevitably called to mind by this moving representation of a dying young Puerto Rican. The work, under the title *Tuberculosis in Harlem,* served as the cover illustration for a catalog of the artist's one-woman exhibition in 1951, with a foreword by the leftist novelist and theorist Michael Gold. While the portrait is a striking example of Neel's social concern, her confrontation with the suffering and deprivation that surrounded her during the period she lived in Spanish Harlem, it is, nevertheless, a unique individual who confronts us — vulnerable, elongated, sensual — not a generalized symbol of the social situation.

During this period of her career, when Neel had gone to live in Spanish Harlem with a Puerto Rican nightclub singer named José, she painted various portraits of neighbors, including the wife and children of this sitter. Rarely has her portrait vision been more unflinching, her empathy more apparent, than in these somberly colored, brooding, expressively drawn representations of victims of

---

1.
A. Neel, doctoral address, Moore College of Art, June 1971, in Athens, 1975, n.p.
2.
Ibid., introduction, n.p.

an unjust order who nevertheless maintain a stoic dignity in the eyes of the artist. This painting might well be compared with the artist's quite different later image of physical vulnerability, *Andy Warhol* (1970), in which the victim, isolated frontally in the center of the canvas — scarred, bandaged, and livid — seems to will himself into a kind of mocking decorum after his near assassination.

150

Isabel Bishop

American, b. 1902

Isabel Bishop was born in Cincinnati, Ohio, and raised in Detroit, where her father was the principal of a public high school. She began Saturday art classes, drawing from life, at the John Wicker Art School at age twelve. In 1918, when she had graduated from high school, Bishop moved to New York City to study at the New York School of Design for Women. The adventurousness of the New York art scene following the 1913 Armory Show stimulated her interest in modern art and led to her enrollment in the Art Students League in 1920. Her intention had been to study with Max Weber, who was then working in a post-Cubist idiom, but his antipathy to her continued interest in drawing from the nude made her unable to function as his student. Her mentor at the League then became Kenneth Hayes Miller, whose Renaissance facture and strong commitment to contemporaneity and urban realism influenced her choice of subject and style for several years. However, Bishop eventually became ill at ease with Miller's ideas of the detachment and anonymity of the artist. With the encouragement of Guy Pène du Bois, whose work is individual and even eccentric, she began to develop a more personal approach to the representation of contemporary life.

Bishop is essentially a New York artist. Her subjects are young women encountered on the subways and streets of New York, on their way to or from work, and relaxing at lunchtime, or derelicts seen from the window of her Union Square studio. Like Reginald Marsh, with whom she is often linked, and Miller himself, Bishop sought to connect the grand manner of classical tradition with contemporary urban subjects.[1] Her multi-figured canvases, such as the early *Dante and Virgil in Union Square*, 1932,[2] or the more recent *High School Students No. 2*, 1973,[3] make use of Renaissance compositional devices, defining space in multi-layered, receding planes and arranging figures in a laterally expanding frieze.

Around the 14th Street area she observed people immersed in their daily lives whose attitudes — both physical and psychological — she found fascinating, often inviting them to her studio to assume a pose that had caught her eye and to model for preliminary sketches. She placed her figures in the settings in which she had found them, sometimes using props for greater authenticity, but she retained a formal, traditional structure. Among the material that she always keeps in her studio are a Chinese mural and a reproduction of a small Rubens. She believes that the juxtaposition of the two answers "the profoundest problems of form."[4]

Throughout her career Bishop has been concerned with the compositional problems that relate to capturing impressions of movement. She has been absorbed by the dynamics of mobility and the representation of the ever present potential for change.[5] She believes that a convincing portrayal of physical movement, given the nature of her subjects and their obviously low social positions, can be a metaphor for the possibility of a shift in social position.[6] Nonetheless, Bishop denies deliberate political or social content in her work.[7] It is the human vitality of her subjects, their kinship with the essential humanity found in traditional genre paintings and in the Baroque grand manner that appeals to her.

Bishop's most successful pictures have women subjects, usually in contemporary dress, sometimes nude, but always in monumental proportions and engrossed in an activity. Her single figures tend to be absorbed in specific physical acts; her dual figures in a mutual response or in a simple act such as reading or eating. She arranges her figures in an endless variety of contrasts and juxtapositions, suggesting a world of multiple possibilities within a feminine syntax. Though not consciously working from a feminist point of view,[8] the vigor and strength of Bishop's vision is revealed in her women.

Isabel Bishop's work first began to attract attention in the 1930s with a one-woman show at the Midtown Galleries in 1932. In addition to the Art Students League, she has been associated with the Whitney Studio Club, later the Whitney Museum of American Art; the National Academy of Design; and the National Institute of Arts and

---

1.
Marsh, Miller, and Bishop went to Europe together in 1931 to study.
Alloway, 62.
2.
Ibid., repr. 61.
3.
Ibid., repr. 62.
4.
Nemser, 15.
5.
Lunde, 60.
6.
Tucson, 1974, 24, and Alloway, 63.
7.
Nemser, 18.
8.
Women were more readily available as subjects than men. Ibid., 18, 20.

Letters. Her work has been continuously exhibited since the 1930s and included in various exhibitions sponsored by the International Exhibition of Painting at Carnegie Institute of Pittsburgh; the 1939 New York World's Fair; the Whitney Museum of American Art; and the Corcoran Biennial in Washington, D.C. One-woman exhibitions of her art include frequent shows at the Midtown Galleries in New York; a 1970 exhibition at the New Jersey State Museum in Trenton; and a major retrospective in 1974 at the University of Arizona Museum of Art, Tucson.

151.
Nude, 1934
Oil on composition board
33 x 40 in. (83.8 x 101.6 cm.)
Signed lower center
New York, Whitney Museum of American Art

151

This *Nude,* one of Bishop's earliest, embodies many of the sensuous, baroque qualities that she admired in the work of Rubens, Rembrandt, Delacroix, Watteau, and Renoir. The twisting forms of the body poised for movement and the breadth of their proportions place this figure in the art historical context of the grand manner. The composition is tightly structured, with solidly modeled forms in a series of interlocking verticals and diagonals carefully aligned with the picture plane. A prevailing animation, which is the result of both active pose and brushstroke, signals the potential for change that is an underlying concern in Bishop's work. Her attempted solution to the problem of giving authenticity to the modern equivalents of the heroic nude is the "mobility" that she considers characteristic of American life.[9]

Bishop found the nude a fascinating subject, "especially for a woman."[10] In selecting models for this theme, she chose women who struck her as possessing a "kind of animality that seemed real."[11] This physical vitality gives Bishop's nudes a sense of immediacy and infuses a subject pointedly free of class or period distinctions with a specifically modern spirit. In each decade of her career Bishop took up the nude along with more explicitly contemporary subjects. Examples such as *Nude by a Stream,* 1938; *Nude Bending,* 1949; *Nude #2,* 1954; and a series of women undressing of the late fifties and sixties demonstrate the richness and variety of the artist's approach to the motive. More recently Bishop has avoided painting the nude, no longer feeling fresh and new impulses toward the subject.[12]

While Bishop was at the Art Students League, the nude had strong currency among artists such as Bernard Karfiol, Alexander Brook, Emil Ganso, and Yasuo Kunyioshi. Bishop was probably not directly influenced by this group, but she was extremely conscious of their work. Her expressed wish to find contemporary relationships to traditional art forms has made the nude an especially credible vehicle for her expression. Commenting on the beauty of Bishop's nudes, John Russell called them "pearly but down to earth, tender but not at all idealized."[13]

9.
Bishop, 1963, 117.
10.
Nemser, 18.
11.
Bishop, 1963, 117.
12.
Nemser, 19.
13.
Russell.

Alice Trumbull Mason

American, 1904-1971

Alice Trumbull Mason was born in 1904 in Litchfield, Connecticut, into an old New England family: among her ancestors were Governor Trumbull of Connecticut, the first governor to support Washington in the American Revolution, and John Trumbull, the famous history painter of the Revolution; on her mother's side was a long line of early conservationists. The family, who were Christian Scientists, were well-to-do, and, in addition to providing an atmosphere of intellectual freedom for their children, were able to afford extensive travel in Europe. It was during a family trip to Italy in 1922 that Mason had her first formal introduction to art at the British Academy in Rome. From 1924 to 1928 she studied at the National Academy in New York with Charles Hawthorne; following this, she enrolled in classes at the Grand Central Art Galleries, taught by Arshile Gorky. This coincided with her initial investigation of abstract painting, and Gorky's classes were therefore particularly stimulating. Mason studied with Gorky for only a few years, but she remained an abstract artist all her life. The only other formal training she had was later, in 1944-47, when she received instruction from Stanley Hayter, at the Atelier 17, in soft-ground etching.

Mason worked in oils, soft-ground etching, and aquatint; she called her style "architectural abstraction." She produced a large body of paintings and prints, but received little more than one-line mentions in reviews of the American Abstract Artists group, of which she was a charter member and a very active participant. The artist served the American Abstract Artists between 1936 and 1963 as treasurer, secretary, and, finally, president. She was also a member of the Federation of Modern Painters and Sculptors and 14 Painters/Printmakers. She was married to Warwood Mason, a ship's captain, and raised two children mainly on her own, as her husband was out to sea much of the time. She sustained great tragedy when her son accidentally died in 1958, yet she continued to paint, although from this time on she withdrew into increasing isolation.

Alice Trumbull Mason died in New York City in 1971, at the age of sixty-seven. She was survived by her daughter, Emily Mason Kahn, also an artist. Although Mason's name is not widely known, her works are in many museums and private collections, including the Whitney Museum of American Art, the Guggenheim Museum, The Metropolitan Museum of Art, and the Museum of Modern Art in New York; The Brooklyn Museum, the Philadelphia Museum of Art, the Walker Art Center, the Hirshhorn Museum, and the Springfield (Mass.) Museum of Fine Arts. She has had several one-woman shows, including those at the Museum of Living Art, New York (1942); the Rose Fried Gallery, New York (1948); the Hansa Gallery, New York (1959); and the Washburn Gallery, New York (1974). Mason was honored with a small retrospective exhibition at the Whitney Museum of American Art in 1973 and has been included in many group shows, including all those of the American Abstract Artists.

152.
L'Hasard, 1948
Oil on masonite
36½ x 28⅜ in. (92.7 x 72.1 cm.)
New York, Washburn Gallery
(See color plate, p. 98)

L'Hasard ("chance") was painted in 1948. The title is taken from Mallarmé's arcane poem "Un coup de dés jamais n'abolira le hasard" ("A throw of the dice never will abolish chance"). Alice Trumbull Mason was raised in a family of word-lovers: they often gathered in the living room at night to play charades and to read poetry, often Mason's own. It was this atmosphere that instilled in Mason a love of words and concepts that endured throughout her lifetime. She wrote a good deal, not only poetry, but a rather abstract form of prose as well. The family religion may have played a part in shaping Mason's lifelong passion for the abstract; at any rate, her interest in abstraction, both in writing and in painting, dates back to the middle of the 1920s. Her paintings developed from biomorphic abstraction, in the manner of Gorky, in the 1930s, to an increasingly geometric form, and finally arrived at the pure, architectural, abstract compositions characteristic of the period extending from the late 1950s to 1969, which is the date of her last paintings.

Composition, color, and craftmanship were of equal importance to Mason in the creation of her paintings. What she strove to achieve was a positive construction, a statement that grew through the freedom of abstract art to combine intellect and feeling, vitality and passion. She once said of her style of architectural abstraction that it was "a building and not a destroying. It is making color, density, dark and light, rhythm and balance work together without depending on references and associations."[1]

At the time *L'Hasard* was painted, Mason had definitively formulated her attitude toward composition. No longer biomorphic, her basic structure was a four-way balance. This balance was very important because she wanted the color and shapes in each painting to exist in a freedom of displacement; by establishing a four-way balance, movement and vitality were assured at each painting's inception. The sense of transition and change she wished to achieve is attained in *L'Hasard*. During the next twenty years, her work became simplified: using fewer shapes and often quieter colors, Mason strengthened the tension and movement among these elements. It is, however, interesting to note that the last dated painting of 1969, *Urban White*, may be viewed as the final statement of a twenty-five year development of the theme of *L'Hasard*.

It was typical of Mason to work in series of ideas: she would learn something from each painting that would be used to solve the problem in a more complete way in the next painting of the series. At times she would hold an idea in abeyance for a few years to investigate it further at a later period. Her color sense is very personal, and she always made her own paints from pigments that she ground and mixed with oil. *L'Hasard* has a typical, rather deep, autumnal color scheme, but she often used color schemes of very pale, evanescent hues.

Mason believed very deeply that making a picture required planning, and she generally made preparatory sketches. The drawing for *L'Hasard,* for example, includes both letters written in to designate the colors and shading of areas to indicate the relation of light and shadow in the colors. Paradoxically, given the title of the work, everything was very clearly conceived in the initial sketch and then faithfully and deliberately carried out in the completed work.

1.
Alice Trumbull Mason Papers, The Archives of American Art, New York, N.Y.

Leonor Fini
French, b. 1908

Leonor Fini is a beautiful, dramatic woman whose personal style has achieved as much celebrity as her work. In an ambience of exotic objects and pampered cats she wears long dresses of sumptuous fabrics and delights in donning masks that transform her into feline or plumed creatures.

Born in the early part of the century in Buenos Aires, Fini spent her childhood and adolescence in Trieste, the city of her mother's family; custody disputes between her parents at times involved Fini and her mother in sudden flights and disguises. When, still in her teens, the tempestuous, whimsical young woman decided to become a painter, she taught herself from her enthusiasms for earlier art. Fini went to Milan, perhaps as early as 1925, and there met Carrà, de Chirico, and Funi. Their interests in a realism derived from various periods in the history of art and their belief in an essential quality beyond the physicality of an object — the heritage of Pittura Metafisica — as well as de Chirico's emphasis on the imagination were beneficial to her development. From what has been written and reproduced of Fini's work before 1939, it varies in style from minutely detailed realism to a free, painterly treatment and reflects a taste for fifteenth-century Germany and Italy, Mannerism, the Hogarth of *The Harlot's Progress,* the Pre-Raphaelites, Art Nouveau, and neoclassical Picasso; its subject matter, which has always been Fini's foremost concern, often involves courtly or theatrical situations in which impertinent young women are the major protagonists.

In 1932 Fini was in Paris, where Surrealism had been gathering momentum since 1924. Her penchant for the unconventional and erotic and her admiration for de Chirico's early paintings coincided with Surrealist attitudes, and by 1936 she had met Max Ernst and Paul Eluard and was experimenting with automatic drawing. Many painters and poets in the Surrealist circle were her friends and she exhibited with them on several occasions but never became a member of the group.

Surrealism proposed to change life by plumbing the unconscious to reveal the rich potential of mankind beyond all present considerations of good and evil, beauty, or the limitations of reason. Fini's realistic treatment of a strange world and the importance she attached to unconscious vision, whether it involves cruelty, erotism, the fantastic, or bizarre metamorphoses, are compatible with Surrealism. Yet, as Fini has noted, her work has juxtapositions that are less arbitrary than the Surrealists',[1] and it is less deliberately iconoclastic, more amenable to historical ties.

When World War II began Fini was in Arcachon, then in Paris and Monte Carlo where she painted portraits. From 1944 to 1947 she was in Rome, and since that time has lived in Paris. It was during the war years that she first designed sets and costumes for the theater. Drama, ballet, film, and book illustration have become important aspects of her career and she is disconcerted when referred to only as a painter. Nonetheless, her painting has continued to evolve. From the 1950s come a series of visionary women guardians reigning over primordial lands of phoenixes or protecting a large pure egg. In about 1958 smooth surfaces and contours give way to more mysterious textures, with iridescent colors forming crushed jewel grottoes and subterranean realms. By the early 1960s svelte women reappear in a world now filled with light and color. A crystalline purity of form often contrasts with an evanescent, textured area and always with the enigmatic psychological purpose of the characters.

153.
The Angel of Anatomy, 1949
Oil on canvas
21⅝ x 13³/₁₆ in. (55 x 33.5 cm.)
Paris, Collection the artist

The somber, wary face of this angel of anatomy belongs to the artist herself; in fact, Fini's features recur in most of her paintings. Here,

1.
Monegal, 12-13. Jelenski, 37.

153

atop eroding flesh and bones, they seem defiant and gain authority from a Baroque wig, courtly robe, and large wings.

The starting point for this painting is an eighteenth-century treatise on anatomy, with engraved and painted illustrations by Gautier d'Agoty, that is in the artist's collection.[2] She has used the last of four plates in which successive layers of muscles are depicted, a series seeming to decompose the body down to the bone. In the engraving, as in the painting, the outer ribs are removed and the fleshy portion of the diaphragm has jagged cuts. The painting is almost the same height as the illustration, but narrower in format; the arms are brought nearer to the body and the outspread hands are given a new function; the upper torso and head receive a slight twist and the living face, the wig, and robe are new additions.

Fini told an interviewer in 1954 of her adolescence in Trieste and her secret rendezvous at the morgue, of her daily, quasi-religious contemplation of the corpses, who stayed on in her spiritual life.[3] She finds death an attractive force, and has equated it with stillness, immobility, and the ideal.[4] Skeletons and bones often appear in Fini's paintings, especially those of the decade following World War II. When presented as part of living beings, as in this work; *The Emerging Ones* (1958, Anvers-Schoten, Collection Plouvier); and the *Sfinge la Morte* (1973), they belong to the realm not only of death, but of metamorphosis, the wondrous changing to something "other." Decomposition becomes the requisite counterpart of transformation, as implied by the title of *Emerging Ones* where diaphanous, skeletal women-torsos sit upright on lion haunches. The sphinx — half-woman, half-lion or sometimes half-woman, half-root — appears most often in her work of the 1940s but continues to inhabit the later paintings as well. This being who poses the riddle of life has Fini's own face united with the beast/root/bone forces of the unconscious. "Night," "stranger," and "unknown" are words Fini once chose for this interior source of art, and in many comments, she has been open about her reliance upon it: "It is the stranger who gives the orders; all works of art obey these strangers."[5]

154.
The Two Skulls, 1950
Oil on canvas
13⅜ x 22¹/₁₆ in. (34 x 56 cm.)
Paris, Collection the artist

154

In 1943-44 Leonor Fini spent six months on the island of Giglio, ten miles off the Tuscan coast, between Italy and Corsica. Here she began a series of still-life compositions of plants, rocks, and debris from the sea, an interest that continues in *Two Skulls,* as well as in such works as *Sphinx Regina* (1946, Turin, Collection Bianca Cavallo), where an eye peers from a cavity in a fallen branch, and *Sphinx philagria* (1945, Rome, Collection Countess Solari), in which a gnarled root sprouts the breasts and head of a woman. In all the color scheme is somber and detail minutely rendered. Jean Genet described this

2.
Gautier d'Agoty, Arnaud Eloi, *Cours complet d'anatomie, peint et gravé en couleurs naturelles par M.A.E. Gautier d'Agoty . . . et expliqué par M. Jadelot,* Nancy, 1773.
3.
Virginia Clément, "Leonor, un souterrain nommé désir," *Aesculape,* 36e année, no. 3, March 1954, 67.
4.
Armand Lanoux, "Instants d'une psychanalyse critique: Leonor Fini," *La table ronde,* no. 108, December 1956, 184.
5.
Ibid., 183.
6.
Jean Genet, *Lettre à Leonor Fini,"* Paris, 1950, n.p.
7.
Alain Jouffrey, "Portrait d'un artiste (IV): Léonor Fini," *Arts,* no. 541, November 9-15, 1955, 9.

period as one of "cruelle bonté" (cruel kindness) and the paintings evocative of "odeurs marécageuses" (swampy odors).[6]

Before *Two Skulls* the viewer must ponder whether one is in an enchanted domain or a haunted underworld. If the skulls alarm in their allusion to death, they are also beyond death, motionless, peaceful. "What attracts me in it [death] is immobility. What exasperates me most is time, change: because I myself am terribly mobile."[7] Those who know Fini note the contrast between the silent, still world of her painting and her own sprightly loquaciousness.

If life has stopped for the skulls, the delicate tendrils of a plant offer four full blooms — welcome touches of pink — and numerous buds. Other plants have withered and dried and catch the low, raking light in craggy forms similar to the bones' contours: a filigree pattern offset by the large areas of light and dark. Convexities and cavities, crevices and points provide satisfying — and erotic — formal relationships.

Seventeenth-century *memento mori* paintings have accustomed us to a human skull contrasted with the ripeness and life of growing things on a table top. Yet here we are out of doors, close to the ground, and the skulls we confront are animal. One was a wolf or dog, but the other is broken beyond recognition; its size and unfamiliarity produce speculations of a prehistoric creature. Fini does not bid us to " 'remember death' and repent," but rather reveals an existence other than we know.

155

Lee Krasner
American, b. 1908

Brooklyn-born Lee Krasner belongs to the New York School of painters whose innovative vision and bold synthesis of European modernism produced new art and moved the center of the artistic avant-garde from Europe to America. She began life as Leonore Krasner, the first American-born child of a large and strongly matriarchal Russian Jewish family. English, Russian, Yiddish, and Hebrew were interchangeable household languages, and a wide range of reading material, from Maeterlinck and Edgar Allan Poe to fairy tales and Russian classics, provided her with an introduction to art and culture. Her earliest training was basically academic, first as an art major at Washington Irving High School and, from 1926 to 1929, at the Women's Art School at Cooper Union — both were schools for women only. She studied life drawing with George Bridgman at the Art Students League in 1928 and spent three years at the National Academy of Design beginning around 1929. Her work from these years is in the Impressionist and Post-Impressionist styles, but her first contact with the School of Paris at the Museum of Modern Art also dates from this period. She was impressed by Picasso, Mondrian, and Matisse; their influence is most strikingly felt in her experimental work of the late thirties.

Krasner's first professional work was making textbook plates for her Cooper Union instructor, Victor Perard, in 1929. During the thirties, she supported herself by modeling for other artists and by working as a waitress in a Greenwich Village café frequented by people in the arts. The latter job provided her an entrance into a circle of avant-garde artists and literary figures, and it was there that she met Harold Rosenberg, who was later to become one of the major critical supporters of Abstract Expressionism. For Lee Krasner, as for many of her contemporaries, the establishment of the WPA and the Federal Arts Project in 1934-35 offered a solution to economic survival, but provided few opportunities for experimentation. Krasner worked as an assistant to the muralist Max Spivak,[1] executing Social Realist cityscapes and factory scenes. She was active in the Artist's Union, and between 1937 and 1940 she studied and worked with Hans Hofmann;

she also came to know the formalist critic Clement Greenberg. Her work began to move toward abstraction, assimilating Hofmann's penchant for flatness, Fauvist color, and Cubist structure.

Krasner's images suggest movement, flux, growth; even in relatively static compositions, irregular, organic shapes float on the canvas surface in readiness for the inevitable consequences of change. The biomorphic forms and vibrant surfaces of her work suggest the shape and mutability of nature and the invisible energies essential to life.[2] During her years with Hofmann she worked in a Cubist style, absorbing and synthesizing European modernism and using nature as a departure point; shortly afterwards she renounced all external models.[3] In a search for a personal idiom, Krasner turned toward internalized images and transcribed them in free, spontaneous, and completely abstract form. Surrealist theories of unconscious creative sources, Jungian concepts, and the ideas of the painter-theoretician John Graham profoundly interested her as they did other abstract artists in the early forties, including Krasner's husband, Jackson Pollock, whom she met in the early forties and married in 1945.

Krasner's imagery is tremendously varied, moving from the thickly impasted surfaces, neutral color, and cuneiform shapes of the Little Image paintings of 1945-50 to the large, open, expressionist canvases of the fifties for which she is best known, to the more recent lyrical color compositions.[4] As she herself has remarked, ". . . change is the only constant."[5] There are, however, certain recurring elements: the rejection of illusionistic space for shallow, unified surfaces and frontal composition; a preference for reductive but richly nuanced color; and an organic work method.[6] She claims to work spontaneously and free of preconceived images, "often astonished at what [she] is confronted with when the major part comes through."[7]

It is in her work method and in her continuously changing imagery that the intensely personal nature of Krasner's art is revealed. The rhythmic flow of paint, the density or transparency of surface, the compositional compression or expansion of forms are products of Krasner's immediate sensations. She claims a biographical basis for her paintings that grows out of the conviction shared with other Abstract Expressionists that the physical process of painting is inseparable from the artist and is an act of self-revelation.[8] Krasner does not discuss the meaning of her images, preferring to let them stand as expressive visual entities.[9] It is, however, in the continuing expansion and diversification of her imagery, the monumental conceptions of even her small-scale work, that her individuality and originality are manifest.

Krasner's work has been exhibited regularly in group shows since her first exhibitions with the American Abstract Artists in the early forties and the important *American and French Painting* show at the McMillan Gallery in 1942. Her first one-woman show was held at the Betty Parsons Gallery in 1951, and her first major retrospective in London in 1965 at the Whitechapel Art Gallery. Recent shows have been held at the Marlborough Gallery in New York and at the Whitney Museum of American Art, both 1973, and at the Corcoran Gallery of Art in 1975.

155.
Red, White, Blue, Yellow, Black, 1939
Oil on paper with collage
24¾ x 19⅛ in. (65.4 x 48.6 cm.)
Signed lower right center: L.K. '39
New York, Marlborough Gallery

Red, White, Blue, Yellow, Black, constructed when Lee Krasner was working and studying with Hans Hofmann, is among her earliest non-representational works. The title of this collage reinforces her growing interest in formal problems[10] and recalls Mondrian's fully saturated primary color schemes of the late twenties and thirties. Under Hofmann's direction, she began to relinquish three-dimensional forms and Renaissance space for flattened, abstract shapes, developing the frontal, close-focus composition to which she still adheres. In *Red, White, Blue, Yellow, Black* the use of collage and shallow space reflects her familiarity with Cubist paintings and her long-standing fascination with Picasso's work. The tight, architectonic structure of this small collage, with its explicit geometric patterns and diagonally opposing forms, already contains the seeds for the monumental, dynamic canvases of the fifties.

Like Hofmann's work during this same period, *Red, White, Blue, Yellow, Black* is a fusion of Cubist structure with explosive color and angular, abstract shapes. Krasner's vision is generally more organic, intuitive, and responsive to the natural world than is immediately apparent in this collage. Her large-scale visionary canvases, upon which her reputation largely rests, and her less well-known small works on paper, are pervaded with a sense of growth, movement, and energy.

Red, White, Blue, Yellow, Black is not yet free of European modernist influences nor is it as innovative and personal as her work was to become. The angularity of its shapes also differs from Krasner's customarily biomorphic or calligraphic imagery; the free-flowing surface texture and the equalization of solid and void of her later collages have not yet emerged here. It does, however, relate to the dense, vertical collages of the early fifties[11] in its basic concern with trapping and retaining dynamic forces. Instead of the thickly textured, vibrant surfaces of her collages of the fifties, however, movement and force depend upon a tightly woven formal structure of closed, sharply edged planes intersecting in a shallow but clearly apparent space. Such concepts derive from European abstraction, by way of Hofmann, and are still far from the entirely personal and lyrical rhythms that Krasner was to uncover, nor is the spontaneity and fusion of imagery and process of Krasner's mature work yet apparent. *Red, White, Blue, Yellow, Black* is, however, an early statement of the problems that were to concern Krasner and for which she was to find an astonishing number of fresh and surprising solutions.

1.
Harold Rosenberg also worked on this project.
2.
See Robertson, 83-87, for nature sources and imagery in Krasner's work.
3.
See Krasner's comments on her relationship to nature during and after her years with Hofmann in Robertson, 84.
4.
See New York, 1973, for the evolution of Krasner's style.
5.
Ibid., 8.
6.
Ibid., 10-11.
7.
Ibid.
8.
Ibid., 12.
9.
Robertson, 84.

10.
Most of Krasner's works bear descriptive or literary titles that are determined only after the completion of each painting. See New York, 1973, 15.
11.
See, for example, Washington, D.C., 1975, no. 37, *City Verticals*, 1953; no. 52, *Milkweed*, 1955; and no. 53, *Shooting Gold*, 1955.

Loren MacIver

American, b. 1909

Loren MacIver was born in New York City. At the age of ten, she entered the Saturday class at the Art Students League, where she remained for about a year: this was her only formal training in art. She continued painting, however, throughout her adolescence and after her early marriage to the poet Lloyd Frankenberg. The couple established residence in Greenwich Village and, after 1931, on Cape Cod. Both New York and Cape Cod provided inspiration for the artist's early works, the former in the case of the abstract, symbolic façade of *Strunsky House* (1935), the latter in the fragile, evocative nature study of *Tern Eggs* or *Beach Plum Landscape* of 1933.

From 1936 to 1939 MacIver worked for the Federal Art Project of the WPA. At this time she also participated in her first public exhibitions: in 1933 or 1934 her work was shown in a group exhibition at Contemporary Arts; in 1935 the Museum of Modern Art bought one of her works; and in 1938 she had her first one-woman exhibition at the East River Gallery, run by Marian Willard. In 1939 the impact of a new experience, the sandy, southern environment of Key West, made itself apparent in MacIver's canvases, and, in 1940, with increasing artistic maturity, she began a series of works at once reflecting and transforming her reactions to New York City. The New York-inspired works are variegated, ranging in subject from the skyline of the whole city to humble objects associated with urban life, like pushcarts, votive lights glimpsed inside a church, an ashcan, a window shade, or the city pavement. During the same period, MacIver turned to themes from nature as well: trees, shrubs, leaves, and snow. Besides works inspired by the more delicate and ephemeral aspects of the natural world, MacIver produced a series of studies of the human figure: portraits of clowns, like those of Jimmy Savo and Emmett Kelly, were her special interest.

In 1948 MacIver and Frankenberg took a trip to Europe, which strongly affected her range of motifs. After her return, in 1949, she painted *Cathedral, Paris*; *Naples Aquarium* (a subject that had, incidentally, fascinated Paul Klee, another twentieth-century artist attracted to the intimate poetry of the small scale in the natural realm); *Venice;* and, in 1950, *Dublin and Environs,* as well as the European clowns, *The Fratellini.* The post-European works are generally bolder in scale and conception than the ones she had painted before her trip. In the fifties, too, she turned to the relatively abstract city phenomena of oil slicks or raindrops on a taxi windshield. The artist was elected to the National Institute of Art and Letters in 1959.

MacIver has an intensely personal, poetic, and delicately nuanced pictorial imagination, a vision that can evoke more universal implications from concrete fragments of experience. In her own words, taken from the *Fourteen Americans* catalog of 1946: "Quite simple things can lead to discovery. This is what I would like to do with paintings: starting with simple things, to lead the eye by various manipulations of colors, objects and tensions toward a transformation and a reward. . . .

"My wish is to make something permanent out of the transitory, by means at once dramatic and colloquial. Certain moments have the gift of revealing the past and foretelling the future. It is these moments that I hope to catch."[1]

As John Baur has pointed out, MacIver's paintings can never be defined as either totally abstract nor as completely representational.[2] They hover, rather, on the brink between realistic recording and poetic invention. Formal sophistication and control are the most essential concomitants of their expressive delicacy and pictorial evocativeness.

1.
New York, Museum of Modern Art, *Fourteen Americans,* ed. D. C. Miller, 1946, 28.
2.
New York, 1953, 11.

Frida Kahlo
Mexican, 1910-1954

156.
Hopscotch, 1940
Oil on canvas
27 x 35⅞ in. (68.6 x 91.1 cm.)
Signed lower right
New York, The Museum of Modern Art
Purchase, 1940
(See color plate, p. 99)

The urban motif, the close-up vision, and the evocative integration of minute observation of humble, everyday reality with firm, knowledgeable abstract pattern on the surface of the canvas make *Hopscotch* a prime example of MacIver's mature style. John Baur has summed up the complex effect of the painting as follows: "The flat, fantastic pattern, somewhat resembling a prehistoric monster consuming numbered chalk squares, is both puzzling and beautiful. As in much of MacIver's best work, one senses first the handsome design and only gradually perceives the poetic motivation. The hopscotch lines are the clue. They lead to a realization that this is pavement, then to the further awareness that this is blistered pavement, not the odd creature of one's first impression. Yet something of that early image lingers, and the mystery of the painting's ultimate meaning grows rather than diminishes. The fragile child's game lying lightly beside the decay of solid asphalt suggests multiple interpretations which are elusive because they are essentially visual, not literary. MacIver achieves here a truly pictorial poetry wrought by a most difficult balance between suggestive design and a concrete image of utmost realism."[3]

Like many of her Mexican contemporaries, Frida Kahlo took inspiration from native popular art in order to find and assert her Mexican identity. Unlike them, Kahlo also used the naive style and fantasy of popular art to distance herself and the viewer from the central subject of her art: her life. A primitivistic style — one full of odd, tart color combinations, static and often frontal figures, irrational space and scale — allowed her to depict the most intensely personal feelings and events without overwhelming or repelling the viewer with her physical and psychological torment.

Frida Kahlo was born in her family's Colonial house in the Mexico City suburb of Coyoacán. Her father was a German-Jewish photographer, her mother a Mexican Roman Catholic of mixed Indian and Spanish descent. One of five children (one boy, four girls), Frida was a bright and lively student. She was thirteen when she first encountered her future husband, Diego Rivera, who was painting a mural in the theater of the National Preparatory School. He became the target of her mischief and her infatuation: she told her friends that her ambition in life was to have a child by Diego Rivera.

When Frida was fifteen and hoping to pursue a medical career, a street car rammed the bus she was riding into a telephone pole. Her spine was fractured, her pelvis crushed, and one foot broken. Doctors in the Red Cross Hospital did not expect her to live, and in fact her remaining twenty-nine years were filled with constant pain that some thirty-five operations did not relieve. Frida's smashed pelvis prevented her from fulfilling what became an obsessive longing to bear children. It is little wonder that physical pain and the despair of several miscarriages and abortions are recurring themes in her art. The confinement of invalidism also led to a confinement in subject matter: almost all of Frida Kahlo's paintings are self-portraits. It is as if by painting her likeness she could exorcise pain as well as confirm and extend her restricted, threatened hold on reality.

3.
New York, 1953, 15.

While convalescing from her accident Frida taught herself to paint, using a specially built easel so that she could work in bed. When she was able to walk again, she took her first three paintings to Diego Rivera. He admired the paintings — and the painter. After a stormy courtship they were wed in 1929, and the vicissitudes of their marriage, separations, divorce, and remarriage are recorded in Kahlo's work with an astonishing candor.

Kahlo's fantastic imagery, sardonic humor, and preoccupation with pain and death appealed to her friend André Breton, who was her guest in Mexico in 1938, along with Leon Trotsky. Later that year Breton claimed Frida as a Surrealist in an essay for the brochure of her first exhibition, at the Julien Levy Gallery in Manhattan. The following year he arranged for a Kahlo exhibition in Paris. Yet Surrealism was not nearly so important an influence to Frida as Mexican Colonial and popular art. (In particular, she admired the ex votos painted on tin, which may help to explain the small size of her paintings and her preference for tin instead of canvas.) Also like these ex votos, and unlike Surrealism, Kahlo dramatized actual events with a highly personal urgency and purpose. Though her contacts with Surrealism did lead her to a more complex involvement with psychological innuendo, there is some justification for the contention of many of her Mexican admirers that Kahlo was a realist. Frida herself said that Breton and his circle "thought I was a Surrealist, but I wasn't. I never painted dreams. I painted my own reality."[1]

In April of 1953 Kahlo had her first major exhibition at the Gallery of Contemporary Art in Mexico City. Ill and in pain, she was carried to the opening on a hospital trolley, then reclined on a four-poster bed to receive her guests one by one. Four months later, her leg had to be amputated. Kahlo's famous *alegría* remained: she ordered a red velvet boot for her false leg and embroidered it with bells. Kahlo's pain ended only with her death on July 13, 1954. Her body lay in state in the hall of the Institute of Fine Arts in Mexico City before being cremated. To make sure that his wife's memory would continue, Diego gave her house in Coyoacán and its contents to the state as the Frida Kahlo Museum.

157.
Portrait of Frida and Diego, 1931
Oil on canvas
39 x 31½ in. (99.1 x 80 cm.)
San Francisco Museum of Art
Gift of Albert M. Bender from His Collection

This painting is typical of Kahlo's work in many regards. Here, as in other paintings, she based her simplified style, with its bright colors, spare stagelike space, and frontal figures, on Mexican Colonial and popular art. Also, Frida appears bedecked in the ribbons, jewels, and Mexican native costume that she habitually wore to draw attention from her injuries. But in this early painting, her features are still soft. They are not yet set in that mask tensed with wariness that came from long years of unflinching composure in the face of pain. More important, the painting is characteristically autobiographical, a fact emphasized by the words on the ribbon held by the dove: "Aquí nos veis, a mí Frieda Kahlo, con mi amado esposo Diego Rivera/pinté estos retratos en la bella ciudad de San Francisco California para/ nuestro amigo Mr. Albert Bender, y fué en el mes de abril del año 1931." (Here you see us, me, Frieda Kahlo, with my husband Diego Rivera/I painted these portraits in the beautiful city of San Francisco California for/our friend Mr. Albert Bender, and it was in the month of April of the year 1931.) In the early 1930s, a period when the political situation in Mexico made it difficult for leftist muralists to find work, the Riveras lived in the United States. Diego painted murals in Detroit, New York, and San Francisco, where his friend and patron Albert Bender helped him land a commission at the California School of Fine Arts.

Unlike most of Frida's portraits which depict her physical or mental pain, this one captures her in a moment of good health and marital felicity. *Portrait of Frida and Diego* was painted less than two years after their wedding in August 1929. Its very composition, with the couple's linked hands placed at the center of the canvas, suggests Kahlo's sense of security in their marriage bond, a sense that proved mistaken for Diego was soon unfaithful to Frida and in the late 1930s he divorced her only to remarry her in 1940. Diego, or "Panzas" ("fat belly"), as she called him, stands as solidly as a triumphal arch. His role is that of the artist, palette and brush in hand, his head turned slightly away from his wife. By contrast, the twenty-year-old Frida looks tiny, delicate, and subordinate — the adoring wife rather than the committed painter. Her head is inclined toward her much older husband. Her tiny beslippered feet barely brush the ground, giving Frida the look of a floating china doll supported by the grip of her monumental mate. (Ironically, because of her primitivistic draftsmanship, Diego's grip on Frida's extended hand is neither tight nor truly sustaining — an example of art prefiguring life.)

Perhaps it was with a secret twinkle that Frida made the general outline of herself and Diego take the same shape as the initial engraved on Diego's belt buckle — the letter *D*. Although both artists were headstrong people, one friend recalls that Frida usually acquiesed to Diego's will. To him, work always came first; to Frida, Diego came before her art. Another friend noting the contrast between Diego's extreme egocentricity and Frida's generous and tolerant loyalty said, "She had to be priestess in Diego's temple."

Portrait of Frida and Diego certainly shows Frida's deference to her husband. Yet the marriage was more complex. Moments of comradely affection alternated with moments of tempestuous passion. Other Kahlo portraits dealing with her marriage proved that Frida was a strong and independent person. Indeed some show that a large ingredient in her marriage was her need to possess Diego, in effect, as the child she was never able to bear. This feeling is evident in

---

1.
Herrera, 43.

Frida's *Portrait of Diego*, 1949, where he appears as a plump naked baby embraced in her Madonna-like lap. Diego echoes such a view in his depiction of himself and his wife in his Hotel del Prado mural (1947-48), where he is a short fat boy in knee pants and she is a woman a head taller than himself, her hand placed on his shoulder in a gesture of motherly possession. For all the solicitousness and femininity of Frida's pose and dress in her charming marriage portrait, *Portrait of Frida and Diego*, Frida's piercing dark eyes stare out at us from under her broad connecting eyebrows with a look of self-knowing strength and even, I think, a glint of that mocking, self-distancing irony that sustained Frida Kahlo through all her travails.

157

Dorothea Tanning
American, b. 1910

Born in Galesburg, Illinois, Dorothea Tanning attended Knox College for two years, then studied art briefly in Chicago before going to New York in 1936. In 1939 she made a short trip to Paris, then returned to New York where she became part of the Surrealist circle, mainly refugees from war-torn Europe, that included André Breton, Marcel Duchamp, André Masson, Yves Tanguy, Kay Sage, Matta, Patrick Waldberg, and, most significantly for Tanning, Max Ernst, whom she married early in the 1940s. References to the latter are both overt and veiled in her work, especially the work of the forties. After the war, Tanning and Ernst lived and worked in Sedona, Arizona, a setting that seems to have had its effect on her imagery of the period. Since 1952 she has lived in France.

In Tanning's most provocative earlier works, the protagonists of her pictorial fantasies are women, sometimes perversely childish, often in the throes of some sexually suggestive action of transformation. In *Children's Games* (1942) two nubile girls in a dark tunnel play with fire that is at once transformed into the streaming hair of one of them while also assuming the forms of a female torso and sex organ as it impinges on the torn wall to the right. In *Eine Kleine Nachtmusik* (1946), a similar pair of girls is placed in a hotel corridor dominated by a torn and writhing sunflower, an image suggesting defloration. Many of Tannings's paintings are haunted by a sinister and provocative Pekingese that appears in a variety of metamorphoses. Her later style, of the fifties and sixties, is more diffuse, loosely painted, and abstract than the finely wrought, meticulously brushed manner characteristic of the forties. In addition to painting, Tanning has designed scenery and costumes for the ballet, has been active as a graphic artist and illustrator, and, in recent years, has created extremely inventive, metamorphic, soft sculpture.

158.
Maternity, 1946
Oil on canvas
56¼ x 43¼ in. (143 x 110 cm.)
Signed and dated lower right
New York, Collection Jeffrey H. Loria
(See color plate, p. 100)

The isolation of woman — the woman artist, or Tanning in particular, perhaps — and the challenge, or existential despair, generated by isolation are suggested by a number of Tanning's works in the forties. In *Hotel du Pavot* (1942), for instance, a small girl is posed in a vista of mysteriously organic architecture; in *Self-Portrait* (1944) a similarly isolated woman, like a doll on a stand, confronts a vast desert dreamscape; in the moving *Birthday* (1942) it is the artist herself who confronts us with her isolation, bare-breasted, barefooted, brilliantly sleeved, growing roots, with her hand on the knob of the first of an infinite series of opening doors and a winged monster on the floor before her. *Maternity* seems a further exploration of a similar theme, weaving together several dominant motifs from Tanning's repertory at this time. The young mother and her identically dressed baby, who may well refer back to an early photograph of the artist's own mother with Tanning in her arms,[1] are isolated in a desert landscape behind one doorway and in front of another; the child's and mother's bodies fuse strongly and the sagging or misplaced breasts and belly of the woman press grotesquely through the fragile shreds of her gown; on a rug at her feet sprawls a baby-faced Pekingese, miniature sphinx of this dream-desert, guardian and portent at once. In the background, framed by the unattached doorway, looms a biomorphic, mechanical construction, related to similar mysterious manifestations in the backgrounds of slightly later works like *Interior with Sudden Joy* (1951) and *The Guest Room* (1950-52). The mood of menace and isolation is reinforced by the smoldering, sulphurous yellow tonality, which suffuses the painting with a deadening glow.

1.
The relationship of the mother and child in this painting to the photograph, repr. 6, Paris, 1974, was pointed out to me by Judith Wolfe. The face of the dog to the left of the painting is almost identical with that of the baby Dorothea Tanning in the photograph.

Artists' Bibliographies, Collections, Exhibitions, Literature

Levina Teerlinc (ca. 1520-1576)
Bibliography

Auerbach, Erna, *Tudor Artists*, London, 1954.

_____, *Nicolas Hilliard*, London, 1961, and Boston, 1964.

Bergmans, Simone, "The Miniatures of Levina Teerlinc," *Burlington Magazine*, LXIV, 1934, 232-36.

Nichols, John Gough, "Notices of the Contemporaries and Successors of Holbein," *Archaeologia*, XXX, 1863, 39-40.

Strong, Roy C., *The English Icon: Elizabethan and Jacobean Portraiture*, London, 1969.

Tufts, 1974, 42-49.

1.
Portrait of a Young Woman
Collections:
Acquired by the museum in 1954; previous history not known.
Literature:
G. Reynolds, "Portrait Miniatures," *The Connoisseur Period Guides: The Tudor Period, 1500-1603*, London, 1956, 131; Auerbach, 1961, 53 and no. 4 (pl. 4); Tufts, 1974, 47 and fig. 17.

Caterina van Hemessen (1528-after 1587)
Bibliography

Bergmans, Simone, "Le problème Jan Van Hemessen, monogrammiste de Brunswick," *Revue belge d'archéologie et d'histoire de l'art*, XXIV, 1955, 133-57.

_____, "Note complémentaire à l'étude des De Hemessen, de van Amstel, et du monogrammiste de Brunswick," *Revue belge d'archéologie et d'histoire de l'art*, XXVII, 1958, 77-83.

Guicciardini.

Thieme-Becker, s.v., entry by F. Winkler.

Tufts, 1974, 50-57.

2.
Young Woman Playing the Virginals
Collections:
Bequest of Mrs. Emmy Schnitzler, Berlin, 1916, to the Wallraf-Richartz Museum; previous history not recorded.
Exhibitions:
Le siècle de Bruegel, Musées Royaux des Beaux-Arts de Belgique, Brussels, 1963, no. 125.

Literature:
J. Poppelreuter, "Vermächtnis an das Wallraf-Richartz-Museum," *Zeitschrift für bildende Kunst*, LII, 1917, 71-72; F. Winkler in Thieme-Becker, XVI, 367; W. Haacke, *Am Klavier*, Königstein, 22; Tufts, 1974, 51 and fig. 22. For a complete list of all museum catalog citations, see I. Hiller and H. Vey, *Wallraf-Richartz Museum: Katalog der deutschen und niederländischen Gemälde bis 1550*, Cologne, 1969, no. 654.

Sofonisba Anguissola (1532/35-1625)
Bibliography

Baldinucci.

Berenson, Bernard, *Italian Painters of the Renaissance: Central Italian and North Italian Schools*, 3 vols., London and New York, 1968.

Bonetti, C., "Nel centario di Sofonisba Anguissola," *Archivio storico lombardo*, LV, 1928, 285-306.

Bonetti, C., *Sofonisba Anguissola*, Cremona, 1932.

Campi, Antonio, *Cremona fedelissima città et nobilissima colonia di Romani . . .* , Cremona, 1585.

Cook, Herbert, "More Portraits by Sofonisba Anguissola," *Burlington Magazine*, XXVI, 1915, 228-36.

Fournier-Sarlovèze, M., "Sofonisba Anguissola et ses soeurs," *Revue de l'art ancien et moderne*, V, 1899, part I, no. 25, 313-24; part II, no. 26, 379-92.

Frizzoni, G., "La pietra tombale di Sofonisba Anguissola," *Rassegna bibliografica dell'arte*, XII, 1909, 53-55.

Haraszti-Takács, Marianne, "Nouvelles données relatives à la vie et à l'oeuvre de Sofonisba Anguissola," *Bulletin du Musée Hongrois des Beaux-Arts*, XXXI, 1968, 53-67.

Holmes, C. J., "Sofonisba Anguissola and Philip II," *Burlington Magazine*, XXVI, 1915, 181-87.

Kühnel-Kunze, Irene, "Zur Bildniskunst der Sofonisba und Lucia Anguisciola," *Pantheon*, XX, 1962, 83-96.

Lamo, 1584: see Zaist.

Nicodemi, G., "Commemorazione di artisti minori — Sofonisba Anguissola," *Emporium*, 1927, 222-23.

Prinz, W., *Die Sammlung der Selbstbildnisse in den Uffizien*, I., *Geschichte der Sammlung*, Berlin, 1971.

Soprani, 411-16.

Tolnay, Charles de, "Sofonisba Anguissola and Her Relations with Michelangelo," *Journal of the Walters Art Gallery*, IV, 1941, 115-19.

Tufts, Eleanor, "Sofonisba Anguissola, Renaissance Woman," *Art News*, LXXI, 1972, 50-53.

Tufts, 1974, 20-29.

Vasari, V, 81; VI, 498ff.; VII, 133.

Zaist, Giovanni Battista, *Notizie istoriche de' pittori, scultori ed architetti cremonesi, opera postuma di Giambattista Zaist data in Luce da Anton Maria Panni*, 2 vols., Cremona, 1774. Appended to the second volume of this work is the *Discorso di Alessandro Lamo intorno alla scoltura, e pittura . . .* , 1584. (There is a facsimile edition of Zaist published by the Societa Multigrafica Editrice SOMU, Rome, 1965, which omits Lamo's *Discorso*.)

3.
Self-Portrait
Collections:
Earl Cadogan; Earl Cadogan Sale, February 14-22, 1726, 2nd day, lot 83, bought by the Duchess of Marlborough for £140; by descent to the present owner.
Exhibitions:
Art Treasures, Manchester, 1857; Women's exhibition, Earl's Court, London, 1900; *Midland Art Treasures*, Birmingham, 1934, no. 456; *Between Renaissance and Baroque*, catalog by F. G. Grossman, City Art Gallery, Manchester, 1965, no. 9.
Literature:
F. G. Waagen, *Treasures of Art in Great Britain*, London, 1854, III, 456; Fournier-Sarlovèze, 383 and 388; Cook, 228 and pl. III E; B. Berenson, *Italian Painters of the Renaissance, A List of the Principal Artists and Their Works with an Index of Places*, Oxford, 1932, 23 (2nd edition, 1953, ibid.); Bonetti, 1932, 145; Venturi, 1933, IX, 923 and 932; Kühnel-Kunze, 86, fig. 5; Haraszti-Takács, 60; Berenson, 1968, I, 14; Tufts, 1972, 50.

Lucia Anguissola (ca. 1540-ca. 1565)
Bibliography

Baldinucci, VIII, 230.

Caroli, Flavio, "Antologia di artisti; per Lucia Anguissola," *Paragone,* 277, 1973, 69-73.

Campi, Antonio, *Cremona fedelissima città et nobilissima colonia di Romani . . . ,* Cremona, 1585.

Kühnel-Kunze, Irene, "Zur Bildniskunst der Sofonisba und Lucia Anguisciola," *Pantheon,* XX, 1962, 83-96.

Vasari, VI, 501.

4.
Portrait of Pietro Maria (Pietro Martire Ponzona?)
Literature:
Vasari, VI, 501; Baldinucci, VIII, 230; Zaist, I, 234; Stirling-Maxwell, 1891, I, 228; Fournier-Sarlovèze, 316 and 318 (see S. Anguissola bibliography); Posse in Thieme-Becker, I, 524; Bonetti, 1932, 146 (see S. Anguissola bibliography); Venturi, 1933, 924, 933-34, and fig. 574; Tolnay, 115 and 118, note 6 (see S. Anguissola bibliography); Tufts, 1972, 50 and 53 (see S. Anguissola bibliography); Caroli, 69, 70, and fig. 66; Tufts, 1974, 22 and fig. 5. In addition, the picture is cited in most of the catalogs of the Museo del Prado published since 1819 (more than thirty).

Lavinia Fontana (1552-1614)
Bibliography

Baglione, Giovanni, *Le vite de' pittori, scultori, architetti, ed intagliatori, dal pontificato di Gregorio XIII del 1572, in fino a' tempi di Papa Urbano VIII nel 1642,* Rome, 1642 (facsimile edition with marginal notes by Bellori, ed. V. Mariani, Rome, 1935).

Galli, Romeo, *Lavinia Fontana, pittrice, 1552-1614,* Imola, 1940.

Malvasia, I, 177-79.

Mancini, Giulio, *Considerazioni sulla pittura,* ed. A. Marucchi and L. Salerno, 2 vols., Rome, 1956-57.

Tufts, Eleanor, "Ms. Lavinia Fontana from Bologna: A Successful 16th-Century Portraitist," *Art News,* LXXIII, 1974, 60-64.

Tufts, 1974, 30-41.

5.
Portrait of Senator Orsini
Collections:
Marquis de Lacaze; bought by the museum from his collection in 1829.
Exhibitions:
Les chefs-d'oeuvre du Musée de Bordeaux, Galerie des Beaux-Arts, Bordeaux, 1952, no. 66.

Literature:
F. Noack in Thieme-Becker, XII, 183; Venturi, 1933, IX, 693; Galli, 67; *Le XVIième siècle européen,* Petit Palais, Paris, 1965, cited on 323; and all catalogs of the Bordeaux museum (fourteen issued from the early nineteenth century until 1910).

6.
Portrait of a Noblewoman
Collections:
J. Pierpont Morgan.

7.
Noli Me Tangere
Collections:
Recorded in the collection of Don Antonio dei Medici in 1632; from thence to the Uffizi.
Literature:
F. Noack in Thieme-Becker, XII, 183; *Catalogo dei Dipinti, Galleria degli Uffizi,* 1926, no. 1383; Venturi, 1933, IX, 693; Galli, 68; Robert Salvini, *La Galleria degli Uffizi, guida per il visitatore, e catalogo dei dipinti,* Florence, 1969, 73.

Fede Galizia (1578-1630)
Bibliography

Bottari, Stefano, "Fede Galizia," *Arte antica e moderna,* no. 24, 1963, 309-60.

_____, *Fede Galizia pittrice (1578-1630),* Collana Artisti Trentini, Trento, 1965.

8.
Portrait of Paolo Morigia (1525-1604)
Collections:
Given to the Ambrosiana in 1670 by Tomaso Buzzi.
Literature:
For most early bibliography and museum catalog references, see A. Falchetti, *La Pinacoteca Ambrosiana,* Vicenza, 1969, 179, to which the following references may be added: F. Bartoli, *Notizia delle pitture, sculture ed architetture . . . d'Italia,* Venice, 1776, 174; Thieme-Becker, XIII, 99; Bottari, 1963, 311 and 317, note 13 and fig. 119b.

9.
Basket of Peaches
Collections:
Harry Sperling, New York, until 1967; John Goelet, Paris, until 1974; New York private collection.
Exhibitions:
La natura morta italiana, Palazzo Reale, Naples, 1964, no. 18 and color pl. I.
Literature:
Bottari, 1965, 20 and pl. 14.

Artemisia Gentileschi (1593-1652/53)
Bibliography

Baldinucci.

Bissell, R. Ward, "Artemisia Gentileschi — A New Documented Chronology," *Art Bulletin,* L, 1968, 153-68.

Cleveland Museum of Art, *Caravaggio and His Followers,* catalog by Richard E. Spear, 1971.

Florence, Palazzo Pitti, *Caravaggio e Caravaggeschi nelle Galleria di Firenze,* catalog by Evelina Borea, 1970.

Fröhlich-Bume, L., "A Rediscovered Picture by Artemisia Gentileschi," *Burlington Magazine,* LXXVII, 1940, 169.

Levey, Michael, "Notes on the Royal Collection — II, Artemisia Gentileschi's 'Self Portrait' at Hampton Court," *Burlington Magazine,* CIV, 1962, 79-80.

Longhi, Roberto, "Gentileschi padre e figlia," *L'arte,* XIX, 1916, 245-314 (reprinted in *Scritti giovannili, 1912-1922,* Florence, 1961, I tome 1, 219-83).

Moir, Alfred, *The Italian Followers of Caravaggio,* Cambridge, Mass., 1967.

Ruffo, Vincenzo, "Galleria Ruffo nel secolo XVII in Messina con lettere di pittori ed altri documenti inediti," *Bollettino d'arte,* 1916, 21ff.

Toesca, Maria, "Versi in lode di Artemisia Gentileschi," *Paragone,* 251, 1971, 89-92.

Tufts, 1974, 58-69.

Voss, Hermann, *Die Malerei des Barock in Rom,* Berlin, 1924, 463.

10.
Susanna and the Elders
Collections:
Acquired by the family of the present owner by 1719.
Literature:
Von Frimmel (see entry, note 10), 75; Voss, 463; Emiliani (see entry, note 11), 42; Moir, I, 100; Bissell, 157.

11.
The Penitent Magdalene
Collections:
First recorded by Inghirami in the Palazzo Pitti in 1826 but presumably already in the Medici collections by the seventeenth century.
Exhibitions:
Caravaggio e Caravaggeschi nelle Galleria di Firenze, Palazzo Pitti, Florence, 1970, no. 47, 74-75.

Literature:
F. Inghirami, *Descrizione dell'Imperiale e Reale Palazzo Pitti*, Fiesole, 1828, 36; Longhi, 1961 ed., 258; Voss, 463; A. Jahn-Rusconi, *La R. Galleria Pitti in Firenze*, Rome, 1937, 138-39; Vincenzo Golzio, *Il seicento e il settecento*, Turin, 1950, 367; Moir, I, 101; Bissell, 156; A.M.F. Ciaranfi, *Pitti Firenze*, Novara, 1971, 11.

12.
Portrait of a Condottiere
Collections:
Agostino Pepoli, Bologna; given to the Palazzo Comunale in 1926.
Literature:
F. Malaguzzi Valeri, "I nuovi acquisti della Pinacoteca di Bologna," *Cronache d'arte*, 3, fasc. 1, 1926, 30 and 33; G. Zucchini, *Catalogo delle collezioni comunali d'arte di Bologna*, 1938, 22; Bissell, 157.

13.
Judith and Maidservant with the Head of Holofernes
Collections:
Prince Brancaccio, Rome.
Exhibitions:
Art in Italy, 1600-1700, Detroit Institute of Arts, 1965, no. 8 (catalog entry by A. Moir); *Caravaggio and His Followers*, Cleveland Museum of Art, 1971, no. 28; *Old Mistresses*, Walters Art Gallery, Baltimore, 1972, no. 7.
Literature:
E. P. Richardson, "A Masterpiece of Baroque Drama," *Bulletin of the Detroit Institute of Arts*, XXXII, 1952-53, 81-83 (reprinted in *Art Quarterly*, XVI, 1953, 91-92); Moir, 101 (dated ca. 1617); Bissell, 157-58 (dated ca. 1625) and fig. 9; Tufts, 1974, 60 and fig. 29.

14.
Fame
Collections:
Oswald T. Falk, Oxford; C. R. Churchill, Colemore, Alton, Hampshire; London and New York art markets, 1943 onwards.
Exhibitions:
Cross-Currents in Baroque Painting, Arcade Gallery, London, 1943, no. 14; *Baroque Paintings*, Arcade Gallery, London, 1948, no. 15; *Exhibition of Works by Holbein and Other Masters of the 16th and 17th Centuries*, Royal Academy, London, 1950, no. 368.
Literature:
Fröhlich-Bume, 169; Bissell, 159, 161, and 162, fig. 12.

15.
David and Bathsheba
Collections:
Dr. Luigi Romeo, Barone di San Luigi, 1743; Carlo Sestieri, Rome, ca. 1960; P. & D. Colnaghi & Co., Ltd., London, 1962; acquired by the museum in 1967 with the aid of the Frederick W. Schumacher Trust Fund.

Literature:
De Dominici, III, 198-99 (cited with its lost companion piece, a *Susanna*, also painted by all three artists); B. Nicolson, "Notable Works of Art Now on the Market," *Burlington Magazine*, CV, Sup. 1, June 1963, no. III; Bissell, 163; B. B. Fredrickson and F. Zeri, *Census of Pre-Nineteenth-Century Italian Paintings in North American Public Collections*, Cambridge, Mass., 1972, 55, 78, 80, 261, and 576; Tufts, 1974, 62 and fig. 32.

Lucrina Fetti (active ca. 1614-ca. 1651?)
Bibliography

Baglione, Giovanni, *Le vite de' pittori, scultori, architetti, ed intagliatori, dal pontificato di Gregorio XIII del 1572, in fino a' tempi di Papa Urbano VIII nel 1642*, Rome, 1642 (facsimile edition with marginal notes by Bellori, ed. V. Mariani, Rome, 1935).

Cadioli, Giovanni, *Descrizione delle pitture, sculture ed architetture che si osservano nella città di Mantove, e ne' suoi contorni*, Mantua, 1763.

Marani, E., and Perina, C., *Mantova: Le arti, III*, Mantua, 1965.

Thieme-Becker, s.v., entry by Mary Endres-Soltmann.

16.
St. Barbara
Collections:
Paul Ganz, New York.

Clara Peeters (1594-after 1657?)
Bibliography

Benedict, Curt, "Osias Beert, un peintre oublié de natures mortes," *L'amour de l'art*, XIX, 1938, 307-14.

Gerson, H., and Ter Kuile, E. H., *Art and Architecture in Belgium, 1600-1800*, Baltimore, 1960.

Greindl, E., *Les peintres flamands de nature morte au XVIIe siècle*, Brussels, 1956.

Hairs, Marie Louise, "Osias Beert l'Ancien, peintre de fleurs," *Revue belge d'archéologie et d'histoire de l'art*, XX, 1951, 237-51.

Hairs, 1965 ed., 241-44 and 398.

17.
Flowers in a Glass Vase
Collections:
Comte de Normand, Nice, France; Galerie J. Charpentier, Paris, June 1, 1951, lot 117; private collection, Belgium; Newhouse Galleries, Inc., New York.

Literature:
Hairs, 1965, 398.

18.
Still Life with Cheese, Bread, and Pretzels
Exhibitions:
Master Paintings, Recent Acquisitions, Thomas Agnew and Sons Ltd., London, 1975, no. 40 in catalog.

Giovanna Garzoni (1600-1670)
Bibliography

Carboni, Giacinto Cantalamessa, *Memorie intorno i letterati e gli artisti della città di Ascoli nel Piceno*, Ascoli Piceno, 1830.

Naples, 27-28.

Pascoli, Lione, *Vite de' pittori, scultori, ed architetti moderni*, 2 vols., Rome, 1730-36.

19.
Dish of Broad Beans
(See next entry.)
20.
Dish of Grapes with Pears and a Snail
Collections:
Probably acquired by the Medici during the seventeenth century though not identifiable with works of Garzoni described in Medici inventories of 1675 and 1692; acquired by the state in 1890.
Exhibitions:
La natura morta italiana, Palazzo Reale, Naples, 1964, nos. 16 (*Beans*) and 17 (*Grapes*).

21.
Still Life with Birds and Fruit
Exhibitions:
Florentine Baroque Art from American Collections, catalog by J. Nissman, Metropolitan Museum of Art, New York, 1969, no. 36.
Literature:
W. Blunt, *The Art of Botanical Illustration*, New York, 1951, 81; Bacci, 53, 77, and pl. XLV, fig. 5 (see note 17, previous entry); Naples, 1964, discussed in text for nos. 14-17.

Judith Leyster (1609-1660)
Bibliography

Harms, Juliane, "Judith Leyster, ihr Leben und ihr Werk," *Oud-Holland*, XLIV, 1927, 88-96, 112-26, 145-54, 221-42, 275-79.

Hofrichter, Frima Fox, "Judith Leyster: A Preliminary Catalogue," Master's thesis, Hunter College, City University of New York, 1973.

————, "Judith Leyster's *Proposition*— between Vice and Virtue," *Feminist Art Journal*, Fall 1975, 22-26.

Hofstede de Groot, Cornelis, "Judith Leyster," *Jahrbuch der Königlich preussischen Kunstsammlungen*, 1893, 190-98, 232.

————, "Schilderijen door Judith Leyster," *Oud-Holland*, XLVI, 1919, 25-26.

Slive, Seymour, *Frans Hals,* 3 vols., London, 1970-74.

Tufts, 1974, 70-79.

Wijnman, H. F., "Het geboortejaar van Judith Leyster," *Oud-Holland*, XLIX, 1932, 62-65.

22.
The Gay Cavaliers (The Last Drop)
Collections:
Sir George Donaldson, London (with the companion picture); Müller Sale, Amsterdam, April 28-29, 1908, lot 70; bought from this sale by John G. Johnson.
Literature:
W. R. Valentiner, [John G. Johnson] *Catalogue . . . Flemish and Dutch Paintings,* Philadelphia, 1913, II, 68 (where the picture is wrongly said to come from the Hoogendyk Collection); A. von Schneider, "Gerard Honthorst und Judith Leyster," *Oud-Holland,* XXXX, 1922, 173; Harms, 237; Brière-Misme in *Gazette des beaux-arts,* 1927, 376; *Johnson Collection Catalogue,* 1941, 31; *John G. Johnson Collection: Catalogue of Flemish and Dutch Paintings* (revision of the 1918 catalog edited by Barbara Sweeny), Philadelphia, 1972, 51; Tufts, 1974, 73 and fig. 36.

23.
The Proposition
Collections:
Münzenberger, Frankfurt-am-Main; Werner Dahl, Düsseldorf; acquired by the Mauritshuis in 1892 as the work of an unknown artist.
Literature:
Hofstede de Groot, 1893, 197; Harms, 145-49 and 237; G. Poensgen in Thieme-Becker, XXIII, 176; Mauritshuis à La Haye, Musée Royale de Tableaux, *Catalogue raisonné de tableaux et sculptures,* The Hague, 1935, no. 564 (with references to catalogs of 1893, 1895, and 1907); Tufts, 1974, 73 and fig. 37.

Louise Moillon (1610-1696)
Bibliography

Faré, Michel, *La nature morte en France; son histoire et son évolution du XVIIe au XXe siècle,* 2 vols., Geneva, 1962.

————, *Le grand siècle de la nature morte en France, le XVIIe siècle,* Paris, 1974.

Wilhelm, Jacques, "Louise Moillon," *L'oeil,* September 6-12, 1956.

24.
At the Greengrocer
Collections:
Acquired by the Louvre in 1955.
Exhibitions:
Natures mortes anciennes et modernes, Musée de Rennes, 1953; *Peintures françaises au XVIIe siècle,* Musée des Beaux-Arts, Tours, 1973.
Literature:
Wilhelm, 8ff.; Faré, 1962, I, 42 and 99, and II, pl. 34; *Musée National du Louvre, Catalogue des peintures, I, Ecole française,* Paris, 1972, 268; *Musée du Louvre, Catalogue illustré des peintures, Ecole française XVIIe et XVIIIe siècles,* Paris, 1974, II, 17 and 206; Faré, 1974, 50-51 and 58-59.

25.
Basket of Apricots
Collections:
François Heim, Paris, since 1953.
Exhibitions:
Natures mortes anciennes et modernes, Musée de Rennes, 1953, no. 18; *Natures mortes de l'antiquité au XVIIe siècle,* Musée d'Art et d'Industrie, Saint-Etienne, 1954, no. 17; *Vier eeuwen stilleven in Frankrijk,* Museum Boymans-van Beuningen, Rotterdam, 1954, no. 17; *Voici des fruits, des fleurs, des feuilles, et des branches,* Bernheim, Paris, 1957, no. 40; *The Grand Gallery,* The Metropolitan Museum of Art, New York, 1974, no. 150.
Literature:
Wilhelm, 13 (repr. in color); Faré, 1962, II, pl. 52; Faré, 1974, 64.

26.
Still Life with Grapes and Vine Leaves
Collections:
François Heim, Paris, 1974; private collection, Paris.
Exhibitions:
La femme peintre et sculpteur du XVIIe au XXe siècle, Grand Palais, Paris, 1975, no. 3.
Literature:
Faré, 1974, 66; M. and F. Faré, "Trois peintres de fruits au temps de Louis XIII," *Connaissance des arts,* no. 272, October 1974, 88-95, repr. 91.

Margaretha de Heer (active in the 1650s)
Bibliography

Thieme-Becker, s.v.

27.
Return from the Hunt
Collections:
Marquis de Lacaze; acquired by the town of Bordeaux in 1829.
Exhibitions:
Chefs-d'oeuvre au Musée des Beaux-Arts de Bordeaux, catalog by M. Martin-Méry, Musée des Beaux-Arts, Ghent, 1970, no. 31.

Literature:
Gilberte Martin-Méry, *La peinture hollandaise du XVIIe siècle dans les collections du Musée des Beaux-Arts,* Bordeaux, 1966, 14 (with full listing of earlier Bordeaux catalogs).

Maria van Oosterwyck (1630-1693)
Bibliography

Houbraken, Arnold, *De groote schouburgh der Nederlantsche konstschilders en schilderessen,* 3 vols., Amsterdam, 1718-20.

Thieme-Becker, s.v.

28.
Vanitas
Collections:
In the Hapsburg collections, Vienna, by 1730.
Exhibitions:
Ijdelheid der ijdelheden, Hollandse vanitasvoorstellingen uit de zeventiende eeuw, catalog by I. W. L. Moerman et al., Leyden, Museum de Lakenhal, 1970, no. 20 (with an erroneous provenance).
Literature:
Eduard Ritter von Engerth, *Kunsthistorische Sammlungen des allerhöchsten Kaiserhauses; Gemälde Beschreibendes Verzeichnis,* 2 vols., Kunsthistorisches Museum, Vienna, 1884, II, 324-25; Würzbach, II, 256; Hofstede de Groot in Thieme-Becker, XXVI, 25; *Verzeichnis der Gemälde,* Kunsthistorisches Museum, Vienna, 1973, 125.

29.
Vase of Tulips, Roses and Other Flowers with Insects
Collections:
Richard Green, London, 1972; acquired from him by the present owner.
Literature:
Unpublished except for an advertisement in *Connoisseur,* September 1972.

Elisabetta Sirani (1638-1665)
Bibliography

Kurz, Otto, *Bolognese Drawings . . . at Windsor Castle,* London, 1955, 133-36.

Emiliani, Andrea, "Giovan Andrea ed Elisabetta Sirani," in Bologna, Palazzo dell'Archiginnasio, *Maestri della pittura del seicento emiliano,* catalog by F. Arcangeli et al., 1959, 140-45.

Malvasia, II, 385ff.

Manaresi, Antonio, *Elisabetta Sirani,* Bologna, 1898.

Tufts, 1974, 80-87.

30.
The Penitent Magdalene in the Wilderness
Collections:
G. B. Cremonese of Bologna, 1660; Zambeccari Collection, Bologna, by 1795; acquired by the Pinacoteca Nazionale in 1883.
Literature:
Malvasia, II, 395; Emiliani, 64 and 66; *Pinacoteca Nazionale di Bologna, Notizie storiche e itinerario illustrativo*, ed. A. Emiliani, Bologna, 1969, 175 (with full references to earlier museum catalogs).

31.
Porcia Wounding Her Thigh
Collections:
Simone Tassi, Bologna, 1664; Bonfiglioli Collection, Bologna; Carlo Sestieri, Rome; Wildenstein & Co., New York.
Exhibitions:
Tableaux italiens: XIVe-XVIIe siècles, L'Oeil Galerie, Paris, 1973, no. 19.
Literature:
Malvasia, II, 399.

Margherita Caffi (active 1662-1700)
Bibliography

Detroit, 1974, 198-99 (nos. 110a-b).

Naples, 1964, 112-13 (nos. 216-65).

32.
Still Life with Flowers
33.
Still Life with Flowers in a Landscape Setting

Maria Sibylla Merian (1647-1717)
Bibliography

Blunt, Wilfred, *The Art of Botanical Illustration*, New York, 1951, 127-29.

Gelder, Jan Gerrit van, *Dutch Drawings and Prints*, New York, 1959.

Lendorff, Gertrude, *Maria Sibylla Merian, 1647-1717, ihr Leben und ihr Werk*, Basel, 1955.

Merian, Maria Sibylla, *Metamorphosis insectorum Surinamsium*, Amsterdam, 1705 (see Schnack).

————, *Erucarum ortus alimentum et paradoxa metamorphosis, in qua origo, pabulum, transformatio, nec non tempus, locus et proprietater erucarum vermium, papilionum, phaelaenarum, muscarum, aliorumque, hujusmodi exsanguinium animalculorum exhibentur . . .*, Amsterdam, 1717.

[Merian], "A Surinam Portfolio," *Natural History*, 1962, 28-41.

Nuremberg, Germanisches Nationalmuseum, *Maria Sibylla Merian, 1647-1717*, catalog by Elizabeth Rücker, 1967.

Pfeiffer, M. A., *Die Werke der Maria Sibylla Merian*, Meissen, 1931.

Quednau, Werner, *Maria Sibylla Merian: der Lebensweg einer grossen Künstlerin und Forcherin*, Gütersloh, 1966.

Schnack, Friederich, *Das kleine Buch der Tropenwunder: kolorierte Stiche . . .* [Maria Sibylla Merian], Leipzig, 1954.

Stuldreher-Nienhuis, J., *Verborgen Paradijzen, Het leven en de werken van Maria Sibylla Merian, 1647-1717*, Arnheim, 1944, 2nd ed. 1945.

Tufts, 1974, 88-97.

34.
Metamorphosis of a Frog
Collections:
History prior to its acquisition by the Minnich Collection unknown.
Exhibitions:
The Minnich Collection, The Minneapolis Institute of Arts, 1970, no. 30.

35.
Study of a Painted Lady Butterfly, a Pink Underwing Moth, a Strawberry, a Pea Pod, Two Shells, and a Sprig of White Currants

Susan Penelope Rosse (ca. 1652-1700)
Bibliography

Foskett, Daphne, *A Dictionary of British Miniature Painters*, London and New York, 1972.

London, National Portrait Gallery, *Samuel Cooper and His Contemporaries*, catalog by Daphne Foskett, 1973.

Long, Basil S., *British Miniaturists*, London, 1929.

Reynolds, Graham, *Samuel Cooper's Pocket-Book*, London (Victoria and Albert Museum, Brochure 8), 1975.

Vertue, George (1684-1756), *The Notebooks, The Walpole Society Annual*, XVIII (1929-30), 116-17; XX (1931), 56-57 and 69; XXIV (1935-36), 21, 41, and 185.

Williamson, George C., *History of Portrait Miniatures*, London, 1904.

36.
Portrait of Eleanor (Nell) Gwyn (1650-1687)
Collections:
Nell Gwyn; Duke of St. Albans (the sitter's son); John Drummond (1723-1774), whose family acquired it when he married the granddaughter of the Duke of St. Albans; then by descent until sold at Christie's, February 1973, lot 131.

Exhibitions:
Samuel Cooper and His Contemporaries, National Portrait Gallery, London, 1973, no. 191.

37.
Self-Portrait of the Artist
Collections:
Edwin Lawrence, by 1862; bought from him by the museum in 1892.
Literature:
Williamson, I, 51-52; Long, 377; Foskett, 1972, 481; London, 1973, 99; Reynolds, 8, 13-14.

38.
Portrait of Robert Wignall
Collections:
Edwin Lawrence, by 1862; bought from him by the museum in 1892.
Literature:
Williamson, I, 51-52; Long, 377; Foskett, 1972, 481; London, 1973, 99; Reynolds, 16-17.

Rachel Ruysch (1664-1750)
Bibliography

Grant, Maurice H., *Flower Paintings through Four Centuries; A Descriptive Catalogue of the Collection Formed by Major the Honorable Henry Rogers Broughton*. Including a dictionary of flower painters from the XVIth to the XIX century by Col. Maurice H. Grant, Leigh-on-Sea, 1952.

————, *Rachel Ruysch, 1664-1750*, Leigh-on-Sea, 1956.

Hofstede de Groot, Cornelis, *Beschreibendes und Kritisches verzeichnis der Werke der hervorragendsten holländischen Maler des XVII Jahrhunderts; nach dem muster von John Smith's Catalogue raisonné zusammengestelt von Dr. C. Hofstede de Groot*, Esslingen, 1907-28.

Renraw, R., "The Art of Rachel Ruysch," *Connoisseur*, XCII, 1933, 397-99.

Tufts, 1974, 98-105.

Valentiner, Wilhelm, R., "An Allegorical Portrait of Rachel Ruysch," *North Carolina Museum of Art Bulletin*, I, 1957, 5-8.

39.
Flower Still Life
Collections:
William Wells by 1835, who sold it with a companion picture at Christie's, May 12, 1848; Edmond de Rothschild (1845-1939); Edward Speelman, London; acquired by the museum in 1956.

Exhibitions:
British Institute, London, 1832, no. 54;
British Institute, London, 1855, no. 68.
Literature:
J. Smith, *Catalogue Raisonné of Dutch, Flemish and French Painters*, London, 1829-42, VI, no. 17; Hofstede de Groot, 1907-28, X, no. 57; Grant, 1956, no. 75 and color pl. 4; K. Lindesmith, "The Good Things in Life," *Toledo Museum News*, n.s., I, no. 3, 1957, 16-18; "Accessions of American and Canadian Museums, October-December 1957," *Art Quarterly*, XXI, no. 1, 1958, 85; Otto Wittmann, "The Golden Age in the Netherlands," *Apollo*, LXXXVI, no. 70, 1967, 474; Mitchell, 224 and fig. 318.

40.
Still Life with Flowers and Plums
Collections:
Sold Amsterdam, July 17, 1782, no. 92 (126 florins); Count Anton Lamberg-Springenstein; given by him to the Akademie with a signed companion (no. 665; lost in World War II) in 1821.
Literature:
C. von Lützow, *Katalog der Gemälde-Galerie*, Vienna, 1889, no. 664; Robert Eigenberger, *Die Gemaeldegalerie der Akademie der bildenden Künste in Wien*, Vienna, 1927, 365-66, no. 664; Hofstede de Groot, 1907-28, X, no. 86; Grant, 1956, no. 50; *Katalog der Gemälde Galerie*, Akademie der bildenden Künste, Vienna, 1961, 112 (and later editions).

Rosalba Carriera (1675-1757)
Bibliography

Carriera, Rosalba, *"Journal" pendant son séjour à Paris en 1720-1721*, trans. A. Sensier, Paris, 1865.

Cessi, F., *Rosalba Carriera*, I Maestri di Colore, Milan, 1967, no. 97.

Colding, 125-37.

Gatto, Gabrielle, "Per la cronologia di Rosalba Carriera," *Arte veneta*, XXV, 1971, 182-93.

Hoerschelmann, Emilie von, *Rosalba Carriera, die Meistern der Pastelmalerei, und Bilder aus der Kunst und Kulturgeschichte des 18 Jahrhunderts*, Leipzig, 1908.

Jeannerat, C., "Le origini del ritratto a miniatura in avorio," *Dedalo*, II, 1931, 767-80.

Levey, Michael, *Painting in XVIII-Century Venice*, London, 1959, 134ff.

Malamani, Vittorio, *Rosalba Carriera*, Bergamo, 1910.

Tufts, 1974, 106-15.

Zanetti, Antonio Maria, *Della pittura veneziana e delle opere pubbliche de veneziani maestri*, 5 vols., Venice, 1771.

41.
Portrait of Robert, Lord Walpole (1700-1751)
Collections:
Robert, Lord Walpole; Horace Walpole at Strawberry Hill by 1784; lot 47, 14th day of the sale of the contents of Strawberry Hill in 1842; bought by Morgan for 3 guineas; Salting Collection; bequeathed to the museum in 1910.
Literature:
B. S. Long, *Hand-List of Miniature Portraits and Silhouettes*, Victoria and Albert Museum, London, 1930, 10; Colding, 137.

42.
Woman at Her Dressing Table
Collections:
Victor E. Pollak, Vienna, 1924; Edward B. Greene, Cleveland; given to the museum by 1950.
Exhibitions:
International Exhibition of Miniatures, catalog by L. Schidlof, Albertina, Vienna, 1924, no. 133.
Literature:
Cleveland Museum of Art, *Portrait Miniatures: The Edward B. Greene Collection*, catalog by L. H. Burchfield and H. B. Wehle, 1951, 20-21 and no. 84 (pl. XXXVII).

Giulia Lama (ca. 1685-after 1753)
Bibliography

Goering, M., "Giulia Lama," *Jahrbuch der Königlich preussischen Kunstsammlungen*, 1935.

Pallucchini, R., "Di una pittrice veneziana del settecento: Giulia Lama," *Rivista d'arte*, 1933, 400.

————, *Piazzetta*, Milan, 1956.

————, "Miscellanea piazzettesca," *Arte veneta*, 1968, 107-30.

————, "Per la conoscenza di Giulia Lama," *Arte veneta*, 1970, 161-72.

Ruggeri, Ugo, *Dipinti e disegni di Giulia Lama*, Bergamo, 1973.

43.
The Martyrdom of St. Eurosia
Collections:
Gatti Casazza Collection, Venice, by 1935; given to the Cà Rezzonico in 1962.
Literature:
Goering, 166; G. Mariacher, "Il lascito Gatti Casazza a Cà Rezzonico," *Bollettino dei Musei Civici Veneziani*, 1962, 31; Pallucchini, 1968, note 3; Pallucchini, 1970, 164; Ruggeri, 20, 21.

Marie Anne Loir (ca. 1715-after 1769)
Bibliography

Bellier-Auvray, s.v.

Lafond, P., "Alexis Loir-Marianne Loir." *Réunion des Sociétés des Beaux-Arts des Départements*, Paris, 1892.

Thieme-Becker, s.v.

44.
Portrait of Gabrielle-Emilie le Tonnelier de Breteuil, Marquise Du Châtelet
Collections:
Given to the museum by the state in 1803 and therefore perhaps in the French royal collection before the Revolution.
Exhibitions:
Les trésors des musées de Bordeaux, Musée des Beaux-Arts, Tel Aviv, 1964, no. 65; *Kunst und Geist Frankreichs im 18 Jahrhundert*, Vienna, Oberes Belvedere, 1966, no. 225; *Exposition des chefs-d'oeuvre du Musée des Beaux-Arts de Bordeaux*, Nagoya, Kamakura, Osaka, Fukuoka, 1971-72, no. 21; *Les femmes peintres au XVIIIe siècle*, Musée Goya, Castres, 1973, no. 21; *Portraits de femmes*, Musée des Beaux-Arts, Bordeaux, 1975, no. 28.
Literature:
L. Clement de Ris, "Musées de province, Musée de Bordeaux" in *Revue universelle des arts*, Paris, 1860, XII, 28; de Ris, *Les musées de province*, Paris, 1872, 95-96; Lafond, 376-77; H. de la Ville de Mirmont, *Histoire du Musée de Bordeaux (1801-1830)*, Bordeaux, 1899, I, 95, 120, and 121; L. Gonse, *Chefs-d'oeuvre des Musées de Province*, Paris, 1900, I, 84; P. de Nolhac, *Jean-Marc Nattier . . .*, Paris, 1905, 139; Thieme-Becker, XXIII, 334; J. Vergnet-Ruiz and M. Laclotte, *Petits et grands musées de France*, Paris, 1962, 243. It is also cited in all published catalogs of the museum issued from the early nineteenth century until 1953.

Anna Dorothea Lisiewska-Therbusch (1721-1782)
Bibliography

Potsdam-Sanssouci, Kulturhaus Hans Marchwitza, *Anna-Dorothea Therbusch, 1721-1782*, catalog by Gerd Bartoschek, 1971.

Thieme-Becker, s.v., entry by C. Reidemeister.

45.
Portrait of Jacob Philipp Hackert (1737-1805)
Collections:
Reception piece given to the Academy by the artist in 1776.
Exhibitions:
Angelika Kauffman und ihre Zeitgenossen, Vorarlberger Landesmuseum, Bregenz, 1968, no. 326.

Literature:
A. Weinkopf, *Beschreibung der K.K. Akademie der bildenden Künste*, Vienna, 1783; C. von Lützow, *Katalog der Gemälde-Galerie*, Vienna, 1889, 274, no. 113; Thieme-Becker, XXIII, 282.

Françoise Duparc (1726-1778)
Bibliography

Auquier, Philippe, "An Eighteenth Century Painter: Françoise Duparc," *Burlington Magazine*, VI, 1905, 477-78.

Billioud, Joseph, "Un peintre des types populaires: Françoise Duparc de Marseille (1726-1778)," *Gazette des beaux-arts*, XX, 1938, 173-84.

46.
The Seller of Tisane
Collections:
Left by the artist in her will to the Town Hall, Marseilles, in 1778; given to the museum in 1869.
Exhibitions:
Les femmes peintres au XVIIIe siècle, Musée Goya, Castres, 1973, no. 5 (with references to five earlier exhibitions).
Literature:
L. Lagrange, "Exposition Régionale des Beaux-Arts à Marseilles," *Gazette des beaux-arts*, 1861, 544; Auquier, 477-78; Auquier, *Catalogue des peintures, sculptures, pastels et dessins*, Musée des Beaux-Arts, Marseilles, 1908, no. 162; Billioud, 178ff.

47.
Head of a Young Woman
Collections:
Rocamir de la Terre; given to the museum before 1884.
Exhibitions:
Les femmes peintres au XVIIIe siècle, Castres, Musée Goya, 1973, no. 6.
Literature:
M. Crouchandeu, *Catalogue raisonné des objets d'art et d'archéologie du Musée de Perpignan*, Perpignan, 1884, 67, no. 30 (attributed to Greuze).

Angelica Kauffman (1741-1807)
Bibliography

Bregenz, 1968.

Busiri Vici, Andrea, "Angelica Kauffmann and the Bariatinskis," *Apollo*, LXXVII, 1963, 201-8.

Manners, Lady Victoria, and Williamson, G. C., *Angelica Kauffmann, R. A., Her Life and Works*, London, 1924.

Mayer, Dorothy Moulton, *Angelica Kauffmann, R.A., 1741-1807*, Gerrards Cross, 1972.

Poensgen, Georg, "Ein Kunstlerbildnis von Angelika Kauffmann," *Pantheon*, III, 1973, 294-97.

Rossi, Giovanni Gherado de, *Vita di Angelica Kauffman, pittrice*, Florence, 1810.

Tomory, Peter A., "Angelica Kauffmann-'Sappho,'" *Burlington Magazine*, CXIII, 1971, 272-76.

Tufts, 1974, 116-25.

Walch, Peter S., "Angelica Kauffmann," doctoral dissertation, Princeton University, 1969.

————, "Angelica Kauffmann and Her Contemporaries," *Art Bulletin*, LI, 1969, 83-85.

48.
Cleopatra at the Tomb of Marc Anthony
Exhibitions:
London, Royal Academy, 1770, no. 118, *German Art 1400-1800 from Collections in Great Britain*, City Art Gallery, Manchester, 1961, no. 197; *Angelika Kauffman und ihre Zeitgenossen*, Vorarlberger Landesmuseum, Bregenz, 1968, no. 52; *The Age of Neo-Classicism*, Royal Academy, London, 1972, no. 160.
Literature:
Manners and Williamson, 188, 223, 236; Michael Levey, *Rococo to Revolution*, New York, 1966, 182f.; Robert Rosenblum, *Transformations in Late Eighteenth Century Art*, Princeton, 1967, 421.

49.
Self-Portrait
Collections:
Johann Peter Kauffman; George Kauffman; The Earl of Morley.
Exhibitions:
Angelica Kauffman, Kenwood, London, 1955, no. 20; *Angelika Kauffmann und ihre Zeitgenossen*, Vorarlberger Landesmuseum, Bregenz, 1968, no. 4.

50.
Cornelia, Mother of the Gracchi
Collections:
George Bowles; Sir Charles Rushout (by inheritance); The Province of Alberta (at 37 Hill St., London, W. 1).
Exhibitions:
Royal Academy, London, 1786, no. 86.

51.
Vergil Writing His Own Epitaph at Brundisium
Collections:
George Bowles; Sir Charles Rushout (by inheritance); The Province of Alberta (at 37 Hill St., London, W. 1).
Exhibitions:
Royal Academy, London, 1786, no. 196.

Anne Vallayer-Coster (1744-1818)
Bibliography

Roland Michel, Marianne, "A propos d'un tableau retrouvé de Vallayer-Coster," *Bulletin de la Société de l'Histoire de l'Art Français*, 1965.

————, *Anne Vallayer-Coster*, Paris, 1970.

52.
The White Soup Bowl
Collections:
Marquis de Marigny, 1771-82; sold Paris, March-April 1782, no. 113; M. Beajon; sold Paris, Hôtel d'Evreux, April 25, 1787, no. 209; private collections, Paris.
Exhibitions:
Hommage à Chardin, Galerie Heim, Paris, 1959, no. 82; *Le cabinet d'un amateur*, Galerie de l'Orangerie, Paris, 1965, no. 100.
Literature:
Salon of 1771, in Diderot, IV, 201; Faré, 1962, I, 178, and II, color pl. XII (see Moillon bibliography); Roland Michel, 1965, 189; Roland Michel, 1970, no. 222.

53.
Vase of Flowers with Bust of Flora
Collections:
Abbé Terray, 1775-79; sold January 20, 1779, no. 92; Le Boeuf Collection; sold April 8, 1783, no. 92; Matthieson Gallery, London, 1959; E. V. Thaw, New York and London.
Exhibitions:
Die Frau als Künstlerin, Kunsthaus, Zurich, 1958, no. 126; *Women: A Historical Survey of Works by Women Artists*, North Carolina Museum of Art, Raleigh, 1972, no. 9.
Literature:
Salon of 1775, no. 99 (for references to critics' comments, see Roland Michel, 1970, 102); Faré, I, 178 and 229, and II, pl. 408 (see Moillon bibliography); Roland Michel, 1970, no. 1.

54.
Still Life with Military Trophies and a Bust of Minerva
Collections:
Mme. Vissitier, 1777; Vicomte G. Chabert and sold from his collection in Paris, Galerie Chabert, June 5, 1909, lot 12; anonymous sale, Hôtel Drouot, Paris, June 9, 1923, no. 15; Mme. P. Potin; sold by her at Galerie Georges Petit, Paris, April 22, 1929, no. 25; anonymous sale, Hôtel Drouot, Paris, March 7, 1941, no. 15; anonymous sale, Galerie J. Charpentier, Paris, December 15, 1959, no. 30; private collection, Paris; Wildenstein & Co., New York.
Exhibitions:
Salon de 1777, Paris, no. 101; *Deux siècles de gloire militaire*, Musée des Arts Décoratifs, Paris, 1935, no. 494; *Hommage à Chardin*, Galerie Heim, Paris, 1959, no. 84; *The Object as Subject*, Wildenstein & Co., New York, 1975, no. 77.

Literature:
Lettres pittoresques à l'occasion des tableaux exposés au Salon en 1777, Paris, 1777, letter 7; E. Dacier, *Catalogue de ventes et livrets de salons illustrés par Gabriel de Saint-Aubin*, III-IV ("Livret de Salon de 1777"), Paris, 1910, 48; Faré, 1962, I, 179, 222, and II, no. 246 (see Moillon bibliography); Roland Michel, 1970, 187-88, no. 264; Nochlin, 1971, 30.

55.
Still Life with Plums and a Lemon
Collections:
Harry G. Sperling, New York; sold 1971.
Exhibitions:
Salon of 1779, no. 105.
Literature:
Roland Michel, 1970, no. 138.

Adélaïde Labille-Guiard (1749-1803)
Bibliography

Passez, Anne-Marie, *Adélaïde Labille-Guiard, 1749-1803*, Paris, 1973.

Portalis, Roger, "Adélaïde Labille-Guiard," *Gazette des beaux-arts*, 1901, II, 476-94; 1902, I, 325-47.

_____, *Adélaïde Labille-Guiard (1749-1803)*, Paris, 1902.

56.
Portrait of Madame de Genlis
Collections:
Bought in France in 1874 by Mrs. Willard Parker; by descent to the present owner.
Literature:
Passez, 232-33.

Marie Victoire Lemoine (1754-1820)
Bibliography

Bellier-Auvray, s.v.

57.
Interior of the Atelier of a Woman Painter
Collections:
Family of Marie Victoire Lemoine; Wildenstein & Co., Paris, by 1926; Wildenstein & Co., New York, 1937-49; Mrs. Thornycroft Ryle, New York; gift of Mrs. Ryle to the museum in 1957.
Exhibitions:
Exposition des femmes peintres du XVIIIe siècle, Galerie J. Charpentier, Paris, 1926, no. 68; *French Paintings of the Eighteenth and Early Nineteenth Centuries*, Cincinnati Art Museum, 1937, no. 14; *Pictures within Pictures*, Wadsworth Atheneum, Hartford, 1949, no. 27; *Portrait of the Artist*, catalog by John Walsh, Metropolitan Museum of Art, New York, 1972, no. 14; *Old Mistresses*, Walters Art Gallery, Baltimore, 1972, no. 15.
Literature:
Livrets des Salons, 1796, no. 284; A. Linzeler, "L' exposition des femmes peintres du XVIIIe siècle," *Gazette des beaux-arts*, 1926, 161; Oulmont, pl. 58; Thieme-Becker, XXIII, 34; D. Ojalvo in *Revue du Louvre*, 1973, 333.

Elizabeth Vigée-Lebrun (1755-1842)
Bibliography

Babin, G., "Mme. Vigée-Lebrun, portrait de Mme. Grand, plus tard princesse de Tally-rand," *L'illustration*, June 1912.

Bischoff, I., "Vigée-Lebrun's Portraits of Men," *Antiques*, January 1968, 109-13.

Blum, André, *Madame Vigée-Lebrun, peintre des grandes dames du XVIIIe siècle*, Paris, 1919.

Bouchot, Henri, "Une artiste française pendant l'émigration, Madame Vigée-Lebrun," *Revue de l'art ancien et moderne*, 1898, I, 51-62, 219-30.

Golzio, Vincenzo, "Il soggiorno romano di Elisabeth Vigée-Lebrun," *Studi romani*, IV, 1956, 182-83.

Hautecoeur, L., *Madame Vigée-Lebrun*, Paris, 1917.

Helm, William Henry, *Vigée-Lebrun, Her Life and Friendships*, Boston, 1915.

_____, *Vigée-Lebrun, Her Life, Works, and Friendships*, London, 1916.

Lebrun, Jean Baptiste Pierre, *Précis historique de la vie de la citoyenne Lebrun, peintre*, Paris, 1794.

Muntz, E., "Lettres de Mme. Vigée-Lebrun relatives à son portrait de la galerie des offices (1791)," *Nouvelles archives de l'art français*, 1874-75, 449-52.

Nikolenko, Lada, "The Russian Portraits of Mme. Vigée-Lebrun," *Gazette des beaux-arts*, LXX, 1967, 91-120.

Nolhac, Pierre de, *Madame Vigée-Lebrun, peintre de la reine Marie-Antoinette, 1755-1842*, Paris, 1908.

_____, *Madame Vigée-Lebrun*, Paris, 1912.

Pillet, Charles, *Madame Vigée-Lebrun*, Paris, 1890.

Tripier-Le Franc, Justin, *Notice sur la vie et les ouvrages de Mme. Le Brun*, extract from *Le journal dictionnaire de biographie moderne*, Paris, 1928.

Tuetey, A., "L'émigration de Mme. Vigée-Lebrun," *Bulletin de la Société de l'Histoire de l'Art Français*, 1911, 169-82.

Tufts, 1974, 126-37.

Vigée-Lebrun, Marie Louise Elizabeth, *Souvenirs de Mme. Vigée Lebrun*, 2 vols., Paris, 1835-37 (Edition cited: Paris, 1869).

_____, *Mémoires*, trans. Lionel Strachey, New York, 1903.

58.
Portrait of Count Shuvaloff
Collections:
Count Ivan Shuvaloff, Moscow; by descent to Countess Elizabeth Vladimirowna Chouwaloff (Shuvaloff) in 1905; Count Karl Lankoronsky, Vienna, by 1908; acquired by the museum in 1952.
Exhibitions:
Portraits russes artistiques et historiques, Exposition Rétrospective de la Ville de Paris, St. Petersburg, Palais de la Tauride, 1905; *From El Greco to Pollock: Early and Late Works by European and American Artists*, ed. Gertrude Rosenthal, Baltimore Museum of Art, 1968, no. 45; *Exhibition Number One from the Permanent Collection*, North Carolina Museum of Art, 1970, 82-83, color repr.; *Women: A Historical Survey of Works by Women Artists*, North Carolina Museum of Art, Raleigh, 1972, no. 12.
Literature:
Vigée-Lebrun, 1869 ed., I, 15-16, and II, 356; Nolhac, 1908, 17, 157, 161; Hautecour, II; Helm, 1915, 13, 216; Blum, 15, 94; W. R. Valentiner, *Catalogue of Paintings*, North Carolina Museum of Art, 1956, no. 162, 72-73, repr.; Nikolenko, 114, no. 46; Bischoff, 109-11; Tufts, 1974, 127 and fig. 70.

59.
Portrait of the Marquise de Jaucourt
Collections:
Marquise de Jaucourt; Steilman Collection by 1909; Jessie Woolworth Donahue by 1942; given by her to the museum in 1954.
Exhibitions:
French and English Art Treasures of the XVIII Century, Parke-Bernet, New York, 1942, no. 65; *Treasured Masterpieces of The Metropolitan Museum of Art*, Tokyo National Museum and Kyoto National Museum, 1972, no. 86.
Literature:
A. Dayot, *L'image de la femme*, Paris, 1899, 309; Nolhac, 1908, 140; Helm, 1915, 202; Blum, pl. XV; Hautecoeur, 61.

60.
Portrait of the Comtesse du Buquoi
Collections:
Prince Paar, Vienna, from whose family the painting was acquired by Wildenstein.
Exhibitions:
O retrato na Franca, Museo de Arte, Sao Paolo, 1952, no. 26; *De Watteau à Prud'hon*, Gazette des beaux-arts, Paris, 1956, no. 90.
Literature:
Vigée-Lebrun, 1869 ed., I, 282, and II, 368; Helm, 1915, 190; Blum, 63-64 and 101.

347

61.
Varvara Ivanovna Narishkine
Collections:
A. Couteaux, Paris, 1863; Boris Serguyev; Wildenstein & Co., New York, 1934-46; Oscar B. Cintas, Havana, Cuba, until 1957; Cintas Fellowship Program, Institute of International Education, New York; Cintas Sale, Parke-Bernet, New York, May 1, 1963, no. 21 (as Princess Tufialkin); bought by the museum with funds from the Lillian Gill Derby Trust Fund.
Exhibitions:
Exhibition of Historical Portraits, St. Petersburg, 1870, no. 735; *Art of the 17th and 18th Centuries*, Cleveland Museum of Art, Ohio, 1934; *La peinture française — collections américaines*, Musées de Bordeaux, Bordeaux, 1966, pl. 16; *France in the 18th Century*, Royal Academy, London, 1968, no. 714; *Six Centuries of Painting from the Columbus Gallery of Fine Arts*, Ohio State University Art Gallery, Columbus, 1973, no. 14.
Literature:
Helm, 1915, 223; "Accessions of American and Canadian Museums: April-June 1963," *Art Quarterly*, XXVI, 1963, 358 and 363.

Gabrielle Capet (1761-1817)
Bibliography

Doria, Comte Arnauld, *Une émule d' Adélaïde Labille-Guiard: Gabrielle Capet, portraitiste*, Paris, 1934.

62.
Portrait of Christian-Georg von Schantz
Collections:
Alexandre von Schantz; given to the museum by 1929.
Literature:
1929 catalog of the Nationalmuseum, no. 157; Doria, no. 53.

Marguerite Gérard (1761-1837)
Bibliography

Doin, Jeanne, "Marguerite Gérard (1761-1837)," *Gazette des beaux-arts*, CIX, 1912, 429-52.

Levitine, G., "Marguerite Gérard and Her Stylistic Significance," *Baltimore Museum Annual*, III, 1968, 21ff.

Perate, A., "Les esquisses de Gérard," *L'art et les artistes*, 1909, 4-7.

63.
An Architect and His Family
Collections:
Doistau Sale, Paris, June 9-11, 1909, no. 46; Eugene Fischoff Collection, Paris; Mary Frick Jacobs Collection, Baltimore.
Exhibitions:
Jewelry and Finery, Herron Museum of Art, Indianapolis, 1967, no. 2; *Old Mistresses*, Walters Art Gallery, Baltimore, 1972, no. 16.

Literature:
H. Barton, *The Collection of Mary Frick Jacobs*, Baltimore, 1938, pl. 24; G. Rosenthal, "Architect Ledoux and His Family," *Baltimore Museum of Art News*, November 1947, 1-3; *Baltimore Sunday Sun*, "Object of the Week," July 21, 1957, Magazine Section, repr. 1; Levitine, 21ff., pl. on 20.

64.
The Piano Lesson
Collections:
Anonymous sale, Paris, April 2, 1857, no. 5; anonymous sale, Paris, April 28, 1857, no. 29; Maulez Sale, Paris, November 29, 1875, no. 36; Tamar Sale, Paris, April 9-12, 1883, no. 34; Pereire Sale, Paris, November 8, 1972, no. 12.

Marie Geneviève Bouliar (1762-1825)
Bibliography

Bellier-Auvray, s.v.

Jouin, Henri, *Mlle. M. G. Bouliard*, Paris, 1891.

Thieme-Becker, s.v.

Trésors des musées du nord de la France: La peinture français, 1770-1830, Musée d'Arras, 1975, catalog entry on Bouliar by Françoise Maison.

65.
Aspasia
Collections:
Recorded in the Musée Napoléon (Louvre); Palais de Fontainebleau, 1837 to 1875; given by the state to the museum at Arras in 1876.
Exhibitions:
Salon of 1795, no. 51; *Trésors des musées du nord de la France: La peinture française, 1770-1780*, Musée d'Arras, 1975, no. 17 (catalog entry by F. Maison).
Literature:
Catalogue . . . du Musée de la ville d'Arras, Arras, 1880, no. 11; Bellier-Auvray, I, 139; Jouin, 10; *Catalogue . . . du Musée de la ville d'Arras*, 1907, no. 27.

66.
Portrait of Chevalier-Alexandre-Marie Lenoir
(See next entry.)
67.
Portrait of Adélaïde Binart (Mme. Alexandre Lenoir)

Collections:
Alexandre Lenoir: Lenoir family by descent to P. Lenoir; bought from him for the museum in 1899. *Adélaïde Lenoir:* Lenoir family by descent to Mme. A. Lenoir; Mlle. Boitte; bought from her for the museum in 1945.
Exhibitions:
Exposition des femmes peintres, organized by Mme. A. Besnard, Hôtel de Lyceum-France, Paris, 1908 *(Mme. Lenoir); Femmes peintres du XVIIIe siècle,* Hôtel des Négociants, no. 7 *(Alexandre Lenoir); Les femmes peintres au XVIIIe siècle,* Musée Goya, Castres, 1973, no. 2 *(Mme. Lenoir).*
Literature:
Jouin, 10 and 14 (409 in the article); Tourneux, 295 and 297.

Jeanne Philiberte Ledoux (1767-1840)
Bibliography

Bellier-Auvray, s.v.

Bénézit, s.v.

68.
Portrait of a Boy
Collections:
Leonce Rabillon (d. 1929); bequeathed by him to the museum.

Constance Charpentier (1767-1849)
Bibliography

Clement, 78.

Ellet, 236.

Paris, 1974, no. 19 and 345-47 in cat. entry by R. Rosenblum.

Sterling, Charles, "A Fine 'David' Reattributed," *The Metropolitan Museum of Art Bulletin*, IX, no. 5, 1951, 121-32.

69.
Melancholy
Collections:
Acquired by the Musée Napoléon in 1801; sent to the Musée de Picardie, Amiens, in 1864.
Exhibitions:
Salon of 1801, no. 58; *Napoléon, Ier*, Musée de Picardie, Amiens, 1969, no. 8; *Equivoques,* Musée des Arts Décoratifs, Paris, 1973; *French Painting 1774-1830: The Age of Revolution*, Grand Palais, Paris, 1974, no. 19, repr. 179.
Literature:
Deloynes Collection of Manuscripts, Cabinet des Estampes, Bibliothèque Nationale, Paris, XXVI, no. 682, 128-29 and no. 690, 326; XXVII, no. 710, 449; F. Benoit, *L'art français sous la Révolution et l'Empire: Les doctrines, les idées, les genres*, Paris, 1897, 339; Catalog of the Musée de Picardie, Amiens, 1911, 19, no. 83; Sterling, 1951, 127, 129-30; J. Foucart, "Compte rendu de l'exposition Napoléon Ier, Amiens, Musée de Picardie, 1969," *Revue de l'art*, no. 8, 1970, 76.

Marie Guillemine Benoist (1768-1826)
Bibliography

Marie-Juliette Ballot, *La Comtesse Benoist, l'Emilie de Demoustier 1768-1826*, Paris, 1914.

70.
Innocence between Vice and Virtue
Exhibitions:
Salon 1791 (no. 273)
Literature:
Le plaisir prolongé, le retour au Salon chez soi et celui de l'abeille dans sa ruche, in the Bibliothèque Nationale, Cabinet des Estampes, Collection Deloynes, XVII, no. 437, 242; *La béquille de Voltaire au Salon, II*, Paris, 1791, Collection Deloynes, XVII, no. 439, 320-21; Ballot, 67-75, repr. opp. 64.

Pauline Auzou (1775-1835)
Bibliography

Cameron, Vivian, "Portrait of a Musician by Pauline Auzou," Currier Gallery of Art Bulletin, 1974, no. 2, 1-17.

71.
The First Feeling of Coquetry
Exhibitions:
Salon of 1804, no. 8.
Literature:
Cameron, 8, 13; Charles Landon, *Nouvelles des arts*, IV, 1804, 131-32; *Lettres impartiales sur les expositions de l'an XIII*, in the Bibliothèque Nationale, Cabinet des Estampes, Collection Deloynes, XXXI, no. 876, 672.

Constance Mayer (1775/78-1821)
Bibliography

Bellier-Auvray, s.v.

Doin, Jean, "Constance Mayer," *La revue de l'art ancien et moderne*, January 1911, 49-60; February 1911, 139-50.

Gueullette, Charles, "Mademoiselle Constance Mayer et Prud'hon," *Gazette des beaux-arts*, May, October, December, 1879.

Guiffrey, Jean, *L'oeuvre de Pierre-Paul Prud'hon*, Musée National du Louvre (Documents d'Art), 1924.

Muther, Richard, *History of Modern Art*, London, 1894, I, 310-13.

Pilon, Edmond, *Constance Mayer*, André Delpleuch, ed., Paris, 1927.

72.
The Dream of Happiness
Exhibitions:
Salon of 1819.
Literature:
Charles Ressort, "Copies, répliques, pastiches" (Dossier du Département des Peintures), *La revue du Louvre*, XXIII, 1973, 399.

Marie Eléonore Godefroid (1778-1849)
Bibliography

Arbaud, L., "Mademoiselle Godefroid," *Gazette des beaux-arts*, XI, 2nd series, 1869, 38-52; 512-22.

Bellier-Auvray, s.v.

Nagler, V, 536.

[De] Sainte-Vallière, *Marie-Eléonore Godefroid, artiste peintre*, Paris, 1847.

73.
The Sons of Marshal Ney
Exhibitions:
Salon of 1810, no. 379.
Literature:
Bellier-Auvray, I, 670; Nagler, V, 536.

Mme. Villers (active late 18th-early 19th century)
Bibliography

Bellier-Auvray, s.v.

74.
Portrait of Mme. Soustras
Collections:
Collection of the artist's husband until 1836 or 1839, entered the Louvre in 1971 from the Mairie de Juvisy.

Antoinette Cecile Hortense Haudebourt-Lescot (1784-1845)
Bibliography

Hautecoeur, L., *Bulletin des musées*, 1925, 324-25 (68-69).

Paris, 1974, 486-87, entry by Sally Wells-Robertson and Isabella Julia.

Sparrow, 179ff.

Valabrègue, A., "Mme. Haudebourt-Lescot," *Les lettres et les arts*, 1887, I, 102-9.

Wells-Robertson, Sally, "A.C.H. Haudebourt-Lescot: 1784-1845," unpublished paper, New York University Institute of Fine Arts, 1973.

75.
Self-Portrait
Collections:
Gift of Mme. Buhner, née Maria Dauby, a pupil of the artist's, in 1867.
Exhibitions:
Les femmes peintres au XVIIIe siècle, Castres, Musée Goya, 1973, no. 12, ill. x; *French Painting 1774-1830: The Age of Revolution*, Grand Palais, Paris, 1974, repr. 273, no. 98, 487.

Literature:
A. Jal, *Salon de 1827*, 1828, 290-91; A. Valabrègue, 1887, 104; G. Lafenestre, *Notice des portraits d'artistes exposés dans la salle Denon au Louvre*, Paris, 1888, no. 41, 27; G. Brière, "Emplacements actuels des tableaux du Musée du Louvre . . . ," *Bulletin de la Société de l'Histoire de l'Art Français*, 1924, 128, no. 407; R. Escholier, *La peinture française, XIXe siècle*, Paris, I, 1941, 102; C. Sterling and H. Adhémar, *Musée National du Louvre. Peintures de l'école française du XIXe siècle*, Paris, 1959, III, no. 1053, repr. 379.

Adrienne Marie Louise Grandpierre-Deverzy (1798- active to 1855)
Bibliography

Bellier-Auvray, s.v.

76.
The Studio of Abel Pujol in 1822
Literature:
Bellier-Auvray, I, 687.

Sarah Miriam Peale (1800-1885)
Bibliography

Baltimore, The Peale Museum, *Miss Sarah Miriam Peale, 1800-1885, Portraits and Still Life*, catalog by Wilbur H. Huntley and John Mahey, 1967.

Born, Wolfgang, "The Female Peales: Their Art and Its Tradition," *American Collector*, XV, August 1946, 12-14.

The Detroit Institute of Arts, *The Peale Family: Three Generations of American Artists*, Charles H. Elam, ed., 1967.

Gerdts, William H., and Burke, Russell, *American Still-Life Painting*, New York, 1971.

Tufts, 1974, 138-45.

77.
A Slice of Watermelon
Collections:
The Peale Family Collections.
Exhibitions:
25 American Paintings from the Revolution to the Civil War, San Francisco, 1942, no. 6; *A. Everett Austin, Jr.: A Director's Taste and Achievement*, Wadsworth Atheneum, Hartford, 1958, no. 61; *Miss Sarah Miriam Peale — 1800-1885, Portraits and Still Life*, Peale Museum, Baltimore, 1967, no. 41, repr. 32.
Literature:
Tufts, 1974, fig. 78, repr. 143; Nochlin, 1974, repr. 73.

Rosa Bonheur (1822-1899)
Bibliography

Bacon, Henry, "Rosa Bonheur," *Century*, XXVIII, October 1884, 833-40.

Bonheur, Rosa, "Fragments of My Autobiography," *Magazine of Art*, XXVI, 1902,
531-36.

Klumpke, Anna Elizabeth, *Rosa Bonheur,
sa vie, son oeuvre*, Paris, 1908.

Masters in Art, Rosa Bonheur, Boston, 1903.

Roger-Milès, L., *Rosa Bonheur, sa vie, son
oeuvre*, Paris, 1900.

Stanton, Theodore, ed., *Reminiscences of
Rosa Bonheur*, London, 1910.

Sterling and Salinger, II, 160-64.

Tufts, 1974, 147-57.

78.
Study of Rams
Literature:
Klumpke, repr. 97.

79.
Oil Sketch for Haymaking in Auvergne
Literature:
Masters in Art; Klumpke, 217-42, oil sketch
repr. 217, *Haymaking in Auvergne* repr.
opp. 228.

80.
Gathering for the Hunt
Exhibitions:
The Horse in Art, Santa Barbara Museum of
Art, 1974, no. 5, repr.
Literature:
L. Roger-Milès, repr. opp. 66,
dated 1857.

Lilly Martin Spencer (1822-1902)
Bibliography

Freivogel, Elsie F., "Lilly Martin Spencer,"
Archives of American Art Journal, XII, no. 4,
1972, 9-14.

Washington, D.C., National Collection of
Fine Arts, *Lilly Martin Spencer, 1822-1902:
The Joys of Sentiment*, introduction by R.
Bolton-Smith and W. H. Truettner, 1973.

81.
The Young Husband: First Marketing
Exhibitions:
National Academy of Design, New York,
1856, no. 86; H. H. Leeds, New York, May
28, 1857 (property of William Schaus), no.
63; *American Painting*, Cincinnati Art
Museum, 1961, no. 18; *American Paintings
of the Nineteenth Century*, California Palace
of the Legion of Honor, San Francisco, 1964,
no. 74; *Lilly Martin Spencer, 1822-1902: The
Joys of Sentiment*, introduction by R. Bolton-
Smith and W. H. Truettner, National Collection of Fine Arts, Washington, D.C., 1973,
171-73, repr. 24; *America as Art*, National
Collection of Fine Arts, Washington, D.C.,
1976.

Literature:
Domestic Manners of the Americans, Frances
Trollope, New York, 1949 (first published in
1832), 85 (Hervieu engraving repr. opp. 41);
The Crayon, III, 146; *The Walters Art Gallery
Bulletin*, XXIV, no. 7, April 1972; *Antiques
Magazine*, July 1973, repr., 110-14; Hermann
Warner Williams, Jr., *Mirror to the American
Past*, 1973, 104, repr. 89; *The History of
Women in America*, Beverly Hills, California,
1975; *Art News*, April 1976, 54.

Emily Mary Osborn (1834-?)
Bibliography

Dafforne, James, "British Artists: Their
Style and Character, No. LXXV — Emily Mary
Osborn," *Art Journal*, XXVI, 1864, 261-63.

Maas, Jeremy, *Victorian Painters*, New York,
1969, 121.

Nochlin, 1974, 74.

"Selected Pictures: *God's Acre*," *Art Journal*,
XXX, 1868, 148-49.

Wood, Christopher, *Dictionary of Victorian
Painters*, Woodbridge, Suffolk, England,
1971, 207.

82.
Mrs. Sturgis and Children
Exhibitions:
Royal Academy, London, 1855, no. 266;
Perfect Touch Gallery, Chicago, 1975.
Literature:
Dafforne, 261.

Elizabeth Eleanor Siddal (1834-1862)
Bibliography

Doughty, Oswald, *A Victorian Romantic:
Dante Gabriel Rossetti*, London, 1960.

Fredeman, William E., *Pre-Raphaelitism: A
Bibliocritical Study*, Cambridge, Mass., 1965;
section 59, 209-11, contains a fairly
complete and annotated bibliography on
Siddal.

Procter, Ida, "Elizabeth Siddal: The Ghost of
an Idea," *Cornhill Magazine*, no. 990, Winter
1951-52, 368-86.

Rossetti, William M., "Dante Gabriel Rossetti
and Elizabeth Siddal," *Burlington Magazine*,
I, May 1903, 273-95.

Troyen, Aimee B., "The Life and Art of
Elizabeth Eleanor Siddal," senior essay,
History of Art Department, Yale University,
1975.

Vitale, Zaira, "Eleonora Siddal Rossetti,"
Emporium, XIX, June 1904, 430-47.

83.
Clerk Saunders
Collections:
Purchased by Charles Eliot Norton in 1857;
given to Dante Gabriel Rossetti in 1869 at the
latter's request; to William M. Rossetti after
Dante's death; bought by Fairfax Murray
in 1884; Fairfax Murray bequest to the
museum in 1910.
Exhibitions:
Pre-Raphaelite Exhibition, No. 4 Russell
Place, Fitzroy Square, London, 1857, no. 65;
Exhibition of Modern British Art, National
Academy of Design, New York, 1857; *Rus-
kin Exhibition*, City Art Gallery, Manchester,
1904, no. 196; *The Pre-Raphaelites, A Loan
Exhibition of Their Paintings and Drawings
Held in the Centenary Year of the Founda-
tion of the Brotherhood*, Whitechapel Art
Gallery, London, 1948, no. 105; *Paintings
and Drawings by the Pre-Raphaelites*, Russell-
Cotes Art Gallery, Bournemouth, 1951;
Pre-Raphaelite Drawings and Watercolours,
Arts Council, London, 1953, no. 65; *Dante
Gabriel Rossetti*, Laing Art Gallery, New-
castle-upon-Tyne, 1971, no. 81, 137;
Präraffaeliten, Baden-Baden, 1974, no. 142.
Literature:
George Birbeck Hill, ed., *Letters of Dante
Gabriel Rossetti to William Allingham, 1854-
1870*, London, 1897, 14, 17, 186; Rossetti,
277; Robin Ironside and John Gere, *Pre-
Raphaelite Painters*, London, 1948, 3-8, pl.
43; Fredeman, 210; John Nicoll, *The Pre-
Raphaelites*, London, 1970, 65, pl. 46; G. H.
Fleming, *That Ne'er Shall Meet Again*,
London, 1971, 212; Nochlin, 1974, 73-74.

Berthe Morisot (1841-1895)
Bibliography

Angoulvent, Monique, *Berthe Morisot*,
preface by Robert Rey, Paris, 1933.

Bataille, M. L., and Wildenstein, G., *Berthe
Morisot — Catalogue des peintures, pastels
et aquarelles*, Paris, 1961.

Fourreau, Al, *Berthe Morisot*, Paris/New
York, 1925.

Mathey, François, *Six femmes peintres*, Paris,
1951, 6-7.

Mongan, Elizabeth, *Berthe Morisot — Drawings, Pastels, Watercolors*, New York, 1960.

Moreau-Nélaton, E., *Manet raconté par
lui-même*, Paris, 1926, I.

Musée National du Louvre, *Peintures, école française, XIXe siècle*, Paris, 1960, III.

New York, Wildenstein & Co., *Berthe Morisot, Loan Exhibition of Paintings*, 1960.

Paris, *Berthe Morisot and Her Circle*, introduction by Denis Rouart, 1952.

Rewald, passim.

Rouart, Denis, *Correspondance de Berthe Morisot*, Paris, 1950 (English translation: *The Correspondence of Berthe Morisot*, New York, 1957).

Sterling and Salinger, III, 163-64.

84.
The Sisters
Collections:
Durand-Ruel, Paris; Mrs. Charles S. Carstairs; acquired by the museum in 1952.
Exhibitions:
Exposition centennale de l'art français, Institut Français, St. Petersburg, 1912.
Literature:
François Monod, "L'exposition centennale de l'art français de St. Petersbourg," *Gazette des beaux-arts*, 4th period, VII, March-April 1912, 318, repr. 319; L. Hautecoeur, "L'exposition centennale de peinture français à Saint-Petersburg, *Les arts*, II, no. 129, September 1912, repr. 30; Bataille and Wildenstein, 24, fig. 106, no. 19; *European Painting: An Illustrated Summary Catalog*, National Gallery of Art, Washington, D.C., 1975, 246, repr. 247, no. 170.

85.
Paris Seen from the Trocadero
Collections:
Georges de Bellio, Paris; Donop de Monchy; J. Doucet; Collection Ryerson, Chicago; Mr. and Mrs. Hugh N. Kirkland, Palm Beach, Florida; Santa Barbara Museum of Art.
Exhibitions:
Boussod et Valadon, Paris, 1892, no. 23; Durand-Ruel, Paris, 1896, no. 117; Marcel Bernheim, Paris, 1922, no. 34; Bernheim-Jeune, Paris, 1929, no. 12.
Literature:
Bataille and Wildenstein, 24, no. 23, pl. III; Rewald, 290, 292, ill. 292.

86.
Mme. Boursier and Daughter
Collections:
Mme. Hitier; purchased by the museum from M. Knoedler and Company in January 1929.
Exhibitions:
Cent Oeuvres de Berthe Morisot, Bernheim-Jeune, Paris, 1919, no. 73; Salon d'Automne, Paris, 1919, no. 137; *Exhibition of French Art, 1200-1900*, Royal Academy of Arts, London, 1932, no. 461 (dated 1873); *California-Pacific International Exposition*, Carnegie Institute, Pittsburgh, 1936; *Leaders of American Impressionism*, The Brooklyn

Museum, 1937, no. 11; *Masterpieces of Art: European and American Paintings 1500-1900*, New York World's Fair, 1940, no. 291 (dated 1878); *Mary Cassatt and Her Parisian Friends*, Pasadena Art Institute, 1951, no. 58; *The French Impressionists, Including Works by Some Earlier Artists Who Influenced the Movement*, Vancouver Art Gallery, 1953, no. 69; *Great French Paintings. An Exhibition in Memory of Chauncey McCormick*, Art Institute of Chicago, 1955, no. 28; *Loan Exhibition of Paintings by Berthe Morisot for the Benefit of The National Organization of Mentally Ill Children*, Wildenstein & Co., New York, 1960, no. 9; *Paintings, Drawings and Graphic Works by Manet, Degas, Berthe Morisot and Mary Cassatt*, Baltimore Museum of Art, 1962, no. 82 (dated 1874-76); *Mary Cassatt, Berthe Morisot*, Huntington Galleries, 1962, no. 35.
Literature:
Fourreau, no. 36; The Brooklyn Museum, *Quarterly*, XVI, no. 3, 1929; *Parnassus*, III, May 1931; Angoulvent, no. 84, 121; Marian King, *A Gallery of Mothers and Their Children*, New York, 1958; Alfred Werner, "Berthe Morisot: Major Impressionist," *The Arts*, XXXII, no. 6, March 1958, 40-45; Bataille and Wildenstein, no. 34, ill. 114.

87.
White Flowers in a Bowl
Exhibitions:
Durand-Ruel, Paris, 1896, no. 161; *Exposition Berthe Morisot*, Galerie Duret, Paris, 1905, no. 28; *Impressionism*, Columbia Museum of Art and Science, 1960; Wildenstein & Co., New York, and California Palace of the Legion of Honor, San Francisco, 1960; *Impressionism: French and American*, Museum of Fine Arts, Boston, 1973, no. 61.
Literature:
Bataille and Wildenstein, no. 182, fig. 195.

88.
Girl in a Boat with Geese
Collections:
Paris, Durand-Ruel; Paris, Denis Cochin; Berlin, Julius Stern (Sale, May 22, 1916, no. 72); Knoedler and Co., New York; Arnold Kirkeby (Sale, New York, Parke-Bernet, November 1958, no. 4); Ailsa Mellon Bruce, New York; acquired by the museum in 1970.
Exhibitions:
Exposition de tableaux, pastels, et dessins par Berthe Morisot, Boussod, Valladon et Cie., Paris, 1892, no. 8; *Berthe Morisot*, Durand-Ruel, Paris, 1896, no. 135; *Exposition Berthe Morisot*, Durand-Ruel, Paris, 1902, no. 51.

Literature:
Angoulvent, 131, no. 273; Bataille and Wildenstein, 39, no. 242, fig. 249; *European Painting: An Illustrated Summary Catalog*, National Gallery of Art, Washington, D.C., 1975, 248, repr. 249, no. 2422.

Mary Cassatt (1844-1926)
Bibliography

Breeskin, Adelyn, *The Graphic Work of Mary Cassatt*, New York, 1948.

———, *Mary Cassatt: A Catalogue Raisonné of the Oils, Pastels, Watercolors, and Drawings*, Washington, D.C., 1970.

Hale, Nancy, *Mary Cassatt*, Garden City, 1975.

Huysmans, Joris-Karl, *L'art moderne*, Paris, 1883.

Segard, Achille, *Mary Cassatt, un peintre des enfants et des mères*, Paris, 1913.

Sweet, Frederick, A., *Miss Mary Cassatt, Impressionist from Pennsylvania*. Norman (Oklahoma), 1966.

89.
Mother about to Wash Her Sleepy Child
Exhibitions:
Fifth Impressionist Exhibition, Paris, 1880; Durand-Ruel, New York, 1895 (no. 9); St. Botolph Club, Boston, 1909 (no. 20).
Literature:
Les modes, IV, February 1904, 4; *La revue de l'art ancien et moderne*, XXIII, March 1908, 175; Segard, opp. 12; *Gazette des beaux-arts*, Series 6, LXI, February 1963, sup. no. 1129, 43.

90.
Young Woman in Black
Exhibitions:
Durand-Ruel, New York, 1924, no. 1; *Exhibition of Works by Cassatt and Morisot*, Durand-Ruel, New York, 1939, no. 11; *Development of Impressionism*, Los Angeles County Museum, 1940, no. 5; Baltimore Museum of Art, 1941, no. 13; Wildenstein, New York, 1947, no. 9; *Sargent, Whistler and Mary Cassatt*, Art Institute of Chicago, 1954, no. 12: *Paintings, Drawings and Graphic Works by Manet, Degas, Berthe Morisot and Mary Cassatt*, Baltimore Museum of Art, 1962, no. 109; *Exhibition of Paintings, Drawings and Graphic Works by Mary Cassatt*, M. Knoedler & Co., New York, 1966, no. 14; *Mary Cassatt Among the Impressionists*, Joslyn Art Museum, Omaha, 1969, no. 19; *Mary Cassatt*, National Gallery of Art, Washington, D.C., 1970; *Old Mistresses: Women Artists of the Past*, Walters Art Gallery, Baltimore, 1972; *Mary Cassatt 1844-1926*, Newport Harbor Art Museum, Newport Beach, California, 1973; *Two Hundred Years*

of *American Painting*, traveling exhibition
— Landesmuseum, Bonn; Museum of Modern Art, Belgrade; Galleria D'Arte Moderna e Contemporanea, Rome; Muzeum Narodowe, Warsaw — 1976.
Literature:
Art News, XXXVIII, November 4, 1939, 9; *Art Digest*, XIV, November 15, 1939, 19; *Magazine of Art*, XXXII, December 1939, 732; *Art News*, LXI, no. 2, April 1962, 30.

91.
Two Children at the Seashore
Exhibitions:
Durand-Ruel, New York, 1895, no. 7, called "Marine"; Manchester, England, 1907, organized by Durand-Ruel, Paris, 1908, no. 13; National Gallery of Art, Washington, D.C., 1966, no. 20, repr. in color.
Literature:
Harper's Bazaar, XLV, November 1911, 490; *Apollo*, n.s. LXXXIII, no. 52, June 1966, 433, pl. 11 (color).

92.
Baby in Dark Blue Suit, Looking over His Mother's Shoulder
Exhibitions:
Art Institute of Chicago, 1934, no. 436, repr.; Durand-Ruel, New York, 1935, no. 8; Art Gallery of Toronto, 1940; Santa Barbara Museum of Art, 1941; Fine Arts Gallery of San Diego, 1941; *Art in Progress*, Museum of Modern Art, New York, 1944, repr. 19; *America and Impressionism*, Birmingham (Alabama) Museum of Art, 1951; *Sargent, Whistler and Mary Cassatt*, Art Institute of Chicago, 1954, no. 15; *John Singer Sargent and Mary Cassatt*, Society of Four Arts, Palm Beach, 1959, no. 41, repr.
Literature:
Figaro artistique, April 28, 1927, 438; *Art News*, XXVII, November 17, 1928, 3; *American Magazine of Art*, XX, January 1929, 42; *Edith Valerio*, 1930, pl. 21; *Margaret Breuning*, 1944, 27; *Cincinnati Art Museum Bulletin*, May 1951, 2; *Art Digest*, XXVIII, January 15, 1954, 6-7; *Cincinnati Art Museum Bulletin*, n.s., II, October 1952, 41.

93.
The Coiffure
94.
The Fitting
95.
Peasant Mother and Child

Lilla Cabot Perry (1848?-1933)
Bibliography

Hilman, Carolyn, and Oliver, J. N., "Lilla Cabot Perry — Painter and Poet," *American Magazine of Art*, XIV, no. 11, November 1923, 601-4.

New York, Hirschl and Adler Galleries, *Lilla Cabot Perry, A Retrospective Exhibition*, essay by Stuart P. Feld, 1969.

New York, Downtown Branch, Whitney Museum of American Art, *19th-Century American Women Artists*, 1976.

Perry, Lilla Cabot, "Reminiscences of Claude Monet from 1889 to 1909," *American Magazine of Art*, XVIII, no. 3, March 1927, 119-25.

Washington, D.C., National Gallery of Art, *American Impressionist Painting*, catalog by Moussa A. Domit, 1973.

Young, William, *A Dictionary of American Artists, Sculptors, and Engravers*, Cambridge, Mass., 1968, 360.

96.
Little Angèle
Exhibitions:
Lilla Cabot Perry, A Retrospective Exhibition, essay by Stuart P. Feld, Hirschl and Adler Galleries, New York, 1969, no. 4, repr. in color; *American Impressionist Painting*, catalog by Moussa A. Domit, National Gallery of Art, Washington, D.C., 1973, no. 44; *19th-Century American Women Artists*, Downtown Branch, Whitney Museum of American Art, New York, 1976.

Eva Gonzalès (1849-1883)
Bibliography

Bayle, Paule, "Eva Gonzalès," *La Renaissance*, June 1932.

Mathey, François, *Six femmes peintres*, Paris, 1951, 8.

Monaco, *Eva Gonzalès exposition*, catalog by Claude Roger-Marx, 1952.

Moreau-Nélaton, E., *Manet raconté par lui-même*, Paris, 1926, I.

Paris, Salons de la *Vie Moderne, Catalogue des peintures et pastels de Eva Gonzalès*, preface by Philippe Burty, essay by Théodore de Banville, 1885.

Paris, Galerie Bernheim-Jeune, *Eva Gonzalès*, 1914.

Paris, Galerie Marcel Bernheim, *Eva Gonzalès, exposition rétrospective*, catalog by Paule Bayle, 1932.

Paris, Galerie Daber, *Eva Gonzalès rétrospective*, catalog by Alfred Daber, 1959.

Roger-Marx, Claude, *Eva Gonzalès*, short essay by Théodore de Banville, Paris, 1950.

97.
Little Soldier
Exhibitions:
Salon of 1870; *Eva Gonzalès rétrospective*, Galerie Daber, Paris, 1959.
Literature:
Karl Bertrand, "Salon de 1870," *L'artiste*, April-June 1870, 319; Roger-Marx, n.p., Rewald, 240-41 and note 4, 268; Geneviève Lacambre and Jacqueline Rohan-Chabot, *Le Musée de Luxembourg en 1874*, Paris, 1974.

Lady Elizabeth Butler (1850?-1933)
Bibliography

Butler, Elizabeth, *Letters from the Holy Land*, London, 1903.

_____, *From Sketchbook and Diary*, London, 1909.

_____, *An Autobiography*, London, 1923.

Clayton, II.

Clement, 68-70.

Meynell, W. (Alice), "The Life and Work of Lady Butler," *The Art Annuals*, XVIII, London, 1898,

Oldcastle, J., "Elizabeth Butler," *Magazine of Art*, II, 1879, 257-62.

Wood, C., *Dictionary of Victorian Painters*, Woodbridge (Suffolk), 1971, 20.

98.
Quatre Bras, 1815
Exhibitions:
Royal Academy, 1875, no. 853; The Guildhall, London, no. 16, 1900.
Literature:
Art Journal, XXXVII, 1875, 220; J. Ruskin, "Academy Notes," 1875, in *The Works of John Ruskin*, ed. E. T. Cook and A. Wedderburn, London, 1904, XIV, 308-9; Butler, 1923, 110-46, passim.

Cecilia Beaux (1885?-1942)
Bibliography

Beaux, Cecilia, *Background with Figures*, New York and Boston, 1930.

Bell, Mrs. Arthur, "The Work of Cecilia Beaux," *Studio*, XVII, no. 78, September 1899, 215-22.

Bowen, Catherine D., *Family Portrait*, Boston, 1970.

Burrows, Carlyle, "The Portraits of Cecilia Beaux," *International Studio*, LXXXV, no. 353, October 1926, 74-80.

Drinker, Henry S., *The Paintings and Drawings of Cecilia Beaux,* Pennsylvania Academy of the Fine Arts, Philadelphia, 1955.

Hill, Frederick D., "Cecilia Beaux, the Grande Dame of American Portraiture," *Antiques,* CV, no. 1, January 1974, 160-68.

Mechlin, Leila, "The Art of Cecilia Beaux," *International Studio,* XLI, no. 161, July 1910, iii-x.

Neilson, Winthrop and Frances, "Cecilia Beaux," *Seven Women: Great Painters,* Philadelphia, New York, and London, 1969, 97-124.

New York, American Academy of Arts and Letters, *A Catalogue of an Exhibition of Paintings by Cecilia Beaux,* by Royal Cortissoz, 1935.

Oakley, Thornton, *Cecilia Beaux,* Philadelphia, 1934.

Philadelphia, Pennsylvania Academy of the Fine Arts, *Cecilia Beaux: Portrait of an Artist,* catalog by Frank H. Goodyear, Jr., and Elizabeth G. Bailey, 1974.

99.
A Little Girl (Fanny Travis Cochran)
Collections:
Fanny Travis Cochran, Westtown, Pennsylvania (along with Beaux's *Portrait of Travis Cochran,* 1887); given by her to the Pennsylvania Academy of the Fine Arts in 1955.
Exhibitions:
The One Hundred Fiftieth Anniversary Exhibition, essay by Walker Hancock, Pennsylvania Academy of the Fine Arts, Philadelphia, 1955, no. 136, 89, and fig. 136, 83; *Face of America,* Brooklyn Museum, 1957; *Portraits of Personalities,* Portraits, Inc., New York, 1958; Fidelity-Philadelphia Trust Co., Philadelphia, 1959; *Two Hundred Fifty Years of Art in Pennsylvania,* Westmoreland County Museum, Greensburg, Pennsylvania, 1959; *Portraits of Children — 1860 to 1960,* Portraits, Inc., New York, 1960; *Family Portrait* (on the occasion of the publication of Catherine Drinker Bowen's book, *Family Portrait*), Charles Sessler Book Shop, Philadelphia, 1970; *Traveling exhibition* — Old Capitol Museum, Jackson, Mississippi; Montgomery Museum of Fine Arts, Montgomery, Alabama; Columbus Museum of Arts and Crafts, Columbus, Georgia; Weatherspoon Art Gallery, Greensboro, North Carolina; Chattanooga Art Association, Chattanooga, Tennessee; The Mobile Art Gallery, Mobile, Alabama; The Charleston Art Gallery, Charleston, West Virginia — 1970; *Held in Trust,* Pennsylvania Academy of the Fine Arts, Philadelphia, 1973, no. 7; *Cecilia Beaux: Portrait of an Artist,* Museum of the Philadelphia Civic Center and the Pennsylvania Academy of the Fine Arts, 1974, no. 24, 60-61.

Literature:
Drinker, 33-35, repr. 35; *Art Quarterly,* XXXIII, no. 1, Spring 1970, detail repr. 82.

100.
Portrait of Bertha Vaughan
Collections:
Bertha Vaughan; bequeathed to Radcliffe College.
Exhibitions:
The Paintings and Drawings of Cecilia Beaux, Pennsylvania Academy of the Fine Arts, Philadelphia, 1955.
Literature:
Beaux, 232; Drinker, 105, repr. 104.

101.
Sita and Sarita
Collections:
Acquired by the museum in 1923.
Exhibitions:
The Ninth Exhibition of Contemporary American Oil Paintings, Corcoran Gallery of Art, Washington, D.C., 1923, no. 105, 38; *Exhibition of Paintings by Cecilia Beaux,* American Academy of Arts and Letters, New York, 1935, no. 17, 14; *The One Hundred Fiftieth Anniversary Exhibition,* essay by Walker Hancock, Pennsylvania Academy of the Fine Arts, Philadelphia, 1955, no. 134, 89; *Women Artists of America, 1707-1964,* catalog by William H. Gerdts, Newark Museum, 1965, 21, repr. 20; *Cecilia Beaux: Portrait of an Artist,* Museum of the Philadelphia Civic Center and the Pennsylvania Academy of Fine Arts, Philadelphia, 1974, no. 42, 76, repr. 77.
Literature:
The American Magazine of Art, XV, no. 1, January 1924, repr. 71; "Six Modern American Portrait Painters," *The Mentor,* XII, no. 9, October 1924, 33ff. repr. 88; Carnegie Institute, *Bulletin,* 1940, 195-96; *Art Digest,* December 15, 1940, repr. 14; Beaux, repr. 88; Drinker, 97.

Marie Bashkirtseff (1859-1884)
Bibliography

Bashkirtseff, M., *Le Journal de Marie Bashkirtseff,* ed. A. Theuriet, 2 vols., Paris, 1887. There are various English translations, including the one by A. D. Hall, 1889 and 1908, cited in note 8 of the biography. See D. L. Moore, 293-95, for other editions.

Blind, M., "A Study of Marie Bashkirtseff," in A. Theuriet, *Jules Bastien-Lepage,* Paris, 1892, 149-90.

Borel, P., "L'idyll mélancolique, histoire de Maria Bashkirtseff et de Jules Bastien-Lepage," *Annales politiques et littéraires,* Paris, 1922, LXXVIII, 535-36, 563-65, 591-92, 617-18, 643-44.

Breakell, M. L., "Marie Bashkirtseff. The Reminiscence of a Fellow-Student," *Nineteenth Century and After,* London, 1907, LXII, 110-25.

Cahuet, A., *Moussia, ou la vie et la mort de Marie Bashkirtseff,* Paris, 1926.

Creston, Dormer (D. J. Baynes), *Fountains of Youth: The Life of Marie Bashkirtseff,* New York, 1937.

Moore, D. L., *Marie and the Duke of H.: The Daydream Love Affair of Marie Bashkirtseff,* London, 1966.

102.
A Meeting
Exhibitions:
Salon of 1884, no. 116; *Exposition rétrospective: Bastien-Lepage, Louise Breslau, Marie Bashkirtseff,* Musée Jules Chéret, Nice, 1939, no. 56 (listed as "réplique du tableau du Luxembourg peinture").
Literature:
L'art français, February 18, 1888, repr. 2; Blind, repr. 169; L. Bénédite, *Ecoles étrangères, le Musée du Luxembourg,* 1898, no. 296, and 1924, no. 385, repr. 116; Clement, 1905 and 1974, 30-32; Sparrow, 293, repr. after 292; J. P. Crespelle, *Les maîtres de la Belle Epoque,* Paris, 1966, repr. 47.

Edith Hayllar (1860-1948)
Bibliography

Wood, Christopher, "The Artistic Family Hayllar," *Connoisseur,* part I, April 1974, repr. 4; part II, May 1974, 6, repr. 7 and in color on cover.

103.
A Summer Shower
Exhibitions:
Royal Academy, 1883, no. 420; *The Art and Mind of Victorian England: Paintings from the Forbes Magazine Collection,* introduction by Melvin Waldfogel, University Gallery, University of Minnesota, Minneapolis, 1974, 22, no. 17 (repr. in color on catalog cover).
Literature:
Christopher Wood, "The Great Victorian Painting Revival," *Auction,* November 1970, 40, repr. 41; Wood, *The Dictionary of Victorian Painters,* London, 1971, 62, repr. 283; Michael A. Findlay, "Forbes Saves the Queen," *Arts Magazine,* February 1973, 30, repr. 27; Wood, 1974, I, repr. 4, and II, 6, repr. 7 and in color on cover; Sarah B. Sherill, "Current and Coming, Victorian Painting," *Antiques,* September 1974, repr. 332; "Major

Exhibit to Key 'U' Victorian Festival," *The Minneapolis Star*, September 18, 1974, repr.; Carole Nelson, "Exhibit Wins Respect for Long-Neglected Victorian Paintings," *St. Paul Sunday Pioneer Press*, Family Life Section, September 29, 1974, 1, repr. 1; Lyndel King, "Heroism Began at Home," *Art News*, November 1974, 45.

Suzanne Valadon (1865-1938)
Bibliography

Beachboard, Robert, *La trinité maudite: Utter, Valadon, Utrillo*, Paris, 1952.

Jacometti, Nesto, *Suzanne Valadon*, Geneva, 1947.

Mermillon, Marius, *Suzanne Valadon*, Paris, ca. 1950.

Paris, Galerie Pétridès, *Suzanne Valadon*, catalog by Jean Bouret, 1947.

Paris, Musée National d'Art Moderne, *Suzanne Valadon*, catalog by Bernard Dorival, 1967.

Pétridès, Paul, *L'oeuvre complet de Suzanne Valadon*, Paris, 1971.

Rey, Robert, *Suzanne Valadon*, Paris, 1922.

Storm, John, *The Valadon Drama*, New York, 1958.

Tabarant, André, "Suzanne Valadon et ses souvenirs de modèle," *Le bulletin de la vie artistique*, December 15, 1921, 626-29.

Valadon, Suzanne, and Bazin, G., "Suzanne Valadon par elle-même," *Promethée*, Paris, March 1939.

104.
The Blue Room
Collections:
Purchased by the French government in 1923.
Exhibitions:
Salon d'Automne, Paris, 1923, no. 1955; *Hommage à Suzanne Valadon*, Musée National d'Art Moderne, Paris, 1948, no. 54; *Charley Toorop, Suzanne Valadon*, Arnhem Gemeente Museum and Groningner Museum, Groningen, The Netherlands, 1955; *Suzanne Valadon*, Musée National d'Art Moderne, Paris, 1967, 62, no. 60.

Käthe Kollwitz (1867-1945)
Bibliography

Berlin, Paul Cassirer Gallery, *Sonder-Ausstellung Käthe Kollwitz zu ihrem 50. Geburtstag,* catalog by Paul Cassirer, 1917.

Bonus, Arthur, *Das Käthe Kollwitz-Werk*, Dresden, 1925.

Bonus Jeep, Beate, *Sechzig Jahre Freundschaft mit Käthe Kollwitz*, Bremen, 1963.

Fanning, Robert Joseph, *Käthe Kollwitz*, Karlsruhe, 1956.

Klipstein, August, *Käthe Kollwitz: Verzeichnis der graphischen Werkes*, Bern, 1955.

Kollwitz, Hans, ed., *Ich sah die Welt mit liebvollen Blicken*, Hanover, 1968.

————, *Käthe Kollwitz: Tagebucherblätter und Briefe*, Berlin, 1949.

————, *Diaries and Letters of Käthe Kollwitz*, Chicago, 1955.

Frau Käthe (Schmidt) Kollwitz. Ten Lithographs, introduction by Elizabeth McCausland, New York, 1941.

Munich, *Käthe Kollwitz, Handzeichnungen und graphische Seltenheiten, eine Ausstellung zum 100. Geburtstag,* catalog by A. von der Becke, 1967.

Nagel, Otto, *Käthe Kollwitz: Die Handzeichnungen*, Berlin, 1972.

New York, St. Etienne Gallery, *Memorial Exhibition, Käthe Kollwitz*, 1945.

Northampton, Smith College, *Käthe Kollwitz*, catalog by Leonard Baskin, 1958.

St. Paul, Minnesota Museum of Art, *Graphic Works of Käthe Kollwitz in the Permanent Collection*, 1973.

Sievers, Johannes, *Die Radierungen und Steindrucke von Käthe Kollwitz Innerhalb der Jahre 1890 bis 1912.* Dresden, 1913.

105.
Whetting the Scythe
Literature:
Sievers, no. 90, n.p.; Klipstein, no. 90, 116-17.

106.
Home Worker
Collections:
Dr. Thelma Moss.
Exhibitions:
Selections from the Permanent Collection, Los Angeles County Museum of Art, 1973; *Prints and Drawings: A Decade of Collecting, 1965-1975,* Los Angeles County Museum of Art, 1975.

Literature:
Berlin, 1917, no. 111, repr.; *Der Weltspiegel,* 1917, no. 32; Nagel, no. 499, 284; Joseph A. Gatto, *Emphasis: A Design Principle,* Worcester, 1975, repr. 23.

107.
Self-Portrait
Collections:
Acquired by Jan Hoowij, Encino, California, from a German refugee in 1934; acquired by the museum in 1969.
Exhibitions:
A Decade of Collecting: 1965-1975, Los Angeles County Museum of Art, 1975, no. 110, repr. 113, 212.
Literature:
Nagel, no. 1246, repr. 442.

Florine Stettheimer (1871-1944)
Bibliography

McBride, Henry, *Florine Stettheimer*, New York, 1946.

Tyler, P., *Florine Stettheimer: A Life in Art*, New York, 1963.

108.
Beauty Contest
Exhibitions:
Florine Stettheimer Retrospective Exhibition, Museum of Modern Art, New York, 1946, no. 32, repr. 22; *Florine Stettheimer Exhibition,* Smith College Museum of Art, Northampton, 1952.
Literature:
Wadsworth Atheneum Bulletin, January 1948, 1, repr.; Tyler, 71, 97, 136.

Romaine Brooks (1874-1970)
Bibliography

Washington, D.C., National Collection of Fine Arts, *Romaine Brooks: "Thief of Souls,"* catalog by Adelyn Breeskin, 1971.

Secrest, Meryle, *Between Me and Life,* New York, 1974.

Young, M.S., "Thief of Souls," *Apollo*, XCIII, 1971, 425-27.

109.
The Crossing
Exhibitions:
Galerie J. Charpentier, Paris, 1925; L'Alpine Club Gallery, London, 1925; Wildenstein Galleries, New York, 1925; *Romaine Brooks: "Thief of Souls,"* National Collection of Fine Arts, Washington, D.C., 1971, no. 13, 20-21, repr. 63.
Literature:
Bazaar, March 1968, 28-29 and repr.; Secrest, 242.

110.
Miss Natalie Barney, "L'Amazone"
Collections:
Natalie Barney.
Exhibitions:
Salon de la Société Nationale des Beaux-Arts, Paris, 1922; Galerie J. Charpentier, Paris, 1925; L'Alpine Club Gallery, London, 1925; Wildenstein Galleries, New York, 1925; *Romaine Brooks: "Thief of Souls,"* National Collection of Fine Arts, Washington, D.C., 1971, no. 19, repr.; *The Fine Arts Society,* London, 1976.
Literature:
L'art et les artistes, May 1923, 313, repr.; *International Studio,* February 1926, 48, repr.; *Romaine Brooks: Portraits — Tableaux — Dessins,* Paris, 1952, repr.; Secrest, 328-29, repr. after 222.

111.
It Makes the Dead Sing
112.
Sorrows of Departure

Gwen John (1876-1939)
Bibliography

Holroyd, M., *Augustus John: The Years of Innocence,* London, 1974.

————, *Augustus John: The Years of Experience,* London, 1975.

John, Augustus, "Gwendolen John," *Burlington Magazine,* LXXXI, no. 475, October 1942, 236-38ff.

London, The Arts Council of Great Britain, *Gwen John, 1876-1939,* introduction by Augustus John, 1946.

London, The Arts Council of Great Britain, *Gwen John,* introduction by M. Taubman, 1968.

New York, Davis and Long Company, *Gwen John: A Retrospective Exhibition,* introduction by C. Langdale, 1975.

Tufts, 1974, 198-210.

113.
Girl with a Blue Scarf
Collections:
John Quinn, New York, until 1924; American Art Galleries, New York, 1927; Miss E. Wetmore; Nelson A. Sears until 1963.
Exhibitions:
Recent Acquisitions: Painting and Sculpture, Museum of Modern Art, New York, 1965; *Gwen John,* Davis Galleries, New York, 1965 (not in catalog); *Gwen John,* The Arts Council Gallery, London, 1968, no. 34, repr.; *British Art 1890-1928,* Columbus (Ohio) Gallery of Fine Arts, 1971, no. 52, repr. 47; *Gwen John: A Retrospective Exhibition,* Davis and Long Company, New York, 1975, no. 16, repr., and 19-21.

Paula Modersohn-Becker (1876-1907)
Bibliography

Bremen, Kunsthalle, *Paula Modersohn-Becker: zum hundertsten Geburtstag,* essays by Günter Busch and museum staff, 1976.

Hetsch, Rolf, *Paula Modersohn-Becker: Ein Buch der Freundschaft,* Berlin, 1932.

Modersohn-Becker, Paula, *Briefe und Tagebuchblätter,* Munich, 1920. (An English translation of this essential source, long overdue, is in preparation.)

Oppler, Ellen C., "Paula Modersohn-Becker: Some Facts and Legends," *Art Journal,* XXXV, no. 4, Summer 1976, 364-69.

Pauli, Gustav, *Paula Modersohn-Becker,* Leipzig, 1919; rev. ed., 1934.

Stelzer, Otto, *Paula Modersohn-Becker,* Berlin, 1958.

Tufts, 188-97.

Werner, Alfred, "Paula Modersohn-Becker," *American Artist,* XXXVII, June 1973, 16-23, 68-70.

114.
Peasant Woman

115.
Old Woman from the Poorhouse
Exhibitions:
Paula Modersohn-Becker, St. Etienne Gallery, New York, 1958, no. 7. repr.

116.
Mother and Child
Exhibitions:
Paula Modersohn-Becker, St. Etienne Gallery, New York, 1958, no. 17, repr.; *Painting and Sculpture from Private Collections in Westchester County,* The Hudson River Museum, 1969; *Paula Modersohn-Becker,* La Boetie Gallery, New York, 1971.
Literature:
Carl Georg Heise, *Paula Becker-Modersohn: Mutter und Kind,* Stuttgart, 1961 (reclam no. 62), pl. 8.

117.
Old Peasant Woman Praying
Collections:
Dr. Hamm, Löhnberg; Kunsthalle, Hamburg, 1919-37; Buchholz Gallery, New York; Robert H. Tannahill Collection, 1939-58.

Exhibitions:
Paula Modersohn-Becker, Kestner-Gesellschaft, Hanover, 1934, no. 52, dated 1905/7; *Contemporary German Art,* Institute of Contemporary Art, Boston, 1939, no. 41; *Landmarks of Modern German Art,* Buchholz Gallery, New York, 1940; *German Art of the Twentieth Century,* Museum of Modern Art, New York, 1957.
Literature:
Curt Stoermer, *Paula Becker-Modersohn,* Worpswede, 1913, no. 71, repr.; Stoermer, *Der Cicerone,* VI, 1914, 7-15, fig. 7; Pauli, 1919 and 1934, no. 38, ill. 12, dated 1906/7; Pauli, *Führer durch die Galerie der Kunsthalle zu Hamburg,* Hamburg, 1924, 200-2, repr.; Pauli, "Die Hamburger Kunsthalle," *Velhagen & Klasings Monatshefte,* Sonderdruck, early color pl., 15; *Art News,* XXXVIII, April 13, 1940, 15; *Magazine of Art,* XXXIII, April 1940, 233; Werner Haftmann, Alfred Hentzen, William S. Lieberman, *German Art of the Twentieth Century,* New York, 1957, 29, repr.; Bernard S. Myers, *The German Expressionists: A Generation in Revolt,* New York, 1957, fig. 98 (concise ed. 1966, fig. 55); Elizabeth H. Payne, *Bulletin of the Detroit Institute of Arts,* XXXIX, 1959-60, 20-21, repr.; Helga Hofmann and Janni Müller-Hauck, *Katalog der Meister des 20. Jahrhunderts der Hamburger Kunsthalle,* Hamburg, 1969, 144; Alfred Hentzen, *Malerei des XX. Jahrhunderts,* Bilderhefte der Hamburger Kunsthalle II/III, n.d., 119 (appendix of works lost through Nazi confiscation).

118.
Still Life with Fruit and Flowers
Exhibitions:
Paula Modersohn-Becker, Etienne Gallery, New York, 1958, no. 1; *Paula Modersohn-Becker,* La Boetie Gallery, New York, 1971.
Literature:
Pauli, no. 227.

Gabriele Münter (1877-1962)
Bibliography

Eichner, J., *Kandinsky und Gabriele Münter vom Ursprüngen moderner Kunst,* Munich, 1957.

Erlanger, L., "Gabriele Münter: A Lesser Life?" *Feminist Art Journal,* Winter 1974-75, 11-13 and 23.

Gollek, R., *Der Blaue Reiter im Lenbachhaus München,* Munich, 1974, 220-46.

Lahnstein, P., *Münter,* Ettal, 1971.

London, Marlborough Fine Art, Ltd., *Gabriele Münter: Oil Paintings, 1903-1937,* 1940.

Munich, Städtische Galerie im Lenbachhaus, *Gabriele Münter, 1877-1962,* 1962.

New York, Leonard Hutton Galleries, *Gabriele Münter, 1877 to 1962. Fifty Years of Her Art, Paintings: 1906-1956,* 1966.

Röthel, H. K., *Gabriele Münter*, Munich, 1957.

119.
Portrait of a Young Woman
Collections:
Acquired from the artist by the Dalzell Hatfield Galleries, Los Angeles; entered the collection of Mrs. Harry Lynde Bradley in 1963.
Exhibitions:
Gabriele Münter Memorial Exhibition, Dalzell Hatfield Galleries, Los Angeles, 1963; *The Collection of Mrs. Harry Lynde Bradley,* Milwaukee Art Center, 1968, no. 359 and repr. 156; *Selections from the Bradley Collection,* Fort Wayne (Indiana) Museum of Art, 1970; *Selections from the Bradley Collection,* Paine Art Center and Arboretum, Oshkosh, Wisconsin, 1970; *Expressionist Revolt,* John Michael Kohler Arts Center, Sheboygan, Wisconsin, 1970.

120.
The Green House
Exhibitions:
The Collection of Mrs. Harry Lynde Bradley, Milwaukee Art Center, 1968, no. 364, repr.

Vanessa Bell (1879-1961)
Bibliography

Clutton-Brock, A., "Vanessa Bell and Her Circle," *The Listener,* LXV, May 4, 1961, 790.

London, London Artists' Association, the Cooling Galleries, *Recent Paintings by Vanessa Bell,* introduction by Virginia Woolf, 1930.

London, Lefevre Galleries, *Catalog of Recent Paintings by Vanessa Bell,* introduction by Virginia Woolf, 1934.

London, Arts Council Gallery, *Vanessa Bell: A Memorial Exhibition of Paintings,* introduction by R. Pickvance, 1964.

London, Anthony d'Offay Gallery, *Vanessa Bell: Paintings and Drawings,* introduction by R. Morphet, 1973.

Rosenbaum, S.P., ed., *The Bloomsbury Group: A Collection of Memoirs, Commentary and Criticism,* Toronto, 1975, 169-77.

121.
Street Corner Conversation
Exhibitions:
Vanessa Bell: Paintings and Drawings, introduction by R. Morphet, Anthony d'Offay Gallery, London, 1973, no. 9, repr.; *Duncan Grant and Bloomsbury,* Fine Arts Society, Edinburgh, 1975, no. 32.

122.
Portrait of Iris Tree
Exhibitions:
Vanessa Bell, The Adams Gallery, London, 1961, no. 11; *Vanessa Bell: A Memorial Exhibition of Paintings,* Arts Council Gallery, London, 1964, no. 27, repr.; *Duncan Grant and Bloomsbury,* Fine Arts Society, Edinburgh, 1975, no. 34; *The Bloomsbury Group,* The National Book League, London, 1976, no. 72.

Nataliia Sergeevna Goncharova (1881-1962)
Bibliography

Apollinaire, Guillaume, "La vie anecdotique-Madame de Gontcharova et Monsieur Larionov," *Mercure de France,* no. 422, January 16, 1916, 373.

Chamot, M., *Gontcharova,* Paris, 1972.

Eganbiuri, Eli (pseud. of I. Zdanevich), *Nataliia Goncharova, Mikhail Larionov,* Moscow, 1913.

_____, "Goncharova i Larionov," *Zharptitsa* [*Jar-Ptiza*], no. 7, 1922, 39-40.

Goncharova, Nataliia S., "Predislovie k katalogu vystavki. 1913 g." [Preface to exhibition catalog, 1913], reprinted in *Mastera iskusstva ob iskusstve,* ed. A. Fedorov-Davydov and G. Nedoshivin, Moscow, 1970, VII, 497-90.

Gray, Camilla, *The Russian Experiment in Art: 1863-1922,* New York, 1972.

Khardzhiev, N., "Pamiati Natalii Goncharovy (1881-1962) i Mikhaila Larionova (1881-1964)" [In memory of Nataliia Goncharova (1881-1962) and Mikhail Larionov (1881-1964)], *Iskusstvo knigi,* V, 1968, 306-18.

Loguine, T., *Gontcharova et Larionov: Cinquante ans à Saint-Germain-des-Près,* Paris, 1971.

Parnak, V., *Gontcharova et Larionov: L'art décoratif théâtral moderne,* Paris, 1920.

Sarab'ianov, D., "Neskol'ko slov o Natalii Goncharovoi" [Some words on Nataliia Goncharova], *Prometei,* VII, 1969, 201-3.

Tsvetaeva, M., "Natal'ia Goncharova" (written 1929), *Prometei,* VII, 1969, 144-201.

Tugendkhol'd, Ya., "Vystavka kartin Natalii Goncharovoi (Pis'mo iz Moskvy)" [Exhibition of paintings by Nataliia Goncharova (Letter from Moscow)], *Apollon,* no. 1913, 71-73.

123.
Fishing
Exhibitions:
Salon 2 Mezhdunarodnaia khudozhestvennaia vystavka, Ustroitel' V. A. Izdebskii, Odessa, 1910, no. 93 (*Rybnaia lovlia*); *Goncharova 1900-1913,* Khudozhestvennyi Salon, Moscow, 1913, no. 438 (*Rybnaia lovlia*) or no. 407 (*Rybolovy*); *Goncharova,* Khud. Biuro N. E. Dobychina, Petrograd, 1914, no. 112 (*Lovlia ryby*) or no. 19 (*Rybolovy*); *Larionov and Gontcharova,* City Art Gallery, Leeds, Arts Council of Great Britain, 1961, no. 94, repr.; *Fauves and Expressionists,* Leonard Hutton Galleries, New York, 1968, no. 24, color repr.
Literature:
Eganbiuri, under 1909 (*Rybolovy*), p. IX; Gray, 1962, 106, repr. fig. 67 (unnumbered page 117), dated 1910; *Art News,* LXVI, no. 9, January 1968, repr. 19; T. Froncek, ed., *The Horizon Book of the Arts of Russia,* New York, 1970, repr. 261; Chamot, color repr. 31 and cover; Gray, 1972, 127, fig. 88 on 128, dated 1910; John E. Bowlt (Review of *Gontcharova* by Mary Chamot), *Art in America,* LXI, no. 6, November-December 1973, 139; *Monthly Art Magazine Bijutsu Techo,* XXVIII, no. 409, July 1976, repr. 49.

124.
Portrait of Larionov
Collections:
Remained in the artist's possession until her death.
Exhibitions:
Goncharova 1900-1913, Khudozhestvennyi Salon, Moscow, 1913, no. 572; *No. 4. Vystavka kartin. Futuristy. Luchisty. Primitiv,* Moscow, 1914, no. 44, repr.; *Goncharova,* Khud. Biuro N. E. Dobychina, Petrograd, 1914, no. 17 or no. 61 (two portraits of Larionov in exhibition); *Natalie de Gontcharowa et Michel Larionow,* Galerie Paul Guillaume, Paris, 1914, no. 43, dated 1913; *Gontcharova et Larionov,* Galerie Beyeler, Basel, 1961, no. 32; *Larionov and Gontcharova,* City Art Gallery, Leeds, Arts Council of Great Britain, 1961, no. 117, repr.; *Gontcharova et Larionov,* Musée d'Art Moderne de la Ville de Paris, 1963, no. 31; *The Heroic Years: Paris, 1908-1914,* Museum of Fine Arts, Houston, 1965; *Selected European Masters of the 19th and 20th Centuries,* Marlborough Galleries, London, 1973, no. 26.
Literature:
Gray, 1962, fig. 81, repr. 155; Gray, 1972, fig. 102, repr. 140; John E. Bowlt, ed., *Russian Art of the Avant-Garde: Theory and Criticism 1902-1934,* New York, 1976, repr. 88.

Alexandra Exter (1882-1949)
Bibliography

Bowlt, John E., "Russian Exhibitions, 1904-1922," *Form,* September 1968.

Compton, Susan P., "Alexandra Exter and the Dynamic Stage," *Art in America,* September-October 1974, 100-102.

Exter, Alexandra, *Décors de théâtre,* preface by Alexander Tairov, Paris, 1930.

Gray, Camilla, *The Russian Experiment in Art: 1863-1922,* New York, 1972.

Hilton, Alison, "When the Renaissance Came to Russia," *Art News,* December 1971, 34-39, 56-62.

Kramer, Hilton, "Bringing Cubism to the Stage," *New York Times,* May 5, 1974, 21.

New York, Leonard Hutton Galleries, *Russian Avant-Garde, 1908-1922,* 1971.

New York, Leonard Hutton Galleries, *Alexandra Exter: Marionettes Created in 1926,* 1975.

New York Public Library, *Artist of the Theatre: Alexandra Exter,* 1974.

Paris, Galerie Jean Chauvelin, *Alexandra Exter,* catalog by Andrei B. Nakov, 1972.

Tairov, Alexander, *Notes of a Director,* trans. William Kulke, Miami, 1969.

Tugendhold, Yakov A., *Alexandra Exter,* Berlin, 1922.

125.
Grapes in a Vase
Collections:
Simon Lissim, New York; Galerie Jean Chauvelin, Paris; M. Nuhume, Paris.
Exhibitions:
Tramway V, St. Petersburg, 1915, no. 88; *Alexandra Exter,* Galerie Jean Chauvelin, Paris, 1972, repr. 16.

126.
Costume for "Entremeses" (?), Farcical interludes, by Cervantes, project for the Moscow Art Theater
Exhibitions:
Dibujos y acuarelas de la vanguardia . . . rusa, Fundacion Eugenio Mendoza, Caracas, Venezuela, 1975, no. 12.

127.
Costume for the Protozanov film "Aelita"
Exhibitions:
Alexandra Exter, Galerie Jean Chauvelin, Paris, 1972, 28-30, repr. 28; *Dibujos y acuarelas de la vanguardia . . . rusa,* Fundacion Eugenio Mendoza, Caracas, Venezuela, 1975, no. 13.
Literature:
New York Public Library, 1974, 15.

Sonia Delaunay (b. 1885)
Bibliography

Cohen, Arthur A., *Sonia Delaunay,* New York, 1975.

Damase, J., *Sonia Delaunay: Rythmes et couleurs,* Paris, 1971; also available in English trans., Greenwich, Conn., 1972.

Mulhouse, Musée de l'Impression sur Etoffes, *Sonia Delaunay: Etoffes imprimées des années folles,* 1971.

Nemser, Cindy, "Sonia Delaunay," in *Art Talk: Conversations with 12 Women Artists,* New York, 1975.

Ottawa, The National Gallery of Canada, *Robert and Sonia Delaunay,* 1965.

Paris, Musée National d'Art Moderne, *Rétrospective Sonia Delaunay,* 1967.

128.
Simultaneous Contrasts
Literature:
Cohen, 61.

129.
Decoration for "La prose du Transsibérien et de la Petite Jehanne de France" (The Prose of the Trans-Siberian and the Little Jehanne of France), by Blaise Cendrars
Literature:
Damase, 21-22, 85, repr. 84 and 86-91; Cohen, 21-35, repr. 6, 7, 11.

130.
The Flamenco Singer (The Large Flamenco)
Literature:
Damase, 102, repr. 117.

Marie Laurencin (1885-1956)
Bibliography

Allard, Roger, *Marie Laurencin,* Paris, 1921.

Apollinaire, Guillaume, *Apollinaire on Art: Essays and Reviews, 1902-1918,* ed. LeRoy C. Breunig, trans. Susan Suleiman, New York, 1972.

Day, George (pseud.), *Marie Laurencin,* Paris, 1947.

Fabre-Favier, Louise, *Souvenirs sur Guillaume Apollinaire,* Paris, 1945.

Laboureur, Jean-Emile, "Les estampes de Marie Laurencin," *L'art d'aujourd'hui,* I, no. 4, Autumn/Winter 1924, 17-21.

Laurencin, Marie, *Le carnet des nuits,* Geneva, 1956.

Lethève, Jacques; Gardey, Françoise; and Adhémar, Jean, "Marie Laurencin," in *Bibliothèque Nationale, Département des Estampes: Inventaire du fonds français après 1800,* Paris, 1965.

Marie Laurencin, preface by Marcel Jouhandeau, Paris, 1928.

Sanouillet, Michel, *Francis Picabia et "391,"* 2 vols., Paris, 1928.

Steegmuller, Francis, *Apollinaire: Poet among the Painters,* New York, 1963.

Strasbourg, Ancienne Douane, *Les Ballets Russes de Serge de Diaghilev, 1909-1929,* 1969, 204-7.

Tokyo, Isetan Gallery, *Marie Laurencin,* 1971.

Wedderkop, H. von, *Marie Laurencin,* Leipzig, 1921.

131.
Group of Artists
Collections:
Gertrude Stein.
Exhibitions:
Dr. Claribel Cone Memorial Exhibition, Baltimore Museum of Art, 1930, no. 10; *Summer Exhibition,* Baltimore Museum of Art, 1934; *Les maîtres de l'art indépandant, 1895-1937,* Petit Palais, Paris, 1937, 42, repr. 43; *A Century of Baltimore Collecting, 1840-1940,* Baltimore Museum of Art, 1941, 82; *Twentieth-Century Portraits,* Museum of Modern Art, New York, 1942, repr. 48; *Pictures for a Picture of Gertrude Stein,* Yale University Art Gallery, New Haven, 1951, 27, repr. 45; *The Cone Collection,* M. Knoedler and Co., New York, 1955; *The Heroic Years: Paris 1908-1914,* Museum of Fine Arts, Houston, 1965; *Four Americans in Paris: The Collections of Gertrude Stein and Her Family,* Museum of Modern Art, New York, 1970, 80, no. 26, repr.; *Women Artists,* Baltimore Museum of Art, 1972; *The Cone Collection from The Baltimore Museum of Art,* Wildenstein & Co., New York, 1974.
Literature:
H. von Wedderkop, "Marie Laurencin," *Der Cicerone,* XIII, 1921, 138; Wedderkop, 1921, 7; André Salmon, "Marie Laurencin," *L'art vivant,* II, 1926, 806, repr. 808; Hans Heilmayer, "Marie Laurencin," *Die Kunst,* LXI, 1930, 294; René Huyghe, introduction to "Le Cubisme" (chap. 8 of *Histoire de l'art contemporain: la peinture*), in *L'amour de l'art,* XIV-XV, 1933-34, repr. 209; Etta Cone, *The Cone Collection of Baltimore,* Baltimore, 1934, pl. 69; René Huyghe, ed., *Histoire de l'art contemporain,* Paris, 1934, repr. 209; Gertrude Stein, *The Autobiography of Alice B. Toklas,* New York, 1934, 76-77; Raymond Escholier, *La peinture française: XXe siècle,*

Paris, 1937, 92; "The Cone Bequest," *The Baltimore Museum of Art News*, XIII, no. 1, October 1949, 11; "Dr. Claribel and Miss Etta, Collectors," *Art News*, XLVIII, no. 9, January 1950, 40; Clive Bell, *Modern French Painting: The Cone Collection*, Baltimore, 1951, 16; Henry McBride, "Pictures for a Picture of Gertrude," *Art News*, XLIX, no. 10, February 1951, repr. 17; *Picasso: Documents iconographiques*, preface and notes by Jaime Sabartès, trans. Félia Leal and Alfred Rosset, Geneva, 1954, fig. 95; Baltimore Museum of Art, *Cone Collection: A Handbook with a Catalogue of Paintings and Sculpture*, Baltimore, 1955, no. 30, repr. 40; "The Cone Collection," *The Baltimore Sunday Sun*, February 24, 1957, Rotogravure section; Pierre Courthion, *Paris in Our Time*, Lausanne, 1957, 96-97, color repr., 97; Elizabeth Sprigge, *Gertrude Stein: Her Life and Work*, New York, 1957, 67-68, repr. following 112; Bernard Dorival, *Twentieth-Century Painters*, New York, 1958, I (trans. W. J. Strachan), 131; Christopher Gray, "Marie Laurencin and Her Friends," *The Baltimore Museum of Art News*, XXI, no. 3, February 1958, 6-15, repr. 7; John Malcolm Brinnin, *The Third Rose: Gertrude Stein and Her World*, Boston, 1959, repr. following 110; "Object of the Week," *The Baltimore Sunday Sun*, December 3, 1961. Rotogravure section; Cecily Mackworth, *Guillaume Apollinaire and the Cubist Life*, London, 1961, 104; Barbara Pollack, *The Collectors: Dr. Claribel and Miss Etta Cone*, New York, 1962, 182-83; John Golding, "Guillaume Apollinaire and the Art of the Twentieth Century," *The Baltimore Museum of Art News*, XXVI, no. 4/ XXVII, no. 1, Summer-Autumn 1963, repr. on cover; Steegmuller, repr. 163; Fernande Olivier, *Picasso and His Friends*, trans. Jane Miller, New York, 1965, 109, repr. following 129; Baltimore Museum of Art, *Paintings, Sculpture and Drawings in the Cone Collection*, Baltimore, 1967, no. 28, repr. 30; Herschel B. Chipp, *Theories of Modern Art: A Source Book by Artists and Critics*, Berkeley, 1968, repr. 195; "The First of the Mixed Media Men," *The Observer Magazine* (London), October 27, 1968, color repr., 64; James R. Mellow, "The Stein Salon was the First Museum of Modern Art," *The New York Times Magazine*, December 1, 1968, 282, repr. in color on cover; Winthrop and Frances Neilson, *Seven Women: Great Painters*, Philadelphia, 1969, 131; Douglas Davis, "Americans in Paris," *Newsweek*, December 14, 1970, color repr. following 80; Joseph T. Butler, "Four Americans in Paris: The Collections of Gertrude Stein and Her Family," *Connoisseur*, CLXXVIII, 1971, repr. 133; Theodore Reff, "Harlequins, Saltimbanques, Clowns and Fools," *Artforum*, X, 1971, repr. 42; Gerrit Henry, "Cone Collection (Wildenstein)," *Art News*, LXXIII, no. 4, April 1974, repr. 95; Herbert Leibowitz, reviews of *Charmed Circle* by James R. Mellow and *Staying on Alone; Letters of Alice B. Toklas*, ed. Edward Burns, *The New York Times Book Review*, February 3, 1974, repr. 1; James R. Mellow, *Charmed Circle: Ger-*

trude Stein and Company, New York, 1974, 12, 346, repr. following 180; Janet Hob-, house, *Everybody Who Was Anybody: A Biography of Gertrude Stein*, New York, 1975, 135; Edward Burns, ed., *Staying on Alone: Letters of Alice B. Toklas*, New York, 1975, 102 n., 217.

Nadezhda Andreevna Udaltsova (1885-1961)

132.
At the Piano
Exhibitions:
0.10, Petrograd, 1915, no. 145(?) *(Muzyka)*; *Erste Russische Kunstausstellung*, Galerie Van Dieman, Berlin, 1922; *Sesqui-Centennial Exhibition*, Philadelphia, 1926; Delphic Studios, New York, November-December 1936; *Anniversary Exhibition of the Société Anonyme, New Forms of Beauty, 1909-1936*, George Walter Vincent Smith Art Gallery, Springfield, Massachusetts, 1939; *Exhibition Inaugurating the Collection Société Anonyme*, Yale University Art Gallery, New Haven, 1942; Connecticut College, New London, October 1943; Mt. Holyoke College, South Hadley, October 1945; *Abstract and Cubist Art*, Duke University, Durham, 1947; *Société Anonyme*, Saginaw Museum, 1950; Institute of Contemporary Art, Washington, D.C., November-December 1951; Annual Exhibition, Lyman Allyn Museum, New London, Connecticut, 1952; *Avant-garde Osteuropa 1910-1930*, Akademie der Künste, Berlin, 1967; *The Cubist Epoch*, catalog by Douglas Cooper, Los Angeles County Museum of Art, 1970, no. 308, pl. 163, repr. 160, 310.
Literature:
L. Lozowick, *New Russian Art*, New York, 1925, repr. 21; *Bulletin of the Associates in Fine Arts at Yale University*, X, no. 3, December 1941, 5; Yale University Art Gallery, *Collection of the Société Anonyme Museum of Modern Art 1920*, New Haven, 1950, 39, repr. 38; Gray, 1962, fig. 144, repr. 207; Camilla Gray, *The Russian Experiment in Art: 1863-1922*, New York, 1972, 197, fig. 172, repr. 196.

Olga Vladimirovna Rozanova (1886-1918)
Bibliography

Betz, Margaret B., "Olga Rozanova: Painting and Theory 1913," master's thesis, Queens College, City University of New York, 1974.

————, "Graphics of the Russian Vanguard," *Art News*, LXXV, no. 3, March 1976, 52-54.

Cologne, Galerie Gmurzynska, *Von der Fläche zum Raum. From Surface to Space: Russland. Russia, 1916-1924*, 1974, 126, 163.

Efros, A., "Vo sled ukhodiashchim" [On one who has gone], *Moskva, zhurnal literatury i iskusstva*, 1919, no. 3, 4-6; reprinted in A. Efros, *Profili*, Moscow, 1930, 228-29.

Katalog posmertnoi vystavki . . . O. V. Rozanovoi, introduction by I. Kliun, Moscow, 1919, I-VI.

Marcadé, V., *Le renouveau de l'art pictural russe*, Lausanne, 1971, 245-46.

Rozanova, O., "Osnovy novago tvorchestva i prichiny ego neponimaniia" [The principles of the new art and the reasons for its misinterpretation], *Soiuz molodezhi*, no. 3, March 1913, 14-22, translated by John E. Bowlt in *Russian Art of the Avant-Garde: Theory and Criticism 1902-1934*, New York, 1976, 103-10.

133.
Man in the Street
Exhibitions:
Union of Youth, St. Petersburg, 1913, no. 105; *Esposizione libera futurista internazionale*, Galleria Sprovieri, Rome, 1914, no. 4; *Il contributo russo alle avanguardie plastiche*, Galleria del Levante, Milan, 1964, no. 1, repr.; *Avant-garde Osteuropa 1910-1930*, Akademie der Künste, Berlin, 1967, no. 104; *Astratlsti russi*, Galleria Vittorio Emanuele, Milan, 1970, no. 27, repr.; *Russian Avant-garde: 1908-1922*, Leonard Hutton Galleries, New York, 1971, no. 110, repr. 76; *Modern Painting: 1900 to the Present*, Museum of Fine Arts, Houston, 1975.
Literature:
L'art moderna, V, no. 44, 1967, repr. 305; Antonio del Guercio, *Le avanguardie russe e sovietiche*, Milan, 1970, repr. 80, pl. 54.

Georgia O'Keeffe (b. 1887)
Bibliography

Eldredge, Charles Child, III, "Georgia O'Keeffe: The Development of an American Modern," University of Minnesota, doctoral dissertation, 1971 (obtainable from University Microfilms, Ann Arbor, Michigan, no. 72-14, 433).

Fort Worth, Amon Carter Museum of Western Art, *Georgia O'Keeffe: An Exhibition of the Work of the Artist from 1915 to 1966*, Mitchell A. Wilder, ed., 1966.

Goossen, E. C., "O'Keeffe," *Vogue*, March 1, 1967.

Kuh, Katharine, *The Artist's Voice: Talks with Seventeen Artists*, New York, 1962, 189-203.

Minneapolis, Walker Art Center, *The Precisionist View in American Art*, catalog by Martin L. Friedman, 1960.

New York, Whitney Museum of American Art, *Georgia O'Keeffe*, catalog by Lloyd Goodrich and Doris Bry, 1970.

Rose, Barbara, "Georgia O'Keeffe: The Paintings of the Sixties," *Artforum*, November 1970, 42-46.

Tomkins, Calvin, "The Rose in the Eye Looked Pretty Fine," *The New Yorker*, March 4, 1974, 40-66.

134-137.
Blue Nos. 1-4
Exhibitions:
O'Keeffe Exhibition Watercolors, 1916-17, The Downtown Gallery, New York, 1958 (nos. 1-4); *Roots of Abstract Art in America, 1910-1930*, National Collection of Fine Arts, Washington, D.C., 1965 (no. 4, no. 134 in ex. cat.); *Georgia O'Keeffe*, Whitney Museum of American Art, New York, 1970 (nos. 1-4, nos. 6-9 in ex. cat.); *Color and Form, 1909-14*, Fine Arts Gallery of San Diego, 1971 (no. 1, no. 65 in ex. cat.); *Forerunners of American Abstraction*, Museum of Art, Carnegie Institute, Pittsburgh, 1971 (no. 2, no. 70 in ex. cat.); *Pioneers of American Abstraction*, Andrew Crispo Gallery, New York, 1973 (nos. 1-4, nos. 85-88 in ex. cat.).

138.
Lake George Barns
Exhibitions:
Reality and Fantasy 1900-54, Walker Art Center, Minneapolis, 1954, 12; *The Precisionist View in American Art*, Walker Art Center, Minneapolis, 1960; *Ten Americans*, Milwaukee Art Center, 1961; *The Stieglitz Circle*, Museum of Modern Art, New York; *Roots of Abstract Art in America 1910-1930*, National Collection of Fine Arts, Washington, D.C., 1965.

139.
Ranchos Church, Taos, New Mexico
Collections:
Mr. and Mrs. Philip J. Wickser, Buffalo, New York.
Exhibitions:
The Room of Contemporary Art, Albright Art Gallery, Buffalo, New York, 1939, no. 38; *Privately Owned*, Albright Art Gallery, Buffalo, New York, no. 57; *New Accessions, USA*, Colorado Springs Fine Art Center, 1972; McNay Art Institute, San Antonio, Texas, 1975; *This Is Your Land*, New Jersey State Museum, Trenton, 1976.

140.
Pelvis with Blue (Pelvis I)
Collections:
Mrs. Harry Lynde Bradley.
Literature:
Personal Selections from the Collection of Mrs. Harry Lynde Bradley, New Orleans, 1975, 71; *Life*, March 1, 1968, 46.

Hannah Höch (b. 1889)
Bibliography

Berlin, Akademie der Künste, *Hannah Höch. Collagen aus den Jahren 1916-1971*, 1971.

Gebhardt, Heiko, and Moses, Stefan. "Ein Leben lang im Gartenhaus," *Stern*, April 22, 1976, 96, 99, 101, 103.

London, Marlborough Fine Art, Ltd., *Hannah Höch*, catalog by Will Grohman, trans. Michael Ivory, 1966.

Mehring, Walter, *Berlin Dada: Ein Chronik*, Zurich, 1959.

Ohff, Heinz, *Hannah Höch*, Berlin, 1968.

Paris, Musée d'Art Moderne, and Berlin, Nationalgalerie, *Hannah Höch, collages, peintures, aquarelles, gouaches, dessins*, with "Interview with Hannah Hoch," by Suzanne Page; "Hannah Höch, ihr Werk und Dada," by Peter Krieger; and "Hannah Höch, Künstlerin im Berliner Dadaismus," by Hanna Bergius, 1976.

Zurich, Kunstgewerbemuseum, *Collagen*, ed. Mark Buchmann and Erika Billeter, 1968.

141.
Tailor's Daisy
Exhibitions:
Hannah Höch, Marlborough Fine Art, Ltd., London, 1966, no. 1, repr.; *Hannah Höch. Collagen aus den Jahren 1916-1971*, Akademie der Künste, Berlin, 1971, no. 8.

142.
The Tamer
Exhibitions:
Hannah Höch, Marlborough Fine Art, Ltd., London, 1966, no. 13, repr.; *Hannah Höch. Collagen aus den Jahren 1916-1971*, Akademie der Künste, Berlin, 1971, no. 50.

Liubov Serbeevna Popova (1889-1924)
Bibliography

Aksenov, I., "Prostranstvennyi konstruktivizm no stsene" [Spatial constructivism on the stage], *Teatral'nyi Oktiabr*, 1926, book I, 31-37.

Cologne, Galerie Gmurzynska, *Von der Fläche zum Raum. From Surface to Space: Russland. Russia, 1916-1924*, 1974, 116, 162.

Etkind, M., "O diapazone prostranstvenno-vremennykh reshenii v iskusstve oformleniia stseny" [On the range of spatio-temporal decisions in the art of stage design], *Ritm, prostranstvo i vremia v literature i iskusstve*, Leningrad, 1974, 209-19.

Popova, L. [Untitled theory], translated by John E. Bowlt in *Russian Art of the Avant-Garde: Theory and Criticism 1902-1934*, New York, 1976, 146-48.

_____, "Poiasnitel'naia zapiska k post-anovke 'Zemlia dybom' v teatre Meier-khol'da" [Explanatory note on the production of "Earth on End" in Meyerhold's theater], *Lef*, 1923, no. 4, 44.

Strizhenova, T., *Is istorii sovetskogo kostiuma* [From the history of Soviet costume], Moscow, 1972, esp. 82-103.

Worrall, N., "Meyerhold's Production of the *Magnificent Cuckold*," *The Drama Review*, XVII, no. 1, March 1973, T-57, 14-34.

143.
Untitled (Human Bust)
Exhibitions:
Dibujos y acuarelas de la vanguarda . . . rusa, Fundacion Eugenio Mendoza, Caracas, Venezuela, 1975, no. 48.

Sophie Taeuber-Arp (1889-1943)
Bibliography

Bern, Kunstmuseum, *Sophie Taeuber-Arp*, 1954.

Paris, Musée National d'Art Moderne, *Sophie Taeuber-Arp*, 1964.

Schmidt, Georg, *Sophie Taeuber-Arp*, Basel, 1948.

Staber, Margit, *Sophie Taeuber-Arp*, Lausanne, 1970.

144.
Little Triptych, Free Vertical-Horizontal Rhythms, Cut and Pasted on a White Ground
Collections:
Marguerite Arp-Hagenbach, Basel.

145.
Activated Circles
Literature:
Schmidt, no. 21; Staber, 72-74, repr. in color 55.

Marlow Moss (1890-1958)
Bibliography

New York, Marlborough-Gerson Gallery, *Mondrian, de Stijl and Their Impact*, catalog by A. M. Hammacher, 1964.

Russell, John. "Moss, Lanyon and Some Modern French," *Art News*, LVII, April 1958, 47.

Seuphor, Michel, "Current and Forthcoming Exhibitions — London," *Burlington Magazine*, C, April 1958, 141.

Zurich, Gimpel and Hanover Galerie, *Marlow Moss: Bilder, Konstruktionen, Zeichnungen*, catalog by Andreas Oosthoek, 1973.

146.
White and Blue
Exhibitions:
Marlow Moss: Bilder, Konstruktionen, Zeichnungen, Gimpel and Hanover Galerie, 1973, Zurich, no. 3, repr.

Agnes Tait (Mrs. William McNulty) (1897-?)
Bibliography

"Agnes Tait in Santa Fe," *Art Digest*, XIX, March 15, 1945, 18.

American Art Today, New York, 1939, pl. 482, 153.

Beall, Karen F., ed., *American Prints in the Library of Congress: A Catalog of the Collection*, Baltimore, 1970, 471.

Collins, J. L., *Women Artists in America: Eighteenth Century to the Present*, Chattanooga, 1973, n.p.

Flint, Ralph, "Around the Galleries," *Creative Art*, VI, June 1930, supplement, 143.

"Geographical Directory of Murals and Sculpture Commissioned by Section of Fine Arts, Public Buildings Administration, Federal Works Agency," *American Art Annual*, XXXV, July 1938-July 1941, 647.

Monro, Isabel Stevenson, and Monro, Kate M., *Index to Reproductions of American Paintings*, New York, 1948, 638.

O'Connor, Francis V., ed., *Register of New Deal Art, National Collection of Fine Arts*, Washington, D.C., 1971, unpaginated checklist.

Park, Esther Ailleen, *Mural Painters in America*, pt. 1, Pittsburgh, 1949, 165.

147.
Skating in Central Park
Exhibitions:
National Exhibition of Art by the Public Works of Art Project, introduction by Edward Bruce, Corcoran Gallery of Art, Washington, D.C., 1934.
Literature:
American Magazine of Art, XXVII, April 1934, repr. 174 as *Winter Afternoon in Central Park*.

Kay Sage (1898-1963)
Bibliography

Breuning, M., "A Kay Sage Retrospective," *Arts*, XXXIV, May 1960, 54.

B[uckley], C. E., "Yves Tanguy and Kay Sage," *Wadsworth Atheneum Bulletin*, May-September 1954, 4.

Soby, James Thrall, "A Tribute to Kay Sage," *Art in America*, LVIII, October 1965, 83.

Waterbury, Connecticut, Mattatuck Museum of the Mattatuck Historical Society, *A Tribute to Kay Sage*, 1965.

148.
Page 49
Exhibitions:
A Tribute to Kay Sage, Mattatuck Museum of the Mattatuck Historical Society, Waterbury, Connecticut, 1965, no. 25.

Franciska Clausen (b. 1899)
Bibliography

Andersen, T., and Hansen, G., *Franciska Clausen*, Borgen, 1974.

Reutersward, O., "Franciska Clausen, constructiviste, cubiste et neoplasticienne danoise," *L'art d'aujourd'hui*, no. 7, 1953.

Stein, M., "La peinture abstraite au Danemark," *L'art d'aujourd'hui*, no. 7, 1953.

149.
Vase with Pipes
Literature:
Andersen and Hansen, color repr., 76.

Alice Neel (b. 1900)
Bibliography

Athens, Georgia Museum of Art, *Alice Neel: The Woman and Her Work*, introduction by Cindy Nemser, 1975.

Mainardi, P., "Alice Neel at the Whitney Museum," *Art in America*, LXII, no. 3, 1974, 107-8.

Nemser, Cindy, "Alice Neel: Portraits of Four Decades," *Ms. Magazine*, II, no. 4, 1973, 48ff.

Nochlin, Linda, "Some Women Realists: Painters of the Figure," *Arts Magazine*, XLVIII, no. 8, 1974, 29ff.

150.
T. B., Harlem
Exhibitions:
Alice Neel, catalog by Michael Gold, New Playwrights' Theatre, New York, 1951, repr. cover as *Tuberculosis in Harlem*; *Alice Neel*, Whitney Museum of American Art, New York, 1974; *Alice Neel: The Woman and Her Work*, Georgia Museum of Art, Athens, 1975, no. 18, repr., n.p.
Literature:
Mainardi, 108; A. Wallach, "*Late in Life, the Moment of Triumph*," *Newsday*, The Arts, pt. II, 20-21 and repr.

Isabel Bishop (b. 1902)
Bibliography

Alloway, Lawrence, "Isabel Bishop, the Grand Manner and the Working Girl," *Art in America*, September-October 1975, 61-65.

Archives of American Art, Smithsonian Institution, "Isabel Bishop Papers."

Bishop, Isabel, "Kenneth Hayes Miller," *Magazine of Art*, XLV, April 1952, 168-69.

_____, "Isabel Bishop Discusses 'Genre' Drawings," *American Artist*, XVII, Summer 1953, 46-47.

_____, "Drawing the Nude," *Art in America*, December 1963, 117.

Canaday, John, "A Certain Dignity for the Figure," *New York Times*, May 11, 1975, 31.

Glueck, Grace, "New Honors for Painter on Union Square," *New York Times*, April 11, 1975, 18.

Harms, Ernest, "Light as the Beginning — the Art of Isabel Bishop," *American Artist*, XXV, February 1961, 28-36, 60-62.

Johnson, Una E., and Miller, Jo, *Isabel Bishop*, American Graphic Artists of the 20th Century series, The Brooklyn Museum, 1964.

Lunde, Karl, *Isabel Bishop*, New York, 1975.

Nemser, Cindy, "Conversation with Isabel Bishop," *Feminist Art Journal*, V, no. 1, Spring 1976, 14-20.

Russell, John, "A Novelist's Eye in Isabel Bishop's Art," *New York Times*, April 12, 1975, 25.

Seckler, Dorothy, "Bishop Paints a Picture," *Art News*, November 1951, 36ff.

Tucson, University of Arizona Museum of Art, *Isabel Bishop: The First Retrospective Exhibition Held in American Museums of Paintings, Drawings, Etchings and Aquatints*, catalog by Sheldon Reich, 1974.

151.
Nude
Collections:
Purchased by the museum in 1934.
Exhibitions:
Second Biennial Exhibition of Contemporary American Painting, Whitney Museum of American Art, New York, 1934, no. 106, 14; *Annual Exhibition of the Art Students League*, New York, 1935-36; *20th-Century American Artists*, Whitney Museum of American Art, New York, 1939, no. 6, repr., n.p.; *Trends in American Painting Today — 36th Annual Exhibition*, City Art Museum, St. Louis, 1942; *Juliana Force and American*

Art, Whitney Museum of American Art, New York, 1949, no. 11, 64; *Isabel Bishop: The First Retrospective Held in American Museums of Paintings, Drawings, Etchings, and Aquatints,* University of Arizona Museum of Art, Tucson, Arizona, 1974, no. 9, 193, ill. no. 7.
Literature:
Bishop, 1963, 117; Russell; Nemser, 18-19, repr. 19.

Alice Trumbull Mason (1904-1971)
Bibliography

New York, Whitney Museum of American Art, *Alice Trumbull Mason Retrospective,* introduction by R. Pincus-Witten, 1973.

152.
L'Hasard
Exhibitions:
Alice Trumbull Mason Retrospective, introduction by R. Pincus-Witten, Whitney Museum of American Art, New York, 1973, repr.; *Alice Trumbull Mason,* A. B. Closson Gallery, Cincinnati, 1973; *Alice Trumbull Mason,* Washburn Gallery, New York, 1974; *Three American Purists: Mason, Miles, von Wiegand,* Museum of Fine Arts, Springfield, Massachusetts, 1975.

Leonor Fini (b. 1908)
Bibliography

Brion, Marcel, *Leonor Fini et son oeuvre,* Paris, 1955.

Carrieri, Raffaele, *Leonor Fini,* Collana di monografie d'arte italiana moderna, VII, 1951.

Fini, Leonor, and Alvarez, Jose, *Le livre de Leonor Fini; peintures, dessins, écrits, notes de Leonor Fini,* Paris, 1975.

Jaloux, Edmond; Eluard, Paul; Moravia, Alberto; Hugnet, George; Ford, Charles Henri; Praz, Mario; and Savinio, Alberto, *Leonor Fini,* Rome, 1945.

Jelenski, Constantin, *Leonor Fini,* Lausanne, 1968 and 1972; New York, ca. 1968.

Monegal, Emir Rodríguez, "La pintura como exorcismo," *Mundo nuevo,* no. 16, October 1967, 5-21.

153.
The Angel of Anatomy
Exhibitions:
Leonor Fini, Galerie Faubourg-Saint-Honoré, Paris, 1951; *Bosch, Goya et le fantastique,* catalog by Gilberte Martin-Méry, Galerie des Beaux-Arts, Bordeaux, 1957, no. 274, 96.
Literature:
Jean Avalon, "A Leonor Fini," *Aesculape,* 36e année, no. 3, March 1954, 49, repr. 51; Brion, n.p.; Brion, *Art fantastique,* Paris, 1961, 67-68; Jelenski, no. 66, repr. only; Fini and Alvarez, 233, repr.

154.
The Two Skulls
Literature:
Carrieri, n.p.; Jelenski, no. 58, color repr. only; Fini and Alvarez, 134, repr.

Lee Krasner (b. 1908)
Bibliography

London, Whitechapel Art Gallery, *Lee Krasner: Paintings, Drawings, and Collages,* catalog by B. H. Friedman, 1965.

Nemser, Cindy, "A Conversation with Lee Krasner," *Arts Magazine,* XLVII, no. 6, April 1973, 48.

_____, "Lee Krasner's Paintings, 1946-49," *Artforum,* XII, December 1973, 61-65.

_____, "Lee Krasner," in *Art Talk,* 81-112.

New York, Whitney Museum of American Art, *Lee Krasner: Large Paintings,* catalog by Marcia Tucker, 1973.

Robertson, Bryan, "The Nature of Lee Krasner," *Art in America,* November-December 1973, 83-87.

Rose, Barbara, "American Great: Lee Krasner," *Vogue,* CLIX, June 1972, 118-21, 154.

Washington, D.C., Corcoran Gallery of Art, *Lee Krasner: Collages and Works on Paper, 1933-1974,* essay by Gene Baro, 1975.

155.
Red, White, Blue, Yellow, Black
Collections:
The artist, New York.
Exhibitions:
Lee Krasner: Collages and Works on Paper, 1933-1974, essay by Gene Baro, Corcoran Gallery of Art, Washington, D.C., 1975, no. 18, repr.

Loren MacIver (b. 1909)
Bibliography

Arb, Renée, "Loren MacIver," *Magazine of Art,* XLI, January 1948, 12-15.

McBride, Henry, "Ladies' Day at the Whitney," *Art News,* LI, January 1953, 30-31ff.

New York, Whitney Museum of American Art, *Loren MacIver; I. Rice Pereira,* ed. John I. H. Baur, 1953.

Soby, James Thrall, "The Fine Arts, Again, to the Ladies!" *Saturday Review,* XXXVI, February 7, 1953, 50-51.

156.
Hopscotch
Collections:
Acquired by the museum in 1940 with Mrs. John D. Rockefeller Purchase Fund.
Exhibitions:
Loren MacIver, Pierre Matisse Gallery, New York, 1940; *Fourteen Americans,* ed. D. C. Miller, Museum of Modern Art, New York, 1946, no. 45, repr. 29; Tate Gallery, London, 1946; *Loren MacIver,* Vassar College, Poughkeepsie, 1950; *Loren MacIver; I. Rice Pereira,* Whitney Museum of American Art, New York, 1953, no. 16, 15, 16, 22, 28, repr. 14.
Literature:
Bulletin of the Museum of Modern Art, New York, VIII, February-March 1941, 14; Alfred H. Barr, Jr., *What Is Modern Painting?* New York, 1943, repr. 10 (3rd. ed. rev., 1946, repr. 14); Barr, ed., *Painting and Sculpture in the Museum of Modern Art,* New York, 1948, no. 459, 313; Arb, 12-15; Barr, ed., *Masters of Modern Art,* New York, 1954, repr. 160; Robert M. Coates, "MacIver, Davis and Corot," *The New Yorker,* XXXII, November 17, 1956, 229.

Frida Kahlo (1910-1954)
Bibliography

Breton, André, "Frida Kahlo de Rivera," brochure for the Frida Kahlo exhibition at the Julien Levy Gallery, 1938, reprinted in Breton's *Surrealism and Painting,* New York, 1972.

del Conde, Teresa, "La Pintora Frida Kahlo," *Artes visuales,* no. 4, October/December 1974, 1-5.

Flores Guerrero, Raul, *Cinco pintores mexicanos,* Mexico City, 1957.

The Frida Kahlo Museum, a catalog containing brief notes on Frida Kahlo by Diego Rivera, Lola Olmedo de Olvera, and Juan O'Gorman, Mexico City, 1968.

Helm, McKimley, *Modern Mexican Painters,* New York, 1941.

Herrera, Hayden, "Frida Kahlo: Her Life, Her Art," *Artforum,* XIV, no. 9, May 1976, 38-44.

Orenstein, Gloria, "Frida Kahlo: Painting for Miracles," *Feminist Art Journal,* Fall 1973, 7-9.

Rivera, Diego (with Gladys March), *My Art, My Life,* New York, 1960.

Wolfe, Bertram D., *The Fabulous Life of Diego Rivera,* New York, 1963.

157.
Portrait of Frida and Diego
Exhibitions:
Modern Mexican Painters, Institute of
Contemporary Art, Boston, 1941, 32, no. 15;
Latin American Painters, San Francisco
Museum of Art, 1956; *Contemporary
Mexican Art, The Adelaide Festival of Arts,*
National Gallery of South Australia,
Adelaide, 1960, no. 10.
Literature:
Magazine of Art, January 1941, p. xxxxv.

Dorothea Tanning (b. 1910)
Bibliography

Bosquet, A., *La peinture de Dorothea Tanning,* Paris, 1966.

Jouffroy, A., "Dorothea Tanning: Le chavire-
ment dans la joie," *XXe siècle,* no. 43,
December 1974, 60-68.

Knokke-le-Zoute, Casino Communal,
*Exposition rétrospective de Dorothea Tan-
ning,* preface by Patrick Waldberg, 1967.

Lebel, R., "Dorothea Tanning," *Cahiers
d'art,* XXVIII, no. 1, June 1953.

New York, Julien Levy Gallery, *Dorothea
Tanning,* preface by Max Ernst, 1944.

Paris, Centre National d'Art Contemporain,
Dorothea Tanning, 1974.

Waldberg, Patrick, "Tanning ou la mémoire
ensorcelée," *XXe siècle,* December 1966,
134-35.

158.
Maternity
Collections:
Formerly in the collection of Mrs. Doris W.
Starrels, Santa Monica.
Exhibitions:
Dorothea Tanning, Centre National d'Art
Contemporain, Paris, 1974, no. 8, repr. 23.
Literature:
Linda Nochlin, review of Tanning exhibition
in *Art in America,* LXII, November 1974, 128.

General Bibliography

Exhibition Catalogs

Amsterdam, *Exposition des dessins exécutés par des femmes*, 1884.

Baltimore, Walters Art Gallery, *Old Mistresses: Women Artists of the Past*, catalog by Ann Gabhart and Elizabeth Broun, *Bulletin of the Walters Art Gallery*, XXIV, no. 7, 1972.

Bregenz, Vorarlberger Landesmuseum, *Angelika Kauffman und ihre Zeitgenossen*, organized by Dr. Oscar Sandner, 1968.

Brussels, Musées Royaux des Beaux-Arts de Belgique, *Le siècle de Breugel; la peinture en Belgique au XVIe siècle*, introduction by Leo van Puyvelde, 1963.

Castres, Musée Goya, *Les femmes peintres au XVIIIe siècle*, catalog by Roger Gaud, 1973.

The Detroit Institute of Arts and Florence, Palazzo Pitti, *The Twilight of the Medici: Late Baroque Art in Florence, 1670-1743*, organized by Frederick J. Cummings and Marco Chiarini, catalog by K. Lankheit, J. Montagu, M. Chiarini, et al., 1974.

London, Geffrye Museum, '*The Excellent Mrs. Mary Beale* ,'catalog by Elizabeth Walsh and Richard Jeffree, 1975.

Naples, Palazzo Reale, *La natura morta italiana*, organized by Stefano Bottari, catalog by Raffaelo Causa, Italo Faldi, Mina Gregori, Anna Ottani, et al., 1964.

New York, The Metropolitan Museum of Art, *The Grand Gallery of the Metropolitan Museum*, 1974.

New York, Downtown Branch, Whitney Museum of American Art, *19th-Century American Women Artists*, 1976.

The Newark Museum, *Women Artists of America, 1707-1964*, catalog by William H. Gerdts, 1965.

Paris, Hôtel de Lyceum-France, *Exposition des femmes peintres*, organized by Mme. A. Besnard, 1908 (see also C. Saunier and M. Tourneux for reviews of this exhibition).

Paris, Hôtel de Lyceum-France, *Exposition des femmes peintres*, 1913.

Paris, Hôtel des Négociants en Objets d'Art, *Explication des peintures, gravures, miniatures et autres ouvrages des femmes peintres du XVIIIe siècle*, 1926.

Paris, Galerie J. Charpentier, *Exposition des femmes peintres du XVIIIe siècle*, 1926.

Paris, Musée des Ecoles Etrangères Contemporaines, Jeu de Paume des Tuileries, *Les femmes artistes d'Europe exposent au Musée du Jeu de Paume*, 1937.

Paris, Bernheim, *Voici des fruits, des fleurs, des feuilles, et des branches*, 1957.

Paris, Grand Palais; The Detroit Institute of Arts; and New York, The Metropolitan Museum of Art, *French Painting 1774-1830: The Age of Revolution*, catalog by Frederick J. Cummings, Pierre Rosenberg, Antoine Schnapper, Robert Rosenblum, et al., 1974-75.

Paris, Grand Palais, *La femme peintre et sculpteur du XVIIe au XXe siècle*, 1975.

Philadelphia, Pennsylvania Academy of the Fine Arts, *The Pennsylvania Academy and Its Women, 1850-1920*, catalog by Christine Jones Huber, 1973.

Poughkeepsie, Vassar College Art Gallery, *7 American Women: The Depression Decade*, catalog by K. A. Marling and H. Harrison, 1976.

Raleigh, North Carolina Museum of Art, and Winston-Salem, Salem Arts Center, *Women: A Historical Survey of Works by Women Artists*, catalog by M. B. Hill, 1972.

Rennes, Musée des Beaux-Arts et d'Archéologie, *Natures mortes anciennes et modernes*, 1953.

Rotterdam, Museum Boymans-van Beuningen, *Vier eeuwen stilleven in Frankrijk*, 1954.

Saint-Etienne, Musée d'Art et d'Industrie, *Natures mortes de l'antiquité au XVIIe siècle*, 1954.

Stockholm, Nationalmuseum, *Kvinnor som målat*, catalog by Görel Cavalli-Björkman, 1975.

The Toledo Museum of Art; The Art Institute of Chicago; Ottowa, National Gallery of Canada, *The Age of Louis XV: French Painting, 1710-1774*, catalog by Pierre Rosenberg, 1975-76.

Musées des Beaux-Arts of Tours, Limoges, and Poitiers, *Peintures françaises au XVIIe siècle*, 1973.

Zurich, Kunsthaus, *Die Frau als Künstlerin*, 1958.

Books and Periodicals

Adair, Virginia and Lee, *Eighteenth Century Pastel Portraits*, London, 1971.

Alesson, J., *Les femmes artistes au Salon de 1878*, Paris, 1878.

Alloway, Lawrence, "Women's Art in the '70s," *Art in America*, May-June 1976, 64-72.

Art Journal, XXXV, no. 4, Summer 1976 (Special issue devoted to Women and Art).

Baldinucci, Filippo, *Notizie de' professori del disegno da Cimabue in qua*, Florence, 1681-1728 (edition cited: *Opere di Filippo Baldinucci*, Milan, 1808-12).

Bell, Quentin, *The Schools of Design*, London, 1963.

Bellier de la Chavignerie, Emile, "Les artistes français du XVIIIe siècle oubliés ou dédaignés," *La revue universelle des arts*, XXI, 1865.

_____, and Auvray, Louis, *Dictionnaire général des artistes de l'école française depuis l'origine des arts du dessin jusqu'à nos jours*, 2 vols., Paris, 1882-85.

Bénézit, E., *Dictionnaire des peintres, sculpteurs, dessinateurs et graveurs*, Paris, 3rd ed., 6 vols., 1924-50.

Benoust, Madeleine, *Quelques femmes peintres*, Paris, 1936.

Bergström, Ingvar, *Dutch Still Life Painting in the Seventeenth Century*, trans. C. Hedström and G. Taylor, New York, 1956.

Bernt, Walther, *The Netherlandish Painters of the Seventeenth Century*, 3 vols., trans. of 3rd German ed., 1969, by P. S. Falla, London, 1970.

Bizardel, Yvon, "Les académiciennes au XVII siècle," *Jardin des arts*, XXXI, 1957.

Blackwell, Elizabeth (fl. 1737), *A Curious Herbal, Containing Five Hundred Cuts of the Most Useful Plants Which Are Now Used in the Practice of Physick*, London, 1739 (Nuremberg, 1757, and Leipzig, 1794).

Boime, Albert, *The Academy and French Painting in the Nineteenth Century*, London, 1971.

Bottari, Giovanni Gaetano, *Raccolta di lettere sulla pittura, sculture, ed architettura*, Milan, 1754 (edition cited: Milan, 1822-25, enlarged by Stefano Ticozzi).

Bowlt, John E., ed. and trans., *Russian Art of the Avant-Garde: Theory and Criticism 1902-1934*, New York, 1976.

Brown, Frank P., *South Kensington and Its Art Training*, London, 1912.

Bye, A. E., "Women and the World of Art," *Art World and Arts Decoration*, X, 1910, 86-89.

Carr, Annemarie Weyl, "Women Artists in the Middle Ages," *Feminist Art Journal*, v, no. 1, Spring 1976, 5-9, 26.

Cavé, Marie Elizabeth, *La femme aujourd'hui, la femme d'autrefois*, Paris, 1863.

Chadwick, W., "Eros or Thanatos — The Surrealist Cult of Love Reexamined," *Artforum*, November 1975, 45-56.

Clayton, Ellen Creathorne, *English Female Artists*, 2 vols., London, 1876.

Clement, Clara Erskine (Waters), *Women in the Fine Arts from the Seventh Century B.C. to the Twentieth Century A.D.*, Boston, 1904.

Colding, Torben Holch, *Aspects of Miniature Painting: Its Origins and Development*, Copenhagen, 1953.

Crelly, William R., *The Painting of Simon Vouet*, New Haven and London, 1962.

Daubié, J. V., *La femme pauvre au XIXe siècle*, Paris, 1866.

Diderot, Denis, *Diderot Salons* [1759-1779], ed. Jean Adhémar and Jean Seznec, Oxford, 1957-67.

Dominici, Bernardo De, *Vite de'pittori, scultori ed architetti napoletani*, 3 vols., Naples, 1742-43.

Duhet, P.-M., ed., *Les femmes et la révolution, 1789-1794*, Paris, 1971.

Edgerton, G., "Is There a Sex Distinction in Art? The Attitude of the Critic Towards Women's Exhibits," *The Craftsman*, June 1908, 239ff.

Ellet, Mrs. Elizabeth Fries Lummis, *Women Artists in All Ages and Countries*, New York, 1859.

Elliott, M. H., *Art and Handicraft in the Woman's Building of the World Columbian Exposition, Chicago, 1893*, Paris, 1893.

Erskine, Beatrice Caroline (Strong), *Lady Diana Beauclerk*, London, 1903.

The Feminist Art Journal, 1970—.

Fidière, Octave, *Les femmes artistes à l'Académie Royale de Peinture et de Sculpture*, Paris, 1885.

Gammelbo, Paul, *Dutch Still-Life Painting from the Sixteenth to the Eighteenth Centuries in Danish Collections*, Leigh-on-Sea, 1960.

Gardner, A. T., "A Century of Women," *The Metropolitan Museum of Art Bulletin*, VII, no. 4, December 1948, 110-18.

Gautier, Xavière, *Surréalisme et sexualité*, Paris, 1971.

Giordani, Gaetano, *Notizie di donne pittrici da Bologna*, Bologna, 1832.

Girodie, André, "Biographical Notes on Aimée Duvivier," *Burlington Magazine*, XXIV, 1913, 307-9.

Goulinat, Jean Gabriel, "Les femmes peintres au XVIIIe siècle," *L'art et les artistes*, XIII, 1926.

Gray, Camilla, *The Great Experiment: Russian Art, 1863-1922*, New York, 1962.

Guhl, Ernest, *Die Frauen in der Kunstgeschichte*, Berlin, 1858.

Guicciardini, Ludovico, *Descrittione dei Paesi Bassi*, Antwerp, 1567 (edition cited: *Guicciardini's Account of the Ancient Flemish School of Painting*, London, 1795).

Hagen, Luise, "Lady Artists in Germany," *International Studio*, IV, 1898, 91-99.

Hairs, Marie Louise, *Les peintres flamands de fleurs au XVIIe siècle*, Paris and New York, 1955; 2nd ed., Paris and Brussels, 1965.

Halle, F. W., *Woman in Soviet Russia*, New York, 1933.

Hamilton, G.-H., *19th and 20th Century Art*, New York, 1970.

Hartley, M., "Some Women Artists," in *Adventures in the Arts*, New York, 1921, 112ff.

Hildebrandt, Hans, *Die Frau als Künstlerin*, Berlin, 1928.

Hirsch, Anton, *Die Frauen in der bildenden Kunst*, Stuttgart, 1905.

Holland, C., "Lady Art Students in Paris," *International Studio*, XXI, 1904, 225-33.

Holmes, C. J., "Women as Painters," *The Dome* (London), n.s. III, April-July 1899, 3-9.

Hutchison, S. C., *The History of the Royal Academy, 1768-1868*, London, 1968.

Jean, René, "Madame de Mirbel," *Gazette des beaux-arts*, XXXV, 1906, 131-46.

Jouin, Henry, "L'exposition des artistes femmes," *Journal des beaux-arts et de la littérature*, Brussels, XXIV, 1882, 66.

Kershaw, J. D., "Philadelphia School of Design for Women," *The Sketch Book*, IV, no. 6, April 1905.

Kramm, Christiaan, *De levens en werken der Hollandsche en Vlaamsche Kunstschilders, Beeldhowers, Graveurs, en Bouwmeesters, van den Vroegsten tot op onzen Tijd*, Amsterdam, 1857-64.

Kuzmany, K., "Die Kunst der Frau," in *Die Kunst für Alle*, XXVI, 1910, 193ff.

Lagrange, Léon, "Du rang des femmes dans les arts," *Gazette des beaux-arts*, VIII, October-December 1860, 30-43.

Laruelle, B., "Marguerite Le Compte," *Bulletin des beaux-arts*, III, 1885-86, 130-35.

Lebrun, d'Albane, "Le portrait de Catherine Du Chemin, femme de François Girardon," in *Mémoires de la Société Académique . . . de l'Aube*, IX, Troyes, 1877.

Leisteungen der Nürnberger Frau auf dem Gebiete der Literatur, Kunst, und Musik, Nuremberg, 1959.

Leris, G. de, "Les femmes à l'Académie de Peinture," *L'art*, XLV, 1888, 122-33.

Lexikon der Frau, 2 vols., Zurich, 1953.

Lindberg, Anna L., and Werkmäster, Barbro, *Kvinnor som Konstnärer*, Stockholm, 1975.

Malvasia, Carlo Cesare, *Felsina Pittrice, vite de pittori bolognesi*, Bologna, 1678 (edition cited: Bologna, 1841).

Marcou, P. F., "Une exposition rétrospective d'art féminin," *Gazette des beaux-arts*, 1908, 297ff.

Merritt, A. L., "A Letter to Artists: Especially Women Artists," *Lippincott's Magazine*, LXV, 1900, 463-69.

Michel, E., *La peinture flamande au XVIIe siècle*, Paris, 1939.

Middleton, M. S., *Henrietta Johnston, America's First Pastellist*, South Carolina, 1966.

Miner, D., *Anastaise and Her Sisters: Women Artists of the Middle Ages*, Walters Art Gallery, Baltimore, 1974.

Minghetti, Marco, "Le donne italiane nelle belle arti al secolo XV e XVI," *Nuova antologia*, XXXV, 1877, 308-30.

Mitchell, Peter, *Great Flower Painters: Four Centuries of Floral Art*, London, 1973.

Munsterberg, Hugo, *A History of Women Artists*, New York, 1975.

Muther, R., *The History of Modern Painting*, 4 vols., rev. ed., London, 1907.

Nagler, G. K., *Neues allgemeines Künstler-Lexikon*, 25 vols., Munich, 1835-Linz, 1914.

Nemser, Cindy, *Art Talk: Conversations with 12 Women Artists*, New York, 1975.

Nieriker, M. (Alcott), *Studying Art Abroad and How to Do It Cheaply*, Boston, 1879.

Nochlin, Linda, "Why Have There Been No Great Women Artists?" *Art News*, LXIX, 1971, 22-39, 67-71.

————, "By a Woman Painted: Eight Who Made Art in the 19th Century," *Ms. Magazine*, III, no. 1, July 1974, 68-75, 103.

Novotny, F., *Painting and Sculpture in Europe, 1780-1880*, Pelican History of Art, Baltimore, 1960.

Orenstein, Gloria F., "Art History and the Case for the Women of Surrealism," *The Journal of General Education*, XXVII, no. 1, Spring 1975, 31-54 (an abridged version of this article appeared in the *Feminist Art Journal*, Spring 1973).

————, "Art History," *Signs: Journal of Women in Culture and Society*, I, no. 2, Winter 1975, 505-25.

Oulmont, Charles, *Les femmes peintres du dix-huitième siècle*, Paris, 1928.

Parada y Santín, Jose, *Las pintoras españolas; boceto histórico-biografico y artistico*, Madrid, 1902.

Pavière, Sydney Herbert, *A Dictionary of Flower, Fruit, and Still Life Painters*, 3 vols., Leigh-on-Sea, 1962-64.

Pérez Sánchez, Alfonso E., *Pintura italiana del siglo XVII en España*, Madrid, 1965.

Pevsner, Nicolas, *Academies of Art, Past and Present*, Cambridge, 1940.

Portalis, Baron Roger, and Beraldi, Henri, *Les graveurs du dix-huitième siècle*, 3 vols., reprint, New York, 1970.

Ragg, Laura, *Women Artists of Bologna*, London, 1907.

Reis-Santos, Luis, *Josefa d'Obidos*, Lisbon, 1955.

Rewald, John, *The History of Impressionism*, 4th ed., rev., New York, 1973.

Rombouts, Philippe, and Lerius, Th. van., *Die Liggeren en Andere historische Archieven der Antwerpsche Sint Lucasgilde*, 2 vols., Antwerp, 1872-76.

Rosenberg, Jakob; Slive, Seymour; and Ter Kuile, E. H., *Dutch Art and Architecture, 1600-1800*, Harmondsworth, 1966.

Rouffaer, G. P., "Vier Kamper Schilders," *Oud-Holland*, V, 1887, 201-9.

Sachs, Hannelore, *The Renaissance Woman*, New York, 1971.

Sanchez-Mesa Martín, Domingo, "Nuevas obras de Luisa Roldán y Jose Risueño en Londres y Granada," *Archivo español de arte*, CLVII, October 1967, 325-31.

Sandrart, Joachim von, *Deutsche Akademie der Edlen Bau-Bild-und Mahlerey-Künste*, Nuremberg, 1675-79, 2 vols. (edition cited: A. Pelzer, Munich, 1925).

Saunier, Charles, "Exposition rétrospective féminin au Lyceum-France," *L'art*, LXXVI, April 1908, 2-7.

Sonnenfeld, Amanda, *Deutsche Frauengestalten: Zehn Lebenbeschreibungen hervorrangender Frauen für die Mädchenwelt*, Stuttgart, 1910.

Soprani, Raffaele, *Le vite de' pittori, scultori, et architetti genovesi . . .*, Genoa, 1674 (edition cited: Genoa, 1768-69, with notes by G. Ratti).

Sparrow, Walter Shaw, *Women Painters of the World*, London, 1905.

Staring, A., "De van der Mijns in Engeland II," *Nederlands Kunsthistorisch Jaarboek*, XIX, 1968, 171-203.

Sterling, Charles, *Still Life Painting from Antiquity to the Present Time*, Paris, 1959.

————, and Salinger, M., *French Paintings in the Collection of the Metropolitan Museum*, New York, II, 1966; III, 1967.

Stirling-Maxwell, William, *Annals of the Artists of Spain*, 4 vols., London, 1891.

Stranahan, C. H., *A History of French Painting from Its Earliest to Its Latest Practice Including an Account of the French Academy of Painting, Its Salons, Schools of Instruction and Regulations*, New York, 1888.

Sullerot, E., *Histoire et sociologie du travail féminin*, Paris, 1968.

Thieme, U., and Becker, F., *Allgemeines Lexikon der bildenden Künstler von der Antike bis zur Gegenwart . . .*, 36 vols., Leipzig, 1907-50.

Tourneux, M., "Une exposition rétrospective d'art féminin," *Gazette des beaux-arts*, XXXIX, 1908, 290-300.

Tufts, Eleanor, *Our Hidden Heritage*, London, 1974.

Vasari, Giorgio, *Le vite de' più eccellenti pittori, scultori ed architettori*, 1568 (edition cited: Gaetano Milanesi, ed., Florence, 1787-1818, 8 vols.).

Vauchon, M., *La femme dans l'art, les protectrices des arts, les femmes artistes*, Paris, 1893.

Venturi, A., *Storia dell'arte italiana*, Milan, 1901-40.

Viallet, Bice, *Gli autoritratti femminili delle R.R. Galleria degli Uffizi*, Rome, ca. 1924.

Vogel, L., "Fine Arts and Feminism: The Awakening Consciousness," *Feminist Studies*, II, no. 1, 1974, 3-37.

Walpole, H., *Anecdotes of Painting in England*, 5 vols., London and New Haven, 1937.

Weese, Maria, and Wild, Doris, *Die schweizer Frau in Kunstgewerbe und bildender Kunst*, Zurich, 1928.

White, H. C., and C. A., *Canvases and Careers: Institutional Change in the French Painting World*, New York, 1965.

Williams, I. A., *Early English Watercolors*, London, 1952.

Williamson, George C., *Richard Cosway, R. A., His Wife, and Pupils*, London, 1905.

Wilson, J. J., and Petersen, Jan, *Women Artists: Recognition and Reappraisal from the Early Middle Ages to the Twentieth Century*, New York, 1976.

Wolff-Arndt, Phillippine, *Wir Frauen von einst; Erinnerungen einer Malerin*, Munich, 1929.

"Women Artists" (Review of E. Guhl's *Die Frauen in der Kunstgeschichte*) in *The Westminster Review* (American ed.), LXX, July 1858, 91-104.

Würzbach, Alfred, *Niederländisches Künstlerlexikon, auf grund Archivalischer Forschungen . . .*, Vienna, 1906-11.

Zarnowska, E., *La nature morte hollandaise*, Brussels, 1929.

Index of Artists

Index of Artists in the Exhibition

Paintings on Limited Exhibition Tour

Los Angeles only
cat. nos. 13, 28, 39, 73, 139
Los Angeles and Pittsburgh only
cat. no. 92
Los Angeles and Brooklyn only
cat. no. 22
Austin and Pittsburgh only
cat. no. 34
Brooklyn only
cat. no. 35

Designed in Los Angeles
by Rosalie Carlson.
All text set in Times Roman
by Ad Compositors, Los Angeles.
Catalog printed on Warren's
Lustro Offset Enamel Gloss
by Murray Printing Company,
Forge Village, Massachusetts.
Color separations
by Chanticleer Press, Inc.,
New York, New York.
Color printing by
Rae Publishing Company, Inc.,
Cedar Grove, New Jersey.